THE SUNDAY READINGS

THE SUNDAY READINGS

"Cycle B" (2)

An Explanation and Application of the Sunday Readings

KEVIN O'SULLIVAN, O.F.M. D.D. L.SS.

FRANCISCAN HERALD PRESS
CHICAGO

NIHIL OBSTAT:
>   VERY REVEREND CANON M. McDONOUGH
>   *Censor Deputatus*

IMPRIMATUR:
>   ✠MICHAEL
>   *Episcopus Galviensis*

GALVIAE 20 Maii 1972

© REV. KEVIN O'SULLIVAN, O.F.M.

Library of Congress Catalog Card Number: 74–141766
ISBN: 8199–0433–3

CONTENTS

ADVENT SEASON:

    FIRST SUNDAY OF ADVENT 1

    SECOND SUNDAY OF ADVENT 8

    THIRD SUNDAY OF ADVENT 16

    FOURTH SUNDAY OF ADVENT 24

CHRISTMAS SEASON:

    CHRISTMAS MASS AT MIDNIGHT 32

    CHRISTMAS MASS AT DAWN 37

    CHRISTMAS MASS DURING THE DAY 41

    SUNDAY IN OCTAVE OF CHRISTMAS (HOLY FAMILY) . 48

    OCTAVE OF CHRISTMAS (SOLEMNITY OF MARY MOTHER OF GOD) 55

    SECOND SUNDAY AFTER CHRISTMAS 61

    EPIPHANY (6th JANUARY) 67

    SUNDAY AFTER 6th JANUARY (BAPTISM OF THE LORD)—FIRST SUNDAY OF THE YEAR 72

    SECOND SUNDAY OF THE YEAR 79

    THIRD SUNDAY OF THE YEAR 87

    FOURTH SUNDAY OF THE YEAR 93

    FIFTH SUNDAY OF THE YEAR 101

    SIXTH SUNDAY OF THE YEAR 109

LENTEN SEASON:

    FIRST SUNDAY OF LENT 115

    SECOND SUNDAY OF LENT 122

THIRD SUNDAY OF LENT 130
FOURTH SUNDAY OF LENT 139
FIFTH SUNDAY OF LENT 147
PASSION SUNDAY (PALM SUNDAY) 155

EASTER SEASON:

EASTER SUNDAY 161
SECOND SUNDAY OF EASTER 167
THIRD SUNDAY OF EASTER 174
FOURTH SUNDAY OF EASTER 182
FIFTH SUNDAY OF EASTER 189
SIXTH SUNDAY OF EASTER 196
ASCENSION OF OUR LORD 204
SEVENTH SUNDAY OF EASTER 211
PENTECOST SUNDAY 219
TRINITY SUNDAY 225
FEAST OF CORPUS CHRISTI 232
SEVENTH SUNDAY OF THE YEAR 241
EIGHTH SUNDAY OF THE YEAR 250
NINTH SUNDAY OF THE YEAR 259
TENTH SUNDAY OF THE YEAR 267
ELEVENTH SUNDAY OF THE YEAR 276
TWELFTH SUNDAY OF THE YEAR 283
THIRTEENTH SUNDAY OF THE YEAR 291
FOURTEENTH SUNDAY OF THE YEAR 299
FIFTEENTH SUNDAY OF THE YEAR 308
SIXTEENTH SUNDAY OF THE YEAR 317
SEVENTEENTH SUNDAY OF THE YEAR . . . 324
EIGHTEENTH SUNDAY OF THE YEAR . . . 332
NINETEENTH SUNDAY OF THE YEAR . . . 340
TWENTIETH SUNDAY OF THE YEAR 347
TWENTY-FIRST SUNDAY OF THE YEAR . . . 355
TWENTY-SECOND SUNDAY OF THE YEAR . . . 363
TWENTY-THIRD SUNDAY OF THE YEAR . . . 372
TWENTY-FOURTH SUNDAY OF THE YEAR . . . 379

TWENTY-FIFTH SUNDAY OF THE YEAR 386
TWENTY-SIXTH SUNDAY OF THE YEAR 394
TWENTY-SEVENTH SUNDAY OF THE YEAR 401
TWENTY-EIGHTH SUNDAY OF THE YEAR 409
TWENTY-NINTH SUNDAY OF THE YEAR 416
THIRTIETH SUNDAY OF THE YEAR 423
THIRTY-FIRST SUNDAY OF THE YEAR 430
THIRTY-SECOND SUNDAY OF THE YEAR 438
THIRTY-THIRD SUNDAY OF THE YEAR 445
THIRTY-FOURTH SUNDAY OF THE YEAR (SOLEMNITY OF
    CHRIST THE KING) 452

HOLY DAYS:

ASSUMPTION OF THE BLESSED VIRGIN MARY (AUGUST 15) 459
IMMACULATE CONCEPTION (DECEMBER 8) 466
ALL SAINTS 475

FIRST SUNDAY OF ADVENT

FIRST READING : Isaiah 63 : 16–17; 64 : 1; 3–8. Thou, O Lord, art our Father, our Redeemer from of old is thy name. O Lord, why dost thou make us err from thy ways and harden our heart, so that we fear thee not? Return for the sake of thy servants, the tribes of thy heritage.

O that thou wouldst rend the heavens and come down, that the mountains might quake at thy presence—thou camest down, the mountains quaked at thy presence. From of old no one has heard or perceived by the ear, no eye has seen a God besides thee, who works for those who wait for him. Thou meetest him that joyfully works righteousness, those that remember thee in thy ways. Behold, thou wast angry, and we sinned; in our sins we have been a long time, and shall we be saved? We have all become like one who is unclean, and all our righteous deeds are like a polluted garment. We all fade like a leaf, and our iniquities, like the wind, take us away. There is no one that calls upon thy name, that bestirs himself to take hold of thee; for thou hast hid thy face from us, and hast delivered us into the hand of our iniquities.

Yet, O Lord, thou art our Father; we are the clay, and thou art our potter; we are all the work of thy hand.

EXPLANATION : Among the prophets of the Old Testament whose writings are extant, Isaiah was the greatest. He spoke as God's mouthpiece to the people of Judah during one of the most critical periods of their history, from 740–700 B.C. Infidelity to, and forgetfulness of Yahweh, the true God who had been a loving Father to them, was rife among the schismatic northern tribes (Israel) and also among the people of Judah. Those latter had Yahweh's Temple in their midst in Jerusalem.

In his attempt to bring about their conversion, the prophet reminds the people of Judah of the dreadful fate their sins are preparing for them. (Israel —the northern tribes—were taken into exile by Assyria in 722; an exile from which they never returned.) Nevertheless, he has words of hope and promises of a glorious future, that is, the messianic age, for the remnant who will repent and remain faithful to God.

Because he was so prominent among God's prophets he had followers and admirers who continued his preaching and added to his writings. It is from one of these later followers (Third-Isaiah) that today's reading is taken. He pleads to Yahweh, the Father of the Chosen People, for mercy. He prays that God will come down among them. This prayer was answered when the Son of

A

God became man in the Incarnation.

Thou . . . Father : This is a wonderful, but a true claim. Yahweh was creator and father of all nations. Ever since the call of Abraham (c. 1800 B.C.) he had revealed his fatherly love in many explicit ways to the Chosen People.

Our Redeemer . . . old : Yahweh elected Abraham to be the father of his Chosen People. This was in preparation for the redemption of all men in the Incarnation. The Exodus, or liberation of Abraham's descendants from the slavery of Egypt, was a foreshadowing of the greater and universal liberation which was to come in the messianic age.

thou . . . err : According to the Hebrew way of thinking Yahweh was somehow to blame because he did not prevent his people from sinning. Yet they realized full well that each one was fully responsible for his own sins. The preaching of the Prophets would otherwise have been in vain.

return . . . servants : The prophet asks Yahweh once more to come amongst them as he did in Sinai. He asks him to fulfill for his faithful ones—his servants —the promise made through the Patriarchs to his Chosen People, "the tribes of his heritage."

rend . . . come down : That Yahweh dwelt above the upper skies was the opinion of the Hebrews. The prophet now asks him to come amongst them in a startling way: by tearing the skies apart and by making the mountains quake. This would be a repetition, on a grander scale, of the theophany on Mount Sinai. Mark evidently sees this fulfilled. He relates that after the baptism of Jesus in the Jordan, John "saw the heavens (skies) torn apart and the Spirit like a dove descending on him" (Mk. 1 : 10).

no one . . . has seen : The goodness and kindness of Yahweh is beyond human comprehension, for he is infinite. St. Paul quotes these words in 1. Cor 2 : 9.

that remember . . . ways : Yahweh will repay those who trust in him and keep his laws.

thou . . . from us : The prophet admits that the present sad state of Yahweh's Chosen People (they are exiles in Babylon) has been caused by their rejection of their merciful God. For generations they have been unfaithful to him. "There is no one that calls upon thy name." As a people they had forgotten God.

hid . . . from us : They had turned away from God and now the prophet and the faithful "remnant" see the disastrous consequences of the people's sins.

Yet O Lord . . . Father : The pious "remnant" realize that unless Yahweh, who is still the Father of the Chosen People, has mercy on them, they will be utterly destroyed by their own iniquities.

clay . . . hand : They remind Yahweh of their lowly nature : they are but clay in relation to him. Because he is their Creator and their Father they call on him for mercy and forgiveness.

APPLICATION : Advent is the holy season in which the Church calls on us to prepare ourselves worthily to commemorate the anniversary of the coming of Christ amongst us. The lesson we have read has many instructions for us. If we take them to heart, they can help us to prepare ourselves for the great feast of Christmas.

The pious Jews—Third-Isaiah was one —looked forward anxiously and eagerly to a second coming of Yahweh amongst them. They had no very clear idea of how this would take place. They hoped and prayed that this coming would be very soon, otherwise the iniquities of the majority would destroy the whole Chosen People.

We are now living in the Christian age and have tthis marvelous advantage over the pious Jews of old : we have seen the realization of all their hopes and prayers. We know that God has come amongst us in a way that they in their wildest dreams could not have hoped for. God the Son became man—one of us. He joined our human nature to his divine nature. This made us his brothers and therefore adopted sons of his eternal Father.

The Jews could call God their Father because he had revealed himself to them and had made them into a chosen race— a people set apart from all the other nations—and had established them in the promised land of Canaan. They called him their Redeemer because he had led them out of the slavery of Egypt and protected them during their long journey toward their homeland.

However, all this was but a shadow when compared with the reality. It was a foretaste of the tremendous act of fatherly love and compassion which the infinite God has since shown, not/ to one race or one people but to the whole human race in the Incarnation of his only-begotten Son. The Jews could call God their Father because he had united them into a Chosen People. With much more right and with infinitely more truth we can and do call him our Father. He has united us to his divine Son and made us his true children, brothers of Christ.

God was the Redeemer of the Chosen People. By his mighty hand he set them free from the slavery of Egypt, and later from other oppressions. He gave them a homeland to live in. But what was this redemption compared with what God has done for us through Christ? Through the Incarnation God has made available to all mankind an eternal home of peace and happiness. There we shall be free from sin and from all earthly limitations, imperfections and dangers. By becoming man the second person of the Blessed Trinity made us children of God and heirs to heaven. By dying for us and rising from the dead he has conquered our death. Because of this, death is not the end of life for us but the beginning of our true life—everlasting life.

The prophet's prayer has been heard, his devout wish has been fulfilled. We are preparing ourselves to commemorate this extraordinary act of divine love for us—the coming of the Son of God as a baby, born of a lowly, human mother in the midst of poverty. We are preparing to celebrate the great feast of Christ, the birth-day of Christ, our divine Redeemer. Like the prophet, we must confess that we too are unworthy of God's love and of God's pardon. How many times have we offended our loving Father during the past year? How often have we forgotten him in our daily pursuit of earthly things?

There is still time to repent of our sins and to make ourselves worthy of all that Christmas means. We are the adopted sons of the Father of infinite mercy. If, truly repentant, we turn to him he will forgive us and make us worthy to be his children and call him by the loving name of "Father."

SECOND READING : 1 Corinthians 1 : 3–9. Grace to you and peace from God our Father and the Lord Jesus Christ.

I give thanks to God always for you because of the grace of God which was given you in Jesus Christ, that in every way you were enriched in him with all speech and all knowledge—even as the testimony to Christ was confirmed among you—so that you are not lacking in any spiritual gift, as you wait for the revealing of our Lord Jesus Christ; who will sustain you to the end, guiltless in the day of our Lord Jesus Christ. God is faithful, by whom you were called into the fellowship of his Son, Jesus Christ our Lord.

EXPLANATION : Corinth, at the time of St. Paul, was a Roman colony, a prosperous port and a notorious center of immorality. The apostle preached the Gospel there for over eighteen months (50–52 A.D.). He had some converts among his fellow-Jews and many among the Gentile population. After he moved from Corinth to continue his missionary activities elsewhere some disputes and difficulties arose among the newly-converted. This present letter is Paul's answer to reports concerning disputes and difficulties which had reached him. The letter was written from Ephesus in 57 A.D.

Grace . . . peace : As in most of his letters the Apostle prays for divine favors (grace) and everything his readers need for their well-being. Peace is the Hebrew "Shalom" meaning well-being, prosperity.

Lord Jesus Christ : The Corinthians could have no doubts as to the divinity of the Christ whom St. Paul had preached to them. He is placed on a level with "God the Father," for he is also God.

I give . . . you : Paul is forever thanking God for the grace, the gift, of Christian faith given the Corinthians.

enriched in him : It was through Christ, to whom they had given their allegiance, that they had received the charismatic gifts which were so numerous in the Corinthian church (see chapters 12 and 14).

testimony . . . confirmed : Paul's preaching concerning Christ and his message for all men was proved to be true by the gifts of the Holy Spirit given to the Corinthian converts.

wait . . . Christ : The Corinthians have been given all the aids necessary to enable them to be found worthy to meet Christ when he comes as judge of the universe.

sustain . . . end : If they remain faithful to their Christian faith, all the necessary graces of God obtained through the Incarnation, death and resurrection of Christ will be available to them throughout their lives.

God . . . our Lord : God gave them the grace of conversion to the faith of Christ, so that they would reach the eternal destiny he had planned for them. He is "faithful"; he does not waver or change his divine interest in them. If they remain faithful to their calling, to their brotherhood and fellowship with Christ—adopted sons of God—then they are assured that Christ's second coming will be a moment of triumph for them and the beginning of the new eternal life.

APPLICATION : On reading these few verses of St. Paul's first letter to his Corinthian converts, our first thought should be to return thanks and heartfelt gratitude to God for the supernatural gift of the Christian faith which he has given us. Like the Corinthians, we were made adopted children of God and brothers of Christ when we received the sacrament of baptism. This Christian faith is not only a satisfactory answer to the questions which our sojourn on this earth raises, but it is the only true answer to the basic question which every thinking man must ask himself : "Why do I exist?"

Our Christian faith teaches us that we were created by God. Through the incarnation we were given the privilege of divine adoption, which means an eternal life with the Blessed Trinity in heaven. Christ, the Son of God has won this for us and has revealed it to us. He has promised us this happy ending to our earthly life provided we keep his commandments and live our earthly lives as faithful followers of his—as true Christians.

During the four weeks of Advent, the Church in her liturgy keeps reminding us of these basic truths of our faith. In helping us to prepare ourselves to welcome the birth of Christ at Christmas, the stress is always on the necessity of living our Christian lives, so that at whatever moment he calls us we shall be ready to meet him and be found worthy to enter eternal life. This is what St. Paul taught the Corinthian Christians. This is what he is teaching each one of us today.

St. Paul may have expected the second coming of Christ, as Judge (the parousia), to take place in the early days of the Church for he had no revelation concerning the when or the how of this coming. Although the géneral judgement did not come then, the particular judgement—meeting Christ as judge—did take place for each Christian at death. Each one's eternity depends on his spiritual state when he meets Christ as Judge.

For us, the end of the world and the last judgement may or may not be far off, but the particular judgement is nearer to each one of us than we might care to admit. It is for this particular meeting with Christ that we must prepare. As the Apostle reminds us today, we have Christ with us sustaining us to the end. The loving God who called us into the fellowship of his Son has put us on the right road to heaven. He will keep us on that road if we follow his instructions, and use the aids Christ left us in his Church.

Let us prepare ourselves to welcome the first coming of Christ amongst us: Had we been there then, knowing what we now know, how gladly, how eagerly, would we not have taken him into our homes and our hearts! But we can still show our appreciation of what Christ has done for us, by welcoming him spiritually into a true Christian home this Christmas, and by receiving him sacramentally into a heart free from sin and from all worldly attachments.

If we do this each Christmas, and if we continue through the year to appreciate what Christmas and Christ's first coming mean to us, then it will not be as a severe judge but as a loving brother and Savior that we shall meet him in his second coming.

GOSPEL : Mark 13 : 33–37. Jesus said to his disciples, "Take heed, watch and pray; for you do not know when the time will come. It is like a man going on a journey, when he leaves home and puts his servants in charge, each with his work, and commands the doorkeeper to be on the watch. Watch therefore—for you do not know when the master of the house will come, in the evening, or at midnight, or at cockcrow, or in the morning— lest he come suddenly and find you asleep. And what I say to you I say to all : Watch."

EXPLANATION : The whole of chapter 13 of St. Mark's gospel is taken up with two topics : the destruction of Jerusalem with its beautiful Temple, and the end of the world. Christ was sitting on the slope of Mount Olivet overlooking the Temple and Jerusalem. One of the four disciples, who were with him, asked when these two events would take place. While Christ gives (in verse 14) some sign which will immediately precede the siege of Jerusalem and its subsequent destruction, he tells the disciples that the moment of the second coming of Christ—the end of the world —is a secret known to God only and not to be revealed (v. 32). It will be sudden and unexpected, but he tells them it will not find them unprepared, if they do what he tells them.

Take heed . . . pray : They are to live in Christian watchfulness, keeping Christ's laws day by day. They are to pray always, that is, honoring God by the faithful performance of their daily tasks and by raising their thoughts to him every now and then in public and private prayer.

like a man . . . journey : In a short parable he now illustrates what this constant watchfulness should be. A householder, leaving home, puts his servants in charge, and warns them to be ready to open to him whenever he returns. That may be midnight or just before dawn (cockcrow) or after sunrise. The servants are to be on the alert all through the night lest he come suddenly and find them asleep (see Lk. 12 : 35).

I say . . . watch : Christ's command to be ever-ready, ever-watchful, is not for the disciples only, but for all who will follow him.

APPLICATION : The end of the world is known only to God. It is his secret. He has not told us for some very good reason. But we do know that the end of this world for each one of us is at the moment of his death. When I breathe my last I shall have ended my stay in this world. I shall enter the new future world which I know exists. However, the knowledge of that moment is also hidden from me, and again for very good reasons. If many Christians knew the day and hour of their death, they would postpone their conversion until that last moment. This, of course, would be extreme foolishness, but the world is full of folly. What guarantee have such "unfaithful servants" that they will be given the grace of conversion at that last moment? What reward could such a selfish servant expect of the good Lord? There have been death-bed conversions

—the good thief on the cross is an example—but such converts did not willingly postpone their conversion.

The moment of our death is kept secret from us so that the naturally lazy and dilatory amongst us will see the need for being ever on the alert. When we realize what God the Father and Christ have done for us we should feel ashamed at our lack of generosity in God's service. We are expected to serve God willingly and faithfully every moment of our lives. But God knows the clay of which we are made, hence Christ's words of warning to all of us. Most of us do what we should out of a sense of gratitude to God, at least for our own self-interest. We all wish to get to heaven, and to do so we must be found worthy at the moment of death. That all-important moment is hidden from us and the only way to make sure of being found worthy then is to strive to be worthy always.

"Watch!" then, is Christ's advice and command. We know not the year or the day or the hour when our master will call us. That year, day and hour will be unexpected, even if we are advanced in years or have been suffering from prolonged illness. We shall not be unprepared for it if we have tried all our lives to be faithful to Christ and to our Christian faith.

This holy season of Advent is an opportune time for each one of us to look into his life and see how he stands with God. Christmas should remind us of the second coming of Christ, which will be very soon for all of us. Let us ask today : how would I fare if I were called from this world today? Could I expect to get honors, or even a pass, in my examination? Would I meet Christ as a loving brother and Savior or as a stern judge who would be forced to condemn me? If, in all honesty, most of us would find much lacking in our preparedness, we have still time to put things right. While we are in this world, God is not a stern judge but a merciful Father. He is ever ready to welcome the prodigal son provided the prodigal returns home. Today is the day to return to God. Today is the day in which to decide our future eternal state. There may be no tomorrow.

SECOND SUNDAY OF ADVENT

FIRST READING: **Isaiah 40:1–5; 9–11.** Comfort, comfort my people, says your God. Speak tenderly to Jerusalem, and cry to her that her warfare is ended, that her iniquity is pardoned, that she has received from the Lord's hand double for all her sins.

A voice cries: "In the wilderness prepare the way of the Lord, make straight in the desert a highway for our God. Every valley shall be lifted up, and every mountain and hill be made low; the uneven ground shall become level, and the rough places a plain. And the glory of the Lord shall be revealed, and all flesh shall see it together, for the mouth of the Lord has spoken."

Get you up to a high mountain, O Zion, herald of good tidings, lift up your voice with strength, O Jerusalem, herald of good tidings, lift it up, fear not; say to the cities of Judah, "Behold your God!" Behold, the Lord God comes with might, and his arm rules for him; behold his reward is with him, and his recompense before him. He will feed his flock like a shepherd, he will gather the lambs in his arms, he will carry them in his bosom, and gently lead those that are with young.

A voice says, "Cry!" And I said, "What shall I cry?" All flesh is grass, and all its beauty is like the flower of the field. The grass withers, the flower fades, when the breath of the Lord blows upon it; surely the people is grass. The grass withers, the flower fades; but the word of our God will stand for ever.

EXPLANATION: These words of consolation and comfort were spoken to the Jewish exiles in Babylon by a follower and devoted disciple of the great Isaiah. The end of their exile was near; Cyrus their liberator was on the horizon. The people would be brought back to Judea and Jerusalem by the power of God. This would be a second Exodus and Yahweh would be to them once more a loving Father and a faithful Shepherd. Following the New Testament writers (Mt. 3:3, Mk. 1:2, Lk. 3:2–6, Jn. 1:23), the Church has seen in these words of the prophet much more than the liberation of the Babylonian exiles, namely, the true and final liberation of all mankind, brought about by the coming of the Son of God as Messiah and Redeemer. It is because of this fuller meaning of the prophet's words that this reading has been chosen for Advent.

comfort my people : God in his mercy has forgiven the past sins and infidelities of his people. He now tells his representative, the prophet, to tell them of the good fortune which is to be theirs.

Jerusalem . . . pardoned : Jerusalem's sins are blotted out by God. She will rise again and see the glory of God and this in a much more sublime way than the prophet or his hearers understood. She will witness the death and resurrection of Christ, the Son of God, and the founding of the universal Church which will include Jew and Gentile.

received . . . her sins : The Babylonian exile was a punishment for the sins of Judah's kings and people. It purified them and made them once more acceptable to Yahweh their God.

in the wilderness . . . prepare : In those days there were no roads or highways in the desert between Babylon and Jerusalem. There were rough camel-tracks followed by traders. When some potentate was coming to Jerusalem workers were sent to mark out the camel-tracks, and to smooth the paths as much as possible. God will be coming with his people across the desert from Babylon. The people are exhorted to make the paths more worthy of his immense dignity. John the Baptist, in whom the Evangelists see this role fulfilled, interpreted the preparation in the spiritual sense. He exhorted his contemporary Jews to prepare their hearts by true repentance of sins, so as to be worthy to welcome their Messiah and Liberator.

glory . . . shall see : The promise went far beyond the liberation of a few thousand Jews in Babylon : "all flesh," all men, will see the glory of God in the new liberation, in the coming of the Son of God.

Jerusalem . . . tidings : The new Jerusalem will be the center from which the good news (the gospel) will go out to all. From the highest mountains it will be announced that God is with us (Immanuel), redeeming and strengthening us (see Revelation 21 : 1–4).

God . . . recompense : God's power liberates the exiles and gives them their reward or recompense, that is, their settlement once more in their homeland. Greater still, but almost incredible, was the power and the loving kindness of God in sending his Son amongst us. He came to earn for us eternal liberation and an everlasting life in our true homeland.

like a shepherd : The prophet deliberately makes no mention of a king, a Davidic descendant who will rule God's people. Yahweh himself will be their ruler, and his rule will be that of a true shepherd. He will cherish his flock and will do everything to ensure the protection and salvation of his flock (see Lk. 15 : 2–7; Jn. 10 : 1–14).

APPLICATION : The prophet's words of comfort and consolation, addressed to his fellow exiles in Babylon, apply to Christians with infinitely greater force and meaning. The exiles were told that their liberation from enemy captivity was at hand. God would bring them back to Judea, to end their earthly days in freedom, but not without much struggle and strife. These same words have their real fulfillment in Christ. For us they have a meaning which goes beyond the confines of this world and of this limited life. The liberation from Babylon was but a shadow of the messianic redemption brought to all men by the incarnation, death and resurrection of Christ.

The knowledge that we are made brothers of Christ and heirs to heaven is surely the most consoling and comforting fact in every thinking man's life. That we must all die and leave this world nobody can ever deny. Death is one of the acknowledged, stark realities of life. For the confirmed atheist and unbeliever (if such exists) death is the end of all our aspirations and hopes; we are nothing any more but a small mound of dust in a graveyard, or an urn of ashes kept for awhile on the family mantelpiece. What an inglorious end, what an unsatisfying finale to life's drama! Man, with all his gifts of intelligence, ambitions and desires to live on, is worse off than the beast of the field or the tree in the forest. They have not intelligence and therefore no thoughts of a future. The cow knows of no tomorrow for it thinks not. Man, because of his highly developed faculties, cannot avoid thinking and planning for the future. What a sad existence, what a cruel fate man's life would be if all were to end in the grave!

But there is comfort and consolation for those of us who accept God's revelation and who know all that God has done through the incarnation of his Son. We were created not only by an intelligent Creator but by a loving Father. He intended an eternal life for us. This eternal life was earned for us by the incarnation. Our death on earth is not the end but the beginning. "Our life is not taken from us but is changed" to the new and glorious form of existence.

The "Lord God has come with might" indeed, and "has brought his reward with him." He has raised us to the status of adopted sons and made us heirs to heaven—if we do our part on earth. And we are not alone in our efforts to merit this rich reward for ourselves; Christ has remained with us in his Church as our Good Shepherd and our divine helper. No sincere Christian need ever despair. Whatever be our temptations and weaknesses, if we call on our shepherd he will be there to help us.

Let us meditate and think often during these weeks of Advent on what the Christmas event means to us. Let us try to show our heartfelt gratitude to God who planned so lovingly our eternity, and to his divine Son who went to such lengths of humiliation and suffering in order to bring us to heaven. It must surely comfort and console us to be assured of an unending life of happiness after death, if only we use, as God wants us, the few short years given us here below. The reward and the recompense are exceeding great. To refuse to strive for that would be the act of a fool or a madman.

The Jerusalem of old rejoiced in the good tidings of the temporal liberation from exile. The new Jerusalem, the Church of Christ, can and should rejoice exceedingly in the good news given it by Christ, the gospel of eternal liberation and exaltation. This is what Christmas means for us. This is what we must ever strive for. Aided by our loving shepherd this is what we shall obtain when our days on earth come to an end.

SECOND READING: 2 Peter 3:8-14. Do not ignore this one fact, beloved, that with the Lord one day is as a thousand years, and a thousand years as one day. The Lord is not slow about his promise as some count slowness, but is forbearing toward you, not wishing that any should perish, but that all should reach repentance. But the day of the Lord will come like a thief, and then the heavens will pass away with a loud noise, and the elements will be dissolved with fire, and the earth and the works that are upon it will be burned up.

Since all these things are thus to be dissolved, what sort of persons ought you to be in lives of holiness and godliness, waiting for and hastening the coming of the day of God, because of which the heavens will be kindled and dissolved, and the elements will melt with fire! But according to his promise we wait for new heavens and a new earth in which righteousness dwells.

Therefore, beloved, since you wait for these, be zealous to be found by him without spot or blemish, and at peace.

EXPLANATION: It is unimportant whether or not this letter was written by St. Peter himself or by one of his disciples. The Church has accepted the epistle as canonical and inspired. Its twofold purpose is to warn against false teachers (ch. 2), and to dispel some anxiety the Christians of that day felt because of the apparent delay of Christ's second coming as judge (ch. 3). There were those (non-Christians) who scoffed at the Christian idea that the world would one day come to an end. Because it had not happened so far, they concluded it would not happen. They laughed at what they thought was a Christian error and delusion. But the writer of the epistle shows the Christians that because Christ seems to delay his second coming, this does not mean that he will not fulfill his promise.

Do not . . . one day: He reminds his readers that God is infinite and transcends time and space. Quoting psalm 90:4 (having inverted it in the first half of his verse) he says: "a thousand years are as one day" with the Lord. He is eternal, and therefore not restricted or measured by time.

Lord . . . count: What may seem a delay to the Christians is not a delay on God's part, but his loving way of giving all a chance to repent and be ready.

will come like a thief: He will come when he is not expected (1 Th. 5:2).

heaven . . . burned up: This is an apocalyptic description of the end of the world. The idea that the heavenly bodies (the stars and planets), the earth, the whole universe, would be destroyed by fire on the last day originated in Persia. Through the Greco-Roman world it passed into Jewish apocalyptic literature. This was the common imagery of the time and need not be taken as scientific fact (see Jerome Biblical Commentary, p. 498).

persons . . . day of God: The end of the world will come sometime. The details and circumstances of its coming are not important for us, but rather the state of preparedness in which it will find us. The author admonishes his readers, and us too, to live lives of holiness and godliness. By so doing we will be ready for God's call whenever it will come to us. **new heavens . . . earth :** This means a new world ("heavens and earth" was the Hebrew way of describing the created universe). There will be a new mode of existence for all men when the world will end, and for each one of us as we end our stay here. Its nature has not been revealed to us, for we have no human concepts in which to describe it.

righteousness . . . at peace : However, we are told it will be an eternal state of existence. We shall be free from all mental and bodily aches or cares. It will be a state of perfect peace and harmony between all men, and between men and God (see Revelation 21 : 1–4).
Therefore . . . be zealous : The reward God has in store for his faithful ones is so great that no human effort can be too much in order to obtain it.

APPLICATION : "We wait for new heavens and a new earth." That is the principal reason for our existence on this earth. We have a number of secondary purposes to fulfill, but each must contribute toward our attaining the primary and principal purpose : our eternal existence in heaven. We are intended by God to be citizens of the "new universe." He has given us our citizenship papers. He has most carefully mapped the road we should travel. He has given us all the material and spiritual helps we need on the journey but, God though he be, he cannot bring us to heaven unless we co-operate with him.

God cannot force us to cooperate in our own best interests. But he does nine tenths of the work for us, and what is left for us to do is relatively easy. He is near us when we dawdle on the road, attracted by some passing fancy. When we turn aside from the prescribed path to seek some forbidden pastures, he waits for us. As soon as we return to the high-road he is ever ready to help us along.

Among the first generation of Christians were many who were so grateful to God and Christ that they felt life on earth was too short to do all the good things they wanted for God, in return for all he had done for them. But there were others too who, through lack of generosity, felt the going hard, and were therefore hoping the end would come soon lest they faint on the way. The words we have just read in this reading were addressed primarily to the latter group. They were evidently disappointed at the delay in the second coming. The author urges them to be patient and to continue to lead holy lives. God is delaying their judgement day precisely to give them a chance to prove the sincerity of their love for him, "not wishing that any should perish."

Down through the twenty centuries of Christianity there have been millions, and thousands of millions, who could not do enough for God and their faith. They lived their lives on earth "in holiness and godliness." The second coming of Christ for them was a happy reunion with their loving brother and Savior. They are now in their new universe, in their new mode of existence in heaven. If we follow their example and strive daily to be as loyal to God and to our Christian heritage as they were, we can, and please God we shall, be with these saintly men and women when Christ calls us to himself. This we can do if we keep our principal purpose in life—our getting to heaven—ever before our eyes. This will not mean that we must neglect the other daily tasks; rather it will mean that we will do these much better. We will use the earthly gifts God has given us in order to earn the one and only gift that matters : eternal life. Our time of waiting, then, will not seem too long—it will rather seem far too short! We have so many returns to make to the Lord for the marvelous gifts he has given us.

Faithfully and diligently, let us use the span allotted by God to us on earth. It is through the proper use, or abuse, of these few short years that we are enabled to earn, or lose, eternal happiness.

GOSPEL : Mark 1 : 1–8. The beginning of the gospel of Jesus Christ, the Son of God. As it is written in Isaiah the prophet, "Behold, I send my messenger before thy face, who shall prepare the way; the voice of one crying in the wilderness : Prepare the way of the Lord, make his paths straight—"

John the baptizer appeared in the wilderness, preaching a baptism of repentance for the forgiveness of sins. And there went out to him all the country of Judea, and all the people of Jerusalem; and they were baptized by him in the river Jordan, confessing their sins. Now John was clothed with camel's hair, and had a leather girdle around his waist, and ate locusts and wild honey. And he preached, saying, "After me comes he who is mightier than I, the thong of whose sandals I am not worthy to stoop down and untie. I have baptized you with water; but he will baptize you with the Holy Spirit."

EXPLANATION : Sts. Matthew & Luke give us a brief account of the conception, birth, and early boyhood of Christ. St. John begins with the eternal life of Christ as God—the Word of the Father. St. Mark opens his gospel, or account of the "good tidings", with the preparation for Christ's public life, in which the chief actor was John the Baptist, whose conception and birth are described in Luke, and taken for granted by Mark.

Jesus . . . God : Mark has not the slightest doubt but that the "man" named Jesus (later the title "Messiah" i.e. "Christ", was added), who was heralded by the Baptist and baptized by him in the Jordan, was also the real Son of God, of divine nature.

Isaiah the prophet : The first verse is from the prophet Malachi, and while this is not a direct reference to the messianic age, Jesus himself adapts these words of Malachi to the Baptist (Mt. 11 : 10).

wilderness . . . Lord : See first Reading for the primary meaning of the prophet's words. Mark (and John 1 : 23) sees the real fulfillment of these words in the Baptist, who sets out in the wilderness, the desert of Judea near the Jordan, to prepare his fellow-Jews to be worthy to welcome the Son of God who as their long-expected Messiah is about to come amongst them.

baptism of repentance : By a true change of heart and a total return to God they could prepare themselves for his arrival.

God would forgive all their past offenses if they would now turn to him with true sincerity.

all . . . Judea . . . Jerusalem : A slight exaggeration perhaps. But a great many people from the whole of Judea (and from Galilee also, see Jn. 1 : 35), must have gone down to the Jordan bank to hear the strange preacher who was speaking about their Messiah. They had had no prophet from God for generations—a fact which worried many of them—and so they went to hear this new prophet, many of them ready to follow his advice and others too hard-hearted and self-centered to do so.

baptized . . . their sins : Among the Jews, external ritual washing was a sign of an internal cleansing of the heart through a true repentance. So John washed, or dipped, in the Jordan those of the people who confessed and repented of their sins.

camel's hair . . . girdle : This was probably the customary dress of a prophet, a mantle made of a camel's hide and tied around the waist with a strap of leather. It may have been the dress of others as well (see 2 Kgs. 1 : 8 on the dress of Elijah).

locusts . . . wild honey : St. Luke tells us that when the Baptist grew up to manhood he left home, and dwelt as a hermit in the desert (Lk. 1 : 80). Locusts were often numerous in the Judean desert and were eaten by many. They still are eaten by people in the Middle East countries. "Wild honey" could be just what it says, but there are those who think it is the name of some edible plant. Mark intends his description of the Baptist to show that he practiced penance all his life and therefore was capable of preaching penance and repentance to his fellowmen.

one . . . mightier : He declares that he is only the messenger, the precursor, who is preparing for one who is about to come, one who surpasses the Baptist in nature and power, for he will confer the Holy Spirit, the Spirit of God, on those whom he will receive into his fold. The Baptist is not worthy to be the most menial servant, one who would untie the sandals of the great one who is coming.

baptized . . . water : John's baptism was but an external symbol of interior conversion, the manifestation of the desire to win God's friendship. The one who was coming could and would give that real friendship with God to all who would accept it.

APPLICATION : "The beginning of the gospel of Jesus Christ, the Son of God." In twelve words St. Mark sums up the initiation of the greatest event that ever occurred in our human history, an event whose culmination would be not on earth but in heaven. God fulfilled the plan he had for us when creation began. He raised us up to the dignity of divine sonship by the incarnation. The eternal Son of God "humbled himself" and joined our human nature to his divinity, thus making us his brothers and capable of sharing with him the eternal kingdom of his Father.

Mark's story was, in fact, the greatest "good news" that man had ever received on earth. It is still the greatest, most astounding and, at the same time, most consoling news for us today. But just as there were those in Palestine who did not accept Christ's claim to be what he manifested himself to be—"he came unto his own but his own received him not" (Jn. 1 : 12)—so today, there are many, too many alas, who do not receive him. The causes for rejecting Christ and his message, and his promise of everlasting happiness are the same today as they were for the Scribes and Pharisees of the first century A.D.

It was their stubborn pride and self-centeredness, the exaggerated sense of their own dignity and perfection, which blinded the eyes of their intellects. The result was that they could not see their Messiah, their Savior, in Christ. He had brought himself down to the level of man, by assuming man's human nature. The Son of God assumed our human nature in order to live amongst us, to teach us how valuable God made us. He did so in order to die for us in that nature and to atone for all the sins of the human race.

The same stubborn pride, that same exaggerated sense of their own dignity, blinds the intellects of many today who not only refuse to accept Christ and his good tidings, but seem impelled also to prevent others from accepting him. The mad rush for earthly possessions and pleasures, the casting-off of all reasonable restraints and restrictions, which are so necessary for human society to survive, the rejection of all things spiritual in man's make-up and life-purpose, the general incitement to the animal instincts in man—all these, and many more, are the evident signs of the rejection of Christ which are so actively propagated by many in our world now.

Let each one of us ask himself today: am I for Christ or against him? Am I on the road to heaven or am I facing in the opposite direction? A brief examination of conscience will give the answer. How Christian is my daily conduct in my home, and in my place of work and recreation? Do I love God? Do I appreciate all he has done for me by sending his Son to raise me up, one day, to heaven? Do I really have my own best interests at heart, by striving always to be ready for Christ's second coming when I breathe my last? Christmas recalls to us his first appearance on earth. Let us use these days of preparation for Christmas to prepare ourselves for his second coming. This will occur for each one of us on the day of our death.

THIRD SUNDAY OF ADVENT

FIRST READING : Isaiah 61 : 1–2; 10–11. The Spirit of the Lord God is upon me, because the Lord has anointed me to bring good tidings to the afflicted; he has sent me to bind up the brokenhearted, to proclaim liberty to the captives, and the opening of the prison to those who are bound; to proclaim the year of the Lord's favor, and the day of vengeance of our God.

I will greatly rejoice in the Lord, my soul shall glory in my God; for he has clothed me with the garments of salvation, he has covered me with the robe of righteousness, as a bridegroom decks himself with a garland, and as a bride adorns herself with her jewels. For as the earth brings forth its shoots, and as a garden causes what is sown in it to spring up, so the Lord God will cause righteousness and praise to spring forth before all the nations.

EXPLANATION : For a description of Isaiah and his disciples see above, 1st Sunday of Advent. These words of encouragement and promise which we read in today's Reading, were uttered by one of Isaiah's disciples, to the exiles in Babylon. As they are very similar in language and thought to the "songs of the Suffering Servant" found in the second-Isaiah (40–55), some authors hold that they form part of the same theme. This may not be correct, but if the consoler and liberator is not the Messiah himself, he is surely a type of the Messiah. His words of consolation and promise are addressed in the first place to the exiles, but they were fully and truly realized only when Christ the Messiah came. Christ applied the first two verses of this text to himself when he first preached in the synagogue of Nazareth (Lk. 4 : 18–19).

Spirit . . . me : The power of God is

necessary for any great work of redemption (see Jgs. 3 : 10; 11 : 19. 1 Sm. 10 : 5–13). It is promised to the messianic king (Is. 11 : 1–2) and to the Suffering Servant (who is the Messiah—Is. 42 : 1). Here it is promised to the Messiah's representative among the Exiles, because he is the type or symbol of the true Messiah who will receive the Spirit in all his fullness (Lk. 4 : 18–19). **anointed me :** He is strengthened internally and is enlightened to know God's revelation and keep it faithfully, while announcing it to others.

good tidings : He is commissioned to bring the good news of their liberation to the prisoners.

year of . . . favor : This signifies a year of jubilee, as prescribed in Lv. 25 : 8. This jubilee year was to be held every 49th year. On its arrival all slaves were set free, loans and mortgages ceased to be binding. The Chosen People and all their property belonged to Yahweh and were returned to him in the jubilee year. The year of liberation from Babylon was such a year, but much more so was the day, or year, of the messianic liberation. **vengeance of our God :** That is, the day when God will punish the enemies of his people.

greatly . . . Lord : Jerusalem, realizing the magnanimous liberation that God has brought her, feels that she is once more the bride of Yahweh, dressed in her nuptial robes, while he is decked with the bridegroom's garland. These images represent the reality : the new Jerusalem will be dressed in the "garment of salvation" and in "the robe of righteousness." The new liberated kingdom will be one of sanctity and true fidelity to God. It had its true fulfillment in the messianic liberation (see Revelation 19 : 7–9).

to spring . . . nations : God gives his word. As surely as the earth brings forth its fruit, so will God fill the new Jerusalem (described in 60 : 1–22) with righteousness and praise, namely, with virtues that will make the nations take notice. This was fulfilled not on the return from Babylon, but when the Messiah established his kingdom on earth, when all nations not only took notice, but took him as their king and leader.

APPLICATION : Whether or not the prophet who spoke these words to his fellow-captives in Babylon foresaw their fuller meaning, their real fulfillment in the future messianic liberation, matters not to us. We have the testimony of our Lord, who applies these very words to himself. After reading 60 : 1–2 of Isaiah in the synagogue of Nazareth he says : "Today this scripture is being fulfilled in your hearing." It was he who was to bring the good tidings to the afflicted, to bind up the broken-hearted, to free the captives, and to proclaim the great year of jubilee, God's liberation of all mankind.

The exile and imprisonment of the Jews in Babylon (587–538) was but an image, a shadow, of the universal exile and self-imprisonment which the human race, through sin, had imposed on itself. Man not only disobeyed God, but forgot him completely. He made his own gods of wood, metal or stone. In these he foolishly put his trust. But they were even more helpless than man himself. In those days before Christ, life for man on earth was harder and more sorrowful than it is for the majority today. Man had nothing to look forward to but the grave. The few who had freedom and riches could enjoy them, but only for all too short a time. For them the thought of death (a thought they could hardly put aside) had more misery in it than for the slave who had nothing to leave behind him.

The Chosen People alone had a knowledge of the true God. They knew he created them. They knew they owed him honor and obedience. They were told to look forward to the day when God's representative, his Messiah, would come and make them (and all nations) members of God's new kingdom. They believed that they would live on in some shadowy way after death and would enter God's kingdom when this Messiah came. We can rightly presume that God, because of his infinite love and mercy, found ways and means too of giving the pagans of good-will every opportunity to merit that same kingdom when it came.

We are the descendants of pagan

ancestors who adored idols and knew nothing of God or of a future life. But we are living in the noonday light of the Christian revelation. We know that God, through the incarnation, has raised us up to the status of sonship with him. He has made us capable of possessing a new, eternal life after death. While our struggles and troubles on this earth may not be as grievous as those of our ancestors, they are still sufficiently serious and severe to make most of us almost despondent at times. However, we have the marvelous advantage that we know the reason for suffering. We can and should appreciate the eternal value of earthly suffering. Suffering is, in fact, part of our training and preparation for our eternal reward. Through the cross we receive the crown.

This morning, let us thank God from our hearts for the "good tidings" of our redemption and exaltation, brought to us by Christ the Son of God and our loving Brother. We are free-men, children of God, on our way to heaven. The road may be rough at times. It may be strewn with many crosses and trials. But if we keep the thought of the happy ending ever before our minds, we shall never falter, never give up. Nothing matters so much to us in this life as the guarantee that we will end it in God's love and friendship. It is only by endeavoring to live in God's love and friendship that we can assure ourselves of this guarantee.

These days of preparation for Christmas are very suitable for us to prepare to meet Christ our Lord when he comes as our Judge.

SECOND READING: 1 Thessalonians 5:16–24. Rejoice always, pray constantly, give thanks in all circumstances; for this is the will of God in Christ Jesus for you. Do not quench the Spirit, do not despise prophesying, but test everything; hold fast what is good, abstain from every form of evil.

May the God of peace himself sanctify you wholly; and may your spirit and soul and body be kept sound and blameless at the coming of our Lord Jesus Christ. He who calls you is faithful, and he will do it.

EXPLANATION: This is St. Paul's second letter. He wrote it during 51/52 to the converts at Thessalonica. At that time he was evangelizing Corinth. On his second missionary journey (50–52), he passed over from Asia Minor, having preached the gospel for some time at Philippi and reached Thessalonica. He made many converts there among the Gentiles and proselytes, but the majority of the Jews stirred up a crowd against him with the result that he had to leave the city after a few weeks. But he had laid lasting foundations for the faith even in this short space of time. The Thessalonica converts not only remained faithful to the Christian gospel they had so gladly received, but they helped very much to spread the Christian message to other parts of Macedonia and Achaia (1 Thess. 4:10). In the eight verses which we read from this epistle today, St. Paul exhorts his converts to thank God always for the gift of faith which they have received. They must respect, while testing, the gifts of the Spirit. This was especially so with regard to prophecy. It was the charism, or gift, which enabled the receiver to clarify the faith and thus improve, encourage and console his fellow-Christians. They are to avoid evil of every kind and do what is good. If they do so, God, who called them to the faith, will enable them to die in his friendship. God is faithful.

pray constantly : The Christian life is more than the keeping of obligations toward God and one's neighbor. It's a way of life directed to God in joy, prayer, and thanksgiving. This prayer and thanksgiving is not just a portion of one's day or life, but rather the sanctifying of one's whole life and worldly tasks. We are to do these tasks cheerfully out of gratitude to God who gave us this life and promises us an eternal one.

quench the Spirit : Not all the converts receive the visible gifts of the Holy Spirit. Those who did not were not to be jealous of those who did. These gifts were useful and necessary for the growth of the early Church, and must not be suppressed.

despise prophesying : There was danger that some who had not been moved by the Spirit would pretend to be so moved and utter their own words of explanation of the faith. The true power of expounding and explaining points of the faith was given to some only, and these should be listened to with every attention.

God of peace : The Christian truths which God had given the Thessalonians were the source and basis of all peace, peace with one's own conscience, peace with one's neighbors, peace with God himself now and forever hereafter.

sanctify you wholly : Paul prays that God will keep on making them holy day after day, until their sanctification is completed at death.

Spirit, soul and body : Paul uses the three nouns here, with the verb in the singular, to describe "man." He is not giving any anthropology of man.

blameless . . . coming : That is, ready to meet Christ, the Son of God when he comes for them.

he is faithful : God will do his part. His purpose in calling them was to bring them to eternal life. He will certainly do so if they cooperate with him.

APPLICATION : Our first impression, on reading these serious exhortations of St. Paul to his Thessalonian converts, could be : as Christians they were away above us in holiness of life and in their daily way of living. Paul certainly seems to demand much of them. Is not the very same demanded of us? We, too, must be ever rejoicing in our good fortune, and ever thanking God for putting heaven within relatively easy reach. We, too, must strive to be found in God's grace—"blameless" when our call to judgement comes. We, too, have St. Paul praying for us in heaven, more effectively now than when he prayed for the Thessalonians. We, too, must abstain from all that is evil.

The Thessalonians, it is true, had the visible gifts of the Holy Spirit to strengthen their faith and to console them in their struggles. But we, too, have at our disposal in the Church all the aids necessary to live truly Christian lives. We have the Church pointing out to us what to believe and what to do. Christ did not leave us orphans; he provided for his followers of all generations.

We have the sacraments to lift us up if we fall and strengthen us with God's grace. We have God's revelation in the written word of the Bible. We have the example of numerous saints who trod the same path we are expected to follow, and successfully reached heaven.

In some ways then, we are better equipped than were the Thessalonians. They had to suffer much opposition from their pagan neighbors, who thought that the Christian religion was at best a form of madness. They were liable to persecution at any moment from the Roman authorities, who thought Christianity was anti-Emperor, anti-Empire. But have we not the same difficulties to face? Our world today is, in fact, more pagan than was the Roman Empire of St. Paul's time. Opposition to Christianity is more rampant today than ever before. Ways and means of secularizing our society, to the exclusion and extinction of all things supernatural, have been multiplied a thousandfold in the present age.

All things considered, it was perhaps easier for the Thessalonians, humanly speaking, to live a truly Christian life and so earn heaven, than it is for us Christians today. However, living a truly Christian life is not a merely human activity. God has a part in it; in fact,

God has the principal part to play in it. What St. Paul told the Thessalonians, he tells us too : "God is faithful." God will do his part, the greater part, of the work of our salvation. So it matters not how many opponents we have. It makes no difference how many machinations they invent to impede us on our journey. Our "God is faithful" and our God is with us, helping us every step of the way.

Rejoice then, nay, exult in joy! Thank God from your heart for the gift of the true faith. Thank him for everything he sends in life. The rough, as well as the smooth, has a part in God's plan for making us worthy of sharing his kingdom. We shall "pray constantly." Our simple, everyday life will be a life of prayer, if we do our daily tasks. They may be humdrum and unimportant, or great affairs of state. But they are prayers, provided we offer them to God and see them as the things we must do on life's journey.

The Christian who lives such a life, who does his duty daily, who is loyal and true to God and to his neighbor, who bears patiently the troubles of life and enjoys the lawful pleasures of life, need have no fear for his future. He will be found "sound and blameless at the coming of our Lord Jesus Christ."

GOSPEL : John 1 : 6–8; 19–28. There was a man sent from God, whose name was John. He came for testimony, to bear witness to the light, that all might believe through him. He was not the light, but came to bear witness to the light.

This is the testimony of John, when the Jews sent priests and Levites from Jerusalem to ask him, "Who are you?" He confessed, he did not deny, but confessed, "I am not the Christ." And they asked him, "What then? Are you Elijah?" He said, "I am not." "Are you the prophet?" and he answered, " No." They said to him then, "Who are you? Let us have an answer for those who sent us. What do you say about yourself?" He said, "I am the voice of one crying in the wilderness, 'Make straight the way of the Lord,' as the prophet Isaiah said."

Now they had been sent from the Pharisees. They asked him, "Then why are you baptizing, if you are neither the Christ, nor Elijah, nor the prophet?" John answered them, "I baptize with water; but among you stands one whom you do not know, even he who comes after me, the thong of whose sandal I am not worthy to untie." This took place in Bethany beyond the Jordan, where John was baptizing.

EXPLANATION : Last Sunday we had St. Mark's account of the Baptist's activity at the Jordan as he prepared the people for the public mission of Jesus. Today, St. John describes the same event for us. He begins by telling us that John the Baptist was "a man sent from God." He does not tell us how this came about, but he knows that his readers knew all about it. St. Luke had described in his gospel how the childless couple, Zachary and Elizabeth, were given a son by God's special intervention. This son was destined by God to be the Precursor—the one who would prepare the way for the coming of Christ among the people (Lk. 1 : 8–24; 57–80). After referring briefly to these facts described in Luke's gospel, John gives some details concerning the Baptist's active role.

A man . . . God : He was a son, given by God to unexpecting and, humanly speaking, incapable parents, because Elizabeth was barren.

name was John : It was God himself who chose this name for the baby, not yet conceived (Lk. 1 : 12; see 57–64). The name "Yohanan" in Hebrew means "Yahweh is gracious"—a most suitable name for the man who was to introduce the greatest act of graciousness and kindness God ever manifested in human history.

witness to the light : John describes his mission. He testifies that the true "light of the world" is coming.

Priests and Levites : Mark told us (last Sunday) that the ordinary people in their thousands flocked to hear the strange preacher and his strange message. In John's vocabulary the "Jews" were those who opposed Jesus. They were the religious leaders of the people at that time. At first they hesitated to pay any attention to the Baptist, but eventually, sent delegates to ask who he was and what right he had to urge people to repentance.

I . . . Christ : The people were evidently saying that John the Baptist was the long-expected Messiah (anointed-Christ). The "Jews," that is, the Priests and Levites, were wondering if this could be so. The Baptist declared without hesitation that *he* was not the Messiah, but that the Messiah was "already in their midst."

Elijah . . . prophet: It was fairly commonly held among the Jews that Elijah, the great prophet of the ninth century (see 3 Kgs. 19 : 1—21 : 27), would return to earth and help to establish God's kingdom (Mal. 3 : 23). Because of Deuteronomy 18 : 15, there were also expectations of a prophet who would take part in the founding of the new messianic age. This is why the delegation asked John if he were Elijah or *the prophet*. John denied he was *a prophet* in the sense that they understood the term.

the voice . . . wilderness: In answer to their further questioning he tells them that he is the fulfillment of Isaiah's prophecy. He is preaching in the desert, trying to prepare the people to meet their Messiah, by straightening out their lives and by true repentance of their past sins.

I baptize with water: It seemed to the Priests and Levites that washing the repentant with water to signify their interior conversion, was a religious function which this John had no right to carry out. He tells them that his baptism is only a symbolic action. But the one who is soon to come ("he stands already among you") will have power greater than the Baptist, and greater than the Priests and Levites.

one . . . not know: The "Jews," those who later bitterly opposed Christ, were already beginning their opposition. Unlike the ordinary rank and file of the Jews, they had not only no intention of repentance but hoped to stop this preaching and talk of a Messiah. This seems to have been the purpose of the delegation. If the Baptist was not Elijah-returned-to-earth, nor the prophet-promised-by-Moses then he had nothing to do with the Messiah and had no right to prepare the people. Because of their stubborn pride, they never got to know their true Messiah.

whose sandal: The Baptist has an inkling of the true dignity of Christ; at least he feels he himself is not worthy to be even his menial servant.

Bethany: This is not the Bethany, near Jerusalem, where Martha, Mary and Lazarus lived but a place on the eastern bank of the Jordan, east of Jericho.

APPLICATION: "There was a man sent from God." In this man we see perhaps the only outstanding example among a multitude, of the workings of God's providence among men. The conception, birth, hermitical life in the desert, and the role of precursor of the Messiah, are all the effects of God's intervention in our behalf. John the Baptist was sent by God: "to bear witness to the Light" of the world, to tell the remnant of the Chosen People (and through them the world) that God's eternal plan for man was being implemented; that the incarnation of his divine Son had taken place. John's testimony was surely world-shaking news. Weak, mortal men were to be changed into sons of God by adoption. Pardon for their many sins would be earned by the bodily sufferings of the incarnate one. His resurrection would conquer death. Men would rise again and enter into the everlasting life of the divine Trinity.

Down through two thousand years or so, God had been preparing the world of man for this staggering event. As a special people, he chose Abraham and his descendants. He revealed to them something of his eternal nature and especially his fatherly interest in the human beings he had created. Through his prophets he gave them some fairly clear indications of the culmination of his eternal plan for men, namely, the fact of the incarnation.

John was the last of the great line of prophets and he was the greatest of them all. It was his privilege to point out to his audience the Son of God in human nature, the "Lamb of God who takes away the sin of the world," and also to hear God's voice from heaven proclaiming Christ to be his "beloved Son." He was surely a man sent from God.

John was sent not only for his contemporaries, for the Jews of his day, but for men of all time. Over the past two thousand years the good news of the incarnation, of our redemption and exaltation, has reached the greater part of mankind. But like the delegates who came down from Jerusalem that day in the year 30 A.D., there have been, in all generations, those who will not hear. These are men who, like the leaders of the Jews in the Baptist's day, are so self-centered and proud that they think they have no need for God or his providence in their lives.

Let those of us who believe in God and who know what he has done to give our life on earth its true purpose and meaning, show him by a faithful service how grateful we are for his infinite mercy and kindness. Let us listen to the call of John the Baptist, and from our hearts repent of our sins. Let us prepare for Christmas, the anniversary of Christ's human appearance on earth, by cleansing ourselves of all sinful attachments, by making a firm resolution to follow the Lamb through life. By so doing we too shall "bear witness to the light." Our living faith will illumine the darkness for others and they, too, will hear the call of God. In that way, each one of us can be another John the Baptist, by giving testimony to God's fatherly interest in all men. Thus can we lead our careless or indifferent brothers back on to the path of salvation, the road to heaven.

FOURTH SUNDAY OF ADVENT

FIRST READING: 2 Samuel 7:1-5; 8-11; 16. When King David dwelt in his house, and the Lord had given him rest from all his enemies round about, the king said to Nathan the prophet, "See now, I dwell in a house of cedar, but the ark of God dwells in a tent." And Nathan said to the king, "Go, do all that is in your heart; for the Lord is with you."

But that same night the word of the Lord came to Nathan, "Go and tell my servant David, 'Thus says the Lord: Would you build me a house to dwell in? Now therefore thus you shall say to my servant David, Thus says the Lord of hosts, I took you from the pasture, from following the sheep, that you should be prince over my people Israel; and I have been with you wherever you went, and have cut off all your enemies from before you; and I will make for you a great name, like the name of the great ones of the earth. And I will appoint a place for my people Israel, and will plant them, that they may dwell in their own place, and be disturbed no more; and violent men shall afflict them no more, as formerly, from the time that I appointed judges over my people Israel; and I will give you rest from all your enemies. Moreover the Lord declares to you that the Lord will make you a house. And your house and your kingdom shall be made sure for ever before me; your throne shall be established for ever.'"

EXPLANATION: When David was anointed king in Hebron by all the tribes of Israel and Judah, his first step was to capture Jerusalem from the Jebusites, and make it the political capital of his kingdom. To ensure the continued loyalty of all the tribes, he determined to make it the religious center also. Having brought the Ark of the Covenant—the symbol of Yahweh's presence amongst his Chosen People—into the city, he decided to build a temple worthy of Yahweh and worthy to house his Ark there. But Yahweh decreed otherwise. David would not build a "house" for Yahweh, but instead, Yahweh would "make him a house"—a house that would last, for there would be forever a successor to sit on his throne.

This promise made to David is but a recapitulation of the patriarchal promises made to Abraham, Isaac, Jacob and Judah. The blessings promised to all nations through the intermediary of Abraham and his descendants, would come sometime in the future, channeled through the Davidic dynasty. The

Angel told Mary (today's gospel) that the son she was about to conceive would sit on "the throne of his father David, and reign over the house of Jacob forever" (Lk. 1 : 32–33). In other words, the promise made to David through the prophet Nathan, although if taken literally is only vaguely messianic, is to be fulfilled in Mary's Son—the Messiah.

David . . . enemies: Having taken Jerusalem and having subdued the hostile Philistines, David built himself a palace of cedarwood in Jerusalem and was living a life of peace and contentment.

Ark of God in a tent: David felt ashamed for providing for himself while the Ark of the Covenant—God's throne —had no lasting abode.

tell my servant David: The prophet Nathan agreed with David's plan to build a temple; this was his own personal opinion, but that night Yahweh told the prophet to inform David that this was not his wish. Yahweh recalls all he has hitherto done for David and promises peace to the king and his subjects for his lifetime. Yet for his own reasons, Yahweh does not want David to build him a temple.

the Lord . . . house: Yahweh promises David a lasting dynasty.

established forever: David's kingdom will last, and a direct descendant of his shall sit on his throne forever. This promise was not fulfilled in the political sense. We know that the last of David's successors on the throne of Judah was Joachin, who died an exile in Babylon, sometime after 560 B.C. There were no further kings after him. Today's gospel tells us that a descendant of David according to the flesh, namely, the Messiah, would re-establish the Davidic throne and reign as King of Kings for ever.

APPLICATION: God's ways are not man's ways. There is a message (apart from the messianic prophecy) in today's reading for all of us. We make plans, even noble plans, with high spiritual ideals. But for some reason, known to God, they are not what he wants. David's plan to build a temple worthy of God in Jerusalem, would seem to us to have been a noble thought, one worthy of David's gratitude to and respect and reverence for the God who had given him Jerusalem and had established his rule there over the Chosen People. Even the prophet Nathan, speaking as a man, not as God's mouthpiece, agreed heartily with this noble intention expressed by David. But, as Nathan learned that night, this was not in accordance with God's will.

David's good intentions, however, did not go unrewarded. God promised to give him a house, a dynasty, that would last forever. And even though David sinned grievously later, God forgave him and did not withdraw his promise. Christ, David's descendant, rules now over the Church, the messianic temple on earth. He is ruling and will rule forever over the Church triumphant in heaven.

How often in our lives have we not felt that God seemed to reject our overtures and our plans to do big things for him? For instance, how many devout parents, who by word and example did everything to foster a religious vocation in a son or daughter, found later that God evidently did not want their child among his religious? God had his reasons, but he did not reveal them to the disappointed parents. How often have we seen a young missionary, who had worked hard for years to learn the language and customs of the mission country, compelled to return home—all his efforts wasted—because of ill-health which God could so easily have averted! How many times has the breadwinner, the ideal husband and father whose ambition it was to give his children all they needed to enable them to take their place in this life, and reap their eternal reward—how often has God taken him before he could put his noble and devout plans into effect?

Our lives are dotted with these question-marks. Again and again we hear of prayers for essential spiritual favors unanswered by God. If given, these answers would bring immense benefits to his pilgrim Church. Yet, his answer is not forthcoming! It would seem as if he did not appreciate our good motives and our good intentions! But today's reading shows that this is not the case. God views this world from eternity; each of us sees a little bit of it from his own tiny corner. God is planning for all time; our view is restricted to a few short years. Although God's view is from eternity, this does not mean that our efforts and our good intentions, restricted though they be, go unnoticed and unrewarded. The fact, like David, that he has not allowed us to carry out our generous plans does not mean that he has no interest in us. He has greater plans for us, as he had for David.

God is weaving a beautiful, colored tapestry of the life story of the human race. Each one of us is but a tiny spot in that picture. But each spot, no matter how tiny, brings out the beauty of the whole canvas. We may want, from the noblest and highest of motives, to be different, but the divine Artist knows better. We may be most anxious to do bigger and better things for him, to occupy more of the canvas, but the darker and smaller spots are as necessary for the total tapestry as are the bright, extended colors. Furthermore, if God chooses us for the less glamorous roles, it is because these roles are necessary and he knows we are the very ones best suited to fulfill them. On the other hand, the bigger and the more honorable tasks may be those which the less willing subjects of God may be moved to carry out. David was, on the whole, loyal to God. He had moments of weakness but he humbly repented when he realized his guilt. Solomon, his son, for whom God reserved the building of his temple, did little else for God. The work and sincerity he put into the construction of the temple may have been for him the means of earning his eternal salvation.

Let us, therefore, gladly accept whatever position God has wisely chosen for us in his tapestry. He is planning for all men. He knows what suits us best and what suits others. We can be certain that none of our good intentions, none of our sincere desires to do greater things for him, will go unrewarded, even though he may not want us to carry out these intentions. David was not allowed to build the house of God in Jerusalem, but God planned to build and establish his house, his dynasty, for all eternity.

SECOND READING: Romans 16:25-27. Now to him who is able to strengthen you according to my gospel and the preaching of Jesus Christ, according to the revelation of the mystery which was kept secret for long ages but is now disclosed and through the prophetic writings is made known to all nations, according to the command of the eternal God, to bring about the obedience of faith—to the only wise God be glory for evermore through Jesus Christ! Amen.

EXPLANATION: St. Paul's letter to the Romans is very different from his other letters. In the others the Apostle is writing to churches which he had evangelized either personally or through one of his companions. The purpose of these letters is generally to answer questions concerning faith or practices which had arisen after he had moved on to another region to preach the gospel. When he wrote this letter he had not as yet been in Rome. The Church there had been founded by others. He intended going there however, and his letter is more or less an introduction of himself to the Christians in Rome and a synthesis (incomplete) of his theology. We read today the concluding verses of this letter. They repeat briefly the main points of doctrine expounded there.

To him ... able: Glory and thanks are due to God the Father who has planned (from eternity) the salvation of all men, Jew and Gentile alike.

according ... gospel: As this letter of mine shows, I have preached Jesus Christ as the God-man, sent by the Father for the eternal salvation of the world.

preaching of Jesus Christ: This is not Christ's own preaching, but Paul's (and the other Apostles'), concerning Jesus.

revelation ... mystery: Generations and generations had lived and died between the creation of man and the coming of Christ, yet God had not revealed his plan for man's eternal happiness until now: "it had been kept secret for long ages" for God's own wise reasons.

the prophetic writings: The Chosen People had been given partial revelation of what God was about to do for mankind. The prophets of the Old Testament had, at least vague, references to the future coming of Christ. But now— Christ having come—God's plan and purpose is "made known to all nations."

command ... faith: It is now God's will and command that his plan of salvation, and the fact of the incarnation of his divine Son, should be made known to all men. The reason for this is that they would accept and follow Christ in obedience to the will of God, by living the Christian faith.

glory ... Christ: Paul asks the Roman Christians to give glory and gratitude to the all-wise God for the infinite kindness and love he has shown toward all men. This glory can be given to God through Jesus Christ, the Savior and Mediator. He was sent by God to raise us up to sonship with himself.

APPLICATION: This is the last Sunday of our preparation for Christmas, the feast which commemorates the birth of Christ. These words of St. Paul have been selected in order to remind us of the sublime facts commemorated at Christmas. In his infinite love and interest in his creatures, God the Father sent his beloved Son in human nature to live amongst us, to tell us of the Father's love and plans for our happiness. More than that, because of our sins he was to suffer and die for us. But he would rise again and conquer death for all. By becoming man Christ elevated our nature when he united it with his own divine nature. He made us adopted sons of God with a claim to eternal life and the possibility of sharing in God's kingdom forever.

This is what our Christian faith means. This is the gospel, the good news that Paul and the other Apostles preached. This is the consolation and strength which gives meaning to our otherwise miserable lives on earth. In our obedience to Christ and his gospel it enables us to rise above our weaknesses and failings and to persevere in spite of adversity.

For every true Christian Christmas is a time of rejoicing. It is a time when we think of our family and friends and show them our love. It is a time when we think of the poor, the needy, and the homeless. We try to do all we can to make things a little brighter for our fellowmen. It is a season in which we should think especially of the really poor and destitute, those namely, who do not know of God's love, who have not heard of Christ or, having heard, refused to accept his story. These are men and women who do not know the great future God has prepared for them, and have nothing to look forward to but the grave.

These are the poorest among the poor of this earth. These are our fellowmen,

our brothers and sisters, who are most in need of our charity at Christmas and all through the year. Unfortunately, we are not like St. Paul. But insignificant and ungifted though we may be, if we have true love of God and neighbor, each one of us will find many ways in which we can help to bring the light of the Christian faith to those who have it not. To live our own Christian lives sincerely and faithfully is the first step we can take in bringing the faith to others. Constant example, day in and day out, will eventually penetrate to the most closed and sealed-off mind. One truly exemplary Christian can edify and inspire a whole parish. Twenty such Christians could convert the whole neighborhood. In a few short years St. Francis of Assisi renovated and revitalized the Christian faith of a great part of Europe.

Finally, St. Paul's words today remind us to give glory to God this Christmas and always, for the marvelous things he has done for us. Our Christian faith is a gift given us by God. The essence and the basis of that faith is the fact of the incarnation : the Son of God humiliated himself and came down to our level, to our lowly human state, in order to raise us up to brotherhood with himself and sonship with his Father. We can never thank God sufficiently for this generosity and love. Eternity itself will not be long enough for us to render thanks. But God will accept the little we can do to show our appreciation. Let us do that little this Christmas, and for the rest of our lives.

GOSPEL : Luke 1 : 26–38. The angel Gabriel was sent from God to a city of Galilee named Nazareth, to a virgin betrothed to a man whose name was Joseph, of the house of David; and the virgin's name was Mary. And he came to her and said, "Hail, full of grace, the Lord is with you!" But she was greatly troubled at the saying, and considered in her mind what sort of greeting this might be. And the angel said to her, "Do not be afraid, Mary, for you have found favour with God. And behold, you will conceive in your womb and bear a son, and you shall call his name Jesus. He will be great, and will be called the Son of the Most High; and the Lord God will give to him the throne of his father David, and he will reign over the house of Jacob for ever; and of his kingdom there will be no end."

And Mary said to the angel, "How can this be, since I have no husband?" And the angel said to her, "The Holy Spirit will come upon you, and the power of the Most High will overshadow you; therefore the child to be born will be called holy, the Son of God. And behold, your kinswoman Elizabeth in her old age has also conceived a son; and this is the sixth month with her who was called barren. For with God nothing will be impossible." And Mary said, "Behold, I am the handmaid of the Lord; let it be to me according to your word." And the angel departed from her.

EXPLANATION : Luke, a Gentile, was converted by St. Paul at Troas about the year 50 A.D. He soon became a fellow-worker with Paul in the spread of the faith. He had learned the gospel story from St. Paul. He had ample opportunity to get information from others also, while he was with Paul in Caesarea (Palestine) and Rome 58–63 A.D. For two years in Palestine he most probably met some of the Apostles and disciples and the Blessed Mother herself. He could have got his story of the infancy from her. Twice Luke tells us that "Mary stored up all these things (concerning the infancy of Christ) and treasured them in her heart" (Lk. 2 : 19 and 52). She could hardly forget these momentous happenings.

Nazareth : Luke, writing for Gentile converts, felt it necessary to explain where the little village of Nazareth was. Even the Jews at the time hardly knew of its existence.

virgin betrothed : The word "virgin" in Greek and Hebrew means a young girl of marriageable age. While Luke clearly indicates that Mary was and would remain a virgin in the strict sense, he is not stressing this here. She was promised in marriage to Joseph. Espousals were a solemn, binding contract among the Jews. They lasted a year. At the end of the year the groom took the bride to his own house and they then became man and wife. This happened only after Mary returned (three months later, at least) from her visit to Elizabeth (Mt. 1: 18–25).

of the house of David : Joseph was descended from David. Mary probably was also. The legal Davidic descent of Jesus is assured through the adopting father, Joseph, if not also through Mary.

Hail . . . with you : The angel's salutation is better translated : "rejoice favored one." God has chosen you for an essential and intimate role in his messianic plan. He "is with you," that is, he will aid you in carrying out this role. That Mary is "full of grace," the closest of all creatures to God, because of the all-important role given her as Mother of the Messiah, follows necessarily, but Luke is not stressing that here.

troubled . . . saying: She is naturally disturbed and surprised to hear herself called God's favored one; she had as yet no idea of why she should be called this.

behold . . . conceive: The angel now explains why she is so favored of God: she will become the Mother of the Messiah. She is about to conceive a son who will be called:

the Son . . . High: In Hebrew terminology this title would not necessarily be taken literally—kings and others were sons of the Most High—but in verse 35 Luke through the words of the angel, gives its literal meaning: "The child to be born will be the true Son of God."

him . . . David: This is a reference to God's messianic promise to David which was given through the prophet Nathan (see today's first reading).

kingdom . . . end: The messianic kingdom would not be of this world, as our Lord told Pilate (Jn. 18 : 36), but an eternal kingdom in the after-life.

since . . . husband: How could this be when she was not yet married? She was betrothed to Joseph but the actual marriage had not yet taken place. She evidently understood the angel's message to imply that the conception of her child would take place immediately. Others

see here a reference to a vow of perpetual virginity, made by Mary before her espousal, and accepted by Joseph. This would be a most unusual occurrence among Jews, but not impossible. The virginal conception of Jesus is clearly stated in Matthew's gospel (Mt. 1 : 25). The fact of Mary's perpetual virginity, with or without a vow, has been the constant teaching of the Church.

Holy Spirit . . . you: The almighty power of God will produce this seeming impossible result: This power is attributed to the Spirit of God. That Spirit hovered over the waters to bring perfection out of the chaos (Gen. 1 : 2) and now hovers over Mary to bring perfection to humanity, which otherwise would remain in a chaotic state.

therefore . . . Son of God: The child who will be born will not be the son of any human father. This is what the angel had explained to Mary: he will be conceived by the power of God alone, and will *therefore* be the "son of God" in an entirely new sense.

kinswoman Elizabeth: As if to prove his statement the angel tells her that her cousin has conceived a son "in her old age" for "with God nothing is impossible." Mary, unlike Zachariah, had not asked for a sign or a proof from the angel, but she got one.

handmaid of the Lord: She who has been chosen from all eternity to be the "Mother of God" humbly accepts and looks on herself as God's handmaid or servant. Gladly will she do whatever God wants of her.

APPLICATION: At the moment our Lady said: "be it done to me according to thy word" the most stupendous event that ever happened, or ever could happen on earth, took place on this planet of ours. The Son of God took on human nature in the womb of the Blessed Virgin. We are familiar with this story from childhood. We often say the Angelus in which this tremendous act of God's love is described. Although familiarity in this case does not breed contempt, it does help to blunt the real impact on our minds of such an extraordinary occurrence. If God had created a very special child, and made him into an outstanding saint, so that he could intercede with God for us, this would be a great act of love for us on God's part. Or, if he had sent an angel from heaven in human form, to teach us all about God and to help us to lead holy lives, this would deserve our deepest gratitude. But neither a saintly man, nor a holy angel could do for us all that God wanted. No man or angel could make us adopted sons of God and heirs of heaven. It was necessary, in God's plan for us, that his divine Son should become man, should share our humanity, so that we could share his divinity.

Could infinite love have gone any further? Our creation, the fact that we exist as human beings on earth, is a great gift to us on the part of God. Of what value could eighty, a hundred, even seven hundred years of a continuously happy life on this earth be for us if we learned that we had to depart this life forever one day? In a world tormented by sin and its evil effects our normal span of life would be less satisfying. However, when God created us, he so planned that our stay here would be but a stage, a stepping stone in fact, toward our everlasting home. We are well aware indeed of the lengths to which God's love has gone in order to make us his children and heirs to his kingdom. Are we, however, grateful to him for the love he has shown us? Are we honestly and sincerely trying to make ourselves worthy of the great future he has in store for us?

Today is a suitable occasion to look right into our hearts, to see how we stand with God. During the week we shall be keeping the feast of Christmas. The Baby in the manger will remind us of what God has done and is still doing for us. What are we doing in return? Have we shown our gratitude by living as true followers of Christ? If most of us must answer: "no," this is the time to change our course and return to the right road once more. God is asking this of us today. Shall our answer be: "behold here I am Lord, your humble and grateful servant, let it be done to me according to your word"?

CHRISTMAS : MIDNIGHT MASS

FIRST READING: Isaiah 9:2-7. The people who walked in darkness have seen a great light; those who dwelt in a land of deep darkness, on them has light shined. Thou hast multiplied the nation, thou hast increased its joy; they rejoice before thee as with joy at the harvest, as men rejoice when they divide the spoil. For the yoke of his burden, and the staff for his shoulder, the rod of his oppressor, thou hast broken as on the day of Midian. For every boot of the tramping warrior in battle tumult and every garment rolled in blood will be burned as fuel for the fire. For to us a child is born, to us a son is given; and the government will be upon his shoulder, and his name will be called "Wonderful Counsellor, Mighty God, Everlasting Father, Prince of Peace." Of the increase of his government and of peace there will be no end, upon the throne of David, and over his kingdom, to establish it, and to uphold it with justice and with righteousness from this time forth and for evermore. The zeal of the Lord of hosts will do this.

EXPLANATION: The prophet Isaiah (765-700 B.C.) has many references to the future Messiah. This prophecy, just read, was spoken very probably soon after the northern kingdom Israel had been destroyed and its inhabitants taken prisoner to Assyria (722 B.C.). The words of the prophet were intended to console the "remnant," those who were left behind. Even though things looked dismal and depressing, a day would come when God would bring joy and happiness once more to the land and to its people—that would be the day of the Messiah.

seen a great light: A complete change has (will) come—the people will rejoice like the farmer rejoices when harvest is plentiful or like soldiers who have won and are dividing the spoils they captured.

yoke . . . oppressor: They will be slaves no longer; they will be free.

day of Midian: As narrated in the book of Judges (7 : 1–8; 28) the Judge Gedeon inflicted a crushing defeat on the Midianites who had been harassing the Chosen People. This victory was remembered and spoken of for centuries.

boot . . . garment: There will be an end to wars.

for . . . a child is born to us: The cause of the great change that will come over the land and its people is the birth of a new King—the birth of a son of David who will establish David's throne forever as the prophet Nathan had foretold (2 Sm. 7 : 14).

Wonderful Counselor : The titles given to the new-born King imply that he will have the wisdom of Solomon, the valor of David and the virtues of Moses and the Patriarchs. In other words, he is the ideal King, the last and true representative of David's line. The description could not apply to any earthly king who held the throne of David; it was fulfilled in the Messiah only.

peace . . . no end : He will bring peace among men and peace between man and God. His Kingdom will be vast.

justice . . . righteousness : The qualities and prerogatives of a wise king.

Lord of hosts : His coming and his gifts will be the work of the all-powerful God—the "God of hosts," who is moved by his love and fidelity to his promises, "his zeal" to do this for us. It is for "us he is born," it is to "us he is given."

APPLICATION : What Isaiah foresaw some 700 years before it happened we are commemorating tonight nearly 2,000 years after it happened, and it will still be commemorated 2,000 years from today if this world will still be in existence. God came on our earth, became one of us so that we could become one with God. This is incomparably greater than any other historical event that ever happened or ever could happen on our planet.

Yet unfortunately there are millions of people who have not yet heard this good news, but its good effects will reach them if their ignorance is not their fault. There are millions of others who have heard this good news but refuse to believe it. The basic reason for their disbelief is not that it couldn't be true, but that it is too good to be true. It is indeed hard to believe that the infinite, all-perfect God should bother with such imperfect, such mean creatures, as we are. But it is because he is infinite and his love is infinite that he can and did go to such lengths for us his unworthy creatures.

While we thank God tonight with true sincerity and heartfelt gratitude, for all he has done for us, and while we promise faithfully to try to make ourselves less unworthy of the infinite love he has shown us in the Incarnation, let us remember all those millions of our brothers who do not really know him yet. Let us beg God to send them the goods news and the grace to accept this great gift of infinite love, so that all his children on earth may know and thank him too. And let us strive by the example of a truly Christian life to make God's love for us known not only to our fellow-Christians but to all men.

SECOND READING: Epistle to Titus 2:11-4. The grace of God has appeared for the salvation of all men, training us to renounce irreligion and worldly passions, and to live sober, upright, and godly lives in this world, awaiting our blessed hope, the appearing of the glory of our great God and Savior Jesus Christ, who gave himself for us to redeem us from all iniquity and to purify for himself a people of his own who are zealous for good deeds.

EXPLANATION: Titus was a Gentile convert of St. Paul to whom he then became a faithful companion and fellow-worker in his missionary labors. Some years after his conversion he was appointed in charge of the church in Crete, its first overseer or Bishop. While there Paul wrote this letter to him calling him his "beloved son in the common faith." In the letter he exhorts him to be zealous for the spread of the faith and gives him counsels and instructions to guide him in his episcopal office. Titus and his Christians must be an example in all things for:

the grace of God: Translations differ here, but the basic meaning is the same, namely, salvation has been given to all men through God's merciful love (his grace) for us. It was Christ who brought us this free gift of God.

renounce irreligion: The following of Christ's teaching forbids the converts to imitate the practices and sexual aberrations of the pagan world; instead the Christian was expected to use the things of this world temperately and justly, that is, with respect for neighbor, and piously, that is, being faithful to God.

awaiting our blessed hope: Keeping an eye fixed firmly on the great day that was to come.

glory . . . Christ: The day of reward when Christ comes in glory to judge the world. St. Paul, since the day of his conversion on the road to Damascus, had never the slightest doubt as to the divinity of Christ. Here as in all his Epistles he expressly calls Christ God.

gave himself for us: This same Jesus Christ who was God was also true man and offered himself (his human nature) as a sacrifice for us on Calvary.

a people of his own: a Chosen People. The Jews were the Chosen People of the Old Covenant. Christians, whether of Jewish or Gentile origin, are the Chosen People of the New Covenant.

zealous for good deeds: The essence of the Christian life.

APPLICATION: Christmas is an occasion for rejoicing, a season of good-will, a time of joy even for those who unfortunately do not know or realize its true meaning. For us Christians it is the second of our greatest annual feasts (next after Easter) in which we call to mind God's infinite love for us and his infinite mercy towards us mortals.

We surely have reason to rejoice and be glad. Christ, the true Son of God, the Second Person of the Blessed Trinity, took to himself our lowly human nature and became one with us in order to raise us up to the dignity of adopted sons of his heavenly Father. If some earthly king or nobleman took the son of one of his servants into his palace, clothed him in costly robes and made him his heir, the world would gasp in amazement. God has taken us, his lowly creatures; has clothed us in the divine garments of grace; has made us one of his family by making his Son one of us, and has made us heirs of an eternal kingdom.

And yet mankind can ignore or forget such an act of benevolence, such a proof of divine love! Of course, we Christians do not ignore or forget this divine benevolence but we just do not remember it as much as we should; we do not thank God often enough for all he has done for us; too often we are ungrateful children.

Tonight, as we call to mind the infinite love of God which sent his Son on earth to be born of the virgin Mary in a stable in Bethlehem so that we could spend our eternity in the mansions of heaven, let us show our gratitude, our appreciation, by resolving to live as adopted sons of God are expected to live.

St. Paul's letter to Titus tells us how. We must reject ungodliness and worldly lusts by living temperately, justly and piously, using the things of this world as stepping-stones to heaven. God has made us his Chosen People; nay more! he has made us his adopted sons. Let us show our true gratitude by striving to live a life worthy of such a sublime vocation.

GOSPEL : Luke 2 : 1–14. A decree went out from Caesar Augustus that all the world should be enrolled. This was the first enrollment, when Quirinius was governor of Syria. And all went to be enrolled, each to his own city. And Joseph also went up from Galilee, from the city of Nazareth, to Judea, to the city of David, which is called Bethlehem, because he was of the house and lineage of David, to be enrolled with Mary, his betrothed, who was with child. And while they were there, the time came for her to be delivered. And she gave birth to her first-born son and wrapped him in swaddling cloths, and laid him in a manger, because there was no place for them in the inn.

And in that region there were shepherds out in the field, keeping watch over their flock by night. And an angel of the Lord appeared to them, and the glory of the Lord shone around them, and they were filled with fear. And the angel said to them, "Be not afraid; for behold, I bring you good news of a great joy which will come to all the people; for to you is born this day in the city of David a Savior, who is Christ the Lord. And this will be a sign for you : you will find a babe wrapped in swaddling cloths and lying in a manger." And suddenly there was with the angel a multitude of the heavenly host praising God and saying, "Glory to God in the highest, and on earth peace among men with whom he is pleased!"

EXPLANATION :

world . . . enrolled : The Roman Emperor Augustus ordered a general census of his empire; this was the whole world in his eyes.

Joseph . . . went . . . Bethlehem : The Jewish family records were kept in the ancestral town or village. As Joseph was descended from David, Bethlehem was the ancestral home.

with Mary : It was only the father of the household who had to register, but Joseph could not leave Mary alone in Nazareth at this critical time for her;

besides it was God's will that she should go to Bethlehem (whether she realized this or not) for Bethlehem was to be the birthplace of her Son, Christ.

first-born son : It does not follow from this that there were other children later. The first-born was a title which emphasized the dignity and rights of the child.

no place for them : Most likely because they were too poor to pay the innkeeper or when they arrived the inn was already full. They found shelter in a stable, and there Christ was born.

shepherds ... in the fields : These humble men who live close to nature were evidently close to God too for it was to them and not the learned or wealthy of Bethlehem that he sent his messenger.

be not afraid : The sudden appearance of this divine messenger, in human form evidently, naturally caused them to be alarmed.

news of a great joy : The shepherds, like all Jews of the time, and perhaps more so than most Jews, were anxiously awaiting the Messiah.

city of David : The divine messenger emphasizes the Davidic descent of the newly-born, for thus the prophecies were fulfilled.

in a manger : The long-promised heir to the throne of David, the royal descendant of the great king was born in a stable and was resting on a bed of straw in a manger! What a test for the faith of anyone who judges by earthly standards. But a greater test was still to come.

Christ the Lord : This baby in these lowly circumstances, poorer even than the poorest who had some little hovel and some poor cradle of his own, was not only the expected Messiah, the heir of the royal David, but he was also the Lord—a title reserved to God in the Old Testament.

Glory to God : Praise and thanksgiving to the great God who is the supreme ruler of all things.

peace . . . pleased : peace to men who are God's friends—who have God's benevolence, "Good-will." Here we have the first verse of the hymn of praise and thanksgiving which is sung or said at every Mass, given to us by the messengers God sent to the shepherds of Bethlehem that first Christmas night. The coming of the Messiah was the beginning of the era in which true praise and thanks could be offered to God. Man alone of his own powers could not offer praise worthy of God, but united to the God-man Christ his acts of praise would have a divine value, for they would be offered in union with Christ. Peace was another consequence of the coming of Christ—man could now be at peace with God and would be at peace with his neighbor if he followed Christ's teaching.

APPLICATION : Tonight as we kneel before the Baby in the Manger in praise and thanksgiving to the Son of infinite love and mercy let not our amazement at the humility and poverty of the stable and manger, touching though they be, prevent us from seeing the greater, the almost incredible, humiliation of the Incarnation itself. Had our Savior been born in Herod's marble palace in Jerusalem and laid on a gilded cot with covers of the finest silk, his becoming man would yet have been a humbling, a lowering of himself, which would stagger the human mind. There are those who puzzle over and try to explain the mystery of the Incarnation—how Christ, namely, could be God and man at the same time, how one Person could have two natures. But mystery though this is, and fully intelligible to God only, the mystery of the love of God who did this *for us* is a greater mystery still and more of a puzzle to our finite human minds. "What is man that God should be mindful of him?" What have we ever done or what could we ever do to merit such love, such mercy, such condescension? No, we did not merit such love but the infinitely unselfish generosity of God, which no human mind is capable of grasping, has done this. We are his creatures who are capable of sharing his own happiness with him for all eternity and he has arranged it that we shall do so.

All we can do is to say from our heart a humble, thank you God, and to resolve to have the sense to avail ourselves of this almost incredible offer. We are "God's friends." He has called us so, then let us do our best to retain this friendship than which there is nothing greater for us on earth or in heaven. If we do, and if we do the little he asks of us, he will do his part; he will give us our share in the eternal happiness the Incarnation has won for us.

MASS AT DAWN

FIRST READING: Isaiah 62:11–12. Behold, the Lord has proclaimed to the end of the earth: Say to the daughter of Zion, "Behold, your salvation comes; behold, his reward is with him, and his recompense before him." And they shall be called the holy people, the redeemed of the Lord; and you shall be called Sought out, a city not forsaken.

EXPLANATION: This second section of the book of Isaiah was written after the return from the Babylonian exile. The lot of the returned exiles was sad, the country desolate, most of Jersualem still in ruins, the people depressed almost to despair. The writer has words of consolation and encouragement for his compatriots. They must trust in God's promise and pray for its fulfillment. There are great things in store for Judah and Jerusalem.
the Lord ... proclaimed: Through the prophet God is making known not only to the Jews but to all people what he is about to do for his Chosen People. This work of his, therefore, was not only for the Jews but for all nations.
daughter of Zion: Zion is another name for Jerusalem. Its citizens, the Chosen People, were God's spouse, their capital city his daughter.
your salvation comes: To the mind of the prophet the Savior, the promised Messiah, is already on the point of coming.

his reward . . . his recompense : He will come as a conqueror carrying the "prize of his victory" and "his trophies" (in Hebrew); his battle already won. It is understood this victory is for his people. **They shall be called :** Those for whom he comes will be

holy people . . . redeemed . . . Lord :

His victory for them is a spiritual victory now brought (or bought) back to the Lord, to God.

not forsaken : People will throng to the new Jerusalem. It will no longer be deserted, it will be renowned, not forsaken.

APPLICATION : These few lines from the book of Isaiah have been chosen to remind us of the blessings the promised Messiah of the Old Testament brought us when he came and formed the New. He redeemed us by his death on the cross. He has made a new covenant with us, an everlasting covenant unlike the old which was only preparatory and therefore temporary. He has made us the new Chosen People, chosen so that we could be holy and near to God. He has won for us and promised to us, not the holy land of Palestine which the first covenant promised, but the abode of eternal happiness, heaven, the new Jerusalem which will be renowned and

glorious forever.

We surely have reason to thank God for sending us our Savior and for having made us members of his Chosen People, the mystical body of Christ, his church. We can never be worthy of such an honor, but let each one of us examine himself and see if he is trying to be less unworthy, trying to get rid of the attractions of this earth which impede his heavenward journey.

Our welcome for Christ this Christmas Day and our thanks to him for coming and doing what he did for us will be sincere if we are sincerely trying to live up to our high vocation as the holy Chosen People of the new covenant.

SECOND READING : Titus 3 : 4–7. When the goodness and loving kindness of God our Savior appeared, he saved us, not because of deeds done by us in righteousness, but in virtue of his own mercy, by the washing of regeneration and renewal in the Holy Spirit, which he poured out upon us richly through Jesus Christ our Savior, so that we might be justified by his grace and become heirs in hope of eternal life.

EXPLANATION : For Titus and this Epistle see above in Second Reading of Midnight Mass.

When . . . kindness . . . our Savior appeared : The coming of the Savior, Christ, and his redemptive work on our behalf, is equated to the "goodness and kindness of God," this is the only explanation for the infinite love which the

Incarnation applies.

not . . . deeds : We did not, we could not, merit such kindness, it was a free gift of God's mercy.

washing of regeneration : The sacrament of Baptism regenerates us—we are given a new life, we share in God's life, for we become members of Christ's body who is God and man.

38 • THE SUNDAY READINGS

renewal in the Holy Spirit : In our Baptism the Holy Spirit enters into us and gives us the gifts of faith, hope and charity (see Romans 5 : 5) together with "abundant grace."

through Jesus Christ : All this Christ has merited for us through his life, death and resurrection. St. Paul in these few lines tells us how each person of the Blessed Trinity plays a part in our sanctification. The Father sends the Son in our human nature to merit heaven for us, the Holy Spirit applies his merits to us in Baptism (and later in the other sacraments).

we . . . heirs : Through Baptism and the grace of the Holy Spirit we are made capable of attaining to heaven, we are made heirs and sons of God. But we must cooperate with God's grace if our "hope of eternal life" is to be fulfilled.

APPLICATION : Christmas is the season of good-will—the season when every Christian worthy of the name strives to be good and kind to all his fellowmen. But this spirit of good-will, of love and kindness, should be active in our hearts all the year round and all our lives. It would be thus if only we reminded ourselves more frequently of the mystery of Christmas, the mystery of the Incarnation which was, and is, the gift of God's goodness and kindness to us. When he created us God gave us existence—he gave existence, life, to the plants and the animals too, but he gave us more than plant or animal life; he gave us the gift of intelligence and free-will which we call our soul, a gift which raises us above all other earthly creatures, makes us the masterpiece of God's creation and in a way, a finite way, like unto himself.

This is surely something we could never be too grateful for, but would it be enough to justify and satisfy these very gifts he has given us? Would sixty, seventy, even a hundred years of peace and plenty on this earth satisfy all our desires, would we want nothing more, would we have made full use of the spiritual powers within us in that short period? And if the answer is "no" even for those whose earthly span was lived in peace and plenty, what of the ninety-nine per cent of the human race whose lot on earth is one of struggle and strain, of hardship and heartbreak? Would their ambitions and desires be fulfilled? The answer of course is no, and the one who says the earthly grave is the end of man is not true to his intelligence and is denying intelligence to his Creator.

God's goodness and kindness in creating us had more in view for us than our span on this earth. He gave us gifts capable of knowing and understanding him and capable of enjoying a share in his own divine happiness. That we could share in that happiness forever, he provided for through his plan of the Incarnation—man could share in the eternal joy of the Trinity because God the Son shared our humanity with us. He raised up, regenerated our human nature, and thereby made us heirs of the everlasting life.

Our real purpose on earth is to get to heaven. This is God's plan for us and the only true explanation of our wonderful human nature. Christmas—the Incarnation of the Son of God—has given us the means and has shown us the way to get to heaven. Would we, could we, be so foolish as to refuse to go there?

GOSPEL : Luke 2 : 15–20. When the angels went away from them into heaven, the shepherds said to one another, "Let us go over to Bethlehem and see this thing that has happened, which the Lord has made known to us." And they went with haste, and found Mary and Joseph, and the babe lying in a manger. And when they saw it they made known the saying which had been told them concerning this child; and all who heard it wondered at what the shepherds told them. But Mary kept all these things, pondering them in her heart. And the shepherds returned, glorifying and praising God for all they had heard and seen, as it had been told them.

EXPLANATION :

when the angels : See Gospel of Midnight Mass.

let us go over : They accepted the word of the angel as the word of God and did not hesitate to do as they were told.

found Mary and Joseph : Luke puts Mary the wife before Joseph because he has already, in his account of the Annunciation (1 : 26–38), narrated the privileged position of Mary in the Incarnation and Joseph's secondary position as foster-father.

when they saw . . . known : The angel had told them they would find the Messiah—the promised Savior, descendant of King David, as a baby laid in a manger, but this baby was also the Lord. They now are convinced of the truth of the angel's good news.

All who heard : There was nothing marvelous about a baby being born, or a baby resting in a manger in those days of poverty. The shepherds had something more to tell that made the people marvel and that was, as the angel had said, that this baby was more than human, that he was divine as well—the Son of God.

Mary kept all . . . in her heart : Luke is hinting here as to the source of his information for the events he is narrating. Who else but Mary, whom he could, and almost certainly did, meet during the years 58-60 when he was in Palestine (while Paul was a prisoner in Caesarea—see Acts 21 : 15), could have known these facts? And was it likely that she could ever forget them?

Glorifying and praising God : Simple, honest, devout men, they returned to their daily task of minding their flocks but they returned, new men, full of praise and thanksgiving to God for the marvelous things he had done for them.

APPLICATION : These simple, uneducated shepherds show us what we should do today when thinking of Christmas and of God's marvelous kindness to us mortal men. They couldn't read or write but they could and did use their natural intelligence. They believed in God, the Creator of the universe; they believed he would fulfill the promises he had made to Abraham and to the Chosen People down through the centuries. They were told now by God's messenger that God had fulfilled his promise and, through grace given them, they saw how far the fulfillment exceeded the hopes of Abraham and of the Chosen People. The Babe in Bethlehem was greater than Abraham, greater than David, greater than all the prophets God had sent them down through the ages, for he was God as well as man. "They returned glorifying and praising God for all they had heard and seen."

Let us imitate those humble shepherds this morning. Let us too return after Mass to our homes, to our ordinary daily tasks, but with renewed spiritual strength, keeping ever before our minds what great things God has done for us. He has raised us up above and beyond our natural human selves. He has given us a supernatural life and a supernatural end and purpose, which is, eternal happiness. Our years on this earth may be short or long, pleasant or difficult, for the vast majority more difficult than pleasant. Whatever they may be, if we but keep our eye fixed on the glorious future that he has prepared for us, we'll use these years as the stepping-stones to get us across the river of life to our everlasting home.

Thank you, Jesus, Son of God, for becoming a Baby in Bethlehem so that I could become a fully-grown supernatural man as God's adopted son in heaven.

CHRISTMAS DAY : MASS

FIRST READING : Isaiah 52 : 7-10. How beautiful upon the mountains are the feet of him who brings good tidings, who publishes peace, who brings good tidings of good, who publishes salvation, who says to Zion, "Your God reigns." Hark, your watchmen lift up their voice, together they sing for joy; for eye to eye they see the return of the Lord to Zion. Break forth together into singing, you waste places of Jerusalem; for the Lord has comforted his people, he has redeemed Jerusalem. The Lord has bared his holy arm before the eyes of all the nations; and all the ends of the earth shall see the salvation of our God.

EXPLANATION : These words were written by a disciple of the great Isaiah, most probably in Babylon, to encourage the exiles. Their God would set them free and return them once more to a clean and purified Jerusalem. But this return, like the Exodus from Egypt centuries earlier, was a type or a foreshadowing of the greater redemption that was to come. The possession of the land of Canaan for a few years; the restoring of Jerusalem and Judah, were but pale shadows of the great restoration and the possession of our eternal "promised land" which were to be given in the days to come, not only to Israel but to all nations.

How beautiful . . . the feet . . . good tidings : The person who brings good tidings is always welcome. The writer sees the announcer of the good news as already present. His good news is that salvation is at hand, that peace has come, that war and exiles are over. The exiles in Babylon would naturally understand this of their return to Jerusalem, but there was much more than that in this message.

Zion, your God reigns: Many of the exiles expected the Davidic monarchy to be restored, because of the promise given to David (2 Sm. 7 : 14). But the returned exiles had no king until the true descendant of David, the promised Messiah, came. He was King as he admitted to Pilate and as the title on his cross proclaimed, but his kingdom "was not of this world."

Hark . . . voice : There were no watchmen on the walls of Jerusalem at the time as there were no walls and no city, but the prophet sees the future day when God will "redeem Jerusalem and comfort his people."

Lord has bared his holy arm : God has shown his power to all the nations.

the ends of the earth : The salvation which the prophet foresees is not just the return from Babylon which was for the Jews alone and did not interest the nations, but the universal redemption of all men in the messianic age.

APPLICATION : Today, Christmas Day, is the day when we commemorate the greatest, the mightiest, the most far-reaching event which ever took place in human history. No wonder we date our years from that event—the period that preceded it we call B.C., "before Christ's coming," the years since as "Anno Domini," the years of the Lord, the years which have elapsed since Christ came to assume the kingship of the world.

The good tidings—the gospel—of peace has been brought to us by no less a person than the Son of God himself. And he came not as a mighty prince in the prime of life, as he could have done, but he came into this world like one of ourselves born of a human mother, "taking the form of a slave," as St. Paul says, "like us in all things save sin." Not alone that but he chose the poorest (though holiest) of mothers who had to give birth to him in a stable. He could have been born in a palace—God could easily have arranged that, but he wanted it this way. He wanted to show us that it is not the things of this world that matter. Wealth and power, the goal and the god of so many foolish men, are empty baubles. We can have them and *perhaps* enjoy them for a few short years but what then? Naked we came into the world and naked we shall go out of it.

Thank God, true Christians, and you are among them, have accepted the good news Christ brought to the world, and are showing their joy and thankfulness for it by following it daily as well as they are able. We fail, yes, maybe often, but we are dealing with a merciful God who sees our good intentions and accepts them often for the good deeds we should have done. We need God's mercy, all of us, but this great and mighty act of God, the Incarnation, which we are celebrating today is such a proof of his love for man and his mercy for us, that we could never and should never despair of receiving that mercy, no matter how black our record, no matter how seriously we have sinned.

Let us therefore "shout for joy and break out in song" as the prophet tells us, together with all the Christians of the earth on this great festival. It is the festival of God's infinite love and mercy, the festival of our salvation and elevation to sonship with God. Nothing greater could have happened to human nature. The Incarnation is *the* event of human history.

SECOND READING: Hebrew 1:1-6. In many and various ways God spoke of old to our fathers by the prophets; but in these last days he has spoken to us by a Son, whom he appointed the heir of all things, through whom also he created the world. He reflects the glory of God and bears the very stamp of his nature, upholding the universe by his word of power. When he had made purification for sins, he sat down at the right hand of the Majesty on high, having become as much superior to angels as the name he has obtained is more excellent than theirs. For to what angel did God ever say, "Thou art my Son, today I have begotten thee?" Or again, "I will be to him a father, and he shall be to me a son?" And again, when he brings the firstborn into the world, "Let all God's angels worship him."

EXPLANATION:

God . . . spoke: On the Epistle to the Hebrews see Cycle C (3)—the 4th Sunday of Advent.

Down through almost two thousand years God spoke to the Chosen People through his deeds and through his mouthpieces—the patriarchs and the prophets.

in . . . various ways: At various times and in various ways. The author is thus bringing out the imperfection of the old revelation when compared with the new which was given *once and for all* by *one* person.

by a son: For the author, following his master and model St. Paul, Christ was unquestionably the Son of God.

heir of all things: In his human nature, after his resurrection, Christ was made heir of all things. As God in his divine nature he was from eternity heir of all things, Son of God.

through whom . . . world: The pre-existence of Christ is stated here, namely, in his divine nature. He cooperated with the Father and the Holy Spirit in the act of creation. In the Old Testament (Wisdom books), wisdom cooperated with God in creation; wisdom is personified and is really the Son (see Prov. 8:30. Wis. 7:22).

reflects the glory: Here the author is possibly using a more ancient liturgical hymn to give some idea of the divine nature of the Son in relation to the Father. He is the reflection, the reflected glory of the Father, as one's face is reflected in a mirror.

bears . . . very stamp: The Greek word translated "representation" is "character," the imprint of a seal, the mark of one thing found on something else. This stresses the exact similarity but at the same time the distinction of one from the other.

upholding . . . universe: The Son maintains all creation in existence and directs their courses "by his word of power," i.e. powerful word. All this stresses his divinity in which he is equal to the Father.

he . . . purification : Through his death in his human nature, the Son, Christ, has redeemed mankind and

sat . . . at the right hand : After his resurrection he has the place of honor in heaven in his human nature.

superior to . . . angels : The aim of the writer of this Epistle was to show the superiority of the new covenant over the old. It was superior because it was given by the Son of God who is superior not only to the prophets, priests and patriarchs but to the angels, the heavenly messengers sent from heaven in the old dispensation.

Thou art my son : The words of Ps. 2 : 7 and of 2 Sm. 7 : 14 refer directly to the king, but in their fuller sense they are fulfilled only in Christ. This is the inspired interpretation of the author of Hebrews.

let all . . . angels worship him : If the angels must adore the Son they are inferior to him (see Dt. 32 : 43).

APPLICATION : The Epistle to the Hebrews was written to show how superior the new covenant was to the old. It was written most probably to converts from Judaism who, because of persecution from Judaizers who were numerous at the time, were tempted to change back to the old law and religion. These six verses of its first chapter were chosen for today's reading because of the clear, definite and emphatic declaration of the divinity of Christ which they contain. The baby who was born in a stable in Bethlehem, lived and died in Palestine, rose the third day from the grave and ascended to heaven forty days later, was also God, equal to the Father in all things. This is a mystery beyond our human comprehension, yet it is a fact, stated by Christ himself, believed and preached by the Apostles and accepted by the Church for almost two thousand years.

To admit the fact of this mystery is no difficulty for anyone who believes in God. If God had no mysteries, if our finite minds could sound the depths of his nature, then he would not be God but a finite being like ourselves. We believe, and we know, because God has revealed it to us, that there are three persons in our one God, and that the Second Person, the Son, became man for our sakes. This may be a mystery to our limited intellectual powers, but it is a consoling fact and a source of joy and rejoicing to us this morning. It is also the basis of our hope of a great future— the Son of God, through his humanity and because of his infinite divine love for us, has made it possible for us to reach heaven when our earthly days are over.

While thanking God this morning for the privilege that is ours, let us not forget our non-Christian fellowmen who also are redeemed by the God-man. He wishes them all to share in this great blessing which his Incarnation brought to mankind. Our prayers can help to bring the light of faith to them. Let us be generous with this help—it will be one very effective way of showing God this morning that we realize how generous he was toward us and that we are truly grateful for his divine generosity.

GOSPEL: John 1: 1-18. In the beginning was the Word, and the Word was with God, and the Word was God. He was in the beginning with God; all things were made through him, and without him was not anything made that was made. In him was life, and the life was the light of men. The light shines in the darkness, and the darkness has not overcome it.

There was a man sent from God, whose name was John. He came for testimony, to bear witness to the light, that all might believe through him. He was not the light, but came to bear witness to the light.

The true light that enlightens every man was coming into the world. He was in the world, and the world was made through him, yet the world knew him not. He came to his own home and his own people received him not. But to all who received him, who believed in his name, he gave power to become children of God; who were born, not of blood nor of the will of the flesh nor of the will of man, but of God.

And the Word became flesh and dwelt among us, full of grace and truth; we have beheld his glory, glory as of the only Son from the Father. (John bore witness to him, and cried, "This was he of whom I said, 'He who comes after me ranks before me, for he was before me.' ") And from his fullness have we all received, grace upon grace. For the law was given through Moses; grace and truth came through Jesus Christ. No one has ever seen God; the only Son, who is in the bosom of the Father, he has made him known.

EXPLANATION: The gospel according to St. John was written long after the other three gospels. The essentials of the Christian faith had already been preached and accepted by thousands of Jews and Gentiles throughout the then-known world—the Roman Empire. The basic doctrine of the faith, that Christ who lived and died in Palestine, rose from the dead and ascended to heaven, was not a mere man but was the Son of God who took human nature for our salvation—this basic doctrine had been preached and believed for over sixty years before John's gospel was written. The other three Evangelists had already given a written synopsis of the faith that had been preached—they too had as their basic tenet the Incarnation. But John's gospel gives a more profoundly theological vision of Christ, the result of years of preaching and of meditating on this wondrous mystery of God's love. And while stressing the divinity of Christ he leaves no doubt as to the reality of his human nature. It was the God-man on whose breast he leaned at the Last Supper of whom he wrote.

In the beginning: While Mark begins with Christ's public life and Matthew and Luke go back to the birth in Bethlehem, John goes back to the beginning of time, when creation began and

was the Word: Christ already was. The Greek imperfect translated "was" means continuous, timeless existence.

the Word: John uses this Greek term "logos"=word to describe the Son as the emanation, the reproduction, the utterance of God. In the Old Testament the word of God meant the revelation of himself in power, in grace, in prophecy.

was with God: This "word" who was divine, was from eternity, was at the same time distinct from the Father (God with the article=Father in New Testament), so there are two persons (at least), two distinct individuals in the Godhead.

Word was God : God here, without the article, means the divinity. A clear statement that this Word was divine.

all things . . . made : This Second Person in the Godhead cooperated in the creation of all things, so he is not only distinct from creatures : he is their co-creator.

In him . . . life : The reference is to the supernatural life and light of revelation. The act of creation mentioned, referred to the natural life given us.

a man . . . name was John : This refers to the Baptist whose preaching prepared for the public ministry of Christ. He spoke of the revelation (the light) of the expected Messiah which was imminent.

He was in the world . . . made : God should have been known through his creatures (see Rom. 1 : 18–23) if men used their intelligence but they did not.

he came to his own : He came in the Incarnation to his own Chosen People and told them who he was, the Messiah and the Son of God, but they (that is, their leaders especially) received him not.

become children of God : The purpose of the Incarnation was to raise humanity to the supernatural level of adopted sons of God—those who accept Christ and keep his doctrine are capable of this divine sonship.

believed in his name : Name stands for person—belief in Christ is belief that he is the Son of God and therefore the source of all *grace* and *truth*.

not of blood . . . God : Those who accept Christ are re-born, regenerated, in a way that is not like the natural conception and birth—it is spiritual, it is "of God."

This verse can possibly refer to the human birth of Christ, too, namely, his birth from a virgin without human father (Jerusalem Bible).

Word became flesh : The Word was divine and continued to be divine, but at a particular moment in history (Greek aorist) it assumed human nature. The word "flesh" which St. John uses here was used in the Old Testament to signify all that was transitory, mortal, lowly and imperfect. John is here stressing the humiliation (the emptying of himself as St. Paul—Phil. 2 : 6—puts it) of Christ in the Incarnation.

dwelt among us : Pitched his tent (in Greek), became one of our tribe, one with us.

beheld his glory : John was one of the first four disciples who followed Christ. He was therefore a witness to Christ's public life from the Jordan to the Ascension.

only Son . . . Father : Having brought the hymn of the Incarnation to its climax —the Word taking flesh, John does not use this term Word any more—he speaks of Jesus Christ, the Son of God.

was before me : Evidently the Baptist knew by revelation of the divinity of Christ. The Baptist was senior to Christ in age—but Christ was (God) from the beginning.

from his fullness . . . received : Of the fullness of "grace and truth" which the God-man brought us, we have all received in the sacraments and in the Church he set up for us.

grace . . . upon grace : One grace brings another, or possibly the new covenant which replaces the old as the following verse clearly states.

no one . . . seen God : He is not visible to earthly human eyes but :

who . . . him known : God is made known to us through Christ; we can grasp the infinite love and mercy of God —his compassion, his understanding of us weak mortals through Christ's loving dealings with us and his gospel of mercy. Christ is God and is in intimate union with the Father, "in the bosom of the Father," hence even in his human nature he reflects the divinity.

APPLICATION : The message the Church wishes us to hear from the readings that are read at the Sunday Masses of Advent and at the three Christmas Masses is surely this : "God so loved the world (i.e. us) that he gave his only-begotten son for us." He gave his divine Son a human nature, to dwell among us, to teach us, and finally to die for us. And "who or what are we that he should be mindful of us?" Why did he go to such lengths for us? This is one of the questions to which we shall, please God, get the answer in heaven.

In the meantime all we can do is admit the fact that God loved us, that he has done wondrous things for us because of that love. One of these things, the greatest of them, is what today's gospel puts so clearly before us : it is the fact of the Incarnation which joined our human nature with the divinity in the Person of Christ, and thereby made us heirs of heaven.

We have forgotten this privilege, this gift, too often in the past and instead of being grateful to God we have insulted and offended him. Through our sinful acts we have told him we did not want him to be our Father, we did not want the eternal heaven his Son earned for us —we did not want his love.

This morning let us tell him we didn't really mean that. We want to love him and we want to go to heaven and with the help of his grace we shall endeavor in the future to be obedient and grateful children of his.

Today's fervor, of course, may not last—but our loving Father foresaw our weakness and left us the means of returning to him any time we fail. Let not our frailty then or our fickleness frighten us. We are dealing with the God of love, among whose sons there is no prodigal who is not welcome back, if he takes the first simple steps on the return journey.

SUNDAY IN THE OCTAVE OF CHRISTMAS.

FEAST OF THE HOLY FAMILY

FIRST READING: Sirach 3:2-6; 12-14. The Lord honored the father above the children, and he confirmed the right of the mother over her sons. Whoever honors his father atones for sins, and whoever glorifies his mother is like one who lays up treasure. Whoever honors his father will be gladdened by his own children, and when he prays he will be heard.

Whoever glorifies his father will have long life, and whoever obeys the Lord will refresh his mother.

O son, help your father in his old age, and do not grieve him as long as he lives; even if he is lacking in understanding, show forbearance, in all your strength do not despise him. For kindness to a father will not be forgotten, and against your sins it will be credited to you.

EXPLANATION: The author of this book was a pious Jew who lived in the second century B.C. He had made a deep study of the law and the revealed religion of his people, and moved by the love of God, of his Law, and of his religion, he wrote a collection of wise maxims to help others live a life pleasing to God. In the verses read today he speaks of the family:

the Lord ... the father: In God's plan for the spread of the human race, the family unit has its foundation. The father has the place of honor and the right to respect and obedience.

right of the mother: The mother shares the authority with the father in the home. It is God's will and decree that their authority be respected by the children.

honors his father ... glorifies his mother:

The children who respect and obey their parents are doing God's will and are thereby giving glory to God and storing up spiritual reward for themselves.

gladdened by ... children: The son (or daughter) who respects his parents will in turn be respected by his own children. God will bless him or her with children who will be dutiful and respectful in turn.

when he prays: Because he is pleasing to God, his prayers will be answered.

glorifies ... long life: A long life was looked on as a divine blessing. It is that, if properly lived. The longer we can work for God (and neighbor) in this life the greater the reward in heaven.

will refresh his mother: The obedient child is a comfort and a source of joy for his mother (and father). He will be obedient to his parents if he is obedient to God—this is one of God's commandments.

help your father in . . . age : It is in his later days a father needs the loving care of his children. Natural instinct and decency would demand this of children, but a greater authority still—the divine will—demands this of them.

do not grieve him : What greater grief could a father have in his old age than to have raised a son of whom he has to be ashamed. The child who has learned to respect his parents is respecting God, and will never cause his parents to be ashamed of him.

if . . . understanding : No matter how feeble, mentally or physically, one's parents may become, it is the children's duty to care for them. Those parents, when they had their health and strength, devoted their energies to their children—the children must now do their part.

kindness . . . not forgotten : God will repay the dutiful child. The kindness he shows his parents in their need is as good as, and better than any sacrifice he can offer in the temple. If he displeases God by neglecting his duty to his parents, no sacrifice of his can be acceptable to God.

credited to you : The full effects of obedience and respect for parents will have a lasting effect on the character of the child and its reward will be everlasting.

APPLICATION : Although all the emphasis, in these verses of holy Scripture just read to us, seems to be on the obligation of children to their parents, there is a profound lesson here for parents too. "Like father like son" is an old and a true saying very often. If the parents fail to do what is right and just in the sight of God they can hardly complain if their children turn out disobedient to God and to them. The young learn more from example than from precept. If parents give their children the example of a life of obedience to the laws of God, and their country—the children will in turn carry out their duties to God, to their parents and to their fellowman. There have been and there will be exceptions, of course, to this rule but they are exceptions; the vast majority follow the pattern laid down for them by their parents.

As you heard during your marriage ceremony: "children are a gift from God to you," a gift for this life to be the joy of your young years and a help and comfort in your old age; but above and beyond that, they are a gift which you must do all in your power to return to God when their hour comes. You must not only strive to make them good citizens of this world but you must never forget that God gave them to you primarily so that you would make them citizens of heaven. You may fail, in spite of your best intentions and endeavors, but God will reward you nonetheless— the failure will not be laid to your door.

Today, on the feast-day of the only perfect family that ever lived on this earth, I would ask all parents to examine themselves and see how they are fulfilling this grave responsibility—which God has placed on them. Are they preparing their children by word and example, especially by example, to be worthy citizens of heaven where they will be their parents' crown and glory?

SECOND READING : Colossians 3 : 12–21. Put on then, as God's chosen ones, holy and beloved, compassion, kindness, lowliness, meekness, and patience, forbearing one another and, if one has a complaint against another, forgiving each other; as the Lord has forgiven you, so you also must forgive. And above all these put on love, which binds everything together in perfect harmony. And let the peace of Christ rule in your hearts, to which indeed you were called in the one body. And be thankful. Let the word of Christ dwell in you richly, as you teach and admonish one another in all wisdom, and as you sing psalms and hymns and spiritual songs with thankfulness in your hearts to God. And whatever you do, in word or deed, do everything in the name of the Lord Jesus, giving thanks to God the Father through him.

Wives, be subject to your husbands, as is fitting in the Lord. Husbands, love your wives, and do not be harsh with them. Children, obey your parents in everything, for this pleases the Lord. Fathers, do not provoke your children, lest they become discouraged.

EXPLANATION : It was Epaphras, a disciple of St. Paul, who preached the Christian message in the town of Colossae. Paul took a keen interest in the work of his disciples. While a prisoner in Rome, Epaphras came to visit him and told him his converts were being disturbed by false teachers. Paul wrote a letter to the Colossians encouraging them to persevere in the true faith, based on the solid foundation of Christ's divinity, and to keep on living a true Christian life according to the teaching of Christ—preached to them by Epaphras. He gave them some very practical rules for an ideal Christian life, a few of which have been read to us today.

put on then . . . patience : These Christian virtues so necessary in a community must be in their heart—part and parcel of themselves. In accepting Christianity they accepted a new life.

forgiving each other : Even Christians could forget their Christian obligations and injure their neighbor but the injured one must always be ready to forgive the offender.

as the Lord has forgiven you : The Lord wiped out all their sins in Baptism and is ever ready to wash away the sins of a repentant sinner. The true Christian must imitate God in this and quickly and willingly forgive a repentant brother.

love . . . perfect : The virtues mentioned above are compared to new garments which are *put on*, but the final outer garment which binds and keeps the others in place is charity—true Christian, brotherly love.

peace of Christ . . . hearts : Christ is the source of unity, harmony and peace. His followers form one compact community —one body, with Christ as its head.

word of Christ . . . you : Christians must not only know the doctrine of Christ, they must live it and produce fruits worthy of it.

teach . . . one another : One member must help the other as in the human body.

in the name of the Lord Jesus : Because they are members of Christ's Body, their every act has a divine value. It is as members of Christ's body that they honor God the Father, their acts give special honor to him.

wives, be subject : Paul gets down to details now. The Christian faith is lived in the Christian home by each member doing his or her duty. It is duty that is stressed here not rights. As "the husband is head of the wife, as Christ is head of the Church" (Eph. 5 : 23), the wife must be subject to him—but in no servile way—it is a loving subjection for the good of the family.

husbands, love your wives : This may sound commonplace today but in the pagan world of St. Paul's time wives were little more than chattels; they were the "property" of the husband and were often treated cruelly and harshly. Christianity changed all that.

children, obey your parents : The family circle is God's place for the spread of the human race. He could have created, and could continue to create human beings in the prime of life, each one capable of running his own life. He chose the better way, we can rest assured. Parents have the responsibility of preparing their children to take their place in life, and what wonderful virtues are developed in parents because of this responsibility! Children on the other hand, have their obligations as soon as they come to the use of reason, the basic obligation of which is obedience to their parents. Through this obedience they will learn to take their place in life and more important still it is through this obedience that they will learn to obey God and reach eternal life.

do not provoke . . . discouraged : Fathers (and mothers too) must teach their children to obey not out of fear but out of love and respect. Obedience given out of fear is not true obedience and is not a training for the child's future life. A loving interest in the child's true welfare must be the motive behind every command and every reprimand.

APPLICATION : Ninety per cent of the first readers of St. Paul's letter—the first Christian converts of the town of Colossae—were pagans before their conversion. To practice the new Christian virtues was no easy task for people reared in the laxity and license of the paganism of their day. Yet they did practice these virtues and produced many saints and martyrs. After twenty centuries of Christianity one would expect that to live a full Christian life today should be less difficult but unfortunately it is not so. For the fact is our world is rapidly sinking back again into paganism—a paganism more inimical to truth and morality than the paganism of St. Paul's day. The pagans of the Roman Empire were tired of vice and worldliness—they were looking for the truth and the real purpose of life. They found it in Christianity and cherished it. Today's neo-pagans are tired of Christianity—they have found it wanting, because they are found wanting in its observance.

What was once the Christian world is today divided into two opposing factions, on one side those who openly deny the existence of God and of a future world; on the other, those who for all practical purposes care not whether God exists and whose only care is for the wealth, pleasure and power of this world. These factions are not in opposition because of any creed or doctrine; it is not dogma that divides them. Both parties have the same idols, *themselves*; their temples are identical, their banks and their stock-exchanges.

No wonder then that true Christians find the practice of their Christian life difficult today, no wonder that the youth of the world is bewildered and baffled, the winds of falsehood are blowing on them from all sides.

But it is not by banner-waving and protest-marching that our world can be saved from itself. Nothing but a return to the gospel of Christ and to the virtues that gospel demands of us can bring sanity back to the world. Where God is forgotten there is no happiness for man. Where the peace of Christ does not reign there is nothing but strife and hostility among men. Where there is no faith and hope in a future life, the present world is already hell.

Let us begin in our own family circle to bring sanity back to our world. Let us have the true peace of Christ in our hearts and in our home, each one carrying out the task God has allotted to him. We shall not convert the world immediately but we shall have made a start. The world is the sum-total of its individual families.

GOSPEL: Luke 2:22-40. When the time came for their purification according to the law of Moses, the parents of Jesus brought him up to Jerusalem to present him to the Lord (as it is written in the law of the Lord, "Every male that opens the womb shall be called holy to the Lord") and to offer a sacrifice according to what is said in the law of the Lord, "a pair of turtle-doves, or two young pigeons." Now there was a man in Jerusalem, whose name was Simeon, and this man was righteous and devout, looking for the consolation of Israel, and the Holy Spirit was upon him. And it had been revealed to him by the Holy Spirit that he should not see death before he had seen the Lord's Christ. And inspired by the Spirit he came into the temple; and when the parents brought in the child Jesus, to do for him according to the custom of the law, he took him up in his arms and blessed God and said, "Lord, now lettest thou thy servant depart in peace, according to thy word; for mine eyes have seen thy salvation which thou hast prepared in the presence of all peoples, a light for revelation to the Gentiles, and for glory to thy people Israel."

And his father and his mother marveled at what was said about him; and Simeon blessed them and said to Mary his mother, "Behold, this child is set for the fall and rising of many in Israel, and for a sign that is spoken against (and a sword will pierce through your own soul also), that thoughts out of many hearts may be revealed."

There was a prophetess, Anna, the daughter of Phanuel, of the tribe of Asher; she was of a great age, having lived with her husband seven years from her virginity, and as widow till she was eighty-four. She did not depart from the temple, worshipping with fasting and prayer night and day. And coming up at that very hour she gave thanks to God, and spoke of him to all who were looking for the redemption of Jerusalem.

And when they had performed everything according to the law of the Lord, they returned into Galilee to their own city, Nazareth. And the child grew and became strong, filled with wisdom; and the favor of God was upon him.

EXPLANATION: St. Luke concludes his detailed story of the Infancy with the presentation of the child Jesus in the temple. When this rite was carried out the Holy Family returned to Nazareth. With the exception of the incident in the temple when Jesus was 12 years old, they remained there in obscurity, as far as the world was concerned, until the beginning of his public life.

this purification: The Mosaic Law, Lv. 12:2–4, prescribed that a mother who gave birth to a son should go through a rite of legal purification, forty days after the birth. The same Law (Ex. 13:2–12) declared that every first-born male (man or beast) belonged to Yahweh, but could be redeemed, bought back, by payment of a certain sum. Luke, combining the two rites here, speaks loosely of " their purification."

Simeon . . . devout: Simeon was a pious Jew who was continually praying for the coming of the messianic age ("the consolation of Israel"). God promised him that he would live to see that day.

inspired . . . Spirit: The Holy Spirit told him to come to the temple on this particular day. Jesus was being "presented" that is, offered to God and bought back. The same Holy Spirit revealed to Simeon that the baby being presented by Joseph and Mary was the "expected one."

the parents: Luke has already made it clear that Mary conceived her child without a human father. By becoming his adopting father Joseph took him as his son, and so Luke can speak of "the

parents."

according . . . law: Neither Mary nor Jesus was bound by the Mosaic Law. Nevertheless, to give example to others, and identify Jesus completely with all humanity, they carried out the law to the letter.

blessed God: On being shown the promised Messiah Simeon's first reaction was to thank God. Then he declared his readiness to leave this life. He had seen with his own eyes the Savior, "the Salvation," not only of Israel but also the revelation of God's mercy and love for all peoples and nations.

marveled . . . about him: They did not have a full revelation concerning the Child; Simeon's recognition of him as the Messiah made them marvel.

said to Mary his mother: He speaks to Mary because Mary is his real parent; the virginal conception is again implied.

fall and rising Simeon prophesies that this Child, the Messiah, will raise up, bring to eternal glory, many of the Jews. But others will refuse him and his message, and will not profit by his coming.

sword . . . soul: Mary herself will suffer with her son. The gospel story will describe that suffering.

thoughts be revealed: There will be no neutrality in relation to the Messiah, men will be openly for or against him. He is the light which cannot be ignored.

a prophetess Anna: Anna was a devout woman who had spent her life (she was now 84) fasting in the temple and there praying for the arrival of the promised Messiah. She too recognized Mary's Baby as the Messiah. She told all the devout Jews she later met that he had arrived on earth.

returned . . . Nazareth: They had gone to Bethlehem, the city of David, because of the census. Jesus was born there. Now having fulfilled all the prescriptions of the Mosaic Law—circumcision, the purification of Mary and the presentation to the Lord of the first-born male child—they returned to a hidden life in Nazareth. There Jesus, again obedient to the Jewish custom of the time, re-mained until he was about 30 years of age, when he began his public life and mission.

grew . . . God: Like any other child, he grew in body and mind, learning the ordinary things of life day by day. The grace and favor of God was ever with him. Luke has indicated the divine nature of Jesus in his infancy narrative, but he stresses the reality of his humanity also. He grew up in Nazareth, from childhood through boyhood, to manhood, like every other human being. But the favor of God was upon him. He was God's Son.

APPLICATION: The Church makes this Sunday the Feast of the Holy Family. She wants all Christian families to look to that special family for inspiration, example and encouragement. We find all three in today's gospel. Their humble, unquestionable obedience to the Mosaic Law, a law to which they were not really bound, is an example and an encouragement for us to keep the laws of God which are binding on us. Mary, because of the virginal conception and birth of Jesus, did not need legal purification. Jesus, being the Son of God, did not have to be redeemed (bought back) from the service of God. His whole life on earth was to be a complete and devoted service of God. Joseph, as father of that family, quietly and humbly accompanied Mary and her Child to Jerusalem.

They then returned to Nazareth to live a life of obscurity and poverty for the next thirty years. They were probably often short of the necessities of life —the earnings of a carpenter in the small village of Nazareth would be meager. Human nature being what it is, there probably were times when Joseph was not paid even what was due to him. Poverty, however, did not mean misery for them. They willingly accepted their lot and thanked God for the little they had. The vast majority of Christian (and other) families today are living on the border-line of poverty. Life is one long struggle for survival. They can and should do all in their power, within the law of God, to better their condition. But if this is impossible then they should accept God's will. He worked no miracle to ease the hard lot of Jesus, Mary and Joseph; we can hardly expect miracles in our case.

It is true that Mary and Joseph were helped by the limited knowledge they had of the role of Jesus in the salvation of the world. It helped them to be docile to God's will and ever ready to suffer for the cause of God. But we have even a more comprehensive knowledge of Christ's role in our regard, and of God's plan for our real eternal happiness. Therefore, we should be ready to bear our lot, and carry whatever cross is sent us. We know that this life is but a stepping-stone to the next life. It is not the difficulty or ease of our lot here below that matters, but rather the use we make of the few years allotted us.

Mothers of families: make Mary your model. Keep the love of God alive and active in your home. The love of neighbor, peace and harmony among the members of the family will follow automatically. Fathers: you have the patient St. Joseph as your model. He labored, day in and day out, often without any temporal reward, often regretting that he could not provide better for his beloved wife and dearly-loved adopted son. But he too accepted God's plan. He was glad to suffer as God's chosen associate in the preparation of the human nature of Jesus for the messianic task that lay ahead.

Children: love, honor and obey your parents, as Jesus loved, honored and obeyed Mary and Joseph. He, the Son of God, the Creator and Lord of all things, was subject to his parents, to Mary his Mother and to Joseph his foster-father. "He went down with them to Nazareth and was subject to them," St. Luke tells us (Lk. 2 : 51). Think of these words if ever you are tempted to complain of your lot. Think of them if ever you feel the restraint of obedience, if your pride should ever move you to rebel against those whom God has placed over you. Christ was subject to his inferiors; you should not find it difficult to be subject to your superiors.

Let us try to make the holy home of Nazareth the model of our homes and imitate the Holy Family in our daily lives. Then when the time comes to bid adieu to this world, we shall be able, like Simeon and Anna, to thank God from our hearts for having been given a vision of the Messiah, not only in our last days, but all through life. We shall be able to say, "now let your servant depart in peace." We shall be ready to face our judge, because we will have obeyed and loved him all through our lives. So may it be.

OCTAVE OF CHRISTMAS: FEAST OF MARY, MOTHER OF GOD

FIRST READING: Numbers 6 : 22-27. The Lord said to Moses, "Say to Aaron and his sons, thus you shall bless the people of Israel: you shall say to them : The Lord bless you and keep you; the Lord make his face to shine upon you, and be gracious to you; the Lord lift up his countenance upon you, and give you peace. So shall they put my name upon the people of Israel, and I will bless them."

EXPLANATION: After the Exodus (or coming out of Egypt) and after God had made a covenant on Mount Sinai with the Chosen People, Moses, on God's instructions, set the tribe of Levi apart so that they would offer the sacrifices and carry out the liturgy in the name of, and for, the rest of the tribes. The direct line of Aaron, head of the tribe of Levi, were to be the priests who would have the principal part in the offering of the sacrifices and in the other liturgical acts. The other male members of the tribe were the Levites whose duty it was to assist the priests. One of the liturgical acts of the priests was to bless the people after the daily sacrifices and on other solemn occasions. The blessing was a reward for the keeping of the covenant by the people, and a guarantee that the blessing promised to all nations through Abraham would be fulfilled one day.

The words of this blessing given by God to Moses are recorded in these verses of the book of Numbers read at today's Mass.

The Lord bless you and keep you : The blessing of God meant peace and temporal prosperity and a renewal of the hope of the great future blessing which was to come.

face shine upon you : May God smile on you, that is, may he be your friend.

be gracious to you : May he grant you his favors.

lift . . . upon you . . . give you peace : May you continue to be his favorites and may he protect you from all enemies so you can live in peace.

I will bless them : This is not just a wish which the priests make on behalf of the people. God promises that he will grant their request which he commands them to make.

APPLICATION : All God's dealings with the Chosen People of the Old Testament, the call of Abraham, the Exodus, the liturgy, this special blessing were part of God's plan of preparation for his greatest act of infinite blessing which was to come in the Incarnation. God's Son was to take our human nature in order to unite us with God. All God's promises, all God's fatherly care for the Chosen People, down through the centuries, all his blessings had their perfect fulfillment and culmination in the coming of Christ on earth.

And the one human being who received the fullness of these promises and blessings was the Virgin Mary when she said : " Be it done unto me according to thy word," for at that very moment she conceived the Christ, the Son of God in her womb. As proof of this we have the Angel Gabriel's words on the occasion of the Annunciation. He salutes her as "full of grace," that is, she has the full friendship of God. He is truly gracious to her, his "face shines on her," he is actually with her as the closest of friends: "the Lord is with thee." He adds : "blessed art thou among women" to show that no woman (or man either) ever received the fullness of God's blessing until now.

The title the Church has always given her, a title confirmed by the Council of Ephesus (431) : "Mother of God," aptly expresses all this. She became the Mother of Christ who was the Messiah and the Son of God, an honor and a dignity which no human imagination could have thought possible. But nothing is impossible to God. As she says herself in her Magnificat : "He who is mighty has done great things for me." And let us not forget it : in honoring Mary, *one of us*, he has honored us all. Through that act of divine love and condescension which brought about the Incarnation, we, the whole human race, with Mary as the most perfect example, have been raised up to a new status, a supernatural condition—we have been made children of God, brothers of Christ and heirs of heaven.

Let us thank God today for all the graces conferred upon Mary, graces through which we all profit. Being the Mother of Christ, she is our Mother too. She will not forget us—she has a greater interest in our true welfare than any earthly mother could have—she will help us on the road to heaven if we place ourselves under her motherly care.

SECOND READING: Galatians 4:4-7. When the time had fully come, God sent forth his Son, born of woman, born under the law, to redeem those who were under the law, so that we might receive adoption as sons. And because you are sons, God sent the Spirit of his Son into our hearts, crying, "Abba! Father!" So through God you are no longer a slave but a son, and if a son then an heir.

EXPLANATION: The people of Galatia, a town in Asia Minor (part of Turkey today), were converted by St. Paul during his second missionary journey (50-52). They accepted the Christian faith gladly and practiced it faithfully until some Judaizers came among them telling them that Paul's doctrine was wrong, that the old law was still in force and must be accepted by Christians. To refute this heresy Paul wrote this letter from Ephesus, showing that the coming of Christ had fulfilled the old law and annulled it. The shadow was removed by the reality. Christians are freed from the slavery of the old law for they have been made children of God.

When . . . time . . . come: The whole history of man on earth, the period of the Old Testament in particular, was a period of promises and preparation. The hour appointed by God from all eternity for fulfilling these promises came when:

God sent . . . his Son: Ever since that day on the road to Damascus (Acts 9: 1-19), when the risen Christ appeared to him, Paul had not the slightest doubt that the Christ who had lived in Palestine and had died on the cross, was the true Son of God as well as the promised Messiah.

born of woman: Paul does not mention Mary. He is not concerned with details here which are known to his converts. What he is stressing is the reality of the human nature of Christ. He has already mentioned his divinity. And especially he is stressing the self-humiliation of the Son of God who deigned to be born of a mother like any human child.

born . . . under the law: Another humiliation. He was the maker of the law but in order to fulfill all the Old Testament prophecies, he took human nature from a descendant of Abraham, and became one of the Chosen Race.

to redeem . . . were under the law: The promises had been given to "those under the law," the Chosen People, so therefore the gospel of redemption was offered to them first.

we . . . adoption . . . sons: The result of Christ's coming was that all men, Jew and Gentile, could become adopted sons of God. All those who accept Christ are by Baptism raised to a new status, a new supernatural life.

Abba (Father): We are adopted sons and can truly call God our Father, as Christ taught his disciples to do. It is the Spirit of his Son, the Holy Spirit given at Baptism, which gives us this privilege.

through God . . . heir: This privilege of sonship which as a consequence makes us heirs of his happiness, i.e. of heaven, is a free gift of God's love and goodness. As human beings we could never earn such a privilege for ourselves. But the Incarnation has earned it for us, and the Incarnation is an act of pure love on God's part.

APPLICATION: The Galatians—pagans recently converted to Christianity by Paul—were being disturbed in their faith by Judaizers, that is, by Jews who pretended to be Christians but were not. These were telling the new converts that Christianity was not something really new, but only a new form of Judaism, and therefore the converts must accept circumcision and other practices of the old law. Paul in his letter reacts strongly to this falsehood. Christianity is not a reform of Judaism, he states, but is its replacement. Judaism was only a preparation, Christianity is the fulfillment; the old law was but a shadow of things to come, Christianity is the reality.

The "fullness of time has come," the period of preparation and promise has ended. Men are no longer slaves of the law or slaves of their past pagan polytheism and its practices. They are now free men and new men, sons of God. They can now truly call God "Abba Father," "for God sent his Son born of a woman." The Incarnation has taken place, men are no longer mere human beings, they have a new life given them in Baptism. They now share in the divine life because Christ has shared their human life with them.

Do we Christians of today really appreciate the privileges the Incarnation has brought to us? Do we really realize what our Christianity means to us? When we say the "Our Father who art in heaven" do we understand even vaguely what we are saying? If we were allowed to salute God as our Creator it would be a reminder of all we owe him, and our duty, but to have the right to call him our Father, the Father who loves us so much, that he has made us his sons, and is gladly ready to share his eternal happiness with us, is so great a privilege that we almost find it hard to believe it.

Yet this is the result and consequence of that great mystery of God's love—the Incarnation, the basic tenet of our Christianity. Today's feast-day—the feast of Mary, Mother of God—recalls to our minds this fundamental truth of our faith. "God sent his son born of a woman"—the woman was Mary "our tainted nature's solitary boast" as Wordsworth describes her. She, among all the daughters and sons of men, was the most closely connected with God's gift of the Incarnation to us. She conceived Christ in his human nature, in her womb. She bore him within her for nine months, she gave birth to him in Bethlehem, she fed him at her breast in his infancy—she provided and cared for him in his boyhood and youth. She finally offered him for us on Calvary. And this son of hers was the Son of God from all eternity.

We Christians are privileged to have been made sons of God by the Incarnation. But how much greater was and is the privilege of the one who was made the Mother of God, and his nearest and dearest human assistant in this mystery of his love for us! God loves us, of that we can have no doubt; Mary too loves us, for we are brothers of the Son of God whom she loves so dearly. She wants us to reap the reward of the Incarnation, in which she played such a privileged part, which reward is to share in the happiness of God for all eternity. This reward she will obtain for us when our moment of judgement comes, if we have tried to love and respect her in life. If we say devoutly, thoughtfully and frequently that simple prayer the Church has taught us: "Holy Mary, Mother of God, pray for us sinners now" we can face "the hour of our death" with confidence. Amen.

GOSPEL : Luke 2 : 21. At the end of eight days, when he was circumcised, he was called Jesus, the name given by the angel before he was conceived in the womb.

EXPLANATION : See the gospel of the "Dawn Mass on Christmas Day" for the explanation of verses 15–20.

At the end of eight days : Circumcision was the outward sign of the covenant God made with Abraham and his descendants (see Gen. 17 : 12, renewed in Lev. 12 : 3). Every male child had to be circumcised on the eighth day after his birth in order to become a member of the Chosen People. It was at this ceremony that the child was given his name.

called Jesus : Joshuah, in Hebrew, which means Yahweh (or God) saves. In Matthew's Gospel the angel explains the meaning of the name to Joseph : "he is the one who is to save his people from their sins" (Mt. 1 : 21).

name . . . the angel . . . in the womb : The angel Gabriel had told Mary that the child who was to be born of her was to be called Jesus, and goes on to state that he will be the Messiah, the Savior of the people (Lk. 1 : 30–33).

APPLICATION : This story of the humble shepherds of Bethlehem coming to find Jesus "in the manger wrapped in swaddling clothes" already read at the Dawn Mass on Christmas Day, is repeated today because of the feast we are celebrating, the Divine Motherhood of Mary. It is the feast of Christmas again, the feast of the Incarnation and birth of our Savior, but it is Mary's part in this wonderful mystery of God's love for men that the Church is stressing today.

There have been Christians who could see no importance in the part played by Mary in our redemption, yet it was God himself who chose her from all eternity for this role and it was God's messenger at the Annunciation who proclaimed she was "full of grace" and that she was God's special friend—"The Lord was with her." The humble shepherds searching for the Savior whose birth

"God had made known to them" found Mary first, then Joseph (the one after Mary who had a very important part in God's plan) and then "the babe lying in the manger."

In following the inspired words of the gospels of Matthew and Luke who stress the importance of Mary's role in the Incarnation, and the constant teaching of the Catholic Church ever since, we need have no fear of taking anything from the honor, glory and gratitude we owe to God, when we honor, as our Mother, the Virgin he first honored by making her the Mother of his Son. Furthermore the last act of our Savior, before dying on the cross, was to make his Mother our Mother, through our representative St. John, to whom he said: "behold thy Mother" (Jn. 1 : 27). It would be disloyalty to Christ not to accept her as our Mother, and it would be disloyalty to the revealed word of God if we denied her divine maternity. God made her Mother of the Messiah, the Savior, who was his divine Son.

Mary was, and is, a human creature, a mere human creature but a human creature selected by God to be the mother of the Savior's human nature, the human nature his divine sonship assumed in order to redeem man and raise him up. It was through no merit of her own that Mary earned this dignity—this honor given her was a sheer gift of God. She was the first to realize and declare this when she said God had "regarded the lowliness of his handmaid" (Lk. 1 : 48). When we honor her therefore we are in fact and in intention honoring and thanking God for the marvelous gifts and privileges he conferred on one of us.

God could have sent his Son on earth without the help of a human mother. He could have created directly for him a human nature in the prime of manhood. He chose instead to make the Son "like unto us in all things except sin" and as man he was born of a human mother, "born of a woman," as St. Paul puts it. That woman was Mary ever-Virgin, she was God's privileged handmaid. And when we honor that privilege of hers we are honoring the loving condescension of God who not only deigned to send us his Son to be our Savior, but deigned that he should be born of one of our own weak human nature to whom he had given and continued to give the necessary graces.

Thank you God, for the Incarnation, thank you God, for the honorable part you gave to "one of us" to play in that drama of divine love. May we ever be worthy of your gifts of infinite love to us!

SECOND SUNDAY AFTER CHRISTMAS

FIRST READING: Sirach (Ecclesiasticus), 24:1-2; 8-12. Wisdom will praise herself, and will glory in the midst of her people. In the assembly of the Most High she will open her mouth, and in the presence of his host she will glory: "The Creator of all things gave me a commandment, and the one who created me assigned a place for my tent. And he said, 'Make your dwelling in Jacob, and in Israel receive your inheritance.' From eternity, in the beginning, he created me, and for eternity I shall not cease to exist. In the holy tabernacle I ministered before him, and so I was established in Zion. In the beloved city likewise he gave me a resting place, and in Jerusalem was my dominion. So I took root in an honored people, in the portion of the Lord, who is their inheritance."

EXPLANATION: On Sirach, the author of this book, see page 48. In the verses read today we have the author's eulogy of Wisdom. Personified Wisdom declares herself as being in union with God and yet distinct from him. She came forth from the mouth of the Most High. She has an important part in the divine council and dwells in the highest heavens. She pre-existed with God and participated in all the works of creation, and will exist for all eternity. From this it is easy to see in personified Wisdom a pre-figuring of St. John's doctrine of the "Logos," the Word which "was with God, was God, and became man and pitched his tent among us" (Jn. 1:1-14).

Wisdom will praise herself: No finite mind could describe the infinite eternal Wisdom. She had revealed herself (partially) to her Chosen People.

In the assembly of the Most High: In the divine council she speaks with authority. All the heavenly hosts recognize her importance.

The creator ... gave ... commandment: Wisdom was then sent to men on this earth by the creator, by God, saying:

In Jacob ... your dwelling: God sends Wisdom to the Chosen People—the children of Israel. Sirach now sees Wisdom on earth in the Thorah—the covenant and law given to Moses. He did not see the fuller and true meaning of his words, which became evident only when the "Word of God came on earth and dwelt among us."

from eternity ... for eternity: Wisdom now declares she is eternal, everlasting, in other words, divine.

In the holy tabernacle ... Zion: Ever since David brought the Ark of the Covenant into that city (about 1000

B.C.), Jerusalem has been God's earthly dwelling place among his people.

I took root ... people ... inheritance : He came to stay among his Chosen People. Unfortunately, they did not remain loyal to him. Jerusalem was destroyed but God's hand was not shortened by their defects. He set up a new Chosen People, a new Jerusalem which would be everlasting, for its real culmination was to be in heaven.

APPLICATION : St. Augustine truly says : "The New Testament is hidden in the Old, the Old Testament is made clear in the New." These verses we have read today from Sirach, an inspired writer of the Old Testament, makes this evident to us. He describes Wisdom—the knowledge and power of God—as someone distinct from God yet equal to God. This was a daring innovation on the part of a Jewish writer for whom the unicity or oneness of God was the basic tenet of the true religion. The doctrine of the Blessed Trinity—three distinct but equal persons in the *One God*—was not openly revealed in the Old Testament. The people of the old dispensation were not ready yet to accept this divine mystery.

But the all-wise God, author of the Old and New Testaments, moves Sirach (as also the writers of the Books of Proverbs and Wisdom) to prepare the minds of the future generations of Chosen People to whom he was to reveal this basic doctrine of the New Testament, for the mysterious but glorious doctrine of the Blessed Trinity, three persons in the One God.

We are surely fortunate. We are truly God's Chosen People, for he has deigned to reveal to us this basic essence of his divine nature, this essential foundation of our Christian faith. Unless we knew of, and believed in, the doctrine of the Trinity our following of Christ would be folly and futile. If Christ was not God, he did not redeem us men; he did not raise us up to give us a share in the divine nature; he could not and did not make us sons of the Father and heirs of heaven; he did not send us the Holy Spirit, a divine person distinct from the Father and the Son, to sanctify and direct his Church and to help us on our road to heaven.

But he did all this because he was true God and true man. He is true God because he is the Second Person of the Blessed Trinity. He is true man because, carrying out the Father's plan for man's glorification, he took real human nature in order to raise us up to the supernatural, divine status God willed for us.

We know, because God has said it, that there are three Persons in the One God. We, with our very limited, finite minds, cannot grasp the full meaning of this mystery—if we could, God would be limited and finite like ourselves. But we can accept it on God's word, and Christ's life and teaching among us confirms this word of God for us. We can therefore rest assured that our Christian faith is on the solid basis of God's truth, that the three Persons of the Blessed Trinity are not only there in some remote heaven, but that they are close beside us, deeply interested and involved in our salvation. The infinite, divine love of the Father for man—the masterpiece of his creation—has sent his Son to become man so that men could become sons of God. The Holy Spirit, continuing the work of the Son among us, is helping us on the road to heaven through his gifts and his inspirations. It is there, please God, in heaven, that the greatest joy of our heavenly existence will be the contemplation of the most Blessed Trinity—the Father, the Son and the Holy Spirit to whom be honor and glory forever. Amen.

SECOND READING: Ephesians 1 : 3–6; 15–18. Blessed be the God and Father of our Lord Jesus Christ, who has blessed us in Christ with every spiritual blessing in the heavenly places, even as he chose us in him before the foundation of the world, that we should be holy and blameless before him. He destined us in love to be his sons through Jesus Christ, according to the purpose of his will, to the praise of his glorious grace which he freely bestowed on us in the Beloved.

For this reason, because I have heard of your faith in the Lord Jesus and your love toward all the saints, I do not cease to give thanks, for you, remembering you in my prayers, that the God of our Lord Jesus Christ, the Father of glory, may give you a spirit of wisdom and of revelation in the knowledge of him, having the eyes of your hearts enlightened, that you may know what is the hope to which he has called you, what are the riches of his glorious inheritance in the saints.

EXPLANATION: This letter was written by St. Paul from his prison in Rome (about 63 A.D.) to his converts in Ephesus. He had already taught them the full Christian doctrine. This letter is a reminder to them to continue as faithful followers of Christ.

blessed be the God and Father: St. Paul has taught the doctrine of the Blessed Trinity to his converts (Jews and Gentiles) who have accepted it without question, although for Jewish converts especially this was not easy.

of our Lord Jesus Christ: The Jesus who had lived and died recently in Palestine was "Christ," that is, the promised Messiah, and was furthermore Lord, i.e. God. We have, therefore, in this single verse the doctrine of the Trinity, the Father and Son (the Holy Spirit is mentioned later), two distinct persons yet one God, and the doctrine of the Incarnation. Jesus, who was the man about whom they all knew, was also the Son of the Father, God.

blessed . . . blessing: The blessings of Christianity have come to them from the Father through (in) the Son, Christ.

before . . . of the world: God's plan for our elevation to sonship with him, through the Incarnation, was from all eternity, as Scotus teaches, and not merely as a remedy necessary because of men's sins.

destined us . . . sons through Jesus: This was God's eternal plan : man would be elevated to the status of adopted son of God through Christ's, his Son's, adoption or assumption of man's human nature.

praise . . . glorious grace: His own glory is God's principal motive in the Incarnation, the secondary motive is our eternal glorification.

APPLICATION: St. Paul in his dungeon prison in Rome could find time to pray for his Ephesian converts. Now that he is in the glorious halls of heaven, he must surely be praying for us too today. And what he prayed and asked God for them is exactly what we need today and need even more so than the Ephesians. He asked God to enlighten their minds so that they would understand the full meaning of their vocation. Do we not all need enlightenment on this very important matter? How often do we stop and think of what being a Christian means? It means we are brothers of Christ, sons of God, and heirs to the eternal kingdom of heaven. We are, as St. Peter (1 Pet. 2: 9) tells us: "a chosen race, a royal priesthood, a holy nation, a purchased people." Do we realize how privileged we are, do we try to live up to our noble calling? We would all be shocked if the son of a king or the son of a president behaved like a thug or gangster, if he forgot his father's and his own dignity and acted like a criminal. Yet our dignity is higher than that of any earthly king's or potentate's sons, we are sons of God, heirs of heaven. And we do forget that dignity of ours, and bring dishonor on our heavenly Father (in as far as we can) when we break his commandments and refuse to do his will.

Another gift Paul asked for his Ephesian converts was that they should learn to realize the riches of the glory of the inheritance God has prepared for his saints. Would that we too could realize this and think often on it! Heaven is ours for the taking, an everlasting home in which there will be nothing but perfect happiness and contentment. There will be no more pains of mind or body—no more strife or quarreling, no shortage of anything that delights us—no more partings from friends, death will be no more. And over and above and infinitely beyond all this, there will be our vision of the Blessed Trinity, the source of all joy and happiness.

Is there a man so foolish who would, even for a moment, run the risk of losing this inheritance, which God has prepared for him, because of some earthly, passing, pleasure or gain?

Let us give ourselves a few moments during today to think seriously on the glorious future which awaits us, and let us see if we are really on the right road toward that inheritance which the Blessed Trinity, the Father, the Son and the Holy Spirit, has prepared for us. These few moments of serious meditation will perhaps mean for some of us here present the turning point in a life that was heading in a wrong, in a fatal, direction.

GOSPEL: John 1:1-18. In the beginning was the Word, and the Word was with God, and the Word, was God. He was in the beginning with God; all things were made through him, and without him was not anything made that was made. In him was life, and the life was the light of men. The light shines in the darkness, and the darkness has not overcome it.

There was a man sent from God, whose name was John. He came for testimony, to bear witness to the light, that all might believe through him. He was not the light, but came to bear witness to the light.

The true light that enlightens every man was coming into the world. He was in the world, and the world was made through him, yet the world knew him not. He came to his own home, and his own people received him not. But to all who received him, who believed in his name, he gave power to become children of God; who were born, not of blood nor of the will of the flesh nor of the will of man, but of God.

And the Word became flesh and dwelt among us, full of grace and truth; we have beheld his glory, glory as of the only Son from the Father. (John bore witness to him and cried, "This was he of whom I said, 'He who comes after me ranks before me, for he was before me.'") And from his fullness have we all received, grace upon grace. For the law was given through Moses; grace and truth came through Jesus Christ. No one has ever seen God; the only Son, who is in the bosom of the Father, he has made him known.

EXPLANATION: These verses of St. John's Gospel have already been explained in the Third Mass on Christmas Day (see above). A brief summary will suffice here. St. John "the beloved disciple," wrote his gospel about sixty years after the Ascension of Christ. The other three gospels had already been for many years in circulation, and the facts concerning Jesus—his doings and sayings—had already been preached to, and lived by, two generations of Christians. The principal purpose John had in writing his gospel was not to retell the story already well known (though he does occasionally repeat some miracles and sayings of Jesus given by the Synoptics) but to emphasize those elements of Christianity most relevant to the Christians of his day and to put them in a language comprehensible to the people of that day.

One of the basic elements of Christianity, of course, was the Incarnation: that the Son of God, who was co-eternal with the Father, took a true human nature and lived among us. The Son of God became the Son of Man. He did this to raise us up and to enlighten us—that is, he, by uniting the human with the divine in his own person, united all of the human race with God; and he "enlightened" us, he gave us the power to see God in him and through him. He who is with the Father and who has pitched his tent among us is the bridge that spans the infinite divide that separates mere man from God.

God had revealed himself in a limited, partial way, to the Chosen People in the law of Moses. But Jesus Christ has brought us "grace," the intimate friendship of God; and "truth," all the knowledge of God and of our relationship with him, which our finite minds can grasp on earth, and which is sufficient for us to enable us to reach our heavenly home where we will see him "face to face."

APPLICATION: We can never fully appreciate the infinite love and condescension God has shown toward us in the Incarnation, but we can and should realize sufficient of its magnitude to move us to do the little he demands of us in return. And that little he demands is more for our benefit than for his. He wants us to earn an eternal life of happiness with him in heaven, by living the few years he gives us in this life, as true Christians, as true followers of his Son whom he sent among us.

Imagine for a moment, the case of an earthly king or nobleman who so loves the family of one of his subjects that he decides to bring them to live with him in his mansion. He sends his own son to live with them in their lowly cottage in order to teach them and prepare them for the day when his father will call them to take up their abode with him and share in all his earthly wealth and comfort. What would you think of their folly, if some or all of that family refused to be taught, and preferred their hovel, their poverty, and their rags to the comforts and honors offered them?

And yet, this is what Christians do who refuse to carry out the law laid down for them by Christ and prefer instead to cling to their earthly attractions, and thus lose their place in the heavenly mansions of their loving Father!

There is no sane man living, of course, who does not want eternal happiness. There is no one (outside of the mental homes) who would wish all his gifts, all his mental abilities, desires and hopes, to end forever in the grave. But there are many, normally sane men, who are so immersed, so taken up, with the fleeting things of this life that they cannot spare the time to think of their final end. Our Lord tells of two such men (there were many others), in the stories of "Dives and Lazarus" and in that of the man building bigger and better barns to store his earthly wealth. He died the night he finished his biggest barn!

We are not forbidden to enjoy and use the gifts God has put in this world for our use. He made man master of all other created things. Man fails in his duty to God and to his own best interest, not while he masters and uses these gifts of God, but when he lets these created things master him and use him.

Let us think again today of the two greatest mysteries and truths of our Christian religion, the Blessed Trinity and the Incarnation. God has raised us by the latter mystery, the Incarnation, so that we could forever enjoy the company of the former—the company of the Father, Son and Holy Spirit in heaven.

FEAST OF THE EPIPHANY

FIRST READING : Isaiah 60 : 1–6. Arise, shine; for your light has come, and the glory of the Lord has risen upon you. For behold, darkness shall cover the earth, and thick darkness the peoples; but the Lord will arise upon you, and his glory will be seen upon you. And nations shall come to your light, and kings to the brightness of your rising. Lift up your eyes round about, and see; they all gather together, they come to you; your sons shall come from far, and your daughters shall be carried in the arms.

Then you shall see and be radiant, your heart shall thrill and rejoice; because the abundance of the sea shall be turned to you, the wealth of the nations shall come to you. A multitude of camels shall cover you, the young camels of Midian and Ephah; all those from Sheba shall come. They shall bring gold and frankincense, and shall proclaim the praise of the Lord.

EXPLANATION : The prophet (second-Isaiah probably) is trying to cheer the exiles by foretelling the glorious future of the new Jerusalem which is not yet rebuilt. The special radiance of God will illuminate it. Gentiles (who once despised it) will bring their riches to it. From East and West peoples will flock to it.

glory of the Lord : The gloom of sadness and despair which enveloped the derelict Jerusalem during the exile will give way to a heavenly brightness, for God will dwell within it once more.

darkness . . . covers the earth : This divine brightness is first and foremost for the Chosen People.

nations shall come to your light : The Gentiles will partake of this divine blessing—their kings will come to share in the light of Zion.

all gather . . . come to you : The glory of Jerusalem will be such that all nations will come to it, and the scattered children of Israel will return home also (see 49 : 22).

abundance . . . sea : The nations of the West (the sea, the Mediterranean) will bring their riches in ships.

Midian, Ephah and Sheba : The eastern nations will come in camel caravans, the usual way of travel through the desert, bearing their gifts.

gold and frankincense : Two of the most valuable means of barter-trading of the time.

proclaim the praise of the Lord : They will come with their gifts to honor the God of Israel, forsaking their pagan idols for the true God.

APPLICATION: The feast of the Epiphany is the feast which commemorates the manifestation of God to the Gentiles. This manifestation began when the Wise Men from the East came to Bethlehem to pay their respects and offer their gifts to the newly-born king of the Jews (see Mt. 2 in today's gospel). Though the words of second-Isaiah were not understood by his hearers as referring to this event, it was only in the coming of the Magi, to welcome Christ, that they were really fulfilled. Jerusalem was in no sense an attraction for the nations in the intervening centuries. But the Magi at Bethlehem were the first-fruits of the thousands and millions of Gentiles who have since then seen the glory of God in the Babe of Bethlehem and who have figuratively come to Jerusalem from the West and from the East to form the new Chosen People, the new Kingdom of God.

Let us thank God today for having called us, Gentiles, to his kingdom, his Church, and for giving us the means to reach heaven. Let us never imitate the Chosen People of the Old Testament who so often forgot how good God was to them, and who often so provoked him, that he allowed them to be taken into exile as slaves of a pagan nation. We too could bring exile on ourselves, an exile much more fatal than the Babylonian one. Whatever else may be my lot, whatever hardship I may have to suffer during the few years I am on earth, God forbid that I should ever, through my unfaithfulness, cause myself to be excluded from my true home, heaven, where "the glory of the Lord will shine" forever.

SECOND READING: Ephesians 3 : 2–3; 5–6. I assume that you have heard of the stewardship of God's grace that was given to me for you, how the mystery was made known to me by revelation, which was not made known to the sons of men in other generations as it has now been revealed to his holy Apostles and prophets by the Spirit; that is, how the Gentiles are fellow-heirs, members of the same body, and partakers of the promise in Christ Jesus through the gospel.

EXPLANATION:
stewardship . . . grace: Paul, writing from a prison in Rome to the Ephesians, whom he had converted to Christianity about 53-56, reminds them of the fact that he was "the Apostle of the Gentiles."
to me for you: This mission to bring the knowledge of Christ to the Gentiles Paul counted as a special grace from God, which it was, both for him and for his converts (see also Rom. 1 : 5; 15 : 15; Gal. 2 : 9).

by revelation: His mission was revealed to him when Christ appeared to him on the road to Damascus (see Acts 9 : 15; 22 : 21).
in . . . generations: The expected Messiah of the Old Testament was understood to be for the Jews only—this was the common opinion of the Jewish people. Even the prophets, many of whom referred to the Gentiles in relation to the Messiah, had no clear understanding of him.
revealed . . . Apostles and prophets:

That Christ the Messiah had come for the Gentiles as well as for the Jews was revealed to the Apostles and prophets—those Christians who in the early Church had special revelations from God for the community. To the Apostles Christ gave the command after his resurrection: "Go therefore and make disciples of all nations" (Mt. 28:19; see Mk. 16:15; 24:47).

members of the same body: The Gentiles are equal members with the Jewish converts in the mystical body of Christ, the Church.

the promise . . . through the gospel: The eternal reward promised by Christ to his followers, in the gospel, and through living up to its teaching.

APPLICATION: St. Paul's thoughts in his prison in Rome are not for himself nor for the fate that awaits him. He is thinking instead of the mission Christ gave him, to evangelize the Gentile nations. He has done much already, and even in prison he does all he can to continue the good work. He writes to his Gentile converts from Rome, to remind them of their great privilege in being called to the Christian faith. They are now God's new Chosen People, they are now members of Christ's mystical body, they are now guaranteed heaven if they appreciate and live up to their vocation.

Today, on the feast of the Epiphany, we are celebrating the coming of the first Gentiles to the feet of Christ. They were the first of the long stream of Gentile peoples and nations that flowed steadily toward Christ's mystical body, the Church, down through the years. We have the privilege of being part of that stream, and St. Paul, who today in heaven is as interested in us as he was in his Ephesian converts, is exhorting us, through these words of his, to appreciate the privilege which is ours. Through the grace of God and not through any merits of our own, we are Christians and are on the road to heaven. "Rejoice and persevere" is St. Paul's advice to us today. If we truly rejoice it means we truly appreciate what the gift of the true faith means. We know where we came from, we know where we are going, and we are certain there is a place, a wonderful, eternal place, to go to. We know too how to get there. This is no mean knowledge in the world of today, where so many seem content to make this world their heaven, and let the future look after itself—if there be a future (and logically to ease their consciences they must hope there isn't one).

Thank God, our faith and our ordinary intelligence tell us there has to be a future life—God would be a cruel joker if he gave us the nature we possess with its spiritual gifts and desires only to have them end in a grave after a few short years. We can rejoice then because we appreciate the great privilege given us, and if we appreciate it we shall hold on to it and follow the path it indicates. We may have to climb some hills and they may look as steep as Calvary, but after Calvary comes the Mount of Olives, the mount of the Ascension.

GOSPEL : Matthew 2 : 1–12. When Jesus was born in Bethlehem of Judea in the days of Herod the king, behold, wise men from the East came to Jerusalem, saying, "Where is he who has been born king of the Jews? For we have seen his star in the East, and have come to worship him." When Herod the king heard this, he was troubled, and all Jerusalem with him; and assembling all the chief priests and scribes of the people, he inquired of them where the Christ was to be born. They told him, "In Bethlehem of Judea; for so it is written by the prophet : 'And you, O Bethlehem, in the land of Judah, are by no means least among the rulers of Judah; for from you shall come a ruler who will govern my people Israel.' "

Then Herod summoned the wise men secretly and ascertained from them what time the star appeared; and he sent them to Bethlehem, saying, "Go and search diligently for the child, and when you have found him bring me word, that I too may come and worship him." When they had heard the king they went their way; and lo, the star which they had seen in the East went before them, till it came to rest over the place where the child was. When they saw the star, they rejoiced exceedingly with great joy; and going into the house they saw the child with Mary his mother, and they fell down and worshipped him. Then, opening their treasures, they offered him gifts, gold and frankincense and myrrh. And being warned in a dream not to return to Herod, they departed to their own country by another way.

EXPLANATION :

Wise men : The term was usually reserved for men learned in the sciences, and among the Persians these were especially the priestly caste.

from the East : From Mesopotamia, of which Persia was the only country of any importance then.

to Jerusalem : Evidently God had revealed to them that a new King of the Jews had been born, and they understood from God that he was a special King; they did not come when Herod or Herod's son was born.

we have seen his star : Astrology was one of the sciences studied by Magi. There was a firm conviction that each human being had his own star and that his fate in life was governed by that star. This was not and is not so, but God made use of their superstition to teach them truth. Some unusual light in the sky aroused their interest; God did the rest.

Herod . . . troubled : He knew the Magi had not come to honor his son—all his sons were grown up at the time, so he immediately thought of an opponent who would oust him from the throne.

all Jerusalem with him : Not because Herod might lose his throne, but for fear of what excess Herod would go to if any opposition arose.

Christ was to be born : Herod, who was a pagan, may have had some idea of the messianic promises which were the kernel of the Old Testament. But when the question of a *special* king of the Jews arose, some of his household must have told him that this must be the expected Messiah (a Hebrew word meaning the Anointed, or the Christ).

the priests and scribes : They knew their bible, they remembered the prophecy of Micah (see Cycle C (3) 4th

BLESSED CANDLE

or

PUZZLED PASTOR

Oh ! Lord ! This street !

Among the urban wilderness of homes, which house ?

They all look just the same.

March on.   What's this ?   A candle's flickering *gleam*

Just visible within a room.

Thrice blessed candle !   Your faint gleam

For who would light a candle in the day

Save the old housebound sinner who's on guard

To greet the gracious visit of the Lord ?

————————————

Sunday of Advent), and so informed Herod that Bethlehem was to be the birthplace of the Christ.

time the star appeared: Herod had already formed his plans—he would destroy that infant. The Magi had probably spent months on their journey. The star may have appeared some months before they left. The Baby could possibly be a year old. But Herod took no chances: when ordering the murder of all the male children of Bethlehem (3 : 16), he said: "from two years and under."

I may . . . come and worship: He may have deceived the Magi but could not deceive God.

star . . . over the place: This heavenly light directed them to the place (not the stable, as it says, they "entered the house") where they found the Child.

with Mary his mother: The omission of Joseph may be due to the simple fact that he was absent because he had found employment in Bethlehem as a carpenter. It is, however, more likely that Matthew who has already (1 : 18-25) told of the virginal conception of Christ, is emphasizing here the fact that Joseph was only the foster-father of Christ.

worshiped him: That is, they paid him reverence by prostrating themselves before him. It does not prove they recognized him as God but they did recognize him as a special King.

gold . . . myrrh: Precious gifts to show their respect and esteem.

departed . . . another way: Herod had told them to return to him but God had other plans—the Magi were instructed to return not via Jerusalem but by another route. This gave time to Joseph to remove the Child before Herod could lay hands on him.

APPLICATION: The Magi are the central personages in today's feast of Epiphany. They were pagans who did not know the true God of the Jews. Yet that true God revealed to them that the King he had promised to the Jews had come. The expected Prince was born. They came to Jerusalem, the capital of Judah, expecting, of course, to find the city and the whole country rejoicing. Instead they found suspicion and hatred in the reigning king—a hatred which in a few days turned to murder. Among the religious leaders they found knowledge of their past history, but utter indifference as regards the present and the future. These leaders knew the Messiah would be born in Bethlehem; they must have realized that the Magi were very sure of the truth revealed to them—they would not have come such a long journey on a "fool's errand." In spite of that, the thought of going to Bethlehem with the Magi never entered their minds. These were the leaders who some years later refused to listen to Christ and in spite of his miracles refused to admit his claim that he was not only the promised Messiah, but the true Son of God. These were the men who rejected him because he had mercy on sinners, and spoke of a future life. What they wanted from their Messiah was political power and earthly freedom and prosperity. Like Herod they ended with murder—the crucifixion of the "King of the Jews." The pagan king was not much worse than the indifferent leaders of God's Chosen People.

We too know the true facts concerning Christ, his mission, and his present and future kingdom. Like the leaders of the

Jews of his day, we also could become absorbed in the affairs of this life and the quest for wealth, pleasure and power. We could become so totally absorbed in such things as to have neither the interest nor the time to pay our respects to Christ or to welcome him into our homes and our hearts, as our true Lord. God forbid it should ever be thus with us. Rather let us resolve this morning to make the Magi our models, to follow them to Bethlehem and offer him all that we have and are. He will accept our offering and we will return by another way, wiser and better men.

FIRST SUNDAY OF THE YEAR

FEAST OF THE BAPTISM OF OUR LORD

FIRST READING: Isaiah 42: 1-4; 6-7. Thus says the Lord; Behold my servant, whom I uphold, my chosen, in whom my soul delights; I have put my Spirit upon him, he will bring forth justice to the nations. He will not cry or lift up his voice, or make it heard in the street; a bruised reed he will not break, and a dimly burning wick he will not quench; he will faithfully bring forth justice. He will not fail or be discouraged till he has established justice in the earth; and the coastlands wait for his law.

"I am the Lord, I have called you in righteousness, I have taken you by the hand and kept you; I have given you as a covenant to the people, a light to the nations, to open the eyes that are blind, to bring out the prisoners from the dungeon, from the prison those who sit in darkness."

EXPLANATION: In second-Isaiah (40-55) there are a series of oracles which describe a "servant of Yahweh" who is to come. He will have the qualities of a king, priest and prophet but to a greater degree. He will suffer for his people and be put to death because he carries out the will of (Yahweh) God to the letter. But God will again raise him up and give him numerous spiritual offspring. The New Testament and Christian tradition have always seen these oracles as messianic prophecies. They were fulfilled in Jesus Christ and in him only.

whom I uphold: God is his support and strength for it is God who has "chosen" him and in him God is "pleased." St. Matthew and St. Mark and St. Luke say these words were repeated from heaven when Christ was baptized by John in the Jordan: "Thou art my beloved (chosen) servant (son, in Greek, can be translated son or servant, like boy in English) in whom I am well pleased." (Lk. 3 : 22; Mk. 1 : 11; Mt. 3 : 17).

I have put my Spirit : In the Old Testament the spirit of God was bestowed on kings, priests and prophets. It is given to the servant because

he will . . . justice to the nations : He shall proclaim the will, the law of God, not only to the Jews but to all nations— his jurisdiction will be universal.

not cry . . . or lift . . . voice : Unlike oriental despots, he will accomplish his missions quietly and kindly.

bruised reed . . . burning wick : Nothing is more useless than a broken reed, nothing more loathsome than a smoking wick as used in the lamps of those days. Yet this servant can and will make something of them—his mercy and power can reach to the very dregs of humanity. Our Lord speaking of "mercy" applies these verses of Isaiah to himself (Mt. 12 : 15–21).

Justice in the earth : To establish the justice, that is, the will of God on earth, is his mission—he will persevere, come what may, until he has done this.

the coastlands : The nations will anxiously wait until he comes to bring them his teaching, i.e. the law of God. The Jews have some knowledge of it already.

I . . . Lord have called you : His mission is from God; his power is from God, "I have grasped you by the hand," and

I . . . the hand : refers to Christ's human nature. The words used are those used in describing Adam's creation.

covenant . . . light : The Jews had already a covenant, a pact with God, but the servant will make a new one and the nations will share in it; they too will have his light.

Blind . . . prisoners . . . darkness : His work is to open the spiritual eyes of people, to free them from the captivity and the darkness of sin and ignorance of God.

APPLICATION : This prophecy of second-Isaiah was chosen for today, the feast which commemorates the baptism of Christ in the Jordan, because on that occasion the Father's voice from heaven proclaimed that Christ was "his beloved servant in which he was well pleased." Following the interpretation of the inspired Evangelists and of the ancient and constant tradition of the Church, we can have no hesitation in seeing in these words of second-Isaiah, written five centuries or so before Christ, a description of the Savior who came on earth to teach Jew and Gentile the new law of God, the law of love and mercy.

He who was the Son of God took our human nature in order to represent us, and *as one of us* to give *our* heavenly Father the perfect obedience and service which no mere man had done ever since the creation, and which no mere man could ever do. This perfect obedience or service of God which Christ, the perfect servant, gave the Father, went as far as the acceptance of the shameful and excruciating death on a cross. But all this he accepted gladly for us—it was in our name he did it—and because he did it, we are all raised to a new relationship with God. He has made us all, Jew and Gentile, the whole human race, adopted sons of his heavenly Father.

As members of his mystical body we

can now, because he is our Head, give a service to God worthy of our new status, a service which God accepts from us because it is given to him and through "Christ our Lord."

Today, as we offer the Mass, the sacrifice of Christ renewed before our eyes, let us try to realize the privilege that is ours. We are able, through Christ, to offer a sacrifice which gives infinite honor to God. We are able in spite of all our weaknesses and all our faults to give a service that is pleasing to God and to make some return for all he has done for us. We have become "good and faithful servants" because Christ the Son of God became the perfect servant of God for our sakes.

SECOND READING : Acts 10 : 34-38. Peter opened his mouth and said: "Truly I perceive that God shows no partiality, but in every nation anyone who fears him and does what is right is acceptable to him. You know the word which he sent to Israel, preaching good news of peace by Jesus Christ (he is Lord of all), the word which was proclaimed throughout all Judea, beginning from Galilee after the baptism which John preached: how God anointed Jesus of Nazareth with the Holy Spirit and with power; how he went about doing good and healing all that were oppressed by the devil, for God was with him."

EXPLANATION : These verses of Acts are read for us today because they contain a reference to our Lord's baptism. This reference occurs in a very interesting event which took place soon after the Ascension and is described in Acts 10 : 1; 11 : 18. Cornelius, a pagan Roman officer stationed in Caesarea in Palestine, a devout man who admires the God of the Jews and the religion of the Jews, is told by an angel to send for Peter. Peter in the meantime has seen a vision from which he learns that the Gentile is as welcome into the fold as the Jew. He comes to Cornelius and baptizes him and his household—the first Gentile family to be accepted into the Christian Church and by none other than by the Prince of the Apostles, Peter himself. Having heard Cornelius's story, Peter has these words to say :

God shows no partiality : Because of the vision he saw and because of the words of Cornelius he has just heard, from which it is evident that Cornelius is dear to God, Peter understands that Christ's salvation is not only for Jews but for Gentiles too.

who fears him . . . to him : He who accepts and respects God does God's will.

the word to . . . Israel : Christ preached to the Jews only, but he gave the order to his Apostles to preach to all nations.

preach . . . by Jesus Christ : This is the essence of the gospel : peace with God and peace between all men brought about by Christ's sojourn on earth.

Galilee . . . John preached : Peter gives a brief summary of Christ's public life in Palestine.

God anointed Jesus : This refers to the descent of the spirit in visible form on Jesus at his baptism in the Jordan, and to the words of the Father proclaiming him his beloved servant—the Messiah. He was the Messiah from the moment of his conception but this was first made evident on the occasion of his baptism and proved apodictically at his resurrection. This was his anointing, i.e. the moment of his inauguration, as the kings and priests were anointed when they actually took on their office.

doing good . . . healing : A reference to the miracles of Jesus of which Cornelius must have heard.

oppressed . . . devil : Epilepsy, madness and most mental illnesses as well as many bodily defects, were attributed directly to the devil at that time. By healing the sufferers, Christ showed his power over the demons.

God was with him : He had the divine power which miracles demand, only God can alter the laws of nature, which he has made. Prophets and holy men in the Old Testament worked miracles by calling on God to give them this power; Christ was God; through his own power he worked his miracles.

APPLICATION : That day, nearly two thousand years ago, when Christ by his baptism in the Jordan, began his public preaching of salvation for all men, is a day—a feastday—no true Christian can ever forget. The baptism of John was for sinners—a sign of change of heart and a turning to God. Christ had no sin, he had never turned away from God, he was God—but he was the representative of sinful humanity. He represented us sinners that day and opened the door of salvation for us. In that ceremony Christ was proclaimed by the heavenly Father to be his son and faithful servant, and the power of the Holy Spirit came upon him.

But this was all for us; as God he already had all things in common with the Father and the Holy Spirit. But in his human nature—our weak human nature which he took on himself in order to be one of us, and our representative—he was on that day proclaimed God's true and faithful servant. At the same moment we human beings were accepted *in him* and *through him* (i.e. through his perfect obedience even unto the death on the cross) as God's adopted children.

The mission of Christ was for us. The Incarnation took place because God's infinite love wanted man, the masterpiece of his whole creation, to have a share in the divine gifts of the Blessed Trinity. God united the divine with the human nature in Christ. We mortal men were raised above our human nature; we would become immortal, not that we would never die on this earth—Christ himself died in his human nature—but "he would raise us up on the last day" to share forever with the Father, the Holy Spirit and the Incarnate Son the eternal bliss of heaven.

How could a Christian, one who knows all this, ever refuse to do the little part he is called on to do—"to fear God, that is, to reverence and respect him and to do what is right"? Reverence and respect for God should come easily from anyone who realizes what God has done for him. But true respect for God is not proved by a few distracted prayers and a grudging attendance at Sunday Mass. It is proved by striving to keep the laws Christ gave us, i.e. doing what is right, every day of our lives. This is difficult at times but if we keep our eternity— the unending life—before our eyes, the few short years of hardship and training on earth, will seem very short indeed. There is no comparison between what God has prepared for us, and promises us, and the trifling conditions he asks us to fulfill in order to earn his promised reward.

GOSPEL : Mark 1 : 7–11. John preached, saying, "After me comes he who is mightier than I, the thong of whose sandals I am not worthy to stoop down and untie. I have baptized you with water; but he will baptize you with the Holy Spirit."

In those days Jesus came from Nazareth of Galilee and was baptized by John in the Jordan. And when he came up out of the water, immediately he saw the heavens opened and the Spirit descending upon him like a dove; and a voice came from heaven, "Thou art my beloved Son; with thee I am well pleased."

EXPLANATION : John's preaching and baptizing near the Jordan had aroused the greatest interest among the Jews of that time. They all associated his mission with the Messiah; many of them thought John was himself the Messiah. This he strongly denied, and he told them that he was only preparing them to greet and welcome the Messiah who was very soon coming amongst them and who was a person superior to him in every way. Mark's gospel today tells us why.

mightier than I : The Baptist had no doubt as to the superiority of the one who was to come. He was one who would be "mighty" with the power of God.

sandals . . . untie : In relation to the Messiah the Baptist felt that he himself was not fit to be a lowly servant.

water . . . Holy Spirit : The baptism carried out by John was an external rite— a symbol of the internal conversion each recipient had brought about in himself. In itself it had no spiritual value. But the Messiah's baptism will confer on those who will receive it the Spirit of God—the grace, friendship and power of God. John's hearers (and probably John himself also) did not understand the "Holy Spirit" to signify the third person of the Blessed Trinity—their understanding would be in the Old Testament sense of the power of God. However, when Mark was writing his gospel the doctrine of the Blessed Trinity and the Holy Spirit's office of sanctifier of men was accepted by all converts. John's words were understood by them in their fuller and real sense.

In those days : When John had baptized all who repented of their sins and once more turned their hearts to God (Lk. 3 : 21), Jesus came down from Nazareth to the Jordan and was baptized by John. Mark does not say so here, but we are told by Matthew (3 : 14–15), that John did not want to do this, but Jesus insisted.

out of the water : The baptism was by total immersion in the waters of the Jordan.

heavens . . . a dove : The Baptist, and

perhaps others present, beheld this vision. In the visible form of a dove the Spirit of God came down from an opening in the sky. According to the Jewish idea God's abode was in the heavens above. This was to signify the beginning of Jesus' messianic mission. In the Old Testament the Spirit (or power) of God is always given for a specific task (Jgs. 3 : 10; 6 : 34; Num. 11 : 7 etc). Christ's task, already indicated by the Baptist (Mk. 1 : 8), is declared also in the "voice from heaven."

Thou art . . . Son : The voice from heaven was that of God the Father. It is generally admitted that God the Father is here proclaiming Jesus as the Messiah foretold by the prophets, but especially by Isaiah in the "suffering servant" prophecies. That this servant of God was also his divine Son was not understood by either John the Baptist or these others who were present that day. By the time the Gospels were written, however, this truth was the basis of Christianity. Hence the three synoptic gospels change the word "servant" used by Isaiah, into "son"—a change which was easy, for the Greek word used in the LXX for servant in Isaiah was "pais," which also means "son." So the one who was greater than the Baptist was not only the Messiah but the Son of God also.

APPLICATION : That Jesus insisted on being baptized by John in the Jordan, just like all the other sinful mortals, was another proof of his love for us and his willingness to undergo any humiliation for our sakes. He had no sins of which to repent; he had no need to show proof that he was changing his sinful ways and returning to God. But that day in the Jordan, he was the representative of all the sinners of the world. God the Father, "made him to be sin who knew no sin so that in him we might become the righteousness of God," as St. Paul tells us (see 2 Cor. 5 : 21. Rom. 8 : 3). By this act of self-humiliation, this acceptance of all our sins, Jesus began his messianic mission of salvation for all sinners. He ended the same salvific mission on Good Friday by nailing all our sins to the cross together with his own body (see Col. 2 : 14).

All of this was for us, for you and for me. God's plan for all men is that they should enjoy an everlasting life with him after their short sojourn on earth. The incarnation has made that possible; it made us brothers of Christ and therefore adopted sons of God. But even though elevated to the status of sonship, we need to be freed from all our sins, and to make adequate atonement for them to God before we can inherit our eternal reward. This we could not do of ourselves, therefore the Son of God incarnate—our brother according to the flesh—has done it for us. Hence his sufferings : the poverty he endured, the insults he bore, the cold-heartedness he met with, the fierce opposition of the leaders of the Jews, an opposition which resulted in the excruciating and shameful death of the cross.

All of this we Christians of today know and admit. Yet, how warm is our gratitude to Christ, how sincere is our thankfulness for all he has done for us? We can ask ourselves, instead, how often are we so ungrateful that we forget and ignore what Christ suffered for us? We not only offend him and "crucify him again" by our serious sins, but we grumble and complain and often openly rebel when he asks us to follow him on the path of humiliation and sufferings, which already he trod to show us the way.

Could a human father who had toiled and labored and mortified himself to give his son an education and a place in life be blamed if he cut out that son forever from his home and family, because that son not only ignored and showed himself ungrateful to his father, but insulted and injured him? Most of us would say that the son more than deserved all he got. But we are just such ungrateful sons, who not only do not thank our divine Savior, but insult and injure him by our sinful lives. However, and thank God for it, Christ is divine as well as human; his mercy, love, understanding and sympathy are not finite and limited like those of men. His love is for sinners as well as for saints, provided the sinners admit their faults and return to him repentant. He is ever sending out to sinners his offers of love and reconciliation. Every day, and every hour of the day, he is recalling sinners to a sense of gratitude, a sense of decency, in fact a sense of their own self-interest in their eternal welfare.

The commemoration of the Baptism of Christ in the Jordan is for all of us today one of those loving calls of Christ. He wants us to be less ungrateful, more appreciative of what he has done for us. He wants us to see this life for what it is : a moment of transit, a short journey toward the glorious future he has earned for us. If we keep this future, our true life, always before our eyes and if we keep in mind all Christ suffered in order to win that true life for us, our earthly troubles, our worldly aches and pains, will then appear in their true light—trivialities, which are well worth bearing because of the reward they will earn for us.

SECOND SUNDAY OF THE YEAR

FIRST READING: 1 Samuel 3:3-10; 19. Samuel was lying down within the temple of the Lord, where the ark of God was. Then the Lord called, "Samuel! Samuel!" and he said, "Here I am!" and ran to Eli, and said, "Here I am, for you called me." But he said, "I did not call; lie down again." So he went and lay down. And the Lord called again, "Samuel!" And Samuel arose and went to Eli, and said, "Here I am, for you called me." But he said, "I did not call, my son; lie down again." Now Samuel did not yet know the Lord, and the word of the Lord had not yet been revealed to him. And the Lord called Samuel again the third time. And he arose and went to Eli, and said, "Here I am, for you called me." Then Eli perceived that the Lord was calling the boy. Therefore Eli said to Samuel, "Go, lie down; and if he calls you, you shall say, 'Speak, Lord, for thy servant hears.' " So Samuel went and lay down in his place.

And the Lord came and stood forth, calling as at other times, "Samuel! Samuel!" And Samuel said, "Speak, for thy servant hears."

And Samuel grew, and the Lord was with him and let none of his words fall to the ground.

EXPLANATION: We have here the account of Samuel's vocation to take over the leadership of the Chosen People —to be Yahweh's prophet and visible representative among them. This was an office to be filled from the death of Eli until Saul was appointed king (c. 1050–1030). The call came while he was still a youth and he served under Eli at the shrine of Shiloh, where the Ark then was, until Eli died. He then became the official leader of the people until God told him to anoint Saul as king and satisfy the people's demand for a king. His birth was God's answer to the prayers of a devout mother who had been barren for years, hence the etymology of his name "I asked Yahweh for him" (1 Sm. 1:20). His mother Hannah was so grateful to God that she dedicated him to serve in the shrine at Shiloh from an early age. It was during his early youth that he was given his special call, his "vocation," to take Eli's place.

Lying down ... temple: He slept somewhere within the shrine very probably in order to re-light the temple lamp should it go out during the night.

the Lord called: Sometime during the

night ("the lamp of God had not yet gone out"—it was extinguished at daylight), Samuel heard his name called. He thought Eli was calling him.

did not . . . Lord : The young boy had never heard the voice of Yahweh. He naturally thought the voice calling him was that of Eli, the only one with him in the precincts of the shrine. He had no expectation that Yahweh would speak to him.

again . . . time : Three distinct times he heard his name called and each time he promptly rose and went to Eli; obedience was one of his virtues!

Eli said : When this call had come a third time Eli grasped its meaning. He told the young boy how to answer if called once more : "Speak Lord for thy servant hears." Samuel replied thus to the fourth call and the Lord then gave him a message for Eli and his own prophetic vocation.

Lord . . . him : The power of God was with Samuel, enabling him to become worthy of the office he was to hold.

words . . . ground : Because of this power of God, Samuel's judgements and decisions as leader of the people were true and solid—they did not fail, they were not proved false. Verse 20 (which is not in the reading) proves this : "All Israel from Dan to Beersheba came to know that Samuel was accredited as a prophet of Yahweh."

APPLICATION : God's ways are surely wonderful! He could govern and regulate this world and all its inhabitants most correctly and successfully all by himself. However, he has decided to give man a chance of co-operating with him in the running of the material and spiritual affairs of his world. Perhaps they are more often a hindrance rather than a help to the Lord. Yet, he not only allows them but he calls them, selects them for various roles in the government of his world.

This is true in the running of the temporal affairs as well as the government of the spiritual life of men on earth. The exercise of power over a nation or community of people is not from man but from God, hence the obligation on subjects to obey the just laws of their rulers. God it is who delegates his authority to earthly rulers.

During the first eight hundred years of God's dealings with his Chosen People, both the temporal and spiritual leadership of the people always resided in one and the same individual. The Patriarchs, Moses, Joshua, the Judges down to the appointment of kings (1030 B.C.), were individually called by God to administer both the temporal and spiritual affairs of the community. Today's lesson tells us how Samuel got his call to fulfill this double task of temporal and spiritual leadership of God's people. Because God was with him in all his doings he carried it out very successfully for about twenty years.

All men have a vocation, a call from God in this life. Each individual has duties to perform which, if faithfully carried out, will earn for him the place God has planned for him in the eternal kingdom. A few are called to be the leaders of their fellowmen. The vast majority are called to follow the leaders by loyally obeying the laws enacted for their just government. Each one of us has a call from God, a part to play in the temporal and spiritual affairs of this life. The future status of each one of us will be determined by the manner in which we carried out our role on earth.

Samuel had not the faintest idea that it was God who was speaking to him when he first got his call, his vocation, in the shrine at Shiloh. But when he eventually realized the truth he immediately offered his humble service to the Lord, "thy servant hears." How few of us have seen a call from God, a divine vocation, in the humdrum activities of our daily lives, and yet these ordinary daily tasks are the road to heaven that God has mapped out for us. These are the "vocations" he has given us. We may say that we ourselves chose our careers in life, we decided what occupation we should follow, but behind our free decisions the wise providence of God, working through parents, neighbors, circumstances of time and place, has so arranged our earthly journey that it would end for us in heaven. Many grumble at their role in life. They think their lot is so inferior and demanding when compared with the life others lead, and even go so far as to say that God could have no part in such a bad arrangement. Yet, God is in charge of his world. He chooses each individual for the role he is to carry to its successful conclusion.

"There is a divinity that shapes our ends, rough-hew them as we will," Shakespeare, the wise Christian tells us. God has a masterplan for the human race; to each one of us he has given a little niche in that plan. If we play the part he has given us, let it be noble or humble in the eyes of this world, we shall make a success of God's masterplan, of this great human drama. Our own eternal success will be assured. With Samuel today, let us accept our vocation and humbly submit ourselves to his divine will: "speak Lord for thy servant hears."

SECOND READING: 1 Corinthians 6:13–15; 17–20. The body is not meant for immorality, but for the Lord, and the Lord for the body. And God raised the Lord and will also raise us up by his power. Do you not know that your bodies are members of Christ? He who is united to the Lord becomes one spirit with him. Shun immorality. Every other sin which a man commits is outside the body; but the immoral man sins against his own body. Do you not know that your body is a temple of the Holy Spirit within you, which you have from God? You are not your own; you were bought with a price. So glorify God in your body.

EXPLANATION: One of the most besetting sins of the pagan port-town of Corinth was fornication, or more precisely prostitution. Some of Paul's converts found the Christian obligation of chastity rather difficult, and, falling back on the ideas of their pagan days, ideas still prevalent among the pagans all around them, they tried to justify fornication as part of the Christian liberty which Paul had preached to them. In this letter, which Paul wrote from Ephesus to his Corinthian converts, he makes it crystal clear that such an interpretation of Christian liberty was wrong. **The body . . . immorality :** These lax converts in Corinth tried to justify their sexual aberrations by saying that sex was a natural desire of the body, and within the Christian code that it should be lawful to satisfy such desires, just as was the bodily desire for food and drink. Paul's answer is an emphatic "no." In baptism the whole man, body as well as spirit, is dedicated and united to Christ. To unite such a body with an illicit partner, which happens in fornication (the use of sex in marriage is, of course, lawful) is a profanation of the union between Christ and the Christian in baptism and is therefore a sacrilege.

God . . . up : The union with Christ, established by baptism, will last forever. We shall die, but just as Christ was raised from the dead, so shall we too be raised by God, and so remain united with Christ forever.

bodies . . . Christ : Paul had taught them this truth : "do you not know," he says, "that your bodies are members of Christ?" As the human body is made up of many and different members, so the body of Christ—his visible Church on earth—is made of all the Christian people. But Paul goes further here and implies that each Christian forms "one flesh," as it were, with Christ : the union is corporal rather than corporate. Hence the malice of fornication.

becomes . . . with him : Christ has sent his Spirit on all the baptized; this will effect the spiritualization of their mortal bodies on the day of their resurrection. **every other sin . . . body :** Although the body plays a part in other sins, for example, gluttony, sins against chastity (fornication and adultery) engage the body more than sins against other virtues. It is an abuse of the body; it separates it from the Lord to whom it was united in baptism.

temple . . . Spirit : Christian baptism confers the Holy Spirit. Every Christian thus becomes a temple of the Spirit— God dwells in a special way within him. **you . . . own :** Christians belong to God. Through the incarnation and death of Christ they were made God's chosen ones, free men and heirs of heaven.

glorify God in your body : By preserving free from immorality their bodies, as temples pure and holy, fit abodes of the Holy Spirit, they should honor God and show their appreciation of his infinite goodness.

APPLICATION : St. Paul wrote these words almost two thousand years ago. Ninety per cent of the world's population was still pagan, knowing nothing of the true God or of his divine plans for them. The only practical philosophy they could and did follow was the enjoyment of every comfort and pleasure. They believed that when they died all was ended forever. St. Paul's converts in Corinth were living in the midst of pagans who practiced this philosophy.

This made Christian living very difficult for some of them. They fell back into the immoral practices in which they had indulged before their conversion.

The Apostle, hearing of this, condemned their conduct in clear and forceful language. "Shun immorality"; "the body is not meant for immorality," he tells them. He then gives the reason why the use of sex, outside of marriage, is not only a sin but a sacrilege. In baptism the Christian has given his body to

Christ. He has become a member of Christ, and therefore, such a body cannot be given to anyone but to a lawful spouse. To join the Christian body to a prostitute in fornication therefore, was a desecration of the sacred, a direct denial of the bond which bound the Christian to Christ. Furthermore, he reminds these immoral converts of a truth he had already told them, namely, that ever since their baptism the Holy Spirit dwelt within them—they were temples of God. They belonged in a very special way to God, for, through Christ, he had brought them out of slavery to be his own heirs for all eternity.

This teaching of St. Paul is, if anything, more necessary today than it was at that time in Corinth. The weak converts of Corinth had the bad example of their local pagan neighbors to contend with. They also had the good example of the majority of their fellow-converts to uplift and encourage them. Today we have to contend, not only with the bad example of local pagan or rather neo-pagan neighbors, but the full force of the world's immorality is blazoned daily before our eyes by the mass-media of television, papers, and scandal-mongering writers.

The campaign for absolute freedom for the individual, the demands of the permissive society, are being daily shouted from the house-tops with such insistence and constancy, that even devout Christians cannot entirely avoid their impact. Sex, or rather the abuse of it, has become the battle-cry of youth. Indeed, it has been raised to the status of a god whose every whim must be obeyed and satisfied. Pornography today has become a billion-dollar industry. As long as there is a demand for it suppliers will not be found wanting. If this sexual extravagance was the invention of the communist countries as a means of reducing the rest of the world to impotency, the democracies of the West would be immediately up in arms. But as it is their own brain-child, they have no word of condemnation for it. If they do not openly encourage it, they at least permit this social cancer to grow and propagate itself. They do not realize or perhaps do not care, that it will eventually corrupt their nations and make social life, and even human existence impossible.

But we Christians can and must stand up and oppose with every means in our power, this pagan immorality. Our bodies are members of Christ's sacred body. We must not desecrate them by indulging in sexual aberrations. We are temples of the Holy Spirit; sin must have no place within us. Parents of families : instruct your children by word and example. Protect them, as far as you can, from this immoral cancer which is being encouraged and developed all around you. Under the guise of liberty our permissive society is demanding more and more license to violate, not only the sacred laws of God himself, but the very nature of humanity. Human intelligence and reason are thrown overboard in the search for sexual pleasure, and man who was made "a little less than the angels" is now debased to the level of the beast of the field.

Listen to St. Paul's advice : "The body is not meant for immorality—it is meant to glorify God."

GOSPEL : John 1 : 35–42. John was standing with two of his disciples; and he looked at Jesus as he walked, and said, "Behold, the Lamb of God!" The two disciples heard him say this, and they followed Jesus. Jesus turned, and saw them following, and said to them, "What do you seek?" And they said to him, "Rabbi" (which means Teacher), "where are you staying?" He said to them, "Come and see." They came and saw where he was staying; and they stayed with him that day, for it was about the tenth hour. One of the two who heard John speak, and followed him, was Andrew, Simon Peter's brother. He first found his brother Simon, and said to him, "We have found the Messiah" (which means Christ). He brought him to Jesus. Jesus looked at him, and said, "So you are Simon the son of John? You shall be called Cephas" (which means Peter).

EXPLANATION : For some months before Jesus came to him at the Jordan, John the Baptist had been preaching and baptizing—preparing his fellow-Jews for the Messiah. As was the custom with the prophets and other holy men, disciples had come to join him. But the Baptist, who knew that his mission was a temporary one, encouraged these disciples to follow Jesus, as soon as he had learned from divine revelation (Jn. 1 : 32–34) that Jesus was the promised Messiah. In today's extract from the fourth gospel, we see four of the Baptist's disciples. Three of them, Peter, James and John, were always among his closest and most privileged Apostles.

Behold . . . God : Calling Jesus the Lamb of God the Baptist points him out to two of his disciples. This title most probably refers to the suffering servant described in second-Isaiah (40–55). In Is. 53 : 7–12, this servant of Yahweh is described as an innocent Lamb who is slaughtered for the sins of all the erring sheep : " taking their faults on himself." These servant poems in Isaiah were accepted as messianic, and the Baptist's disciples understand that their prophet is pointing out the Messiah to them.

they followed Jesus : They had come from Galilee thinking, as many other Jews did, that the Baptist himself was the Messiah. Now the Baptist has made it clear to all (Jn. 1 : 19–34) that he is as nothing compared to the Messiah. From the Baptist's words, the two disciples understood that Jesus was the Messiah foretold by Isaiah. So they left John and followed Jesus.

what do you seek : He wants them to declare their reason for following him. **come and see :** Clearly, their reason was to know more about him, and so they hinted that they wished to live with him. He invites them to come along. **one . . . was Andrew :** It is generally accepted that the other was the Evangelist. He never mentions his own name in his gospel, but speaks of the "beloved disciple" or the "son of Zebedee."

his brother Simon : Simon was at the Jordan and evidently was a disciple of the Baptist also. Andrew, who recognized Jesus as the Messiah, told Simon who then also came to follow him. The statement "he (Andrew) *first found his brother*" seems to imply that the other (John) found his brother (James) also and brought him to Jesus. In the synoptic gospels Peter, Andrew, James and John are the first four disciples to be called by Jesus (see Mk. 1 : 16–20).

you shall . . . Cephas: The Aramaic name, Cephas, means "rock." On his very first encounter with Simon, Jesus promises him that his name will be changed to "Rock," which means strength, solidity. A change of name among the Chosen People meant a change of position or function. This change of position or function took place later, when Simon was given the primacy of the Church. He was then made the Church's solid foundation on which it was to stand for all time (Mt. 16 : 18). He was to be the Rock (Petros or Peter=Cephas or Rock) on which Christ would build his Church.

APPLICATION: In the eight short verses read to us today from St. John's gospel we have an account of the vocation of the first four Apostles who followed Jesus. It was a momentous event in the history of salvation. It was the beginning of a stream of vocations that would grow and spread down through the ages until the end of the world. It was momentous, firstly, in that Christ, who had come to open heaven for all men and who could find means of bringing them all to that eternal home without help from any man, decided instead to let men co-operate with him in this divine task. He decreed to set up a kingdom in this world—his Church —which would be run by mere mortals for their fellow-mortals, but which would be under his protection and assisted by his divine aid until the end of time. Christ chose this very human way, in order to make his Church more acceptable to our limited, human understanding and more approachable for sinful, human nature.

Christ, as God, could deal directly with every human being on earth. He could teach the infallible truth; he could pardon sins; he could give all the graces needed to travel successfully to heaven. There would then be no need for a Church with its teaching magisterium, no need for the sacrament of initiation, baptism, or of reconciliation, penance, nor of the Holy Eucharist itself or of any other such aids. Christ could do all that his Church does for the salvation of mankind, and more successfully, of course, but yet he chose the way which divine wisdom saw was best.

We mortals know that God can speak directly to our hearts, and actually has done so to many men in the past. We know that he can do directly all that is done by his Church, to whom he gave the power, with its teaching magisterium and sacraments. If he were to act in this way we should be open to continuous doubts about the source of our inspirations and the objectivity of the graces we thought we were receiving. It was to remove such doubts, and the possibility of self-deception that Christ left to us the external visible kingdom to which he gave all the powers necessary for men's salvation. It was for the security and peace of men's consciences that he set up a visible Church founded on the Apostles, men like ourselves, but transformed by his assisting grace.

Another momentous fact in Christ's choice of the Apostles on whom he was to build his Church, is that he "chose the lowly and the humble to confound the wise." The first four Apostles, as well as the other eight, were simple, lowly fishermen from Galilee. They may possibly have been able to read and write a little, but they were certainly not men of education or any social standing in their communities. He could have converted and chosen some of the more highly educated scribes of Jerusalem, or some of the Roman centurions then in Palestine, or some of the many philosophers in Greece, or even Roman senators whose influence as Christian teachers would carry such weight with the educated elite of the empire. But he did not. The instrument he chose to carry his message to all men, was not dependent on human ingenuity or on the educational or social standing of his witnesses. Rather was it to stand on the power of God, of which it was the expression and proof.

We can see clearly the divine wisdom governing Christ's choice of Apostles! Had his message of salvation been spread and promulgated by men of learning and social standing, the cry would soon go up on all sides: "This religion is the invention of philosophers; it is a clever plan of the upper classes to keep the poor and humble workers in subjection." But it was the poor and working classes who spread Christ's message, and who suffered imprison-ment and death itself at the hands of the educated and upper classes for so doing.

Today, let us thank our blessed Lord who provided so humanly- and yet so divinely for our eternal welfare. In the Church, which he founded on the lowly but solid foundation of simple fishermen of Galilee, he erected an institution against which the gates of hell, the power of all the enemies of our salvation, cannot prevail, for his divine guidance and help will be with it forever. It has had enemies and opposition from the beginning; they may be more numerous and more destructive than ever, today. But the promise of Christ still holds good, his word cannot fail. Therefore, neither the opposition of materialistic enemies from without, nor the even more insidious attacks from faint-hearted and worldly-minded members from within, can affect the safety and permanence of the building which Christ built on the Rock. "If God is with us," it matters not "who is against us."

THIRD SUNDAY OF THE YEAR

FIRST READING: Jonah 3:1–5; 10. The word of the Lord came to Jonah, saying, "Arise, go to Nineveh, that great city, and proclaim to it the message that I tell you." So Jonah arose and went to Nineveh, according to the word of the Lord. Now Nineveh was an exceedingly great city, three days' journey in breadth. Jonah began to go into the city, going a day's journey. And he cried, "Yet forty days, and Nineveh shall be overthrown!" And the people of Nineveh believed God; they proclaimed a fast, and put on sackcloth, from the greatest of them to the least of them.

When God saw what they did, how they turned from their evil way, God repented of the evil which he had said he would do to them; and he did not do it.

EXPLANATION: The book of Jonah is not an historical account of the life and preaching of a prophet called Jonah who lived in the eighth century B.C. (see 2 Kgs. 14:25), but rather a fictional, didactic composition written after the return from the Babylonian exile, some time in the fifth century. The book is a sermon in the form of a story. The theme of the sermon is that Yahweh is the God of all nations, not of the Jews only, and that the Jews who have knowledge of him should spread that knowledge among the Gentiles. The returned exiles (the Jews back from Babylon) refused to do this. Instead their ambition and hope was that all Gentiles would be severely punished, if not annihilated, by Yahweh.

According to the story, a man called Jonah was told by God to go to a pagan city and preach repentance to the sinful people there. He refused and tried to escape. God punished him but spared him (the storm at sea and the fish which swallowed him), and eventually made him go.

word . . . Jonah: The command had already been given in 1:1, here it is repeated.

message . . . you: The message was already given in 1:1. The wickedness of Nineveh was known to Yahweh, he would punish them if they did not repent.

Nineveh: This was the capital city of Assyria, the arch-enemy of Israel in the eighth century. Jonah would naturally prefer to see them punished by Yahweh rather than that they should be converted and spared. This city was no longer standing when the book was written; it was razed to the ground in 612 B.C.

a great city . . . journey : There is some slight exaggeration here. It is said to have been three miles in width. But the larger the city the more wondrous its conversion.

forty days : If the people of Nineveh do not repent Yahweh will destroy them and their city after forty days.

people . . . God : They accepted as true what the God of this Jewish prophet had said. They believed that he had dominion over them also, and that they should cease to offend him. This they did.

put on sackcloth : They immediately began to do penance "in sackcloth and fasting," mortifying their flesh.

God repented : There was no change in God, but because the sinners of Nineveh had changed God accepted them back in his favor once more.

he did not . . . them : Because of their conversion neither they nor their city would be destroyed.

APPLICATION : The lesson of this story should have been very clear to the writer's Jewish contemporaries. They could see from it that God did not approve of their narrow-minded religious and nationalistic outlook. Even if they were God's Chosen People, he was not their God to the exclusion of all other races. He owned them but they did not own him, and this was exactly what they were trying to do. Yet, had they known the history of God's dealings with them, they should have understood that God had chosen them in order that the blessings of the incarnation would come through them to all nations. Abraham, their Father, was called to be a blessing for his descendants and for the whole world (Gen. 12 : 3). Too often many of them forgot this.

These verses from Jonah have not been chosen for today's reading so that we should condemn the narrow-mindedness of the Jews of past ages. They have been chosen to remind us of our duty to look on all men as adopted sons of God and our brothers, toward whom we have a grave obligation to help on the road to heaven. God has destined all men for heaven. He sent his divine Son as man to make heaven available for all. He expected his Chosen People of old to share their special knowledge of him with their pagan neighbors. So too does he expect every Christian worthy of the name to do all in his power to spread the greater knowledge of Christ the Savior among all peoples, so that they too can share in the blessings he brought and avail of the happy future which is in store for them.

Have we been doing this? Have we really been interested in our fellowmen? How often have we given them a thought or prayed for their conversion? How often have we donated a dime or a dollar to help the missionaries who, at home and abroad, have dedicated their lives to the conversion of pagans and sinners? There are Christians who excuse themselves from this obligation because they say : "we have more than enough to do to work out our own salvation." Their statement is more true than they realize. They will never succeed in reaching their own eternal salvation if they refuse to help their fellowmen. No one who does not love God can get to heaven. The proof of real love of God is love of our neighbor, St. John tells us. So, to know if we are on the right road to heaven let us examine our consciences as regards our love of neighbor. Have we been practicing the corporal and spiritual works of mercy, especially the spiritual works? It is they that are in question in today's reading.

Pope Pius XI used to say: "The Christian who is not an Apostle is on the way to becoming an apostate." The reason is that the very essence of Christianity is love, and love like heat diffuses itself automatically. The Christian who is not spreading the love of God has not got that love within him. His heart is full of self. There is no room in it for God. Down through the ages we have more than enough proof of this, but more so perhaps in recent times. We have men and women today who at one time gave themselves wholeheartedly to the service of God and their neighbor. But through overconcentration on them-

selves, on their rights and freedoms, they have forgotten their neighbor, and to all intents and purposes therefore, they are forgetting God and their own eternal welfare.

While we beg of God to keep us on the right road to heaven, let us realize that if we want to stay on that road we must help all our brothers that we meet on the way. We must help our next-door neighbors by example and word. Those who are far off too, we must help financially, and by our prayers and penances. There is abundant room for all in God's heaven. Because of the good influence he had, directly or indirectly, on their lives on earth, each one's own personal happiness will be intensified and increased by seeing and knowing the happiness these others are enjoying in heaven.

SECOND READING: 1 Corinthians 7 : 29-31. Brethren, the appointed time has grown very short; from now on, let those who have wives live as though they had none, and those who mourn as though they were not mourning, and those who rejoice as though they were not rejoicing, and those who buy as though they had no goods, and those who deal with the world as though they had no dealings with it. For the form of this world is passing away.

EXPLANATION: Christ clearly revealed to his disciples that he would return to this earth in his glory to judge the living and the dead (see Mt. 24; 1 Th. 4 : 13-17; 5 : 2-11; 1 Cor. 15, etc.). However, he did not reveal to them when this would be, so some of the first Christians (including, perhaps, St. Paul himself) thought and hoped it would be during their own lifetime. In these three verses of his first letter to the Corinthians, St. Paul does not say,

for he does not know, whether the end of the world is near or far off; all he does is to admonish his converts to do what our Lord himself advised his follower—always to be ready for the judgement (Mt. 24 : 43-44; 25 : 13 : "so stay awake because you do not know either the day or the hour").

appointed . . . short: The appointed time for Paul is the messianic era. It has already begun, is of a limited duration and is of its nature short.

who have wives : The moment of judgement, that moment on which each one's eternity depends, is unknown. It behoves all to be always ready to answer the call when it comes. To be able to do this, we must be detached from persons and things in this world. He mentions wives, joys and sorrows, the goods and affairs of this world. He does not forbid them the lawful use of matrimony or of the goods and joys, as well as the sorrows of this life, but they must use and possess them in a way in which they can be ever ready to leave them when Christ calls them to judgement.

form of this world : The Christian era, just begun, is moving toward its culmination : the end of time and the beginning of eternity.

APPLICATION : St. Paul is speaking to each one of us here today and is giving us the very same sound, spiritual advice which he gave to his converts in Corinth. Unlike them, we are not expecting the general judgement in our lifetime; but what is worse, most of us are giving little thought to the particular judgement, to the fact that each one of us will soon be called to meet Christ in a judgement that will decide our eternal future. It is a strange, human phenomenon that while we plan and provide for future probabilities, some of which will never happen, few of us plan and provide for the one certain, future fact in our lives, which is that we are certain to die some day.

Men train for occupations and professions. Men build houses for themselves and their families. Men take out insurances against illness and unemployment. Men put money into businesses or investments which are likely to give them a sound income later. And all the while they are speculating, perhaps wisely, on future probabilities, but failing to face and prepare for the one certain future happening : their departure from this world.

Someone may say : must we take no interest then in temporal affairs? Of course, we must! It is by taking an interest in, and honestly and fully carrying out, our temporal duties that we are making ourselves ready at all times to meet our Judge. Each one's daily task faithfully carried out is a devout prayer to God, it is an honor given by man to his Creator; it is the Christian's way of saying "thank you" to Christ our Savior.

Preparing for heaven does not mean removing oneself from association with the world. Some devout Christians did this in the early Church. It means using the world as the stairs on which we can climb to heaven. Men can have wives, and women can have husbands, they can have homes and property, investments and insurances, provided all these things are accepted as God's gifts and used for their own and their neighbor's sanctification. It is the abuse of these gifts that can make us all unfit and not ready to meet our Judge. A healthy bank account —the fruit of honest labor—will be no hindrance to entering heaven, whereas the rags and poverty of the idler are no *open sesame* for the heavenly portals.

Let us remember this always : the time in which we can earn the everlasting life after death is very short even for the youngest amongst us. But be it thirty days or sixty years, whatever length of time it is, each one of us can make sure that we shall be found ready when our last moment comes. We can indeed assure ourselves of this, if we begin today to live a Christian life, loving God and neighbor. This is indeed the word of the Lord coming to us through the great Apostle St. Paul.

GOSPEL: Mark 1:14-20. After John was arrested, Jesus came into Galilee, preaching the gospel of God, and saying, "The time is fulfilled, and the kingdom of God is at hand; repent, and believe in the gospel."

And passing along by the Sea of Galilee, he saw Simon and Andrew the brother of Simon casting a net in the sea; for they were fishermen. And Jesus said to them, "Follow me and I will make you become fishers of men." And immediately they left their nets and followed him. And going on a little farther, he saw James the son of Zebedee and John his brother, who were in their boat mending the nets. And immediately he called them; and they left their father Zebedee in the boat with the hired servants, and followed him.

EXPLANATION: St. Mark's gospel, which he calls "the Good News about Jesus Christ the Son of God," abruptly enters into the public life of Christ. He takes it for granted that his readers know all the facts of his human origin (they were already described by Luke and Matthew) and the fact of his divinity. In thirteen short verses he mentions the Baptist (without describing his origin or his call, except the fact that he fulfilled a prophecy of Isaiah), the baptism of Jesus and his temptation in the wilderness. Then he comes directly to the public ministry of Christ in Galilee.

after John . . . arrested: The precursor had finished his work. The One for whom he was preparing had come. The Baptist had publicly denounced Herod Antipas for taking, in unlawful wedlock, Herodias, the wife of his brother Philip who was still living. Herod had John cast into prison where he was later beheaded because of the hatred Herodias (not Herod) bore toward him. **The time is fulfilled:** From all eternity God had decided the when and the where of the messianic era. This new kingdom of God which would embrace all men on earth, if they accepted it, would make them worthy of sharing eternal happiness with him. Christ tells his audience in Galilee that the time has now come. During his public life he unfolds this mystery and his own part in it.

repent . . . gospel: The first essential for becoming members of the messianic kingdom on earth is conversion—a change of life from one of sin to one of sanctity, a true return to God. Secondly, those who would enter the kingdom must believe in the message Christ is bringing to them: it is the message of salvation which tells them how they can earn the eternal life in heaven which Christ's coming on earth will win for them.

Simon . . . John: In last Sunday's gospel, taken from St. John (1:35-42), we saw that certainly Peter and Andrew and most probably John and James, left the Baptist and followed Jesus after the baptism in the Jordan. That some (if not all) of the Apostles were with him ever after his baptism by John, was the firm belief of the first Christian community, as expressed in Acts 1 : 22. By inserting this account of the call of the first four Apostles at the very beginning of Christ's public ministry, St. Mark is following this tradition. As he does not tell us of what happened at the Jordan or of the wedding feast in Cana as John does, he inserts the call of the first Apostles at the earliest opportunity. **They were fishermen:** The four Apostles mentioned here earned their livelihood by fishing in the sea of Galilee. Jesus promised to make them fishers of men; they would bring their fellowmen to the shores of heaven.

left . . . father: Peter and Andrew left their nets, their means of livelihood; John and James left their father as well. All four left everything to follow Jesus. This was, and is, what true discipleship of Jesus means for those to whom he gives a special call.

APPLICATION: "Jesus came into Galilee preaching the gospel of God." Jesus came to announce to all men the good news of God's eternal plan for them. He spent his public life convincing the Jews of Palestine of the truth of this message, and he died on the cross because he claimed to be what he was—God's divine Son, who had come in human nature to raise all men to the standing and status of adopted sons of God. That very death, cruel and unjust though it was, was part of the divine plan. He conquered death and was raised from the grave to prove that we too, if we accept his divine gospel and live by it, will be raised from the dead and reign with Christ in the kingdom of his Father forever. Christ preached this doctrine in Palestine. It is the doctrine for which he gave his human life and which he gave to his Apostles to hand down to all future generations. This is the self-same doctrine preached by Christ's Church to all men today. It is the good news of God's mercy and love toward us weak, mortal creatures. To some it seems too good to be true; it would indeed be so if God were a limited, finite being like us, but he is Being itself. He is without limit, his goodness and love are limitless as is his nature. What God can see in creatures has ever been a puzzle to thinking man. One of the psalm-writers said centuries ago: "what is man that you should spare a thought for him, the son of man that you should care for him?" (Ps. 8 : 4). Many a saint too, has repeated this remark ever since.

We cannot hope to fathom the mind of God, nor do we need to. He has gone to such a length as the humiliation of his divine Son in the incarnation in order to give us a new standing in relation to himself and a new mode of eternal living after death. We are still God's creatures, "the work of his hands," but through accepting Christ and his gospel—his message of divine truth—we are no longer mere mortals. We shall die, but death is the beginning of the true life which God has arranged for us. It is no wonder that St. Paul could cry out: "O death where is your victory, O death, where is your sting?"

We Christians should be the happiest people on earth. We know why we are here, we know where we are going and we know how to get there. There are trials and troubles which beset us on our journey; there are rough parts of the road and weaknesses in our human nature which often lead us off the right road, but we are not left to our own human resources. We have help from above to strengthen and comfort us on our journey. We have divine aids in the Church which Christ set us and we have the guarantee of our Good Shepherd that he will keep us in his fold or bring us back should we foolishly wander from it (Jn. 10 : 14; Lk. 15 : 4–7).

We Christians can indeed be the happiest people on earth, if we live according to the divine good news revealed to us through Christ. "Repent and believe in the gospel," Christ told the people of Galilee. The same call goes out from our loving Savior to each of us today : repent—change your outlook on life—see it, as God sees it to be for us, a short journey toward heaven. If we really believe in the gospel of Christ, the revelation of God's plan for our eternal happiness, our earthly troubles will look small, our trials and temptations will appear to us as they really are—a means of earning the eternal victory. Christ, the innocent victim for our salvation, has gone before us, carrying his heavy cross; can we refuse to carry the relatively lighter cross which he places on our shoulders as our means of making atonement for our own failings and for those of our fellowmen? God forbid that we should! If we have failed in the past, let us repent today and show our belief in the truth of the Christian gospel, by living as true Christians who are on their way to heaven.

FOURTH SUNDAY OF THE YEAR

FIRST READING : Deuteronomy 18 : 15–20. Moses said to the people, "The Lord your God will raise up for you a prophet like me from among you, from your brethren—him you shall heed—just as you desired of the Lord your God at Horeb on the day of the assembly, when you said, 'Let me not hear again the voice of the Lord my God, or see this great fire any more, lest I die.' And the Lord said to me, 'They have rightly said all that they have spoken. I will raise up for them a prophet like you from among their brethren; and I will put my words in his mouth, and he shall speak to them all that I command him. And whoever will not give heed to my words which he shall speak in my name, I myself will require it of him. But the prophet who presumes to speak a word in my name which I have not commanded him to speak, or who speaks in the name of other gods, that same prophet shall die.' "

EXPLANATION : This central section of the book of Deuteronomy (16 : 18–18 : 22) describes the various offices and officers of the theocratic society which Yahweh, through his servant Moses, is setting up for the Chosen People. Judges, kings, priests and prophets are promised to the people, to regulate their civil and religious life. The prophet was to be the mouth-piece of Yahweh among the people. He was to be listened to because he brought the word of God, Yahweh's revelation, to them. And just as there had to be a line of kings, judges and priests, so there had to be a line of prophets, who would interpret previous revelation and add some new truths, when necessary for each generation. After the return from the Babylonian exile (c. 538 B.C.) however, the people began to interpret this text of Deuteronomy as referring to one individual eschatological prophet, the Messiah who was to come. The New Testament followed this interpretation and saw these words of Moses "a prophet like me" verified in Christ (Acts 3 : 22; 7 : 37). That this was the opinion of our Lord's contemporaries is clear from Jn. 1 : 21; 6 :14; 7 : 40. These verses, therefore, have been chosen for today's first reading because they refer to the "preacher with authority" who is mentioned in today's gospel.

for you a prophet : Moses promises the people that after his own death God will send one of themselves ("from your brethren") to take his place as God's interpreter or mouth-piece.

him . . . heed : They must obey his commands and advice because he is taking God's place in their regard.

at Horeb . . . you said : The reference is to the giving of the ten commandments on Mount Sinai or Horeb. The people heard the voice of Yahweh which was accompanied by thunder and lightning: "they shook with fear" (Ex. 20 : 18) and begged that Moses should speak to them rather than that Yahweh himself should address them. Moses now says Yahweh will grant their request. He will speak to them only through his prophets.

put my words in his mouth : Yahweh will reveal to the prophet all he wants him to tell the people.

whoever . . . heed : Whoever disobeys or refuses to do what the prophet commands is disobeying Yahweh and will have to answer to him.

prophet who presumes : Any man claiming the office or charism of prophecy who has not received it from Yahweh, is guilty of serious deception and is to be put to death. Likewise any Israelite who would encourage the cult of a false god deserves death.

APPLICATION : That God fulfilled his promise to send prophets to speak in his name and with his authority is evident from the pages of the Old Testament. Beginning with Joshua, the immediate successor of Moses, there was a continuous line of representatives of God, who directed the people, corrected their faults and filled them with hopes for a better future, right down to John the Baptist who was the precursor of the final and greatest of all prophets. God could, of course, have spoken directly to his people, but through Moses the people had asked him not to do so, because the hearing of his voice on Mount Sinai had struck terror into their hearts. In his mercy and love Yahweh granted their request.

Had the Chosen People listened to those prophets and obeyed their instructions, their history would have been different. They would have avoided much temporal suffering, and more important still, their large percentage who lost faith in God and his promises of future happiness would have remained faithful and would now be enjoying that promised happiness. But when they got full possession of the land God gave them, they began to get too interested in the economic and political affairs of their world. They forgot God who had been so generous toward them, and took credit to themselves for all that they were and had.

Who are we, living as we are in glasshouses, to throw stones? The prophets of the Old Testament were but foreshadowings or types of the real prophet, God's divine Son. He humbled himself to share in our humanity so that we could share in his divinity. Of this astounding fact every Christian is aware, and yet how many millions of "ex-Christians" are there in our world today? How many live their lives in total disregard of Christ's teaching and complete oblivion of what he did and suffered for them, or, what is worse still for themselves, with complete disinterest in their own future state. Yet this is the sad fact of history. More than half the people of what were once the Christian nations are no longer interested in the Christian message today. Their days and their lives are so given to acquiring things and pleasures that every thought of a future life is blotted from their minds.

This neo-paganism which has been developing over the past centuries, has reached frightening proportions today. God has little, if any, place in the councils of nations. Man-made laws have replaced the ten commandments, and the result is, of course, a world in turmoil. There is not and there cannot be any brotherhood of man if we exclude the Fatherhood of God. There will never be "peace on earth among men" until all men make their peace with the God of heaven. False prophets and promoters of false gods, advertisers of pornography and permissiveness surround us on all sides today. There are those who are trying to prevent the pollution of land, water and atmosphere but too few, if any, who oppose the mental and moral pollution of people which is being propagated daily in our midst. All would like this world of ours to be a beautiful place to live in, only very few think to provide for a beautiful place to which they can go after they leave this world.

Please God we are among that few, but instead of clapping one another on the back for this, let us rather beat our breasts in repentance for our past faults and resolve to let the light of our Christian faith shine before our neighbors in future. Every good-living Christian is a prophet, a representative, of God among his neighbors. His example will speak and its message will be the word of God and it will produce fruit in God's good time. We are our brothers' keepers in that they are God's adopted children too, and he wants them. He is looking to us to give them a helping hand. Would we refuse him, the all-loving Father who sent his Son to open heaven for us? Would we be so ungrateful as to refuse the little he asks of us in return?

SECOND READING : 1 Corinthians 7 : 32–35. I want you to be free from anxieties. The unmarried man is anxious about the affairs of the Lord, how to please the Lord; but the married man is anxious about worldly affairs, how to please his wife, and his interests are divided. And the unmarried woman or girl is anxious about the affairs of the Lord, how to be holy in body and spirit; but the married woman is anxious about worldly affairs, how to please her husband. I say this for your own benefit, not to lay any restraint upon you, but to promote good order and to secure your undivided devotion to the Lord.

EXPLANATION : St. Paul devotes the whole of chapter seven of this Epistle to answering questions he was asked concerning marriage and virginity. Because the first Christian converts, not only in Thessalonika and Corinth, but everywhere, believed or strongly hoped that the end of this world and the second coming of Christ as Judge were imminent (and St. Paul himself must have, at least, encouraged this belief and hope), many of them thought they should not enter into marriage, lest marriage should interfere with their whole-hearted service of God. As regards those already married when they became converts, the Apostle tells them marriage is a holy state ordained by God and it is a lifelong partnership according to the teaching of the Lord (see Mt. 5 : 32; 19 : 3–9). To those not yet married he recommends a life of virginity but only if they feel they can live that life in all fidelity. In today's extract St. Paul emphasizes freedom to serve God fully, freedom from earthly cares which those who choose a life of celibacy have.

The unmarried man : The celibate can give all his undivided attention to living his Christian life and pleasing God.

married man . . . divided : The married man on the other hand has to give a lot of his attention to pleasing his wife and to providing for her needs as well as his own. He has less time therefore for the things of God.

unmarried . . . woman : The same applies to women.

lay . . . way : St. Paul says he had no direction from the Lord as regards virginity (7 : 25). Our Lord's words in Mt. 19 : 12 are not a command but only a counsel or recommendation, and so Paul is making only a recommendation. He does not wish to restrict their choice.

your . . . attention : He tells those as yet unmarried that they will be in a better position to serve the Lord if they remain single.

APPLICATION : While it is true that St. Paul recommended a celibate life to those who were still single, because of the general feeling at the time that the end of this world was at hand, his recommendation of celibacy and its advantages have been accepted through the ages down to our own day. The truth of his statement : "the unmarried man (or woman) is anxious about the affairs of the Lord, the married man (or woman) is anxious about worldly affairs (as well as about the affairs of God) and his interests are divided," needs no demonstration, it is self-evident. For this reason we have had a line of men (and later of women also) through the nineteen centuries of the Church's life who gladly deprived themselves of earthly comforts in order to devote their lives exclusively to God's service. The voluntary celibates of the early Church were followed by the Fathers of the Desert, later by the Eastern and Western monks, then the religious orders and in more recent centuries by various congregations for men and women.

These celibates, of course, were always a small minority of the body of the faithful and it was always understood (as it was by St. Paul) that while their vocation was a call to the exclusive service of God it was by no means the only way of serving God and earning heaven. The married life is also a Christian vocation, a vocation indeed ordained by God for the vast majority. For the Christian who is sincere in his service of God, it entails many difficulties and trials from which his celibate life sets the religious free. On the other hand the life of a religious, of a celibate for God, has its own difficulties. But for both the married and the religious there is always available for the asking, the grace of God to help them over life's hurdles. When God calls a man or woman for a task, he gives him or her the strength to carry it out, he fits the shoulder for the cross.

While the married life is indeed a vocation, a means of earning heaven, and an ordinance of God necessary for the procreation of citizens of heaven, the religious life, this voluntary abstention from marriage, by those so called, is a divine plan to help the married (as well as the religious themselves). Apart from the spiritual and material help which religious give to their married neighbors—teaching their children, caring for the disabled, running homes for the aged, helping families in need and the thousand other ways in which the spiritual and corporal works of mercy are joyously done in our midst each day —the special value of this total dedication of self to God, which the religious life demands and gives, is that it is a sign, a reminder, not only to all Christians but to all men, of the real purpose of life on earth.

God created us in order to raise us up after death to a new and endless life of happiness. Our few years on this earth are but the apprenticeship we must serve in order to earn our eternal standing or status as heirs of God in the eternal kingdom. But because man's human nature can, and does so often, get so enmeshed in the things of earth we need reminders. We need signs and sign-posts to keep our true purpose in life before our minds. This is exactly what the few of our members who dedicate their whole life to God's exclusive service, do for us. They remind us, urge us on by their noble example to serve God in our own limited, but sufficient, way so that we too can reach the future life prepared for us.

Both the married life and the religious celibate life are vocations from God. While the religious help the married and their families on the road to heaven, the married can and must help the religious to continue their exclusive and devoted service to God, by providing them with the material necessities of life. This is part of their own devoted service of God, this is one of the ways in which they fulfill their vocation. Heaven is the goal of both religious and married people. Where each of the parties devotedly and loyally fulfills the duties arising from each one's vocation, that goal will be successfully reached by both.

D

GOSPEL: Mark 1:21-28. They went into Capernaum; and immediately on the sabbath he entered the synagogue and taught. And they were astonished at his teaching, for he taught them as one who had authority, and not as the scribes. And immediately there was in their synagogue a man with an unclean spirit; and he cried out, "What have you to do with us, Jesus of Nazareth? Have you come to destroy us? I know who you are, the Holy One of God." But Jesus rebuked him, saying, "Be silent, and come out of him!" And the unclean spirit, convulsing him and crying with a loud voice, came out of him. And they were all amazed, so that they questioned among themselves, saying, "What is this? A new teaching! With authority he commands even the unclean spirits, and they obey him." And at once his fame spread everywhere throughout all the surrounding region of Galilee.

EXPLANATION: St. Mark enters abruptly into the public ministry of Christ. He describes very briefly the preaching of the Baptist, the temptation in the desert place, the call of the first four Apostles and then tells of Jesus beginning to preach the good news in Galilee. It was in east Galilee that he called the first Apostles and it was in the town called Capernaum, a day or two later, that he preached one of his first sermons to his fellow Jews. It was in their synagogue on the Sabbath day that he also worked a miracle.

Jesus . . . synagogue: Every town of any size in Palestine had a synagogue, a sacred building where all pious Jews gathered on the Sabbath day (Saturday) to recite prayers and to hear the scriptures read, and explained by the local rabbi or teacher.

he taught them: Jesus was probably invited by the local rabbi to address the people because it seems to have been the custom of the time to invite any stranger present to speak to the congregation (see Acts 13:15).

taught as . . . authority: Unlike the scribes and the rabbis, he did not quote others to prove his words. He laid down the law himself on his own authority (see Mt. 5:21: "You have heard that it was said . . . *but I say* to you"). He was the Messiah and the Son of God but the people did not grasp this though the "unclean spirit" did.

man . . . spirit: A devil or evil spirit dwelt in this man. This seems clear from the remarks that follow. The others present in the synagogue did not recognize Jesus as the Messiah. The evil spirit could have this knowledge, and he used it with the hope of embarrassing Jesus in some way.

you . . . us: That the Messiah would put an end to the reign of Satan and sin in the world was the general expectation among the Jews. This particular spirit is aware of this and realizes that he and his fellow fallen angels are about to be conquered.

you come . . . us: To end our reign, is what is implied. This is what Christ did, for by his incarnation, death and resurrection, he gave all men the means of becoming sons of God, free from the snares of Satan and sin.

the Holy . . . God: One very close to God. To the unclean spirit and to Mark and his Christian readers, the title equalled "the Son of God," but the Jews of Capernaum did not attach such a meaning to it.

Be silent . . . out: As Jesus does not

want his true relationship with God known as yet, he forbids the spirit to say anymore, but orders him to leave the man whom he had possessed.

They were all amazed : Exorcisms were often practiced by their rabbis but a long liturgical formula was used. Here, by a simple word of command, Jesus makes the spirit depart.

a new teaching : The authority with which he expounded the Scriptures in his sermon, and the same super-human authority exercised over the unclean spirit, gave the people food for thought. They would understand it later.

his fame . . . Galilee : The people of Capernaum told their fellow-Jews in the other towns of Galilee what had happened in their synagogue. Therefore before he left Capernaum to preach and work miracles in other parts of Galilee, his fame as a man with super-human power had reached these outlying districts and towns.

APPLICATION : St. Mark makes it clear that, from the very first day of Christ's public ministry, his messianic power began to be manifested to those who saw and heard him. The Jews of Capernaum were "astonished" at his teaching and "amazed" at his power over the evil spirits. "What is this," they asked one another, "a new teaching and the unclean spirits obey him!" But they were still a long way from recognizing him for what he was, the Messiah and Son of God. This is as might be expected, the astounding mystery of the incarnation was away beyond human expectation or human imagination. And it was our Lord's own plan to reveal this mystery, slowly and gradually, so that when the chain of evidence had been completed by his resurrection, his followers could look back and see each link in that chain. Then they would be ready to accept without hesitation the mystery of the incarnation and realize the infinite love and power of God that brought it about. We look back today through the eyes of the Evangelists, and, like them, know that Christ was God as well as man—two natures in one person. We should not therefore be "amazed" at the teaching of Jesus or at his power over the unclean spirits. What should amaze us really is the love that God showed mankind in becoming one of our race.

We are creatures with nothing of our own to boast of. We were created by God, and every talent or power we possess was given us by God. God's benevolence could have stopped there and we would have no right to complain. But when we recall the special gifts he gave man, which raise him above all other created things, we see that he could not, because of his own infinitely benevolent nature, leave us to an earthly fate. What thinking man could be content with a short span of life on earth? What real purpose in life could an intelligent being have who knew that nothing awaited him but eternal oblivion in the grave? What fulfillment would man's intellectual faculties find in a few years of what is for the majority of people perpetual struggle for earthly survival? No, God created us to elevate us, after our earthly sojourn, to an eternal existence where all our desires and potentialities would have their true fulfillment. Hence the incarnation, hence the life, death and resurrection of Christ, who was God's

Son, as the central turning point of man's history.

Today, while amazed at God's love for us, let us also be justly amazed at the shabby and grudging return we make for love. Many amongst us even deny that act of God's infinite love, not from convincing historical and logical proofs, but in order to justify their own unwillingness to co-operate with the divine plan for their eternal future. This is not to say that their future, after death, does not concern them; it is a thought which time and again intrudes on all men, but they have allowed the affairs of this world which should be stepping stones to their future life, to become instead mill-stones which crush their spirits and their own true self-interests.

While we sincerely hope that we are not in that class, we can still find many facets in our daily Christian lives which can and should make us amazed at our lack of gratitude to God and to his in-carnate Son. Leaving out serious sin which turns us away from God if not against him, how warm is our charity, our love of God and neighbor? How much of our time do we give to the things of God and how much to the things of Caesar? How often does our daily struggle for earthly existence and the grumbles and grouses which it causes, blot out from our view the eternal purpose God had in giving us this earthly existence. How often during the past year have we said from our heart: "Thank you, God, for putting me in this world, and thank you a thousand times more, for giving me the opportunity and the means of reaching the next world where I shall live happily for evermore in your presence"? If the true answer for many of us is "not once," then begin today. Let us say it now with all sincerity, and say it often in the years that are left to us.

FIFTH SUNDAY OF THE YEAR

FIRST READING : Job 7 : 1-4; 6-7. Job said : Has not man a hard service upon earth, and are not his days like the days of a hireling? Like a slave who longs for the shadow, and like a hireling who looks for his wages, so I am allotted months of emptiness, and nights of misery are apportioned to me. When I lie down I say, "When shall I arise?" But the night is long, and I am full of tossing till the dawn. My days are swifter than a weaver's shuttle, and come to their end without hope. Remember that my life is a breath; my eyes will never again see good.

EXPLANATION : The book of Job is a didactic book—a story with a moral. It is a book with a lesson to teach. It tells the story of a good-living, upright man, who was blessed by God with the possessions of this world as well as a large family. But ill-fortune struck him and he not only lost his possessions and family but was himself struck with bodily sores. The author of the story, a post-exilic Israelite, gives us a picturesque explanation of these misfortunes. Satan, the enemy of man and God, tells God that Job's fidelity and uprightness will last only as long as the temporal blessings he has remain. And he asks God to put Job to the test. God does so but Job remains faithful and after a long period of mental and bodily suffering is finally given back his family, and twice the possessions he had lost. The lesson the author intended to teach was that the belief prevalent among the Jews for centuries that God rewarded the good in this life and punished the

wicked was not well-founded. The author shows that Job was not a sinner and yet he suffered much in this life : this was proof that this commonly held belief was wrong. The author did not solve the problem, because in common with his contemporaries, he had only very vague ideas about the future life. With the example of Christ's sufferings and cruel death before us, we can now see the value of suffering in this life, and the full meaning of the didactic story of Job.

a hard . . . earth : Three friends of Job came to visit him when ill-fortune hit him. Being convinced of the traditional teaching that it was sinners only who suffered, each one of the three tried to get Job to admit that he was a great sinner but Job answered each of his accusers by asserting his innocence. In today's lesson he is answering the first speaker and having declared his innocence he admits the severity of the trials by which he is afflicted. He compares his life to the three most wretched states of life then known—those of the conscript, the hireling and the slave. He says a man's life on earth (his own especially) is like the life of a conscript ("pressed service" in the Jerusalem Bible).

days . . . hireling : He has no freedom but must be at the beck and call of his master.

slave . . . shadow : Working under the scorching sun the poor slave would love to get some shady place wherein to rest.

hireling . . . wages : He has no interest in his work and no comfort in it, and all he gets out of life is his wages and they were not very much.

emptiness . . . misery : Apart from the grief over the loss of his family, Job has been for months suffering from bodily sores and ill-health—his days are empty of value to himself or to anybody and his tortured mind finds no rest even at night—nothing but misery.

When I . . . down : Knowing his night will be sleepless he keeps hoping that dawn will come soon, but the night drags on while he tosses and turns in pain.

my days . . . shuttle : But when day comes it brings no relief, it passes too quickly. It has the speed of a weaver's shuttle.

my life . . . breath : His life is but a brief, transitory moment. It is like the breath one breathes out, it is gone in an instant.

eyes . . . good : His eyes would soon close in death and that was the final end for him. Remember Job, or the author, had no knowledge of a future life so for him everything ended in death.

APPLICATION : While the book of Job points out that earthly sufferings are not always a punishment for previous sins committed by the sufferer—Job was an innocent man—it does not solve the problem of human pain. The author could not solve this age-old problem because his world-view was restricted to life on this earth. It was only when the full revelation of man's purpose in life and God's loving plans for him, were made known through Christ that the full answer to this question was given. When life on this earth was thought to be the sum total of a man's existence it seemed hard and cruel that his few short years should be marred and saddened by bodily and/or mental ailments. But with our new knowledge and certainty that this life is only a preparation, an apprenticeship, for the eternal life that awaits us after death, we are able to see our earthly sufferings in their proper perspective. They may be punishment for past sins—God's loving way of giving us an opportunity of making atonement for our offenses—or these sufferings may be laid on our shoulders to atone for fellowmen who are incapable of carrying their own saving cross.

For whichever reason these trials are sent us, we Christians should, with the example of Christ before us, be able to accept them with good will and bear them patiently because they come to us from God. But the objection can be raised : it is not God but sinful men, wicked neighbors or even wicked members of our own family who are the cause of my ill-health, my mental and bodily sufferings. Granted that this is often true and that many, if not most of the pains and hardships people have to suffer, are caused by wicked fellowmen, yet all of this is happening with God's knowledge. He could prevent it but he will not because out of evil he can produce good. The sufferings of the innocent bring down God's grace not only on themselves but on the very wicked who caused their sufferings.

God wants all his adopted children in heaven. His all-wise way of bringing this to pass may often seem to our limited intellects to be almost unjust to the innocent while the guilty ones seem to be favored. But it is not so. God's innocent children will be rewarded where the reward will be everlasting, and when they reach that reward they will have an added source of joy in the knowledge that it was their patient endurance of suffering brought on them by wicked men, which earned for their one-time oppressors a place in the eternal kingdom. In heaven there will be no narrow-mindedness, no sense of resentment or desire for revenge. Remember the words of Job : "man has a hard service upon earth . . . he is like a hireling and a slave." Most of us can see this fulfilled in our own lives. However, our conscription, our military service or slavery, is of relatively short duration. If we put up patiently with our tribulations (having done all that is humanly and lawfully possible to ameliorate our condition), we will soon see that what looked like the heavy hand of an enemy was instead the caressing hand of the eternal Father, who loved us and so sent us crosses which he would turn into eternal crowns.

Knowing, then, that this life is only an apprenticeship through which we can earn our eternal life of happiness, we should all be able to face "the slings and arrows of outrageous fortune" which come our way. We should, in fact, be able to welcome them for they are reminders kindly sent us by God, lest we forget our real purpose in life. What is more : they are means given us to make us apostles in our own homes. Through patiently-borne sufferings, we can bring God's grace down on fellowmen who have no time or no thought of asking for it.

Christ suffered for us and died the excruciating death of the cross, so that we might have eternal life. He asks us to take up our cross daily and follow him. That daily cross of ours can never be as heavy as his, for he was the innocent God-man. If, however, we carry our cross patiently, it will be turned into our crown of glory when we meet Christ at the moment of our death.

SECOND READING: 1 Corinthians 9:16-19; 22-23. If I preach the gospel, that gives me no ground for boasting. For necessity is laid upon me. Woe to me if I do not preach the gospel! For if I do this of my own will, I have a reward; but if not of my own will, I am entrusted with a commission. What then is my reward? Just this: that in my preaching I may make the gospel free of charge, not making full use of my right in the gospel.

For though I am free from all men, I have made myself a slave to all, that I might win the more. To the weak I became weak, that I might win the weak. I have become all things to all men, that I might by all means save some. I do it all for the sake of the gospel, that I may share in its blessings.

EXPLANATION: In this section of his letter St. Paul is encouraging his Corinthian converts to be always ready to forgo their own rights when the edification or spiritual welfare of a neighbor is at stake. To emphasize this teaching, he tells them how he has given up rights and privileges, which he certainly could claim, in order to give himself fully and entirely to the spreading of the gospel among them, and to be seen to be free from any personal interest or gain.

preach . . . boasting: The fact that Paul is an Apostle, a preacher of the gospel, is in no way due to himself. He did not choose the office, Christ imposed it on him (see Acts 9:15), so he cannot boast of it.

woe . . . gospel: This apostleship is his vocation in life, the task Christ gave him to do. Should he fail in it, his future life would be in jeopardy.

not of my own will . . . commission: He compares himself to the slave who is given a position of authority in the household "a commission." If he fulfills the position well and faithfully, he will get no reward because he is only a slave, but if he fails, he is punished: "woe to him."

gospel . . . charge: This is something Paul is doing of his own will and he can expect a reward for it. He did not burden the converts with his upkeep, but worked with his hands to earn his bread (see Acts 18:3; 1 Cor. 9:1-15), even though he had a right to material support from them.

a slave to all: Though a free-man and a Roman citizen he made himself a slave amongst them, getting no wages, no material reward for his work of evangelizing them. This was so that nobody, friend or foe, could charge him with working for his own benefit. He acted thus in order to win all the more to Christ.

all . . . men: St. Paul tried (and succeeded admirably) to put himself on an equal footing with all those with whom he came into contact. With the simple he was simple, with the learned he showed his learning, with the weak he spoke of his own weaknesses, with those who boasted of heavenly gifts he spoke of the great gifts he had himself received, hence, the success, under God, of his missionary activity.

save some: Notwithstanding all his efforts, he sadly admits that not all of those who heard him and knew him would follow the gospel, but the fault lay in them, not in him.

may share . . . blessings: However, he is still going to give his all in order to spread the "goodness" of Christ, so that as many as possible may share with him in its eternal blessings.

APPLICATION : St. Paul is the single Apostle about whom we know most. From the accounts of him given in the Acts, and from his own letters to the various churches, we have not only the principal events of his life but clear glimpses into his character. He was never a man of halfmeasures but put his whole heart and mind into whatever cause he espoused. As a young Pharisee —a student of the Mosaic law in Jerusalem—he exceeded in zeal even his teachers and elders. To the Pharisees Christ was a false Messiah. He was not what they expected and what was worse, he was a blasphemer for he claimed to be God, so they had him condemned to death. But his followers began to proclaim that he had risen from the dead and was not only Messiah but the Son of God. For this they were persecuted and imprisoned—this heretical sect had to be wiped out.

In this persecution of the infant Church Saul of Tarsus took a leading part. But Christ intervened on behalf of his Church. On his way to Damascus, with authority to arrest any believers in Christ that he found there, and bring them prisoner to Jerusalem, he was converted. The vision of the risen Christ gave him a new outlook on life, the persecutor was turned into an Apostle of the new faith. Baptized in Damascus, he spent some time in solitary meditation in the desert and later in his native Tarsus. Then he began his mission to the Gentiles, the mission given him by Jesus (Acts 9 : 15). From Antioch in Syria he traveled through Cyprus (where he changed the name Saul into Paul), Asia Minor, Greece and as far as Rome. He spent the last twenty-four years of his life bringing the message of Christ to the Gentiles. In doing so he suffered hardship after hardship. Apart from fatiguing journeys during which he frequently suffered from hunger and thirst, he was often beaten up by mobs. Five times he was scourged by the opposing Jews. He was stoned, ship-wrecked and imprisoned at least three times (see 2 Cor. 11 : 23–29).

The vision of Christ which Paul had on the road to Damascus remained his guiding-light all through these years. He gladly and completely became the slave of Christ and put every ounce of energy he possessed into serving his master. Because his fellowmen were brothers of Christ, Paul made himself their slave also. For him there was neither Jew nor Gentile, Greek nor Barbarian, slave nor freeman—all were brothers of Christ, adopted sons of God, and his all-burning desire was to help them all reach the eternal inheritance that God, through Christ, had in store for them.

We can hardly hope to emulate the true brotherly-love, the total dedication, the complete self-giving of Paul, but we must all try to follow him if only from afar. We cannot and need not take on distant missionary journeys, we cannot and need not give up all our earthly cares and responsibilities, but we all can and must take an active interest in the temporal and spiritual welfare of our fellowmen. Some of this obligation, which is on every true Christian, we can fulfill by helping missionary societies, but nearer home, in our own very neighborhood, there are works of charity which each one of us can carry out. There are neighbors, fellow-sons and daughters of God who are in dire need of the ordinary necessities of life—we can spare a little from our own resources to help them out. There are many heirs to heaven who, alas, are leading lives which will not bring them to their everlasting home. A word of advice, an encouraging example, a few devout prayers, can still work miracles. Let us try to imitate St. Paul, if only from afar. Every least effort, every smallest sacrifice for Christ and our fellowmen, will have its reward when our day of reckoning comes.

We can all be apostles in our own limited surroundings; we must all be apostles if we hope to reign one day soon with Christ in heaven.

GOSPEL : Mark 1 : 29–39. Jesus left the synagogue, and entered the house of Simon and Andrew, with James and John. Now Simon's mother-in-law lay sick with a fever, and immediately they told him of her. And he came and took her by the hand and lifted her up, and the fever left her; and she served them.

That evening, at sundown, they brought to him all who were sick or possessed with demons. And the whole city was gathered together about the door. And he healed many who were sick with various diseases, and cast out many demons; and he would not permit the demons to speak, because they knew him.

And in the morning, a great while before day, he rose and went out to a lonely place, and there he prayed. And Simon and those who were with him followed him, and they found him and said to him, "Every one is searching for you." And he said to them, "Let us go on to the next towns, that I may preach there also; for that is why I came out." And he went throughout all Galilee, preaching in their synagogues and casting out demons.

EXPLANATION : St. Mark began (last Sunday's reading) to describe Christ's first day of missionary activity in Galilee. He preached "as one who had authority" in the synagogue of Capernaum and by a simple command he drove an unclean spirit out of a man. Later that same day, after sundown, he worked many more miracles of healing, beginning with Peter's mother-in-law, and he drove out many other demons. But very early next morning, he left Peter's house and went to a lonely place to pray. Here Peter and his companions found him and told him that all the people were waiting to see him in Capernaum. But he pointed out to them that his plan was to travel through the towns and villages of Galilee, to bring them all the good news of the messianic kingdom, as this was the purpose of his coming on earth.

Simon and Andrew : Although Peter was married, there is no mention of his wife in the whole gospel story. It is very probable that she had already died by this time; this would explain why her mother was living in Peter's house, to care for him and Andrew.

lifted her up : With the simple action of lifting her up by the hand, he cured her of her fever.

and she . . . them : St. Mark adds this little detail to show the immediateness and the complete effectiveness of the cure. She was straight away able to provide a meal and serve it to Christ and his four followers.

that evening at sundown : As it was a Sabbath day no loads could be carried and so the neighbors waited until the Sabbath was over at sundown. Then they brought their sick and their possessed ones on stretchers or pallets to the door of Peter's house where Christ was staying.

the whole city : It hardly could be called a city and the inhabitants both of Capernaum and its neighborhood would not be very numerous, but they all came to see miracles and the miracle-worker.

he healed ... diseases : The people were not disappointed; he healed all kinds of diseases—there was no limit to his power —and he cast out many demons.

permit ... speak : The people had as yet no idea as to what or who he was, but the demons knew him to be the Messiah and they would have spread this news about but he forbade them, and they had to obey. Christ wanted to manifest himself gradually, first preparing the minds and hearts of his hearers to understand the true nature of his mission. The people had the wrong idea of what the Messiah would be—a political leader who would free Israel from the hated Roman and pagan government—this wrong idea Christ gradually corrected. His "kingdom was not of this world."

a great ... day : Next morning very early, he went to a deserted place outside the town to pray to his Father in solitude. Christ prayed daily but the gospels mention special occasions like the present one—the beginning of his preaching and healing mission—when he put himself in his Father's hands.

go ... towns : He informs the four disciples now of his plans for the future. The good news has to be brought to all towns and all people.

that ... came out : This was the purpose of his incarnation, of his coming from heaven on earth in human form, namely, to tell all men of God's plan for them.

throughout all Galilee : He began that very day to fulfill the role his Father had destined for him.

APPLICATION : Surely the people of Capernaum saw enough that first day of Christ's public ministry among them to make them realize that this man from Nazareth who had come amongst them was no ordinary preacher, no ordinary rabbi, no ordinary man. They saw that he preached as one having authority; they saw that by a simple command he cast out demons and removed all bodily ailments. Yet though they were astonished and amazed at his power, their worldly outlook did not let them rise above their own small interests. Our Lord did not blame them or criticize them, he knew and fully understood their slowness of mind in regard to things spiritual, and he knew also that they would eventually give themselves wholeheartedly to his kingdom.

While he was prepared to wait for the desired effects which his miracles and preaching would eventually have on them, he hastened the arrival of that day by praying to his heavenly Father to send the graces necessary for their conversion into their hearts. When the four Apostles found him praying in a lonely place, they told him that all Capernaum was searching for him, but he knew why they were searching for him. They wanted to see more miracles and very likely they were hoping that he would stay on in Capernaum and the sick and the maimed from the whole of Galilee would be brought there for healing. This would increase their earthly business and prosperity. His answer to the Apostles, while not directly condemning this worldly outlook, shows that his mission had an entirely different objective. He had come on earth not to bring earthly prosperity to any town or country but to bring spiritual salvation and blessing on all people. That very morning he began to carry out his mission and for the remaining two years or more he went from town to town preaching the kingdom of God.

We Christians of today have many advantages over the people of Capernaum of that day. They saw Christ with their bodily eyes as a man of power amongst them; we see him with the eyes of faith as he really was and is—the Son of God who came on earth as man in order to make us sons of God. We know who he really was and we know the full meaning of his mission. We have seen that mission completed amongst us by his death on the cross and his resurrection. By his death he conquered death for us; by his resurrection he opened the gates of heaven for us and led the way there for all who will follow him.

This is the good news Christ brought to our world. This is the meaning of Christianity; this is why we are Christians. We are members of Christ's kingdom on earth, so that when our life here ends we shall be members of his everlasting heavenly kingdom. Yet, with all of this knowledge and with the example of the thousands and millions of saints who have lived according to this knowledge over the past nineteen hundred years and more, and who are now enjoying the reward Christianity promised them, how active and how effective is our Christian faith in our daily thoughts and deeds? In my daily dealings with my fellowmen would I be picked out as a Christian? Do I, by my words and deeds, prove to those with whom I live and work that I am convinced there is a future life after death, that reaching that life is the most important thing in this world for me, and that it is through living my short earthly life as a true Christian that I can earn that eternal life?

If I can say yes to these questions I am, thank God, on the right road. But if my answer is "no" then it is time I had another good look to see where I went off the road, and to find out that I can return to that right road once more. God is merciful; Christ is patient with followers who straggle and wander, but it could be fatal to postpone for too long our call to the God of mercy. It will be too late if we delay turning to our patient Christ until we are about to die. Stop straggling and wandering off the highway today and the patient Christ will welcome you and help you back. There may be no tomorrow for you, you have no guarantee of it.

SIXTH SUNDAY OF THE YEAR

FIRST READING : Leviticus 13 : 1–2; 45–46. The Lord said to Moses and Aaron, "When a man has on the skin of his body a swelling or an eruption or a spot, and it turns into a leprous disease on the skin of his body, then he shall be brought to Aaron the priest or to one of his sons the priests.

"The leper who has the disease shall wear torn clothes and let the hair of his head hang loose, and he shall cover his upper lip and cry, 'Unclean, unclean.' He shall remain unclean as long as he has the disease; he is unclean; he shall dwell alone in a habitation outside the camp."

EXPLANATION : This book which is concerned with the regulating of Israelite worship, gets the name Leviticus because this worship was to be carried out by the tribe of Levi. It was the Septuagint, the Greek translation, which first gave the book this name. As well as laws regulating worship, the ordination of priests, their duties and rights, it has rules concerning food, legal purity and impurity. It also lays down regulations as regards certain bodily diseases which made a person unclean and a menace to the health of his neighbors. Leprosy was one such disease. It was the duty of the priests to declare a man infected or not by leprosy. The priest examined a patient and declared him a leper; the patient had then to live in isolation outside the camp or the dwelling-place of the people, to prevent the spread of the dreaded disease. In this chapter 13, other skin diseases are included for the possibility of a cure occurring is mentioned, but real leprosy at that time and for cen-

turies after was deemed incurable. But any infectious skin disease made the patient unfit to take part in the religious rites, and, to protect the others, he was isolated until cured.

swelling . . . spot : Any of these symptoms could be the beginning of leprosy.

Aaron . . . priests : Aaron was the first Chief Priest and all his sons were associated with him in the priesthood. All the male members of the other families of the tribe of Levi were "Levites" whose office and duty was to help the priests in the offering of sacrifices and other acts of divine worship.

wear torn clothes : The poor unfortunate had not only to live in isolation but he had to warn anyone approaching him both by his dress and by word of mouth, that he was unclean and should be avoided.

cover . . . lip : The patient had to let the hair of his head grow long and also cover his face with a beard so that nobody could mistake him for a healthy person.

as long . . . disease : As said above, the fact that one could gradually get rid of this skin-affection indicates that it was not leprosy in the strict sense.

dwell alone : The man pronounced a leper had to live away from his fellowmen. He could take no part in their life or their liturgy, for according to the Hebrew mentality, one having such a disease was struck by God and therefore unfit to worship him.

APPLICATION : Man was made to live in the society of his fellowmen. His nature needs the comfort and the sustaining support of his family and neighbors. To be isolated from them, to be compelled to live a life apart must be the hardest lot that could befall a human being. This was the sad lot of lepers in the Old Testament times and well into New Testament days as well. Thanks to the progress of medicine and of Christian charity there are hardly any cases of complete isolation today. There are cures for all infectious and contagious diseases, including most forms of leprosy, today. There are medical means of protection against infection and contagion which means that no patients need to be in strict isolation. They can be visited and consoled by their relatives, friends and charitable neighbors, and their cross of suffering in loneliness is lightened for them.

There are, however, other cases of isolation not caused by any disease but rather resulting from lack of thought or lack of true fraternal charity on the part of fellowmen. There are elderly people in hospitals and in homes for the aged whose relatives are all dead and who have no one to visit them or to cheer them and help them to carry their cross. Here is an occasion for the true Christian to put his religion into practice. "I was sick and you visited me," Christ says to the just on the last day. Yes, if we visit and console a fellowman, a brother of Christ, we are visiting and consoling Christ. There are, thank God, a few who practice this very necessary form of charity, but many more are needed.

There are also individuals and sometimes families in almost every community, who seem to be isolated or left coldly to themselves. It may be partly their own fault—they show no inclination to mix with their neighbors, they may even resent any intrusion on their privacy—but this does not excuse the truly Christian neighbor from trying to make such individuals or families feel at home and welcome in their neighborhood. The charitable person will find ways and means of integrating such people into their local community, and of making life less solitary and therefore, more bearable for them.

Think again on the sad fate of the lepers of old, cut off from all human fellowship, compelled to warn all to keep at a safe distance, lest they become infected. If you had been there, would you not have tried to help those poor unfortunate people, if only with a word of encouragement and consolation from afar? You were not there, but you have today plenty of opportunities to exercise charity toward lonely or isolated neighbors, who are within the reach of your kindness, if you are truly kind. You need not fear any contamination of body or mind, in fact, the kindly, friendly encounter with such people who are so much in need of friendship and kindness will have an elevating effect on your own life and cannot but bring you closer to God. "I was a stranger and you made me welcome; I was sick and you visited me; I tell you solemnly insofar as you did this to the least of these brothers of mine, you did it to me" (Mt. 25 : 35-40).

SECOND READING : 1 Corinthians 10 : 31-11 : 1. Whether you eat or drink, or whatever you do, do all to the glory of God. Give no offense to Jews or to Greeks or to the church of God, just as I try to please all men in everything I do, not seeking my own advantage, but that of many, that they may be saved. Be imitators of me, as I am of Christ.

EXPLANATION : There were pagan temples in Corinth in which animals were sacrificed to the gods. The meat which was not burned in the sacrifice was often sold in the market-place. Some of St. Paul's converts, both Jews and Gentiles, had scruples regarding the eating of such meat—it could mean participating in the honor given to a pagan god. St. Paul's general answer was that as "the earth and all that is in it is the property of the Lord" a Christian can lawfully eat any meat placed before him and need not be concerned as to its origin. But if the use of this lawful freedom should scandalize a weaker brother who would think this Christian was intending to honor the pagan gods, then the Christian should deny himself this freedom. This discussion on meat offered to pagan gods or idols, in 10 : 23-30, leads up to today's exhortation which is to do everything for God's glory, giving offense to nobody. In doing this they will be imitating St. Paul their Apostle, who himself was a close imitator of Christ.

eat or drink : The ordinary everyday actions of men, human actions like eating or drinking, if done in moderation and for God's glory, will merit a reward for the one so acting.

offense . . . Greek : As Christians they had an obligation to give good example by doing what was right, and to abstain from any act which would prevent any Jew or Gentile from becoming members of Christ's Church.

Church of God : If, through some offense of theirs, a Jew or Gentile is prevented from becoming a Christian, they are offending against the Church of God, the universal community of believers, for they are impeding its expansion.

please all men : Paul tried always to be all things to all men (see last Sunday's second reading).

my own advantage : He wanted nothing for himself in this life, not even the things he might lawfully have had.

but . . . be saved : His one and only ambition was to bring God's good news, the gospel of Christ, to as many as possible, so that they would inherit the eternal kingdom that Christ had earned for them.

be imitators of me : Paul asks his converts to be all things to all men, as he was.

I am of Christ: In giving his all for his fellowmen, Paul was surely imitating Christ, who became a slave so that men would be free; who became man so that men could become sons of God; who died a shameful death so that men could have eternal life. This was self-giving to a degree that neither Paul nor any other mere human could ever equal, but they could follow him from afar.

APPLICATION: If I were to ask each one of you: "what did you do for God's honor and glory since last Sunday?" would you have to stop and think and maybe answer: "I did nothing except a few hurried prayers said at night." Those who would answer thus have not a proper understanding of what living the Christian life means. From the moment of his baptism a Christian's life is a life dedicated to God's glory and leading to his own eternal reward on his last day. Every act of a Christian's day, his recreation as well as his work, his joys as well as his sorrows, his sleeping as well as his waking hour, gives honor and glory to God, and earns heaven for the Christian. This is the real meaning of living a Christian life. This is what St. Paul tells us today when he says: "whether you eat or drink or whatever you do, do all to the glory of God." This is how St. Paul himself lived and acted and became a great saint. Undoubtedly, he gave most of his time to teaching the gospel to others, but he also worked with his hands, ate some meals, slept some hours at least each night, had moments of recreation or relaxation with friends, but he offered it all to God and it all added to God's glory and to his own sanctification. God lived more and more in him and with him each day that dawned. There are millions of saints in heaven who did nothing extraordinary in their whole lives but they lived their ordinary lives honestly and well. It should not be too hard for the weakest of us to do this. It will help us to do our daily tasks more faithfully if each morning we offer our day to the honor and glory of God. This morning offering can be made while dressing, or while on our way to work and if sometimes we forget it, God will understand.

So the true answer to what did you do for God's honor and glory since last Sunday is: I have given him seven days' service; I have honored him in all my doings. This will be true for every Christian who has been honest in all his doings and who has lived within the laws of God, of his Church, and of his country. We cannot honor God with a dishonest act, we can give no glory to God while wilfully disobeying in serious matters the commandments of God or of his Church, or the lawful enactments of the State. But our merciful God knows how weak our human nature can be at times, and has given us an easy means of rising again should we fall into disobedience. The sincere Christian who realizes that our daily tasks, if they are carried out while we are not in God's friendship, are not capable of honoring God or earning our own eternal salvation, will rise quickly from sin and return to God's friendship. To sin is partly human frailty and partly human folly; to remain deliberately in sin is criminal injustice to God and to ourselves, because all those days, weeks, and months perhaps, are squandered and wasted as far as God and our eternal destiny are concerned.

Let us try, from now on, to imitate St. Paul by devoting twenty-four hours each day to the honor and glory of God. We do not have to say any extra prayers; we do not have to do any unusual mortifications but if we do each task of each day faithfully and truly, we shall be honoring God daily and storing up a priceless reward for ourselves in heaven.

GOSPEL: Mark 1:40-45. A leper came to Jesus beseeching him, and kneeling said to him, "If you will, you can make me clean." Moved with pity, he stretched out his hand and touched him, and said to him, "I will; be clean." And immediately the leprosy left him, and he was made clean. And he sternly charged him, and sent him away at once, and said to him, "See that you say nothing to anyone; but go, show yourself to the priest, and offer for your cleansing what Moses commanded, for a proof to the people." But he went out and began to talk freely about it, and to spread the news, so that Jesus could no longer openly enter a town, but was out in the country; and people came to him from every quarter.

EXPLANATION: During the first day of his public ministry in Galilee Jesus cured all sorts of diseases and cast out demons (Mk. 1:21-34). On the next day he performed what was looked on as the greatest miracle of all, he healed a leper. Although at least some of the cases called leprosy in Leviticus (see first reading) were not real leprosy but some other form of skin-disease, at the time of Christ in Palestine leprosy was looked on as incurable. According to the rabbis "the healing of leprosy was as difficult as the raising of the dead." But Christ was able to raise the dead too. There were many lepers in Palestine (as well as in all countries) at that time. This man was most probably living near Capernaum and through some friend or relative had heard of the miracles of healing which Christ had worked there on the previous day. Filled with hope and faith, he approached Christ as he was leaving Capernaum, and asked for a miracle. His request was granted.

kneeling said to him: Putting himself in the most humble posture—on his knees —he made his request.

if you . . . can: He shows absolute faith in Christ's power to heal him even from this incurable disease. All that is needed is that Christ deigns to befriend him.

I will; be clean: Moved with pity for the poor sufferer, who was cut off from all human intercourse because of his disease, Christ answered: "I will," and then touching him with his hand he gave the command "be clean" or "be made clean." As leprosy was a decaying of the skin and eventually of the flesh and bones, the term used for healing it was a *cleansing*—a removal of the filth of rotting flesh and a restoration of clean flesh and skin.

was made clean: The cure was instantaneous.

say . . . anyone: Christ warned the cured leper to say nothing to the people about this miracle but to go to Jerusalem (or wherever the nearest priest could be found) and get a declaration of complete health from him. Only the priests could give this declaration.

offer . . . cleansing : Moses (Leviticus 14 : 1–32) ordered that certain ceremonies should be performed by the priest who declared a leper free of his disease, and certain offerings for sacrifice should be made by the cured leper.

a proof . . . people : The people who had known a man as a leper would now have the priest's guarantee that he was free of the disease and was no longer a danger to their health.

talk . . . it : It would seem ungrateful if this cured leper were immediately and openly to disobey his benefactor, but most likely he felt an obligation to spread the fame of this generous miracle-worker. This often happened during Christ's public life.

Jesus . . . town : The result of the publishing of this extraordinary miracle as well as of the others performed in Capernaum, was that everybody gathered into any town Jesus was approaching, and so it would be impossible to preach to them or to cure their diseases.

out in the country : He therefore stayed in the open country where large crowds could and did gather from every quarter. Even then it was sometimes difficult to address the throngs that came to hear him (see Lk. 5 :3).

APPLICATION : We see both the divine power and the divine compassion of Jesus in this act of healing. The divine power was necessary in all instantaneous cures. Even if the diseases were curable, the ordinary process of nature took time to fight off the causes and to return to normality. Therefore, where there was an instantaneous recovery some power above nature, some supernatural cause brought it about. But where the disease was incurable, as real leprosy then was, to remove it by a simple word of command was more emphatically still the result of divine power. This divine power Jesus had, for he was himself divine, the Son of God.

His compassion for suffering humanity was, however, co-terminous with his power, it was also divine. It was out of compassion for the sad lot of the human race on earth that he descended to man's level, becoming man, equal to us in all things except sin, in order to suffer with us and for us. By his human sufferings he made an atonement, a satisfaction for all the sins of the world—a satisfaction which all mankind could never make—to his heavenly Father, and so obtained for us God's pardon. At the same time, by joining our human nature to his divine nature, he brought us into the divine orbit and made us adopted sons of God and heirs of the eternal life of the Blessed Trinity. Because this seems almost too good to be true, there are men who deny it or refuse to accept it. Such men make the mistake of measuring the infinite compassion of God with the limited yardstick of their own finite and puny compassion.

Thanks be to God, for his infinite compassion! Thanks be to God, for Christ his Son, who came and dwelt amongst us! He put heaven and a share in the life of God within our reach; he has shown us how to attain them, giving in his Church and the sacraments, all the necessary aids. But we still need all of Christ's compassion if we are to get there. Because of our inclination to sin and because of the many times we unfortunately give in to that inclination, nothing but the mercy of God can save us from our own folly. However, that mercy is available, if only we ask for it. What we sinners need is the faith and confidence of the leper in today's gospel reading. He believed firmly in the power and the mercy of Jesus. "If you will, you *can* make me clean," was his approach to Jesus.

This should be our approach too, if we have the misfortune to fall into serious sin. Jesus does will and does want our salvation. His incarnation, and death on the cross, proves that. The fact that he left the power to forgive sins to his Church is another proof of both his will and desire to help us. "All power has been given to me in heaven and on earth," he stated. Part of that power which he left to his Church is in the sacrament of penance where the leprosy of sin can be washed away and the sinner restored to new and perfect spiritual health. What folly for any Christian then, to commit sin and isolate himself, like the unclean leper, from God. But it is greater folly still, to remain in this unclean state when the cure for his disease is so easily available to any sincere penitent.

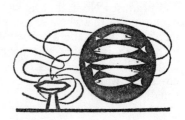

FIRST SUNDAY OF LENT

FIRST READING : Genesis 9 : 8–15. God said to Noah and to his sons with him, "Behold, I establish my covenant with you and your descendants after you, and with every living creature that is with you, the birds, the cattle, and every beast of the earth with you, as many as came out of the ark. I establish my covenant with you, that never again shall all flesh be cut off by the waters of a flood, and never again shall there be a flood to destroy the earth." And God said, "This is the sign of the covenant which I make between me and you and every living creature that is with you, for all future generations : I set my bow in the cloud, and it shall be a sign of the covenant between me and the earth. When I bring clouds over the earth and the bow is seen in the clouds, I will remember my covenant which is between me and you and every living creature of all flesh; and the waters shall never again become a flood to destroy all flesh."

EXPLANATION : The story of the Flood given in Genesis, chapters 6–8, is part of pre-history. It is similar in many respects to other mid-eastern accounts of a like catastrophe, but the biblical version is strictly monotheistic and the cause of the catastrophe is the sinfullness of men which compels God to repurify the human race. The pagan stories of the Flood attribute it to jealousies and disagreement among the many gods—there is no moral lesson to be learned from this catastrophe. In the Genesis account, all men (in the region where the deluge occurred) were destroyed, except Noah, his wife, his three sons and their wives. These were preserved by God because of Noah's innocent way of life, and were now to carry on the knowledge of God down to Abraham's day.

Noah offered a sacrifice of thanksgiving to God for having spared him and his family. God accepted the sacrifice and promised Noah that he would never again punish the whole earth because of man's sins. He made a covenant or pact with Noah in which this promise was enshrined.

covenant with you: A covenant is usually between two parties. Here it is unilateral. God promises to spare mankind in future even if men are sinful.

every . . . creature: According to the deluge story, the waters destroyed all living creatures except those that were in the Ark with Noah. In future, all creatures will share in the promise of security that God is giving to Noah and, through him, to all men for all time.

never . . . flood: This was the substance of the covenant.

my bow . . . cloud: In future the rainbow would be a sign, a reminder of this promise. The rainbow, a natural phenomenon, was always there in certain cloud formations, but henceforward it would remind both God ("I will remember my covenant") and man of the covenant.

water . . . all flesh: There would never again be a universal flood, to destroy all flesh as this deluge is supposed to have done.

APPLICATION: The holy season of Lent began last Wednesday. It should be a season of penance, during which we look into our hearts, and see how ungrateful, how mean we have been to our loving God, and having seen our meanness, try to make some atonement for our past ingratitude. The lesson from Genesis that we have just read reminds us of these two facts: man's disobedience and disloyalty to the divine Benefactor who made man and gave him all the gifts of body and mind which he has, and on the other hand the magnanimity, the infinite forgiving mercy of God who puts up with his creatures, who not only forget him but who positively offend and insult him.

The deluge story was intended to show this divine mercy. Men had become so wicked and so sinful that God decided to wipe them off his universe. Yet he decided to spare one innocent family from whom the human race could grow and spread once more. This he did by getting Noah to build the Ark. When the deluge had ended and Noah had offered his thanksgiving sacrifice, God made a pact with the human race through Noah, a covenant in which he solemnly promised never again to send a similar flood on this earth.

God in his mercy gave the human race a second chance. We are here on earth today because of this divine mercy and we have his guarantee, his covenant, to assure us that we will not be struck down suddenly because of our sins. But the fact that God does not want the sinner to die in his sins should never be an excuse for a continuation in sin but rather a motive, an inspiration to the sinner to return to his loving Father. While God does not will the death of a sinner in his sins, but rather that he be converted and live, every sinner knows that death may be around the corner at any moment and if it finds him in sin, it will not be God's fault but his own. There is only one guarantee we can give ourselves of dying in God's friendship and that is: to live always in God's friendship.

Now, in this covenant that God made with all of us through Noah, all the giving was done by God himself. It was a unilateral, magnanimous covenant on the part of God. He did not demand promises from Noah in return, but yet from the very nature of the case such promises were expected of Noah and of us too. If God is ready to forgive man his sins, it follows that men must ask

for that forgiveness. To ask for forgiveness implies and includes the intention of turning away from sin.

Lent is the special occasion for all Christians to turn away from sin and to do penance for all of their past offenses against God. We can fulfill our part of that pact that God made with Noah, by resolving to be faithful in future. Thus we can ensure that we shall not be cut off in our sins, as all those drowned in the deluge were, but that we shall die, as we were living, in God's friendship. You may have another Lent next year, in which to repeat this resolution and you may not, but if you make it with all sincerity now and live up to it, you are giving yourself a guarantee that when death calls you, you will be found in God's friendship.

SECOND READING : 1 Peter 3 : 18–22. Christ also died for sins once for all, the righteous for the unrighteous, that he might bring us to God, being put to death in the flesh but made alive in the spirit; in which he went and preached to the spirits in prison, who formerly did not obey, when God's patience waited in the days of Noah, during the building of the ark, in which a few, that is, eight persons, were saved through water. Baptism, which corresponds to this, now saves you, not as a removal of dirt from the body but as an appeal to God for a clear conscience, through the resurrection of Jesus Christ, who has gone into heaven and is at the right hand of God, with angels, authorities, and powers subject to him.

EXPLANATION : In the passage from which these five verses are taken, St. Peter is exhorting the newly converted Christians to live according to the Christian faith, no matter what trials they may have to endure because of it. In many places Christians were being persecuted by Gentiles and Jews because of their new faith. They should accept

and bear these persecutions willingly, for they know they are not guilty of any crime except that of honoring the true God and his Son, Jesus Christ. Therefore "to suffer for being good you will count as a blessing" (3 : 4). Peter sets before them the example of the Innocent Christ who was put to death and who accepted his sufferings and torments for our sakes, for our sins. Through his death we have eternal life available to us. We are saved through the waters of baptism (which cleanses us of sin and makes us one with Christ) just as Noah and his family were saved at the time of the deluge.

Christ . . . for all : Because Christ was God in human nature, the atonement his death made to God was good for all time and for all the sins of all men.

righteous : Christ was innocence itself, but he took on himself the sin of the world; he made himself a sin-sacrifice for us.

bring us to God : This was the divine purpose of the incarnation : to make all men adopted sons of God and worthy of heaven if they die in the state of grace.

made alive . . . spirit : Christ died on the cross but God raised him from the dead in a glorified body which could never again die.

preached . . . not obey : Peter now refers to the deluge and Noah, for he saw in the waters of the flood, the life-giving waters of baptism. The spirits who did not obey are very probably the "sons of God," the rebellious angels who, according to the deluge story, were the principal cause of the sinfulness which caused the deluge (Gen. 6 : 1–4). When Christ had triumphed over death and sin he announced this victory to these rebellious angels who were henceforth subjected to him.

God's patience waited : The long interval between God's resolve to send a deluge (Gn. 6 : 7) and the beginning of the flood (Gn. 7 : 11), was an opportunity given the sinners to repent, but they did not.

few . . . persons : The few is stressed probably to show the similarity with the Christian Church at this time. The number of Christians in relation to the pagan population, was relatively very small.

baptism corresponds : Peter compares the waters of the deluge to the waters of baptism. As Noah was saved in or from the deluge, so Christians are saved in the baptismal water.

not . . . dirt : Probably a reference to circumcision, but it can also mean : the washing in baptism is not for a cleansing of the body but a cleansing, a new form of life for the baptized.

appeal . . . conscience : "A pledge" would seem to be a better translation here (as in J.B.). The baptized pledges himself to live according to the new life which faith in the resurrection of Christ promises him.

gone into heaven : Christ the man-God now in his glorified body is in heaven, in the next place of honor after the Father, "at the right hand of God."

angels . . . powers : The reference is to the disobedient spirits, the evil powers, who are now forever subjected to the glorified Christ. In causing his death they brought about their own undoing (see Phil. 2 : 10; Rom. 8 : 38; Col. 2 : 10–15, et passim in St. Paul).

APPLICATION : "Christ died for sins," *for our sins.* This is the thought which should dominate every true Christian's mind always, but especially during this Lenten season. The climax and culmination of these forty days during which we are constantly reminded of all God has done for us, comes on Good Friday with the commemoration of the excruciating death of our Savior on the cross. If only men would let the true significance of Good Friday sink into their minds, sin would disappear from our world, true love of God and neighbor would take over. Think of it; God so loved "the world" that is, us that he sent his only begotten Son, to suffer and die in our stead. The Son of God, the Creator and Lord of the universe became man, became one of us, so that he could take our sins on himself and nail them, with himself, to the cross. The innocent Lamb of God elected to take the whole load of all the sins and infidelities of all of us "lost sheep," on his own back, so that we could be set free.

Five centuries before that first Good Friday the prophet described the humiliations and sufferings of him who was to come: "He was despised and rejected by men, a man of sorrows and acquainted with grief; surely he has borne our griefs and carried our sorrows . . . he was wounded for our transgressions; he was bruised for our iniquities . . . and with his stripes we are healed. All we, like sheep, have gone astray . . . and the Lord has laid on him the iniquity of us all. Like a lamb that is led to the slaughter . . . he opened not his mouth. They made his grave with the wicked although he had done no violence and there was no deceit in his mouth. Yet it was the will of the Lord to bruise him . . . he offers his life in atonement" (Is. 53 : 3–10). Here we have the first twelve Stations of the Cross described in words, more poignant than any painter ever succeeded in depicting them, for the prophet puts before

our minds that it was for us that Jesus suffered his tortures. St. Peter reminds us today to meditate, to think seriously, on this almost incredible act of divine love for us, which moved God to send his own Son on earth as man, to suffer and die so that we might have true, everlasting life. Our finite minds can make no attempt to grasp this mystery of God's love for us, but we have before our eyes, in words and in picture, the terribly real sufferings of the human Jesus. We know the reason for his sufferings, our very real sins. This we can grasp and it is on this we should act. The future life in heaven which God has planned for us from all eternity, must be for us a good so great, so exalted that it is worth all the sufferings and humiliations his incarnate Son had to endure. Surely, then, we should gladly and willingly co-operate with God in procuring for ourselves this marvelous future life.

We are Christians. We have been put on the road to heaven by the reception of baptism. We shall get there if we follow Christ as closely as we can during our time on earth. Noah and his family were saved in the deluge because they listened to God's advice and built their Ark. We are being advised today by the inspired writers of the Old and New Testaments to spend this Lent well, to turn away from sin, to do daily some little acts of mortification, to meditate often on the one and only thing that really matters—our attainment of that union with God which is so important that the Son of God suffered and died so that we could have it everlastingly.

GOSPEL : Mark 1 : 12–15. The Spirit drove Jesus out into the wilderness. And he was in the wilderness forty days, tempted by Satan; and he was with the wild beasts; and the angels ministered to him.

Now after John was arrested, Jesus came into Galilee, preaching the gospel of God, and saying, "The time is fulfilled, and the kingdom of God is at hand; repent, and believe in the gospel."

EXPLANATION : The reason why the first two verses of this short extract from Mark are chosen for the First Sunday of Lent is obvious. The Church appointed for us a Lent of forty days of penance and of war against our evil inclinations in imitation of the forty days of struggle which Christ waged in a desert place (which implies mortification) against Satan, the recognized leader of the forces of evil. Mark does not mention that Christ fasted for the forty days and nights but the "desert" seems to imply this; nor does he specify the various "temptations" as Matthew and Luke do. But his very brief account clearly implies that Satan lost in the struggle or rather that Satan was made to realize that this Jesus was the Messiah who would eventually conquer him and his assistant evil spirits. The mention of his being among wild beasts who did not harm him, and also of the angels coming to minister to him, most probably meant to Mark that in this first encounter, Jesus had reversed Adam's defeat and had begun the process of restoring paradise. Having briefly described Christ's victory, the Evangelist then goes on in the next two verses to outline the public ministry in Galilee where according to the Synoptics, most of Christ's public life was spent. Verse fifteen gives the essence of Christ's preaching in a very brief summary.

Spirit . . . wilderness : The Holy Spirit which descended on Jesus when he was baptized in the Jordan, moved him to join battle with Satan in the desert. The word "drove" seems to imply some compulsion, but Matthew and Luke in parallel places use the word "led."

forty days : Moses before receiving the Old Law on Mount Sinai fasted for forty days (Ex. 34 : 28); Elijah, the first of the great prophets, sent to Israel, fasted for forty days on his journey to Mount Horeb (1 Kgs. 19 : 5), so Christ also, the lawgiver of the New Covenant, the Prophet of God's mercy and love, spent forty days in the wilderness before beginning his mission of redemption.

tempted by Satan : The current belief of the Jews was that the Messiah would put an end to the sway of evil which had prevailed over good since sin entered the world. Satan was the name for the leader of the forces of evil—the enemies of God and of the good. Jesus, proclaimed Messiah at the Jordan, was moved by the Holy Spirit immediately to open his campaign of conquest. He did so and Satan's kingdom began to totter. Satan could still win some local battles but his day of tyranny over men was ended when Christ came.

wild beasts . . . angels : Harmony between all creatures was a sign of the messianic age (see Is. 11 : 6; Hos. 2 : 18; Ez. 34 : 25–28) and the ministering angels would imply that the gates of paradise were about to reopen—"the cherubim with flaming swords" have become the assistants of the Messiah (see Gn. 3 : 24).

after John was arrested : It was only when the Precursor, the herald of the Messiah, had left the stage that Christ began his final battle with the powers of evil.

the gospel of God : The good news of God's eternal plan for the elevation and the redemption of mankind.

the time is fulfilled : The moment of the coming of Christ, the beginning of the kingdom of God on earth—a kingdom which would end in heaven—had been decreed by God from all eternity. It is now here, Christ tells the people of Galilee.

repent . . . gospel : The first necessary step was to turn from sin and return to God, to change one's outlook on life and one's conduct (see Joel 2 : 12). Having turned from sin to God it will be easier for men to accept the good news of God's plan for them.

APPLICATION : The very thought of our divine Lord's suffering hunger, loneliness, and humiliation at the hands of his enemy—and that all this was for us—should make us feel ashamed at the little bits of suffering and humiliation we are willing to suffer for our own selves. He had no sin to atone for. He was making atonement for us and for our sins. He was the Son of God and his home was heaven, but he left it for a while to assume human nature, so that he could through his humiliations and sufferings bring us to share his eternal home with him. What is the thanks he gets from us? Ingratitude, forgetfulness, and even worse : insults and disobedience.

While the Church has eased the strict fastings and penances of Lent, we are still expected to do some private fasting and penance. It need not be fasting from food, but we can all do some daily penance which will help to keep our unruly minds and bodies in check while at the same time it will show that we are grateful to our loving Savior for all that he suffered for us. A few extra prayers each day, control of our temper in the home, less talk and especially less uncharitable talk among our neighbors, a little helping hand to a neighbor in need, a fervent prayer and where we can spare it (perhaps by doing without some luxury) a donation toward helping the starving millions in other lands. The sincere Christian will find a hundred such ways in which to thank and honor Christ during this holy season of Lent. We can all keep the last verse of today's reading before our minds with great profit. "Repent and believe in the gospel." This is the essence, the marrow, of Christ's teaching. Turn away from sin and come back to God. Anyone who believes in the gospel, who believes that there is an everlasting life after death prepared by God for all those who do his will while on earth, should not find it hard to give up offending that loving God who thinks so much of him. This life is only a passing shadow, every step we take, every breath we breathe is bringing us nearer to our earthly end and to the grave. But the believing Christian knows the grave is not the end. Rather, is it the beginning of the true life—provided we use this passing shadow, these few years, properly.

Now is the time to take these words of Christ to heart. He is asking each one of us today, to repent and to believe the gospel, that is, to act according to its teaching. Christ, in his mercy, will make this appeal to men again and again, but will we be here to hear it? If we answer his appeal now and start living our Christian faith in all sincerity, we need not care when death calls us. It will find us ready to pass over to the future, happy, unending life.

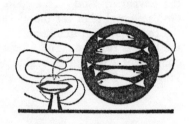

SECOND SUNDAY OF LENT

FIRST READING: Genesis 22 : 1-2; 9-13; 15-18. God tested Abraham, and said to him, "Abraham!" And he said, "Here am I." He said, "Take your son, your only son Isaac, whom you love, and go to the land of Moriah, and offer him there as burnt offering upon one of the mountains of which I shall tell you."

When they came to the place of which God had told him, Abraham put forth his hand, and took the knife to slay his son. But the angel of the Lord called to him from heaven, and said, "Abraham, Abraham!" And he said, "Here am I." He said, "Do not lay your hand on the lad or do anything to him; for now I know that you fear God, seeing you have not withheld your son, your only son, from me." And Abraham lifted up his eyes and looked, and behold, behind him was a ram, caught in a thicket by his horns; and Abraham went and took the ram, and offered it up as a burnt offering instead of his son.

And the angel of the Lord called to Abraham a second time from heaven, and said, "By myself I have sworn, says the Lord, because you have done this, and have not withheld your son, your only son, I will indeed bless you, and I will multiply your descendants as the stars of heaven and as the sand which is on the seashore. And your descendants shall possess the gate of their enemies, and by your descendants shall all the nations of the earth bless themselves, because you have obeyed my voice."

EXPLANATION: Abraham had promptly obeyed the true God, left his pagan kith, kin and country and come to Canaan. God told him he would be the founder of a great race, the Chosen People, from whom God's blessing—the Messiah—would eventually come (Gn. 12 : 1-3). To be the founder of a race, Abraham needed to have a son. God let him wait for twenty-four years before he blessed Sarah, his wife, and himself with a son. In all of that time Abraham was faithful to God, but God had one more test for him. When his son Isaac had grown to boyhood, God asked Abraham to offer him in sacrifice at an appointed place. Abraham obeyed promptly once more, but God intervened as Abraham got ready to slay his son. He told Abraham how pleased he was with his ready obedience. He renewed to him once more the promise of a great race, through which the whole world would receive the blessing of God—divine adoption through the incarnation.

God . . . Abraham : God knew the answer, but he wanted Abraham's faith and trust in God to be an example for his descendants for all time.

only son . . . love : There were two reasons which made it so difficult for Abraham to obey. First, he loved his only son, as only a father who begot a son in his old age could love and secondly, how could he be father of a great race if his only son was put to death? However, Abraham's love of God overcame his natural love for his son, and his firm faith in the power of God told him that God could still find a way to fulfill the promise of a great race, which he had made to him in his pagan homeland thirty or so years earlier.

a burnt offering : This seems an extraordinary request on the part of God. But in the surrounding pagan lands at that time and for long after, children were offered in sacrifice on pagan altars. God by no means approved of this crime, but the fact that it was happening made it possible for Abraham to think that God really wanted him to sacrifice Isaac.

Abraham, Abraham : As Abraham was just ready to slay his son before burning him on the altar God's messenger calls on him to stop.

you fear God : It was now clear that Abraham was willing to obey God in all things even a thing so difficult and repugnant as this.

a ram . . . thicket : As the altar was ready, Abraham felt he should offer some sacrifice to God because he had spoken to him there, and so he offered the ram which happened to be within reach.

by myself . . . sworn : Because of Abraham's fidelity and trust God now renews his promise in a most solemn way—he swears by himself. There was nothing, or no person higher, by whom he could swear or guarantee fulfillment of his promise.

all . . . themselves : All the peoples of the world would come to know in time that it was through Abraham and his descendant, Christ, that God's privilege of sonship was made available to them (see Heb. 11 : 12; Rom. 4). They will see Abraham as the human intermediary in God's plan for all men.

APPLICATION : The faith and trust of Abraham in the true God whom he had got to know only late in life, and about whose power and love he did not know a fraction of what we know, should well put us to shame. Abraham left his country, his home, and his kin at a time when one's life depended on the strength of one's clan. He came to a foreign land about which he knew nothing. There he lived among strangers who had no time for invaders and "foreigners." All of this looks easy on paper but what a sacrifice it must have been for Abraham to leave his own people, to travel the long desert journey from Haran in Assyria to Canaan, and then to try to earn his daily bread in unfriendly, if not positively hostile, surroundings. All of this Abraham did because he was convinced of this true God's omnipotence and fidelity to his promises. Abraham was glad of the role that God had chosen for him—the human agent through whom the great divine blessing for all peoples would come.

Abraham's second test of obedience and trust, of which we have just read, was even a more severe trial than the first. He was asked to give up forever his only real son and thereby be unable to fulfill the role God had promised him. Here again Abraham's trust in God gave him the strength and the courage to do what he was told. Abraham's prompt, unquestioning obedience pleased God—he did not have to sacrifice his only Son. His goodwill, his desire and readiness to obey God's command, were proof enough of his justice, fidelity, sanctity.

How many of us could imitate Abraham? How many of us who have seen God the Father sacrificing his beloved Son in his human nature, offering him as sacrifice for our sins on the cross, could or would measure up to Abraham's prompt obedience when God demands some sacrifice of us? How many of us who can devoutly make the Stations of the Cross, and see and feel the insults, degradation, tortures that the innocent Lamb of God suffered for our sins, will turn around soon after and refuse to give up some sinful association, some personal and unlawful gain, some habit of gluttony, or personal animosity against a neighbor? Such unwillingness to sacrifice something much less important than an only son, for the sake of God and our own eternal welfare, is far indeed from the prompt and ready obedience of Abraham.

We all have much to learn from this saintly man who lived nearly four thousand years ago. He is our father in the faith, for it was through his descendants that the knowledge of the true God was preserved on earth, and it was from one of his descendants that our Savior—the Messiah—took his human nature. We should, therefore, remember him with gratitude and we should show that gratitude especially by our endeavors to imitate his spirit of obedience and submission to God's will. Let each one of us look into his or her own heart today. There are desires and plans and attachments there, which God is asking us to sacrifice, to burn up, to destroy during this Lent. They are trifling sacrifices compared with that demanded of Abraham, but they are big enough to keep us from true loyalty to God in this life and are a very positive impediment to our entrance into heaven in the next.

SECOND READING: Romans 8 : 31–34. If God is for us, who is against us? He who did not spare his own Son but gave him up for us all, will he not also give us all things with him? Who shall bring any charge against God's elect? It is God who justifies; who is to condemn? Is it Christ Jesus, who died, yes, who was raised from the dead, who is at the right hand of God, who indeed intercedes for us?

EXPLANATION: Unlike his other Epistles, which were letters written by Paul to churches that he, or one of his assistants, had evangelized, this letter is to a church that he had not even visited. It is, therefore, less personal and more in the form of an exposition of part (not all) of the Christian message which he had preached in Asia Minor and Greece, and was now anxious to preach to the Romans also. In the section of the letter from which this extract is taken, St. Paul is emphasizing the indwelling of the Spirit in Christians and their freedom from sin, eternal death and the Jewish law. The liberating act of Christ had made them children of God, destined for glory. The Christian is a freeman who lives in hope. His hope is founded on the infinite love of God for men. That love was made manifest in Christ Jesus.

If God . . . us: He has demonstrated that God is clearly on the side of man. The salvific plan of God which Paul has expounded so far is sufficient proof of this.

who . . . us: With God on our side, all enemies are powerless against us.

who did . . . Son: What greater proof of his love for us could God have given us than this, that he handed over his own Son to the death of the cross for our sakes (see 5 : 5–8).

all things with him: If he gave his beloved Son to us and for us, he will give everything else that is necessary for our eternal salvation.

bring . . . against: Christians are God's chosen ones. God is the supreme Judge; who shall dare to bring any charge against them in God's court?

It is God who justifies: The same idea is here repeated.

Is . . . Jesus: Christ who has made us his brothers by his incarnation, and died on the cross for our sins will not bring a charge against us.

raised . . . intercedes: Christ who died has been raised from the dead and is now in his glorified humanity in the principal place in heaven. He is interceding for us, that is, he is continuing his activity as Savior. Could he then become our opponent? The answer, of course, is "no."

APPLICATION: These four short verses of St. Paul's letter to the Romans are among the most encouraging and consoling scripture passages in the whole Bible. He tells us God and Christ are entirely in favor of admitting us to heaven. He admits that there are some enemies who would try to prevent us from getting there, but he logically concludes: what can any enemy or number of enemies do if God and Christ are our defending Counsels and Judges? In brief "if God is for us who is against us?" Paul's whole letter is full of proofs that God is for us, the greatest proof of all being the fact of the incarnation and crucifixion of his Son, for us sinners. If God went to those lengths in order to bring us to heaven it is more than logical that he will give us the lesser gifts and the assistance that each one of us needs in order to get there.

The Christian who keeps vivid this consoling knowledge of God's love for him and God's interest in his eternal welfare should never have a sad moment in his life. The things that cause us worry and trouble in life are trifles, when compared with the assurance and certainty we have of final triumph. That assurance comes from God's infinite love, so definitely proved to us by the incarnation. St. Paul goes on in the very next verse after the text which is read today (8 : 35) : "who shall separate us from the love of Christ? Shall tribulation, or distress or persecution or famine or nakedness or peril or sword" . . . No, in all these things we are more than conquerors through him who loved us . . . no created thing can ever come between us and the love of God made visible in Christ Jesus our Lord."

This is the assurance that St. Paul gives the newly converted Christians of Rome and it was not based on any speculation or wishful thinking, but on the solid proofs of God's love for us which the incarnation so definitely demonstrated. Let no one say : this might be all very true as regards the early Christians, they were full of zeal and full of the love of God; they were not likely to feel all the weaknesses of the flesh and all the attractions of the world which we feel today; life was easier then,

they could give more time to the things of God than we can today, the struggle for existence was not so hard for them. St. Paul who knew human nature very well and who had dealt with thousands of converts would deny such statements absolutely. He knew the Roman converts were subject to the same human weaknesses as are all men of all ages. He knew they could, and very likely did, sin occasionally but he also knew that they had been instructed on how to repent of their sins and had enough interest in their eternal welfare to do so.

They had the same weakness that we have, they had the same enemies opposing their salvation. We have the same remedies and protections as they had; they used these remedies and were saved. Shall we not be as active in our own best interests as they were? God is as much for us as he was for the Romans, he wants us in heaven and he has done all that was necessary (and much more) to get us there. If we fail in our final examination one of our greatest causes of grief will be that the fault is completely and entirely our own. We can blame no person or thing in heaven or on earth for our dreadful failure except ourselves. Pray God today, that you shall avoid such grief. You will, if you try always to keep before your mind what God, the Father, Son and Holy Spirit, has done and continues to do daily for you. "If God is with us who is against us?" God is ever with us if we do not deliberately and seriously separate ourselves from him.

GOSPEL : Mark 9 : 2–10. Jesus took with him Peter and James and John. and led them up a high mountain apart by themselves; and he was transfigured before them, and his garments became glistening, intensely white, as no fuller on earth could bleach them. And there appeared to them Elijah with Moses; and they were talking to Jesus. And Peter said to Jesus, "Master, it is well that we are here; let us make three booths, one for you and one for Moses and one for Elijah." For he did not know what to say, for they were exceedingly afraid. And a cloud overshadowed them, and a voice came out of the cloud. "This is my beloved Son; listen to him." And suddenly looking around they no longer saw any one with them but Jesus only.

And as they were coming down the mountain, he charged them to tell no one what they had seen, until the Son of man should have risen from the dead. So they kept the matter to themselves, questioning what the rising from the dead meant.

EXPLANATION : A few days previous to the event narrated here by St. Mark, Jesus had told his disciples of the sufferings and death that awaited him in Jerusalem. "He began to teach them that the Son of Man must suffer many things and be rejected by the elders and the chief priests . . . and be killed and after three days rise again (Mk. 8 : 31). This statement greatly depressed the Apostles. They still had the wrong idea of their Messiah. They still hoped he would establish an earthly kingdom, that he would use his great powers to subdue all his earthly enemies and that he would set up a triumphant kingdom in Israel. It was while they were in this mood of deep depression that he took Peter, James and John—the same three who were to witness his Agony in the Garden a few months later—to the top of a high mountain. Here he gave them a glimpse of the divine glory which was his, but of which he had "emptied himself," as St. Paul puts it, "taking the form of a servant being born in the likeness of men, though he was in the form of God" (Phil. 2 : 6–7) so that he could, through his life and sufferings as man,

redeem and elevate all men.

was . . . before them : The appearance of Jesus was completely changed; He had become someone entirely different, someone glorious. Even his garments shone with a brilliance and whiteness not of this world : "no fuller on earth could bleach them thus." Jesus allowed his three Apostles a momentary prevision of what his glorified body united to his divinity will be like in heaven.

Elijah, Moses : These were the two outstanding representatives of the Law and the prophets, that is, of the Old Testament. Their presence was an indication that Christ was the promised Messiah.

talking to Jesus : Mark does not mention the subject of this talk but Luke (9 : 29) tells us they were speaking of "his departure", his passion and death in Jerusalem.

Peter said : Always the leader and always ready to speak. Peter, beside himself because of the glorious vision, suggests that this should continue forever. Hence the idea of erecting three booths (or tents) in which Jesus, Moses and Elijah could remain. There may have been the thought in his mind that in the eschatological age God would pitch his tent among men (see Ez. 37 : 27; Zech. 2 : 10–11).

did not . . . say : This is an indication of the folly of Peter's suggestion.

exceedingly afraid : They knew that they were in the presence of something supernatural and were therefore afraid.

a cloud . . . them : In the Old Testament a cloud was always the symbol of the presence of the divine majesty. God spoke to the Israelites in the desert from a cloud (Ex. 16 : 10). He gave the ten commandments to Moses from a cloud (Ex. 19 : 16). He manifested his presence in the newly-built temple of Solomon in a cloud "which filled the house of the Lord" (3 Kgs. 8 : 10).

a voice came : From out of the cloud God proclaimed that Christ was his beloved Son whom the Apostles must hear and obey: "listen to him."

no longer . . . Jesus only : St. Matthew tells us the Apostles fell on their faces when they heard the voice of God from the cloud—they were terrified and wanted to hide themselves. Matthew also adds that Jesus then came to them and told them to rise up and not to be afraid. The only one they saw when they stood up and opened their eyes was Jesus in his ordinary human appearance.

he charged them : On their way down from the mountain Jesus commanded the three Apostles to tell nobody what they had witnessed until :

the Son . . . dead : After the resurrection they would understand that Jesus was more than man and more than a human Messiah. This vision would then have a clear meaning for them and for those to whom they would tell it.

rising . . . meant : They kept this secret from all others but they discussed it among themselves, and they were especially puzzled by Jesus' mention of his resurrection from the dead. This puzzlement was not about the possibility of the resurrection of all men—for like the vast majority of their contemporary Jews, they had no doubts about an eventual resurrection from the dead—but how could Jesus rise from the dead when they were convinced that he could not die. He had power over all things, he had raised others from the dead, and this vision they had just seen proved how close to God he was, so how could he die? Nothing else but the actual death of Jesus on the cross was able to convince his Apostles that he would or could die.

APPLICATION : This vision of Christ glorified, given to these Apostles on Mount Thabor (the traditional site of Transfiguration) was surely a very special privilege, and it was one they did not forget. "We saw his glory," St. John says in his gospel, written over sixty years later. In his epistles John also refers to this privilege (1 Jn. 1 : 1–4). St. Peter, writing from Rome to the churches in Asia Minor about thirty years later, mentions this outstanding experience : "For we were not following fictitious tales when we made known to you the power and coming of our Lord Jesus Christ, but we had been *eye-witnesses of his majesty*. For he received from God the Father honor and glory, when from out the majestic glory a voice came down to him saying : 'this is my beloved Son in whom I am well pleased.' And this voice *we ourselves heard* borne from heaven when we were with him on the holy mountain" (2 Pt. 1 : 16–18).

Yes, the three Apostles were privileged and we too are sharers in their privilege. The Transfiguration of Christ is but one among many of the incontrovertible proofs of the divine Sonship of Christ which we have in the gospel narratives and in the twenty centuries-long history of the Church which he founded. Were he not divine, that Church would long since have crumbled and fallen under the many vicious assaults from outside which it has undergone, as well as from the many human weaknesses which have beset it from within. But Christ is God and the Church has his divine protection and assistance. Therefore, it will go on to the end of time to continue his work of elevating and redeeming mankind.

This enlightening glimpse of Christ's future glory—a glory in which they would share—was given to these Apostles to strengthen and encourage them in the terrible test of their faith which the passion and death of Jesus would be for them very soon. It is for a similar reason that the Church orders this story of the Transfiguration to be read to us during this season of Lent. We are or should be mortifying ourselves during this season. This mortification can earn for us a glorious and unending future life. To encourage us to continue it, we are reminded that the One we are following, the One whose voice we listen to, is none other than the Son of God. There are the voices of many false prophets shouting around us, telling us to enjoy ourselves in this life, to "eat, sleep, drink and be merry for tomorrow we die," but there is the rub—tomorrow we shall die, but where shall we go then?

Let us thank our divine Lord today, for giving this consoling and encouraging vision of his glory to his Apostles and through them to us. It was for them, and it is for us, a guarantee and a foretaste of the joys and the glory that will be ours for eternity, if we but persevere in our struggles against the world, the flesh and the devil. This struggle is not easy for our weak nature, but our loving Savior is ever beside us to "raise us up and tell us not to fear" if we but rely on him. When we are tempted to give way to our human weaknesses, or to give way under the weight of the crosses that sometimes are about to crush us, let us think of Mount Thabor, and the glorified Jesus, who a few weeks later faced his own real passion and cross cheerfully for our sakes. This thought will help us to carry our crosses as the thought of the future glory which will be ours should make us thank God that we have been created and thank his beloved Son for setting us on the road to that future glory.

E

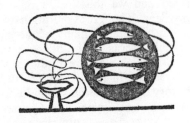

THIRD SUNDAY OF LENT

FIRST READING : Exodus 20 : 1–17. God spoke all these words, saying, "I am the Lord your God, who brought you out of the land of Egypt, out of the house of bondage. You shall have no other gods before me. You shall not make for yourself a graven image, or any likeness of anything that is in heaven above, or that is in the earth beneath, or that is in the water under the earth; you shall not bow down to them or serve them; for I the Lord your God am a jealous God, visiting the iniquity of the fathers upon the children to the third and the fourth generation of those who hate me, but showing steadfast love to thousands of those who love me and keep my commandments. You shall not take the name of the Lord your God in vain; for the Lord will not hold him guiltless who takes his name in vain. Remember the sabbath day, to keep it holy. Six days you shall labor, and do all your work; but the seventh day is a sabbath to the Lord your God; in it you shall not do any work, you, or your son, or your daughter, your manservant, or your maidservant, or your cattle, or the sojourner who is within your gates; for in six days the Lord made heaven and earth, the sea, and all that is in them, and rested the seventh day; therefore the Lord blessed the sabbath day and hallowed it. Honor your father and your mother, that your days may be long in the land which the Lord your God gives you. You shall not kill. You shall not commit adultery. You shall not steal. You shall not bear false witness against your neighbor. You shall not covet your neighbor's house; you shall not covet your neighbor's wife, or his manservant, or his maidservant, or his ox, or his ass, or anything that is your neighbor's."

EXPLANATION : When God had freed the Chosen People, the descendants of Abraham, from the slavery of Egypt, he led them to Mount Sinai in the southern sinaitic peninsula. There, amidst awe-inspiring manifestations of his presence, he made a Covenant or pact with the Israelites through which he promised to make them his own people, to lead them into the Promised Land, and to protect them from their enemies there. The Israelites, on their part, were to reverence him and him only as their Lord, and they were to obey the moral and cultic laws which he laid down for them. The Ten Commandments which we have just read are the essence of the moral obligations imposed on the Israelites. These commandments governed their duties to God and to their neighbor. While it is true that there were similar codes of law in Egypt, Babylon and Assyria at the time of Moses (about 1350 B.C.) governing the obligations towards neighbors, the strict monotheism of the sinaitic code distinguishes it from all these others. It is God himself, the master of the universe ("all the earth is mine" Ex. 19 : 5) who imposes these apodictic laws ("thou shall, thou shalt not") on the Israelites. The commandments governing their relations with their neighbors are derived from the "natural law" and are to be found in all the pre-Mosaic social laws, but God makes them part of his Covenant with Israel. They must obey them if they accept him as their God and their protector.

I am . . . God : The Israelites knew this. Yahweh was their God and the power he had shown in liberating them from Egypt proved that he was a universal God unlike the national and local deities of the nations whose powers (if any) were restricted to their local territory.

no other gods : All the other so-called gods were mere idols, the Israelites have the true God and must therefore have nothing to do with imitations.

graven image : The pagan gods were represented by images of wood and other materials. All such idols must be excluded. Neither must the Israelites represent Yahweh by any man-made image or statue.

iniquity . . . generation : This was in the form of a threat and was fulfilled only where the sons and grandsons imitated their fathers' infidelity. At the time of Christ, when all bodily defects were looked on as a punishment for sin, defects from birth were attributed to the sins of parents (see Jn. 9, the man born blind) and were seen as a fulfillment of this threat, a conclusion denied by our Lord.

take . . . in vain : The sacred name was not be be profaned by perjury or by its use in magical incantations or curses, a common practice with the names of the pagan idols. Later, the Jews carried this so far that the name Yahweh was never to be pronounced. While the name was written in their scripture it was always read as Adonai (=Lord).

the sabbath day : The custom of resting from work on the seventh day of each week was already practiced by the Israelites. In Ex. 16 : 23, a double portion of manna had to be collected on the eve of the Sabbath, to avoid the labor of collecting on the Sabbath. Other nations also had this regulation. The Israelites were not only to abstain from all labor on the seventh day but they were to sanctify it to God, as God himself had done when creating the universe (Gn. 2 : 2–3 taken literally).

Honor . . . mother : While natural instincts and inclinations would move the vast majority to obey, reverence, and provide for their parents if they were in need, there would always be those who would be found wanting. God commands all of them to keep this regulation.

kill . . . steal : The rights of each individual to his life and to his possessions must be respected. The foundation of these rights is that each individual human being is a child of God and it is God who has given him all that he is and all that he (rightly) possesses. Therefore no creature can usurp God's authority.

false witness : This includes not only legal perjury committed in a court of law but the damaging of a neighbor's character outside of a court by telling untruths about him.

covet . . . or anything : What it is unlawful to take, it is unlawful seriously to desire to take. Adultery and stealing are forbidden and any serious plans or desires relating to them are also forbidden. Internal acts of the will and intellect of man are known to God who makes men take responsibility for them.

APPLICATION : The Ten Commandments of God were the basis of the religious life of the Chosen People of the Old Testament. They are still the foundation of the spiritual life of the new chosen people—the Christian Church. Unfortunately, the Israelites too often forgot all that they owed to God, and failed to show their gratitude by keeping his commandments, as the Covenant made on Sinai expected them to do. For this reason many of them lost their faith and with it the eternal reward that God was anxious to give them. There are Christians too who forget all that God has done for them and who ignore the Covenant he has made with them—"if you would enter into life (eternal) keep my commandments." In this respect Christians are far more blameworthy than the Israelites, because they have greater proofs of God's love for them, including the outstanding proof which he gave us in the incarnation.

The Ten Commandments can be summed up in two, as our Lord summed them up when questioned by the Pharisees. "Thou shalt love the Lord thy God with thy whole heart and thy whole mind, this is the first and greatest of the commandments, and the second is like unto this : thou shalt love thy neighbor as thyself; on these two depend the whole law and the prophets." In other words, he who truly loves God and his neighbor fulfills the whole of God's law and will earn heaven as his reward.

The command to love God is more a privilege than an obligation for any thinking man. It was out of his infinite goodness and love that God created us and raised us to the status of his adopted sons. Could we ever show God how much we appreciate these privileges, and the goodness and love he has shown toward us? Even if we lived a thousand years on this earth, we could not of ourselves alone make any return which would remotely repay God for all that he has done for us. But once we have been made brothers of Christ by the incarnation, a new and superior value has been added to all our good acts, and these acts are therefore acceptable to God as signs and proofs of our desire to return love for love, within our human limits. As adopted sons of God, our heavenly Father is pleased with our filial love. He appreciates and rewards every proof, that we give in our daily lives, of our desire to thank him for all that he has done for us.

The second commandment, the obligation to love our neighbors as ourselves, includes all from the fourth to the tenth of the Decalog given on Mount Sinai. It is here that most of us are more liable to be found wanting. How can we love those who injure us, or those who are so thankless when we help them, or those who seem to have no interest in their own welfare, or those who deny the very existence of the true God who has imposed this obligation on us? Humanly speaking, it would indeed be impossible to love such people with the same love that we have for ourselves, but neither we nor these unattractive neighbors are any longer *mere humans*. We have been given a much higher status because of the incarnation. Our unlikeable neighbors are also sons and daughters of God by adoption. They have the same destiny as ourselves. Their inheritance is heaven and they too are on the way there. Therefore, the more they falter on the way, the more they refuse to recognize their duties of gratitude to God, and even deny his very existence, the more need they have of a helping hand from us who know where we are going and know how to get there.

We must overcome any natural antipathy which comes between us and the true love of all neighbors, because our own eternal salvation depends on this. All our declarations of love for God, and all the good acts we think we are doing to prove that love, are empty and false if we refuse to love our neighbor. St. John is very emphatic on this when he says : "If anyone says 'I love God' and hates his brother, he is a liar; for he who does not love his brother whom he has seen cannot love God whom he has not seen" (1 Jn. 4 : 20). Therefore, it is by the love that we show our neighbor that the true love of God is made manifest in our lives. We must show respect for what he is and what he has. We must be willing to help him in his temporal and especially his spiritual needs. There is no saint in heaven who hated or despised his neighbor. There is no one damned in hell who really fulfilled the command to love and help his neighbor during his time on earth.

Ask yourself today : "Do I really love God; am I on the right road to heaven?" The answer will depend on a truthful answer to this other question : "Do I love my neighbor as myself?"

SECOND READING : 1 Corinthians 1 : 22–25. Jews demand signs and Greeks seek wisdom, but we preach Christ crucified, a stumbling block to Jews and folly to Gentiles, but to those who are called, both Jews and Greeks, Christ the power of God and the wisdom of God. For the foolishness of God is wiser than men, and the weakness of God is stronger than men.

EXPLANATION : In a few sentences St. Paul gives us the basic reasons which motivated opposition to the gospel message on the part of Jews and Gentiles. The Jews who did not accept Christ as their promised Messiah, refused because he did not fit the pre-conceived ideas they had formed of the Messiah. The Messiah they were looking for was to be a political leader, a national liberator who would not only rid Palestine of the hated Romans but set it over all the pagan nations. God, they thought, would help him to do this, by giving him the power to work some spectacular miracles or signs (see Mt. 12 : 38; 16 : 4; Jn. 4 : 48; 6–30). The Greeks or Gentiles on the other hand looked to philosophy or human "wisdom" for the solution of man's problems. Christianity had no such earthly wisdom and so the intelligentsia among the Greeks had no time for the gospel of Christ.

preach . . . crucified : Crucifixion was the death given to a public criminal. That the one who posed as their Messiah should allow himself to suffer defeat in such a shameful manner was something revolting and abhorrent to their ideas. In fact it amounted to evident proof Christ was not the promised Messiah but a fraudulent usurper of the title.

folly . . . Gentiles : The intellectual Greeks could see nothing but folly in a man dying for his friends. There was no future life. What then was Christ gaining for others? Why shorten the too-brief life which could be his?

to those . . . called : Those Jews and Gentiles who have heard the gospel of Christ and answered its call. For these, Christ the God-man, who died so that they might live, proves the power and the wisdom of God. The incarnation, death and resurrection of Christ were the greatest of "signs" which only the infinite power and love of God could work. These acts of God's love for us give the one and only satisfying explanation of man's life on this earth—a philosophy, a wisdom that the Greeks could not comprehend, much less discover for themselves.

foolishness of God : What to mere men looks like foolishness (the Son of God suffering for men, for instance) is instead an act of the divine wisdom.

weakness of God : The enemies of Christ thought they had won when Christ was crucified, but his resurrenction showed the power of God over death, and over all enemies. In what looked to men like weakness, the strength of God was shown forth.

APPLICATION : These few lines from St. Paul's letter to the Corinthians should make us stop and think how fortunate and blessed we are to have the gift of the true faith. We know that Christ was and is for us the power and the wisdom of God. Through that power and wisdom God proved his infinite love for us. In creation he made man the masterpiece of his work and the master of all other created things on earth. He gave us the gifts of intellect and will by means of which we can see the good and the beautiful and come to love both. This in itself was a marvelous privilege but the fact that we are finite, that our span of life on earth may be all too short could spoil and mar our enjoyment of the good and the beautiful and render earthly sufferings almost unbearable. Man might well envy the beasts which have no knowledge of the good and the beautiful, and no remembrance of happy days gone by nor any desire for future happiness—if he had all these and saw no fulfillment for them. But the wisdom of God was at work when creating us. He planned to raise us above merely human status so that we could have our natural desire for everlasting enjoyment of the good and beautiful fulfilled. This he did through Christ—his divine Son who "was made man." By joining our human nature to his divine nature he made us his brothers and heirs to the eternal life.

We must still die, as Christ himself died in his humanity, but like him, we shall be raised from the dead to begin our new eternal life in the presence of the Good and the Beautiful—God himself—who will be the source and cause of happiness to us for all eternity. This is what the power and wisdom of God has arranged for us. This is for us the true philosophy of life. It explains our sufferings as well as our joys; it answers all our hopes and explains our earthly disappointments. The coming of Christ was surely the proof of God's power and wisdom for us and should be so for all men.

Yet, unfortunately, there are millions alive today, who have the same innate desire for lasting happiness and the same dislike for life's trials and disappointments, but have not the light of the Christian faith to answer their basic question : " what is it all for? Why am I here? Must all my desires and ambitions and hopes end in the grave?" The answer is there. But they will not heed it. The crucified Christ, whom St. Paul preached in Corinth, is still a stumbling block and a folly to too many, Jews and Gentiles, who will not open their eyes to look beyond earthly interests or who have long since closed their ears to the pleading voice of conscience. They think they are stronger than God and can do without him. They imagine themselves wiser than God, and consider that they do not need any solution to their problem from him. But there is only one real wisdom, there is only one who is powerful. To reject him is to reject hope, and to face a very short but a very bleak future. Far better to be an animal who does not remember yesterday and has no idea of, or thought for, the morrow.

We appreciate then, the gift of the true faith which we have received, and see the folly of those who deliberately reject that gift of God. Let us, however, not forget that God wants all men in heaven, and that a big part of our duty as Christians is to help by every means in our power, to bring our fellowmen to a knowledge of their loving Father. The willing apostle will find many ways of spreading the gospel message, but for all of us there is the simple but effective means of good example. The follower of Christ who lives his daily life in a truly Christian manner is a constant reminder to his family and neighbors of the true meaning of life. His example may not be copied immediately but it will eventually have its effect.

Today, let us say two short prayers. First, a prayer of sincere thanks to God for being so good as to give us the gift of the true faith. Second, a prayer of petition, let us ask God to open the eyes and ears of those of our fellowmen who have shut them against God and his Son, Jesus Christ. Lord, that they may see; Lord that they may hear!

GOSPEL : John 2 : 13–25. The Passover of the Jews was at hand, and Jesus went up to Jerusalem. In the temple he found those who were selling oxen and sheep and pigeons, and the money-changers at their business. And making a whip of cords, he drove them all, with the sheep and oxen, out of the temple; and he poured out the coins of the money-changers and overturned their tables. And he told those who sold the pigeons, "Take these things away; you shall not make my Father's house a house of trade." His disciples remembered that it was written, "Zeal for thy house will consume me." The Jews then said to him, "What sign have you to show us for doing this?" Jesus answered them, "Destroy this temple, and in three days I will raise it up." The Jews then said, "It has taken forty-six years to build this temple, and will you raise it up in three days?" But he spoke of the temple of his body. When therefore he was raised from the dead, his disciples remembered that he had said this; and they believed the scripture and the word which Jesus had spoken.

Now when he was in Jerusalem at the Passover feast, many believed in his name when they saw the signs which he did; but Jesus did not trust himself to them, because he knew all men and needed no one to bear witness of man; for he himself knew what was in man.

EXPLANATION : St. John puts the cleansing of the temple at the beginning of our Lord's public life. The Synoptics place it at the end. There could very well have been two such cleansings, though it is also possible that St. John is anticipating the time for theological reasons (see Mal. 3 : 1). But it is not the chronology of the event, so much as its meaning, that is important. Jesus intended to make his claim to be the Messiah known to the leaders of the Jews, the priests and Pharisees, who were always around the temple. He also foretold his resurrection, even though neither his enemies nor his friends understood his prediction then. They both did later. He drove the leaders and the money-changers from the temple precinct and nobody dared to stop him. The Jews (i.e. his opponents in John's usage of the word) suspected he was the Messiah because they asked for a "sign," a miracle from God to prove that he was the Messiah. He gave them a sign. They did not understand it and they gradually lost even this "suspicion" and in time turned completely against him and his claims. He worked some miracles during this stay in Jerusalem but had very few real converts.

Passover . . . Jews : This is the feast which commemorated the liberation of the Jews from the slavery of Egypt, thirteen hundred years earlier. The feast got its name from the fact of the avenging angel who struck down the first-born in every Egyptian house, but *passed over* the homes of the Israelites whose door-posts were stained with the blood of the lamb sacrificed that evening. When St. John adds "of the Jews" it shows that the Christian feast of the same name was long in use at the time he wrote.

"went up" : This is a term meaning : "went on pilgrimage" to Jerusalem, irrespective of what part of the country the pilgrim lived in.

oxen, sheep, pigeons : These were necessary for the sacrifices which pilgrims would offer in Jerusalem. It would have been very difficult if each pilgrim had to bring his own beasts or birds. But it was an abuse to have these for sale in the precincts of the temple.

money-changers : Only Jewish shekels could be used for buying animals for sacrifice. The coinage in use in the country at the time was the pagan Roman coinage. This had to be changed. Hence, the money-changers.

my Father's house : He calls the temple his Father's house, signifying a special relationship with God. The temple should be a place of worship, not a market-place.

zeal ... house : The disciples remember psalm 69, where it was written : "zeal for thy house will consume me." This psalm was quoted frequently as messianic in the New Testament. The disciples saw it as fulfilled that day. The cleansing of the temple by the Messiah was foretold by Zechariah also (14 : 21).

the Jews then : This same thought must have come to the "Jews," his opponents, also, for they ask him to prove he is the Messiah that he is pretending to be.

destroy ... temple : He meant "you will destroy my human body but in three days I will raise it from the grave." But the Jews thought that he was speaking

of the temple of Jerusalem and he was accused of this later.

when ... dead : The disciples, like the Jews, thought that he was speaking of the material temple. It was only after they were convinced of his resurrection that, looking back, they remembered what he had said in the temple precinct on that day.

believed the scripture : In Acts 2 : 31 (St. Peter) and 13 : 35 (St. Paul), the words of psalm 16 verse 10 are interpreted as referring to the resurrection of Jesus.

the word ... spoken : Our Lord had foretold his death and resurrection several times. This occasion in the temple precincts was one such.

many ... name : The "name" stands for the "person." Belief here means commitment to Jesus, not simply the acceptance of some truth.

saw the signs : Because they saw the miracles he worked they concluded that he had God with him in some way.

trust ... to them : Their acceptance of him was only half-hearted. Thus, he did not see them as true followers. He did not trust them, for their ideas of a political Messiah were well known to him, and this outlook he wished to discourage.

needed ... man : With the divine revelation given him, he could read the secrets of men's hearts.

APPLICATION : If we had only the Synoptic gospels (Mt., Mk., Lk.) we could easily conclude that Jesus spent almost all his public life and did all his preaching in Galilee and its neighborhood. St. John who wrote his gospel several years later corrects this false impression by mentioning visits made by our Lord to Jerusalem. He gave the

"leaders of the people" in Jerusalem plenty of opportunity of hearing his message and his claims. He also worked some astounding miracles in or near the city. For instance, the man crippled for thirty-eight years (Jn. 5); the man born blind (Jn. 9), the raising of Lazarus; who had been four days buried (Jn. 11). St. John makes it very clear that the leaders (the priests and Pharisees) in Jerusalem were given every opportunity to learn who Jesus was, and every help to believe in him, but they would not. The fault was theirs, therefore, and the loss.

On this particular visit he made it clear to them that he was someone special, someone close to God whose house they were desecrating, and whom he even called his Father. In hidden language he told them that they would put him to death but that that would not be the end, for he would rise again. Some of them seem to have remembered this saying of his after they had put him to death, for they asked Pilate to place a guard on his tomb lest his disciples should remove the body and pretend he had risen for: "we recall," they said, "that this impostor said while he was still living, 'after three days I shall rise again'" (Mt. 27 : 63). But even the miracle of his resurrection did not affect the majority of them. They had made up their minds and "there are none so blind as those who will not see."

The reasons for their blindness were the same as those that keep millions of the neo-pagans of today from accepting and living the Christian faith. These, like the priests and Pharisees of Jerusalem in the year 28, are so immersed in the affairs of this world that they can give no thought to their own future. Their eyes are so fixed on the earthly objectives that they have set themselves, that they can see nothing else. The priests and Pharisees wanted more than political freedom from Rome. They had hopes that their Messiah would give them a great world empire, and with it

wealth and power without limit. Our contemporaries' aims may not go so far, but worldly aims are important enough in their eyes to make them exclude from their minds the thought of anything higher. Yet, they have more than enough reminders whichever way they turn to recall their minds to the historical facts of Christianity. This is 1972 A.D., that is 1972 years since the birth of Christ. Who was he, why was he born, why does the world divide its history into before he came, B.C., and after he came, A.D.? In every town and village of our once Christian western world there is a church or two with steeples pointing to the sky. Why? What do churches mean to men? Near every town there are cemeteries or "sleeping places," according to the meaning of that Greek word. Are those buried there only sleeping and waiting to be called, if not already called, or are they finished forever just like the ox or the unthinking cow that may be buried in the next field.

The agnostics and free-thinkers of our day should start to think about the real facts of life—the central ones of which are that Christ, who was the Son of God, took our human nature and lived for some time on this earth, so that he would raise us up to sonship with God. He suffered crucifixion, because the world was full of sin when he came. But his death made atonement to the heavenly Father for all the sins of the world. His resurrection from the dead was the prelude and the guarantee that we shall all rise to a life of glory in heaven, if only we have followed him faithfully during our years on earth.

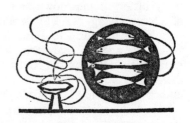

FOURTH SUNDAY OF LENT

FIRST READING: 2 Chronicles 36:14-16; 19-23. All the leading priests and the people likewise were exceedingly unfaithful, following all the abominations of the nations; and they polluted the house of the Lord which he had hallowed in Jerusalem.

The Lord, the God of their fathers, sent persistently to them by his messengers, because he had compassion on his people and on his dwelling place; but they kept mocking the messengers of God, despising his words, and scoffing at his prophets, till the wrath of the Lord rose against his people, till there was no remedy. The Chaldeans burned the house of God, and broke down the wall of Jerusalem, and burned all its palaces with fire, and destroyed all its precious vessels. He took into exile in Babylon those who had escaped from the sword, and they became servants to him and to his sons until the establishment of the kingdom of Persia, to fulfill the word of the Lord by the mouth of Jeremiah, until the land had enjoyed its sabbaths. All the days that it lay desolate it kept sabbath, to fulfill seventy years.

Now in the first year of Cyrus king of Persia, that the word of the Lord by the mouth of Jeremiah might be accomplished, the Lord stirred up the spirit of Cyrus king of Persia so that he made a proclamation throughout all his kingdom and also put it in writing: "Thus says Cyrus king of Persia, 'The Lord, the God of heaven, has given me all the kingdoms of the earth, and he has charged me to build him a house at Jerusalem, which is in Judah. Whoever is among you of all his people, may the Lord his God be with him. Let him go up.'"

EXPLANATION: The Book of Chronicles (now divided into two books) is an historical summary of the history of the Chosen People. Although it begins with Adam, and covers the same ground as that covered from Genesis to 2 Kings, its chief emphasis is on David and on the Levites. Hence, of the descendants of Abraham, the tribes of Judah (David's tribe) and Levi figure with greater prominence than all the others. Of all the kings of Judah, David and Solomon have pride of place (the northern kings being omitted), and after them the "good" kings only, Jehosaphat, Ezechiah, and Josiah, who promoted or reformed the observance of the law and the divine cult in the temple. This summary history comes down to the decree of Cyrus giving the Babylonian exiles permission to return to Jerusalem. It is generally agreed that the books of Ezrah-Nehemiah are the continuation of the same work written by the same author around 400 B.C. Today's extract refers to the edict of Cyrus, the king of Persia, permitting the exiles to return to Jerusalem and rebuild the temple, which had been burned by the Chaldeans as a punishment from God for the infidelities of the Chosen People.

leading . . . people : The last three kings of Judah were unfaithful to God and his law. The priests were no better. Pagan practices were allowed in Jerusalem and even in the temple of the true God "the abominations of the nations polluted the house of the Lord in Jerusalem."

Lord . . . messengers : In his mercy God kept sending his messengers, his prophets, pleading with them to mend their ways, but they ignored and even scoffed at his interventions "till there was no remedy."

The Chaldeans : King Nebuchadnezzar of Babylonia (also called Chaldaea) invaded Palestine, captured Jerusalem, destroyed the temple and took the king and most of the citizens off to Babylon as prisoners of war (597-587 B.C.). In this the chronicler saw the hand of God whose wrath had been aroused by the stubborn disobedience and disrespect of his Chosen People.

until . . . Persia : The Jews remained prisoner in Babylon for almost seventy years.

land . . . sabbaths : The sabbath law which prescribed rest for the people and the land (for no servile work could be done in it) had been ignored. Now this same land will have seventy years of rest for there will be no Jew to till it. Jeremiah the prophet had foretold this (see Lv. 26 : 34; and Jer. 25 : 11; 29 : 10).

first . . . Cyrus : Cyrus set free all foreign prisoners of war in Babylon including the Jews. In doing this he fulfilled the prophecy of Jeremiah mentioned above.

the Lord . . . Cyrus : The God of the Jews, who was God of the Universe, was able to influence the new ruler of Babylon to set his people free, as he had influenced the previous king to punish them for their offenses against himself and his temple.

The Lord . . . heaven : These words do not mean that Cyrus recognized the God of the Jews as his own God and Benefactor. He respected all gods for he knew that a people obedient to their god would be obedient to himself too. Cyrus anticipated by centuries the syncretism of the Roman empire.

Let him go up : The Jewish prisoners were now free to return to their homeland and encouraged to rebuild their temple in Jerusalem. Now that they had no king and no intention of having one, the temple would be the focal point round which the nation would gather; in it their faith and their hopes for a glorious future would be centered.

--- --- --- --- ---

APPLICATION : When this world of ours shall end and we shall see the complicated and multicolored tapestry that the history of men on earth has woven, we shall clearly recognize the hand of God putting the varied and intricate strands of that history into their proper place. "The old order changeth giving place to the new and God fulfills himself in many ways," says the great poet Tennyson. Yes, even those who now think that they are running this world themselves, without any assistance or what they call interference, from God, will see who moved them—for his own long-distance purpose. The history of the Chosen People of the Old Testament is evident proof of God's big part in the regulating of their world. He worked extraordinary miracles to bring them into Canaan, the land he promised Abraham. But on the way and during their sojourn there, again and again, he used their enemies, and his, in order to make them realize their dependence on him. God's plan was that the future Messiah would come from his Chosen People in the land of Canaan, yet he allowed the northern tribes, because of their disloyalty, to lose all ownership of their part of the territory. As we saw in today's reading, Judah (Benjamin) and Levi almost suffered the same fate. "Almost" only, for here God's plan steps in. While they had to be punished for their infidelities, the punishment was to be a purification, they would be chas-land and Bismarck of Germany unwit-to come from them in Judea.

The history of the Christian era is no different. God's Chosen People of the New Testament have often been disloyal to him. They have often provoked his wrath, and God allows their enemies and probably his own enemies to purify and cleanse them. There have been times too when God allowed sinful despots to torture and kill innocent Christians for their own criminal motives, but out of the sufferings of his faithful ones God built a bigger and more loyal following. Nero, Caligula and Diocletian, for instance, sent more martyr saints to heaven than even the great Apostle St. Paul—saints, perhaps, who might otherwise not have got there.

In later days, we see Cromwell of Eng-that first Good Friday the Son of God tingly doing more to spread the Catholic Church in the western continent than all the zealous Catholic missionaries who had gone there up to that time.

What holds true of people and nations is true also in the life of each individual. God is working in our lives in a way that we do not always realize. He has an active interest in each one of us from the cradle to the grave. The devout Christian family which was ever loyal to God is suddenly deprived of the breadwinner, the mother of a young family is called away leaving a helpless father to face the difficult future. The young boy or girl in whom the parents had set their hopes and on whom they had spent much of their limited income, and most of their love, is stricken down as he or she graduates from college. These do not look like the doings of a loving and benevolent God when seen from our side of eternity. But when we shall see the tapestry of our life on the last day, we shall then see why such "misfortunes" had to happen. In fact, we shall see that they were blessings from God in disguise—someone or other of the actors in the scene would not have reached heaven had these so-called misfortunes not occurred in the family.

God is looking after us; he can write straight with "crooked" lines; the crookedness indeed is the result of our angle of view. When the whole picture is painted we shall see how necessary it was for our salvation that we should take the rough with the smooth. Fair-weather sailors are not fit for long and difficult voyages. Our journey to heaven is a long and often stormy voyage—we need to be trained in dealing with storms if we are to arrive safely in the place that God has destined for us. While very often we can attribute the storms of life to the wickedness of evil neighbors or anti-religious governments, let us not forget it, God is using these crooked lines and these worldly agents to write for us that beautiful sentence: "well done, thou good and faithful servant . . . enter into the joy of the Lord." So may it be for all of us!

SECOND READING: Ephesians 2:4–10. God, who is rich in mercy, out of the great love with which he loved us, even when we were dead through our trespasses, made us alive together with Christ (by grace you have been saved), and raised us up with him, and made us sit with him in the heavenly places in Christ Jesus, that in the coming ages he might show the immeasurable riches of his grace in kindness toward us in Christ Jesus. For by grace you have been saved through faith; and this is not your own doing, it is the gift of God—not because of works, lest any man should boast. For we are his workmanship, created in Christ Jesus for good works, which God prepared beforehand, that we should walk in them.

EXPLANATION: St. Paul preached the gospel in Ephesus during his third missionary journey. He spent over two years in that city (54–57), and had a very large group of converts there. This letter was written from prison (most probably Paul's Roman imprisonment 61–63), and is a calm, studied exposition of the Christian doctrine he had already taught them. The doctrine of the Blessed Trinity and the part each of the divine persons plays in our salvation is stressed. The mutual love between Christ and his Church is compared to the mutual love between husband and wife. The kingdom of Christ is already here on earth, each member shares in it through baptism, but it is only in the future age that it will be a full reality. In today's extract from this letter, St. Paul is emphasizing the gratuitousness of the gift of faith which the Ephesian converts have received. This gift which God gave them, *even when they were sinners*, had united them to Christ, and has given them the

right to share in his glorious resurrection and inherit heaven with him and through him.

God . . . mercy: This infinite mercy or goodness of God is the explanation of everything we have and will have.

he loved us: What a startling idea this must have been for the Gentile converts especially. Their pagan gods never loved them—they were always a threat and had to be placated by sacrifices but the true God loves his creatures, "even when dead through trespasses."

alive . . . Christ: Through being united to Christ, that is, to the God-man, human beings are made to live with a new life, a higher life, a life of adopted sonship with God.

raised up with him: St. Paul sees Christians as already participating in the blessings of the resurrection of Christ. They have through baptism the qualifications necessary to obtain for them, after death on this earth, a place with Christ Jesus in heaven. They have their citizenship papers and their passport, all they need is to travel on the right road.

in . . . ages : At a future date all true Christians will share in "the immeasurable riches" that God has prepared for us in and through his incarnate Son.

by grace . . . saved : He now stresses the gratuitous character of the heavenly gifts which Christ and their Christian faith will earn, and has already earned in part, for them.

not because of works : No natural powers or works of man are able to merit the supernatural gifts—eternal life in glory with all that follows from that —but God alone in his infinite goodness makes a free gift of these blessings to us.

his workmanship : As he created us in the natural order, so he has now created us in the supernatural order.

created in Church Jesus : Through the incarnation we have been made "a new creation," this truth occurs often in St. Paul (see 2 Cor. 5 : 17; Gal. 6 : 15; Tit. 3 : 5; Col. 3 : 10; Eph. 4 : 24).

for good works : Our natural works cannot merit anything supernatural for us, but because we are raised by baptism to a supernatural state our good works are meritorious.

that we . . . them : God himself has laid down for us in our Christian religion a certain line of action, a form of life that we must follow in our living. Through our fidelity to these prescriptions, we shall reach the rewards prepared for us by God's gratuitous love.

APPLICATION : The holy season of Lent ends with the great drama of the "Triumph of Failure" on Calvary. On that first Good Friday the Son of God as man died the most shameful and painful death on the cross. He did so that we men might live forever. It is, therefore, most fitting that in our preparation during Lent for the worthy commemoration of that world-shaking event, we should be reminded of the immense and almost incredible love of God for us which caused this to happen. Think on it as we may, and meditate on it as often as possible, we could still never fathom the depths of pure, unalloyed love which made God go to such lengths for our sakes. But we can see and understand enough of that divine love to make us utter frequently a heartfelt and sincere "thank you" to our heavenly Father.

Having created us and having given us the intellectual gifts which raise us above all other created things on earth,
God could have left us in that natural state. We could have a certain amount of happiness, mixed with suffering of course, and we should be grateful for this, but could we really have any true happiness, any real contentment in a life which moved irrevocably and swiftly toward its eternal end in the grave? The merciful and loving Creator saw this before he ever created us. We were never intended for a mere natural life on this earth. The special faculties that he intended giving us deserved and, one could say, almost demanded something immensely greater than a few fleeting years of joy mixed with sorrow on this little planet. Therefore, our loving Creator ordained from eternity that we should share his eternal happiness with him.

That God could have found many ways of doing this, there is no sound reason to doubt, but the way he chose— the uniting of our human nature with the divine in his incarnate Son—was surely the way that expressed his true and fatherly love in the most emphatic manner possible. This is what our heavenly Father has done for us. He did so, as St. Paul says today : " out of the great love with which he loved us." The superior intellectual faculties which he gave man in creation can now have, as their object, infinite love and happiness, infinite truth and beauty. Multiply any earthly joy and happiness you have ever experienced, by infinity (if that can be done) and you have some vague idea of what your future life in heaven will be.

To help us appreciate how privileged we are—God's friends on our way to God's home—let us think often during Lent of our unfortunate neighbors, who have no such faith, no such hope, no such consolation in their day after day struggles. This may be their own fault or that of their parents or grandparents, but it matters not who is responsible, these neighbors of ours were created for heaven, God wants them there and unless they get there, their life on earth has been a dreadful failure. We can help them in many ways and if we really appreciate all that God has done and is doing for ourselves, we will gladly do a little bit for him in return, by assisting his prodigal sons on the road back to their Father. This act of true charity toward our fellowmen in need will not impede us on our journey to heaven. It will be an immense help to keep us closer to God and more faithful to our Christian calling. A very special additional joy for us in our eternal life will be to have with us in heaven those whom we helped to bring there with us.

GOSPEL : John 3 : 14–21. Jesus said to Nicodemus, "As Moses lifted up the serpent in the wilderness, so must the Son of man be lifted up, that whoever believes in him may have eternal life. God so loved the world that he gave his only Son, that whoever believes in him should not perish but have eternal life. For God sent the Son into the world, not to condemn the world, but that the world might be saved through him. He who believes in him is not condemned; he who does not believe is condemned already, because he has not believed in the name of the only Son of God. And this is the judgement, that the light has come into the world, and men loved darkness rather than light, because their deeds were evil. For every one who does evil hates the light, and does not come to the light, lest his deeds should be exposed. But he who does what is true comes to the light, that it may be clearly seen that his deeds have been wrought in God."

EXPLANATION : In chapter three of his gospel, St. John tells us of a nocturnal conversation which Jesus had with a leading Jew, a man of wealth and position. This man, whose name was Nicodemus, had been impressed by Jesus' preaching and miracles, but being afraid of his fellow-Jews, in the circle in which he moved, he came to speak to Jesus at night. Nicodemus is told that to enter into the kingdom of God, a man must believe in Christ and be baptized. He is born anew of the Spirit in baptism. Jesus also tells him that it is God's will that he himself should be lifted up on the cross and die so that those who believe in him may have eternal life. It would seem that Nicodemus believed in Jesus to a limited degree. He tried to defend him later on when the Pharisees were condemning Christ (Jn. 7:51), and he assisted Joseph of Arimathea in the burial of Jesus and supplied expensive aloes and myrrh for the embalming of his body (Jn. 19:39).

serpent . . . wilderness : During their wanderings in the desert the Chosen People often rebelled against God. On one such occasion, described in the Book of Numbers (21:4–9), God allowed poisonous serpents amongst them. Anyone bitten by one of these serpents died. The people then repented, and God told Moses to make a bronze image of a serpent and raise it aloft on a pole. Anyone bitten by a serpent who looked on the elevated bronze serpent was instantly healed of his poisoning.

so must . . . Man : The "Son of Man" (the half-hidden messianic title that Jesus used of himself) must also be raised aloft (on the cross) in order to earn eternal life for all who will believe in him. In John's gospel the phrase "to be raised up" referring to Jesus has always a double meaning, to be raised up on the cross and to be raised up in glory at the resurrection and ascension.

gave . . . Son : These are most probably John's interpretation and explanation of the role of Jesus in our salvation. It is entirely due to the incredible love of God for us. He did not spare his own Son but sent him as man amongst us to live and die for us.

shall not perish : Death will not be the final end of those who truly believe in Jesus.

not . . . world : Neither God nor his incarnate Son condemns men. Men condemn themselves by their refusal to accept God and his Son whom he sent to open heaven for them.

He who believes : Belief in Christ put into daily practice is indicated here. Saying "Lord, Lord" will save no man, "but he who does the will of my Father, he shall be saved."

condemned already : The atheist, agnostic and disbeliever who persevere in this frame of mind are already writing their own sentence of condemnation, just as the true believer who perseveres in his faith is already writing his sentence of approval.

believed in the name : That is, in the person of Jesus, who was God's divine Son.

light has come : Christ as the light of the world is an image frequent in St. John. Christ himself says : "I am the light of the world, he that follows me shall have life and will not walk in darkness" (Jn. 8:12, see also 9:5; 12:35–45; 12:46). Christ has come to illuminate, to give light to the minds of men, so that they can know the true facts regarding their purpose in life.

men loved darkness : That is, the negation of light and what it means. Men preferred not to know their destiny lest they should have to go to the trouble, the self-restraint necessary to reach it.

deeds were evil : They were sinners and loved their sins.

does . . . light : The vast majority of evil deeds are done in secrecy and in the darkness.

he who . . . light : The innocent man who does what is right has no fear of being seen by everybody.

deeds . . . God : Good works are done by the aid and under the inspiration of God, if they are truly good and meritorious. Works good in themselves, can lose all merit and spiritual value because of the evil or wrong intention of their author.

APPLICATION : This man Nicodemus had a half-open mind as regards Jesus. He was moved by his teaching and miracles. He defended him when his companions were out to have Jesus arrested. He helped to have him properly buried when his enemies had him put to death, but that was as far as he went, apparently. There is no mention of him in the first Christian community of Jerusalem. What held him back, what kept him from giving himself fully to Jesus who spoke so kindly and told him so clearly that he himself was indeed a teacher who had come from God, that he had been offered by God as the sacrificial victim who would save the world? All Nicodemus had to do was to accept his word, "believe in him" and be baptized and he too would have eternal life.

Why did he not do this? The answer is given in the beginning of his story : "He came to Jesus by night." He was one of the leading Pharisees and evidently was afraid of what they would think of him had they seen him associating with Jesus. How much more so did he dread what their reactions would be had he become a follower of him whom they called "this impostor." Nicodemus had only half of his mind open to the truth, the other half was closed and barred by his fear of what his own class—the leaders of the Jews —would think of him. He risked his own future happiness in order not to lose the present respect of his sinful associates.

What a foolish man we would all say! Yet, are not many of us often like Nicodemus, when it comes to living up to our following of Christ? There are Catholic men who would like to, and should, go much more often to Holy Communion but are afraid of what their fellow-parishioners, who receive but rarely, would think of them. There are many, far too many, Christians who will not defend or stand up for their religion when it is insulted and attacked in their place of work or in a saloon. There are Christians who stand idly by, and give at least tacit approval, when grave injustices are being carried out by individuals or by local or national groups. These and many more like them are Christian types of Nicodemus, who through fear of losing the approval, the worthless esteem, of their sinful associates, are prepared to forfeit the esteem of God and their own eternal welfare.

Nicodemus probably thought he had made reparation for his lack of openness to Jesus when he assisted at his burial. What value, however, had that work of mercy for one of his frame of mind? There are amongst us today, humanists, most of them ex-Christians, men and women who make assisting their neighbor, while excluding Christ and God, the essence of religion. While the assistance the neighbor receives will benefit him materially, what spiritual or religious value can it have for the humanist who excluded God and our Savior Jesus Christ? Humanism or concentrating on our neighbor *to the exclusion of God*, is an imitation of religion and a very false imitation at that. Helping our neighbor because he is a son of

God is part of our true religion, and the second of the two great commandments of love; but helping a neighbor from whom we have effaced the image of God has not and cannot have any religious value or significance whatever. It is as meaningless as lighting a candle before the photograph of a wife one has deliberately deserted.

Thank God, we have accepted Christ with our whole heart and our whole mind. It is through him that we have been made sons of God. It is through him that we have learned to love God and learned of God's infinite love for us. Because all men are God's sons also, and our brothers in Christ, we will gladly help them whenever and wherever we can because God has commanded us to do so. This is true humanism which sees in the neighbor the workmanship of the almighty Creator, and what is more important still, the elevating effects of the divine Savior, as well.

FIFTH SUNDAY OF LENT

FIRST READING: Jeremiah 31:31-34. Behold, the days are coming, says the Lord, when I will make a new covenant with the house of Israel and the house of Judah, not like the covenant which I made with their fathers when I took them by the hand to bring them out of the land of Egypt, my covenant which they broke, though I was their husband, says the Lord. But this is the covenant which I will make with the house of Israel after those days, says the Lord: I will put my law within them, and I will write it upon their hearts; and I will be their God, and they shall be my people. And no longer shall each man teach his neighbor and each his brother, saying, "Know the Lord," for they shall all know me, from the least of them to the greatest, says the Lord; for I will forgive their iniquity, and I will remember their sin no more.

EXPLANATION: At the very early age of 23 Jeremiah was called by God to be a prophet. He spoke the word of God in Jerusalem during the most critical period of Judah's history (627–587). The kings, priests and people of that time were more interested in politics than in serving Yahweh, their God. They had been made subjects of Babylon and had to pay yearly tax to that foreign power. They hoped that Egypt (another pagan power) would free them from Babylon. Jeremiah opposed this intrigue, foreseeing that Egypt would not help and that rebellion would bring nothing but the devastation of Judah and the deportation and exile of its people. Abuses in the temple and in Jerusalem reached an alarming point. The prophet spoke out fearlessly against the sins and disloyalty of the Chosen People of God, and foretold the destruction of the city and temple and also the long Babylonian exile. Because of this he was imprisoned and maltreated. Later it was decided to kill him. He was placed in an empty cistern, but a Cushite, a servant of King Zedekiah, released him with the king's permission, but unknown to the court officials. Eventually, he was forcibly taken down to Egypt and, according to tradition, was murdered there by his own people.

In today's extract, the prophet is foretelling the setting up of a New Covenant, to replace the Old Covenant made between God and his Chosen People on Mount Sinai, a covenant which the Chosen People had not kept. The New Covenant would not be written on tablets of stone but on each individual's heart. It would be a covenant of love rather than one of obligation.

the days are coming : Jeremiah is seeing into the future, into the Messianic age.

Israel and Judah : Israel as a kingdom (the northern kingdom) had long since disappeared (722 B.C.), but remnants still remained. These, together with what would remain of Judah (after the Babylonian exile), would come under God's special care and would be part of the new Chosen People of God.

covenant ... broke : In the first covenant the Chosen People had promised to be loyal to God and to keep his commandments. They had failed miserably in this, especially in the years immediately preceding and during the life of Jeremiah.

I was . . . husband : God called the Chosen People his spouse, his bride, but they forgot that and went after false gods; hence idolatry is often called adultery in the Old Testament (see Jer. 3 : 8–9; Ez. 23 : 7; Ho. 2 : 1–13; 4 : 12–14).

law within them : This new covenant or pact between God and his new Chosen People will be a true consensus of mind and will. Each individual will give himself with his whole heart to God, and God will give himself to his chosen ones.

teach his neighbor : Intermediaries, such as Moses, will not be necessary. God will speak directly to all men. He will be known by all of his Chosen People. (The incarnation, the coming of the Son of God as man on earth, made the love and wisdom of God known in a way that the people of the Old Covenant could not even dream of.)

forgive . . . sin : The age of the New Covenant will be an era of real forgiveness of sin. The "sin of the world" will be taken away by the Lamb of God (Jn. 1 : 29).

APPLICATION : It must have grieved and offended a devout lover of God, and an appointed prophet as Jeremiah was, to see the laws of his God broken and trampled on day after day, and this by the leaders of the people who were especially bound to give good example to their followers. The kings and people of Judah were facing a terrible trial. However, instead of relying on the good God who had so often helped them out of impossible difficulties in the past, they were seeking earthly aid from a pagan neighbor—a pagan neighbor who would not help them. Having chastized them in the strongest language for this gross infidelity, he now promises that even though they have deserted God, God will not desert them. The Chosen People were elected by God with the incarnation in mind. Abraham and his descendants were chosen to prepare the way for the coming of God's Son. Unworthy though they had proved themselves for this noble role, God would still carry out his eternal purpose for all men. The Chosen People would be decimated. Their temple, his visible abode amongst them, would be razed to the ground, for they had despised and betrayed him. But a remnant would be saved—a purified remnant from which would come God's Son in human nature.

We are the beneficiaries of this infinite act of God's mercy toward, and patience with, sinful humanity. We have seen the New Covenant established between God and all men (not Abraham's descendants only). We have seen the depth of God's love for us, as illustrated on Mount Calvary. Our New Covenant was not mediated to us by any mere human being like Moses, but by the Son of God himself in his human nature. The blood with which this Covenant was ratified was not the blood of sheep and oxen which Moses used for the ratification of the first Covenant. It was the precious blood of Jesus Christ : "This is the blood of the New and everlasting Covenant which will be shed for you and all men so that sins may be forgiven." This is a universal covenant "for all men." It is not made between God and one race or people but between God and all men of all races and nations.

This is what we mean when we speak of the "New Testament." It is not merely the books which describe what happened, but the happening itself. The Messiah promised in the Old Covenant and for whom the Old was a preparation, has come on earth and has proved to be not a mere messenger or delegate from God but his own dearly-beloved Son. This Son of God has brought about a pact, an agreement, between God and all men—an agreement through which all men are now elevated to the position of sons of God and heirs to God's eternal kingdom. By the sacrifice of himself on the cross, the Son of God has removed any impediment (sins) which could prevent us from possessing that promised inheritance. This is the happy lot of man on earth today. But how many know of this pearl of great price, which is theirs for the taking? How many who do know of it are willing to "sell the few possessions they have" in order to acquire this treasure? How many, in other words, are willing to live the Christian life on earth in all sincerity, so that they can be Christians and brothers of Christ for all eternity in heaven?

Let each one of us ask these questions today, and give an honest answer. Living in the Christian era now will mean nothing to us hereafter, if we do not live as true Christians. Having the new pact with God written in our hearts by baptism will not help us to get to heaven unless we observe the two great commandments, love of God and love of neighbor. The fact that Christ has left a means for washing away our sins will not cleanse us unless we repent and confess our sins. The fact that we were made "spouses" of the Lord when we became Christians will give us no rights or privileges if we have divorced ourselves from him by unworthy conduct.

There is still hope. We are still alive. Lent is a very suitable occasion to examine ourselves : to see our faults and failings, to repent of them and ask from God forgiveness and the necessary grace to remain his true spouses, his true "chosen ones" for the future.

SECOND READING: Hebrews 5:7-9. In the days of his flesh, Jesus offered up prayers and supplications, with loud cries and tears, to him who was able to save him from death, and he was heard for his godly fear. Although he was a Son, he learned obedience through what he suffered; and being made perfect he became the source of eternal salvation to all who obey him.

EXPLANATION: The Epistle to the Hebrews was written by some disciple of St. Paul, who wrote under the influence of the preaching and writings of the great Apostle of the Gentiles. This letter was written to Jewish converts as the title (given in the 2nd century), and especially the contents, clearly indicate. The author's purpose is to confirm the converts in the Christian faith which they have accepted. To do this, he proves from the Old Testament that Christ was the promised Messiah, that all the rites and ceremonies of the Old Testament were but shadows and types of the future true liturgy of the Church. The high priest in the Old Testament went into the Holy of Holies on the day of atonement to intercede for his own sins and the sins of the people. The new High Priest, Jesus, has entered into heaven to intercede for us (he had no sins of his own) and his prayer will certainly be answered.

In the days ... flesh: That is, while he was here on earth in his human nature.
prayers ... tears: Our Lord's Agony in the Garden was caused by the thought of the torments and sufferings which were about to befall him. He prayed to his Father "who was able to save him from death." This prayer, as is clear from St. John (12:27-32; 17:5; Acts 2:25-31) and from the present context ("he was heard"), was not a request to be saved from the cruel death which he saw awaiting him, but from the lasting hold of death. In other words, he was praying for his glorious resurrection and exaltation.

sin ... obedience: In his human nature he obeyed his Father's plan for redemption, and learned the full meaning of that obedience in his intense sufferings.
being ... perfect: That is, being exalted in glory. After he had endured the torments of his passion and death he became the:
source ... salvation: Through him all men are now heirs of the eternal kingdom of God if they:
obey him: Each one must apply the means of salvation won for him by Christ. In other words, if he is to reach his eternal inheritance he must carry out the commandments of Christ and live his Christian life in all sincerity.

APPLICATION: When we are asked to live as true Christians we are being told to be obedient to the will of a heavenly Father who wants us to go to heaven. It is through obeying that divine will that we shall be working toward our best and truest interest. We all have sins and failings to atone for; we all have weaknesses and evil inclinations which we want to overcome. Hence the need for the self-mortification which living the true Christian life imposes on us. God gave us the marvelous gifts of intellect and free-will and we are all—without exception—tempted to dislike being ordered or commanded by another. We can easily get the foolish idea that we are masters of our own destiny, whereas the truth is that our eternal destiny depends on God's good-will toward us. That good-will is promised and secured by those who obey him.

This reading from Hebrews today sets before us the inspiring example of the perfect obedience of Christ, who was the Son of God. He had no sins, he had nothing to atone for, eternal happiness was his by virtue of his sonship. Yet God the Father asked him to undergo the tortures and torments of crucifixion in his human nature for our sakes, and he obeyed! This is the sublime model of perfect obedience, the unparalleled example of complete submission to God's will. It is set before us in this short reading. How could we be expected to imitate the perfect Christ? Yet St. Paul not only says we are expected to do so, but commands his Philippian converts to do so when he says: "In your minds you must be the same as Christ Jesus . . . who was divine but emptied himself to assume the condition of a slave, being born in the likeness of men. And being found in human form he humbled himself and became obedient unto death even death on a cross (Phil. 2 : 5–8). St. Paul and his disciple, the author of Hebrews, call on Christians to imitate the obedience of Christ. In doing this they are asking no more than he himself asked when he laid down the condition for discipleship : "If any man would come after me, let him deny himself and take up his cross and follow me" (Mt. 16 : 24, see today's gospel also).

The truly sincere Christian must be ready to suffer torture and crucifixion, if called on for the sake of Christ. Many have done so but true obedience for most of us consists in carrying our own crosses, our sicknesses, our loneliness, our struggles for earthly existence, our sorrows and bereavements. These may not lead to the Calvary of martyrdom, but they lead us over very rough roads —roads, however, which bring us, in God's good time, to the reward won for us on Calvary.

Are we on that rough road of true obedience, or have we sought the smoother path of giving in to our weaknesses? Lent is a suitable time to examine ourselves and then to return to the road of true obedience if we have strayed off it.

GOSPEL : John 12 : 20–33. Among those who went up to worship at the feast were some Greeks. So these came to Philip, who was from Bethsaida in Galilee, and said to him, "Sir, we wish to see Jesus." Philip went and told Andrew; Andrew went with Philip and they told Jesus. And Jesus answered them, "The hour has come for the Son of man to be glorified. Truly, truly, I say to you, unless a grain of wheat falls into the earth and dies, it remains alone; but if it dies, it bears much fruit. He who loves his life loses it, and he who hates his life in this world will keep it for eternal life. If any one serves me, he must follow me; and where I am, there shall my servant be also; if any one serves me, the Father will honor him.

"Now is my soul troubled. And what shall I say? 'Father, save me from this hour'? No, for this purpose I have come to this hour. Father, glorify thy name." Then a voice came from heaven, "I have glorified it, and I will glorify it again." The crowd standing by heard it and said that it had thundered. Others said, "An angel has spoken to him." Jesus answered, "This voice has come for your sake, not for mine. Now is the judgement of this world, now shall the ruler of this world be cast out; and I, when I am lifted up from the earth, will draw all men to myself." He said this to show by what death he was to die.

EXPLANATION : St. John has just described Jesus' last coming to Jerusalem. It was a triumphant entry : he was met by many local people and also by several pilgrims who had come from many parts of the Mediterranean world to celebrate the feast of Passover in Jerusalem. They saluted him as the Messiah—the king of Israel. They did not salute him as a political king now, as other enthusiasts had done on a previous occasion (Jn. 6 : 15). What moved the local inhabitants (who had witnessed this miracle) and the foreign pilgrims who had now heard of it, was the raising of Lazarus from the tomb. They were honoring him as the conqueror of death. The Pharisees were shocked but could do nothing but exclaim : "there is nothing you can do, the whole world is running after him" (12 : 19). The request of the Greek pilgrims to see Jesus (that is, to learn

from him more about himself) was proof of what the Pharisees said. The Evangelist does not tell us if they spoke to him, but the following words of Jesus are a manifestation of himself and his mission for all to see : by his death he will conquer death. He will be glorified in his resurrection and be the Savior who will bring a similar eternal glory to all men.

Some Greeks : These were not Greek-speaking Jews, but Gentiles who had learned of the true God of the Jews. They had heard of the raising of Lazarus (see 12 : 17) and were anxious to know more about Jesus.

Jesus . . . them : Whether the Greeks got near to him or not is not important. What matters is Jesus' answer, which should prepare both his disciples, and those admirers from afar for the shock which the next Friday would give them.

The hour has come : He has come to

Jerusalem to let his enemies do their worst against him. They are but fulfilling the plan of God.

Son of man . . . glorified : His death on the cross was the door to his resurrection and glory. As God he would display once more all the glory of his divinity (he had hidden this during his sojourn on earth, "he had emptied himself of it," St. Paul says—Phil. 2 : 7), and as man he would enter heaven in a glorified humanity.

grain . . . dies : He now shows the necessity for his death by an example familiar to all his hearers : the grain of wheat must be buried in the earth and lose its own individual life in order to produce new wheat in abundance.

loves . . . it : The man whose whole concern is to get the last ounce out of his life here on earth will find that he has ignored and lost the real life which could have been his.

who hates his life : "hates," when contrasted with "loves" is a semitic way of saying "loves less." The man who uses his life not solely for pleasure but with the future in view will continue to live a much more happy life when he leaves this world.

serves . . . me : The man who would be a true member of Christ's family must be ready to imitate him, even in his painful death, if necessary.

where I am : He promises his followers a share in the glory which is soon to be his, as he said above.

Father . . . him : Eternal glory is God the Father's reward for all those who serve his divine Son faithfully.

now . . . troubled : Here we have an anticipation of the Agony in the Garden, which St. John does not describe in his gospel. The thought of the harrowing scenes of his passion and death which he foresaw in all their dread details troubles his human mind immensely, but knowing the reason for which he came into this world, he does not ask his Father to save him from these sufferings, for in God's plan they are necessary.

glorify . . . name : Instead, he is praying for his triumph over death, his resurrection and eternal glory in his human nature, and in this glorification of the Son the Father is himself glorified. God's infinite power and love for sinful men are manifested in the triumph of the cross.

a . . . heaven : God the Father answered his prayer. He has already glorified Christ in his life and miracles. A glimpse of his divine glory was given at the Transfiguration, at which John the Evangelist was a witness. Christ's glory will be more manifest still in his resurrection.

The crowd . . . heard : They did not understand what the voice said.

voice . . . sake : Just as the Transfiguration was intended to give courage to the three chosen Apostles to face the soul-disturbing events of Holy Week, so now these words of the Father are intended to help both disciples and other followers present to understand that the cross would be a stumbling block for many.

judgement . . . world : The crucified Christ will decide the future fate of all men. Those who accept him in all sincerity will be saved, those who knowingly and deliberately reject him will be condemned.

ruler . . . out : The cross of Christ will also put an end to the reign of evil of Satan and his satellites, in this world.

I . . . earth : His purpose in dying on the cross is to make eternal salvation available to all men. His salvific will is universal. If any man is excluded it is because he has excluded himself. Christ wants to "draw all men to himself," he wants no man eternally lost.

to show ... death : John explains what Christ means by being "lifted up."

APPLICATION : On the first Palm Sunday, as Christ entered Jerusalem not as a conquering king on a charger but "riding on an ass" to show that he was the humble servant of all men, he clearly foresaw the sufferings and torments that would be his in that city, before the week was out. Among those who waved palm branches to honor him and who sang aloud : "Hosanna to the son of David, Hosanna in the highest," there were perhaps some who, urged on by the leaders, would be shouting the following Friday, "away with him, crucify him," and "we have no king but Caesar." Such was the fickleness of human nature then. Unfortunately it has not changed much, if at all, in the two thousand years that have since elapsed. We are still fickle when it comes to choosing between Christ and the things of this world. Yet he knew all of this, and was still willing to carry the cross for us who are such unworthy mortals!

This very thought should put us all to shame, for what repayment does the very best of us make for the incredible love he has shown for us? We grumble and complain when some small cross is laid on our shoulders; we are full of laments if life is not running smoothly for us; we cannot understand why God should let certain things happen to us, his friends! But see for a moment what the lot of his beloved Son was on earth. Born and reared in extreme poverty; insulted and offended by those he wanted to teach; quickly forgotten by those he benefited by his miracles; hounded by his enemies and betrayed by one who had been his disciple for over two years and who had sat at table with him that same night;

deserted in his moment of trial by those very ones who had sworn undying allegiance to him. Then followed the torments wished on him by his enemies —those he had come to save; the mock trial and illegal condemnation; the scourging at the pillar; the crowning with thorns; the carrying of the cross and finally the three hours of intense torture and agony while his body hung on the cross! The next time we are tempted to grumble and complain about our sad lot, let us look thoughtfully at a crucifix for a few moments!

"He who loves his life loses it," this is a truth stated by Christ at the solemn moment when he was speaking of the purpose of his own painful death. He died so that we might live, not for sixty or even a hundred years on earth, but forever in heaven. We can, we know, lose the eternal life Christ won for us if we are too attached to our transitory, earthly life. If we love our own comforts, pleasures, temporal gains, our own worldly will, more than we love our unending, happy future, then we are loving our earthly lives wrongly, and we are gravely risking the loss of the future, true life.

If, on the other hand, we do our best to be faithful servants of Christ, we shall always judge all our actions with eternity in view. We can use the things of this life which God gives us, and still be close followers of Christ. The lawful possession of the goods of this world, the enjoyment of the licit pleasures of life, are allowed to the fervent Christian. If these possessions and pleasures are accepted with Christian gratitude, they will become stepping-stones that will help us across the river of life to our everlasting home beyond.

Each one of us should look fervently and devoutly on the crucifix today, and try to compare our willingness to suffer those crosses sent to us by God, with the crushing cross and passion our Savior Jesus Christ gladly accepted for us and not for his own sake. Do not let the conclusion you draw stun you into inactivity, but rather let it shock you into a new outlook on life; a new resolve to serve, follow and imitate our loving Christ more closely in future. So may it be for all of us.

PASSION SUNDAY

FIRST READING: Isaiah 50 : 4-7. The Lord God has given me the tongue of those who are taught, that I may know how to sustain with a word him that is weary. Morning by morning he wakens, he wakens my ear to hear as those who are taught. The Lord God has opened my ear, and I was not rebellious, I turned not backward. I gave my back to the smiters, and my cheeks to those who pulled out the beard; I hid not my face from shame and spitting. For the Lord God helps me; therefore I have not been confounded; therefore I have set my face like a flint, and I know that I shall not be put to shame.

EXPLANATION: The second-Isaiah describes in these verses how the suffering servant—the Messiah—accepts the role of suffering which the Father had designated for him. He is to preach the message of God's mercy to men. Many will reject him and torture him, but God is on his side and he will not be moved from his resolute purpose by their insults and injuries.

The Lord has given me: It is God who has appointed him teacher of the people and has given him "a well-trained tongue," the gift necessary for his task.

how . . . word: His preaching will touch both friend and foe. The former will be moved to listen and obey—the latter will grow stronger in their opposition.

morning by morning: His was a daily task, a difficult task, but:

I . . . rebellious: He continued notwithstanding the difficulties.

I gave my back . . . my cheeks: Literally fulfilled in the scourging at the pillar and the mocking of the Roman soldiers.

shame and spitting: In the presence of Caiphas (see Mt. 26 : 67–68).

The Lord God . . . me: The source of his strength.

set my face like a flint: No insult or

suffering would weaken his resolve (see Ez. 3 : 8, when God promises the same strength to Ezekiel).

I shall not be put to shame : All their insults and injuries (even crucifixion) will be in vain. He will triumph in the end.

APPLICATION : The sufferings and crucifixion of our divine Lord in his humanity are the Christian's source of strength and encouragement in his daily struggles against the enemies of God and of his own spiritual progress. Because of our earthly bodies, and because of the close grip that this world of the senses has on us, to keep free from sin and to keep close to God on our journey to heaven is a daily struggle for even the best among us. But we have the example before our eyes, the example of our true brother. He was one of ourselves, the truly human Christ. He not only traveled the road before us and made the journey to heaven possible for us, but he is with us every day, close beside us, to encourage and help us on the way.

We need to remind ourselves daily of this. We have the crucifix in our Christian homes, on our rosary beads, on our altars, on the very steeples of our churches. These crucifixes are not ornaments, but stark reminders that our Savior's path to heaven led through Calvary and through all that preceded Calvary. They are also stern reminders to us that the carrying of our crosses on the road to heaven is not an unbearable burden for us, but an essential aid to our progress.

When you are tried by temptations, when you are tested by bodily pain or mental suffering, worried to death perhaps by the bodily needs of yourself or your family or by the disobedience and insults of ungrateful children, stop and think on the Leader and his humiliations and sufferings. He came to open the road to heaven for us, to make us all sons of God, to preach the message of divine forgiveness and mercy to mankind. What did he get in return? He was scourged, tied to a pillar, spat upon and insulted, jeered at and mocked. He was nailed to a cross on Calvary between two thieves!

How light is my cross in comparison, how easy my Calvary. But he was sinless: his obedience, as man, to the Father was perfect. Can we or should we complain, we whose life up to now has often been far from perfect? Stop, think and listen to today's lesson.

SECOND READING : Philippians 2 : 6–11. Christ Jesus, though he was in the form of God, did not count equality with God a thing to be grasped, but emptied himself, taking the form of a servant, being born in the likeness of men. And being found in human form he humbled himself and became obedient unto death, even death on a cross. Therefore God has highly exalted him and bestowed on him the name which is above every name, that at the name of Jesus every knee should bow, in heaven and on earth and under the earth, and every tongue confess that Jesus Christ is Lord, to the glory of God the Father.

EXPLANATION : It is generally admitted that Paul is here quoting an earlier liturgical hymn in which the Judeo-Christian Church expressed its faith in the true humanity and the true divinity of Jesus Christ. He who was God, humbled himself to become a man like us, hiding his divine glory but receiving it back at his resurrection, or exaltation. Because of this, everyone must confess and adore his equality in divine glory with his Father.

in the form of God : He was divine and did not cease to be divine when he became man but :

emptied himself : He did not let the divine glory appear. Instead his humanity, the same as that possessed by all men, was what was evident. He was a truly obedient servant (slave) of God however, as all men should be, but were not. This true obedience led him to the humiliating death on a cross (see Isaiah in first reading).

God exalted him : By raising him from the dead on Easter morning God restored to him the glory of the divinity that he had hidden during his earthly life (see Eph. 1 : 21), and glorified his human nature.

name above every other name : Name stands for "person." He is exalted to the right hand of the Father in his humanity as well as in his divinity, the chief place in heaven after God the Father.

at Jesus' name : The man who walked the roads and hills of Palestine, who ended his life on a cross, is none other than the Lord. Adonai is the name for God used by the Jews to avoid saying the sacred name Yahweh. It is God the Father who has proclaimed this, who "bestowed upon him the name" therefore :

every knee must bend : All men are bound to pay him reverence as God and :

every tongue confess : To proclaim their faith in the divinity of Christ the Savior is the basis of their Christian faith and the only hope of salvation for all.

to the glory of God the Father : His human nature also is sharing in the divine glory in heaven, the guarantee that our finite human nature can partake in some measure in this same divine glory if we have been his faithful brothers on earth.

APPLICATION : As Christians we have no doubt as to the two natures of our Savior. He was the God-man. He humbled himself so low in order to represent us before his Father and by his perfect obedience ("even unto the death on a cross") earn for us not only God's forgiveness but a sharing in the divinity, through his being our brother but also the Son of God. These words of Paul, or rather of the early Christian hymn he is quoting, are for us today a consolation and an encouragement.

Surely every sincere Christian must be consoled by the thought of God's infinite love for him, as shown in the Incarnation. We are not dealing with some distant, cold, legal God of justice who spends his time marking up our sins and failures against us. We are dealing with a loving Father who sent his own beloved Son to live among us and die for us in order to bring home to us the greatness of divine love. Could any human mind, even the minds of the greatest of this world's philosophers, have invented such a humanly incredible story of true love? No, it was only in the infinite mind of God that such a proof of love could have its source.

What encouragement this should and does give to every sincere Christian. We know we are weak. We can and do sin often. We know we are mean and ungrateful and that we seldom stop to thank God for the love he has shown us.

If we were dealing with a human, narrow-visioned God, we should have reason to despair, but when our Judge is the all-loving, all-merciful God how can even the worst sinner ever lose hope?

No, there is no place for despair in the Christian faith. But there is room for gratitude and confidence. We can never thank God sufficiently for all that he has done for us. Eternity itself will not be long enough for this, but we must do the little we can. Let us face this coming Holy Week with hearts full of thanks to God and to his divine Son for all they have done for us. When meditating on the passion of Christ on Good Friday let us look with gratitude and confidence on the Son of God who died on the cross in order to earn eternal life for us.

He did not die to lose us but to save us. He has done ninety per cent of the work of our salvation. And, even as regards the remaining ten per cent that he asks us to do, he is with us helping us to do it. Could we be so mean and so foolish as to refuse the little he asks of us?

GOSPEL : Mark 14 : 1–15; 47.

EXPLANATION: Because of the length of this gospel (119 verses) the text is not printed here. Nor shall we give any detailed explanation of the text, for the Passion, death and burial of our Lord is well known to all Christians.

St. Mark begins his account with a meal in a house in Bethany, a village south-east of Jerusalem. During the meal a woman entered and anointed the head of Jesus with costly precious oint-

ment. When someone (Judas, according to John) objected to this "waste," our Lord defended the woman's action : he said it was done in preparation for his burial. Judas planned to betray Jesus, his Master, to the chief priest. Arrangements were made in Jerusalem for the Last Supper, at the end of which the Holy Eucharist was instituted. During and after the meal, Jesus foretold that one of them would betray him and that all would desert him in his tragic sufferings. "Not I," says Peter, but our Lord said that the opposite would be the case, and so it was.

Then follows the account of the Agony in the Garden of Gethsemane, the arrest of Jesus, his trial before the Sanhedrin, the High Court of the Jews, his answer to the high priest that he was the Messiah and the Son of the Blessed one for which he was declared a blasphemer and guilty of death. He was spat upon, blindfolded and hit with fists. All of this happened during Thursday night.

Early on Friday morning he was brought before Pilate, the Roman governor, to have him condemned to crucifixion—the death sentence for criminals and outlaws. Pilate, who could see no guilt in him, condemned him to be scourged and crucified, because he wanted to "placate the mob" yelling for his crucifixion. Pilate was more concerned with keeping his own job than in seeing justice observed. Having been mocked by the Roman soldiers, scourged, crowned with thorns (for he claimed to be a king), and spat upon and beaten, Christ, carrying his own cross, was led to Calvary, the public place for crucifixion. There he was nailed to the cross in the company of two thieves. While he was enduring the slow torture of this kind of death, with his life-blood slowly draining from his body through the nailed hands and feet, his enemies mocked him saying: "he saved others, now let him save himself. If he is the Christ, the Messiah, let him prove it to us now by coming down from the cross." The passers-by also jeered him, the place was just outside one of the main gates of the city.

After three hours of agonizing suffering on the cross Christ uttered a loud cry: " Father, into your hands I commit my spirit" (Lk. 23 : 46), and then breathed his last. The Roman centurion in charge of the crucifixion was amazed at what he had seen and declared : "truly this man was the Son of God."

Pilate was surprised that Jesus had died so soon. It was not unusual for one crucified to linger on in agony for a whole day or even more. When, however, he got confirmation from the centurion that Jesus was really dead, he gave Joseph of Arimathea permission to bury the body of Jesus. He was buried in a stranger's tomb.

APPLICATION : The story and most, if not all, of the details of our divine Lord's sufferings at the hands of his fellow-Jews, his Father's Chosen People, on that first Holy Thursday night in Jerusalem and the subsequent sentence of crucifixion pronounced by a pagan Roman judge on one he had declared innocent of any crime, is well known to any Christian, worthy of the name. But theoretical knowledge is not what makes a Christian or a follower of Christ. Down through the ages great men have lived and died and their lives and deeds have benefited others in many ways, for greater or lesser periods. But the life and death of Christ has not only benefited man's life on earth, it has changed the very purpose of man's existence, for it has changed his relationship with God and with his eternal destiny.

Through and by the Incarnation, death, resurrection of Christ, we, mere human mortals, have been made sons of God by divine decree, and heirs of God's eternal kingdom of heaven. This was God's original plan in creating the universe. Man was to be the masterpiece of the divine act of creation and the master of the universe. He contains within himself a part of every created being and has the necessary faculties to dominate all the lesser creatures. But he was to be more than that. His human nature was to be raised to union with the Godhead in the Incarnation. This completed plan was eventually fulfilled in Christ.

Therefore, the life and death of Christ is not just some recorded bit of history of the past, rather it is for all men, not Christians only, a fact of the past which dominates and basically affects rational man's purpose in life today and always as well as his day-to-day mode of living that life. There are millions on our earth today who, through no fault of their own, have not yet heard of God's infinite love for them as proved in the Incarnation, but God will find ways of extending its benefits to them if they do their part. There are millions too who have heard the good news but refuse to believe it or to act according to it; those too we can safely leave to the all merciful God. But for ourselves, professed followers of Christ, who during this Holy Week will be reminded daily of what God has done and is continuing to do for us, our only answer is to beat our breasts in humble contrition like some of the crowds returning from Calvary on that first Good Friday.

We know we are utterly unworthy of the unfathomable love that God has shown us. When we look at the crucifix and see the Son of God nailed hands and feet to that cross, slowly shedding his heart's blood for us, what can we do but bow our heads in shame? If we did not jeer at him and mock him openly as the Pharisees did that day on Calvary, we did so indirectly by our coldness, our forgetfulness, and worse still by our many deliberate sins against God and neighbor. Pilate condemned the innocent Christ "for fear of the Jews, for fear of losing his job" (St. John says); Judas betrayed him for 30 pieces of silver; the Pharisees forced Pilate to crucify him because of their pride. If we look into our past, how often have we offended him, that is, condemned him for similar reasons, and we are less excusable than these people were. We do, or should, know so much better than they did what Christ means to us.

But while we have reason, all of us, to repent of our past faults during this Holy Week, we have also every reason not to despair but to hope. In the very height of his agony on the cross, our loving Savior uttered a fervent plea to his heavenly Father, asking for forgiveness for all those who had brought his death-agony on him. The words, "Father, forgive them for they know not what they do," hold for all time; we too were included there, and God's merciful answer to his dying Christ is for us too if we avail of it.

Holy Week will be truly a holy week and a turning point in our lives if we repent of our past and turn to our loving God. Through the life, sufferings and resurrection of his beloved Servant and Son, he has made us his adopted sons and heirs of heaven. He will not fail us now.

EASTER SUNDAY

FIRST READING : Acts 10 : 34; 37–43. Peter opened his mouth and said : "You know the word which was proclaimed throughout all Judea, beginning from Galilee after the baptism which John preached : how God anointed Jesus of Nazareth with the Holy Spirit and with power; how he went about doing good and healing all that were oppressed by the devil, for God was with him. And we are witnesses to all that he did both in the country of the Jews and in Jerusalem. They put him to death by hanging him on a tree; but God raised him on the third day and made him manifest; not to all the people but to us who were chosen by God as witnesses, who ate and drank with him after he rose from the dead. And he commanded us to preach to the people, and to testify that he is the one ordained by God to be judge of the living and the dead. To him all the prophets bear witness that everyone who believes in him receives forgiveness of sins through his name."

EXPLANATION : These verses are part of the story of the conversion of Cornelius, a Roman army officer. Stationed in Caesarea, Cornelius believed the God of the Jews was the true God, but though a good-living man, he had not become a Jew. Advised by a divine messenger, he sent to Joppa for St. Peter, whose antipathy to pagans had been corrected by a vision seen that same day. Peter came to Caesarea and, contrary to his life-long custom, entered the pagan home of Cornelius, who explained to him why he had been asked to come (10 : 1–33). Peter then speaks : **You know . . . which was proclaimed :** Peter gives a synopsis of Christ's public life and mission in Palestine, of which Cornelius, a man in a position of authority, must have heard already.

anointed . . . with the Holy Spirit : a reference to the descent of the Holy Spirit on Jesus during his baptism by the Baptist in the Jordan.
and . . . power : proved by his many miracles and by his teaching.
God was with him : In his human nature divine power was given him. He was God the Son, but in his human nature, as man, he emptied himself of his divine glory, as St. Paul tells us (Phil. 2 : 6; see last Sunday).
"hanging him on a tree" : a figurative expression for crucifixion (see Dt. 21 : 23).
only to have God raise him . . . third day : The resurrection of Jesus is attributed to the Father in almost all the texts that refer to it in the New Testament. The verb in Greek is passive "was

F

raised." St. Jerome translated this with the active voice *surrexit* "he rose." As the Father and Son are one God, there is no theological difference.

not to all . . . witnesses: He appeared to the Apostles, disciples and others (see 1 Cor. 15 : 1–8), during forty days after his resurrection.

and drank with him: Jesus had eaten with the Apostles—not that the risen, glorified body needed food but to convince them of the reality of his risen human body.

to preach to the people: The commission given to the Apostles on Ascension Day.

judge of the living and the dead: Judge of all men. This will be the role of Christ the God-man (see 17 : 31).

prophets . . . witnesses: No prophets are quoted, but in a true sense the whole Old Testament was a preparation, and a prophecy in fact, concerning him who was to come (see 3 : 19–26).

through his name: The purpose of the Incarnation was to make men not only friends but sons of God. Where sin had intervened, its remission was necessary and available for all who believed in Christ (see 3 : 19–26).

APPLICATION: This passage from Acts has been selected for Easter Sunday not only because the resurrection is mentioned in it, but especially because St. Peter in his first discourse to a Gentile makes the resurrection the basic doctrine and the crowning proof of the truth of the Christian faith. As St. Paul says: "If Christ has not risen vain is our preaching, vain too is your faith" (1 Cor. 15 : 14). And like Paul, St. Peter stresses the truth of the resurrection by citing witnesses, including himself, who had not only seen the risen Jesus but had spoken to him and actually eaten with him.

There is no room for doubt but that Apostles and disciples had thought that the sad events of Good Friday had put an end forever to the mission of love and mercy of their beloved Master. In spite of his previous references to his resurrection, they had completely forgotten it and were convinced that the tomb near Calvary was the end of all their hopes. They had locked themselves into the room of the Last Supper for fear of the Jews—two of them had set off for home on the Sunday morning, down-hearted at the Master's failure; the others were waiting for an opportunity to slip out of the city quietly. But the resurrection changed all this. The unexpected, the unhoped-for happened. Even the most skeptical of them all, doubting Thomas, was eventually convinced of its reality. Had they been hoping for it, or even thinking of it, there might be some reason to suspect it was only an hallucination, the result of their "wishful thinking," but the very opposite was the case. They were hard to convince even when it happened.

All this was intended by God—the basis of our Christian faith was proved beyond doubt. Christ, who had died on the cross on Good Friday, was raised from the dead by his Father on Easter morning. He returned to heaven in the full glory of the divinity which he had hidden while on earth, together with his human body, now also glorified. There (in heaven), as God and Man, he pleads for us at the right hand of the Father until the day when he who redeemed all men will come to judge them all.

The Alleluia is repeated often during the Easter ceremonies. It is a Hebrew word which means "praise ye the Lord." It is our attempt to give verbal expression to our joy and gratitude for all that God has done for us. We are no longer mere humans living on this planet for a few short years. We are citizens of heaven, made children of God the Father by Christ our Brother. And he has gone before us to his and our kingdom to prepare a place for us. He conquered death. Our earthly death has, therefore, now no real fears for us: it is not the end but the beginning of our true lives. It is only after our earthly death that we truly begin to live.

There is only one death now which we can fear—the spiritual death of serious sin which can keep us from our true heavenly life. But while this is a possibility for all of us, it is only a possibility. The sincere Christian who realizes what God has done for him and what is in store for him, will never be so ungrateful to God or so forgetful of his own best interests as to let some temporal and passing pleasure, pride, or profit, come between him and the eternal home which God's love has prepared and planned for him.

SECOND READING: Colossians 3:1-4. If you have been raised with Christ, seek the things that are above, where Christ is, seated at the right hand of God. Set your mind on things that are above, not on things that are on earth. For you have died, and your life is hid with Christ in God. When Christ who is our life appears, then you also will appear with him in glory.

EXPLANATION: The method of administering Baptism in the apostolic days was by immersion. Those who heard the story of the gospel and were ready to believe in the one true God, the Father, the Son and the Holy Spirit who had cooperated in man's redemption and elevation to divine sonship, were immersed in water to be cleansed from their sins and their previous worldliness. Immersion in water symbolized being buried in the tomb with Christ. By immersion, therefore, the new Christian died with Christ to all earthly attachments and desires. He was raised again from the water (the tomb) to be with the Risen Christ.

If you have been raised . . . Christ: The physical act of immersion and rising again from the baptismal bath was not enough unless the convert meant what he was doing. The Christian life was a *new life*, a life of unity with Christ. Therefore, the new Christian must:

set your mind . . . things above: His thoughts must now be on the things of the spirit, the everlasting truths which he has just learned. His past evil practices must be forgotten.

where Christ is seated: He must strive to earn heaven where Christ is now in glory, having gone through death and resurrection to make heaven available to us.

not on things that are on earth: The things of earth insofar as they are sinful, or occasions of sin, are now forbidden. Insofar as they are necessary for the sustenance of earthly life they are not forbidden, but they must always be used so that they do not impede the journey to heaven.

You have died ... your life ... Christ: The Christian has died in baptism to all sinful earthly concerns. He is now living a new life; it is hidden because it is a spiritual life. Externally, in bodily appearance, he has not changed, but since his baptism, he is a *new man*. He is with God, a brother of Christ and a member of God's family.

When Christ ... appears: Christ lives in the Christian. The Christian lives in Christ and through Christ. Christ is the source of our new life, and the essence of it, by faith and the sacraments, especially the Eucharist.

you shall appear ... glory: Christ will appear in glory at the particular and the general judgements. The loyal Christian will appear, will return with Christ from the grave, in the glorified state which will be his for all eternity.

APPLICATION: Children at boarding schools draw up calendars and mark off each day which brings them one nearer to the end of the term. Fiancés mark off the months, the weeks, the days that separate them from the great day when they will be united forever, they say, to their beloved one. Seminarians count the years, months, weeks to the great day when they will be ordained and say their first Masses. Parents look forward anxiously to the day when their children will be educated and safely settled in life. In fact, we are all always looking forward to a happier day which is to come some time. All this is very natural and very human, because our present life is not our permanent life; our present home, this earth, is not the real home destined for us by our loving Creator.

We were created for unending happiness in heaven, and it is only when we get there that our desire and our quest for some greater happiness will end. From then on, we will always enjoy and possess that all-satisfying happiness.

Today, Easter Sunday, St. Paul reminds us that we have this happiness within our grasp. We are moving steadily and more quickly than we realize toward it. The Holy Trinity, God the Father, the Son and the Holy Spirit, have already done, and are daily continuing to do for us, all within their power. All that is needed is that we do the little that is asked of us.

St. Paul tells us we must "mind the things that are above not the things that are on earth." We must never let the "things of earth," the pleasures, the power, the possessions which we can or could have in this life, block or impede us on our upward journey. Does this mean that we must all return to the deserts of Egypt, as some early Christians did? By no means. We are not forbidden to have the lawful pleasures of life. We are not forbidden possessions or power if they are used justly. All we are forbidden is the unlawful use of the things of this world.

And as regards minding the things that are above, this is not something calling for extraordinary self-sacrifice or unnatural mental activity. All we are asked to do is to try to stay in God's grace, and do our daily chores whatever they be, as well and as diligently as we can. We are expected to recognize our natural weakness and to turn to God frequently for pardon and for help.

Whilst there are saints in heaven who lived lives of extreme self-mortification and did extraordinary things for God and for their neighbor, it is an encouraging and consoling thought that there are millions of unknown saints in heaven who lived normal lives, unnoticed by the world and maybe even by themselves. They are people who kept in God's friendship all their lives, or got back quickly to it, if they sometimes forgot or offended their heavenly Father.

What millions of others have done I can do too. We are aided by God's grace as they were. God wants me in heaven. He has an Easter resurrection planned for me.

GOSPEL : John 20 : 1–9. On the first day of the week Mary Magdalene came to the tomb early, while it was still dark, and saw that the stone had been taken away from the tomb. So she ran, and went to Simon Peter and the other disciple, the one whom Jesus loved, and said to them, "They have taken the Lord out of the tomb, and we do not know where they have laid him." Peter then came out with the other disciple, and they went toward the tomb. They both ran, but the other disciple outran Peter and reached the tomb first; and stooping to look in, he saw the linen cloths lying there, but he did not go in. Then Simon Peter came, following him, and went into the tomb; he saw the linen cloths lying, and the napkin, which had been on his head, not lying with the linen cloths but rolled up in a place by itself. Then the other disciple, who reached the tomb first, also went in, and he saw and believed for as yet they did not know the scripture, that he must rise from the dead.

EXPLANATION : The accounts of Christ's resurrection on Easter morning as given by the four Evangelists vary in details but agree on the essential points. Some women, the leader among them being Mary Magdalene, came to the tomb early on Sunday morning to anoint the dead body with spices, in order to help preserve it. This anointing had been done very hastily on the Friday because of the Sabbath which began at sundown. The tomb was found open and empty. The first thought of the women was that somebody had stolen the corpse. This shows how far resurrection was from their minds. They went in haste to tell the disciples. Peter and John ran to the tomb. Later that day Christ appeared to Mary Magdalene, to ten of the Apostles, to Peter separately (according to St. Paul, 1 Cor. 15 : 5), to two disciples on the road to Emmaus (Lk. 24 : 13); and, later on, he appeared often to the Apostles and disciples in Galilee, for a period of days.

First day of the week : The Sabbath was the last day of the Jewish week, so the first day corresponds to what is now called Sunday.

Mary Magdalene : John mentions only Magdalene by name but the "we don't know" in verse 2 implies there were others with her.

stone had been moved away : The tomb was raised above the ground and its entrance was closed by rolling a large stone, cut for the purpose, across the entrance (see Mk. 16 : 3).

they have taken the Lord . . . : Magdalene's only possible explanation of the absence of the body.

Peter and the other disciple : Peter and John ran to the tomb. When they found the winding sheet and the cloth that covered the head lying there, they realized that the body had not been stolen or taken away : why should the linen coverings have been removed?

He saw and believed : That Peter had been the first to believe and then John, seems to be the meaning here, not that John believed in contrast to Peter.

as yet they did not understand : Until this moment they had not understood the Scriptures which had foretold his resurrection. In fact neither had they believed Christ's own prophecies of his resurrection—it seemed to be something which could not happen.

APPLICATION : As we said above, the accounts of the resurrection of Christ differ in many details in the different writings of the New Testament, but the fact of the resurrection stressed in all of them, was the basis of the new Christian Faith. Had it not happened, Christianity would have been stillborn. It would have disappeared from Jerusalem and the world on that first Easter Sunday. Peter and his companions would have returned to their fishing-nets and boats on Lake Genesareth, and Christ the good and the kind man who had helped so many, would have been forgotten in half a generation.

But Christ was no mere man of kindly acts and words of wisdom. He was the Messiah promised for centuries. He was the suffering servant foretold by Isaiah, whose perfect obedience to his Father had led him to the Cross and the grave. But above all, he was the Son of God who had emptied himself (St. Paul) of his divine glory in order to be the perfect human servant of the Father, and who was now raised by the Father with his divine glory restored, and his glorified resurrected body sharing in that glory. This was the divine plan of God for mankind, through Christ, and because of Christ's (the new Adam's) per-

fect obedience, all mankind would be made worthy of divine sonship, and worthy of one day rising like Christ from the grave in glorified bodies.

Is all this too good to be true? It is, if we make God to our image and likeness, as so many opponents of Christianity do. He is God and his love is infinite and incomprehensible to us. What God can see in me and my fellowmen will always be a mystery to me, but then I have not the mind of God. All I know and all I need to know is that I have sufficient proofs that God loves all men. The Incarnation, death and resurrection of his Divine Son for man's sake is the greatest proof of love for us that even the omnipotent God could give. He has given it. As a necessary consequence from this act of divine love, we are guaranteed our resurrection from the dead to a life of unending happiness and glory if we do not, in extreme folly, reject God's offer.

Today, let us thank God once more for Easter and for all that it means for us. Our personal Easter morning is not far away from even the youngest among us. We have a few Calvaries to climb perhaps in the meantime but what are they when we see our glorious Easter on the horizon?

SECOND SUNDAY OF EASTER

FIRST READING : Acts 4 : 32–35. The company of those who believed were of one heart and soul, and no one said that any of the things which he possessed was his own, but they had everything in common. And with great power the Apostles gave their testimony to the resurrection of the Lord Jesus, and great grace was upon them all. There was not a needy person among them, for as many as were possessors of lands or houses sold them, and brought the proceeds of what was sold and laid it at the Apostles' feet; and distribution was made to each as any had need.

EXPLANATION : The Acts of the Apostles is a book which gives a brief history of the infant Christian Church, from the Ascension of our Lord until the year 63 A.D.—period of about 30 years. Its first twelve chapters deal with the beginnings of the Church in Jerusalem and its neighborhood before the Church moved out to the Gentile lands. Today's four verses of Chapter Four describe the fervor of the first Jerusalem Christians, who were so filled with the love of God and neighbor that everyone shared with his fellow-Christians all that he had. The Christian community in Jerusalem had all things in common; it was the ideal Christian family while it lasted.

who believed ... soul : The newly converted lived in a truly fraternal charity atmosphere.

had ... common : There was a complete sharing amongst them of all earthly possessions.

great ... testimony : The Apostles from the day of the Descent of the Holy Spirit convincingly and effectively preached the truth of Christ's resurrection. Miracles confirmed their preaching (see 3 : 12; 4 : 7; 6 : 8 etc).

great grace ... all : "They were all given great respect" (by the people in general). Thus the Jerusalem Bible. That this is the meaning is clear from 2 : 47; 4 : 21 and 5 : 13.

possessors ... them : This was a free act done out of love of God and neighbor at a time when Christian idealism was at its height.

laid ... feet : Those who sold their lands or houses gave the proceeds to the Apostles to be distributed among the needy members of the community.

APPLICATION : In this brief glimpse of the life of the first Christian community in Jerusalem, St. Luke (the author of Acts) emphasizes the ideal of Christian brotherhood, which animated the first Christians so much that many of them gave their possessions gladly for distribution among those of their brothers who were short of the necessities of life. As is clear from the incident of Ananias and Sapphira nobody was compelled to sell his possessions or to give all he possessed to the community (see 5 : 4), but those who did so were setting a lofty and praiseworthy ideal for all time.

While the vow of poverty, taken by religious, is an imitation of this early Christian ideal—the religious gives all that he or she has or may have to the community—such an act of abdication is of necessity restricted to relatively very few. The vast majority of men and women need personal possessions to support themselves and their dependants. The life of religious is governed by two other vows, obedience and chastity, which make the observance of poverty not only feasible but desirable. The life of a religious is regulated by obedience : he can be moved not only from one occupation to another but from one place to another, even from one country to another. Personal property would be a serious impediment here. The vow of chastity means that the religious will have no spouse and/or family to provide for, and so the chief need for personal possessions is removed.

But, granted that our Christian religion does not demand of all of us that we should follow the example of the first Christian community in Jerusalem, we still have an important lesson to learn from today's reading. While we can, and the vast majority of us must, retain our personal possessions, we must still be always ready to share them with those in need. We are not the real owners of what we possess; we are only the administrators of the property God has given us. He is the real owner, and he expects us to use what he has given us justly and charitably.

We use our possessions first and foremost to provide for our own needs and the needs of those depending on us. That charity and justice begin at home is true in this sense, but they do not end at home. While we provide for the needs of the home let us not exaggerate these needs; let us not indulge in luxuries for ourselves and our family, while there are neighbors on the brink of starvation. We need, today especially, a revival of that wonderful spirit of fraternal feeling which led many of the first Christians to sell all they possessed and distribute the proceeds to the needy. However, instead of selling our possessions, we need to use them well and wisely, so that we can give a helping hand not only to our fellow-Christians but to men and women of every nation and creed who are in need of help.

Four-fifths of the world's population today are living in poverty, and some on the starvation line, through no fault of their own. One-fifth are living a life of comfort and sufficiency, many of them actually in luxury. While we may not be and most likely are not, among the latter, there are things we too could and should do without if we allow Christian charity to govern our lives.

Have a good look at your home, your way of dressing, your meals, your recreations and entertainments and you may find many occasions for saving a dollar to give to relief organizations. When you put on your heavy winter overcoat think of the poor, naked children in Africa and elsewhere who have not even a little shirt to keep out the cold. When you sit down to your four-course dinner think of the unfortunates who would be glad of one bowl of rice a day. When tempted to spend a night drinking with your friends stop and think of the thousands of children dying for want of a bottle of milk.

The Christian community in Jerusalem earned the respect of all for their charitable behavior. All you can do for your needy neighbor may not earn you any headlines in the daily papers, but if you do what you can you will be printing your name where alone it matters. You will be inscribing yourself in the Book of Life which is kept in heaven.

SECOND READING : 1 John 5 : 1–7. Every one who believes that Jesus is the Christ is a child of God, and every one who loves the parent loves the child. By this we know that we love the children of God, when we love God and obey his commandments. For this is the love of God, that we keep his commandments. And his commandments are not burdensome. For whatever is born of God overcomes the world; and this is the victory that overcomes the world, our faith. Who is it that overcomes the world but he who believes that Jesus is the Son of God? This is he who came by water and blood, Jesus Christ, not with the water only but with the water and the blood. And the Spirit is the witness, because the Spirit is the truth.

EXPLANATION : This first Epistle of St. John is an encyclical letter written between 90 and 100 A.D. to all the churches of Asia Minor, when the gnostic heretics were trying to undermine the Christian faith. These Gnostics claimed to have a special knowledge of God and to be sinless, without keeping his commandments. They ignored the commandment of fraternal charity. It is doubtful if they admitted the divinity of Christ. St. John exhorts the Christians to continue to know and love God—this knowledge and love of God are shown by keeping his commandments. All men are sons of God. If, therefore, we love God we must love all of God's children. "Anyone who says : 'I love God' and hates his brother is a liar" (4 : 20). Through Jesus Christ we know God is our Father; we know Christ is the promised Messiah and the Son of God. Let us live then as God's children in obedience and love.

believes . . . Christ : This is the basis of the Christian faith. The Messiah was promised to Abraham and to his descendants. This promise was repeated many times in the Old Testament. The one who would bring blessings on all nations came at last in the person of Jesus who was, therefore, called the Anointed or the Christ.

a child of God : Everyone who accepts Jesus as Messiah becomes an adopted son of God. We, therefore, became his brothers and God's sons.

loves . . . child : Anyone who really loves God must love God's children, that is, all mankind, for it is God's commandment.

keep his commandments : The man who keeps God's commandments proves that he loves God.

not burdensome : What is done out of love is not a burden but a pleasure.

born . . . world : Having been made sons of God "born of God," we are no longer subject to any forces hostile to God; we have been given the power to overcome them. The "world" in St. John, invariably means the sinful forces opposed to the truth and the light of God.

victory . . . faith : Those who accept Christ as Messiah and Son of God overcome the allurements to sin. Christ conquered death, sin, and the world by his death and resurrection. This victory was won for us and not for himself. Therefore, if we live according to our Christian faith, the world will have no hold on us.

by water and blood : When Christ insisted on being baptized in the water of the Jordan he was taking on himself the sins of the world (the sins of all time); he became our passover lamb. When he shed his blood on the cross he washed away all those sins and won the victory over evil for all those who would believe in him.

not . . . water only : The Gnostics, against whose false doctrines John is warning his fellow-Christians, held that the baptism of Jesus alone was significant for giving the Holy Spirit to believers. John insists that the shedding of his blood on the cross was a necessary part of the work of our redemption. The water and blood which came from the side of Christ when pierced with a lance (Jn. 19 : 34) were for John a proof of the redemptive value of Christ's death and the bestowal of the Holy Spirit. They were also symbols of the sacraments of baptism and the Eucharist, the principal sacraments of the Christian church.

spirit . . . witness : The same Spirit which descended on Jesus at his baptism in the Jordan remained with him all through his death. This the Agnostics denied, saying the Spirit left him before his death.

Spirit . . . truth : Christ promised the Holy Spirit to his Church : "that Spirit of truth whom the world cannot receive" (Jn. 14 : 17) "but the Advocate, the Holy Spirit whom the Father will send in my name" (14 : 26), "when the Advocate comes . . . the Spirit of truth who issues from the Father, he will be my witness" (15 : 26). Now that witness, who was with Jesus all through his life, is with his Church, a testimony to the eternal truth of the Christian faith.

APPLICATION : "This is the victory that overcomes the world, our faith." In one short sentence, St. John, the beloved disciple of Christ, expresses the profoundest philosophy ever put before thinking man. We have had many philosophers and many searchers after the meaning and purpose of rational life on earth. We have had many attempts at explanations, but all have failed, for none of them satisfied the innate desires and total capacity of human nature. Of all the beings on our planet, man alone has the faculties for perceiving the truth and for enjoying the beautiful. While he shares with the animal kingdom the impulse to self-preservation and the perpetuation of the species, he has within him powers that surpass all animal instincts and raise him above the material world where he lives and moves. He can perceive beauty, truth, love, joy and happiness. With his will, which is motivated by the good, he can and does desire to possess these supramundane "goods," not only for a few short years but forever.

How can man do this? How can he

fulfill that desire for perpetual happiness, that longing for unending love, that craving for eternal beauty and joy especially if his life is to end forever in the grave and if the same dreary fate is to await him as awaits the dumb animals? This is where the goodness and infinite generosity of God steps in. It was he who gave us these spiritual faculties. Of their very nature they seek for spiritual fulfillment, and therefore he has planned for us an existence after our earthly death, in which all our rational desires will be fulfilled.

This is the message of the Christian faith. St. John says that it conquers and puts in its proper place, in relation to man, our world and all its false attractions. This is the good news which Christ came on earth to establish and announce to men. God has planned a future life of perfect happiness for all who will accept it. Through sending his divine Son in our human nature, he has elevated our nature and given us a new status, the status of adopted sons. It gives us a right to the eternal kingdom of the Father. Our mortal life, if left to itself, would end naturally in the grave. But through the incarnation it is transformed into a new and everlasting life. As the preface of the Mass for the dead says: "life is not taken away (from us) rather it is changed." Death for the adopted son of God is not the end but the beginning of the true, beautiful and happy, unending life.

This is surely a story of victory and the true philosophy of life. Our Christian faith alone gives the answer to all the problems which have disturbed men down through the ages. We, therefore, have the truth. We know the real facts of life and death. We have God's revelation through Christ, but we must put our knowledge into daily practice. It is not enough to be a Christian, nor enough to know where we are going; "it is not those who say to me 'Lord, Lord' who will enter into the kingdom of heaven but the person who does the will of my Father in heaven" (Mt. 7 : 21). We must live as Christians, and travel the road marked out for us by Christ. We must do the will of God every day of our lives.

We must love God, then, and love our neighbor who is a fellow-child of God like ourselves. We must keep God's commandments. When we truly realize what reward awaits us, the keeping of the commandments will not be a burden but, as St. John says, a pleasure and a privilege. Our Christian faith is surely the victory which overcomes the world.

GOSPEL : John 20 : 19–31. On the evening of that day, the first day of the week, the doors being shut where the disciples were, for fear of the Jews, Jesus came and stood among them and said to them, "Peace be with you." When he had said this, he showed them his hands and his side. Then the disciples were glad when they saw the Lord. Jesus said to them again, "Peace be with you. As the Father has sent me, even so I send you." And when he had said this, he breathed on them, and said to them, "Receive the Holy Spirit. If you forgive the sins of any, they are forgiven; if you retain the sins of any, they are retained."

Now Thomas, one of the twelve, called the Twin, was not with them when Jesus came. So the other disciples told him, "We have seen the Lord." But he said to them, "Unless I see in his hands the print of the nails, and place my finger in the mark of the nails, and place my hand in his side, I will not believe."

Eight days later, his disciples were again in the house, and Thomas was with them. The doors were shut, but Jesus came and stood among them, and said, "Peace be with you." Then he said to Thomas, "Put your finger here, and see my hands; and put out your hand, and place it in my side; do not be faithless, but believing." Thomas answered him, "My Lord and my God!" Jesus said to him, "Have you believed because you have seen me? Blessed are those who have not seen and yet believe."

Now Jesus did many other things in the presence of his disciples, which are not written in this book; but these are written that you may believe that Jesus is the Christ, the Son of God, and that believing you may have life in his name.

EXPLANATION : Last Sunday's gospel, also taken from St. John, described the first hint at the resurrection which the Apostles received. Peter and John, convinced that the body had not been taken away, because the winding sheets were left behind, were beginning to believe. But the others were skeptical, the two disciples on the way to Emmaus paid no heed to the women's story, and Thomas refused to believe the testimony of the other ten, even when this present appearance of our Lord had convinced them.

evening of . . . first day : The evening of the Sunday.

the doors being shut . . . : He came through the closed door, which shows the spiritual qualities of the resurrected body (see 1 Cor. 15 : 44–48).

came and stood among them : To prove that he was the Christ who had been crucified and who was now alive once more.

Peace be with you : Jews saluted one another by wishing peace, that is, health and prosperity both in the material and spiritual sense. Here Christ is not only wishing "well-being," especially the spiritual well-being, but he is *giving* it (see 14 : 27).

so I send you : He is now conferring on them the mission he had promised them before his death (see Mt. 4 : 19; Jn. 17 :

18 etc.), which was the continuation of the work of divine salvation inaugurated by himself.

Receive the Holy Spirit : He breathed on them and said these words—the sacramental action. He had promised them the Holy Spirit when he had returned to his Father in glory (7 : 39; 16 : 7). This condition had been fulfilled that Easter morning.

If you forgive . . . sins : Catholic tradition has rightly seen in this act the institution of the Sacrament of Penance.

Thomas, one of the twelve, . . . : He stubbornly refused to believe the word of the other ten Apostles and perhaps of disciples also who may have been with them. He needed personal evidence and the merciful Savior gave him that evidence.

eight days later : For Thomas's sake the risen Jesus appeared again in the very same place and circumstances. He asked Thomas to prove for himself that his body bore the marks of the crucifixion.

Thomas answered : Whether Thomas did touch the sacred wounds we are not told but his statement :

My Lord and my God : Proves how convinced he now was. And his statement goes further in expressing the divine nature of Christ than that of any other person in the four Gospels. "Lord and God" were the words used in the Old Testament to stress the true God "Yahweh Elohim."

Blessed . . . who have not seen : Christ is not belittling Thomas's expression of faith, but rather his slowness in accepting it on the testimony of others. Far greater, therefore, and more meritorious, Christ says, is the faith of all those, including ourselves, who have not had the privilege of seeing the risen Christ with our bodily eyes, but yet have believed in him on reliable testimony.

Many other things : These last two verses were the original ending of John's gospel. Chapter 21 was added later. His reason for writing his gospel was that men might believe that the Jesus who lived and died in Palestine was the promised Messiah and the true Son of God. He who believes this and lives up to his belief will have everlasting life because of what this Jesus has done for all men.

APPLICATION : It may surprise and amaze us that the Apostles were so reluctant to believe that Christ had risen from the dead, to live forever in glory with his Father in heaven. But we must remember that during their two or three years with him they saw nothing in him but a mere man, one with divine powers, but yet a man; certain prophets of the old covenant had some such powers also. Christ had "emptied himself" of his divine nature, and he had foretold his resurrection many times. But that he could be really God, as well as man, was something they could not then grasp, and if he was a mere man death had to be the end.

Their slowness of faith had its value for the future Church and for all of us. If they had been expecting the resurrection, and anxiously looking forward to it, people could say that they imagined it, that they persuaded themselves it had happened. Indeed, there have been men proud of their acuteness of judgement, who have said that the story of the resurrection is a story of mass hallucination, although all the evidence proves the opposite. Their conviction that it could not happen, could not be removed from their minds except by impressive evidence that it had. Hallucination is born in a mind already expecting and hoping for the *imagined fact*.

We can thank the Apostles and especially Thomas, the last to give in, that our faith in the resurrection and divine glorification of Christ is that much the stronger. Our Christianity which would have ended before the first Easter week had passed, if Christ had not risen in glory, spread rapidly to the then known world and is still spreading, because its author was none other than Christ "our Lord and our God." How prophetic were the words of Gamaliel at the meeting of the Sanhedrin which tried to prevent the Apostles from preaching the new Christian faith: "If this plan or work is of men, it will be overthrown; but if it is of God, you will not be able to overthrow it" (Acts 5: 38–39).

THIRD SUNDAY OF EASTER

FIRST READING: Acts 3: 13–15; 17–19. Peter said to the people: "The God of Abraham and of Isaac and of Jacob, the God of our fathers, glorified his servant Jesus, whom you delivered up and denied in the presence of Pilate, when he had decided to release him. But you denied the Holy and Righteous One, and asked for a murderer to be granted to you, and killed the Author of life, whom God raised from the dead. To this we are witnesses.

"And now, brethren, I know that you acted in ignorance, as did also your rulers. But what God foretold by the mouth of all the prophets, that his Christ should suffer, he thus fulfilled. Repent therefore, and turn again, that your sins may be blotted out."

EXPLANATION: Peter and John, on their way to the temple, met a man crippled from birth. He asked them for alms. Peter said he had neither gold nor silver, but he would give him something better. He told the man: "in the name of Jesus of Nazareth" to "stand up and walk." The man stood up and followed Peter and John into the temple, "walking and jumping and praising God" (3: 8). The people recognized the man as the cripple who used to be at the gate each day begging for alms. The crowd, full of curiosity and excitement, gathered around the Apostles and the man who had been cured. Peter spoke to the crowd and told them that it was not through their own power or holiness that they had cured this man, but through the power of Jesus.

God . . . our fathers : Peter emphasizes that he also is a son of Abraham, Isaac and Jacob and that their God was also his God.

his . . . Jesus : Second-Isaiah had described the future Messiah as the Suffering Servant (Is. 52 : 13—53 : 12), who would be obedient to his Father unto death. The Apostles and the Christians saw in Jesus this suffering servant (see Acts 8 : 32ff). Peter tells the crowd that God had glorified this servant Jesus in his resurrection.

delivered . . . Pilate : Peter now reminds them that a short time previously they had handed over this Jesus to the Roman governor to be crucified and had denied that he was their king or Messiah. They had forced Pilate to condemn him even though Pilate "could find no guilt in him."

Holy . . . One : The Suffering Servant of Isaiah was holy, righteous and innocent of any crime. Like an innocent lamb he was led to the slaughter. This was Jesus whom they, the Jews, had been forcing Pilate to condemn and crucify.

murderer . . . life : This refers to their choice of Barabbas, whom Pilate thought could save Jesus (Mt. 27 : 20). Barabbas had committed murder and was awaiting trial. Jesus was about to give the true and everlasting life to all men.

whom God raised : God was able to undo all their wickedness. He raised Jesus from the dead. Peter and all the Apostles and disciples were witnesses of the resurrection. They had seen and spoken with him, and eaten with him after his resurrection.

acted in ignorance : His master, when nailed to the cross, had begged his Father to forgive them " for they do not know what they are doing" (Lk. 23 : 34). Following that example Peter says that the mob that howled for the death of Jesus, as well as the leaders who incited it, acted in ignorance. They did not know that Christ was God, nor did they believe him to be the promised Messiah. They had a built-in prejudice against his claims and were unable rightly to judge.

God foretold : The Jews were acting as God's agents in carrying out what he had foretold concerning Jesus.

repent . . . blotted out : The Jews must return to God; they had drifted away from him through their pride and prejudices. If they but return to God, abandoning their prejudices and pride, Peter now tells them that they will obtain forgiveness for all of their sins.

APPLICATION : In the early days of the Church in Jerusalem the resurrection was the topic of conversation among the friends and enemies of Jesus. The latter did their best to deny the fact, but in vain; the followers of Jesus kept claiming that it was a fact, and worked miracles in proof of that claim. In today's reading the cure of the cripple-from-birth is one such miracle. Peter worked this miracle " in the name (that is, the person and power) of Jesus of Nazareth (3 : 6), whom the God of the Jews had glorified and had raised from the dead." If Christ had been an impostor, as the Pharisees and scribes had stated (Mt. 27 : 63), God would not have raised him from the dead and glorified him. Before a large gathering in the temple precincts in Jerusalem, Peter makes this claim only a few weeks after Christ's death on the cross. The people were impressed. In spite of the opposition of their leaders the number of Jews who became followers of Christ increased daily, "the total number of whom had now risen to something like five thousand" (see 4 : 4, the same day this miracle took place). This was a large percentage of the inhabitants of Jerusalem at that time.

No true Christian can have the slightest doubt about the fact of the resurrection of Jesus. The growth of the infant Church in Jerusalem and in Gentile lands is sufficient proof of it. Men and women do not attach themselves to one who has failed, nor do they take on a new and demanding form of life without sufficient conviction. Yet, there are men and women who, like the leaders of the Jews, still refuse to open their eyes to the light and who shut their minds against the most convincing evidence. Such people need help. One of the best ways of showing how grateful we are for the true faith is a willingness and eagerness to spread that faith to our fellowmen. Christ became man for them too, he died on the cross for their sakes, and God the Father raised him from the dead so that they too may rise in glory one day. As true Christians, and true lovers of Christ, it is our duty to give a helping hand to those brothers of ours who are sorely in need of help.

However, you may say : "What can we do; we are not missionaries nor preachers? We are not theologically equipped to enter into dialog and con-vince unbelievers." The fact is, that without becoming missionaries, preachers or theologians every Christian can act as a missionary, or preacher, or theologian without leaving his home and employment and without opening a book. The Christian who prays often and fervently for his fellowmen and who lives his Christian life to the full, is a preacher and a missionary wherever he lives and works. In his daily actions he is showing forth Christ. His abounding faith and charity, his unshakable hope in the eternal future which awaits him, will do more to enlighten the mind and will of unbelievers than all the skill of preachers and all the theology of great writers.

Are we not grateful to God and Christ? We are convinced that heaven is the pearl of great price compared with which everything this world has to offer is but as a grain of sand to the desert. We know that God wants all his adopted children in heaven. For that purpose we know that Christ humbled himself even to the death of the cross. We know also that Christ is counting on us to help him to bring them to heaven. Would we refuse him this return for all he has done for us? Would we be true Christians who love God above all things if we did not love our neighbor as ourselves? We want heaven for ourselves; we must want it for them too. Through the grace and mercy of God our prayers and the good example of our Christian lives will be the means of converting many sinners and unbelievers to Christ. He in turn will reward them and us with eternal life.

SECOND READING: 1 John 2:1-5. My little children, I am writing this to you so that you may not sin; but if any one does sin, we have an advocate with the Father, Jesus Christ the righteous; and he is the expiation for our sins, and not for ours only but also for the sins of the whole world. And by this we may be sure that we know him, if we keep his commandments. He who says "I know him" but disobeys his commandments is a liar, and the truth is not in him; but whoever keeps his word, in him truly love for God is perfected. By this we may be sure that we are in him.

EXPLANATION: About this first Epistle of St. John, see the second reading of last Sunday. In today's extract from this letter, the Apostle is urging his fellow-Christians to avoid sin. If they should sin, they are to admit their fault and seek pardon, which will be given in abundance. He has in mind, evidently, the Gnostic heretics of the time who, among other things, did not keep God's commandments and yet held that they were not sinning by violating them. John exhorts his Christians not to imitate these heretics.

My little children: St. John uses this affectionate term seven times in his first Epistle, and six times the term "dearly-beloved," as a proof of his real affection for all the followers of Christ.

you ... sin: In the preceding verses the Apostle says that we are all inclined to sin and are at times guilty of sin. This is a defect of our human nature. The Jerusalem Bible translation is: "to stop you sinning" and may better translate the Greek and fit in with the context.

advocate ... Father: We have an advocate in heaven who has pleaded, and is always pleading for us, Jesus Christ, the just one. The Father will hear him.

expiation ... sins: By his death on the cross Christ has already made atonement, "expiation," for all our sins and "for the sins of the whole world." Those only who by repentance ask to participate can receive expiation.

know ... commandments: Although they claimed that they had special knowledge of him the Gnostics did not know him, because they did not keep his commandments. True knowledge brings love and obedience with it. Sincere Christians keep God's commandments. They know God, all he is and all he means to them.

disobeys ... liar: He who violates God's commandments is saying by his actions that he does not know God as a Father who loves him and deserves every reverence man can give.

who ... his word: The faithful service of God—the keeping of his laws—will bring each faithful servant of God to the perfection of love which is the essence of true sanctity. The cause of perfect sanctity must be the true love of God, not the false love of God (shown by ignoring and violating his commandments) preached by the Gnostics.

APPLICATION: It is a consolation for us to hear the saintly St. John, the beloved disciple, declare that any one of us, even the best of us, can sin. He loved God and fully realized what lengths God has gone to in order to share heaven with us. The very thought of offending God must have been something abhorrent, something detestable. Yet he knew that all Christians had not received as many graces as he had, and he, therefore, understood that their love could grow cold at times and that they could occasionally offend God. Coming from so great a saint as the beloved disciple, this understanding is consoling. He is but reflecting the mind of Christ, his Master, whom he loved so much. John had lived with Jesus for about three years. He saw how kindly he treated sinners.

The Mary Magdalenes of Galilee, the adultress of Jerusalem, the tax-collectors all over Palestine, were all treated with kindness and understanding. If they but asked for forgiveness, even if only indirectly, they were forgiven their sins. In the apostolic circle too, Jesus had been merciful and patient with his worldly-minded disciples. Many months after they had joined him, John himself and his brother James were angling for positions of power (and maybe wealth) in the earthly messianic kingdom which they thought he would set up (Mt. 20:20). All the Apostles deserted Jesus when he was arrested in Gethsemane. That night Peter denied that he ever knew him. However, when they later realized their faults and repented they were freely forgiven. Even Judas would have been forgiven his act of betrayal had he but repented.

We sinners—and we are all sinners in many ways—are dealing with a forgiving God. What is more we have the forgiving Christ as our Advocate in heaven. Through his passion and cross he has already earned for us the right of forgiveness. On our part all that is needed is the humility to admit that we are sinners and the resolve to turn away from our sins. God and Christ will do the rest. Our Lord has left to his Church his sacrament of mercy. From a delegate empowered by Christ to do so, we can not only receive forgiveness for our sins but a declaration that they are forgiven us. This mercy of God and his divine Son should arouse in us a desire and urge to try to return a little bit of love for all that had been and is being done for our salvation. "Whoever keeps his word," St. John says, "in him truly the love of God is perfected." If we strive to keep the laws of God, if we try to live the Christian life, we will have the true love of God in us, we will be moving towards the state of perfection which will be ours in heaven.

Should some over-powering temptation, or some unexpected assault of the enemy make us lapse momentarily, we have the guarantee that God will accept us back, if we but avail ourselves of the means his mercy has placed so easily within our reach—sincere repentance and, where possible and as soon as possible, the placing of our sins at the feet of his representative in the sacrament of penance.

What earthly mother was ever so kind, so patient, so tolerant toward the children of her womb as our God in heaven is tolerant, patient, kind and merciful toward us his weak mortal children?

GOSPEL : Luke 24 : 35–48. The disciples told what had happened on the road, and how Jesus was known to them in the breaking of the bread.

As they were saying this, Jesus himself stood among them, and said to them, "Peace to you!" But they were startled and frightened, and supposed that they saw a spirit. And he said to them, "Why are you troubled, and why do questionings rise in your hearts? See my hands and my feet, that it is I myself; handle me, and see; for a spirit has not flesh and bones as you see that I have." And when he had said this, he showed them his hands and his feet. And while they still disbelieved for joy, and wondered, he said to them, "Have you anything here to eat?" They gave him a piece of broiled fish, and he took it and ate before them.

Then he said to them, "These are my words which I spoke to you, while I was still with you, that everything written about me in the law of Moses, and the prophets and the psalms must be fulfilled." Then he opened their minds to understand the scriptures, and said to them, "Thus it is written, that the Christ should suffer and on the third day rise from the dead, and that repentance and forgiveness of sins should be preached in his name to all nations, beginning from Jerusalem. You are witnesses of these things."

EXPLANATION : This is the continuation of the appearance of the risen Lord to the two disciples on the road to Emmaus. When these two disciples eventually recognized that the "stranger" who had explained the messianic prophecies to them on the way to Emmaus was none other than Christ, they hurried back to Jerusalem to inform the Apostles. They discovered that the Apostles were now convinced of the resurrection, for Simon had seen him. While they were discussing these things Christ appeared in the midst of them. **Peace . . . you :** This is the usual Hebrew salutation. Coming from Christ it was more than a pious wish.

saw a spirit : Even though they had believed Simon and the two disciples they still were startled to see him there in their midst especially as St. John adds that he came through the closed door (Jn. 20 : 19). Was he a ghost, then, or was he real? They had seen Lazarus raised from the dead, but it was the self-same Lazarus back on earth to continue life where he had left off. The resurrection of Jesus was different. He had risen to a new life, a life of glory which would last forever. A glorified body is not visible to human eyes, but Jesus took on a human form which could be seen. In this appearance the form was the same as the body that was crucified; on other occasions it was a different form, as was the case on the road to Emmaus (Lk. 24 : 13–35), and at Tiberias (Jn. 21 : 1–12).

questionings arise : The Apostles did not believe our Lord's prophecies regarding his resurrection; they did not believe he could die, so how could he rise again? Now, presented with the fulfillment, they were still slow to admit the fact.

hands . . . bones : He now asks them to see for themselves that it is Jesus who is there. They can see the marks of the nails on his hands and feet. He is not a mere spirit; a spirit has not flesh and bones as he had.

disbelieved for joy : It was too good to be true; they could not believe their eyes.

anything to eat : A risen, glorified body does not need food, but to convince his Apostles, Jesus appeared in a body similar to that which was crucified and ate some food to prove that he was really alive again—in a new mode of life, yes, but really alive.

Thus . . . written : Jesus goes on to remind them of the prophecies of his resurrection which he had given them so often. He spoke also of the necessity of his death and resurrection. This was the plan of God as foretold in "the Law, the prophets and the writings" (psalms), which was the usual Jewish description of the Old Testament.

forgiveness of sin : Beginning in Jerusalem the Apostles were to preach repentance to the world. Christ by his incarnation, death and resurrection had obtained eternal life (salvation) for all men; this Christian gospel must be preached to all nations. For this he had chosen his Apostles; they had been witnesses of his public life, his teachings, his death and resurrection.

APPLICATION : Our Lord's glorious resurrection is the crowning miracle of his sojourn on earth among men. It is the foundation and cornerstone of our Christian religion. His death on Calvary proved that he was really human; his resurrection proved he was also divine. During his public life he had claimed to be God. Had that claim been untrue God the Father could not have raised him from the dead. By his death he made atonement for the sins of the world—"he nailed them to the tree of the cross"; by his resurrection he opened the gates of death for all men and made them heirs to the eternal life.

We need hardly delay to prove the fact of the resurrection of Christ, for without it there would have been no Christianity, no Christian Church. In the story of the appearance which precedes today's Gospel, we are told how two of Christ's disciples were so depressed and disorientated by his death that they were giving up all interest in the dead Master and were returning home at the first opportunity (the Sabbath, Saturday, had intervened and they could not travel on that day). The Apostles were no better since Good Friday. They had remained behind locked doors for fear of the Jews. They had no hope left. They too would have left Jerusalem that Sunday were it not for the story brought by Mary Magdalene that Christ's body had been taken from the tomb. When the risen Christ appeared to the ten Apostles (Thomas was absent) they thought he was a ghost, so far were their thoughts from a possible resurrection.

When the truth sank into their minds, however, they became changed men. After Pentecost day they fearlessly proclaimed to the Jews, of whom they had been frightened, that Christ whom those same Jews had crucified, had risen and was now glorified by the Father. Thousands of Jews in Jerusalem had come to believe in Christ, because they were convinced he had risen and was the Messiah and the Son of God, as he claimed to be. The four Evangelists testify to the truth of the resurrection and we have the exceptional witness of St. Paul whose radical change of life can have only one explanation—he saw the risen Christ on the road to Damascus.

Of the fact of the resurrection we can

have no doubts; Christianity is inexplicable without it, and Christianity has existed for almost two thousand years. A more important point for consideration today is what this resurrection means to us. "If Christ has not risen," says St. Paul (1 Cor. 15 : 17), "vain is your faith, for you are still in your sins." But "Christ has risen from the dead, the first fruits of those who have fallen asleep." Our faith then is not in vain, for the founder and foundation of our faith is the Word of God who cannot deceive or be deceived, and his resurrection is the guarantee of our resurrection. He is the "first fruits," the earnest of the full harvest that was to follow after our earthly death. We shall all rise again, in glory if we have been faithful during our time on earth, in a less pleasant state, if we have not followed Christ here below.

Human life has always been the great enigma for philosophers down through the ages. The resurrection of Christ, which causes and guarantees our resurrection, is the one and only explanation of that enigma. If death were the end of man, with all his gifts of intellect and will; if the grave were to enclose forever this noble being whom God has raised above all other earthly creatures and has endowed with super-mundane gifts and aspirations, then indeed man's sojourn on earth would be an inexplicable enigma. But the gifts God gave to man were not simply to help him to make a precarious living and enjoy a fleeting happiness, interspersed with much sadness, for sixty, seventy or even a hundred years. No, they were intended to last for eternity and to reach their real fruition in eternity.

With St. Paul then, we may well sing out today: "O death where is thy victory, O death where is thy sting? . . . thanks be to God who has given us the victory through our Lord Jesus Christ" (1 Cor. 15 : 55–57). Yes, Easter time is a time of rejoicing for every true Christian. It is a time for Alleluias, for praising and thanking God. Our happy future is within our reach. Our eternal happiness has been won for us by Christ and is within our grasp, if only we hold fast to the true faith of Christ, taking the rough with the smooth, going through our lesser Gethsemanes and Calvaries as Christ went through his great ones. If we do this we can hopefully await the angel who will roll back the stone from our grave one day, and allow us to enter into the glory of the eternal Easter in heaven.

FOURTH SUNDAY OF EASTER

FIRST READING: Acts 4 : 8–12. Peter, filled with the Holy Spirit, said to them, "Rulers of the people and elders, if we are being examined today concerning a good deed done to a cripple, by what means this man has been healed, be it known to you all, and to all the people of Israel, that by the name of Jesus Christ of Nazareth, whom you crucified, whom God raised from the dead, by him this man is standing before you well. This is the stone which was rejected by you builders, but which has become the head of the corner. And there is salvation in no one else, for there is no other name under heaven given among men by which we must be saved."

EXPLANATION: This excerpt from Acts is a sequence of what was described in last Sunday's first reading. Peter had cured a cripple-from-birth. He told the people that it was not by his own power that he did this, but through the power of Jesus of Nazareth, whom the Jews had, in ignorance, crucified. But the God of the Jews had raised Jesus from the dead. While the ordinary Jews were very impressed, and many of them accepted the faith of the Apostles, the leaders, the priests and Pharisees of the Sanhedrin, were anything but pleased. They had Peter and John arrested and kept in prison overnight. Next day they were interrogated and Peter answered for them both.

filled . . . Spirit: This was as Christ had promised his Apostles while he was still with them: "they will hand you over to the Sanhedrin . . . do not worry . . . the Spirit of your Father will be speaking in you" (Mt. 10 : 17-20). Before the highest authorities and in the highest courtroom of the Jews in Jerusalem Peter, who only a short while before had locked himself, together with the other Apostles, in the upper-room "for fear of the Jews," now fearlessly proclaims his belief in the risen Christ.

done . . . cripple: This was the miracle that started it all. The healed cripple is evidently produced in court—"this man *is standing* before you healed."

name . . . crucified: It was through the power of Jesus that this miracle was worked—through the power of one whom this Sanhedrin had thought was silenced forever when they forced Pilate to crucify him. Peter courageously tells this to the arch-enemies of Christ and of his followers, and he wants all the Jews of Palestine to hear of it.

whom God raised: Their plan to put an end to Christ was in vain, for God had raised him from the dead.

stone . . . builders: Peter says that by rejecting Christ as the true Messiah they had fulfilled the messianic prophecy of

Psalm 108, verse 22. This stone, rejected by the builders, the leaders of the Jews, has become the cornerstone which would unite firmly the two walls of the house, the Gentiles and the Jews.

salvation . . . else : There is only one Savior, one Messiah, sent by God.

no other name : "name" stands for person, and also the name Jesus, or Joshuah in Hebrew, means "God saves." There is no salvation for those who will not accept and follow Jesus.

APPLICATION : Clear and logical as was this discourse of Peter, and moved as he was by the Holy Spirit to deliver it, it fell on deaf ears as far as the vast majority in that Jewish highcourt was concerned. They had long since desired a political Messiah who would set up a world-wide kingdom for them. Not only did they want to be free from the hated Romans, but were ambitious to govern all the Gentile nations. Their ambitions and desires were of this world—worldly. Christ's talk of repentance, mortification and preparation for the world to come found no responsive chord in their hearts. He was not the Messiah they wanted; hence he was an impostor, a perverter of the people, and so they called on the hated Romans to nail him to a cross.

Now his followers were claiming that God had proved that he *was* the Messiah and, what was more, that he was divine, by raising him from the dead. They were working miracles to back up this claim, and surely it is well known that God does not work miracles for impostors and sinners (see Jn. 9 : 31). The reasonable attitude for them to take, even at this late hour, would surely have been to check the evidence. But no, they had already made up their minds and would not change them. No evidence could shift the wall of personal pride which they themselves had built. "There is none so blind as he who will not see," was surely verified in the case of the leaders of the Jews.

Let us leave their judgement to God and turn our scrutiny on ourselves and on our acceptance of Christ. Do we ever allow temporal interests and worldly ambitions to come between us and our Savior? Are all our dealings with our neighbor strictly according to the commandments of God? Do we ever succumb to the temptation to make an easy dollar to the detriment of our neighbor, forgetting our Christian obligations? If we are employers, do we pay our workers a just wage and respect their rights as fellowmen? If we are workers, do we work honestly and fairly giving a right return for the wages paid us? Do we accept all men as our brothers, as sons of God, who like ourselves are on the road to heaven, and are we always ready to give them a helping hand when and if they need it? Finally are we, by our faithful observance of the Christian life, a lamp shining brightly, helping the many unfortunate ex-Christians who have left the path of Christ, to return to their Savior and to the true road to heaven?

"There is no other name under heaven by which we can be saved." We Christians are dedicated to the sacred name of Jesus Christ by baptism, but it is only those who live up to the obligations of their Christian baptism who are worthy to bear that name and to share in the eternal salvation which it guarantees.

SECOND READING : 1 John 3 : 1–2. See what love the Father has given us, that we should be called children of God; and so we are. The reason why the world does not know us is that it did not know him. Beloved, we are God's children now; it does not yet appear what we shall be, but we know that when he appears we shall be like him, for we shall see him as he is.

EXPLANATION : St. John here sets out in a couple of sentences the basic effect of the incarnation. Already in this life men are made children of God. Because we are God's children here below we shall see him as he is in the future life.

love . . . given us : The infinite love of God is beyond the comprehension of our finite minds. Why should God love us since he does not need us? Our love has always something of the selfish in it; that is, even we find it difficult to recognize absolutely unselfish love.

called children of God : "Called," because we are. God decided, before creating us, to share his own eternal home with us—to adopt us. To do this he decreed the incarnation of his Son : "Yes, God loved the world (mankind) so much that he gave his only Son, so that everyone who believes in him may not be lost but have eternal life" (Jn. 3 : 16). By joining our human nature to his divine person Christ united us all in a special relationship to God the Father. We are the adopted children of God, as John emphatically says.

would . . . know us : Christians need not be surprised that the world, that is, the forces of evil in the world, does not recognize them nor show any inclination to imitate or respect them, for this world (of evil) treats God in the same manner.

God's . . . now : Already on this earth we are numbered among God's adopted children. This we realize only through faith. When this life is over we shall have a more direct and intimate knowledge of our good fortune.

when he appears : John is referring to this perfect stage of our sonship here. When the Parousia, or the second coming of Christ, takes place, we too shall be glorified like Christ. We shall be raised to a higher supernatural state.

we shall . . . he is : Referring to God the Father, John says that in our glorified state we shall see God "as he is." St. Paul expresses the same truth thus : "For our knowledge (of God) now is imperfect . . . once perfection comes all imperfect things will disappear . . . Now we are seeing a dim reflection in a mirror (the bronze mirrors used in those days) but then we shall be seeing *face to face*. The knowledge that I have now is imperfect, but then I shall know as fully as I am known" (1 Cor. 13 : 12). After our resurrection we shall see God as he is, face to face.

APPLICATION : During this holy season of Easter, while our thoughts center on the glorious Christ who rose from the dead and returned to heaven, our thoughts should follow him there, and dwell for a while on that happy place for which we were prepared by God and elevated by the incarnation of his divine Son. St. John gives us a little glimpse of that future home of ours in today's reading: we shall be glorified like the risen Christ he tells us, and we shall see God as he is, not through the veil of faith as we now see him, but in reality. In another book, "Revelation," John gives us a further glimpse into the heaven which awaits us: "Behold the dwelling of God is with men. He will dwell with them and they shall be his people and God himself will be with them" as a Father among his children, "he will wipe away every tear from their eyes, and death shall be no more, neither shall there be mourning nor crying, nor pain any more, for the former things have passed away" (Rev. 21: 3-4).

Heaven, therefore, as St. John describes it, is a state wherein every happiness a man can desire will be attainable; the vision of the infinitely perfect God is the guarantee of this, and every sadness and cause of sadness will be forever removed. In heaven man will have no sorrow, no pain, no regrets; instead he will have everything that is pleasing, beautiful, and good. We all have experienced some moments of happiness in our lives, moments when everything was going smoothly and happily for us, when we had no pain or sorrow or fear. We knew, however, that these were but fleeting moments, they could not, and they did not, last, for that is of the very nature of our temporary life on earth. In heaven, however, these happy moments will be turned into an eternal state, a state that will have no end.

It is hard for us, in fact it is impossible, to form any complete concept of the joys of heaven. All our ideas, all our images are derived from our earthly surroundings. St. Paul, who was given a vision of heaven, tells us that he could not describe to his converts in Corinth what he had seen, because human language had no words or images to describe it. "I knew a man in Christ," he says, "who fourteen years ago, was caught up into paradise and heard things which must not and cannot be put into human language" (2 Cor. 12: 2-3). That vision of St. Paul, that glimpse of what awaited him, made him willing to sacrifice everything on earth, even his very life, in order to reach the heaven God had prepared for him. "For Christ I have accepted the loss of everything and I look on everything as so much refuse if only I can have Christ and be given a place in him . . . I have not yet won but I am still running, trying to capture the prize for which Christ Jesus captured me" (Phil. 3: 8-12).

Without having the privileges which St. John and St. Paul had we have a sufficient idea of heaven to make us all desire it. But like these Apostles, and all the other millions of saintly men and women, we know that we must "work our passage" to reach that abode of God. We must stay on the path of the Christian commandments, ever ready to count as nothing any earthly thing that would lure us off their path. During our earthly life we must keep God and Christ daily before our eyes if we hope to live in perfect happiness with them in the hereafter.

GOSPEL: John 10:11–18. Jesus said to his disciples: "I am the good shepherd. The good shepherd lays down his life for the sheep. He who is a hireling and not a shepherd, whose own the sheep are not, sees the wolf coming and leaves the sheep and flees; and the wolf snatches them and scatters them. He flees because he is a hireling and cares nothing for the sheep. I am the good shepherd; I know my own and my own know me, as the Father knows me and I know the Father; and I lay down my life for the sheep. And I have other sheep, that are not of this fold; I must bring them also, and they will heed my voice. So there shall be one flock, one shepherd. For this reason the Father loves me, because I lay down my life, that I may take it again. No one takes it from me, but I lay it down of my own accord. I have power to lay it down, and I have power to take it again; this charge I have received from my Father."

EXPLANATION: The Jews were a pastoral people, and it was only natural that their literature, the Old Testament books, should have many references to pastoral life. Our Lord and his Apostles continued this tradition and used pastoral images familiar to the people to illustrate for their hearers the spiritual truths of Christianity. In today's reading St. John gives us our Lord's description of himself under the well-known image of the good shepherd who not only cares for his flock but is willing to die to protect the life of that flock.

I am ... shepherd: He was the owner of the flock; they belonged to him, and he would prove himself a worthy leader and defender of his flock.

lay ... life: In those days wolves, lions and robbers often raided the sheepfolds. The true shepherd should and would defend them with his life. Jesus laid down his life for his flock.

hireling ... flees: The hired hand who does not own the sheep will flee when danger threatens. He thinks only of his own safety; he leaves the helpless flock to its fate. It was in Jerusalem, the stronghold of the Scribes and Pharisees, that our Lord preached this sermon. His cure of the man born blind (mentioned in the previous chapter of John) had caused an uproar among the Pharisees. When they could not deny the miracle, they said that Jesus worked it by some demoniacal power. The blind man, now healed, answered this very tellingly: "We know that God does not hear sinners ... if this man (Jesus) were not from God he could do nothing" (Jn. 9: 31-33). The Scribes and Pharisees were the legal shepherds of the Jews, but actually they were far more interested in their own gain and glory than in the spiritual welfare of their flock. The mass of the people were being attracted to Jesus; there was a danger that these leaders would lose their position and the substantial profit it entailed. Hence one of the reasons for their fierce opposition to Jesus. In this sermon, quoted by St. John, Jesus contrasts himself, the true, good shepherd, with these hirelings who were working only for personal gain.

I know my own: As the true shepherd knows every sheep in his flock, and every sheep knows him, Jesus knows each of his followers with a knowledge arising from love, and his followers likewise know him. Unless they do they are not true followers.

Father ... the Father: The mutual

knowledge of the Father and Son is infinite, since each is a divine Person. The Christian's knowledge of Christ can never be infinite, but it can and should be as great as possible. Based on true love, it will be as complete a knowledge as the finite mind is capable of reaching. On the other hand Christ's knowledge and love for his followers is infinite because of his divine nature.

I lay . . . sheep : He said the good shepherd would defend his flock with his life. Now to prove that he is such a shepherd he states that he is about to do just that.

I have . . . sheep: Most of the Jews had the erroneous idea that they alone would be God's flock always, that the messianic kingdom would be for them only. The universality of the promised messianic kingdom was frequently foretold in the Old Testament. Abraham was called to bring a blessing not only on his descendants but on all nations (Gen. 12 : 3). The Gentiles, therefore, were also to be part of the good shepherd's flock.

will . . . voice : This prophecy of Christ began to be fulfilled within a short time after his resurrection. St. Peter received the first Gentile, Cornelius of Caesarea, into the Church within a year of the resurrection. Before the last of the Apostles died the Church had been firmly established in the principal cities and towns of the Roman empire.

one flock . . . shepherd : All the followers of Christ form one fold, one Christian Church. As St. Paul puts it to the Colossians : "here (that is, in the Christian Church) there is no Gentile and Jew, no circumcised and uncircumcised, no Barbarian and Scythian, no slave and freeman; but Christ is all things and in all" (Col. 3 : 11).

reason . . . loves me : The Father's love is poured out upon the Son because, in obedient love, he lays down his life for mankind in fulfillment of the Father's design.

I may . . . again : By his death he nailed our sins to the cross; by his resurrection he opened the door from death to heaven for us and proved that he was the Son of God and the Messiah.

no one . . . from me : He chose death freely, his enemies did not take his life from him (as they thought they were doing) against his will. This freedom is frequently emphasized by Jesus during his public life (17 : 4; 18 : 4; 19 : 30).

this . . . father : His voluntary death followed by his glorification in his resurrection was the Father's purpose in sending him on earth. He freely and willingly accomplished this mission.

APPLICATION : The image of Christ as our Good Shepherd has always appealed to human nature. One of the earliest paintings of Christ in the Roman catacombs represents him as carrying an injured sheep on his shoulders. This is a manifestation of love which touches our innermost feelings. We do not mind being likened to sheep in this context. There is something guileless about a sheep, and at the same time a lot of foolishness. Does not this describe the vast majority of men, even many of those who openely oppose Christ? Is there not something very sheeplike about the man who, because God gave him a limited intellect, thinks he knows all things and needs no further help from God? The sheep who thinks it knows as much, and even more, than the shepherd and sets out to fend for itself, is no more foolish than the man who thinks he can do without God's revelation and God's Church.

Indeed we all act like sheep on many occasions, when it comes to the things that concern our spiritual welfare. We often ramble off from the flock to nibble at little bits of forbidden pasture. However, we have a Shepherd who understands us, one whose patience and love are infinite. He is always ready to go after us when we stray too far; his voice is constantly reaching out to us— in missions, retreats, sicknesses, crosses and other various ways. How many times have we already felt his loving grace calling and helping us back to the safety of his fold?

There are many who are not so fortunate as we, who either through no fault of their own or through their own fault do not hear his voice and do not know or follow him. This is an opportunity he gives us to show how we appreciate all he has done for us. He died on the cross for all men. He wills all men to profit by his death, and his statement "them also I must bring" is a direct appeal to us to cooperate with him in this work. Every Christian is a missionary. The very fact of living the Christian life in its entirety, in the midst of our fellowmen, is of itself a powerful example to outsiders. It influences for good the lax Christian and the non-Christian. It makes them stop and think

and look into their consciences. This is generally the first step on the road back to God.

The devout Christian will not stop at good example only. If he truly loves God, he must truly love his neighbor and must want him to have a share in his own good fortune. He knows there is welcome and room in heaven for all men, and he knows that the greater the number there the greater will be God's eternal glory. He will strive then by every available means to help his neighbor into Christ's fold.

After good example, prayer will be his most potent weapon. Day in, day out the devout Christian must pray for the conversion of his fellowmen who are wandering aimlessly in the barren desert of this life far from God. He must also learn all he can about the truths of his faith in order to be able to help honest enquirers. He must also cooperate with any parochial or diocesan societies for the propagation of the faith, insofar as his family and financial state allow him.

The sermon preached by our Savior nearly two thousand years ago is still echoing and re-echoing around the world, calling on his faithful flock to do all in their power to help those other children of God who are still outside the fold. Do not shut your ears to this call of Christ today. Give him a helping hand by helping your fellowman to see the light of the true faith.

FIFTH SUNDAY OF EASTER

FIRST READING: Acts 8 : 26–31. When Saul had come to Jerusalem he attempted to join the disciples; and they were all afraid of him, for they did not believe that he was a disciple. But Barnabas took him, and brought him to the apostles, and declared to them how on the road he had seen the Lord, who spoke to him, and how at Damascus he had preached boldly in the name of Jesus. So he went in and out among them at Jerusalem, preaching boldly in the name of the Lord. And he spoke and disputed against the Hellenists; but they were seeking to kill him. And when the brethren knew it, they brought him down to Caesarea, and sent him off to Tarsus.

So the church throughout all Judea and Galilee and Samaria had peace and was built up; and walking in the fear of the Lord and in the comfort of the Holy Spirit it was multiplied.

EXPLANATION: Saul, who later changed his name to Paul, was born of Jewish parents in Tarsus in Cicilia. He came to Jerusalem as a youth to study the Law (of Moses) and become a rabbi. He had qualified as a rabbi about the year that Jesus was crucified. He took a firm stand against the young Christian Church, looking on it as an heretical sect which had to be crushed. Having harassed the Christians in Jerusalem, he set out for Damascus to arrest and bring to Jerusalem any Christians he found there. On the road to Damascus he was converted by a vision of the risen Christ. Having spent some time in Damascus preaching to the Jews of the city that Jesus was the Son of God, he paid his first visit to Jerusalem. This visit is the subject of today's reading.

join the disciples: Saul wanted to join with the Christians of Jerusalem at their prayers and meetings, but, remembering too well his past conduct in the city they did not trust him, for they thought he had not become a disciple of Christ, but was there to spy on them.

Barnabas . . . Apostles: Barnabas, a man of standing in the church in Jerusalem (Acts 4 : 32-37), was convinced that Saul had become a sincere Christian. He, therefore, introduced him to the Apostles telling them about Saul's conversion on the road to Damascus when "the Lord spoke to him," and about his great work for the spread of the Christian faith in Damascus. Barnabas could have had contacts with

Damascus and heard of the conversion and work of Saul there, and could even have had confirmation of this from Saul himself.

went . . . them: The result of Barnabas' intervention was that Saul was fully accepted by the Christians in Jerusalem.

against the Hellenists: Jerusalem had many Jews who had been born outside of Palestine and spoke only Greek. These were called Hellenists. Paul was a native speaker of Greek, and was well qualified to argue about Christ with them, which he did.

seeking . . . him: Not all of these Hellenists were willing to accept Christ. Some, unable to answer his arguments, were planning to put him to death. They probably knew his past history and looked on him as a traitor, and traitors, they thought, deserved death. The other Apostles had not been Pharisees or rabbis, and so were not as guilty, in their eyes, as Saul.

Caesarea . . . Tarsus: To save him from death by stoning, the death Stephen suffered a few years previously (Acts 6 and 7), the Christians of Jerusalem saw him safely to the port of Caesarea in Palestine, from whence he went by ship to Tarsus, his native town.

church . . . built up: The open persecution of the Christians during the first years seems to have ceased. The leaders of the Jews may have grown tired of arrests and trials, or perhaps they had paid heed to the wise words of one of their members, Gamaliel, who said at one of their trial sessions: "If this enterprise (Christianity) is of human origin it will break up of its own accord; but if it does in fact come from God you will not only be unable to destroy them (the Christians) but you might find yourself fighting against God" (Acts 5 : 39). Whatever the reason, the Christians in Jerusalem were allowed to live in peace. Their numbers increased daily, not only in Jerusalem but throughout Judea, Samaria and Galilee, that is, in all of Palestine.

walking . . . Lord: This is living the full Christian life, giving offense to neither God nor man.

comfort . . . Spirit: The visible effects of the descent of the Holy Spirit in baptism on the converted were there to strengthen and encourage the Christians and to attract other converts. Hence the great growth of the Church.

APPLICATION: Although the verses of today's reading, taken from the Acts of the Apostles, begin with Saul and his first visit to Jerusalem, the point of interest for us is the growth, and marvelous spread of the Christian faith among the Jews of Palestine. "The Church throughout all Judea and Galilee and Samaria had peace and was built up." If we were dealing with human achievement and human endeavor only, we would have an incredible story in those few words. During his public life of over two years Christ had traveled around Palestine. He had worked many miracles, but evidently these were soon forgotten. He had stated that he was the promised Messiah, but very few, if any, believed him. On many occasions he had referred to his sonship with the Father, but even his disciples did not grasp that. The leaders of the Jews were against him from the very beginning, and the people followed their leaders. Like their leaders, the Jews of that day were looking not for a spiritual kingdom after death, but a prosperous, wealthy kingdom here on earth in their own lifetime. So, with the few exceptions, all his calls to repentance and to love of God and neighbor fell on deaf ears. His death at the hands of his enemies was the last straw—that proved the absurdity of his claims to be the Messiah and the Son of God.

Yet what do we find a few years later, after the apparent failure of Calvary? Thousands of those same Jews who ignored or derided Jesus while he was amongst them, were becoming his fervent followers and ardent admirers. They were spreading his teaching among their neighbors. There is no natural explanation for such a change of attitude in a whole people. There is, of course, a supernatural explanation for this change of mind : the resurrection. This fact alone explains the change of outlook on the part of thousands of Jews : this alone explains the fearless courage of the Apostles—the one-time timid group who huddled in an upper-room behind locked doors "for fear of the Jews." Now they were confronting the very Sanhedrin in their stronghold, preaching the risen Christ in the streets of Jerusalem and throughout the land of Palestine. Their power of working miracles, and the visible assistance of the Holy Spirit was moving not only the ordinary laity but many of the priests and leaders in Jerusalem itself, to accept Christ and Christianity (see Acts 6 : 7).

This fact, the resurrection of Christ, is the very foundation stone of our Christian religion. If it had not happened, no Jew would have been converted in Palestine, no Apostle would have the foolhardiness to preach of one who had failed. The Church which Christ promised would have been still-born and would never have survived. But it did exist and it spread. It is still in existence and will be, as long as men are on earth who must be directed to heaven.

The resurrection of Christ is not only the solid basis of our faith, it is also the guarantee for us that we too shall rise, in glorified bodies like his, one day. That day will be our real birthday, the day we are born to unending life. Let us thank God for his love and mercy; he could have ignored us and left us to our fate, but his infinite love did not let him do so. His goodness moved him to share his eternal happiness. That we shall do, if we do what is asked of us while we are here below. When the crosses of life come our way (and who can avoid them?), let us grasp them firmly. We want, and we hope, to be like the risen Christ hereafter; we shall if we, like him, carry our cross cheerfully whenever he asks us to do so.

SECOND READING : 1 John 3 : 18–24. Little children, let us not love in word or speech but in deed and in truth. By this we shall know that we are of the truth, and reassure our hearts before him whenever our hearts condemn us; for God is greater than our hearts, and he knows everything. Beloved, if our hearts do not condemn us, we have confidence before God; and we receive from him whatever we ask, because we keep his commandments and do what pleases him. And this is his commandment, that we should believe in the name of his Son Jesus Christ and love one another, just as he has commanded us. All who keep his commandments abide in him, and he in them. And by this we know that he abides in us, by the Spirit which he had given us.

EXPLANATION : See second Sunday of Easter for an explanation of the first Epistle of John. In today's seven verses, the Beloved Disciple is urging his readers, and all Christians, to believe firmly in Jesus Christ the Son of God, and to love their neighbor with a practical love, a love which will help him in his corporal and spiritual needs.

not . . . in deed : Our love of God and neighbor must prove itself by good deeds. Actions, not declarations, are needed.

we . . . truth : Our charity—love of God and neighbor—alone will prove to us that we have the true faith of Christ, that we are children of God.

reassure our hearts : "hearts" stand for conscience here. If a Christian has doubts about the sincerity of his faith, his practice of true charity should reassure him. He may have some defects but :

God . . . hearts : God's mercy and love are infinite; where one has true charity, his smaller offenses will be generously forgiven—"charity covers a multitude of sins."

he knows everything : Because of his infinite knowledge God is certainly better able to examine our consciences than we ourselves are.

confidence before God : The Christian

whose conscience tells him that he is living in true faith and charity, can feel assured that God will answer all his lawful requests for divine grace and help.

keep his commandments : To keep God's commandments is to please God and when God is pleased with us he will, like a kind Father, help us on our way to heaven.

believe . . . name : This means : to accept Jesus for what he is, not the Messiah only, but the true Son of God himself. This has been the foundation-stone of the Christian religion from its very beginning.

love one another : Fraternal charity for all our fellowmen was the command of Christ and the proof of the sincerity of Christians : "By this will all men know that you are my disciples if you have love one for another" (Jn. 13 : 35).

abide in him : All who keep Christ's commandments are assured of continued communion with God.

by the Spirit : The Holy Spirit, the third person of the Blessed Trinity, dwells in the Christian who is loyal and true to God. The effects of the presence of the Holy Spirit were especially noticeable in the early Church. Wherever the Holy Spirit is there also are the Father and the Son.

APPLICATION: The sincere, active faith and charity which St. John demanded of the first and second generation of Christians in Asia Minor is still demanded of all of us today. Nineteen centuries have elapsed since John wrote that letter, but the essence of the Christian faith has not changed in all those years. If anything, the need today for a living faith, that is, a faith lived daily, and an active charity, is greater than it was in the first century after Christ. The opponents of the Christian faith (the unbelievers, the Agnostics and the humanists) are more numerous in our world today than they were then in Asia Minor. What these opponents of our faith need is not rhetoric or apologetics or logical arguments, but the living example of sincere Christians. There is far too much counterfeit Christianity —a nominal adherence to Christ—while he and everything he taught are denied in practice. Perhaps, therefore, unbelievers and others have some excuse today for despising the Christian religion.

But what they are despising is the counterfeit, the false currency, which is being passed around as Christianity. Some of them, it is true, may not accept the real faith if it is put before them in the lives of true Christians, but many will, and we have, therefore, a grave obligation to put it before them. Instead of denouncing atheistic communism, humanism and all the other substitutes for the truth which men have invented, let us show them the truth by living it to the full. Let us convince them that the future life which God has planned for us, and made available to us through his divine Son Jesus, is a fact of which we are certain and for which we are ready to sacrifice every earthly power,

pleasure and gain. If we are true Christians we must desire and hope that all our fellowmen will become obedient to God, for this is God's desire. That is why his divine Son became man. But, as St. John tells us today, it is not enough to desire and hope for this blessing for all our neighbors, we must show our true desire "in deed and in truth."

This we shall do if we ourselves live up to the teaching of our Christian faith. There are many historical explanations for the loss of the true faith in many of the once Christian nations of the Western world, but the basic cause is the lack of a living, active faith and charity in those who by their position, education and influence, were the leaders of the people. The "isms" of today, the substitutes for true religion, would never take root in a truly Christian soil; they took root and they spread where Christianity was but a name, or worse still a veneer which covered injustice and corruption.

We Christians owe a debt of reparation to all lapsed Christians. We have a grave obligation to bring our brothers who have been led astray by lax and false Christians, back on the true road to heaven. Let us begin today to put our own house in order. Let us see to it that our conscience is right with God and resolve to keep it so. Then we can hope to exercise a quiet but effective influence on our neighbors who have wandered off the highway. Christ told his followers to let their light (of faith and good works) shine before men. If we have not been doing so let us begin today. There are millions groping in the darkness of spiritual despair; we can light their way to God. In God's name let us do so!

GOSPEL: John 15: 1–8. Jesus said to his disciples, "I am the true vine, and my Father is the vinedresser. Every branch of mine that bears no fruit, he takes away, and every branch that does bear fruit he prunes that it may bear more fruit. You are already made clean by the word which I have spoken to you. Abide in me, and I in you. As the branch cannot bear fruit by itself, unless it abides in the vine, neither can you, unless you abide in me. I am the vine, you are the branches. He who abides in me, and I in him, he it is that bears much fruit, for apart from me you can do nothing. If a man does not abide in me, he is cast forth as a branch and withers; and the branches are gathered, thrown into the fire and burned. If you abide in me, and my words abide in you, ask whatever you will, and it shall be done for you. By this my Father is glorified, that you bear much fruit, and so prove to be my disciples."

EXPLANATION: Today's excerpt from St. John's gospel is part of the long discourse our Lord delivered to the Apostles at the Last Supper. It was in the form of a farewell address delivered on the eve of his death. Its purpose was to console and strengthen them to face the ordeals of the coming days. He told them not to be troubled, but to trust in God. Where he was going they would follow him later. He is the Way, the Truth and the Life. He is in the Father and the Father is in him, "if you knew me you would know the Father too." His death will not be the end; he will still live, and they too shall live. His life is not being taken from him, he is laying it down in obedience to his Father. Keeping his commandments will be the proof that they love him: "and anybody who loves me will be loved by my Father" (Jn. 14).

Christ goes on (in chapter 15) to describe the intimate union that must exist between him and his followers, under the image of a vine and its branches. His Father is the vinedresser who will encourage the good and cut off the useless branches. The fruit produced by the vine and branches, by Christ and his followers, will be to God's eternal glory.

I am ... vine: The image of a vine or a vineyard to represent the Chosen People of God was often used in the Old Testament (Is. 5: 1–7; Jer. 2: 21; Ez. 15; Ps. 80: 9–16). Here Christ says that he and his followers will form the new Chosen People. He is the *true* vine, the vine that will bear fruit; the Old Testament was only a shadow, a type of what was to come.

Father ... vinedresser: Christ frequently stresses that he is only the instrument used by his Father. His success as a vine depends on his Father who planted the good vine and cares for it.

takes away: Useless branches are lopped off, the fruit-bearing branches are pruned so that they will produce more fruit.

clean ... spoken: The revelation of God, which he has already given to them, has pruned them, that is, cleansed them from useless growths.

abide in me: As branches, they will wither and die unless they remain attached, that is, united with, the vine.

apart ... nothing: No purely human act can have any salutary value, any value for eternal life, but if it is done under the influence of grace, then it can and is effective. Christ, by his incarnation, death and resurrection, opened the channels of divine grace for man. Because of the foreseen merits of Christ, the effects of the incarnation were retroactive and grace was obtainable before he came.

cast . . . withers : If they persevere in this sinful attitude Christ's followers who fail in their duty will be cut off from the life-giving vine and must of necessity wither and die (spiritually).

ask . . . will : The follower of Christ, who is in intimate union with him, will have every request he makes in prayer granted. Such a Christian's prayer will always be according to the will of God. my Father is glorified : The followers of Christ will add to God's external glory by the good works they do and the fruit they produce. They will produce such fruits only because they are united to the vine who is Christ. They are his true disciples. Through him they glorify the Father.

APPLICATION : The words of consolation and encouragement which our Lord spoke to his Apostles on Holy Thursday night were intended to console and encourage all his followers for all time. They encourage and console us today, and we need encouragement to persevere on the road to heaven. Living a truly Christian life is never easy. We have always the attraction of the world, and the temptations by the agents of evil, to make that life less easy still. But in our own day these difficulties have increased a hundredfold. The attractions of this world have been multiplied by the increased comforts, pleasures and means of self-indulgence which science and technology have put within our reach. Human nature, always inclined to choose the easiest way out, has been given so many means of escape from the strain of self-control that even for a fervent Christian it is frequently very difficult to avoid these worldly allurements.

Having the ordinary comforts of life and the possession of some of this world's goods, is not wrong or anti-Christian, but the natural temptation is to get more and more of these comforts

and riches, and the point is soon reached where this becomes the only purpose in life. When this sad stage is arrived at God and our future life are forgotten; this world becomes our idol and our prison. The temptations which the agents of evil put in Christ's way are also multiplied today. The communications media are now very technically improved and perfected and can be, and sometimes are, a means for good. Unfortunately more frequently they are the channels of bad example. The evil deeds of men have more "news value" than their good deeds. And it is so much easier to follow the bad example! Permissiveness, rejection of authority, glorification of unlawful sexual indulgence, drug addiction, and other such crimes are placed before the minds and the eyes of the youth of today, and are unfortunately copied by far too many.

It is indeed hard to swim against the current; it is so much more pleasant to allow oneself to be carried along without effort by the rushing tide. But when there are rocks and shoals ahead, the thoughtless and ease-seeking swimmer will end in grief. Our Lord has warned us today, as he warned his first followers, to abide in him, to remain closely united with him, as is the branch to the vine, if we hope to bear fruit worthy of heaven. He promises us that if we remain closely united to him, that is, if we strive daily to keep his commandments, he will be ever ready to answer our requests, and to heed all our prayers. The sincere prayer today of every man who is trying to lead a Christian life is for the grace to overcome the allurements of the world, the flesh and the devil. Let us take courage, then. Christ has promised to remain beside us during life if only we stay close to him. While we remain healthy branches of the vine, Christ, we will be on the road to heaven. Our daily tasks, our work as well as our prayer, our recreations as well as our rest, our joys as well as our sorrows, will give glory to God and prove that we are worthy to be called disciples of Christ.

SIXTH SUNDAY OF EASTER

FIRST READING: Acts 10 : 25–26; 34–35; 44–48. When Peter entered, Cornelius met him and fell down at his feet and worshiped him. But Peter lifted him up, saying, "Stand up; I too am a man."

And Peter opened his mouth and said : "Truly I perceive that God shows no partiality, but in every nation any one who fears him and does what is right is acceptable to him."

While Peter was still saying this the Holy Spirit fell on all who heard the word. And the believers from among the circumcised who came with Peter were amazed, because the gift of the Holy Spirit had been poured out even on the Gentiles. For they heard them speaking in tongues and extolling God. Then Peter declared, "Can any one forbid water for baptizing these people who have received the Holy Spirit just as we have?" And he commanded them to be baptized in the name of Jesus Christ. Then they asked him to remain for some days.

EXPLANATION : Today's text from the Acts of the Apostles describes the reception of the first Gentiles into the Christian Church. Cornelius, a Roman centurion stationed in Caesarea, had been an admirer of the God of the Jews. He gave alms generously and prayed much. God told him through an angel to send for Simon Peter who was in Jaffa. Peter, already prepared by a vision of clean and unclean animals (10 : 8–16) in which he was taught that what God had made clean must not be called unclean, came to Caesarea. The vision given him in Jaffa became clear on seeing the religious faith of Cornelius. He had no hesitation in entering a pagan household, something strictly forbidden to a Jew. He preached Christ's life, death and resurrection to the assembled Gentiles and while he was preaching the Holy Spirit descended on them and they began to praise God in various languages, just as the Apostles and disciples had done on Pentecost day in Jerusalem. What greater proof was needed to convince Peter and his companions that God wanted the Gentiles, as well as the Jews, in his Church? Thus Cornelius and his household were baptized in the name of Jesus Christ and became the first Gentiles to enter the Church.

Cornelius . . . feet : The Roman centurion wanted to honor Peter as a God, but Peter made him stand up telling him that he, Peter, was a mere man and should not be honored thus.

Peter said : Having learned from Cornelius about the vision of the angel and the command to send for Peter, the Apostle declares that he now understands that all men, Gentiles as well as Jews, are acceptable to God, if they turn to him. His own vision in Jaffa had prepared him for this.

still . . . this : While Peter was explaining Christ and his teaching (10 : 36-43), the Holy Spirit came upon all the Gentiles present.

believers . . . circumcised : The converted Jews "brothers from Jaffa" (10 : 23) who had accompanied Peter "were amazed that the gift of the Holy Spirit had been poured out even on the Gentiles," for they still had the idea that Christ was the Messiah of the Jews only. Although Peter had no hesitation in accepting Cornelius and his household into the Church, the Council of Jerusalem had to be called to correct this wrong Jewish idea (Acts 15 : 1-29).

Can . . . baptizing : With the incontrovertible evidence that the Holy Spirit had descended on these Gentiles, Peter rightly declared that no man-made opinion could or should prevent them from full membership of the Church. They were then baptized with Christian baptism.

APPLICATION : "God shows no partiality but in every nation anyone who fears him and does what is right is acceptable to him." These inspired and inspiring words of Peter, the head of the Apostles, removed any doubts which his fellow-Jewish-Christians from Jaffa had as to the right of Cornelius and his household to be baptized and become Christians like themselves. They should also have opened the minds of all Jewish converts to the mission of Christ as a mission of salvation for all nations and not for Jews only. Unfortunately, there were some who exaggerated their own claims on God and who still looked down on the Gentiles. There were among the Jewish-Christians those who grudgingly admitted that Gentiles could be received into the Christian Church, but only if they became Jews first by accepting circumcision.

These people were a serious embarrassment to St. Paul in his missionary activity among the Gentiles. They followed him through Asia Minor telling the converted Gentiles that they were not really members of the Christian Church for they had not first become Jews. These "Judaizers" as they were called, were causing such upsets among the Gentile converts that Paul and Barnabas were forced to ask the Apostles, assembled in the first Council of the Church in Jerusalem, to give a definitive answer to this question (Acts 15 : 1–2). They did, and the false teaching of the Judaizers was condemned. Gentiles could and should be received directly into the Church, without passing through any form of Judaism or without accepting any of the Jewish ritualistic practices.

God, through the Holy Spirit, has been with his Church right down through the ages and from its very beginning. The case of conversion of Cornelius, narrated in today's reading, happened in order that Peter, the head of the Apostles and the principal speaker at the Council of Jerusalem, should have visible proof from God that he wished Gentiles to be taken directly into his Church without any of the Jewish ritual observances. Peter's address to the Council, describing what happened at Caesarea, silenced all opposition and settled this question for all time. But before the vision of the clean and unclean animals shown him in Jaffa, and the proofs of the presence of the Holy Spirit which he witnessed in Caesarea, Peter too had his narrow judaizing tendencies.

The lesson for all Christians is that God has been, and will be, always with his Church. Christ has committed it to the care of mortal and fallible men but he has given them (and us) the assurance that he will be with them always even unto the end of time (Mt. 28 : 20). Today, many devout and sincere Christians are worried because of evident dissension between theologians on moral and dogmatic questions. Since the second Vatican Council there has

been a flood of writings from the pens of reputable theologians and sometimes from men with less depth of knowledge and less balanced judgement. This is but a natural consequence of the winds of change to which the saintly Pope John opened the windows of the Church.

Ever since Trent (1546), when the cold-war with the Reformers began, the Catholic Church had remained rather static in its exposition of faith and morals. While the world around us had made giant strides in the study of man and the world in which he lived, and also in the study of ancient literature and culture, our seminary text-books were faithfully copying the sixteenth century expositions of the theologians of that day. This in itself was right as far as it went, since the defined dogmas of the Church remain fixed for all time. However, it did not go far enough; it paid little or no heed to the immense growth in secular knowledge, or to the change in terminology and linguistics which the new philosophies had introduced. Scripture especially which, with Tradition, is the basis of all theology, was very much neglected, to the detriment of our people's knowledge of the revealed world of God.

Thanks to the Holy Spirit, who worked through Pope John and Vatican II, that has all been changed, or rather is being gradually changed. As in all change, there must be upsets and a disturbance of the *status quo ante*. There will be naturally men who oppose change, and on the other hand there are likely to be men who want to change too much. We are going through this period of change at present, and some people are surprised, if not shocked, at some of the moral and dogmatic pronouncements of present-day writers. Knowing, as we do, that the Holy Spirit is with the Church we need have no fear. She has had similar experiences in the past—nearly all her great General Councils were preceded by disputes between theologians and would-be theologizers. The Councils, guided by the Holy Spirit, defined and expounded the true faith.

Truth will prevail; we can look forward confidently to the day when present disputes will end. Our Christian faith and morals will continue to be expounded authoritatively with the backing of the Holy Spirit, by the successors of the Apostles whom he sent to teach all nations.

SECOND READING: 1 John 4:7–10. Beloved, let us love one another; for love is of God, and he who loves is born of God and knows God. He who does not love does not know God; for God is love. In this the love of God was made manifest among us, that God sent his only Son into the world, so that we might live through him. In this is love, not that we loved God but that he loved us and sent his Son to be the expiation for our sins.

EXPLANATION: On this Epistle see above, the second Sunday of Easter. In today's four verses, St. John is urging us to love one another, for we are sons of God whose very essence is love. He proved this when out of the infinity of his love he sent his own divine Son to give us eternal life and make expiation for the sins of the world.

let . . . another: The love St. John urges us to have for our fellowmen is not the natural attraction which has its basis in family bonds, or sex, or some qualities we hold in common. It is that supernatural respect, interest and esteem which we have for all men. It is based on our knowledge of God as our common Father.

love is of God: This supernatural love of neighbor derives from God, whose very nature is love, and it is a free gift which he has instilled into us together with faith and hope in our baptism.

born . . . God: The man who has this supernatural love is a son of God by adoption; it was in his adoption cere-

mony that he was given this gift. He therefore knows God, not in the sense of the Gnostics but in the true sense; he is intimately associated with God through participation in the very nature of God which has been given him in baptism, in the divine gift of love.

God . . . Son: This is the manifestation of God's love for us: he sent his only Son to live and die among us.

might . . . him: Through the incarnation, the coming of God the Son as man among us, we have been made sons of God and heirs of eternal life.

not that we loved God: John is stressing the gratuitousness of God's love for us. He loved us when we were incapable of loving him; even before we existed. His Son died for us while we were still sinners. As St. Paul says: "for someone really worthy a man might be prepared to die—but what proves that God loves us is that Christ died for us while we were still sinners" (Rom. 5: 7–8).

APPLICATION: It is told that when St. John was too old and feeble to say Mass, he insisted on being carried to the Church on Sundays to preach to the congregation. Sunday after Sunday his sermon consisted of one short sentence: "Little children, love one another." After some weeks of this repetition, the presiding priest had the courage to say to the Apostle: "Father, could you not say something more?" The answer that he got was: "No, for if they do this they are doing everything." Undoubtedly the Beloved Disciple was the Apostle of love. His gospel and Epistles are dominated by the thought of "the Word made flesh," the mystery of God's love for us which brought about the incarnation. Having been made children of God, we must, of course, love God for this gratuitious gift; but the real proof of our love of God is our love for our neighbor.

"He who does not love (his neighbor) does not know God." This hardly needs proof. If we do know God we know the marvelous thing he has done for us in making us his children and heirs to heaven through the incarnation, and the natural and supernatural reaction to such knowledge should be the desire to do something for God in return. And God himself through Christ has told us what we can do for him—we can be charitable toward his little ones, our fellow-children of God on earth. Everything kind and good we do for them, we are doing it for himself, he tells us (Mt. 25 : 40).

Therefore, we are expected, and what is more, we are commanded to love all God's children. This is the way in which the good God allows us to make some little return for all he has done for us. Generous souls would not need a commandment, they would rejoice at the opportunity of doing something for God, but most of us are not too given to generosity, and so God has given us a commandment to do our duty. On the fulfilling of that commandment our own eternal welfare will depend. "I was hungry and you fed me, I was naked and you clothed me, I was sick, I was in prison, and you visited me; well done good and faithful servant enter into the joy of the Lord."

These are words we all would like to hear when called to judgement. We shall hear them if we keep our part of the contract. If we carry out the spiritual and corporal works of mercy, whenever and wherever we can, we need have no fear about God doing his part. We may not have much of this world's goods, and we may not be able therefore to help our neighbor much in his bodily needs, but we can help him with our prayers, with words of consolation and encouragement. There is a little poem on kindness written by Father Faber which brings out what a help even the poorest of us can be to his neighbor, if only true charity inspires us. It runs like this:

"It was but a sunny smile and little
    it cost in the giving,
But it scattered the night like the
    morning light
And made the day worth living.

It was only a kindly word, a word
    that was easily spoken,
But it was not in vain for it chilled
    the pain
Of a heart that was nearly broken.

It was but a helping hand and it
    seemed of little availing,
But its clasp was warm and it saved
    from harm
A brother whose strength was failing."

Which of us is so poor in spirit, so weak in charity, that he cannot give a sunny smile to his neighbor whenever he meets him; or speak a kind word to someone in need of consoling, or give a helping hand, be it ever so little, to one in greater need than himself?

GOSPEL: John 15:9-17. Jesus said to his disciples, "As the Father has loved me, so have I loved you; abide in my love. If you keep my commandments, you will abide in my love, just as I have kept my Father's commandments and abide in his love. These things I have spoken to you, that my joy may be in you, and that your joy may be full.

"This is my commandment, that you love one another as I have loved you. Greater love has no man than this, that a man lay down his life for his friends. You are my friends if you do what I command you. No longer do I call you servants, for the servant does not know what his master is doing; but I have called you friends, for all that I have heard from my Father I have made known to you. You did not choose me, but I chose you and appointed you that you should go and bear fruit and that your fruit should abide; so that whatever you ask the Father in my name, he may give it to you. This I command you, to love one another."

EXPLANATION: Today's verses are a continuation of last Sunday's quotation from our Lord's Last Supper discourse to his disciples on Holy Thursday night. In last Sunday's gospel, our Lord used the image of the vine and the branches to describe the intimate association between himself and his followers that was necessary if his disciples were to produce fruit for eternal life. Today, our Lord urges his followers to abide in his love and to love one another. This love for neighbor must have as its model and exemplar Christ's love for his disciples, which made him lay down his life for them. The disciples are not Christ's servants but his intimate associates: they will bear lasting fruit in their life-work if they trust in God and are motivated by true love of God and neighbor.

As the Father has loved me: The Father loves the Son with an infinite love. As God, Christ's love for his followers (represented by the disciples) is infinite; as man, it is as complete as human love can be.

if . . . commandments: God's commandments were Christ's also. Keeping the commandment's is man's way of proving his love for Christ.

I have . . . commandments: As man, he obeyed every wish and command of the Father in every detail, "not my will but thine be done."

greater . . . friends: There is nothing greater that a man can do for those he loves, than to give his life for them. Christ did this.

servant . . . know: His relationship with his disciples was not that of master and servant, for he had brought them into the intimacy of the divine family. He had revealed the Father to them during his years with them; he had made them adopted sons of the Father.

I chose you : Their vocation was Christ's free gift to them. He chose them, not they him.

bear fruit : That fruit for heaven was the number of their brothers who would be brought to eternal life. This fruit will last forever.

ask . . . name : He is their (and our) mediator with God. All our petitions to the Father, made through him, will be answered because by his life, death and resurrection he has earned for us all spiritual and where necessary for the spiritual, temporal rewards.

This I command you : Christ ends by repeating the second of the greatest commandments : love of neighbor.

APPLICATION : It is only a few weeks since Good Friday when we commemorated the agonizing death of Christ on Mount Calvary. This was an excruciating, shameful death even for hardened criminals who deserved it. But for our loving Savior, the innocent lamb of God, one who had never offended God or neighbor, it was something of which the whole human race should be ashamed forever. What caused Christ that torment and death on the cross was our sins, the sins of all mankind and not the spite and hatred of his Jewish opponents, who were only instruments in the tragedy. Atonement had to be made to God for the sins of the world, so that men could reach the eternal inheritance which the incarnation made available to them. However, not all the acts of the entire human race could make a sufficient atonement to God. A sacrifice, an expiation of infinite value was needed. The death of the Son of God in his human nature was alone capable of making such an expiation.

That Christ willingly accepted crucifixion for our sakes, that he gave the greatest proof of love which the world has ever known, by laying down his life for his friends, did not make his suffer-

ings any less, did not ease any of the pains of Calvary. His agony in the Garden before his arrest shows this : he foresaw all the tortures and pains which he was to undergo and sweated blood at the thought of what awaited him. But he was to keep his Father's commandment : "not my will but thine be done." We Christians must have hearts of stone, hearts devoid of all sense of gratitude, when we forget what Christ has done for us and deliberately offend him! Alas, this is what all of us do sometimes, and many of us do all the time. Christ died to bring us to heaven but we tell him, by our sins, that he was wasting his time. We do not want to go to heaven, we are making our happiness here!

How far can human ingratitude and thanklessness go? Christ told us, through the disciples on Holy Thursday night, that he had made us his friends, his intimates. We are no longer servants in the household, who merely earn their daily wage and have no intimacy with the family and no hope of ever sharing in the family possessions. Instead, we have been adopted into the family by Christ becoming man, we have been guaranteed all the rights of children : intimacy with the Father, Son and Holy

Spirit and the future sharing in the eternal happiness of that divine household. Christ's incarnation made us God's children; Christ's death on the cross removed sin. Sin is the one obstacle that could prevent us reaching our eternal inheritance.

Because God gave us a free will we can in a moment of folly, a moment of madness really, deprive ourselves of the privileges and possessions which Christ has made available to us. We can choose to exchange an eternity of happiness for a few fleeting years of self-indulgence on earth. We can fling Christ's gift of love back in his face and tell him we don't want it. God forbid that we should ever act like this, that we should ever forget God's purpose in creating us. It is a marvelous thing to be alive, if we have hope in a future life. If nothing awaited us but the grave, then to live on this earth, which is a valley of sorrow and tears for the vast majority, would be the cruelest of jests. But of this we need have no fear. Life on earth is but a short prelude to our real existence. If we use this brief period as Christ has told us how to use it, death for us will be the passage into the eternal mansions. Be grateful to God, Father, Son and Holy Spirit; love the Blessed Trinity; prove your love by loving your fellowmen. By doing this you are fulfilling the whole law and the prophets; and you are assuring yourself of the place in heaven which Christ has won for you.

THE ASCENSION OF OUR LORD

FIRST READING : Acts 1 : 1–11. In the first book, O Theophilus, I have dealt with all that Jesus began to do and teach, until the day when he was taken up, after he had given commandment through the Holy Spirit to the Apostles whom he had chosen. To them he presented himself alive after his passion by many proofs, appearing to them during forty days, and speaking of the kingdom of God. And while staying with them he charged them not to depart from Jerusalem, but to wait for the promise of the Father, which, he said, "you heard from me, for John baptized with water, but before many days you shall be baptized with the Holy Spirit."

So when they had come together, they asked him, "Lord, will you at this time restore the kingdom to Israel?" He said to them, "It is not for you to know times or seasons which the Father has fixed by his own authority. But you shall receive power when the Holy Spirit has come upon you; and you shall be my witnesses in Jerusalem and in all Judea and Samaria and to the end of the earth." And when he had said this, as they were looking on, he was lifted up, and a cloud took him out of their sight. And while they were gazing into heaven as he went, behold, two men stood by them in white robes, and said, "Men of Galilee, why do you stand looking into heaven? This Jesus, who was taken up from you into heaven, will come in the same way as you saw him go into heaven."

EXPLANATION : St. Luke begins his second book, called Acts of the Apostles, with a brief description of our Lord's bodily ascension into heaven, after he had given his Apostles their final instructions. He identifies the exact location of this event as Mount Olivet, both here and in his gospel (24 : 50). In Acts he seems to imply that forty days elapsed between the resurrection and ascension. All the other writings of the New Testament assume that the ascension took place immediately after the resurrection, which would be according to the nature of things. This was also the belief of the Church for the first three centuries; the ascension was then closely associated with the resurrection ceremonies. It was only from the fourth century that a special feast of the ascension, forty days after Easter (following the Lucan date), came to be celebrated.

That our Lord, in his glorified body,

took his place at the right hand of the Father is the dogmatic and historical fact, and the time, most likely, if not certainly, was resurrection day. Luke's forty days is most likely a round number, not to be taken literally, for our Lord's "appearances" in human form to his disciples. These appearances were repeated over a period of two weeks or so (see Jn. 20 : 19; 26; 21 : 1).

the first book . . . day: In his gospel Luke describes the resurrection, the appearances to two disciples on the road to Emmaus, an appearance to Simon (Peter), an appearance to the eleven Apostles and some disciples (all apparently on the resurrection day), and finally his ascension from the outskirts of Bethany which is part of Mount Olivet.

to them he presented . . . alive: Christ proved he had risen—"he was alive again,"—by his appearances to them over a period of time (see above on the forty days).

while staying . . . depart . . . Jerusalem: They were to wait in Jerusalem to receive the Holy Spirit whom he had promised to send them from the Father, when he had returned to the Father (Jn. 14 : 26; 16 : 6ff).

you . . . be baptized . . . Holy Spirit: The Baptist's baptism with water was an external sign of internal change of heart, the descent of the Holy Spirit will bring about a complete change of mind and heart in the Apostles.

restore the rule of Israel now: The Apostles were still expecting a messianic kingdom for Israel, or perhaps a theocratic kingdom here on earth, to be established when Christ would return in glory.

my witnesses . . . earth: Our Lord's answer seems to be that he understood their question to refer to his second coming, the time of which was a secret God was not revealing. The second part, however, the missionary activity of the Apostles from Jerusalem to the ends of the earth, implied that his kingdom was not for Israel alone and that the second coming was in the far distant future.

lifted up . . . their sight: Each time he appeared to his Apostles, he disappeared again. Luke, perhaps because he is describing the last appearance here, describes his departure as an ascension, as heaven the abode of God, was thought to be above the skies.

why do you stand . . . heaven: This is probably a reprimand for those Christians who, instead of earning their daily bread, were awaiting in idleness for the second coming of Christ, at the time Luke was writing (see 2 Thess.).

Jesus who was taken up from you: Their beloved master will return (some day) as Judge of all. In the meantime they had their apostolic life-work to fulfill.

APPLICATION: The ascension or the return of Christ to heaven, in his human but glorified body, is the culmination, the sign and seal of the accomplishment of his salvific mission on earth. He, the Son of God, the second divine Person of the Blessed Trinity, became man, lived and died on this earth so that we men could live with God forever in heaven. By his death on the cross, he reconciled sinful man with his divine Creator. His human death earned for us a share in the divine life. His resurrection is the divine guarantee that we too shall rise again, and his ascension to the Father is the prelude to our entrance into God's everlasting kingdom.

Christ, our Savior, our intimate friend, who suffered hardships, humiliations, and finally the painful and degrading death on the cross for our sakes, while here on earth, is now seated in the place of honor at the right hand of the Father in heaven. He is there as our representative and as our intercessor. He has gone to heaven to prepare a place there for us. He said to his Apostles (and through them to all of us) at the Last Supper: "In my Father's house there are many dwelling places . . . I am going to prepare a place for you and then I shall come back to take you with me, that where I am you also may be" (Jn. 14 : 2–3).

What a consolation, what a source of joy this feast of the ascension is for any true believer! It is the natural desire (indeed the supernatural desire, for it is instilled in our very nature at creation)

of every human being to keep on living —death is the negation of everything we love and have. However, we know that earthly death awaits every one of us. Our human make-up is of its nature mortal. How sad it would be, and how dreadful it must be for those who do not believe in God, if the grave were the final end for us.

We Christians know it is not the end but rather the beginning and today's feast is the reminder of this consoling fact. We shall all leave this world some day soon, but for a true Christian, this thought should be a cause for joy rather than sadness. We leave this valley of tears to go on an eternal holiday. Christ has won this divine heritage for us; he has promised he is preparing a place in his own heavenly home for us and he is helping us on our way there. What have we to fear from earthly death? It is not the entrance to a perpetual prison but rather the door to our eternal happiness.

SECOND READING: Ephesians 1 : 17–23. May the God of our Lord Jesus Christ, the Father of glory, give you a spirit of wisdom and of revelation in the knowledge of him, having the eyes of your hearts enlightened, that you may know what is the hope to which he has called you, what are the riches of his glorious inheritance in the saints, and what is the immeasurable greatness of his power in us who believe, according to the working of his great might which he accomplished in Christ when he raised him from the dead and made him sit at his right hand in the heavenly places, far above all rule and authority and power and dominion, and above every name that is named, not only in this age but also in that which is to come; and he has put all things under his feet and has made him the head over all things for the Church, which is his body, the fullness of him who fills all in all.

EXPLANATION: St. Paul is praying God to give his Ephesian converts an ever deeper insight into the mercy and love of God the Father who made them members of Christ in the Church and called them to share in the divine heritage. They have been made members of the mystical body of which Christ is the

Head. The Father raised Christ from the dead and gave him the principal place in heaven. The Church continues daily to increase in numbers and in grace until it completes the fullness (pleroma) of Christ who himself, by his resurrection and ascension, fills and fulfills the divine plan for the universe (see 1 : 10).

God of our Lord Jesus Christ : Paul is praying to the Holy Trinity; to God the Father of Jesus, who is "Lord," i.e. God also, that he may send the Spirit of wisdom on the Ephesian converts.

the hope to which he . . . called you : The real meaning of the Christian faith they have received.

riches . . . inheritance : They have been called to partake in the eternal happiness of the Trinity.

immeasurable . . . of his power : What God does for those who believe in Christ, is to raise them to a supernatural state—to sonship with God—only divine power could do this.

great might . . . accomplished : The resurrection and exaltation of Christ in his human nature was an act of divine power. Christians will also be raised and given a place of honor by the same divine power.

far above . . . dominion : Christ in his human nature is next to God in heaven, above all other creatures.

all things under his feet : The Father has subjected all creatures to Christ, whether past, present or future. Not only man but also all other created beings insofar as they share in the cosmic rebirth brought about by the Incarnation.

APPLICATION : St. Paul reminded the Ephesians nearly nineteen and a half centuries ago of the marvelous generosity and goodness of God who had made them Christians and sharers-to-be in the glory of Christ, which was the eternal glory of God. The words the Apostle wrote to those first converts were written for us also and are as applicable to us today as they were in the year 61 A.D. He prayed that God would enlighten their minds to try to understand and appreciate the marvelous things God had done for them through the Incarnation, death, resurrection and ascension of our Savior, Jesus Christ.

Which of us can say that we really appreciate, as we should, these same marvelous things God has done for us? Because Christ came on earth we have been given the power to go to heaven. As mere creatures we have no such power and not even the slightest claim

to any such extraordinary gift. We, as creatures, are by our very nature, mortal. Death on earth should be our final end. But because the infinitely good and generous God wished to raise us up to the status of adopted sons of his, and to make us capable of sharing, in as far as our limited nature could, in his eternal life and happiness, he sent his divine Son on earth to share in our humanity.

This is the mystery of the Incarnation, the mystery of God's love for us, a love of which we are utterly unworthy. Today we are commemorating the final act in this drama of divine love. God the Son, returning to his Father, bearing our human nature and guaranteeing to each one of us that we too, when we leave this earth, will find our true life, our unending life, in the home of the Father with Christ, our true Brother.

Cast your eyes heavenwards today, where Christ now dwells surrounded by millions of our fellowmen, and say to yourself : There is my true home, there is where I shall be forever at peace with God, with neighbor and with myself. Millions of my fellowmen have already got there. I have the same weaknesses which they had. I have the same strength and helps that they got. Why should I not make it? The one and only person who could stop me from getting to my heavenly home is myself. Could I ever be so foolish? God forbid!

GOSPEL : Mark 16 : 15–20. Jesus said to the eleven, "Go into all the world and preach the gospel to the whole creation. He who believes and is baptized will be saved; but he who does not believe will be condemned. And these signs will accompany those who believe : in my name they will cast out demons; they will speak in new tongues; they will pick up serpents, and if they drink any deadly thing, it will not hurt them; they will lay their hands on the sick, and they will recover."

So then the Lord Jesus, after he had spoken to them, was taken up into heaven, and sat down at the right hand of God. And they went forth and preached everywhere, while the Lord worked with them and confirmed the message by the signs that attended it.

EXPLANATION : Much has been written over the centuries on the ending of Mark's gospel. Some hold that it ends at verse 8, but the abruptness of this ending and the use of "gar"="for" as the concluding word makes this very improbable. The most plausible solution to this question is that the last page of the original manuscript of Mark's gospel got lost and the present ending was composed by some later writer to fill out the picture. As far as we are concerned, whether or not it was Mark himself who wrote verses 9 to 20, they are inspired. Trent decreed expressly that all our present text was written under inspiration. The ending of Mark was explicitly discussed at the Council. In the last six verses of the present closing chapter of Mark, we have Christ's appearance to the eleven after his resurrection, their apostolic commission, Christ's Ascension to the right hand of God, and the Apostles carrying out their commission of preaching aided by miraculous powers from God.

appeared . . . eleven : The unfortunate Judas had taken his own life, so the Apostles were reduced to eleven. Mark (or his continuer) does not tell where this vision took place, but as Christ ascended after he had given them their apostolic commission it would seem to be somewhere outside of Jerusalem. In St. Luke's Gospel and Acts, the Ascension took place from the Mount of Olives, which overlooks the city of Jerusalem.

Go . . . world : Christ had come, as he had said and as the prophets of the Old Testament had foretold, for the salvation and elevation of all men, so now he gives the same universal mission to his Apostles, and necessarily also to their successors, because the Apostles could not and did not fulfill his command in their lifetime.

whole creation : That is, to all men of every race and nation. Only men could accept and profit by the message.

believes . . . saved : The 'man who accepts the story of Christ, that is, the Christian message, and receives baptism which incorporates him in the body of Christ his Church, is on the road to heaven. He still has some essential duties to perform to get there.

who . . . believe : The man who is offered the knowledge of Christ with proofs of its authenticity and truth, and deliberately refuses to accept Christ and Christianity, is condemning himself.

these signs : Christ promises miraculous powers not only to his Apostles but to all who believe in him. The power to cast out demons, speak foreign languages, escape poisoning and the power to cure the sick, are some of the miraculous powers promised. That the early Church had such powers is clear from the Acts and from the Letters of St. Paul.

was taken . . . heaven : According to the Jewish ideas of the time heaven, the abode of God, was above the skies. Christ disappeared in the direction of the sky to convince his Apostles of his return to the Father. The father it was who "took him up" in his glorified human nature.

sat . . . God : This was the chief place of honor.

went forth everywhere : In one verse this gospel gives us the missionary activity of the Apostles. They set out, eventually, from Jerusalem and carried the message of Christ, the good news of the gospel, as far as they could.

Lord . . . them : Their preaching was confirmed by the miracles which Jesus worked through them, miracles which confirmed the faith of the Apostles and of their converts.

APPLICATION : Christ came on earth to carry out his Father's eternal plan of salvation for all mankind. Having fulfilled his Father's will, he returned with his risen, glorified body to take his place of honor in heaven as God and man. But before taking this last step in the process of salvation, Christ solemnly commissioned his Apostles, and through them their successors, to bring the good news of what had been done for them to all men. Lest they should be frightened at the thought of such a difficult and indeed tremendous task, he promised to be with them always, encouraging and confirming them.

Christ, the Son of God, not only won salvation for all men, he put the means of salvation within the easy reach of all men of all time. That day on the Mount of Olives, when commissioning his Apostles, Christ had you and me before his eyes. Thousands of years and thousands of miles intervene, but to the Lord a thousand years is but a day, for everything is present to his infinite mind. He saw the saints and the sinners of all ages and nations, and he saw the innumerable millions in between, who, like ourselves, are neither great saints nor great sinners. Weak, fickle and ungenerous though we be, on that day he arranged that his message of hope and encouragement would reach us.

We have received the faith of Christ which gives us a full explanation of life and death. From it we learn where we came from and whither we are going. We have received the sacrament of baptism, which he instituted on that

Ascension day, as the door which admits us to brotherhood with himself and therefore to sonship with God. He had already left to his Church, which he had founded, all the other aids necessary for our journey, including the greatest gift of them all: himself in the Blessed Eucharist to be our spiritual nourishment on the way.

Only an infinite mind could make such long-range plans, only infinite love could make such preparations for our eternal happiness. Christ was God, and his knowledge, his power and his love as God are infinite. He used that infinite power on our behalf in order to share the happiness of the Blessed Trinity with us forever. But how do we react to this love and benevolence shown to us by Christ. Very often, I fear, coldly and ungratefully. "Thank you, dear God, for all you have done for me, and thank you especially for the great future you have in store for me!" How many times did any of us say that since last Sunday? But we were so busy over the daily chores we did not really have time! How long does it take to say: "Thank you, God"? What is more, the daily chores whether they be in the kitchen, factory, office or the field, are means of thanking God if only we do them with the intention of honoring him. He knows we have to earn our daily bread, but by earning it honestly and faithfully we are turning it into bread for heaven.

Look up to heaven today. See Christ ascending to his Father and our Father. Say from your heart a sincere solemn: "Thank you, God, for creating me. Thank you especially for giving me, through the incarnation of your beloved Son the honor of being adopted by you and of being made an heir to your eternal happiness. Give me, O loving Father, the grace and the strength to keep your commandments, to be a loving, grateful child while here on earth, so that I may be found worthy to receive my promised inheritance when my day of reckoning comes." For every prayer I say for success in life, I should say three for a successful death, a death free from sin and at peace with God.

SEVENTH SUNDAY OF EASTER

FIRST READING: Acts 1:15-17; 20-26. Peter stood up among the brethren (the company of persons was in all about a hundred and twenty), and said, "Brethren, the scripture had to be fulfilled, which the Holy Spirit spoke beforehand by the mouth of David, concerning Judas who was guide to those who arrested Jesus. For he was numbered among us, and was allotted his share in this ministry. For it is written in the book of Psalms, 'His office let another take.' So one of the men who have accompanied us during all the time that the Lord Jesus went in and out among us, beginning from the baptism of John until the day when he was taken up from us—one of these men must become with us a witness to his resurrection." And they put forward two, Joseph called Barsabbas, who was surnamed Justus, and Matthias. And they prayed and said, "Lord, who knowest the hearts of all men, show which one of these two thou hast chosen to take the place in this ministry and apostleship from which Judas turned aside, to go to his own place." And they cast lots for them, and the lot fell on Matthias; and he was enrolled with the eleven apostles.

EXPLANATION: According to the account of the Ascension given in Acts, Christ told his Apostles to wait in Jerusalem for the descent of the Holy Spirit before beginning their missionary activity. The eleven Apostles, together with a large number of disciples as well as Mary the Mother of Jesus and some of his cousins and some other women, met frequently for prayer. During the ten days that they awaited the coming of the Holy Spirit, Peter, the recognized head of the group, decided it was necessary to elect a man who had been with Christ during his public life, to fill the apostleship vacated by Judas.

Peter ... brethren: Brothers or brethren was a title for Christians; it was in use at the time Acts was written, and perhaps from the very beginning (see Acts 11:1; 12:17-18).

about one hundred and twenty: Most, if not all, of the seventy-two disciples who had followed our Lord were still faithful to him and some others had evidently joined since.

scripture ... fulfilled: The verses from two psalms quoted by St. Peter refer to the treatment an enemy deserves, and

God is invoked to see that this punishment is carried out.

Holy Spirit spoke : Peter accepts these psalms as Davidic and as inspired by the Holy Spirit.

Judas guide : Peter sees Judas as the enemy who deserves God's punishment.

His office . . . take : Psalm 69 : 25 is omitted in the reading here, but psalm 109 : 8 is given. It is interpreted by Peter as requiring to be fulfilled, for Judas lost his position as a member of Christ's Apostles. That place must be filled.

beginning . . . John : The man to be chosen to take the place of Judas must be one who has been with Christ from the very beginning of his public life.

witness to his resurrection : This was to be the central and basic point of the apostolic preaching, as it was the crowning point in the Christian event. If Christ had not risen there would have been no apostolic ministry and no Christian Church. The candidate to be chosen then must be able to testify to the resurrection and also to the preaching and miracles of Jesus.

put forward two : Those present presented two men who fulfilled the qualities demanded by Peter.

prayed and said : They now request the Lord (Christ) to decide for them which of the two men : "thou hast chosen" as Apostle.

Judas . . . place : The reference is to the desertion of Judas, who turned aside from the ministry and went his own way.

they cast lots : This would be in accordance with ancient Jewish custom. When an answer was wanted from God, the high priest cast lots for a "yes" or "no" with the Urim and Thumim. It was firmly believed that God would bring out the right answer. Here the Apostles and disciples had no hesitation in attributing the choice to Christ. The lot fell on Matthias and he was immediately enrolled with the eleven Apostles.

APPLICATION : The only activity (apart from prayer) taken by the Apostles and disciples between the Ascension and the descent of the Holy Spirit was, according to Acts, this election of a successor to Judas. It was an important step, for the Apostles saw themselves as chosen by Christ to be the twelve Patriarchs of the New Israel. Christ had for this reason (so they understood) chosen twelve and it was necessary that that number should be complete. Secondly, what was very important in this action taken by Peter as head of the Apostles was the question of who should replace Judas. It was necessary that he should have been an eye-witness of Christ's public ministry from the baptism by John until his Ascension. The reason for this was that this new Apostle should, like the other eleven, be able to teach all that Christ had said and done, be an eye-witness, in other words, to the Christian faith, the basic truth and proof of which was the resurrection.

Here we have the solid basis for teaching by Tradition, a doctrine always held by the Church, laid down from the very beginning of Christianity. There were not as yet, nor for years afterwards, any written accounts of the teaching and the doings of Jesus. But the facts and the truths of the Christian faith were preached by men who had been eye-witnesses of what they preached—the first and second generation converts accepted their word without questioning, and rightly so. These Apostles had nothing to gain, but everything to lose, by preaching this gospel. They brought on themselves hardships, imprisonment, tortures because they preached Christ. No sane men would take on such a campaign unless absolutely convinced of the truth of what they preached and the necessity of its acceptance by all who heard them.

One by one, the Apostles gave their lives gladly for their faith in Christ, but before their departure the torch had been handed on to others who in turn devoted their lives to carrying it further. At least thirty-five years later the first gospel, and almost seventy later St. John's gospel, incorporated this teaching of the Apostles. It was but a faithful account of what Jesus said and did, put in abbreviated form into our four gospels under the guidance of the Holy Spirit and so we got the double stream that flows from the same source— Sacred Scripture and Tradition. In order to fulfill their commission of preaching the true Christian message to all nations the Apostles had, of necessity, the power and authority to interpret and explain what they preached, as well as the compelling duty to correct or condemn any false meaning attributed to what they preached. This power, essential in the Church of Christ for all ages, was handed on by them to their successors and so we have the living teaching authority of the Christian Church stemming from Christ himself. Such an authority was necessary during the first two generations—the age of oral tradition alone when at least some of the Apostles were alive. However, it was even more necessary when the written word came into common use. By then the authoritative voices of the Apostles themselves were silenced. But Christ had provided for the safe-keeping of his doctrine in his Church.

In itself the election of Matthias to replace the traitor Judas, may not be of great interest to us. There is not a single mention of this Matthias after that. But the providence of God which, working through Peter, assured us and the Church of Christ for all time that the true faith would be handed down to the Church and preserved in all its purity, is of the greatest importance to us and is a convincing proof that while we follow the definite teaching of the Church we are on the right road laid down for us by our Savior.

In an age like ours, an age of doubt, vacillation, agnosticism in matters of faith and morals, it is surely a consolation and a security to know that while we believe and act with the Church, we are believing and acting with Christ. We are living our lives as Christ wants us to live them, in a way, that is, which leads eventually but securely to heaven.

SECOND READING: 1 John 4:11-16. Beloved, if God so loved us, we also ought to love one another. No man has ever seen God; if we love one another, God abides in us and his love is perfected in us.

By this we know that we abide in him and he in us, because he has given us of his own Spirit. And we have seen and testify that the Father has sent his Son as the Savior of the world. Whoever confesses that Jesus is the Son of God, God abides in him, and he in God. So we know and believe the love God has for us. God is love, and he who abides in love abides in God, and God abides in him.

EXPLANATION: These verses read today are a continuation of those from the same Epistle read on the Sixth Sunday of Easter—see above.

If God ... us: John has described how God's love for us went to the extreme of sending his beloved Son on earth as man. He concludes from this that surely we should give our little bit of finite love to God in return, but the way to prove this gift of ours is to love our fellowmen.

has ... God: God is a pure Spirit not visible to human eyes. We shall be able to see him in our glorified bodies, after our resurrection, with the aid of the grace of the beatific vision.

if we ... another: Even though we cannot see God on this earth, we can experience his presence and feel the true love for him expand in our hearts *if we love one another.*

God ... us: God is in our wills and intellects, urging us on to live according to the truth and to choose what is good always. He is thus proving his loving interest in us and moving us to love him more and more.

given ... Spirit: On the first Pentecost day the Holy Spirit descended on the Apostles and made his presence manifest not only to them but to all the Jews who gathered around the Cenacle. He came (visibly by his powers) on all the early Christian converts (see Acts passim; 1 Cor. 12). He is still present to every Christian who is in the state of grace, urging him to what is right and good.

Son ... world: This is the highest imaginable act of love for us. The Father asked his divine Son to endure the humiliation of the incarnation and the torture of crucifixion so that we, his creatures, could have everlasting life.

Jesus ... God: To confess this, the central doctrine of the Christian faith, requires the gift of faith which God alone gives. He who makes this confession of faith does so because he is moved to do so by the special gift of God—faith.

God is love: His very nature is to love with an infinite, an unlimited love.

who ... love: The Christian, or he who through no fault of his own has not heard of Christ and his message, who loves his neighbor out of unselfish love, or because he is a fellow-child of God on the road to heaven, is in close intimacy with God.

APPLICATION: This teaching of St. John on the necessity of loving our fellowmen is well known to all of us but how many of us really and truly practice this kind of unselfish love? Is there one among us who really loves his neighbor as he loves himself? Yet, this is the criterion by which our love is judged. Far too many Christians are so preoccupied with their own difficulties in life that they have little or no time to stop and help a fellowman who is lying idly or helplessly by the roadside. Yet it is exactly by helping our fellowman in need that we successfully overcome our own difficulties. For when we practice charity toward our neighbor "we abide in God and God abides in us," as St. John tells us, and if God is with us it matters not who is against us?

Yes, it is God's plan that we travel to heaven in groups, in pre-arranged parties. God wants the whole group there, and in his plan some are less capable of making the journey so that the able-bodied members and the more qualified ones, should have an opportunity of paying for their own passage by helping their needy fellow-travelers. This is part of God's love for us; he puts in our way the opportunity to prove our love for him by bestowing loving help on our neighbor.

Let us look around us and see who are those that God in his mercy has put in our particular traveling party. First comes our own family. Not only are we bound by ties of flesh and blood to help them in this life, we are also bound by the commandment of charity to cherish them as we do ourselves. If we ourselves want to be saved—and that is why we are Christians—we must also want to have our families reunited with us later on. Husband and wife must help one another to live according to the Christian standards every day of their lives. Both parents must work in close and fervent cooperation to prepare their children not only to make a living in this world but especially and above all to make them good citizens of heaven.

After the family come relatives, nearest neighbors, those we meet at work or casually. They have next claim on our sincere Christian love. We cannot exempt ourselves from carrying out the spiritual works of mercy on the ground that we cannot go on the mission fields. If we are truly charitable, occasions can be found for exercising these good works without ever leaving our own home-town, or maybe our own street. Generous souls will, while carrying out their duties of charity nearer home, also find ways of helping the spread of the faith in foreign lands.

We all want to be saved; we shall, if we help our fellow-travelers on the way. These are not only the people who need bodily help, but also and especially those in need of spiritual light and encouragement—the sinners, the lax, the careless and the lapsed Christians. These need our help. It is with these that our Lord would associate if he were among us today, as he did in Palestine. Mary Magdalene. Zachaeus and the thousands of other sinners of that day, are now in heaven because Christ had an encouraging word, a word of love and hope, for them. They reacted to his sincere love. Let us try to imitate that love of Christ, if only from afar, and our sinner neighbors too will react to the little ray of divine love which our charity sheds on them.

GOSPEL: John 17:11-19. Jesus lifted up his eyes to heaven and said, "Holy Father, keep them in thy name, which thou hast given me, that they may be one, even as we are one. While I was with them, I kept them in thy name, which thou hast given me; I have guarded them, and none of them is lost but the son of perdition, that the scripture might be fulfilled. But now I am coming to thee; and these things I speak in the world, that they may have my joy fulfilled in themselves. I have given them thy word; and the world has hated them because they are not of the world, even as I am not of the world. I do not pray that thou shouldst take them out of the world, but that thou shouldst keep them from the evil one. They are not of the world, even as I am not of the world. Sanctify them in the truth; thy word is truth. As thou didst send me into the world, so I have sent them into the world. And for their sake I consecrate myself, that they also may be consecrated in truth."

EXPLANATION: Our Lord's long discourse at the Last Supper ends with the priestly prayer of Christ for his Apostles and for all those who through the preaching of the Apostles would believe in him—the Christians of all ages. Today's verses deal with the Apostles. Jesus, who knows he is about to finish the work given him on earth and return to his Father in heaven, prays that the disciples the Father has given him will remain united in true faith and love in order to carry out the mission he has given them. Their task will be hard, for though living in this world their activities will be directed to the other world, and the worldly-minded opponents of things spiritual will hate them as they hated him before them.

keep . . . name: Christ appeals to his heavenly Father to protect and keep true to their vocation the disciples he had given Christ.

one . . . one: God the Father and Son were one by nature and divine perfection. The disciples could only imitate this unity from afar, but they could have perfect human unity among themselves.

none . . . but: All his Apostles had remained faithful to him, and continued to remain so in spite of the shock his crucifixion and death caused them. One, however, had defected; this was foreseen, "that the scripture might be fulfilled," but not pre-ordained. Judas acted with full freedom. The fact that God *foresaw* what he did in no way impeded Judas' freedom of action. God sees now where I shall end up on my judgement day, but I shall end up there because of my own free decision. It is the sum-total of these free decisions that God already sees.

I am . . . thee: As Jesus is very soon to return to his Father, the disciples will be left alone in the world, but Christ prays the Father to let them also share in the joy of his reunion with his Father.

given . . . word: He has revealed God to them, and his own intimate connexion with God in as far as they were, as yet, able to grasp all this.

world . . . them: As nearly always in St. John, the term "world" is used in the sense of the evil that is in this world. This evil wanted to have nothing to do with Christ or his talk of a future spiritual life. This same hatred included his Apostles, especially after his departure.

out . . . world : To carry out their mission the Apostles must remain and work in the midst of this evil world and, therefore, Christ's request to the Father is not to let them be overcome by this evil.

sanctify . . . truth : The Apostles are the priests of the New Law, and as priests of the temple were consecrated before beginning their functions, Christ now asks the Father to consecrate his disciples to the ministry of preaching the word of God which is "truth" itself.

didst send me : The Father had sent Christ in the incarnation into this world; so now Christ sends his Apostles to preach the truths about God and men, which he had given them. In Jn. 20 : 21 their mission is given to the Apostles, but Christ's prayer, as given here, foresees the future as already accomplished.

I consecrate myself : Jesus' sacrificial act on Calvary next day was the culmination of his sacerdotal ministry among men on earth. The Apostles are now to begin where Christ left off in his visible activity.

APPLICATION : Our divine Lord closed his discourse at the Last Supper with his priestly prayer for the unity of his Apostles in the bond of Christian charity, and for the true Christian brotherhood of all who would accept from them the message of Christ's gospel. During the first six centuries of the Church's history the Father answered this prayer of Christ; a few heresies raised their heads now and then, but the successors of the Apostles, with Peter's representative at their head, condemned these errors and the Church went on in peace and fraternal unity. Later on there were more widespread breaks with the successor of Peter in both the East and the West, and most of these divisions have continued down to our own day. Where was the efficacy of Christ's prayer then; why did God not answer him? Christ's prayer was efficacious and God did answer, but, like God's answer to all prayer, it is given as and when it is of the greatest value. God could not prevent men from exercising the gift of free-will which he himself had given them. When creating man he foresaw that that gift would often be misused to man's own disadvantage, but without it man would not be man; he would be incapable of any single act of merit and of enjoying the future eternal life.

So God could not prevent Christians from separating from one another, nor could he force them to return to Christian unity against their free-will. But he is ever ready to assist them by his grace and encouragement to co-operate once more in giving glory to God and in spreading the message of the gospel of love to all men. We are fortunate to be living in an age when the complete reunification of the Christian Church is the aim of all Christians, and has the evident assistance of our heavenly Father. It was not by accident that Pope John ascended the throne of Peter; it was not by chance that he called a Council—a Council which took its own share of the blame for the divisions in the Church and spoke of those outside it not as "schismatics" and "heretics" but as "separated brethren."

All this did not happen by accident. God saw the opportune moment and inspired the parties concerned with feelings of regret for past errors and with resolutions to do all in their power to put right the past. Our leaders and theologians are doing this. Theirs is no easy task; it is not the work of a few months, or even of a few years, but a beginning has been made and with God's grace and good-will on the part of our leaders it is a task that will have a successful and blessed ending.

However, the ordinary Christians in the various churches are not to be idle onlookers; we too have a part, and a big part, to play in bringing about this desired and most desirable unity of all Christians. First of all, we can assist in this noble work, and in a very effective way, by sincere and constant prayer. The grace of God, through our fervent prayers for our leaders and theologians, can and will open their eyes to see ways and means to unification without sacrificing any of the revealed truths of Christianity. There are some human accretions to the basic doctrines of faith in all the various churches which can be jettisoned without loss to the faith, but the revealed dogmas cannot and will not be bartered for any temporary gain. No church can sacrifice the truth, and no church will be asked to do so, for truth is God's gift to us and is necessary for the whole Church. Let us pray frequently, and fervently, that God will show our superiors the way, the one and only way, the way of truth to unity.

After prayer, each one of us will in his neighborhood or place of employment, meet members of the other Christian churches. It is our duty to show them by word and deed that we are their brothers in Christ. Some of them may show no interest at first in any kind of brotherhood of Christ or of man, but constant charitable contact will wear down this barrier. We can, if we are unity-minded, that is, Christian-minded, find topics for discussion that involve the Christian faith, and through these discussions our desire and our hope for a united Christian Church can be introduced. Charity will open the best-locked door; true Christian charity will soften the hardest heart. If we have the welfare of all our neighbors, Christian and non-Christian, at heart, we will gladly do everything in our power to bring about the existence of one, holy, catholic and apostolic Church which will have the true light of Christ to illumine its members and lead those fellow-sons of God who are still outside it, to enter it and share in its faith, its hope, and its charity.

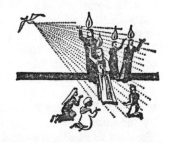

PENTECOST SUNDAY

FIRST READING: Acts 2:1–11. When the day of Pentecost had come, they were all together in one place. And suddenly a sound came from heaven like the rush of a mighty wind, and it filled all the house where they were sitting. And there appeared to them tongues as of fire, distributed and resting on each one of them. And they were all filled with the Holy Spirit and began to speak in other tongues, as the Spirit gave them utterance.

Now there were dwelling in Jerusalem Jews, devout men from every nation under heaven. And at this sound the multitude came together, and they were bewildered, because each one heard them speaking in his own language. And they were amazed and wondered, saying, "Are not all these who are speaking Galileans? And how is it that we hear, each of us in his own native language? Parthians and Medes and Elamites and residents of Mesopotamia, Judea and Cappadocia, Pontus and Asia, Phrygia and Pamphylia, Egypt and the parts of Libya belonging to Cyrene, and visitors from Rome, both Jews and proselytes, Cretans and Arabians, we hear them telling in our own tongues the mighty works of God."

EXPLANATION: "Pentecost" which means "fiftieth" was the second of the three most important of the annual feasts in the Jewish calendar. It occurred seven weeks after Passover and was primarily a feast of thanksgiving for the harvest : the first-fruits of the wheat crop were offered to God on that day. Later on the giving of the Law to Moses on Mount Sinai was also commemorated on this feast day. All Jewish men, not legitimately impeded, were expected to come to Jerusalem, to the temple, for the feast. Hundreds of Jews from outside of Palestine also came, and the city was usually full to overflowing. It was very fitting therefore that this feastday was chosen for the descent of the Holy Spirit on the Apostles.

The Christian religion was to be universal, and the gift of tongues showed its universality. The law given by God to Moses was for the Jews only; the new law, given by Christ, and confirmed by the power of the Holy Spirit, was for all men. The vast gathering of Jews from Palestine and from all nations was a very suitable occasion on which to proclaim publicly the message of Christ given through the mouth of Peter.

Suddenly . . . a sound came: The Apostles had been told by our Lord to wait in Jerusalem (Lk. 24:49), until the Holy Spirit came on them. They were all in one place, probably the room of the Last Supper where Jesus had appeared to them twice after his resurrection.

like the rush of a mighty . . . : Spirit means breath or wind, so it was fitting the Holy Spirit made his presence felt by the noise of a strong driving wind.

Tongues as of fire appeared : Something that looked like a flame rested on each of them. When God gave the law to Moses, peals of thunder and lightning flashes signified God's presence and made the people tremble (see Ex. 19 : 18ff). The loud noise and the flames signified the presence of the Holy Spirit.

to speak in other tongues . . . : The first signs of the power of the Spirit. They were given foreign languages and a new superhuman courage to proclaim their faith. Hitherto they had sheltered from the Jews.

and at this sound : This sound "like a driving wind" was heard all over the city, and by devout Jews from "every nation under heaven," a pious exaggeration and a way of saying that they came from most of the known nations of the Roman empire, which was the whole world then known to the Jews.

each one heard : Each foreigner who spoke the language of the country he came from heard one or other of the Apostles speaking his language.

amazed . . . wondered : Little wonder they were amazed. They had enquired of the local Jews, and knew that the Apostles were simple men, with little education, from Galilee. Where did they learn all these foreign languages?

Parthians . . . : These foreigners say they are from Mesopotamia, Greece, Asia Minor, Egypt and North Africa, Crete and Arabia. There are even Romans present, most of them Jews, but Gentile proselytes also among them.

we hear . . . tongues : This was the cause of their amazement, these simple folk from Galilee speaking all kinds of languages.

the mighty works of God : The Apostles were speaking of Christ, his teaching, and his resurrection. St. Peter develops this theme later (2 : 14ff).

APPLICATION : Pentecost day is called the "birth-day" of the Church. The Apostles had already received the Holy Spirit on Christ's first appearance to them after his resurrection (Jn. 20 : 22). But on Pentecost day the descent of the Holy Spirit was a public manifestation intended to impress and amaze the crowds of local and foreign Jews who thronged Jerusalem on that great festive occasion. The signs and wonders that manifested his coming brought these Jews in huge crowds to the place where the Apostles were staying, and immediately the gift of tongues was used by the Apostles to explain the occurrence.

It was a marvel wrought by God, a necessary consequence of the sojourn of Christ among them. He was the Christ whom the Jews had crucified but whom God had raised from the dead, thus proving he was the promised Messiah and his own beloved Son. Christ had chosen the Apostles to bring his good news to all nations—the good news that all men were once more reconciled to God their Creator, and were now adopted sons of God and heirs to heaven.

Today was the day chosen for the opening of this mission of the Apostles. That they were backed by the divine power of the Holy Spirit was proved not only by the gift of tongues but more especially by the change his coming wrought on the Apostles. From this day forward they were men dedicated to one purpose and to one purpose only, to bring the good news, the Gospel of Christ, to the world.

When Peter, representing the eleven, preached Christ, crucified, raised from the tomb by the power of the Father, and now seated at his right hand in heaven, he raised the Christian standard aloft. He and his fellow-Apostles (including Matthias and Paul later) gave their lives gladly to plant it throughout the Roman empire. The remaining twenty-six chapters of the book of Acts and the inspired letters of the Apostles tell the story of the growth of the infant Church. It was brought about by frail and mortal men, turned into spiritual heroes by the power of the Holy Spirit.

Twenty centuries separate us from those heroic men of God, but the truth of their labors is with us still thanks to the same Holy Spirit who has remained with the Church down through the years. From generation to generation the message and the means of salvation have been handed down, sometimes through periods of peace and evident progress, but more often through years of persecution and apparent near-extermination. The Church survived because men of God valued eternal life, and the Church as the means of reaching it, more than their own comfort or personal safety.

Our own generation too needs men of principle, men of generosity, men who will put the eternal values before personal conveniences or earthly gain. The Church today has her enemies. They shout loud and long—the same centuries-old themes are put to some of the present-day pop music. But we need not fear. The voice of the Holy Spirit is still as strong as it was on that first Pentecost day in Jerusalem. His powers are divine and will never diminish. He is still at the helm of the barque of Peter and will continue to bring millions to the shores of the eternal kingdom as he has done during the past two thousand years.

"Come, Holy Spirit, enkindle in the hearts of the faithful the fire of divine love."

SECOND READING : 1 Cor. 12 : 2–7; 12–13. No one speaking by the Spirit of God ever says "Jesus be cursed!" and no one can say "Jesus is Lord" except by the Holy Spirit.

Now there are varieties of gifts, but the same Spirit; and there are varieties of service, but the same Lord; and there are varieties of working, but it is the same God inspires them all in everyone. To each is given the manifestation of the Spirit for the common good.

But just as the body is one and has many members, and all the members of the body, though many, are one body, so it is with Christ. For by one Spirit we were all baptized into one body—Jews or Greeks, slaves or free—and all were made to drink of one Spirit.

EXPLANATION : The gifts of the Holy Spirit were very evident in the infant Church. This was necessary to prove to the pagans that the Christian religion was from the real God who controlled all things. As pagans they had their local god or gods to whom supernatural powers were often falsely attributed. But the God of the Christians had real powers and they were distributed freely by the Holy Spirit when occasion demanded. St. Paul in this part of his first letter to the Corinthians is emphasizing that these gifts are not given to an individual for his honor or glory but to help to build up the Church.

No one . . . the Spirit : One of the first tests of the genuineness of a gift from the Holy Spirit was conformity with the Christian faith. If any man claimed he was moved by the Holy Spirit to blaspheme Jesus, he was evidently a liar and a fraud. On the other hand he who sincerely professed that Christ was God was moved by the Holy Spirit. Faith is a gift from God.

varieties . . . same Spirit : All the gifts given to the early Christian converts were from the same Holy Spirit and each had its special purpose. It is possible that Paul wished to prevent any

temptation for one to boast that he had a better gift than his neighbor. All were from the same source.

varieties . . . service : The ability to help in administering the affairs of the early Christian communities was a gift of God—each one receiving the gift necessary for his particular task. Helping the sick, feeding the poor, calling the assemblies together, explaining the faith, powers of healing, are all examples of these different ministries, but they all came from the same God.

given for the common good : These gifts were given for the good of the whole community—to help build up the Church, and so that no one should refuse to use the gift he got or claim it as his own.

The body is one : St. Paul now introduces the simile of the human body made up of many members, to describe the Church of Christ. From this we get the title of "Mystical Body of Christ" to describe the Church.

for by one Spirit : It was the Holy Spirit, sent by Christ on his ascension to heaven to direct and inspire his newly-founded Church, who gave us the grace to become members of Christ's Body.

Jews or Greeks : Meaning all men.

Greek stood for Gentile, that was the rest of the world apart from the Jews. **were baptized :** The sacrament instituted by Christ to make men members of his Church, his body.

APPLICATION : These verses of St. Paul are very suitable on this the feast-day of the descent of the Holy Spirit on the Apostles. Not only did he make his presence felt by the external exercise of his powers, on that first Pentecost day, but he continued to do so for some years until the Church had laid solid foundations in the Gentile world.

These gifts of the Spirit were foretold in the Old Testament as signs of the Messiah's arrival (see Joel 3 : 1ff; Acts 2 : 16ff), and were manifested in the early Church in Jerusalem (Acts 2 : 4), Samaria (8 : 17), Ephesus (19 : 6), Rome (Rom. 12 : 6), Galatia (Gal. 3 : 5), and in Corinth. St. Paul has much to say of the gifts given in Corinth because there was evidently some abuse of them or some dissensions because of them in that city.

But for us the important point to bear in mind today on this, the anniversary of the public manifestation of the descent of the Holy Spirit on the Apostles, is the infinite love of God for us, his Chosen People of the new covenant. Through the Incarnation men are empowered to become adopted sons of God; through baptism we become members of Christ's body, his Church. Through the direct reception of the Holy Spirit in the Sacrament of Confirmation, we are made active members of the Christian Church, with all the strength and powers necessary to be effective members, on active service daily, true soldiers of Christ.

Let each one of us take an honest look at himself today, and ask himself : Am I really an active member of the body of Christ? Am I spiritually healthy, living in God's grace and thus helping the whole body to be healthy? Or am I a diseased member, and not only sickly and weak through my personal sins, but spreading that sickness and weakness to my neighboring members by my bad example? But perhaps I can claim I have no very big sins and give no grave scandal, but I am lukewarm in the practice of my religion. I haven't much time for things of that sort. If I am one of these two types—a diseased member or a lukewarm one, I could hardly call myself a soldier of Christ on active service. Deserters and dishonest draft-dodgers are not at the front.

Thank God, a large percentage of Christians do strive to remain healthy members of his mystical body—they may weaken now and then but they call on their divine physician and put things right again. This is as it should be, but is it all that is expected of us?

The Holy Spirit came to us in confirmation with his gifts and graces to enable us to work for the whole Church, for the whole body of Christ. We are made soldiers to form an army that will work together for the protection of our nation and our freedom. No man is put into military uniform in order to look after his own interests. We too are not made soldiers of Christ in order to save our own souls only—we are soldiers in order to help our fellow-Christians and all men in their common fight against sin and Godlessness. We must then take an active part in the battles of the Church, against everything that impedes the practice of the Christian virtues.

There is a place for everyone in the

Church's line of battle. We need not search far to find it. We need not be physical or intellectual giants in order to fulfill the role destined for us. What we need is sincerity and a bit of moral courage; sincerity in our belief that it is the future life that counts—the present is only a few years of training; moral courage to face opposition and criticism from enemies and often from false friends. When God and the Holy Spirit are on our side, we need not worry about the opinions or sneers of worldly-minded men. If we are true soldiers of Christ we shall win our battles, not by crushing our enemies but by making them too children of God and our brothers for all eternity.

GOSPEL : John 20 : 19–23. On the evening of the first day of the week, the doors being shut where the disciples were, for fear of the Jews, Jesus came and stood among them and said to them, "Peace be with you." When he had said this, he showed them his hands and his side. Then the disciples were glad when they saw the Lord. Jesus said to them again, "Peace be with you. As the Father has sent me, even so I send you." And when he had said this, he breathed on them, and said to them, "Receive the Holy Spirit. If you forgive the sins of any, they are forgiven; if you retain the sins of any, they are retained."

EXPLANATION : For the explanation of these five verses of St. John, see the second Sunday of Easter. They are repeated here today, the feast of the Holy Spirit, because on that first appearance of the risen Lord he conferred the Holy Spirit on the Apostles. Today's feast commemorates the solemn public and publicized conferral of the same Holy Spirit.

APPLICATION : The liturgical cycle, which each year represents to us God's mercy and kindness in our regard, closes today with this great feast of Pentecost —the public solemn descent of the Holy Spirit, the Sanctifier, on the Christian Church. During Advent we try to prepare ourselves for the coming of the Son of God to dwell as man among us. Christmas recalls to our minds and hearts the great act of divine love. Lent prepares us for the sufferings endured by Christ during Holy Week on our behalf. Easter is the feast of triumph, Christ's triumph over death, the guarantee of our final triumph and union with him in his eternal glory. Pentecost crowns Christ's work among us. The Holy Spirit comes to abide with the Church, directing and effectively aiding its leaders to preserve, explain and spread the gospel of hope and love which Christ had brought on earth. This same spirit helps and aids each member of the Church to live a life of holiness by following the teaching of Christ and by helping his fellowmen to do likewise.

Briefly, this annual series of Church feastdays recalls to our minds the infinite love of the Blessed Trinity for us finite, mortal men. At the same time it shows us the part played by each of the divine Persons in the eternal plan to share with us the perfect peace and the unending happiness which they enjoy in their heavenly kingdom.

God the Father created us with the intention and plan to raise us up to adopted sonship with him. God the Son took human nature so that we might share in the divinity. Representing all men he gave perfect obedience and reverence to the Creator "even unto death on a cross," and thus merited sonship for us. The Holy Spirit, the

"fruit of divine love," came from the Father and the Son to bring to perfection the work of our sanctification. Thus the three divine Persons of the Blessed Trinity have cooperated in the great work of infinite love and condescension which opens for us a future of unending happiness, if only we have the common sense to appreciate what has been done for us, and the simple common decency to do in return the few relatively easy little tasks asked of us.

May the Holy Spirit today fill us with gratitude for all that God has done for us.

TRINITY SUNDAY

FIRST READING: Deuteronomy 4:32–34; 39–40. Moses said to the people: "Ask now of the days that are past, which were before you, since the day that God created man upon the earth, and ask from one end of heaven to the other, whether such a great thing has ever happened or was ever heard of. Did any people ever hear the voice of a god speaking out of the midst of the fire, as you have heard, and still live? Or has any god ever attempted to go and take a nation for himself from the midst of another nation, by trials, by signs, by wonders, and by war, by a mighty hand and an outstretched arm, and by great terrors, according to all that the Lord your God did for you in Egypt before your eyes?"

"Know therefore this day, and lay it to your heart, that the Lord is God in heaven above and on the earth beneath; there is no other. Therefore you shall keep his statutes and his commandments which I command you this day, that it may go well with you, and with your children after you, and that you may prolong your days in the land which the Lord your God gives you for ever."

EXPLANATION: On the Book of Deuteronomy see the Fourth Sunday of the Year. According to the author of this book, Moses has led the Chosen

People from Egypt to the Transjordan and now addresses his last instructions to them before they cross over into the Promised Land. Today's reading is taken from the first of the three long discourses which the author puts into the mouth of Moses. The Chosen People have been privileged beyond all nations that ever were; the true God led them out from slavery by signs and by wonders in order to make them his own people. He is about to give them a homeland of their own. As Lord of the universe, he has every right to demand obedience of them. Yet, if they obey his commandments they and their children after them will be rewarded by being happy in their homeland forever.

ask . . . past: Moses challenges the people to search the history of man on earth to see if they can find anything to compare with the privileged experience they had with God in the Exodus from Egypt and the revelation on Mount Sinai.

hear . . . live: It was the common opinion then that any mortal who saw or heard God would die immediately. The Chosen People had heard God's voice on Mount Sinai and did not die (see Exodus 19 : 1–20 : 21).

any . . . attempted: God took the Chosen People out of the midst of powerful Egypt. The conviction among the pagans was that the god of one nation had no power in another nation. The God of the Chosen People proved that he was God of all nations by displaying his power in Egypt.

signs . . . terrors: Moses is referring to the great power he used to free the Israelites from the slavery of Egypt. He is referring to all that is described in the book of Exodus (1–14).

before your eyes: The Chosen People, or Israelites, were witnesses to this great power and the loving benevolence of Yahweh their God.

know . . . your heart: He warns them never to forget that Yahweh their God is the one supreme God. *"There is no other."*

keep . . . commandments: These are the moral and liturgical laws God had given them on Mount Sinai, which Moses is now going to repeat once more to them in the following chapters.

it may . . . you: If they keep his commandments God will provide for them in their needs.

land . . . forever: They and their children after them, down through the generations ("forever") will continue to possess the country (Canaan) that he is giving over to them.

APPLICATION: The mystery of the Blessed Trinity was not revealed in the Old Testament because God saw that his Chosen People were not yet ready to accept such a mystery. Living, as they were, surrounded by adorers of many gods, any knowledge of the Trinity of persons in the one God, might have weakened their monotheism. It was only when Christ came on earth claiming (and proving his claim) that he was the divine Son of God, and promising to send the Consoler, a third Person in God, to strengthen and guide his disciples that this doctrine was fully revealed. It was accepted without question from the very first days of the Christian Church, first of all because it was Christ who revealed it, and, secondly, because it was felt that the Church had proof of the existence of three distinct Persons in the one God in that each of them played a part in the founding and spreading of Christianity. The Father sent his Son on earth in human form, and raised him from the dead when he had carried out his Father's will. The Father and the Son sent the Holy Spirit to direct and govern the Church founded by the Son.

While we admit the fact that there are three distinct Persons in the one God and have valid reasons for doing so, we still do not understand how this is. Of course, if God could be fully understood by our finite minds, he would not be God, but a limited being like ourselves. Let us be content today to say how privileged we are to know of this doctrine and even more so to know that each of the three divine Persons has played a part in giving us a share in their life. When we get to heaven we shall see and understand it all more clearly with the added light of the Beatific Vision, which will be given to our glorified bodies.

In today's reading from the book of Deuteronomy we see how privileged the Chosen People of Israel were, how wonderful God had been in his dealings with them, and how all he asked for in return was that they should keep his commandments. These were for their own good. Sad to relate, they did not keep his laws! They quickly forgot all that he had done for them and turned to adore lifeless idols, pagan "gods" who could not help either themselves or anyone else. This was ingratitude and meanness of a high order, but let us remember that everything that God did for the Jews, he did for us too. Through his dealings with them he was preparing the way for the incarnation.

Do we return due thanks to God the Father, Son and Holy Spirit for this immensely greater love? Before we criticize or judge the Jews of old, let us see if our own consciences are in order before God. We owe him obedience for far weightier reasons than the Jews had. He set them free from the slavery of Egypt; he has set us free from Satan's power. He gave them Canaan as their homeland; he has prepared heaven, the place of unending life, for us. He made Moses, one of themselves, the mediator between himself and the Israelites; he has given his own Son to be our mediator. In return for it all and as a token repayment, we are asked to keep his commandments!

God is surely not asking too much of us. Any generous Christian would not only do this, he would look for further means of showing his gratitude to the Blessed Trinity. All the saints did so and earned the honor of God and the respect of man. We all want to be saints. Let us begin today not merely to keep the commandments but also to do some extra bit each day to show our sincere gratitude to God. God will never be outdone in generosity.

SECOND READING: Romans 8:14-17. All who are led by the Spirit of God are sons of God. For you did not receive the spirit of slavery to fall back into fear, but you have received the spirit of sonship. When we cry, "Abba! Father!" it is the Spirit himself bearing witness with our spirit that we are children of God, and if children, then heirs, heirs of God and fellow heirs with Christ, provided we suffer with him in order that we may also be glorified with him.

EXPLANATION: On the Epistle to the Romans, see the second Sunday of Lent. In today's four verses, St. Paul stresses the change which Christianity has brought to Jew and Gentile. Man is no longer a slave of sin or of the world: he has been made a son of God through Christ's life, death and resurrection and is therefore a freeman. This image of slave and freeman was much more telling when St. Paul wrote, for real slavery was then practiced. If we can—and we can and should—call God our Father, Abba, it is because the Holy Spirit moves us to do so and the Holy Spirit does this because we have indeed been made sons of God by the incarnation of his Son. Because we are adopted into God's household, heaven is our inheritance provided we obey Christ's commands.

led . . . God: Anyone moved by the Spirit of God, anyone, that is, who has received the Holy Spirit in baptism has now a new life in him, a supernatural life. He has been made a son of God.

not . . . but sonship: The Christian is not a slave of God but an adopted son and heir. It is the Spirit that unites men to Christ and thus puts them in a special relationship with the Father. They have now the status of "sons."

Abba (my) Father: Christ used this familiar name when calling on Father in his moment of extreme agony (Mk. 14:36). It became the Christian invocation for the Father among the Jewish Christians. Even among the Gentiles Paul uses it. The Christian, because of his adoption, can speak of God and to God in the very terms used by Christ, his real Son.

fellow heirs with Christ: If Christians are children of God then they are heirs and will share heaven with Christ, who made them his brothers.

we . . . him: As Christ suffered in order to enter into his glory in heaven, and as the servant is not above the master, we too must earn our reward by carrying whatever cross God sends us. Only if we do this, can we expect to share his inheritance with Christ in the hereafter.

APPLICATION: About the year 57-58 that is to say, less than thirty years after the resurrection, St. Paul wrote this letter to the Christians in Rome. It was a church he was very anxious to visit (he had had nothing to do with the spread of the faith there). The Roman Christian community was made up of Jew and Gentile converts. It is evident from St. Paul's words that they were quite familiar with the doctrine of the three divine Persons in one God. We know, of course, that they had received baptism in the name of the Blessed Trinity. Therefore, they had accepted the fact about the true God before becoming Christians. To do this was not, humanly speaking, easy for a Jew or a Gentile, but we must remember that the early Christians did not rely on human logic or human thinking. The grace and the power of God was with them in generous measure.

For a Jew, the very essence of whose religion was strict monotheism, there was one God and one God only. The three Persons must at first mention have sounded like many gods, something abhorrent to his nature. Yet, thousands of Jews accepted this doctrine from the very first days of the Church (all the first Christians were Jewish converts). They were convinced that God, although he was strictly one God, had revealed that there were three Persons in that one divine nature. If God revealed this knowledge of his innermost nature and if it did not contradict the unity, the oneness of God, how could they refuse to accept this revelation? For the Gentiles also, this doctrine must at first sight have seemed a stumbling block. They were sick and tired of their own pagan gods. Was Christianity offering them three instead of many gods? Again, aided by God's grace, they realized that Christianity was not preaching three Gods but three Persons who in some mysterious way are in the one and only God.

We Christians of today are no more advanced than the early Jew and Gentile converts were as regards the mysteries of faith. We cannot examine the Godhead scientifically, and prove to ourselves from cold logic that there are three Persons in God. But like them, we too know that we have the word of God for it and God is the God of truth. His word is stronger and more convincing than any human proof or logic can ever be. Like the early Christians, we also

have had the experience of the three Persons, each performing a distinct role in the work of our salvation. The Father created us and planned an eternal life for us. He sent the Son to enable us to fill the role his Father had planned for us. After the Son's ascension, both the Father and the Son sent the Holy Spirit to sanctify, give courage and strength to the Apostles and those who would join them.

This threefold activity is still going on in the life of each one of us—the three Persons of the Blessed Trinity are co-operating to bring us to heaven. Why? We may well ask. The Blessed Trinity is infinitely perfect, infinitely happy in heaven. God needs nothing from us. Here again is where our small, finite intelligence fails us. We can understand human love and human generosity which at their greatest are but temporary, passing things and of necessity very limited in quality and quantity. But God's love for us is infinite. It is completely and entirely without self-interest. God does not act out of need but out of nature. His very nature is goodness and so he is moved by that nature to share his goodness, his happiness with those who are able to appreciate it, that is, with us men.

It has been very clearly and very definitely revealed to us that God loves us with an infinite love. This is the basic message of the New Testament. The three Persons of the Blessed Trinity are still proving this fact to us. In this life we cannot understand why, but we can and we must show our gratitude for this fact of divine generosity and love.

Today, on this special feastday of the Blessed Trinity, let us resolve to make ourselves less unworthy of their divine love : by doing what is asked of us, by living our faith in charity, and by keeping ever before our minds the eternal future that awaits us. The day is not far off when, please God, we shall meet the Blessed Trinity face to face. Then we shall understand a lot more about the three divine Persons in God, and the infinite love and mercy shown to us by these three Persons.

GOSPEL: Matthew 28 : 16–20. The eleven disciples went to Galilee, to the mountain to which Jesus had directed them. And when they saw him they worshiped him; but some doubted. And Jesus came and said to him, "All authority in heaven and on earth has been given to me. Go therefore and make disciples of all nations, baptizing them in the name of the Father and of the Son and of the Holy Spirit, teaching them to observe all that I have commanded you; and lo, I am with you always, to the close of the age."

EXPLANATION : Omitting the other appearances of the risen Savior to the Apostles, and others which are described in Mark, Luke, John and St. Paul (1 Cor. 15), St. Matthew mentions only the appearance to the women in Jerusalem and this last appearance to the eleven Apostles somewhere in Galilee. On this occasion, Christ commissions his Apostles to bring his gospel, "to make disciples of" all men. He adds that they were to be made disciples of Jesus by being baptized in the name of the Father, Son and Holy Spirit. They were to keep his commandments and he promised to be with them always, to the close of the age.

went to Galilee : After a week of appearances by the risen Savior in Jerusalem (Jn. 20 : 19–21 and 21 : 1), the Apostles went to Galilee, as Christ had told them to do (Mt. 28 : 10).

to the mountain : Evidently he had specified the place where they were to meet him.

some doubted : In all of the resurrection stories there is the candid admission that some did not recognize him. The fact is that the risen Christ, in his glorified body, could not be visible to human eyes on earth, so he assumed a visible human form on each occasion. Twice in the supper room (Jn. 20 : 19–28), he evidently had a body similar to the body he had on earth together with the marks of the nails and the spear on it. But on the other occasions it was a different type of body. This doubting on the part of some, as well as the fact that not one of them expected the resurrection, is a greater proof of its reality. All did eventually recognize him as the risen Christ.

all authority . . . earth : The Father has given Christ, the God-man, power over all creation and all created beings, in heaven and on earth.

Go therefore : With this power he commissions them to preach his gospel, his good news, to all people.

baptizing them : This was to be the sacrament of introduction of the new Chosen People into the kingdom of God on earth.

in the name of . . . Spirit : Those who accepted the Apostles' preaching of Christ, were to be given the possession of the Blessed Trinity. They were to be dedicated, given to the service and honor of the Father, Son and Holy Spirit.

to observe all: If the initiated, by baptism, are to honor the Blessed Trinity they must do so by obeying all that Christ had laid down, during his public life, as necessary to salvation.

with you always: His final word is one of encouragement and strength. In all their doings he will be with them with his power, and not only with them but with their successors until the end of this world.

APPLICATION: The reason why these five verses, that conclude the final chapter of St. Matthew's gospel, were chosen for today's Mass is evident. The three Persons of the Blessed Trinity are mentioned by name in this pericope.

All those who would enter the new kingdom of God, the Church, were to be dedicated in the ceremony of baptism to the Blessed Trinity; they were to enter into a fellowship with the three divine Persons. Whether Christ himself gave the exact words for the form of baptism does not concern us here, but from 2 Cor. 2 : 21, it would appear that this form was in use from the earliest days of the Church. We are aware that we ourselves were dedicated to God in our baptism and destined to have an eternal fellowship with the Trinity in heaven. We are aware, too, of the part played by the three divine Persons in making that eternal happiness and friendship with the Trinity available to us. While the essence of the Trinity, or the way in which there can be three Persons in the one God, is a mystery which our limited minds cannot even begin to solve, we have no hesitation in accepting the existence of this deepest mystery of our religion. It was no less an authority than Jesus Christ himself who revealed it to us. With his guarantee for its truth, we are left in no doubt as to the existence of this mystery. We can safely wait for a greater, if not a complete understanding in heaven.

Today, as we honor the Blessed

Trinity, our predominant thought must be one of gratitude to each of the three Persons for all they have done and are still doing for us. First, to God the Father, who in his love planned not only our creation as intelligent human beings, the highest and noblest of his creatures on earth, but planned to give us adopted sonship as well. Secondly, let us show our deepest gratitude to the all-obedient, all-loving Son of God, who carried out to the letter the divine Father's plan for our adoption, by sharing with us our humanity so that we could share in his divinity. Thirdly, let us be eternally grateful to the Holy Spirit—the fruit of the love of Father and Son—who has come to dwell in the Church and in each member of the Church, in order to fill our hearts with a true love of God, and to direct our faltering steps toward the everlasting happiness which awaits us beyond the grave.

We know only too well how unworthy we are of this love of the Blessed Trinity which has been poured out on us. The greatest saints were unworthy of this infinite love. Our unworthiness should not, and must not, stop us from availing ourselves of this divine love and from doing what we can to prove how we value and sincerely appreciate the love and goodness of the Blessed Trinity for us. In return for this love, Christ asked us, his followers, to keep his commandments. This is the one genuine proof we can give of our gratitude for all that these three Persons have done for us.

We are so weak that we often let the passing things of this world turn our thoughts and actions away from God and from our own eternal interests. We forget Christ and his commandments at times and let the world rule our hearts and minds. However, even for sinners like us there is hope and encouragement in the infinity of God's love. Let us not forget it : the Father, Son and Holy Spirit know all our weaknesses, they knew them before they arranged to make us sharers in their own eternal happiness. They know, also, that those of us who try and try again to rise above our human weakness will finally share with them their heaven.

This possibility is open to all of us. The Blessed Trinity will exclude nobody from heaven. If some fail, the fault will be entirely and completely their own. May God the Father, Son and Holy Spirit grant us the courage and strength to overcome our human weaknesses! May they give us the grace to live and die in their love so that we may share their eternal kingdom of happiness!

FEAST OF CORPUS CHRISTI

FIRST READING : Exodus 24 : 3-8. Moses came and told the people all the words of the Lord and all the ordinances; and all the people answered with one voice, and said, "All the words which the Lord has spoken we will do." And Moses wrote all the words of the Lord. And he rose early in the morning, and built an altar at the foot of the mountain, and twelve pillars, according to the twelve tribes of Israel. And he sent young men of the people of Israel, who offered burnt offerings and sacrificed peace offerings of oxen to the Lord. And Moses took half of the blood and put it in basins, and half of the blood he threw against the altar. Then he took the book of the covenant, and read it in the hearing of the people; and they said, "All that the Lord has spoken we will do, and we will be obedient." And Moses took the blood and threw it upon the people, and said, "Behold the blood of the covenant which the Lord has made with you in accordance with all these words."

EXPLANATION : The second book of the Pentateuch is called Exodus or the "going out," for it describes the liberation of the Israelites from the slavery of Egypt. For this historic event God appointed Moses to be the leader of the people. God made a covenant or pact with the Israelites, when they reached Mount Sinai. Moses was the intermediary. The people were to keep the commandments (the Decalog and various cultic laws). If they did, he would lead them into the Promised Land of Canaan, and would establish them there. Today's extract describes the solemn signing of this pact on the part of the people.

words . . . ordinances : Moses was given the Decalog and the other laws on top of Mount Sinai. The people remained at the foot of the mountain. Moses came down and told the people what God had commanded.

one voice . . . do : The people accepted the commands of God and promised to keep them.

altar . . . pillars : A covenant or pact was ratified in those days by sacrifices offered to the gods of the parties. Here the covenant or pact was made between the true God and his Chosen People. Moses built an altar and got young men, the representatives of the people, to offer burnt offerings and peace offerings to God. Around the altar he had twelve dolmens, or stones, one for each of the twelve Tribes of Israel.

half . . . blood : Moses sprinkled around the altar half of the blood drawn from the animals that were sacrificed.

book of the covenant : That is, the Ten Commandments, with probably the prescriptions laid down in Exodus 20 : 22 —23 : 19. Moses read these laws to the people—they promised to obey all of God's commandments.

threw . . . people : Parties ratifying a covenant sprinkled the blood of the sacrifices on themselves, the implication being : if we do not observe the terms of the covenant may the fate of the sacrificed animals befall us. Moses, having already sprinkled half of the blood of the victims on the altar which represented God, now sprinkled the other half over the Israelites. The covenant was thus solemnly ratified.

the blood of the covenant : That is, the blood which ratifies and seals the covenant.

all these words : What the covenant demands of the Israelites is expressed in the words that Moses read to them— they knew their obligations and accepted them.

APPLICATION : God called Abraham from his home in Mesopotamia and promised him and his descendants a homeland of their own in the land of Canaan. God's purpose in doing this was to enable him to fulfill his eternal plan of elevating man to divine sonship, through the incarnation of his own divine Son. Christ, the Son of God made man, who would bring this blessing of sonship to all mankind, was to take his human nature from a descendant of Abraham. Hence's God's very special interest in the Chosen People. The detailed covenant he made with the Israelites, after he had miraculously freed them from the slavery of Egypt, was the first pact he made with the people as a whole. On his part, he promised to lead them into the land he had promised to them through Abraham; there he would protect them from their enemies and prosper them, provided they were loyal to him and to his commandments. This pact, or covenant, was solemnly sealed and ratified with the blood of the sacrificial victims, sprinkled on the people and on the altar.

Like the whole of the Old Testament this was a representation and a preparation for the real, the new Testament, the new Covenant which God was to make not only with Abraham's descendants, but the whole human race through Christ. When he came, he made a new pact between God and all men. In this pact God promised an ever-lasting home in heaven to all men and divine assistance on their way, provided they kept his commandments. This new and eternal covenant was signed and sealed with the precious blood of Christ who offered himself to God the Father as a propitiatory sacrifice for the sins of all mankind.

We are celebrating today in this annual feast of Corpus Christi the second and final covenant. The story of the first covenant is read for us to show us how the whole Old Testament, the whole of God's dealings with Abraham and his descendants, were a preparation and a foreshadowing of the greater things he was to do for us, the Chosen People of the New Testament. God promised to lead the Israelites into Canaan and make them prosper there in their earthly concerns. That they would share in the future blessing, the incarnation, was only very vaguely hinted at. He gave them Moses, one of themselves, a son of Abraham, to be their leader. He agreed to accept the sacrifice of sheep and oxen and farm produce as a token of their reverence and respect. To us, on the other hand, he has opened his own heavenly kingdom and has given us all the necessary means to merit it. He has guaranteed us an eternal happiness. He has given us as our leader his own divine Son. The sacrifice with which we can show our reverence and gratitude to him is not a token. It is a sacrifice which gives God full honor and glory, for it is the sacrifice of his own beloved Son.

What return are we asked to make for these extraordinary privileges and promises? Nothing more than was asked of the Israelites. We are to keep the laws laid down by Christ. They include the Decalog and the cultic laws of the New Testament. One might say : surely, no sane man would refuse to pay so little for so great a reward! Yet, unfortunately, there are many Christians who do not keep the commandments. They forget all that the good God and his only begotten Son has done for them. They become so immersed in the pleasures and things of this passing world, that they have no time to think of the real world which lies ahead. They are willing to risk their own eternal future for the sake of some passing pleasure or some trifling gain.

The Chosen People at Mount Sinai unanimously and willingly promised to keep God's commandments. Within a few weeks they forgot their solemn promise and rebelled against God. Because of their rebellions, their journey from Sinai to Canaan was so prolonged that none of the adults who were led by God out of Egypt reached their Promised Land. Christians, too, forget their baptismal promises, promises often repeated in adult life. Should they continue in this state of revolt against God, they too would find entrance to the eternal home denied them.

However, God is ever merciful, ever ready to forgive and forget our past. On this feastday of the precious Body and Blood of our Savior, let us revere that sacred Blood while we renew once more our firm resolve to do all that our heavenly Father asks of us.

SECOND READING : Hebrews 9 : 11–15. When Christ appeared as a high priest of the good things that have come, then through the greater and more perfect tent (not made with hands, that is, not of this creation) he entered once for all into the Holy Place, taking not the blood of goats and calves but his own blood, thus securing an eternal redemption. For if the sprinkling of defiled persons with the blood of goats and bulls and with the ashes of a heifer sanctifies for the purification of the flesh, how much more shall the blood of Christ, who through the eternal Spirit offered himself without blemish to God, purify your conscience from dead works to serve the living God.

Therefore he is the mediator of a new covenant, so that those who are called may receive the promised eternal inheritance, since a death has occurred which redeems them from the transgressions under the first covenant.

EXPLANATION : This Epistle was written by a disciple of St. Paul to Christians—the majority of whom were converts from Judaism. He is encouraging them to persevere in their faith in spite of persecutions. From the frequent use of the Old Testament, which is shown as so much inferior to the new dispensation, the Christian religion, it would seem that many of the readers were converts tempted to return to the old dispensation, with its temple worship. The author shows the emptiness of the old ritual when compared with the reality of the New Testament sacrifice and ritual. Today's excerpt from this Epistle compares the sacrifice offered by the high priest in the temple on the very solemn day of Atonement, with the sacrifice of true and infinite atonement offered by Christ for us.

On the day of Atonement the high priest alone offered the sacrifices for his own sins and the sins of all the people. He entered the innermost sanctuary— the holy of holies—to sprinkle the blood of the sacrifices on the Ark of the Covenant, God's throne. This was the only day in the year when the blood was sprinkled there. The Epistle is referring to this.

Christ . . . priest : Christ is the High Priest of the New Testament "the good things that have come."

more perfect tent : On the great day of real atonement—Good Friday—he entered, not through the veil in the temple, but through the veil of death and resurrection into heaven, the real Holy of Holies.

once for all : In the temple ritual the ceremonies of Atonement day had had to be repeated each year. Christ made his perfect atonement for the sins of the world to his Father "once and for all."

blood ... calves : Unlike the Jewish high priest, it was not the blood of animal victims that Christ offered but his own blood—by his own sacrifice of his life he secured eternal redemption for all men.

if . . . goats : This temple ritual had value because it was a foreshadowing of the real purification which was to come.

much more . . . Christ : There is no comparison between the two ceremonies. Christ's sacrifice had infinite value, because he was God as well as man.

through ... Spirit : Not the third Person of the Blessed Trinity, but the divine nature of Christ gave his act infinite value.

without blemish : All the animals offered

in the temple sacrifice had to be without defect or blemish. Christ's human nature was sinless and pure in God's sight.

purify your conscience : This sacrifice of Christ will remove any sin, "dead works", which leads to death and make each one fully acceptable to the Father —"the living God," the true God.

mediator . . . covenant : Christ, the Son of God in human nature, brought about this new and perfect covenant or pact between God and all men. The old covenant (see first reading) made on Mount Sinai was a preparatory temporary covenant. It prepared the way for this new and everlasting covenant.

eternal inheritance : The old covenant promised a life-time inheritance to the Israelites in the land of Canaan. The new covenant promises eternal life in the land of everlasting happiness.

a death . . . redeems : Christ's death on the cross obtained forgiveness for all the disobediences which men had committed against the first covenant.

APPLICATION : If any of the first readers of this Epistle felt any temptation to return to the Jewish religion, the comparison between the value of the sacrifices offered on the day of Atonement by the Jewish high priest and the sacrifice offered by Christ on Good Friday must surely have put their minds at rest. The Jewish high priest was a man; Christ was the Son of God in human nature. The high priest had to atone for his own sins as well as those of his people; Christ was sinless. The high priest offered as sacrifice sheep and calves, things in themselves that had no value for making atonement or for honoring God; Christ offered his own human body, an offering that had infinite value in atoning for sin and in giving honor to his Father : for he who made the offering was the Son of God. The high priest had to repeat this ritual of atonement each year; Christ's offering was made once and for all, for it had infinite value for all men for all time.

Do we really appreciate how fortunate we are to be members of the new Chosen People, rather than to be living under the old dispensation? The Old Testament was the only true religion, the one religion that in its day taught a knowledge of the true God, but how limited was its knowledge, how empty of power and efficacy were its ritual observances, how little did the Israelites know of the infinite love and mercy of God compared with what our Christian religion teaches us?

Today's feastday is a striking reminder of this infinite love of God. Not only did the Son of God die on the cross for our salvation, but through his divine power he arranged to leave to his Church the power to repeat that selfsame death in an unbloody manner each time the holy sacrifice of the Mass is celebrated. Every Mass said renews the efficacy of Calvary. The high priest of Christianity enters once more into the heavenly holy of holies; infinite glory is given to God; infinite atonement is made for the sins of men, and the flood-gates of heaven are opened to pour down a superabundance of divine grace on mankind. We surely have " the supreme high priest who has gone through to the highest heaven " and one who at the same time understands and sympathizes with us in all our human needs and weaknesses. Therefore, not only did he open heaven for us and show us the way but he bequeathed to his Church for all time his precious Body and Blood, to be offered to God as an infinite atonement. At the same time his Body and Blood are our spiritual food in this life.

The Blessed Eucharist is a sacrifice and a sacrament. Corpus Christi is the feastday of the Blessed Eucharist. Both sacrament and sacrifice are closely united. In the Old Testament times, the priest offering some animal to God as sacrifice and the person or persons for whom he offered the sacrifice, ate part of the victim as a sign of their close intimacy with God. It is the same with the Blessed Eucharist. The receiving of the Body and Blood of Christ is an essential sequence to the offering of Christ in the sacrifice of the Mass. Jesus Christ becomes present on our altars to re-enact the sacrifice of Calvary and also to be our spiritual nourishment. This is his intention for he said, when instituting the Eucharist : "take it and eat ; this is my body," and of the cup he said : "Drink all of you from this, for this is my blood" (Mt. 26 : 27).

While it is the priest alone who is empowered to consecrate at Mass, all who are present are the offerers of the sacrifice and should, therefore, partake of the sacrifice. They should, in other words, receive under one or both species during the Mass. This community participation in the eucharistic sacrifice was stressed and practiced very much in the early Church and down through the first centuries. In recent years the faithful have been urged to renew this very spiritual practice. We give infinite honor to God by being present and by participating in the offering of the Mass. But we participate fully and receive the full benefits of this sacrificial act only when we partake of the sacrifice with our fellow-worshipers by receiving Christ in Holy Communion.

For those who feel they are seriously unworthy to receive Christ in the Holy Communion, the merciful means of obtaining forgiveness is within easy reach. For those who feel unworthy of such an honor because of minor faults and failings committed during the week, a heartfelt act of love of God will cleanse them of such minor faults and failings. God is the God of love and mercy. His presence in the sacrifice and sacrament of the Eucharist is proof of this. Let us strive to be always ready to welcome him into our hearts when he is present with us on our altars.

GOSPEL: Mark 14:12–16; 22–26. On the first day of Unleavened Bread, when they sacrificed the passover lamb, his disciples said to him, "Where will you have us go and prepare for you to eat the passover?" And he sent two of his disciples, and said to them, "Go into the city, and a man carrying a jar of water will meet you; follow him, and wherever he enters, say to the householder, 'The Teacher says, Where is my guest room, where I am to eat the passover with my disciples?' And he will show you a large upper room furnished and ready; there prepare for us." And the disciples set out and went to the city, and found it as he had told them; and they prepared the passover.

And as they were eating, he took bread, and blessed, and broke it, and gave it to them, and said, "Take; this is my body." And he took a cup, and when he had given thanks he gave it to them, and they all drank of it. And he said to them, "This is my blood of the covenant, which is poured out for many. Truly, I say to you, I shall not drink again of the fruit of the vine until that day when I drink it new in the kingdom of God."

And when they had sung a hymn, they went out to the Mount of Olives.

EXPLANATION: In these ten verses (verses 17–21, which refer to Judas' betrayal are omitted), we have St. Mark's brief account of what happened in Jerusalem on the first Holy Thursday night. Jesus evidently had a Passover meal with his disciples, at the end of which he instituted the Blessed Eucharist. Matthew (26:17–29), Luke (22:7–20), and St. Paul (1 Cor. 11:20–27), have similar accounts. St. John, who alone has given the promise of the Eucharist (6:34–58), does not describe the actual institution at the Last Supper. This fact was so well known at the time he wrote, and so clearly documented in the synoptic gospels and St. Paul, that he saw no need to repeat it.

first . . . bread: Passover, which takes its name from the fact that God's avenging angel in Egypt passed over the houses of the Israelites whose doorposts were marked with the blood of a lamb offered in sacrifice (Ex. 11 and 12), was one of the greatest of the Jewish religious festivals. It commem-orated the departure of the Chosen People from Egypt after the tenth plague, when the first-born of every Egyptian family was struck dead. The feast lasted seven days from the 14th to the 22nd day of Nisan. Only unleav-ened bread was eaten during these seven days. In St. Mark's account, the first day was the vigil of this festival for he specifies:

when . . . lamb: The passover lamb, commemorating the lamb slain in Egypt, was killed before sundown on the vigil. It was eaten that night, which was in fact considered to be the next day, for the Jews measured their days from sundown to sundown. Each family had a one-year old male lamb killed—its blood was sprinkled on the lintel and doorposts; it was then roasted whole with none of its bones broken (see Jn. 19:36). The family ate the meal in haste, dressed for a journey. With the lamb they took bitter herbs and unleavened bread to remind them of the slavery of Egypt and of the haste with which they left.

prepare . . . passover : Evidently, Christ was accustomed to celebrate the Jewish festivals with his disciples.

go into the city : He gives the two disciples a clear sign as to how they will find the supper room which he has already ordered. A man carrying a jar of water was something unusual. Women did this, men would carry water-bottles or skins, but not jars.

there . . . for us : Jesus kept the place selected a secret, most likely because of Judas. He knew he had planned his betrayal and Christ did not want his enemies to find them in the upper room. He had to eat the passover meal, institute the Blessed Sacrament and give a long discourse to his disciples.

as he had told them : The disciples found everything as he had said and they prepared the passover meal.

As . . . eating : Mark is not concerned with the passover meal, he mentions how Christ foretold the betrayal and then goes on to the point that interests him. He notes it was Passover night because Christ was about to celebrate his own passover, his own sacrifice of self, to set all men free from the slavery of sin.

took bread . . . broke it : Jesus as the head of the group took a loaf of unleavened bread, pronounced a blessing on it, a thanksgiving to God, broke it into little pieces and gave a piece to each saying :

Take . . . my body : In the passover meal the father of the family had to explain the meaning of the unleavened bread—"the bread of emergency for it was in great haste that you came out of the land of Egypt" (Dt. 16 : 3). Now Jesus as head of the household tells his disciples the meaning of the bread he is giving them. It is his body, his very self.

By his divine power he has made himself present in what looks like a morsel of bread. Although the Greek verb *estin* used in Mark can mean *"this is in reality"* or *"this represents,"* the verb was used by him in the first sense as the earliest tradition of the Church proves (see St. Paul, 1 Cor. 11 : 24–27, where the reality of Christ's presence after these words of consecration is clearly affirmed).

blood of the covenant : Giving each of the disciples the cup to drink, Jesus declares it to be **his blood** and this ratifies the new Covenant. As the old covenant on Mount Sinai which made the Israelites God's own people was ratified by the pouring of the blood of the sacrifices (see first reading), so now the blood of Christ which is being shed in sacrifice for all men, ratifies and seals the covenant between God and his new Chosen People.

is poured . . . many : He is about to shed his blood for many, that is, for all, or an indefinite multitude; it is the fulfillment of the "suffering servant" prophecies in second-Isaiah (Is. 42 : 6; 49 : 6; 53 : 12). Whether the disciples fully grasped the meaning of his words on that Thursday night is doubtful, but next day when they witnessed the events of Calvary, and especially after the resurrection, his meaning became crystal clear to them. The cup which he distributed among them contained his blood which was to be shed next day on Calvary. It was now being shed mystically in order to form a new Chosen People and make a second and a greater covenant than that of Sinai, which the feast of the Passover partly represented.

I shall . . . again : The food and drink his own body and blood, which he was leaving them would sustain them spiritually until they came to the messianic banquet in heaven. This eucharistic food was partaken of by the early Christians in joyful expectation of the final coming of Christ and the definitive establishment of the kingdom of heaven (see 1 Cor. 15 : 24; Eph. 1 : 22; Mt. 13 : 43; 26 : 29; Apoc. 21 : 1–5), when the unending messianic banquet would be held.

APPLICATION : Our divine Lord said : "greater love has no man than this that a man lay down his life for his friends" (Jn. 15 : 13). Christ carried out this act of love when he laid down his life for us on the cross. Because he was more than man, he was also capable of greater love than any man could show, and this he proved on the first Holy Thursday night. As man he could die for us only once, but being God as well, he ordained that this death of his could be repeated sacramentally time and again under the form of the separation of his precious blood from his body (what happened on Calvary) by means of the separate acts of consecration of bread and wine. This he did himself in the first instance. He then gave the power and the command to repeat this supernatural transformation when he said to his disciples : "do this as a memorial of me" (Lk. 22 : 19; 1 Cor. 11 : 24).

Our Savior not only became man, lived among us and died on the cross for our sakes, but in his love for us, and because of his divine power, he arranged to leave to his Church the power to re-present once more to his heavenly Father and ours, his fully-atoning sacrifice of the cross under the Eucharistic form. He thus enabled us to partake of that sacrifice as our spiritual nourishment during life. This is what our Savior did for us on Holy Thursday night in Jerusalem. That he could do it we have no doubt, because we admit he was God and man. He hid his divinity under the cloak of humanity while he was on earth as the incarnate Son. That he could hide his humanity, his body and blood, under the appearance of bread and wine is hardly any more difficult for divine power.

We have his own infallible word as witness and we have the indisputable fact that his disciples and their converts took him at his word, in the full literal sense, from the very beginning of the Church. The Eucharist, or the Mass as it was called later, was the one and only corporate act of worship which the Christian community offered to God, from the very first days of the Church. And, it must be remembered, all the first Christians in Palestine and many of them outside of Palestine, were Jews. Into them were instilled from childhood the need and grave duty to offer sacrifices of thanksgiving, petition and placation to God. On becoming Christians, they ceased offering the Jewish sacrifices, for they were convinced that they had in the Eucharist the true sacrifice which replaced all the offerings prescribed in the Old Law. It was a true sacrifice, which of its very nature, gave infinite honor, infinite thanksgiving and infinite atonement to God.

With such evidence from sacred scripture, and from the tradition of the Church from its very infancy, it seems strange that some who still claim to be Christians say they cannot admit that Christ left us his real body and his real blood in the blessed Eucharist. If he did not, he deceived the Church, a statement which is blasphemous for anyone who admits Christ's divine nature. The Church was not deceived.

"Thou hast said it, O Lord, and thy word is true," this is the solid basis of our belief in the Blessed Eucharist as a sacrifice and as a sacrament. As a sacrifice : every time we participate in the celebration of the Mass we are offering a perfectly acceptable sacrifice to God; we join together as his Chosen People to render him the thanksgiving, the honor and atonement we owe him. When we partake of that adorable sacrifice and when we eat of the bread and drink of the wine which has become the body and blood of Christ, we receive Christ within us and we become intimately united with him and with one another.

"What return can I make to the Lord for all he has done for me?" The answer is : almost nothing or very little indeed. My finite love is puny indeed beside the infinite love of God. But that does not exempt me from doing what I can. The widow's mite was appreciated. I can attend the sacrifice of the Mass devoutly as often as I possibly can, and I can and should receive my Savior into my heart every time I participate in the Mass. I know that I am not worthy and never will be worthy to receive him under my roof. I am more unworthy perhaps than the Roman centurion who first said this to Christ, but it is not the healthy who have need of the physician but the sick. I need all the spiritual help I can get in this life. What greater source of help and strength could I get than Christ himself, the very author of my salvation?

SEVENTH SUNDAY OF THE YEAR

FIRST READING : Isaiah 43 : 18–19; 21–22; 24–25. Thus says the Lord : Remember not the former things, nor consider the things of old. Behold, I am doing a new thing; now it springs forth, do you not perceive it? I will make a way in the wilderness and rivers in the desert, that the people whom I formed for myself might declare my praise.

Yet you did not call upon me, O Jacob; but you have been weary of me, O Israel! But you have burdened me with your sins, you have wearied me with your iniquities. I, I am He who blots out your transgressions for my own sake, and I will not remember your sins.

EXPLANATION : The prophet is in Babylon with the exiles and is encouraging his fellow sufferers with words of hope and consolation. Soon they will be set free, to return to their native land. This liberation—second Exodus—will be even greater and more astounding than the first Exodus from Egypt.

Thus ... Lord : The prophets frequently use such words to show that they were speaking for God, not from themselves.

remember not : All through their history the Jews looked back with longing on the great things God did for them in the past; the liberation from Egypt was among the greatest of these past favors.

I ... new thing : The same true God is still there and active. He is about to perform another liberation—a new proof of his love and his power. He will soon set them free from Babylon.

perceive it : This Exodus from Babylon is already in God's mind, and he implies that the exiles also should see it.

a way ... wilderness : The exiled Jews had to cross over miles of empty desert to return to Palestine, but God would prepare a road for them on which they could travel with all security.

rivers ... desert : One of the chief hazards to life in desert travel is lack of water. God would provide abundant water for his travelers.

people I formed : These are the Chosen People, the descendants of Abraham who had been his special concern for about twelve centuries (from the eighteenth to the sixth century B.C.).

declare my praise : His Chosen People alone know him as the true God. They alone can, therefore, give him honor and praise. Did they always do so?

not call upon me : God now reprimands them for their negligence in the past. They did not call on him, they did not rely on him, but instead relied on the help of pagans. Thus they lost their freedom and were sent into exile.

I am he ... sake : He who is Yahweh, God of all, pardons their transgressions, not because they deserve this mercy but because of his infinite forgiveness, and because they have a part to play in his plans for the future liberation of the human race—in the incarnation.

APPLICATION : Because of their forgetfulness of their vocation as God's Chosen People and on account of their utter worldliness, God allowed the Jews to be driven from their homes and fatherland by the king of Babylon in the year 597. Their temple and city of Jerusalem were razed to the ground. Strangers came and lived there. They remained as serfs in Babylon from 597 to 538. King Cyrus captured Babylon in 539 and, inspired by God, one of his first acts was to give the Jews permission to return to their homeland and rebuild their temple and city. Many of them returned. Because of this there were descendants of Abraham and of David in Palestine when God's appointed

time came for sending his divine Son on earth.

This past history of the Jews is not something which does not concern us; it was part of God's merciful and loving plans for our redemption. Twelve centuries earlier he had chosen Abraham and revealed himself to him. He made the descendants of Abraham his own special people; he heaped love and kindness on them; but their response was far from generous. However, he tolerated them even when they ignored and insulted him, for in the incarnation which he had planned from eternity, his divine Son was to take his human nature from a descendant of Abraham.

Therefore, the liberation from the

Babylonian exile which happened through God's loving intervention twenty-four hundred years ago, was a necessary step toward our salvation. If the prophet idealizes and exaggerates the happy conditions of the returning exiles, for example, "roads in the wilderness and rivers in the desert," it is because he sees in his mind's eye the true liberation of all men for which this was but a remote preparation. The life, death and resurrection of Christ not only brought men back from exile from God which sin had imposed on them, but it laid down a direct road through the desert of life to the homeland, which Christ won for us through his incarnation. Through the shedding of his blood Christ has made the treasures of divine grace available to all who seek them—rivers of life-giving water flow through the wilderness of this world for all who will drink of them.

Reflect for a few moments today on all that God has done for our salvation. Bringing back the Jewish exiles from Babylon was but one small incident in the long chain of events which he set in motion in order to make us Christians and his adopted children. The call of Abraham, thirty-eight centuries ago, the Exodus from Egypt thirty-two hundred years ago, the return from Babylon in 538 B.C., the coming of Christ on earth nearly two thousand years ago, were all links in the golden chain of God's salvific plan for all of us. He intended heaven to be our eternal home. To do this he raised us up through the incarnation of his divine Son to the status of adopted children. This gives us a claim to a share in his kingdom; this makes us heirs to heaven.

Unfortunately, there is but one thing that can spoil this plan of God as far as we are concerned, abuse of the free will which God has given us. Our free will which should follow what is right, which should choose the greatest good can, and sometimes does, choose instead what is not only not good but what is positively evil. We know from experience that this is so. We have been ungrateful, disloyal, disobedient and insulting to God in the past. But we know also that we do not have to continue in such a state. We can use our free will to choose what is right and avoid what causes offense to God. We owe so much to God that we should never hesitate in future to do what he asks of us. The eternal happiness of heaven is worth all the crosses and sufferings and mortification of a million lives on this earth. Let us not begrudge sixty or seventy years of loyal service to him, who has prepared a place for us since the beginning of time.

SECOND READING : 2 Corinthians 1: 18–22. As surely as God is faithful, our word to you has not been Yes and No. For the Son of God, Jesus Christ, whom we preached among you, Silvanus and Timothy and I, was not Yes and No; but in him it is always Yes. For all the promises of God find their Yes in him. That is why we utter the Amen through him, to the glory of God. But it is God who establishes us with you in Christ, and has commissioned us; he has put his seal upon us and given us his Spirit in our hearts as a guarantee.

EXPLANATION: St. Paul wrote this second letter from Ephesus or from Philippi, to his Corinthian converts toward the end of his third missionary journey (53–57). There were a few among his converts, or some others who had come among the converts, who were belittling Paul and boasting of their own superiority. He does not mince his words to show that he is no mean Apostle. He has suffered and labored to spread the message of Christ and God has been generous to him with his divine revelations. He "needs no letters of recommendation" as some do (3 : 1). He has words of praise and affection for his converts while he warns them against heeding the dogmatic errors of his opponents. In today's excerpt from his letter we find the Apostle asserting under oath that he was not fickle and changeable. He and his companions taught the truth for they taught Jesus Christ who is absolute, existing truth. Paul's commission to preach the gospel to the Corinthians came from God himself, and the Spirit of God was with him in his missionary activities guaranteeing success.

God is faithful : This was the introductory formula of an oath : "as true as God"; so true is my statement.

our . . . no : His teaching was always consistent, without deception or vacillation.

Son of God : What Paul, Silvanus and Timothy had preached to the Corinthians was Jesus Christ, who was the Son of God. There could be no contradictions, no hesitations, in such a doctrine, for :

in him . . . yes : Jesus Christ is truth itself.

All . . . in him : All the promises of God in the Old Testament were fulfilled in Christ. He was the one of whom God spoke, therefore he was the truth incarnate.

amen . . . glory : Christ is our sole mediator with God : through him alone are we able to give glory to God. It is by our acceptance of Christ, our saying "amen" to him, that we can glorify God.

God establishes . . . Christ : It is God who gave Paul and the Corinthian converts the grace and strength to become followers of Christ.

commissioned us : Paul reverts to the defense of his apostleship. It was God who appointed him for this task (see Acts 9 : 15–16) of preaching Christ to the Gentiles. "Anointed us," as the Jerusalem Bible has it, is a better translation, but the meaning is the same.

seal . . . guarantee : God has marked Paul (and his converts) as his own property. He has made a down-payment on the reward in store for them in the future, by giving him, and them, the Holy Spirit whose presence was made evident by his gifts to Paul and the converts. How could Paul be insincere or vacillating while the Holy Spirit dwelt in him? The Blessed Trinity is mentioned here : the Father gives the grace to men to accept Jesus, his Son and on acceptance the Spirit dwells in the converts.

APPLICATION : St. Paul's principal purpose in these five verses from his letter was to prove to the converts of Corinth that he was faithful in every way to his office of preacher of the Gospel of Christ. This was an office given him by God the Father. At the same time, he stresses the Christocentric dogma of our faith. Christ, the incarnate Son of God, is the fulfillment of all God's promises, of all God's plans for the elevation and sanctification of mankind. It is through him alone that we all can give to God the honor and glory which is his due. It is through the Son's incarnation that we are made capable of sharing in God's eternal kingdom of happiness.

We men are mere creatures whose habitat, like that of all other creatures, is this earth. We are mortal like all other earthly creatures. But we have special gifts which differentiate us very clearly from all other earthly creatures —we have the spiritual gifts of intellect and free will. With our intellect we can form abstract ideas, we can reason, see truth, remember the past and to a limited extent we can foresee the future and provide for it. With our free will we can admire and love the good and beautiful; we can pick and choose; we can decide what to do or not to do whenever a time for decision presents itself.

Now these special gifts raise us above all other earthly creatures. Because of them we can master and subdue all other creatures, and make them serve our purposes. However, if these special gifts were to help us only in this world, they would be of doubtful value. If our intellect which empowers us to remember the past, plan for the present and future, enables us to build and produce objects which will outlast us by centuries, and if this same intellect were to tell us that we had only a few years to enjoy our life and faculties, it would hardly be a source of comfort. If our free will, which sees the good things that follow from life, and which of its very nature seeks the lasting good and happiness, were to learn through the intellect that such longings and desires were in vain, would we then not be better off without such a faculty?

In other words, if man's end is the grave, if all the satisfaction he can derive from his intellect and will, from his superior faculties, must be crammed into comparatively few years would he not be far better off without these faculties? The dumb beast in the field is content with satisfying its animal needs. It has no thought for the future because it has no thoughts at all. It does not fear its grave because it does not foresee the grave. It sheds no tears at parting with its fellow beasts because it does not know of its departure, nor are the others its *fellow-beasts*. Man, indeed, would have good reason to regret being a man, and not a cow or an ass, if life ended for him in the grave.

This is where we see God's love and goodness. Out of his sheer goodness he created us and gave us these superior faculties because he meant us to enjoy them forever in his own eternal kingdom. The means he adopted to raise us from the status of creatures and make us capable of sharing his kingdom was the incarnation. His Son was to share our human nature with us and thus give us the right to share with him his divine nature. Christ "adopted" our human nature so that God the Father would adopt us as his sons. This was God's plan, and was put into operation when Christ became man. "All the promises of God find their yes (their fulfillment) in him," says St. Paul. Not only the prophecies in the Old Testament, but the whole story of the Old Testament was God's preparation for this supreme act of love and benevolence toward mankind. The incarnation is the supreme culmination of God's love in his dealings with men.

We can, therefore, give glory and honor to God for we are brothers of Christ and adopted as sons by God.

Without this elevation to sonship we could give no acceptable honor to God, could expect no divine reward. The grave would be our end. But the incarnation has changed all for those who lived before Christ, as well as for those who have since entered this world. The eternal benefits of the incarnation are not restricted to Christians only, they are available to all who do not knowingly and deliberately reject Christ and his Father.

Our knowledge of the incarnation and of the infinite love of God who planned it put us in a privileged position. If we appreciate the privileges, as we should, we ought to be ready to do all in our power to share them with our fellowmen who, through no fault of their own, are still ignorant of Christ and his incarnation. Our resolution today should be to do so.

GOSPEL: Mark 2:1-12. When Jesus returned to Capernaum, it was reported that he was at home. And many were gathered together, so that there was no longer room for them, not even about the door; and he was preaching the word to them. And they came, bringing to him a paralytic carried by four men. And when they could not get near him because of the crowd, they removed the roof above him; and when they had made an opening, they let down the pallet on which the paralytic lay. And when Jesus saw their faith, he said to the paralytic, "My son, your sins are forgiven." Now some of the scribes were sitting there, questioning in their hearts, "Why does this man speak thus? It is blasphemy! Who can forgive sins but God alone?" And immediately Jesus, perceiving in his spirit that they thus questioned within themselves, said to them, "Why do you question thus in your hearts? Which is easier, to say to the paralytic, 'Your sins are forgiven,' or to say, 'Rise, take up your pallet and walk'? But that you may know that the Son of man has authority on earth to forgive sins"—he said to the paralytic— "I say to you, rise, take up your pallet and go home." And he rose, and immediately took up the pallet and went out before them all; so that they were all amazed and glorified God, saying, "We never saw anything like this!"

EXPLANATION: St. Mark describes an incident which occurred in Capernaum during the early days of Christ's public ministry. Friends brought a paralytic on a stretcher to Jesus to be cured. They had to go to great lengths to get him to Jesus, because the crowd was so great. Jesus admired the strong faith they and the paralytic showed, and he told the paralytic that his sins were forgiven him. This shocked the Scribes. Only God can forgive sins, they said to themselves, this man is a blasphemer, for he is claiming to have divine power. To prove to them that he had divine power, Jesus told them that to cure the paralytic also required divine power. There and then he cured him. The Scribes were confounded; the crowd glorified God.

many gathered: The news that he was a miracle-worker very quickly had spread through Galilee. Most of the crowd had come, hoping to obtain or see a miracle—they listened to his preaching but to them that was of secondary importance.

carried . . . men: Four men brought on a stretcher a man unable to walk. When they could not get near enough, because of the large crowd, they went up on the flat roof of the house, taking the paralytic with them. They removed the matting and a few branches. This was the usual type of roof on houses in Palestine at that time. They lowered the stretcher inside the door of the house where Jesus was standing as he taught.

saw their faith: These men were definitely expecting Jesus to cure their friend—they had no doubt that he could. They would not have gone to such trouble otherwise. The paralytic also must have had the same strong faith or he would not have allowed them to do what they did.

your sins are forgiven: The man probably felt how sinful and unworthy he was when he found himself so close to the sinless one. Jesus' statement was meant to put his mind at rest: "your sins are forgiven."

Scribes . . . there : They were, evidently, nearest to the door—"they always chose the first places."

it is blasphemy : Their statement would have been right if their premise had been right. If Jesus was not God, then he was a blasphemer if he claimed divine power. But he was God and he proved it.

which . . . say : Jesus now answers their unspoken criticism. To cure a paralytic requires divine power, and the miracle-worker who does not call on God to work the miracle, but does it on his own authority and as of right, must be God. This is what Jesus did.

take . . . home : "That you may know that the Son of man has authority on earth to forgive sins," Jesus said; this I shall prove to you by showing you that I have also on my own, the power of miracles. Thereupon he commanded the paralytic to stand up and walk, fully healed.

never . . . like this : Jesús had worked other cures before this, but this was probably the most striking miracle they had seen so far. "They glorified God," that is, they thanked God for the presence of such a person among them. As yet, they were far from recognizing him as the Son of God. That would come in time.

APPLICATION : In this incident we have the fundamental dogma of our Christian faith, namely, that Christ was the Son of God, stated by no less an authority than Christ himself. He had said to the paralytic: "your sins are forgiven"; straight away the Scribes, who knew their Old Testament, objected. This was blasphemy. They said: only God can forgive sins, for all sins are committed against God and it is only the offended person who can forgive an offense; this *man* is claiming to be God. This was surely blasphemy, for according to them *this man* was not and could not be God. Christ, in his answer, proved to them how wrong they were. First, he showed them that he knew the thoughts they had in their minds—they had not expressed their feelings openly. Secondly, he asked them which was easier to say and to say effectively: "your sins are forgiven," or "rise, take up your pallet and walk?" Both effective statements required divine

power. To prove that he had that power, and to prove it in a way that was visible to them (they could not see whether the man's sins were forgiven or not) he went on: "But that you may know that the Son of man has authority on earth to forgive sins"—he said to the paralytic—"I say to you rise, take up your pallet and go home." The sick man arose immediately, took up his stretcher and walked away in the presence of that huge crowd.

Whether the Scribes were among those who "were amazed and who glorified God" because of what they had witnessed, is doubtful. They were hard-hearted and full of pride and therefore, found the reversing of the judgements more than difficult. But we can leave them to the mercy of God. For ourselves, we can thank our divine Lord for giving us this clear proof of his divinity. He claimed to be God, when he forgave sins; he proved that claim by an outstanding miracle. He would have worked this miracle of mercy even if the Scribes had never interfered, but he tells them that he is about to work it to prove to them that he is divine. By a single word of command, given on his own authority, the paralysis leaves the sick man and he is healed instantly—a visible proof of Christ's claim to be God.

This is but one of the many proofs of his divinity which Christ gave to his disciples, and through them to us, during his public ministry. His claim to be divine was well known to his enemies, it was in fact the principal charge on which they had him crucified. "The Jews answered Pilate : we have a law and according to that law he must die because he made himself Son of God" (Jn. 19 : 7). They did not say that he was God, they could never admit that, all the evidence notwithstanding; but only that he, *falsely of course*, claimed to be Son of God.

We who already are firm believers in the divinity of Christ our Savior have no new doctrine to learn from today's gospel. It can, however, fill us with an ever deeper gratitude to God who sent his Son as man on earth, to make us his own adopted sons and heirs to heaven. It should also make us have a greater appreciation of our own value in the sight of God. He wants us in heaven with himself and so he sent his Son among us to make us capable of going there. Christ, his Son, humbled himself so that we should be glorified. Christ bore the cross so that we might get the eternal crown. Christ died an agonizing death that we might have an unending life of happiness.

Is there anything more that God could have done for us? Like the crowd that day in Capernaum, we are amazed at the love God has shown us and the fatherly interest he has in our eternal welfare. Let us imitate the same crowd by glorifying God and his divine Son, who has made us his brothers.

EIGHTH SUNDAY OF THE YEAR

FIRST READING : Hosea 2 : 14-15; 19-20. Thus says the Lord, "Behold, I will allure her, and bring her into the wilderness, and speak tenderly to her. And there she shall answer as in the days of her youth, as at the time when she came out of the land of Egypt. "And in that day, says the Lord, I will betroth you to me for ever; I will betroth you to me in righteousness and in justice, in steadfast love, and in mercy. I will betroth you to me in faithfulness; and you shall know the Lord."

EXPLANATION : After the death of Solomon in 931 B.C., the northern part of his kingdom revolted and set up a separate kingdom which was called Israel. Ten of the twelve Tribes lived in the northern half; Benjamin only remained with Judah in the southern kingdom. The schism, at first political, very soon became a religious one also. Yahweh was forgotten in Israel; idolatry spread from the kings to the people. But Yahweh did not desert his people even though they had deserted him. He sent one prophet after another to recall them to their senses. It was in vain, as far as the kings and leaders were concerned. The result was that Israel eventually, in 721, disappeared as a nation and as a people, never to rise again.

One of the earliest prophets whose works we have in writing was Hosea. He was called by Yahweh to bring the northern people back to their God. He preached around the middle of the eighth century B.C. It was a period of irreligion, political turbulence and gen-eral discord. Regicide became the order of the day—no less than six kings reigned in Israel between 743 and 724. The prophet's theme was the disloyalty of Israel. She was Yahweh's spouse. He had led her out of the slavery of Egypt and had given her a homeland, but she played the harlot, she was unfaithful. Today's four verses bring out the essence of this general theme.

Thus says the Lord : This is the customary introduction of the prophetic work. It is God who is speaking through his mouthpiece, the prophet.

allure . . . wilderness : Yahweh is quite willing to forgive the infidelity of his spouse, Israel. All he wants is that Israel should come back and begin once more to be loyal. She was loyal and faithful when first he made her his spouse in the desert of Sinai; she had no other gods then. He would bring her back there to the desert to enable her to recapture her first fervor and fidelity.

and in that day : The prophet is referring to the messianic age, "that day," when God will take back Israel once more and this time it will be a faithful marriage.

betroth . . . forever: It will not be a temporary or temporal union, it will be eternal.

righteousness and justice: The new alliance, or marriage, or covenant, will be based on true uprightness, true justice, true love on the part of Israel, and on God's part steadfast love and mercy.

know the Lord: The Israel of old did not know the Lord. The people were selfish and self-seeking. They forgot God's blessings as soon as they had received them. The new Israel will be different. Through Christ they will really get to know the infinite love and mercy of God. The incarnation brought God down among us, and put the knowledge of God's nature, which is love, within the reach of even the lowliest.

APPLICATION: For any Christian reader of the Old Testament, the infidelity, the ingratitude and the lack of love which the Chosen People showed toward God, and which is apparent in almost every page of their sacred writings, is an insoluble enigma. They were the one people on earth to whom he had revealed himself. While their neighbors on all sides, men far more intelligent and more skillful than they, were still adoring idols and offering valuable sacrifices to sacred bulls or to images of wood or stone, the Israelites knew and adored the Creator of heaven and earth, the first cause and the final end of all things that exist. They knew not only that he was existence itself but that it was he who gave existence to all that was or ever will be. That knowledge was more than theoretical, he had made himself their special protector. He had proved his special interest in them and when he led them out of Egypt, proved that he had the power to do so.

They appreciated this for the moment. When he made a pact or covenant with them on Sinai they "with one voice" agreed and promised to carry out their part of the pact. He would be their God; they would ignore all false gods;

they would keep all his commandments. But this resolution did not last long. Many times in the journey through the desert they rebelled against him and against Moses, the leader whom he had appointed over them. Aided by God's mighty hand, they took over the land of Canaan and settled there. Here, too, they quickly forgot that it was he who put them there, and began to pay attention to the Canaanite idols. With the fatherhood of God forgotten by the vast majority of them, it was not long until their own brotherhood of the tribes was forgotten. The schism came—the north first fell away completely and was lost to history in 721. The south survived for some two hundred years longer, but Judah, too, was taken into exile. In Judah, however, there were always a faithful few and the faithful few saved her from extinction. A remnant, as the prophets had foretold, returned to the homeland and God's reason for choosing the descendants of Abraham was fulfilled: the incarnation took place as he had planned it from eternity.

This is, in brief, the sad history of the Chosen People—a people he had espoused, made his own wife, as it were, but this people were unfaithful to him and again and again left him and played the harlot with pagan gods. Yet, time out of number, God pardoned them and was ever ready to take them back whenever they repented of their folly. We know not which to wonder at most —the gross ingratitude of that stiff-necked, hard-hearted people, or the infinite patience and pity of the good God who was ever ready to forgive in order to bestow his blessings on them.

While we must, and do, feel ashamed for the manner in which the Chosen People of old treated the all-merciful, the all-loving God, it might be no harm for us to take a good look at our own relationship with the same all-merciful, all-loving Father. True, we can declare straight away that we are still Christians, but does this make us loyal spouses of the Father and faithful followers of Christ? Most, if not all of us, can find that there is much lacking in our relationship with God. We may not be bending our knee to Venus, Mars or Jupiter, but how many worthless idols have we set up in our own hearts? Officially and publicly we have not abandoned God but how much of our thoughts and time do we really give to him? We may still be Christians in name but that is not living the Christian life. Our Lord made this very clear to us when he said: not everyone who says to me "Lord, Lord" shall enter into the kingdom of heaven, but rather he who does the will of my Father in heaven" (Mt. 7 : 22). Are we obeying the will, that is, keeping the commandments of God? Are we known as Christians in our daily dealings with our neighbors? Does our Christian religion influence our whole lives or is it a little show reserved for Sunday mornings?

The Chosen People of old had many, far too many faults, but even though we Christians have a greater knowledge of God and greater proofs of his infinite love for us, many of us are little better than these people of old. The Jews of the Old Testament had no clear knowledge of the future life, the time was not yet ripe to reveal it. On the other hand, we know that reaching eternal life, which Christ has won for us, is the one thing that really matters. We may be rich or poor in this life; we may have successes or failures; we may be sick or in good health, but none of these things will matter when we face the future life. To be with God, then, alone matters. I know what I want when I die. I, and I alone, can assure for myself what I want. Christ has given me the key to the happy future that I desire. Will I have the sound sense to use that key each day of my life, and so assure my entrance into eternal happiness?

SECOND READING: 2 Corinthians 3:1-6. Are we beginning to commend ourselves again? Or do we need, as some do, letters of recommendation to you, or from you? You yourselves are our letter or recommendation, written on your hearts, to be known and read by all men; and you show that you are a letter from Christ delivered by us, written not with ink but with the Spirit of the living God, not on tablets of stone but on tablets of human hearts.

Such is the confidence that we have through Christ toward God. Not that we are sufficient of ourselves to claim anything as coming from us; our sufficiency is from God, who has qualified us to be ministers of a new covenant, not in a written code but in the Spirit.

EXPLANATION: Today's reading is a continuation of last Sunday's reading from St. Paul's second letter to the Corinthians—see above. He is still defending his apostleship, his divine commission to preach the gospel of Christ to all nations. The faithful and sincere Corinthian converts are the best testimony, and the only testimony he needs, of his ministry among them. But it was God, not he, who made them what they are.

need . . . to you: He is, evidently, referring to the false preacher who had tried to belittle the work of Paul as an Apostle of Christ. He must have come into the Corinthian community with letters of recommendation—a guarantee from somebody that he was a true Christian. Paul does not condemn this practice—the Church in Ephesus recommended Apollos as a Christian teacher to the Corinthians (Acts 18 : 27), but he, Paul, needs no such recommendation: it is Christ himself who appointed him an Apostle.

you . . . our letter: "From their fruits you shall know them." The faithful Christians of Corinth are the proof and the recommendation of his work among them.

read by all men: Their upright Christian lives are evident to all.

from Christ . . . us: He was only Christ's messenger in bringing the Christian faith to them; he was Christ's mail-man in the bringing of that letter.

not . . . but Spirit: This letter, this Christian message, was written not with ink but with the Spirit whose presence was evident from the numerous gifts bestowed on them (see 1 Cor. chapters 12–14).

not . . . hearts: Unlike the covenant of the Old Law, the covenant of the New Testament is not written on stone tablets but on the actual human hearts of those who accept the covenant. This was foretold by the prophet Jeremiah (31 : 31–34).

such . . . confidence: "Before God, we are confident of this through Christ" (Jerusalem Bible) is a better translation. Paul can testify, before God, that his ministry in Corinth inscribed the true Christian faith in the hearts of his converts, because Christ gave him this ministry and the Holy Spirit testified to its fruitfulness.

not . . . ourselves: Paul immediately disclaims any credit for himself in this successful ministry. It was the grace of God which made a success of Paul's mission.

God who qualified: God converted Saul from being a persecutor of the

Christian Church, into a great apostle of the new covenant, the new Christian religion.

not . . . code : Unlike the old covenant, the new is written in the hearts of the believers, by the Holy Spirit.

kills . . . life : The Decalog was composed of "do" and "don't," but it was ineffective for it did not give the power to accomplish. The Spirit who inscribes the new Covenant in the hearts of men gives them the power, the necessary strength, to carry out its commands.

APPLICATION : The marvelous growth of the Christian Church from the first Pentecost day was nothing less than a miracle of reciprocal love. The infinite love of God, seen in the incarnation, life, death and resurrection of his own divine Son, together with the visible presence of the Holy Spirit sent by the Father and the Son, moved the hearts of those who witnessed these marvels and those who heard of them from witnesses, to give their all in order to become sharers in this divine banquet of love. Once the unprejudiced Jews of Jerusalem listened to the story of the divine benevolence of God, as narrated by the Apostles, their immediate reaction was to make some return for that love. They did so by repenting of their sins and by becoming, in their thousands, followers of Christ. Three thousand Jews became Christians on the first Pentecost day (Acts 2 : 41); within a few weeks this number had risen to five thousand (Acts 4 : 4), and continued to increase daily (see Acts 5 : 14; 6 : 1–7).

Soon the Christian faith spread to all Judea and from there to Samaria, Galilee, Phoenicia, Cyprus and Syria (Acts 8 : 4–8; 9 : 31; 11 : 21; 24; 16 : 5). From Antioch in Syria, Paul began his three great missionary journeys that brought the faith to Asia Minor and Greece. In the meantime, others (most probably St. Peter at their head) had taken the gospel message to Rome itself, the capital of the empire—the then-known world. By the time the last of the Apostles, St. John, had died there was scarcely any town of any size in the Middle East, Asia Minor, North Africa or the Mediterranean provinces which had not a flourishing Christian Church. And this happened in spite of strong opposition from the Jews, and official persecution and pogroms from the Roman authorities.

The Christian religion was not then (and never was and never will be) the opium of the people, or the religion of the soft. For a Jew to become a Christian at that time meant breaking with centuries of tradition, breaking with one's family and incurring excommunication from the synagogue with the certainty of being imprisoned and persecuted by one's fellow-Jews whenever these had the power to do so, or to be denounced to the Roman authorities when the Jews could not themselves punish him. Things were no easier for the Gentiles; if anything, conversion meant more difficulties for them. Their pagan life had been one of completely lax morality; to curb their animal passions and to mortify their senses, therefore, was demanding a great deal of them. Add to that, the jibes and the sneers of their pagan neighbors, as well as the possibility and often the strong probability of official persecution, imprisonment and death. This was no opium, no glorious pipe-dream for Jew or Gentiles; becoming a Christian had no earthly or material attraction. Christianity was not something to be adopted by the weakling or the self-seeker, it did not play up to the weaknesses of human nature.

Christianity, however, had what no other religion ever had or could have, it was based on the infinite love of God for man, a love manifested through the Son of God becoming man, so that men could become sons of God. As St. Paul puts it : "God loved us with so much love that he was generous with his mercy . . . he brought us life with Christ . . . and raised us up with him and gave us a place with him in heaven" (Eph. 2 : 4–6). St. John says : "Think of the love that the Father has lavished on us, by letting us be called God's children, and that is what we are" (1 Jn. 3 : 1). It was this infinite love of God for man manifested in the incarnation that attracted followers to Christ. It was the desire of all generous hearts to make some return to God for all he had done and continued to do for them, that prompted the first Christians to abandon kith and kin where necessary, and their own human inclinations, and dedicate themselves to the following of Christ. It was the same spirit of generosity, aroused by the evidence of God's love, that made the thousands of martyrs go singing joyfully to their execution and made millions of saints live a life of self-mortification and penance, in order to say thanks in the best way they could.

We are part of that long procession of Christians wending our way to heaven, which began on that first Pentecost day and will end only when the love and mercy of God have brought the last inhabitants of this earth to heaven. We may not be asked to imitate the hardships of the first Christians, but we are asked to pay our sincere thanks to God : by living our Christian life to the full every day of our lives. Ours is a religion of love and generosity; God gave himself to us and we are trying to make some return for that generosity by striving to love God with our whole heart, and our neighbor for love of God.

GOSPEL : Mark 2 : 18–22. John's disciples and the Pharisees were fasting; and people came and said to him, "Why do John's disciples and the disciples of the Pharisees fast, but your disciples do not fast?" And Jesus said to them, "Can the wedding guests fast while the bridegroom is with them? As long as they have the bridegroom with them, they cannot fast. The days will come, when the bridegroom is taken away from them, and then they will fast in that day. No one sews a piece of unshrunk cloth on an old garment; if he does, the patch tears away from it, the new from the old, and a worse tear is made. And no one puts new wine into old wineskins; if he does, the wine will burst the skins, and the wine is lost, and so are the skins; but new wine is for fresh skins."

EXPLANATION : In this section of his Gospel (1 : 40–3 : 6), St. Mark has placed side by side a series of controversies which the Pharisees had with Jesus. It began with Jesus' claim to forgive sins (last Sunday's gospel), then came the call of Levi, a tax-gatherer and, therefore, a sinner according to the Pharisees. Not only did Jesus ask Levi (Matthew) to follow him but he had a meal in Levi's house at which other tax-gatherers and sinners took part. Then comes to-day's dispute about fastings, to be followed by the plucking of the ears of corn and the healing of a withered hand on the sabbath day (next Sunday's gospel). This was the climax. The Pharisees then "began to plot . . . discussing how to destroy him."

In today's incident Jesus and his disciples are accused of not fasting. Moses had prescribed only one day of fasting each year—the day of Atonement—but the Pharisees multiplied their fastings and made sure that everybody knew this (see Mt. 6 : 16; Lk. 18 : 12) : "they got their reward in this life," Jesus told them. The Baptist's disciples, like the Pharisees, were still Jews and relied very much on external observance. They, too, kept many fasts. Our Lord's answer to those who questioned him was : while

I am with my disciples they are celebrating the new covenant, the nuptials of God with the new Chosen People (Hos. 2 : 16–20; Is. 54 : 5–6; Jer. 2 : 2; Ez. 16). Therefore, this was not a time for fasting. Furthermore, the new covenant cannot and must not be fitted into the confining limits of the Old Law— the new wine in the old wineskins, the new patch on the old garment.

John's disciples : When the Baptist began to preach at the Jordan many devout Jews came to him and stayed with him as his disciples. Four of these, at least : Peter, Andrew, James and John had joined Christ, when the Baptist pointed him out to them. Others remained with John. John's life was one of strict fasting, his disciples naturally tried to imitate him.

Pharisees fast : Fasting from food, within reason of course, is in itself a neutral act. It derives its value from the motive which inspires it. The Pharisees, unfortunately, seem to have been moved by a desire to be admired by the people. Thus their fasting had no spiritual valve.

wedding guests : Jesus compares his disciples with wedding guests, as explained above. A wedding is a time for feasting not fasting.

the days will come : When Jesus leaves them, the days of feasting will end; they will have their share of fasting and other mortifications.

piece . . . cloth : Jesus now brings in two similes or parables to show that the new covenant which he is founding is not a mending, or a repairing of the old. It is entirely distinct. A patch of new cloth on an old garment will render the garment and the patch useless.

new wine . . . skins : Bottles or containers, made of goat- and sheep-skin, were the usual containers in use at that time. An old wine-skin container was already stretched to its limit. New wine expands as it ferments—if the container cannot expand with it, it bursts and the wine and container are lost. The message here was : the new covenant was not to be inserted into the old or confined within the limits of the old. It went much further than the old. It established a new relationship of love and sonship between man and God.

APPLICATION : The Old Testament, the religion of the Jews, was a preparation for the New, the Christian religion. It had many factors which raised it far beyond and above any of the other pagan religions of that time, but nevertheless it was very imperfect. The Israelites (later called Jews) knew the true God, the God who made heaven and earth and was Lord of all, but their knowledge of him was very limited and their response to that knowledge was still more limited. They knew him as their Father and Benefactor, but the vast majority of them did not regulate their lives according to that knowledge. They looked to him for material benefits and when they had these they promptly forgot him. They called on him to win their wars for them, but in their days of peace and plenty they forgot he was there. While the essence of their religion and the reason God made them his Chosen People was to prepare for the Messiah—the one who was to come—they frequently forgot this and set their whole heart and interest in getting all they could out the present life. It is true that God for his own wise reasons, had revealed very little to them as regards life after death, but they did not know that their future hopes were tied up with the one who was to come. They did not know that if they served God faithfully, keeping his commandments, that he would provide for them. But their idea of God's providence, or providing, was nearly always restricted to earthly benefits. By the time the promised Messiah came, their idea of him was purely secular—he would be a political leader who would free them from the hated Roman rulers and give them an extensive worldly empire.

When Christ came there were some who were zealous for the Law. They set out to keep it strictly according to the letter, but their motive for keeping it, pride and self-glory, ruined their otherwise good deeds. They forgot God whose Law they were keeping; they despised their neighbors, their fellow-Jews, who did not observe the Law so strictly as they; they shut their eyes and their ears to Jesus' claims that he was the promised Messiah. Even more, that he was the Son of God himself. How could he be? They argued : he is friendly with sinners, his disciples don't fast as we do, he does not keep the Sabbath, he

I

has made one of the tax-gatherers, the vilest sinners, a disciple of his?

Christ answers them in today's gospel. He is the Bridegroom of the new covenant. His new pact with those who will follow him, is a cause for joy and happiness. His coming is the culmination and crowning act of God's love for mankind. The old covenant or pact with the Chosen People was but a shadow or foretaste of the reality. The new covenant, the Christian religion is not a reparation, an amending, or a refilling of what was missing in the old—it is a new and independent entity. It is a new wedding, with new wedding garments. It is a new container capable of holding safely the new wine of mutual love between the Father and the sons he has adopted through Christ.

This is our religion, the religion formed by the bonds of divine love which bind us to the Trinity. God the Father gave us Christ to be our brother. He thereby made us his own adopted sons. The Father and Son have sent the Holy Spirit into the hearts of each one of us at Baptism to enable us to recognize that God is our Father and we his beloved children. We are no longer servants, therefore, we are no longer out-siders, we are members of God's family and our duties are not obligations imposed on us, but duties which arise from being members of God's household, duties deriving from love. We keep God's laws, then, and the laws of his Church, not as something we have to do, but as something which gives us an opportunity of showing him our love and gratitude for all he has done for us. The good Christian does not inquire how much he is obliged to do in order to go to heaven, rather he seeks extra ways and means of proving how grateful he is to God for giving him the chance of reaching heaven. He finds this life far too short to do all he would like to do for God.

If that is the criterion on which we are judged, many of us may truly say that we are not good Christians. Perhaps we have not been always good Christians, but while there is life there is hope. We can always mend our ways. Begin, today, to serve God out of love and very soon you'll find that what you looked on before as a burden will be changed by love into a privilege and a joy. God will never be outdone in generosity.

NINTH SUNDAY OF THE YEAR

FIRST READING : Deuteronomy 5 : 12–15. Thus says the Lord, "Observe the Sabbath day, to keep it holy, as the Lord your God commanded you. Six days you shall labor, and do all your work; but the seventh day is a Sabbath to the Lord your God; in it you shall not do any work, you, or your son, or your daughter, or your manservant, or your maidservant, or your ox, or your ass, or any of your cattle, or the sojourner who is within your gates, that your manservant and your maidservant may rest as well as you. You shall remember that you were a servant in the land of Egypt, and the Lord your God brought you out thence with a mighty hand and an outstretched arm; therefore the Lord your God commanded you to keep the Sabbath day."

EXPLANATION : On the Book of Deuteronomy see the Fourth Sunday of the year. Today's four verses treat of the observance of the Sabbath day.

observe . . . day : The name Sabbath is most probably derived from the verb **Shebath**=to cease from work, to repose, and not from the noun **Sheba** which means the number seven. That the observance of the day of rest was prescribed every seventh day does not justify the second derivation which is contrary to the laws of Hebrew phonetics.

to keep it holy : This day of rest was to be dedicated to the Lord.

six . . . labor : Man must work the other six days of the week, but the seventh day he is free from work and so can think of the Lord and thank him.

son . . . maidservant : Every individual in the household, both the members of the family and the servant or slaves, must be free from work on that day.

ox . . . sojourner : The animals used for carrying loads or tilling the land must also be allowed rest, as must any strangers who happen to be staying in the camps or the towns of the Israelites.

a servant . . . Egypt : In Exodus (20 : 11), the reason why the seventh day should be a holy day and free from all work was that God himself rested from his work of creation on the seventh day and blessed that day and made it sacred. Here, in Deuteronomy, the Israelites are commanded to rest from labor and to allow all their household to rest, because they were slaves in Egypt when God set them free, and gave them rest from the hard labor they were forced to do there. They are to imitate this mercy of God and give freedom from labor one day a week to themselves and especially to their slaves.

not do any work: This was the negative side of the day of rest; the positive and most important side was the making of the day holy to the Lord.

APPLICATION: It is very probable that the custom of keeping the seventh day of the week holy goes back to pre-Mosaic times. In Exodus (20 : 18), the Israelites are told to "remember the Sabbath day" and here in Deuteronomy "the Sabbath day" is introduced as already known to the people. Among the other commandments which he gave them on Mount Sinai God made this seventh day of rest a command. The motive given in Exodus was to imitate their Creator. Here the reason is gratitude for the deliverance from the slavery of Egypt. This gratitude is best shown by freeing their own servants and slaves from hard labor once a week; the reason in both cases is a religious one. "The seventh day is a sabbath to the Lord your God"—that day is given to God as a thanksgiving for the other six days of the week which he has given them to work for themselves.

This command to keep the Sabbath holy was one of the best observed of the Ten Commandments among the Israelites. During the Babylonian exile and later in the Diaspora, when they dispersed around the Greek empire, without temple or other place of worship, they were distinguised from the Gentiles by their observance of the Sabbath. Early in the Maccabean war the Jews refused to defend themselves against the Syrians who attacked them on the Sabbath; they preferred to die rather than violate the Sabbath (1 M. 2 : 29–38). Mattathias, however, thought that this zeal for the Sabbath observance was going too far, and he decided that the Jews had a right to defend themselves on the Sabbath. Even those who did so refused to pursue a defeated enemy on that day (2 M. 8 : 25). Later the Scribes and Pharisees added so many additions and interpretations to the law of abstention from work that even the most necessary personal needs could not be attended to.

However, the commandment was observed in all its rigor at the time of Christ, as we shall see in today's gospel. The Christian Church accepted this commandment with the others from the beginning, but instead of the seventh day, the day of prayer and rest from work was changed to the first day of the week—from Saturday to Sunday. This change was most probably brought about among the Gentile Christians outside of Palestine by St. Paul. Sunday was chosen in place of Saturday because Christ rose from the dead on Sunday, the Holy Spirit descended on the Apostles on Sunday and God the Father began his work of creation and sanctification on Sunday. Thus our Sabbath day is a day dedicated to the Blessed Trinity.

While we abstain from work on our Sabbath day our abstention is rather from unnecessary servile or hard labor. In this, we are following our Lord's own interpretation and the tradition of the Church from the very earliest ages. Abstention from labor is the negative side of the commandment as it was laid down by God for the Jews. Our principal observance is the honoring of God by dedicating one day of the week to his service. This we do primarily by participating in the offering of the sacrifice of the Mass and also by some extra prayer and meditation. But to be a true Christian, our service of God sanctifies our whole week. Our daily work and our daily recreation give honor and glory to God if done with that intention. Our religion is not and must not be put into separate and distinct compartments, our whole life is dedicated to the service of God by baptism. Our Sunday Mass and private devotions are oases at which we refresh ourselves on our desert journey through life. The devout Christian will find that his Sunday has given him new courage and a new resolve to spend his working week honestly, knowing well that his work is giving honor to God, while providing a livelihood for himself and his dependants.

While we must avoid the casuistry of the Pharisees in deciding what one could or could not do on the Sabbath, it might be well for all of us to have a close look at our Sunday observance. Freedom from work is not leisure for sin. A half-hour in Church can hardly be called dedicating the day to God. The Sabbath is truly sanctified through some extra prayers in the church or in the home, the reading of books of instruction on our Christian religion, acts of kindness and charity toward our neighbors. It is by these deeds that we are laying up stores for ourselves in heaven. Lawful recreation is allowed, because it rebuilds our energies and makes us better able to serve God in our work during the following week.

Sunday should be a day of joy—it is a gift of God to us, and a reminder of all the marvelous gifts we Christians have received from the Father, Son and Holy Spirit.

SECOND READING : 2 Corinthians 4 : 6–11. It is the God who said, "Let light shine out of darkness," who has shone in our hearts to give the light of the knowledge of the glory of God in the face of Christ.

But we have this treasure in earthen vessels, to show that the transcendent power belongs to God and not to us. We are afflicted in every way, but not crushed; perplexed, but not driven to despair; persecuted, but not forsaken; struck down, but not destroyed; always carrying in the body the death of Jesus, so that the life of Jesus may also be manifested in our bodies. For while we live we are always being given up to death for Jesus' sake, so that the life of Jesus may be manifested in our mortal flesh.

EXPLANATION : St. Paul tells his converts of Corinth that it was the light and grace of God which made him, a weak mortal agent, capable of bringing them the truth of the gospel of Christ. God chooses such earthen vessels to show his transcendent power. "It was to shame the wise that God chose what is foolish by human reckoning and to shame the strong that he chose what is weak by human reckoning" (1 Cor. 1 : 27). Paul in his weakness showed forth the power of God.

Let . . . darkness : Paul is referring to the story of creation where God said : " let there be light . . . he divided the light from the darkness" (Gen. 1 : 3).

who . . . hearts : This same God is still creating light, he illumined Paul on the road to Damascus and enabled him to see :

the glory . . . Christ : In that vision Paul saw and realized that Christ was the incarnate Son of God who had come on earth to show to the world the infinite love and glory of God. The vision of God which Moses had, remained reflected on his face for some time (Ex. 35 : 29), but the glory of God as reflected in Christ and in his followers is for all time. The knowledge of the glory of God which Paul has learned from Christ and which he has communicated to his converts, is the light which illuminates his and their hearts. It is like the first creation of light.

earthen vessels : Paul himself especially, and his converts too, were very weak vessels, incapable of the task given them, but :

transcendent power : The infinite power of God shines out all the more brightly because of this. It is God who is working through Paul, hence the success of his missions.

afflicted not crushed : He goes on now to describe his trials and his weaknesses. Of himself he would have failed miserably but he was sustained in all his trials and weaknesses. He was not forsaken— God was with him.

in the body . . . Jesus : His vocation and the vocation of all Christians is to bear the mortifications, the sufferings of Christ in their own lives as an example to those outside. The fact that Paul, and his converts, survive all of these mortifications proves that Christ is still living and has power to save them.

while we live : Paul and all other preachers of the gospel live a life of slow death, a life of continual mortification, for the cause of Christ. By so doing, they are a living example to all others of the purpose of the life and death of Christ. By their likeness to Christ's death, they are the means of bringing the Christ-life, the life of grace and salvation, to their fellowmen.

APPLICATION : The God who created light, without which natural life on our planet could not exist, is, as St. Paul tells us today, the same God who gave to the world the light of faith, the source and sustenance of all spiritual life. God had already given some of this spiritual light to the Chosen People of old, but it was not until he sent Christ on earth that he gave to men the full light, the knowledge of his infinite love and mercy. The incarnation was a new creation. "We are God's work of art, created in Christ Jesus to live the good life as from the beginning he had meant us to live it." Thus St. Paul to the Ephesians (2 : 10), and again: "Your mind must be renewed by a spiritual revolution so that you can put on the new man that has been created in God's way, in the goodness and holiness of truth" (Eph. 2 : 23); "For anyone who is in Christ, there is a new creation, the old creation has gone and now the new one is here" (2 Cor. 5 : 17).

It is clear that to St. Paul the incarnation was the beginning of a second creation and one infinitely more important than the first creation. In the first, God made the perishable things of the universe—things that had to end one day. Man, of his nature, was among these perishable things, but God had higher plans for him. These plans were to be revealed in the incarnation of Christ. They were. Christ came and by his life, death and resurrection in our human nature made us new creatures—adopted sons of God, heirs to an eternal life after our natural life ends. What was perishable in us became everlasting; what was natural became supernatural: "the old creation is gone and now the new one is here." The first creation was an act of God's omnipotence, and omniscience; the second creation is an act of infinite love and mercy shown by God to unworthy men.

Do we grasp the full meaning of what God has done for us through Christ? Do we realize what being a Christian means? It means the possibility (and the certainty, if we do our part) of having an eternal life after we leave this world, a life without pains of mind or body, a life of unbroken contentment and true happiness. This is the treasure of which St. Paul reminds us today: the treasure of the Christian faith. However, as he tells us, we carry this treasure in earthen vessels, vessels of clay that are easily broken. If Paul felt so about himself, how much more earthly are our vessels, how many more human weaknesses have we not got? We are not called on to suffer all that he suffered, but our dangers are not so much from outside enemies who want us to abandon our faith, as from our own internal evil inclinations which prefer the present and the passing pleasure to the lasting and

real pleasure that is to come.

However, it should console us to know that millions of Christians who, like us, had the same human weaknesses gradually succeeded in overcoming these evil inclinations and reached heaven. As St. Paul tells us today, many of these weaknesses are left to us so that the power of God would be shown in us. It is his grace, and not any natural gift that we may have, which will supernaturalize us and our actions.

Let us imitate St. Paul. He was afflicted in many ways but not crushed. We have afflictions from ourselves and others but we must not let them crush us. He was perplexed; he often saw no immediate answer to his problems, but he waited hopefully for a solution. We, too, must try to do as he did. We all have many problems. God will solve them in his own good time. Paul was persecuted but not forsaken. He suffered many persecutions at the hands of the Jews and the Romans (see chapter 11 of this Epistle), but he had some faithful friends. He had, too, what was all important, God was with him. He was struck down but not destroyed. Paul lost many a battle, but he finally won. So shall we, too, if we realize what a gift of God the Christian religion is to us. If we try to bear with our weaknesses and our defects, as St. Paul did, we, too, shall win our war with God's gracious help.

GOSPEL: Mark 2:23–3:6. One Sabbath Jesus was going through the grainfields; and as they made their way his disciples began to pluck ears of grain. And the Pharisees said to him, "Look, why are they doing what is not lawful on the Sabbath?" And he said to them, "Have you never read what David did, when he was in need and was hungry, he and those who were with him: how he entered the house of God, when Abiathar was high priest, and ate the bread of the Presence, which it is not lawful for any but the priests to eat, and also gave it to those who were with him?" And he said to them, "The Sabbath was made for man, not man for the Sabbath; so the Son of man is lord even of the Sabbath."

Again he entered the synagogue, and a man was there who had a withered hand. And they watched him, to see whether he would heal him on the Sabbath, so that they might accuse him. And he said to the man who had the withered hand, "Come here." And he said to them, "Is it lawful on the Sabbath to do good or to do harm, to save life or to kill?" But they were silent. And he looked around at them with anger, grieved at their hardness of heart, and said to the man, "Stretch out your hand." He stretched it out, and his hand was restored. The Pharisees went out, and immediately held counsel with the Herodians against him, how to destroy him.

EXPLANATION: The two incidents described in today's gospel are part of a series of conflicts which the Pharisees had with Jesus. St. Mark has placed these five incidents together (see last Sunday's gospel); it is very likely that they did not happen one after the other. Today's two events, two violations of the Sabbath according to the Pharisees, made Jesus denounce their too strict interpretation of the Sabbath rest. Instead of listening to his reasoning, however, they held counsel and planned with the Herodians how best they could destroy him.

disciples . . . corn: As they walked along a path through a cornfield the disciples began to pluck some of the ripe grain and eat it. This, according to the Pharisees, was tantamount to reaping the grain, a work forbidden on the Sabbath, so they complained to Jesus.

Have . . . read: In answer to their complaint Jesus quotes from the Old Testament, an example of a greater violation of the Law. King David was regarded as a model upholder of the Law of Moses, his personal lapses notwithstanding, even by the Pharisees. He did not hesitate, when hungry, to eat the sacred bread in the sanctuary which the priests alone were permitted to eat. He ate this bread himself and gave it to his companions. This incident occurred when David was escaping from the clutches of King Saul (see 1 Sm. 21:1ff). "If the pious David and his companions ate the bread consecrated to the Lord in the sanctuary what my followers are doing is hardly unlawful," this is the meaning of the reference to David, but Jesus adds:

Sabbath . . . man: It was for man's good that God instituted rest from all labor on each seventh day. It gave man an opportunity to give one day a week back to God and, at the same time, a repose which would restore his bodily energies. Therefore, this Sabbath rest from labor must not be an impediment to man, it was intended to help.

Son of man . . . Sabbath: This claim that he is the Lord of the Sabbath and, therefore, can dispense his disciples, is a new reason for justifying the action of the disciples and does not fit in with the context. Some authors say it was added by Mark, not said by Jesus. But the following story shows Jesus acting on this claim. "Son of man" was a not-obvious messianic title frequently (80 times) used of himself by Jesus during his public life, but by nobody else—one exception is St. Stephen in Acts 7:56, where the reference is directly to Daniel 7:13. By using this term Jesus could slowly introduce his hearers into the secret of his person. At the same time he could keep them from the mundane-political ideas about the Messiah which most of his contemporaries entertained and which he wanted at all costs to avoid.

withered hand: It is evidently taken for granted by friends and foes that Jesus can perform miracles of healing; the big question here is whether he will use that power on the Sabbath day. If so, the Pharisees will be up in arms again.

Is it . . . Sabbath: He challenged the Pharisees before working the miracle. Healing by a physician was regarded as work and forbidden on the Sabbath according to the Pharisees. Therefore, according to them, healing by miracle would also be work.

to do good . . . harm: From the context the meaning, according to the mind of Mark is: the Pharisees are about to plan the death of Jesus on this a Sabbath day, yet they are waiting to accuse

him of violating the Sabbath, if he heals this man's withered hand. Planning a murder was surely a violation of the Sabbath—and sinful, any day of the week. Doing good was not.

they were silent: Most likely they realized what he was referring to—their own sinful scheming on the Sabbath.

looked . . . anger: Mark is the only Evangelist who speaks of Jesus' anger. The reason for his anger was the stubborn opposition they had built up in their hearts against him. He "was grieved at their hardness of heart," at the intellectual blindness which their stubborn pride brought on them.

immediately held counsel: The Herodians, with whom the Pharisees took counsel, were a political party, followers of Herod Agrippa and very probably hoping to have a peaceful settlement with Rome and get back the throne of Herod. To these Jesus was a danger: he might have himself proclaimed king and bring the anger of Rome on them all. That the Pharisees, a religious group, should join forces with such a party, which was more pagan than Jewish, can be explained only by their hatred of the common enemy, Christ.

how . . . him: The Pharisees evidently understood that he was claiming to be the Messiah and more than a mere human Messiah. He was forgiving sins and claiming to be Lord of the Sabbath. The Herodians were afraid lest he should arouse the anger of Rome. So both agreed that the only solution to their problem was to cut short his life. The Pharisees remained steadfast in their evil intention and finally carried it out. There is no mention of the Herodians in the account of the condemnation of Jesus.

APPLICATION: In this conflict between the Pharisees and Christ—a conflict which began very soon after his presence in Palestine became known to them—we see the dark wall of intellectual blindness which stubborn pride and ingrained prejudice can place before even an intelligent man's mind. The Pharisees were well-educated men; they had a good knowledge of the sacred writings of the Old Testament; they specialized in the interpretation of the Decalog and of the cultic laws. In this they went to a rigoristic extreme and added all kinds of additions to the original laws. About 130 B.C., when they first became known as a group, their strict observance of the Law was admired by the ordinary people. Unfortunately, they prided themselves in this and gradually put themselves on a pedestal, away above the ordinary citizens. All others except themselves were "sinners," and to be shunned. When walking through the streets of Jerusalem they gathered their long robes tightly around them, lest they touch a passing sinner and become contaminated. As they had such an attitude of mind toward their fellowmen, it was little wonder that they misjudged Christ. He was the friend of sinners, he spoke to them, he ate with them, he healed their maladies, he even made them his disciples. Only one who was a sinner could act like this. He said he had come to save sinners but to them this was absurd, sinners did not deserve to be saved. The future life, in which they believed, was for the good only, for such as themselves, therefore, he could not be from God as he claimed to be, God does not deal with sinners. They could have nothing to do with him; and they even felt obliged to put an end to his deceptive practices, for the ordinary people were believing that he was from God, and were following him in their thousands. The Pharisees forced the Roman Governor, Pilate, very much against his will and sense of justice, to have Jesus crucified. They could have stoned him to death themselves but they wanted him to die the most excruciating and shameful death then known. This would put an end, they thought, not only to his heresy but to any hopes his followers had. Things turned out differently. Christ's death opened the door of eternal life for all men; Christ's cross became the banner which led many Jews and countless Gentiles to the heavenly victory. It was pharisaism that died.

The sect of the Pharisees is long-since dead. But the basic vice which ruined these otherwise good men, is still far too much alive and rampant among us. Pride, or over-estimation of self, is still exercising a destructive influence among nations and individuals. Not all the followers of the humble Christ are immune to it. We are living today in a world which is in turmoil. Nations are arming against nations, not in defense of any ideal, but to defend their own imagined superiority. Their pride cannot tolerate an equal, much less a superior. Wealth is being poured into armaments, while people are dying of starvation. Within nations, there is race-hatred and class hatred, again the poisonous fruit of pride and of false self-esteem. We human beings, who are gifted with free will and intelligence, seem willing and even anxious to make life miserable for ourselves, as well as for others. This is so when we think that we have not been treated as we should, according to pernicious pride and exaggerated self-esteem.

This, of course, is to act irrationally.

But we are continually acting irrationally and, therefore, our world is falling around our ears, as it is pulled down by ourselves. Their own reason and rational judgements should convince non-believers in God and in Christ that a pleasant, peaceful journey to the grave is better than a journey marred with fighting, strife and sorrow. If there is nothing awaiting them beyond the grave, they have at least a right to peace and happiness in this life. However, for the Christian who believes in God and Christ whom he sent, there is the extra knowledge that God has made us all brothers in Christ. We are all on the same road to heaven—to arrive there is our biggest and most important ambition in life. But we do so not by obstructing one another, not by despising or injuring one another, but by carrying one another's burdens.

Pride can have no place in a truly Christian heart. Any over-esteem of our nation, our race, or ourselves is a sin against Christ who was all things to all men. There are no saints and sinners, no goodies and baddies, in the true Christian's catalog of people. We are all sinners. Were it not for the grace and mercy of God we would all be lost. Let us show our appreciation of this divine mercy by being merciful and kind to all of our fellowmen with whom we come into contact. Let us banish pride forever from our hearts and install humility and true brotherly love there.

TENTH SUNDAY OF THE YEAR

FIRST READING: Genesis 3:9-15. The Lord God called to the man, and said to him, "Where are you?" And he said, "I heard the sound of thee in the garden, and I was afraid, because I was naked; and I hid myself." He said, "Who told you that you were naked? Have you eaten of the tree of which I commanded you not to eat?" The man said, "The woman whom thou gavest to be with me, she gave me fruit of the tree, and I ate." Then the Lord God said to the woman, "What is this that you have done?" The woman said, "The serpent beguiled me, and I ate." The Lord God said to the serpent, "Because you have done this, cursed are you above all cattle, and above all wild animals; upon your belly you shall go, and dust you shall eat all the days of your life. I will put enmity between you and the woman, and between your seed and her seed; it shall bruise your head, and you shall bruise its heel."

EXPLANATION: The first eleven chapters of Genesis were written not to give details of history in our present-day sense, but to give the basic doctrines of the faith of Israel, and to explain the need for salvation history which begins with the call of Abraham in chapter 12 : 1. By an act of his omnipotent will the one true God had created all things that are, including man. He created all things "good," yet man at the time that Genesis 3 to 11 were written and for centuries before, was far from good— he was doing what was evil and dishonoring his Creator. This "doing of evil," or sin as it is called, had come into the world because man, whom God had endowed with intellect and free will, became proud of himself and his "gifts." He did not see why he should thank God for anything, or reverence him as his Maker. He made himself his own master and did as he pleased. The result was chaos. Not only did man insult God but he insulted and injured his neighbor —even the members of his own family, as the murder of Abel by his brother Cain, described in chapter 4 of Genesis, brings out. In today's incident, as the sacred author sees it, we are given a poetic description of what happened when the first parents sinned.

where are you : The man thought that he could hide from God. He evidently realized that he was guilty and felt that God would demand a sanction.

eaten of the tree : This refers to the command given by God in 2 : 17. Because he had disobeyed the divine command, man realized he had brought humiliation and shame on himself. He had not become like a god, he found himself less a man. To be naked or nude was a sign of subjection and slavery (Dt. 28 : 48); prisoners of war were stripped naked to disgrace them (see Is. 20 : 4; 47 : 3, also Jer. 13 : 26; Ez. 16 : 37; Os. 2 : 5); so instead of winning freedom for himself, his disobedience caused by his pride had brought disgrace and humiliation on

him. That the disobeyed command had to do with sex, suggested by some authors, seems excluded by the sacred author in 2 : 24, where monogamous marriage was already instituted by God. **The woman . . . me :** The man puts the blame on his wife, but also indirectly on God himself : it was God who gave him a wife!

serpent . . . me : The woman in turn tries to excuse herself by putting the blame on the serpent. That the serpent, introduced into this story by the author, was some evil spirit and an opponent of God, who wished to make man also an enemy of God, seems clear from the context. He speaks to the woman; he tells lies; he makes absurd and false promises : "You will be like gods." His purpose was to injure God and man insofar as he could.

upon . . . eat : The natural characteristics of the animal are used to symbolize the punishment of the evil spirit. The animal always crawled and seemed to eat dust; but to crawl on one's belly before a conqueror was a sign of subjection, as likewise was the expression : to eat dust, that is, to be face downward on the ground, while the conqueror placed his foot on the conquered one's neck.

enmity . . . woman : Enmity can exist only between rational beings, another indication that the serpent was only a cover for some intelligent being. The enmity God is placing between the woman and the serpent is not the natural fear a woman would have in the presence of a serpent. It is a moral opposition between the woman and what the serpent represents—evil-doing.

your . . . seed : This enmity, this opposition, would continue between the descendants of the woman and the forces of evil which were to continue harassing the human race.

bruise . . . head: The head of the serpent is his most vulnerable part. Here it means: a victory sometime, for the descendants of the woman— the human race.

bruise its heel: The human race, or the member representing it, will be injured in the final battle. But the injury will not be fatal—victory at some future date is promised.

APPLICATION: As we said above, the author of this section of Genesis is giving the background and reason for the call of Abraham. The Father of the Chosen People was told by God to leave his home and country, his kith and kin, and go to a far away land. There God promised to make him into a great nation: he would be blessed and be a source of blessing to all the tribes of the earth (Gn. 12:1-3). What this blessing was to be was still very vague, but at least one facet of it is clarified a little in today's reading. It was evident to all that sin abounded in the world which God made. This state of sin, or disobedience to God, must have been suggested and induced in the very first human inhabitants of the earth by some evil power—here called a serpent and later identified with Satan the leader of the evil spirits (fallen angels). This sad state of the world would be corrected one day— a descendant of Abraham and of the first sinners, would break the vicious power that Satan had over mankind. The serpent's head would eventually be crushed even though the victor too would suffer much in the combat.

This victory over the serpent, the enemy of God and man, is the first indication of the meaning of the blessing which Abraham's vocation would bring to the world. It is the first hint at the good news: that God intended to set the world right once more. It is, therefore, called by Christian writers the proto-evangelium or the "first good news, or tidings." It was the beginning of those preparations by God which were to make men his friends once more and what was more basic still: to make them his adopted sons. That was why God called Abraham. This first promise was vague and in fact is not referred to again in the Old Testament. But as time went on, God, through his prophets, clarified his message to the Chosen People, so that when Christ the Messiah came on earth, claiming to be the one promised by God, he was eventually, after his resurrection, recognized by almost all men of unprejudiced minds, to be not only Messiah, but God's own divine Son.

While it is a sad commentary on the weakness and folly of our human nature that sin has been in the world from the first days of man on earth, we can at the same time find great consolation in the thought that God's infinite love and mercy for us was infinitely greater and stronger than our sins. It was God's plan from all eternity to send his divine Son in human form to raise us up to sonship with himself and thus make us heirs to his eternal kingdom. Man's foolish desire to be independent of God, even to be equal to him, was really childish pride and the cause of all sin. It did not, however, prevent God's plan from being fulfilled. He still wanted us to go to heaven. Because of sin and Satan, his Son would now have to suffer the torments of a cruel death, but this he willingly underwent for our sakes. Surely not even God could have greater love than this. He gave his only-begotten Son as a victim to atone for us wayward, ungrateful creatures.

Because of this love of God, we Christians have the door of heaven fully opened to us. Nothing and no one can keep us out except our own selves. We can still sin, we can let our foolish pride, our impulse to be independent stop us dead on our road to heaven. Could we be so foolish, so forgetful of our own best interest, as to shut the door of eternal happiness on our own faces? It has happened to others. Our gratitude to God should not only keep us from sin but should urge us to do

all in our power to make some return to him for his infinite love. Yet, the possibility of a moment of weakness cannot be excluded. But for this God has prepared. He has left us a sacrament to wipe out sins. Where or when this sacrament is not available, an act of sincere love of God will put our conscience right with him. So we need never remain "out" with God. He is ever ready to forgive our human folly, and welcome us back into his friendship.

Remember, heaven is waiting for you and neither a wife, nor a husband, nor Satan himself can keep you from getting there. Only you yourself can do this. God forbid that you should.

SECOND READING: 2 Corinthians 4:13–5:1. Since we have the same spirit of faith as he had who wrote, "I believed, and so I spoke," we too believe, and so we speak, knowing that he who raised the Lord Jesus will raise us also with Jesus and bring us with you into his presence. For it is all for your sake, so that as grace extends to more and more people it may increase thanksgiving, to the glory of God.

So we do not lose heart. Though our outer nature is wasting away, our inner nature is being renewed every day. For this slight momentary affliction is preparing for us an eternal weight of glory beyond all comparison, because we look not to the things that are seen but to the things that are unseen; for the things that are seen are transient, but the things that are unseen are eternal.

For we know that if the earthly tent we live in is destroyed, we have a building from God, a house not made with hands, eternal in the heavens.

EXPLANATION: In last Sunday's reading, from this Epistle, we heard St. Paul describe his own life as an Apostle and the life of the Christian converts as lives of suffering and continual mortification. In this they are re-enacting the sufferings and death of

Christ, for as Christ triumphed over his sufferings and death, so too will his followers. For a Christian to be able to see his life in this light he needs faith, and it is of this faith and confidence in God's plans for us that St. Paul speaks today.

same . . . faith : Paul quotes the psalmist (Ps. 116 : 10), according to the Septuagint, where it is said : "I spoke because I believed," that is, he has fully believed the word of God; therefore, he is sure to overcome his enemies. Likewise, Paul has complete trust in God and in his promises.

who . . . Lord : God the Father, who raised Jesus from the dead, will raise Paul and his converts too and bring them to heaven "into his presence."

all . . . sake : The Corinthians have received the true faith through the sufferings of Paul. His solid faith enabled him to endure these sufferings. That faith has spread to them, and from them to others, and so God's grace has increased. The primary purpose of the spread of the gospel, however, is the glory of God.

do not lose heart : In spite of all he has to endure, Paul is full of courage when he sees the harvest that is being reaped for God.

outer . . . wasting : Gradually his physical strength is waning, and the end is drawing closer, but his inner strength, his faith and trust in God's promises, grows stronger by the day.

slight . . . affliction : He calls the constant trials he has had to endure slight and momentary (for a list of his sufferings, see chapter 11 of this epistle), because he is comparing them to "the eternal weight of glory beyond all comparison" which they are earning for him.

things . . . unseen : Paul is looking at the eternal things, not at the transient joys or pleasures of this life.

earthly . . . destroyed : He compares his life on earth to a temporary dwelling, a tent, something not very durable, whereas God has prepared for us a new body—a new, glorious and permanent dwelling or mode of living in heaven.

We know : He introduces this statement with an assertion based on the firmness of his Christian faith. He is certain of it.

APPLICATION : If only our faith were as firm as that of St. Paul, and our vision of the beauty and the perfection of what awaits us in the next world as clear and as definite as his was, our earthly troubles would look small indeed. Paul could call his sufferings "slight and momentary." Ours, in comparison, are not even worth mentioning. At the time he wrote this letter, he had traveled on foot (he could not afford any other means) well over two thousand miles, to bring the gospel to the towns of Asia Minor and Greece. He had been scourged five times by the Jews—39 lashes each time; stoned once; beaten with sticks three times; shipwrecked three times—spending a day and night adrift once in the open sea. At night, often with no sleep, he had to work with his hands at tent-making so that his upkeep would not be a burden on his converts. He tells us that he was frequently hungry and starving at times and sometimes frozen for want of sufficient clothing. Later he spent four years in prison, was released, rearrested and finally beheaded in Rome for his faith.

Paul could call this catalog of calamities a "slight and momentary affliction," only because he was comparing it with the " eternal glory, beyond all comparison " which awaited him in the next life. Truly, for a man like St. Paul, who kept the eternal happiness of heaven always before his eyes, no earthly sufferings could seem of any importance. His appreciation of what the innocent Christ had suffered for us sinners, made him anxious to emulate, if only from afar, the example of the Master. Nothing he could do or suffer for his Lord and Master could in his eyes be called much, not to say *too* much, and the reward Christ had won for him was so great and so worthwhile that he would have spent ten such lives of sufferings and trials in order to reach it.

What about our attitude to suffering! We have not been given the missionary vocation of St. Paul, nor all the graces that went with that vocation, but we have the same faith as he had. We, too, know that God who raised Jesus from the dead will raise us up also and give us a place in his eternal home. We know too, as Paul knew, that Christ has asked for each one of us to carry our personal cross daily and follow him. Do we do so? Do we see in the trials that come to us a cross sent by Christ to enable us to rise above earthly ambitions and worldly entanglements? Do the hardships and struggles of life make us fix our gaze on the future home which God has prepared for us? Do we welcome these things for what they are —messengers from God to remind us that we have not on this earth a lasting home?

Compared with the sufferings of St. Paul, our trials are indeed relatively trivial. If we accept them, however, with a grumble and with reluctance, and if we fail to see them in relation to the reward that awaits us, we can indeed make huge mountains out of our little mole-hills; we can not only make our earthly life miserable but we can put it in jeopardy. St. Paul tells the Corinthians that his bodily strength was wasting away, and little wonder, but, and this was what mattered to him, his inner nature, his heartfelt desire for the things of God and for the future that was in store for him was renewed and grew stronger with each day that passed. If we could imitate St. Paul in this, if we could keep the future, that awaits us, ever fixed before our minds, our earthly troubles and our daily crosses would not be stumbling blocks for us on our journey to heaven, but stepping-stones that would make it easier for us to get safely over the morasses of life. If we could see our life from the viewpoint of our death-bed we, too, would gladly say with St. Paul: "I consider that the sufferings of this present time are not worth comparing with the glory that is to be revealed to us" (Rom. 8 : 18).

GOSPEL : Mark 3 : 20–35. Jesus and his disciples went home; and the crowd came together again, so that they could not even eat. And when his friends heard it, they went out to seize him, for they said, "He is beside himself." And the scribes who came down from Jerusalem said, "He is possessed by Beelzebub, and by the prince of demons he casts out the demons." And he called them to him, and said to them in parables, "How can Satan cast out Satan? If a kingdom is divided against itself, that kingdom cannot stand. And if a house is divided against itself, that house will not be able to stand. And if Satan has risen up against himself and is divided, he cannot stand, but is coming to an end. But no one can enter a strong man's house and plunder his goods, unless he first binds the strong man; then indeed he may plunder his house.

"Truly, I say to you, all sins will be forgiven the sons of men, and whatever blasphemies they utter; but whoever blasphemes against the Holy Spirit never has forgiveness, but is guilty of an eternal sin"—for they had said, "He has an unclean spirit." And his mother and his brethren came; and standing outside they sent to him and called him. And a crowd was sitting about him; and they said to him, "Your mother and your brethren are outside, asking for you." And he replied, "Who are my mother and my brethren?" And looking around on those who sat about him, he said, "Here are my mother and my brethren! Whoever does the will of God is my brother, and sister, and mother."

EXPLANATION : Up until now the Scribes and Pharisees, as we saw for the past three Sundays, had been accusing Jesus of claiming to be God and of violating the Sabbath. In today's incident they go a step further : they accuse him of being possessed by a devil, in fact, of being in league with Satan the chief of the devils, from whom he has received the power of miracles. This is blasphemy of the worst kind : to say that he, the Son of God, is under the power of the evil one. Jesus shows them that not only is such an idea absurd but it is an unforgivable sin, the worst insult they could offer to God.

went . . . disciples : He had been preaching around the shores of Lake Tiberias, had spent a night in prayer on a mountain near the lake and had just appointed the twelve as his Apostles. He most probably came back to Simon's house and entered there with the twelve to rest and eat.

crowd . . . eat : A huge crowd gathered around the house anxious to see or obtain a miracle. Some must have pushed their way into the house so that Jesus and his disciples could not rest or eat.

his friends heard it : Following the Vulgate, nearly all modern translations have misconstrued the Greek here. The Greek *auton* refers back to the crowd *ochlos*, a masculine noun. As "turba," the latin for crowd, is feminine, the Vulgate should have *eam* not *eum*. The crowd was so large that it got out of hand. The disciples went out to quieten, "restrain," the crowd because they said the people had grown excited. From the previous verse, it is clear that Jesus is *in* the house. Therefore, "his own," his friends, did not go out to quieten *him*. The question of Jesus being "beside himself" (RSV) or "out of his mind" (JB) does not arise (the above is gratefully borrowed from *A New Catholic Commentary*, p. 962 : no. 751e).

Scribes from Jerusalem : The chief officials of the party of the Pharisees had come down to Galilee to enquire into Jesus' behavior. They had heard all the enthusiastic reports of his miracles; they now saw the huge crowd in Capernaum waiting for him. They sought an explanation.

possessed by Beelzebub : A pagan God of Ekron, meaning "Baal the prince" but changed to Beelzebub "God of the flies" in 2 Kgs. 1 : 2, to show the Israel-contempt for a pagan god, who to them was a demon.

casts out demons : According to the Scribes it is with the power and authority of the prince of demons, the authority of Beelzebub that Jesus casts out demons. That this was absurd as well as blasphemous Jesus shows them.

Satan . . . Satan : Jesus had been exorcizing demons from the very beginning of his public ministry and the demons realized that the Messiah, who would put an end to Satan's reign, had come. "Have you come to destroy us?" was their usual comment to him. But if, as the prejudiced Scribes said, he was doing this as a delegate of Satan then Satan was agreeing to the destruction of his own power which would be absurd. No kingdom or house divided against itself can survive.

strong man's house : Notwithstanding the strength of Satan's power up to the present, one stronger than he had come, one who was able to enter his house and despoil him of all he possessed. This is

Jesus. He had now begun the despoliation of Satan and would soon put a total end to his kingdom.

blasphemies . . . Spirit : Accusing Jesus of being in league with Satan was blasphemy against God, through whose Spirit Jesus worked his miracles. It was the worst of sins and coming from men versed in God's revelation, it could not be excused on the plea of ignorance. It would never be forgiven, for most probably the ingrained pride of the Scribes would not let them change their minds and repent.

mother and brethren : Mary, the Blessed Mother of Jesus, had no other children. Therefore, Jesus had no brothers, or sisters. That is clear from the infancy narratives in Matthew's and Luke's gospels, and from the constant tradition in the Church. It is confirmed also by John's gospel (19 : 26). Jesus would not have had to commend his Mother to John's care if she had other sons or daughters. The "brothers" or brethren of Jesus are mentioned here, and in the parallel passages in Matthew and Luke and in Acts 1 : 14, because there was no other word in Aramaic or Hebrew to describe cousins or close relatives.

came . . . him : They had evidently come down to Capernaum from Nazareth and they wished to see him. The house in which he was, was surrounded by so huge a crowd that they had no chance of entering. Somebody told Jesus they were anxious to see him.

Who are . . . brethren? : The question asked by Jesus was not a denial of interest in his mother and relatives. He was stressing that it was not to form human relationships that he came, but spiritual brotherhood. All who learn from him to do the will of God will be his real brothers and kinsmen. That his blood relations, especially his Mother, could become members of his new spiritual family is by no means excluded.

He is emphasizing the wider and more important brotherhood.

APPLICATION : The truth of the saying "pride goeth before destruction" (Prov. 16 : 18) is clearly demonstrated in the first and third readings today. Pride indeed induced the First Parents to disobey God. They wished to be independent of him, in fact, they hoped to be his equals. The evil results of their folly are still among us. It was their sinful pride, their sense of superiority, their utter contempt for all who did not conform to their standard of observance, that led the Scribes and Pharisees to oppose Jesus. Blinded as they were by this deep-rooted pride, they could see nothing good in him. Absurdly, they explained as the work of Satan the miracles he worked. To any honest mind these miracles proved that he was, at least, a friend of God. That most of the Scribes and Pharisees continued in their blind pride even after their attempt to silence him for ever had failed, is most likely, as Jesus' reference to the unforgivable sin would indicate. They could not be forgiven while they refused, through pride, to ask for forgiveness.

While we can thank God that perhaps none of us has the same exalted opinion of himself as had the Scribes and Pharisees, there is still much pride in even the best of us. It is still the root of all the evil that is in our world. If faithfully observed the Ten Commandments of God would make the journey of all men to heaven easier, safer and surer. But they are violated daily. Why? Because proud men refuse to be restricted in their actions. They cannot admit that any higher power has the right to regulate their lives; they are the sole arbiters of their fate; they will do as they please.

Which of us would admit to violating the first commandment? "I am the Lord your God, you shall not have strange gods before me." We never even thought of adoring a false god, we will say, we would never think of setting up a statue of Mars or Jove or Venus and bowing the knee before it. Yet, every time we break the law of God, we are setting up an idol—one more absurd than any false god of the pagan world. We are setting up our own self, our own will, our own authority in the place of God. We will not have *him* rule over us!

We are living today in what is politely called the permissive age—the age when God's laws are shamelessly flouted and despised; the age when men and women, old as well as young, do what they like regardless of whether or not their actions offend God and neighbor. This is a false philsophy, not of life, but of death; this is a philosophy or whim which has the ripe seeds of destruction of human society breaking through its crust. How long can we go on living together on earth, if each one claims the right to do as he pleases? If, with impunity, we can lay our hands on all the wealth and property we feel we want, what of our neighbors whom we despoil? If we can drive a coach and four through the laws of the state, which are themselves applications of the laws of God, how long can our state last? If, outside of marriage, we have every right to enjoy all the sexual pleasure of which we are capable, who is going to take on himself the responsibilities of married life: Who will produce the next generation of citizens and who will feed and educate them! If we have the right to all possible comfort, pleasure and ease in this life, then abortion, euthanasia for the old and defectives, in fact, the quiet removal of anyone who stands in our way, who interferes with our absolute freedom, is not only lawful but absolutely necessary! How many will survive this regime?

Of course, those who approve of and demand permissiveness, do not encourage going to such extremes—except when it suits them. But if there is no divine authority the state laws will have to be enforced with the gun. They will collapse, however, once a sufficient number of citizens opt for permissiveness.

He who does the will of God is the brother and kinsman of Christ and only his true brothers will get to heaven. We must keep the commandments of God. not only are they the guides that will keep us on the road to heaven, but they are our only guarantee of survival during our short sojourn here on earth.

ELEVENTH SUNDAY OF THE YEAR

FIRST READING: Ezekiel 17:22–24. Thus says the Lord God: "I myself will take a spring from the lofty top of the cedar, and will set it out: I will break off from the topmost of its young twigs a tender one, and I myself will plant it upon a high and lofty mountain; on the mountain height of Israel will I plant it, that it may bring forth boughs and bear fruit, and become a noble cedar; and under it will dwell all kinds of beasts; in the shade of its branches birds of every sort will nest. And all the trees of the field shall know that I the Lord bring low the high tree, and make high the low tree, dry up the green tree, and make the dry tree flourish. I the Lord have spoken, and I will do it."

EXPLANATION: Up until the year 597 B.C. Ezekiel was a priest of the temple of Jerusalem. Then he was deported to Babylon with King Jehoiachin and the first deportees. Among the exiles in Babylon, he denounced the sins of the people which brought on the exile. He foretold greater misfortunes still for Judah: Jerusalem and its temple would be destroyed by the Babylonians and the remainder of the people taken into captivity. They had deserted Yahweh, their God; he would not desert them for awhile. But Ezekiel, like his contemporaries Jeremiah and second-Isaiah, had words of encouragement also. Better days were to come when Yahweh would take back his people once more, and dwell in their midst forever (37 : 25). Today's extract is a messianic prophecy in which God says that he will raise up a descendant —a sprig from the lofty cedar David, who will yet be the glory of Israel.

sprig from . . . cedar : In the previous 21 verses of this chapter, the prophet has described in allegorical form what has already befallen Judah and the greater punishment which is yet to come. The eagle, Nebuchadnezzar, has come and plucked the top branch of the cedar and carried it off to Babylon. The cedar is the Davidic dynasty; the top branch was the reigning king Jehoiachin. The eagle planted a mere vine in its place : Nebuchadnezzar appointed Zedekiah, Jehoiachin's uncle, to the throne of Judah. Instead of keeping the treaty he had made with Babylon, he began to intrigue with Egypt and thus brought destruction to Jerusalem with its people and its temple, in 587. In all of this Zedekiah was disloyal to Yahweh his God, and the whole population of Judah suffered for they too had been disloyal. Yahweh, however, would not be angry with Judah forever. A day would come when, in view of all, he would plant in their midst on a lofty mountain a sprig from the top of the cedar—a descendant of David who would bring glory and blessing to the Chosen People and to all men.

become . . . cedar : From being a shoot, a cutting from the Davidic cedar, this sprig, planted by God, will become a noble cedar in its own right.

all kinds of beasts : This noble cedar will attract all living beings, birds of the air will safely make their nests in its branches, the beasts of the field will find shelter and security under its shade. Here the universality of this new Davidic kingdom is described.

all . . . field : The cedar is a king, so the other trees of the field are kings.

I . . . high tree : All the kings of the earth will learn through the "one who is to come" that God is Lord of all. He can bring down the proud and raise up the humble. He will let those who are self-sufficient wither away, while in his mercy he will give new life to the needy who recognize their need.

I . . . have spoken : God has promised this messianic restoration, he will fulfill his promise.

APPLICATION : God had planned from all eternity to make all men his adopted sons and, therefore, heirs of his heavenly kingdom, by sending his divine Son as man on earth. He selected the descendants of Abraham to co-operate with him in carrying out this plan. He made them his Chosen People and showered benefits on them time out of number. But again and again they proved themselves unworthy of his paternal interest. Their own misconduct, their own long infidelity and that of their kings ever since Solomon (with a few noble exceptions), finally brought the Babylonian exile on them. This should have been the end of them as a people and a nation, but the infinite mercy of God stepped in and saved them. He brought them back to Judah once more. They rebuilt Jerusalem and the temple and in spite of their many lapses and many interferences from outside powers, he protected and kept them there until the time came for the incarnation of his divine Son. In spite of opposition from his enemies and disloyal friends—his Chosen People—God fulfilled his eternal plan for man.

Centuries and centuries ago God was quietly but surely setting in motion the chain of events which eventually led to the incarnation. The leaders and the majority of his Chosen People proved unworthy of the honor which he had conferred on them. They were ungrateful for his many benefits. Yet, a remnant was faithful and cooperated with him in his plans. Though the throne of David had been vacant for five centuries, when the "fullness of time" arrived, there were still descendants of David in Judah—living, it is true, in humble circumstances, but still descendants in the direct line. In spite of all opposition God brought his eternal plan to fruition and fulfilled all his prophecies and promises. The words of Ezekiel spoken in Babylon about the year 590 B.C. were fulfilled in Christ. He was the sprig from the Davidic cedar; God planted this sprig on a lofty mountain and it became a noble cedar —a refuge and shelter for all men for all time.

We Christians of today are the beneficiaries of this infinite love and mercy of God which was at work in the world down through the ages. From our faith we know that we have been adopted by God as his sons. We are going to inherit a place in heaven because God's Son came on earth to make us his brothers. We know that our life on this earth is a training-ground for the eternal life. We must all die, but we shall rise from the dead and return to life in a new glorified form, to enjoy unending happiness with God. It is God's infinite love that has arranged all this for us. Just as of old he made Abraham's descendants his Chosen People, he has now made all men his own adopted sons. As his friends of old so often proved disloyal to him, so too his adopted sons can, and unfortunately they often do, prove unfaithful. And in so doing their infidelity is more serious than was that of the Jews because their knowledge of God and of the lengths he has gone to in order to give them an eternal home, is much greater than the Jews' knowledge of him.

He came to the Chosen People in a cloud on Mount Sinai, but they could not dare see or approach him. He worked many wonders among them to save them from their pagan neighbors and to bring material benefit to them. But to us he has sent his only-begotten Son, in human form, visible and approachable to all. His Son died for us in his human nature, to make atonement for our sins. He has opened the treasure-house of divine grace, putting heaven within the reach of the weakest of us. The Christian who can forget all of this and be disloyal and disobedient to such a God of love, is heartless and utterly ungrateful, far more ungrateful and disloyal than any Jew ever could be. What is more, the Christian who would persevere in this frame of mind is his own worst enemy. It is his own future which is put at risk. God does not need him but he badly needs God. Without such a disloyal Christian, heaven will be the happy abode of God and his faithful friends; but where will the disloyal Christian be if he fails to reach heaven?

SECOND READING: 2 Corinthians 5:6–10. We are always of good courage; we know that while we are at home in the body we are away from the Lord, for we walk by faith, not by sight. We are of good courage, and we would rather be away from the body and at home with the Lord. So whether we are at home or away, we make it our aim to please him. For we must all appear before the judgement seat of Christ, so that each one may receive good or evil, according to what he has done in the body.

EXPLANATION: On this Epistle see Seventh Sunday of the Year. In today's reading, St. Paul tells his Corinthians that his constant desire and motive in life is to please God. In this he wants them to imitate him. While on earth this is his aim and when he goes to God in heaven this will be his purpose and his delight.

of good courage: St. Paul's faith is such that even though he is living on earth, yet he is so certain of heaven that depression or despair, have no place in his mind.

away . . . Lord: While living in this world we are separated from the Lord who is in heaven.

we . . . faith: We live our daily lives,

"we walk," knowing from our faith that we are moving ever nearer to the day when we shall be with God.

whether . . . away: Like every sincere Christian, Paul was anxious to be safely with God; but while he was still "away," still on this earth, his one aim was to please God.

judgement . . . Christ: God is infinitely merciful to us while we are on this earth. When, however, we close our earthly eyes in death we close our account books also. These account books —the record of our behavior during our years on earth—will decide our future eternal fate. If we have imitated St. Paul, we have nothing to fear.

APPLICATION: The thought that "we must all appear before the judgement seat of Christ" the moment that we die is a thought which should never be far from our Christian minds. Our days on this earth are days of training, days of preparation, for that most important moment in our life. Our eternity depends on how we stand in relation to God at that—all-important moment. As St. Paul tells us in today's reading, and says more clearly still in his letter to the Romans: "God will award to every man what his acts have deserved; eternal life to those who have striven for glory and honor and immortality, by perseverance in doing good; the

retribution of his anger to those who are contumacious, rebelling against truth and paying homage to wickedness" (Rom. 2:6–8). God's judgement will be absolutely fair: those who will be condemned will be the first to admit that they got what they deserved. The very fact that they have no one but themselves to blame will add to their suffering. Those who will be rewarded with eternal happiness will be amazed at how far the reward exceeds the little they did during life.

They will also be amazed to find that they are rewarded for doing the same daily tasks as their neighbor who was condemned; the reason is that they did their daily tasks for the honor and glory of God "to please the Lord," as St. Paul says, while the condemned neighbor ignored God and had no spiritual profits from his earthly chores. While there have been great saints like St. Paul who have done extraordinary things for God, the vast majority of the human race will reach heaven through doing the ordinary things of life in the ordinary human way, provided they intend to please God and serve him by doing these things honestly and willingly.

This is all God asks of us. He created us to live on this earth and then enter into the real life, the eternal life. He gives us gifts of mind and body to work our way through this earthly life. They enable us to earn our daily bread. He also gave us an abundance of spiritual gifts—his revelation and his Church through Christ. By the use of these we can make our earthly journey the means of reaching the eternal goal which he has planned for us. This seems an easy and a very reasonable program. But for many it is made difficult and in some cases impossible, because of the demon of pride which they allow to dominate their lives.

"Why should we be subject to God?" the men of pride say. "Why should we believe in his promises, or fear his threats? We have our intellects and free wills, we can do as we will." From whom did they get their intellects and free wills? Where will they find true satisfaction for these gifts in the few years they have here below? Man's intellect is ever searching for more truths; man's will is always seeking for more and more of the good and beautiful. All the pleasure and happiness he gets out of this life will never be sufficient to satisfy his longing for true and lasting joy. God gave man the intellectual faculties, capable of enjoying unending truth and lasting joy because he intended him to be with him forever. If man, in his foolish pride, rejects God's offer and settles for the paltry and the passing joys of this life it is he alone who will be the loser.

Most Christians do not reject God's offer of a life of unending happiness after their sojourn on earth, but not all of them do what is asked of them in order to earn it. Nothing extraordinary, no outstanding works of penance, no prolonged prayer or meditations are demanded of the vast majority of us. What is expected of us is the daily living of our lives, honestly and faithfully, within the commandments of God; and living this ordinary life with the intention and motive of pleasing God. That is little when compared with the eternal reward which will be ours.

GOSPEL: Mark 4:26-34. Jesus said to the crowds, "The kingdom of God is as if a man should scatter seed upon the ground, and should sleep and rise night and day, and the seed should sprout and grow, he knows not how. The earth produces of itself, first the blade, then the ear, then the full grain in the ear. But when the grain is ripe, at once he puts in the sickle, because the harvest has come."

And he said, "With what can we compare the kingdom of God, or what parable shall we use for it? It is like a grain of mustard seed, which, when sown upon the ground, is the smallest of all the seeds on earth; yet when it is sown it grows up and becomes the greatest of all shrubs, and puts forth large branches, so that the birds of the air can make nests in its shade."

With many such parables he spoke the word to them, as they were able to hear it; he did not speak to them without a parable, but privately to his own disciples he explained everything.

EXPLANATION: When speaking to the crowds about the kingdom he was about to found, our Lord generally used parables—stories about possible and obvious facts which would illustrate and explain the less obvious truths. His reason was because the minds of the populace were centered on a worldly kingdom. They wanted a political Messiah who would set them free from Rome and give them a great empire. Gradually he was to wean them away from this wrong idea. In the meantime, he described the kingdom he was founding in a way that they would later understand. His stories or parables are taken from the everyday life of Palestine, and concern farmers, fishermen, shepherds and housewives. Today's two parables are drawn from agricultural experience. The kingdom he is founding will grow and increase quietly and almost imperceptibility—no uproar or rebellion, no war or turmoil will be necessary. It will grow from the very smallest beginnings but will become so great that the birds of the air— the people of the earth—will flock to it for food and protection.

a man . . . ground: A farmer having plowed his field scatters grain on it. Then he leaves it and goes about his other daily tasks. He does not have to assist it any further—the soil does the rest, the ripe crop will come in due time. Then the farmer will return to his field and reap his harvest.

mustard seed . . . seeds: The smallness of the mustard seed was used as a comparison by the rabbis in Palestine before the time of Christ. Absolutely speaking, it is not the smallest of all seeds, but for the size of the plant it produces it is relatively smaller than any other seed.

greatest . . . shrubs: In Palestine and other warm climates the plant reaches a height of ten feet or more and it has wide-spreading branches. Its seed is very much liked by birds which flock to it when it is in seed.

as they . . . hear it: Because of the people's ingrained prejudices, he could not, as yet, tell them openly that he was the Messiah and was about to set up the messianic kingdom. The danger of an uprising against Rome was always there. He did not look like the

Messiah now but later they would see that the tree was present in the tiny seed.

privately . . . everything : To his dis- ciples he explained what he meant in his parables, but even they were very slow to grasp the full meaning of his words.

APPLICATION : One of the proofs of the divine origin of the Church of Christ is its growth from very humble beginnings. Christ could have come on earth in the prime of manhood, without the cooperation of any human ancestry. He could have preached his gospel to the whole world himself without any help from men. By extraordinary miracles he could have astounded the world into believing. If he wished to have the assistance of men he could have chosen the outstanding philosophers and orators of Greece and Rome.

Instead, he chose to come into this world as a baby, the son of a poor mother and of a carpenter foster-father. He was born in a stable; was forced into pagan Egypt before he was a year old; he lived thirty or so years in Nazareth in poverty, earning his meager daily bread by the sweat of his brow. Then for three years he trudged the highways and by-ways of Palestine, often weary, hungry and footsore, preaching the good news of redemption. For assistants he chose fishermen, shepherds and tax-gatherers, twelve of the most ordinary of the ordinary people of his day.

When the time came for him to lay down his life for the world as prearranged by his Father, he allowed his enemies to capture him and to condemn him to the death of the cross. These were surely humble beginnings for a kingdom which was to span the earth and the ages. The mustard seed in comparison was large. Yet, this was God's plan and therefore it succeeded as he said it would. The story of his humble origins among us, of his equality with us in all things, sin alone excepted, and of his self-immolation for us, touched human hearts wherever it was told and the grace of God did the rest.

It was not the eloquence of the Apostles, nor their gift of persuasion, nor their fame for learning that moved the pagan world to forsake its idols and its vices. No, nothing but the moving grace of the Holy Spirit and the objective truth of the gospel story can explain the conversion of the Roman empire.

Therefore, the spread of the Church is a proof of its divine origin—it is from God and God is with it. Knowing this, how grateful should we not be to him who has made us members of his kingdom on earth, with the assurance of a place in his eternal kingdom in heaven, if we remain his loyal subjects here below. How good God has been to us! To what lengths of humiliation did he not go to in order to open heaven for us! When we think of Bethlehem, Nazareth, Calvary, can we dare complain because he sends us a few crosses to help us to atone for our own past sins? When we wipe the sweat of honest labor from our brow, we will think of the carpenter of Nazareth. When we feel the pinch of poverty, hunger, debt, we will think of Bethlehem and its stable and of the poor home of Nazareth. If or when the injustice of others should drive us from our home and fatherland, as is the lot of so many today, we will think of the exile in Egypt. If we are saved this humiliation we will do all in our power to help "displaced" persons wherever they may be.

The tiny mustard seed has grown into a tree but it has yet to gather many more under the shelter of its branches. Christ asks every one of his followers to help him to bring all men into the safety of his kingdom on earth, so that they may be enabled to enjoy happiness forever in his heavenly kingdom. Realizing all that God and his divine Son have done for us, would we be so mean and ungrateful as to refuse to lend a helping hand? God forbid! God has already put us on the right road to heaven; we will help him to get in the stragglers, the lazy, the "couldn't-care-less" ones on that same road, by every means available to us.

TWELFTH SUNDAY OF THE YEAR

FIRST READING: Job 38:1; 8–11. The Lord answered Job out of the whirlwind: "Who shut in the sea with doors, when it burst forth from the womb; when I made clouds its garment, and thick darkness its swaddling band, and prescribed bounds for it, and set bars and doors, and said, 'Thus far shall you come, and no farther, and here shall your proud waves be stayed' "?

EXPLANATION: On the Book of Job, see above on the Fifth Sunday of the Year. The point in the story of Job, an inspired didactic novel, is that God has plans and purposes which mortal men cannot grasp. While Job's three friends try to persuade him that he must be guilty of some crime, otherwise he would not be suffering as he is, Job insists on his innocence. God now comes on the stage. By correcting Job's friends he indirectly proves that Job is innocent, but at the same time, he does not proclaim Job's *right* to complete happiness on earth. The author of Job, like his contemporaries, had hardly any idea of vicarious suffering on earth. A future eternal life of happiness did not loom very large in their calculations. God does not, therefore, give a satisfactory answer to the problem raised in this sacred novel, for the author did not have sufficient revelation at the time, but in the chapter (38-41) from which today's short reading is taken, he makes it clear to Job that he is not in a position to judge the doings of God.

who shut . . . sea: In these last chapters of the book, God is showing to Job how little he knows about creation and how much less, therefore, does he know about the Creator. So what right has he to question God's justice?

burst . . . womb : When the sea was created, or as it were, born, who but God set limits to it? (Gn. 1 : 9).

clouds . . . bands : The sea like a new-born babe was wrapped in the swaddling clothes of cloud and darkness.

thus far . . . come : God appointed limits beyond which the sea might not extend.

proud . . . stayed : The sea's fury is beyond the power of men to control but it is under the power of its Creator.

APPLICATION : The question which agitated the mind of the author of the Book of Job : "Why should God let the good suffer and the wicked prosper in this world?" is no longer a problem for true Christians. We are followers of the innocent Christ, who suffered and died for the sake of mankind. We know that God's retribution is not always, and never fully, given in this life. We know that the good can and do suffer many hardships on this earth. As members of the mystical body of Christ, they are carrying the burdens of weaker members who are too weak to carry their own. And the good, those who are truly sincere Christians, will only rejoice if God chooses them to carry some extra burdens. They realize what the future life holds for them. They know that reaching that future life is worth all and anything they may have to suffer on this earth.

There are, however, weaker members among us, members whose outlook is not as fixed on the after-life as it should be. These are often puzzled by the ways in which God's providence works. When some calamity strikes them, when the father of a young family is taken, leaving a helpless wife and children; when the mother so necessary for her young children dies; when the only son or daughter, the hope and expected consolation of loving parents, is lost, it is perhaps only human to question God's goodness, God's interest in us. But it is a human and not a Christian reaction. Our Christian faith tells us very clearly and definitely that we are not in this world in order to be rich or comfortable or truly happy—we are here in order to reach heaven where we shall be forever truly rich, truly comfortable, and truly happy.

This is where the loving goodness of God comes in. He is providing for our eternal happiness, not for a few passing years of comfort here on earth. When he takes a loved one, it is to assure true eternal happiness to that one, or to those left behind who would not otherwise reach the goal which he has in store for them. From a human point of view, the loss of one sorely needed can and generally does bring out the best in those left behind and in their charitable neighbors. It is for these that God is planning when he allows death to strike a family. If life on earth should run smoothly, sweetly and happily for everybody up to extreme old age, how many would think of God or of their future life? By nature we are mean; we can easily forget God who gives us everything we have; we can even forget our own best interests and become so entangled in this present life that we would not be prepared for the after-life even in extreme old age.

So the good God, the loving Father who wants all of us to have the true, eternal life, keeps sending us messages to remind us that we have not here a lasting city—that our real home is in heaven. His messages are sent through sicknesses, sorrow, disappointments and deaths. These are intended to make us sit up and take notice, to realize that we are only pilgrims on a journey, liable to suffer many mishaps and inconveniences before we reach our final destination. We can, and should if we are truly Christian, see the loving hand of God in our sorrows as well as in our joys, in our heart-aches as well as in our moments of pleasure. We may be tempted to ask : why should we and not others be picked out as the ones who have to suffer? But if we give in to this temptation, we are making the mistake that Job made : we are trying to measure the infinite mind and plans of God with our infinite minds. We are like the child who tried to bail the ocean into the hole he had made in the sand.

Instead, let us ever keep before our minds the final words which the inspired author puts in the mouth of Job :

"I know that you are all-powerful. What you conceive you can perform; I am the man who obscured your designs with my empty-headed words. I have been holding forth on matters I cannot understand, on marvels beyond me and my knowledge" (Job 42 : 1-3).

SECOND READING : 2 Corinthians 5 : 14-17. The love of Christ controls us, because we are convinced that one has died for all; therefore all have died. And he died for all, that those who live might live no longer for themselves but for him who for their sake died and was raised.

From now on therefore we regard no one from a human point of view; even though we once regarded Christ from a human point of view, we regard him thus no longer. Therefore, if any one is in Christ, he is a new creation; the old has passed away, behold, the new has come.

EXPLANATION : St. Paul is here urging his converts never to forget what being a Christian means. They have been given a new mode of life—they are new creations—because Christ died and rose from the dead for them. Therefore, they already have the seeds of immorality in them. They, too, will rise from the dead. However, to bring these seeds to flower, they must now live, not for themselves, not for this world but for Christ—by keeping his commandments.

love . . . us : Ever since his vision of the risen Christ on the day of his conversion, St. Paul's life has been regulated by the love of Christ for him. In return, he tried to reciprocate that love.

one . . . for all : He is convinced, without the slightest doubt, that Christ died for all men. The Son of God became man and like any man died in his human nature. His death was indeed a cruel death, because of his sinful opponents, but he would have died in any case, in order to be like us in all things. He rose from the dead—to open the gates of death for all men. These he has made sons of God with a right to eternal life.

all have died: In his death Christ represented all men and so, legally, all men died *in him*. This means that death is conquered for them; they will still have to die their own death, but this death will no longer have any hold on them.

those who live: That is, first and foremost, Christians who have learned the facts of Christianity, and all others who, through no fault of their own, have not had the gospel preached to them.

no . . . themselves: Those who know the facts of the Christian faith must now live for Christ, that is, they must live according to the rules he laid down. Therefore, they must no longer live for their own personal pleasure or gain, they belong to Christ.

human point of view: Christians are no longer mere human beings. The same holds for all men of good-will, as we said above. They are raised to a supernatural status, they are adopted sons of God and brothers of Christ.

once . . . Christ: Before his conversion Paul looked on Christ not only as a human being but a wicked human being who pretended to be the promised Messiah; according to Paul and his friends the Pharisees, he was not.

regard . . . no longer: The vision on the road to Damascus (Acts 9) changed it all. He, a bitter opponent, was changed into a passionate supporter and promoter.

in Christ . . . creation: Any baptized Christian is a new being. He has a new principle of life—a principle of eternal life—in him. By the grace of the Holy Spirit, sent by the Father and the Son, he is in Christ and Christ is in him.

old . . . away: The old law of Moses has passed away; it has fulfilled its purpose. But the old status of the pagan world has also ended. By Christ's incarnation all men are now made adopted sons of God. Externally things may seem the same but the world after Christ is entirely different from the world before Christ. The new order, planned by God from all eternity has come to stay forever.

APPLICATION: In these few verses, the words of St. Paul ringing down through the centuries, are a clarion call to us to live our Christian life to the full. We Christians, and all others who do not refuse to see the light, are on our way to an everlasting life. By his incarnation Christ has made us his brothers and heirs to heaven. The one and only reason why we are living today on this earth is to make our way to heaven and live there in happiness forever. We all know that, in theory. It is at the back of our minds, but that is not enough. This thought of our purpose in life, this reason for being Christians, must be ever the motivation of our whole life and every day and hour of our life.

When one asks: what about all the things we have to do on earth, what about families and dependants, what about our daily tasks, our struggle to provide for our bodily needs? St. Paul understood all these responsibilities to the full; he was a man of outstanding common sense; he understood very well the daily cares and worldly anxieties of all his converts. When telling them to live no longer for themselves but for Christ, he was not asking them to enter a monastery, or to go into the desert to spend all their time in prayer. He was asking them to do their daily tasks, to earn a livelihood for themselves and their dependants, but to do this for God's honor and glory. What he was warning them against was the danger, as common then as it is today, of becoming so attached to this world and its passing attractions, that they should forget God and their Christian status.

The true, sincere Christian today, just as the first Christians of Corinth, can remain in the world and work his way to heaven, while doing the ordinary things that all men do, sin excepted. The forty-hour week spirit in the factory, or the office, or in household duties are forty hours which are earning reward in heaven, if they are honestly spent, and spent with the intention of honoring God. The fifty or so hours a week spent in sleep are not fifty wasted hours, but hours which are totted up in our favor in the book of life, if again we offer them to God. Likewise, the hours spent in legitimate recreation can be to our credit in heaven, if only we have the right motive.

God put us on this earth. He could have permitted this earthly life to be our complete span of existence. We would still have to work for our living, we would still have to struggle and strive against the trials of life and then have nothing for it all in the end, but the grave. No hope, no future to look forward to, no chance of ever meeting our beloved ones again—what a sad, gloomy existence that would be. Suicide in such circumstances would surely be

the order of the day, and the only reasonable response for an intelligent being to such a cruel fate. But God's infinite goodness, his divine nature's inclination to share his own happiness with those who could appreciate and value it, made him plan an unending life for man. His divine Son did the needful, he shared in our human nature so that we could share in the divine. Our earthly death which could have been our end forever, becomes instead the gateway which opens into eternity.

The next time we are tempted to bewail the crosses and sufferings which befall us, let us remember that there is a reward, an eternal, unending, reward, awaiting us at the moment of death. This will be so if we bear crosses and live our years on earth in peace with God, our conscience and with our neighbor. Let us do our daily tasks honestly and faithfully, enjoy the passing sunshine of life when it comes our way, bear with the shadows and the dark clouds of life and offer it all in thanksgiving to God the Father and his beloved Son, Christ. God has given us a future to which we can look forward, an eternal home where cares and troubles will be no more, where sorrow will not enter and all tears will be wiped away. With such a Christian outlook on life and death, with such a bright future ahead and which can be so easily reached, what Christian, worthy of the name, could be so foolish as to let himself forget the goodness of God and risk losing his eternal home.

GOSPEL: Mark 4:35–41. When evening had come, Jesus said to his disciples, "Let us go across to the other side." And leaving the crowd, they took him with them, just as he was, in the boat. And other boats were with him. And a great storm of wind arose, and the waves beat into the boat, so that the boat was already filling. But he was in the stern, asleep on the cushion; and they woke him and said to him, "Teacher, do you not care if we perish?" And he awoke and rebuked the wind, and said to the sea, "Peace! Be still!" And the wind ceased, and there was a great calm. He said to them, "Why are you afraid? Have you no faith?" And they were filled with awe, and said to one another, "Who then is this, that even wind and sea obey him?"

EXPLANATION: Our Lord had spent the day preaching and healing the sick at Capernaum where great crowds had gathered. Many had come out of curiosity to see miracles, and many others, who had the idea of a political Messiah in their minds, were ready to raise the standard of revolt against the Romans and proclaim Christ as king of Palestine. This our Lord always avoided by hiding from them (Jn. 6:15), or by dispersing the crowd or by leaving them as in the present instance.

when . . . had come: Matthew introduces the same story with: "When Jesus saw great crowds about him he gave orders to cross the sea (of Galilee) to the other shore," as if to avoid the impetuous crowd.

just as he was: Mark has told us in 4:1 that because of the huge crowd that had gathered Jesus had got into a boat and had it moved a little distance from the shore so that he could see and speak to the huge crowd. He has now told the Apostles that he wants them to take him across the sea and they obey him immediately. Neither he nor they return ashore for anything, they went "just as they were."

other . . . him: There were other fishermen besides Peter, Andrew, James and John living around Capernaum. They were probably sitting in their boats close by while Jesus was preaching, and now decided to cross the lake with the Apostles. We are not told what became of them, but they witnessed the storm and its calming and would thus be witnesses later on of the divine power exhibited by Jesus.

great . . . arose: A sudden and violent storm arising in the sea of Galilee is no rare occurrence. The sea or lake is 600 feet under sea-level, it is surrounded on almost all sides by high hills, so it is a natural place for violent storms.

boat . . . filling: As the waves were so high, they broke over the bow and sides of the boat frequently. The fishermen kept bailing out the water but eventually they realized that the boat would soon sink, unless Jesus could help.

he . . . asleep: This simple remark brings out the true humanity of Jesus. He was so tired after the hard day that neither the noise of the storm nor the waves breaking over the boat awakened him. A few minutes later, the same Jesus who was human, tired, and sleepy, proved himself Lord of the elements—proved himself to be God. The two natures in Jesus, the human and divine, were so perfectly united in the one person that the divinity took nothing away from the humanity. His human nature was, as St. Paul says, like unto ours in all things save sin—nor did his humanity impede his divinity in any way.

they woke him: While they thought that their last moment had come, he was soundly asleep in the stern which was the steadiest and driest part of the boat.

Teacher . . . perish: Despite all the miracles they had already seen him perform, despite the many proofs that God was with him, they now thought that their boat would sink and that he and they would drown. They did not yet realize that he was the promised Messiah and the Son of God, and therefore that his life could not end yet and that they too were safe in his presence.

rebuked . . . sea: This act of Christ recalls God's absolute command of the elements, especially the sea, in the Old Testament (see today's first reading, also Job. 9 : 8; 26 : 12–13; Ps. 89 : 9; 104 : 7; 106 : 25).

was a great calm: Immediately the wind and waves obeyed. The most violent storms abate eventually and the disturbed waters settle down gradually, but here the wind and the water calmed instantly.

have . . . faith: He is surprised at their lack of trust in his power after all the miracles they have already seen him perform. He could save others, could he not save himself and them, whom he had chosen to be his helpers only a short time previously?

they . . . awe: They were not yet convinced believers in his Messiahship or much less his divinity, but the power he proved to have over the elements had evidently something of the divine in it. As Jews they would have known something of the Old Testament.

who then is this? They ask one another who can he be and the remark:

Even . . . obey him: is tantamount to answering their question with the statement: he is God, for God only can command the elements he created. This may have been added later by Mark.

APPLICATION: There is a very important lesson for every one of us in today's gospel story. Our lives are really a journey across the sea of time to the shore of eternity. During that crossing all who comes to the use of reason encounter some storms. There is no smooth, calm crossing for anyone. This is the will of God. Our Lord knew that a storm was going to blow up that night in the Sea of Galilee. He allowed his disciples to face that terrifying ordeal, because he wanted his future Church to have confidence in his divine power and assistance, when tribulations and persecutions would seem to be on the point of ending her forever. Down through the centuries the Church of God has had to face storms and trials which would have swamped her if she had not a divine Founder and Protector. Christ, however, kept his promise: the gates of hell cannot prevail against her. She survived the storms and as a consequence of them gained new vigor and strength.

That same divine guarantee which Christ gave his Church will be with her until the last human being on earth has entered heaven. It is with her today. It will save her from internal weaknesses which could do more damage to her spiritual vitality than open persecution from without could ever do. We know Christ is in the barque of Peter. He is

K

waiting to be called. If we realize that of ourselves we are not able to weather this storm, and call on him, he will rebuke the winds of pride and calm the waves of turbulent self-assertion. The barque of Peter will enter calm waters once more.

What is true in the life of the Church is true also in the life of each member of the Church. God foresees all our life's storms. He permits them, because he is to use them as means to help us in our struggle to reach heaven. If we use these storms or trials of life to come closer to Jesus, to throw ourselves on his mercy, they will serve the purpose for which he permits them. Unfortunately, there are Christians who question not only the goodness of God, but his very existence, when some heavy seas break across their life's barque. "How could God, if he be good," they ask, "allow me to suffer like this, I who have been so faithful? Why should he let me bear all this poverty, all these pains, all this dishonesty of my fellowmen, when a small act of his will could remove it all and make me healthy, happy and prosperous?"

What such a Christian forgets is that God's purpose in creating him was not to make him healthy, happy and prosperous in this life, but to give him a share in his own eternal happiness in heaven. If this life were the end and sum-total of man, if all ended with death, then certainly that complaint would have some foundation. However, our human intelligence, and divine revelation, prove to us conclusively that this life is not an end for man but a *means* with which to attain his real end, perfect happiness.

Therefore, we must not expect to get from life what it cannot give. Instead, we must use what it gives us, the unpleasant as well as the pleasant, the rain as well as the sunshine, the pain as well as the pleasure, as means which will help us to reach our perfect ending, our eternal dwelling-place in heaven. Too often like the disciples that night in the storm, we think that God has forgotten us, that he is not interested in us when storms break around us. In fact, it is then that he is nearest to us. We think he is sleeping and that all is lost, when he is but using this storm to rekindle our faith, and make us realize that we are pilgrims on our way across this earth and not permanent residents here.

THIRTEENTH SUNDAY OF THE YEAR

FIRST READING: Wisdom 1 : 13–15; 2 : 23–24. Because God did not make death, he does not delight in the death of the living. For he created all things that they might exist, and the generative forces of the world are wholesome, and there is no destructive poison in them; and the dominion of Hades is not on earth. For righteousness is immortal. God created man for incorruption, and made him in the image of his own eternity, but through the devil's envy death entered the world, and those who belong to his party experience it.

EXPLANATION: The Book of Wisdom was written by a Greek-speaking Jew, very probably in Alexandria in Egypt, in the first half of the first century B.C. That he was a Jew is evident: he is loyal "to the God of the Fathers" (9 : 1), and proud to belong to the " holy and blameless race " (10 : 15). He quotes the Old Testament from the Greek translation (the Septuagint), is well versed in the Greek language and knows something of Greek philosophy. His book was written to commend wisdom which comes from God, the source of all wisdom. In wisdom God created the world and in wisdom he governs it. Wisdom is the basis of all virtue. It is the way to God and to the future life. The present life is but the preparation for the life to come in which the virtuous live with God and the wicked are punished (3 : 9–10).

In today's reading from this book, we have a reference to a truth which is clearly stated for the first time in the whole Old Testament: man's real destiny is an unending life with God. Hitherto the only hint at a future life was some pale existence in Sheol separated from God. Man's reward for loyalty to God was a long life, prosperity, a large family and prestige *in this world*. This did not always work out as it should and many questions are raised. Wisdom was the first and only book to express categorically and clearly man's real purpose in life: to reach eternal life with God after death.

God . . . death: The reference is to spiritual death, as verse 24 shows. In the preceding verse the author says: "Do not court death by the error of your ways." The death he refers to, therefore, is death to God by sin. This is not part of God's plan for man.

death of the living: God does not delight in, or want, any of his human creatures to die to him, but having given man a free will he cannot prevent him from acting foolishly.

all things . . . exist : When God created things they were " good " and " wholesome "—there was nothing evil in them. To the lower creatures he gave a temporary existence on this earth. For man, who alone among earth's creatures could enjoy and appreciate an unending life, he planned an eternal life of happiness after he had earned it by the proper use of his temporary existence on earth.

dominion . . . earth : Hades stands for death in the context. It has no right of its own on earth, it is a usurper brought in by an enemy, its sway will be ended one day.

righteousness is immortal : It is sin that brings eternal death but justice, upright living, leads to immortality in the future life.

God . . . incorruption : This is the first categorical statement in the Bible of man's real purpose in life. This immortal life does not exclude man's

natural death, it will begin after he has passed through the portals of natural death.

image . . . eternity : God gave man faculties which raise him above all earthly creatures. These faculties are a limited reflexion of God's own intelligence and free will. They make man, alone among earth's creatures, capable of eternal life.

the devil's envy : Very probably this is an allusion to Genesis 3, the story of the fall. If so, the author interprets the threat of death there (Gn. 3 : 3) as referring to spiritual death. Wisdom is the only Old Testament book to identify the serpent of Genesis with the devil (see Jn. 8 : 44; Ap. 12 : 9; 20 : 10).

those . . . party : Spiritual death which implies a perpetual separation from God, is the lot of all those who belong to Satan and who live in sin. There can be no question here of natural death— for all men experience that.

APPLICATION : That God created us for immortality, that is, for an unending life after we die is not news to us Christians. It is our reason for being Christians; it is the reason why we follow Christ. As St. Paul says : " If our hope in Christ has been for this life only, we are the most unfortunate of all people " (1 Cor. 15 : 19). What would be the purpose of self-mortification, of obeying commandments, of trying to serve God and neighbor if all ended in death? But, of course, human life does not end in death, natural life does, but our natural death is only the beginning of our eternal existence.

Christ came on earth, as we Christians know, in order to put into action God's

eternal plan for us men. God could have found other ways of sharing his heaven with us after the end of our life here, but he chose the way and the means that would best show forth his infinite love and his infinite interest in us. He sent his Son to become man on earth, in order to make us his brothers and co-heirs to heaven. We now have a claim on God. Eternal life is a free-gift to us on his part but because Christ is our brother, we now have a legal claim, as it were, to it. Once the incarnation took place all men, except those who deliberately exclude themselves, become heirs to heaven, co-heirs with Christ. Being an heir gives one a legal right to the inheritance.

We Christians who know this, who know that we shall go to heaven when we breathe our last on earth, provided we are loyal to Christ and the faith he gave us, do not think enough about this. It is the most important event that can ever happen to us and we do not meditate on it sufficiently often. The terrifying thought is that we could lose our inheritance, that we could exclude ourselves from that one place that can satisfy our every desire and find ourselves at the judgement seat unfit to There have been such unfortunate Christians in the past; there will be others in the years to come and we could be among them. Whatever about the nature of the fires of hell, there can be no doubt about the reality of the heart-burning regret and remorse which will keep gnawing at the Christian who will then realize what he has lost—and irrevocably lost forever.

However, we can insure ourselves against such a dreadful calamity. We can make sure that we shall be found worthy when our call to judgement comes: simply by trying always to be in God's friendship. Let each one of us ask himself how he would fare if he were called to judgement this moment. Am I worthy of heaven as I stand here and now? If there are black marks against me, I have the means and the divine helps left to me by Christ to erase these marks. If whole pages of my book of life have been smeared and spattered with ugly sins and dreadful offenses against God and neighbor, I can tear out all these pages and begin to write my life story anew. While I am alive, God's infinite mercy is available to me for the asking. He cannot force his mercy on me against my will, but he is pleased to give it, if asked.

"God created me for incorruption," that is, for the unending, happy life of heaven. He wants me there. He sent his Son on earth to endure humiliations and sufferings so that I would get there. I would be ungrateful, thankless to God and so forgetful of my own best interests if I failed to get there. God forbid that this should happen to me!

SECOND READING: A2 Corinthians 8:7; 9; 13–15. As you excel in everything—in faith, in utterance, in knowledge, in all earnestness, and in your love for us—see that you excel in this gracious work also. For you know the grace of our Lord Jesus Christ, that though he was rich, yet for your sake he became poor, so that by his poverty you might become rich. I do not mean that others should be eased and you burdened, but that as a matter of equality your abundance at the present time should supply their want, so that their abundance may supply your want, that there may be equality. As it is written, "He who gathered much had nothing over, and he who gathered little had no lack."

EXPLANATION: In chapters 8 and 9 of this letter, St. Paul is urging the Corinthians to give generously toward the collection he is organizing for the poor Jewish converts in Palestine. He had already sent alms from Macedonia and Galatia to the poor in Jerusalem, but this was a general collection from all the Gentile churches to the needy Christians in Palestine. This was an occasion for the Gentile converts to show their solidarity and union with their Jewish brethren and also an opportunity for them to practice the virtue of charity. The Jews of the Diaspora used to show their solidarity with their fellow-Jews in Palestine and retain their bonds of fraternity with them, by sending their annual temple-tax to Jerusalem. St. Paul wanted his Gentile converts to show the same regard and love and attachment to the mother Church in Jerusalem, by sending this financial gift to the Palestinian church. There was no distinction between Jew or Gentile, Greek or Barbarian, all were one in Christ.

as you excel . . . utterance : St. Paul reminds the Corinthian converts of the great gifts they have had from God : their great faith, their gifts of tongues and their power of expounding the doctrines of the faith, their sincerity and loyalty to the faith in the face of opposition, their love for their Apostle and Father in the faith. They excelled in all these gifts. He now expects them

to excel also in this work of charity— the collection for the poor Christians in Jerusalem.

grace of our Lord : Grace here stands for graciousness, generosity. Christ who was God, rich in all things, made himself man, that is, poor. "He emptied himself" of his divine glory for their sakes. He became man so that they could become adopted sons of God.

others . . . burdened : Paul does not want the Corinthians to reduce themselves to poverty while making the Judeo-Christians rich. What he wants is a sharing of their abundance to relieve the wants of the others.

their abundance . . . want : The Judeo-Christians will share their abundance in things spiritual with the Corinthians in return for the material gifts sent them. Thus there will be equality of distribution.

as it is written : Paul quotes Exodus (16 : 18) to prove that God wants his gifts divided equally among his children. The Corinthians, therefore, must be ready to share their earthly goods with the poor of Jerusalem who, in turn, will share their spiritual goods with the Corinthians.

APPLICATION : In the midst of all his trials and troubles, bowed down as he was with worry and care for his many newly-founded churches, the big-hearted and generous St. Paul found time to think of the needy church of Jerusalem. He had not labored in the formation of that church but, having visited Jerusalem more than once, he knew the dire poverty in which most of the Christians of Jerusalem and Palestine lived. Many of them, including many priests and Levites had lived off the temple revenues before their conversion. They now had

lost that means of support and could find no means of a livelihood in that poor country. Though Asia Minor and Greece were not affluent countries by today's standards, they were rich when compared with Palestine. St. Paul knew this, and his Christian love for all of Christ's brothers moved him to take practical steps to help them in their need. That the result was good we can be sure; it brought material help to the needy of Palestine and it brought the blessing of God on the charitable Gentiles.

In organizing this good work of mercy, St. Paul was but carrying out the teaching of our divine Lord. He himself, as St. Paul tells us today, set us an example of infinite charity, infinite giving to the destitute human race. "Though he was rich, yet for your sake he became poor, so that by his poverty you might become rich." He was God in the infinite glory and happiness of heaven. "He emptied himself of this divine glory to assume the condition of a slave and became as men are . . . humbler yet, even to accepting death on a cross" (Ph. 2 : 7–8). Christ came to us in our desperate need. Depriving himself of his right to divine glory, while here on earth, he willingly sacrificed also the humanity he had assumed and died the shameful death of the cross, in order to raise us up from our mere natural state to the privileged position of sons of God and heirs to heaven.

This was, of course, infinite charity, infinite love of others in need—a charity from which we all have profited. He expects us all to imitate this love even if only in our own limited way. He expects us to help our neighbor, that is our fellowman, whenever he is in need. This is made crystal clear in his description of the judgement day. "The king will say (on that day): come you blessed, possess the kingdom prepared for you since the world was made. For when I was hungry you gave me food,

when thirsty you gave me drink . . . naked you clothed me . . . for anything you did for one of my brothers here, however humble, you did for me " (Mt. 25 : 34–40). It is true, of course, that the other virtues will be on the credit side for the just on judgement day; the other vices will be on the debit side for the wicked. But what Christ is stressing here is the basic law of charity, love of God and neighbor. Love of neighbor is the proof that God is loved. If this law is not kept, then keeping the rest of the Commandments will not help us when our account books are checked on judgement day.

This judgement is an examination awaiting all of us, and on it our eternity will depend. In preparing for examinations it is very helpful to know what kind of questions were asked in previous years. After hearing our Lord's own description of the judgement day, we can be in no doubt as to the basic question he will put to us. Were we or were we not charitable to our needy fellowman? Did we do all we could to alleviate his sufferings and his want? If we did, it was to Christ himself that we were giving help and thus we can expect full marks on that question. But if we turned a deaf ear to all the charitable appeals we turned a deaf ear to Christ and we can hardly expect him to hear our "Lord, Lord" and our appeal for mercy on our fateful examination day.

GOSPEL : Mark 5 : 21–43. When Jesus had crossed in the boat to the other side, a great crowd gathered about him; and he was beside the sea. Then came one of the rulers of the synagogue, Jairus by name, and seeing him, he fell at his feet, and besought him, saying, "My little daughter is at the point of death. Come and lay your hands on her, so that she may be made well, and live." And he went with him.

And a great crowd followed him and thronged about him. And there was a woman who had had a flow of blood for twelve years, and who had suffered much under many physicians, and had spent all that she had, and was no better but rather grew worse. She had heard the reports about Jesus, and came up behind him in the crowd and touched his garment. For she said, "If I touch even his garments, I shall be made well." And immediately the hemorrhage ceased; and she felt in her body that she was healed of her disease. And Jesus, perceiving in himself that power had gone forth from him, immediately turned about in the crowd, and said, "Who touched my garments?" And his disciples said to him, "You see the crowd pressing around you, and yet you say, 'Who touched me?'" And he looked around to see who had done it. But the woman, knowing what had been done to her, came in fear and trembling and fell down before him, and told him the whole truth. And he said to her, "Daughter, your faith has made you well; go in peace, and be healed of your disease."

While he was still speaking, there came from the ruler's house some who said, "Your daughter is dead. Why trouble the Teacher any further?" But ignoring what they said, Jesus said to the ruler of the synagogue, "Do not fear, only believe." And he allowed no one to follow him except Peter and James and John the brother of James. When they came to the house of the ruler of the synagogue, he saw a tumult, and people weeping and wailing loudly. And when he had entered, he said to them, "And they laughed at him. But he put The child is not dead but sleeping." And they laughed at him. But he put them all outside, and took the child's father and mother and those who were with him, and went in where the child was. Taking her by the hand he said to her, "Talitha cumi"; which means, "Little girl, I say to you, rise." And immediately the girl got up and walked; for she was twelve years old. And immediately they were overcome with amazement. And he strictly charged them that no one should know this, and told them to give her something to eat.

EXPLANATION : In today's reading from St. Mark's gospel, the Evangelist describes two of our Lord's miracles, one a healing, the other a raising from the dead. Both took place near the west- ern shores of the Sea of Galilee and during the first months of our Lord's public ministry. Jairus, one of the rulers or supervisors of the synagogue (prob- ably of Capernaum), met Christ and falling on his knees begged him to come and heal his young daughter who was on the point of death. While most of the Jewish religious authorities looked on Jesus as an impostor, here was one who, when faced with a calamity, had the good sense to admit that Christ had supernatural power and begged for its exercise with a public display of humility. He fell on his knees, which showed that he really recognized the character and source of the supernatural power. Jesus did not refuse his request; "he went with him." While on their way, a woman who had suffered from an internal hemorrhage for twelve years, touched his garment and was instantly healed. She has done this secretly and furtively, but Jesus showed that he knew what had happened. He asked who it was that had touched him. The woman, in fear and trembling, confessed it was she and he told her that her faith —her trust in his power to heal her— had made her well.

Before the party reached the house of Jairus, some messengers met them with the news that the girl was dead and so according to them, there was no purpose in bringing Jesus any further. They could believe he had the power to heal the living, but to raise one dead was out of the question (see Jn. 11, where Martha and Mary had the same idea: "If you had been here my brother would not have died"). Jesus told Jairus not to fear but to believe. He went to the house, put out the neighbors and friends who were weeping and wailing, and taking Peter, James and John, as well as the father and mother of the girl, he entered her room and raised her from the dead. All were overcome with amazement.

who touched my garments? : With a huge crowd surging and pushing around him and trying to get near him, this seemed a strange question, as the disciples remarked, but Jesus wished to show that he was able to distinguish a touch which brought healing—because of the faith that inspired it, from all the other casual touches.

the woman . . . truth : The frightened woman confessed what she had done and announced the good result which she knew it had already produced. One touch of the hand of Jesus had effected what many physicians had been unable to do for her over a period of twelve years.

people . . . loudly : Besides the mother and relatives, the official mourners had already come to lament loudly over the dead person. This was a Jewish custom and was practiced by other races as well. It survived in the country districts of Ireland until the early decades of this century.

not dead but sleeping : It has sometimes been suggested that this is to be taken literally. But how should Jesus have known that she was only in a deep sleep, he had not yet entered the room where the girl lay? Besides, even in those days, people knew when one had ceased breathing—people were not buried because they were in a coma. The mourning people were not sent for until it was certain that the girl had died. Would St. Mark have recounted this story with all its details, if all Christ did was to raise a girl from a deep sleep? Sleeping, as a euphemism for death, was common among the ancients. The Christian usage of "sleeping" for death is based on the certain fact of the resurrection. All those who are now in our "cemeteries" will be awakened one day. Our word "cemetery" comes from the Greek word for dormitory or sleeping-place.

they laughed at him : The neighbors

and mourners knew that the girl was dead. Thus thinking that he meant "she is sleeping" in the literal sense, they laughed at what they thought was his ignorance.

immediately . . . walked : This was the proof that she was once more alive and well.

something to eat : Here is another proof that she was her real self and not a ghost.

no one . . . this : At this stage Christ did not want his miracles to be published to all and sundry. There were the political fanatics who would want to proclaim him king of Palestine.

APPLICATION : Today's gospel gives us two further proofs of the divine power and the infinite mercy of our Savior. Apart from the primary purpose of proving his claim to be the promised Messiah, all his miracles had as their aim and end : the benefit of suffering human beings. He worked no miracle for the sake of astonishing people. or to satisfy idle gossip. Each one was performed in order to help someone in distress. All who were helped by his miracles of mercy had one thing in common—they were motivated by trust in his mercy and power. The leper in Matthew (8 : 2) expressed the sentiments of them all : "Lord, if only you will you can cleanse me (of my leprosy)." In many cases, as for instance that of Jarius above, it was a relative or friends who showed this faith and confidence. It was always present either in the fortunate person or in the relative or friend who asked for the miracle.

The Gospels give us only some of the many miracles our Lord worked. They give them to prove that he was what he claimed to be : the Son of God and the long-expected Savior; and also to prove his compassionate understanding and sympathy for suffering humanity.

We must not forget, however, that the meaning of his miracles and his mission was lost on thousands of his contemporaries in Palestine, small though the country was. While great throngs followed our Lord and listened to his message and were interested in his mission, still great throngs remained at home, stolidly immersed in their worldly tasks and thoughts. They heard rumors about the man from Nazareth who was said to be the Messiah, and was supposed to be able to work miracles, but they were too practical, too sensible to listen to such rumors. Anyway they had no interest in the Messiah, or in silly spiritual things, they were fully occupied with their financial and worldly interests.

Has the world changed much in nineteen centuries? How many millions of nominal Christians ignore Christ and his Gospel today, millions who are too practical, too down-to-earth to waste time on such a silly thing as their eternal salvation! How many millions are spiritually sick and dying but who have not the faith, humility and confidence of Jairus, to cast themselves at the feet of Jesus and ask him to cure them? How fortunate would not people be if they would repeat the leper's prayer : "Lord, if only you will you can make me clean"; if they could, like the suffering woman in today's Gospel, break through the throng of worldly pride, worldly interests and worldly associates and touch the hem of his garment; if they had the faith of Jairus; if only they could say to our Lord :

"come and lay your hands upon me so that I may be made well and live."?

Today, let us say a fervent prayer of thanksgiving to God for the gift of active faith which he has given us and beg of him to keep that faith ever alive in our breasts. Let us think, too, of our fellowmen, our brothers in Christ, who are so busy with their worldly occupations and pleasures that they cannot find time to listen to his message. They are spiritually anemic and almost spiritually dead, but cannot push their way toward Christ through the throngs of earthly, worldly barricades which they have built about themselves. Our sincere prayers can help them to overcome these obstacles; frequently and fervently let us ask God to send them his efficacious grace so that these brothers in Christ will also be with him in heaven.

FOURTEENTH SUNDAY OF THE YEAR

FIRST READING: Ezekiel 2:2-5. The Spirit entered into me and set me upon my feet; and I heard him speaking to me. And he said to me, "Son of man, I send you to the people of Israel, to a nation of rebels, who have rebelled against me; they and their fathers have transgressed against me to this very day. The people also are impudent and stubborn: I send you to them; and you shall say to them, 'Thus says the Lord God.' And whether they hear or refuse to hear (for they are a rebellious house) they will know that there has been a prophet among them."

EXPLANATION: Ezekiel, one of the four major prophets of the Old Testament, carried out his office of God's mouthpiece to the Chosen People from 593–571 B.C. In 597 he was among the nobles of Judah carried into exile by Nabuchadnezzar of Babylon, together with king Jehoiakim. Some four years after his arrival in Babylon, God appointed him to speak to his fellow-exiles. The burden of his preaching was that Judah had brought this exile on herself by her infidelity to Yahweh, her God. Worse was still to come. Jerusalem and its temple, which had been desecrated by unworthy priests, would be razed to the ground. Judah would cease to exist as a nation and all the able-bodied people would be taken as slaves to Babylon. As he, and Jeremiah also, had foretold: all of this happened in 587.

Then in the latter half of his ministry, he began to console the exiles and to promise them that, having undergone their just punishment, they would be restored to their homeland. A new Jerusalem and a new temple would be built. The people, purified by the exile, would serve God with a new heart and a new spirit. The heart of stone, which they had up to now, would be replaced by a heart of flesh (see 11 : 18-19). This part of the prophecy was not completely fulfilled until the coming of Christianity. The verses taken from Ezekiel today, treat of his appointment as prophet—God's representative—among the exiles in Babylon.

The Spirit . . . me : Ezekiel is conscious that God, through his Spirit whom he has received, has chosen him as his prophet or mouthpiece.

heard the Lord : He has no doubt about the authenticity of his vocation—it is God himself who speaks to him.

Son of man : This simply means "man," or human being. When used by our Lord of himself it has a vague messianic connotation. It is not easily recognizable and that is why he used it.

Israel . . . rebels : This is a true description. With a few notable exceptions since the time of king Jehoram 848, the kings of Judah had been disloyal to their God and the people as a whole followed the bad example of their kings. It was this disloyalty to Yahweh which brought on them the Babylonian exile.

impudent and stubborn : They positively insulted their God not only by forgetting to thank and serve him but by turning to false gods. Again and again he sent his prophets to correct them but in vain. They remained hardhearted and stubborn.

I . . . them : Even in the exile of Babylon, brought on them by their sins against God, he did not leave them uncared for. He sent his representative to them. He raised up one of their number to be his mouthpiece among them.

whether they hear : They neglected God but they could never accuse God of neglecting them. He sent them Ezekiel and later he would send second-Isaiah. They would lose if they did not listen to his word.

APPLICATION : As we read it in the historical books of the Old Testament, the history of the Chosen People is a sad commentary on the meanness of human beings in their dealings with God. God had been a Father to the Israelites, ever since he brought them out of the slavery of Egypt. But even during the desert journey to the Promised Land which he had arranged to give them, they murmured and rebelled against him. When they eventually settled in Canaan, with the help of his almighty hand, they very soon forgot him. Harassed by the neighboring pagan people, they remembered him and called on him. He sent them the Judges to free them from their enemies. He allowed them to establish a monarchy and he aided and assisted the first occupants of the throne, but as their temporal affairs prospered their spiritual interests declined. For over four hundred years, from the death of David to the fall of Jerusalem, only four of the eighteen kings in Judah were loyal to Yahweh and encouraged the people to serve him.

As God said in today's reading : the Chosen People, to whom he was sending Ezekiel, were a "nation of rebels." The very fact that he was sending a prophet, his own representative, to them notwithstanding their unworthiness, makes us marvel at this infinite mercy and love. Who but the infinite God could keep on sending prophet after prophet, giving chance after chance to this stubborn rebellious people to change their mind? He could have abandoned them and found some people more worthy of his paternal interest, but he did not. He was God and was able to use their very disloyalty for his purpose. The Babylonian exile, which they had now brought on themselves, saw the end of their kingdom and their kings. The Messiah, the "blessing" promised to Abraham and the descendant foretold to David who would make his throne glorious forever, would now be born not in a palace but in a stable, not in wealth and luxury but in the direst poverty.

All this was foreseen and fore-planned by God. He used the disloyalty of his Chosen People to bring his plan to fulfillment. Would we want it otherwise? Had Christ been born in a king's palace in Jerusalem, had he grown up as a prince surrounded by courtiers and noblemen, would he have had the effects he had on the minds and hearts of ninety-nine percent of those who became his followers? If agnostics and rationalists try to pick flaws in the eternal truths he proclaimed, when humanly speaking, he was only a carpenter from Nazareth, what faults could they not find in his teaching if he had been one of the earthly nobility? All of these "ifs," however, are futile, because God planned things the right way and the best way. The Son of God, the King of kings, not only humbled himself by taking our created human nature, but he took that human nature and became as one of the lowest and the poorest of that time.

Just as the Chosen People, on whom he had lavished his love, proved to be unfaithful to him and unworthy of their election so will it be until the end of time. Of the hundreds of millions of Christians in our world today, how many are loyal and truly grateful for all that God has done for them? How many cherish the eternal inheritance Christ has won for them? Are not many imitating the Chosen People of old; ignoring and insulting God, forgetful of all he has done for them, and forgetting their one and only purpose in life? These Christians are foolishly and sinfully preparing to lose the inheritance Christ won for them. They are ready to sacrifice their King and their eternal kingdom.

It could happen to any one of us. God forbid that it should. If it should, the loss would be ours, a fatal and eternal loss. God will not suffer—we shall. God sent his prophets to speak to his Chosen People even when they were in exile. He will not, and cannot, send any prophet to us in our eternal exile, for our judgement at the moment of death will seal our fate forever. Daily he is sending his messengers to us while we are still alive. Turn aside today from the bustle and noise of this empty world, and listen to God's whisper in your heart: "Where would you like to be a hundred years from today?" The decision is in your own hands.

SECOND READING : 2 Corinthians 12 : 7–10. To keep me from being too elated by the abundance of revelations, a thorn was given me in the flesh, a messenger of Satan, to harass me, to keep me from being too elated. Three times I besought the Lord about this, that it should leave me; but he said to me, "My grace is sufficient for you, for my power is made perfect in weakness." I will all the more gladly boast of my weaknesses, that the power of Christ may rest upon me. For the sake of Christ, then, I am content with weaknesses, insults, hardships, persecutions, and calamities; for when I am weak, then I am strong.

EXPLANATION : St. Paul preached the Gospel in Corinth for eighteen months (50–52 A.D.), and founded a flourishing church there. He left for Jerusalem and returned via Antioch to visit the churches founded in Asia Minor and Greece. While he was away from Corinth some "intruders," some other self-appointed preachers, had come there and were upsetting the Christians. They evidently were belittling Paul and boasting of their own superior qualifications. In this letter, which Paul sends to the Corinthians from Ephesus or Macedonia (about 57 A.D.), he feels forced to prove that he was a true Apostle : who suffered much for Christ and his Gospel and who also had been given the privilege of special visions and revelations. He devotes chapters 10 to 12 : 6 to this subject. As if to make atonement for speaking so boastfully about himself, he goes on now to describe some weakness he had which troubled him very much. He prayed fervently to have it removed, but was told by the Lord that he would get the grace necessary to bear with it. He concludes that he is content with weakness and sufferings because the power and strength of Christ, working through a weak instrument, will be all the more visible and convincing.

abundance of revelations : In the previous verses he has referred to the many revelations he had from God. Now he says that he had some special weakness, and he sees in this an occasion to keep him humble in the midst of the many blessings and gifts he had from God.

a thorn ... flesh : The grammatical construction would suggest that this affliction was relatively permanent. Whether it still persisted is not clear.

a thorn ... flesh : A better translation would be : to the flesh (dative in Greek). The weakness or defect therefore does not come from the flesh, so the suggestion made by some that St. Paul suffered from continual concupiscence of the flesh is ruled out. This weakness, which impeded him in his work for Christ, was some bodily defect or recurring disease like malaria.

messenger of Satan : According to the Jewish mentality, all sicknesses and bodily defects came from sin and therefore finally from Satan. In any case, Paul sees this defect or disease as an agent which is impeding his missionary activity, and can therefore be attributed to Satan who would prevent all missionary activity, if he could.

Three times ... Lord : Like our Lord's three-fold prayer in Gethsemani he begged Christ, the Lord, to remove this hindrance.

he ... to me : On his third request he got an answer. That answer is still effective, as the Greek perfect implies.

my grace . . . weakness : Christ tells him that his work will be successful notwithstanding this bodily weakness; in fact, it will be all the more successful, because it will be seen as principally the work of Christ himself who can successfully use such a weak instrument.

boast . . . weaknesses : Paul, therefore, wants everybody in Corinth to know of all his weaknesses, for through them the power of Christ will be made evident. He is happy to face any calamity for :

when I . . . strong : The weaker he is as an agent of Christ, the more will Christ's power (as he was promised in answer to his prayer) be evident in his successful ministry of the gospel. His strength is in Christ.

APPLICATION : There are few, if any, of us who have not questioned at one time or another God's way of dealing with us. This is so when he allows some sickness, or bodily ailment or some calamity to interfere with our work for him or for our fellowmen. The upright and devout Christian businessman, who helps so many worthy and charitable causes loses his profits and eventually his business because some more powerful rival moves into his district. The devout Christian mother, the moral support of her husband and the exemplary religious teacher of her young family, is struck down with sickness and becomes a chronic invalid. The young, zealous missionary, who has just learned the language and customs of the pagan country for which he volunteered, develops some disease which compels him to return home. Again and again we hear, or witness, these things and are tempted to wonder if God does look after his own.

Today's reading should give us the answer. St. Paul, one of the greatest of Christ's apostles, had some bodily infirmity which he thought impeded his success in his ministry. He felt he could be much more effective without it and, saint that he was, he prayed to Christ and asked him to remove this defect. For two reasons his devout and reasonable request was not granted. St. Paul himself gives us the first reason : "to keep him from becoming proud." Had he been free from this defect he might possibly have taken the full credit for all his success. The second reason is given by Christ : "my power is made perfect in (your) weakness"; whatever weakness St. Paul had, it should have impeded his success in evangelizing the Corinthians, but it did not, because Christ was working with him and through him, and so the divine truth of the Christian gospel shone all the more clearly through the defects in the human instrument.

God allowed the great Apostle to suffer from some infirmity which St. Paul thought to be adversely affecting his work for God. On the contrary it was a great help to the saint's spiritual life and the progress of the Gospel. Have we, therefore, any grounds for questioning God's dealings with us? If the Apostle who gave his life for Christ, felt there was a danger of his developing a spirit of pride because of the good work he was doing, how much greater is that danger of pride in us? We are far from the heights of holiness reached by St. Paul. Down through the centuries, there have been men of great standing in the Church of Christ who became proud of their attainments and ended up by abandoning the Church. The leaders of all the heresies, which the Church had to condemn, were men of learning. Unfortunately, their esteem for themselves was greater than their love of truth. Their pride could not let them see any errors in their theological speculations; they refused all correction and rather than admit the authority of those over them they apostatized from the faith.

This dreadful vice of pride is hidden away in each one of us. It is looking for an opportunity to raise its head. Of all the known forms of pride, spiritual pride or pride in our spiritual progress, is the most satanic of all. It cuts the very basis from true spirituality, for it attributes to human endeavor that which can come only from a divine source. We cannot take one single step on the road to heaven without the active cooperation of divine grace. "What have you," says St. Paul, "which you have not received and if you have received it why glory in it as if it were your own?" Any gifts of body or mind which we have were given us by God. To him alone is glory due for them.

We need to be careful then in acts of charity to our neighbors, lest pride should rob our good deeds of all spiritual value. The Pharisees of the time of Christ were devout religious men; they fasted and observed the law of Moses very strictly; they gave alms liberally but took personal pride in all their doings and earned some very harsh comments from our divine Lord. He dealt mercifully and gently with all type of sinners and they repented, but for the Pharisees he had nothing but condemnation. Their pride, which was their basic vice, would not let them admit that they were guilty of any sin.

In future, if ever we are tempted to question God's way of dealing with his faithful children, let us think of St. Paul and how Christ dealt with him. If we feel that we are asked to carry some cross which interferes with our spiritual activity we will pray and ask to have that cross removed—if that should be according to God's will. But we should always remember that it may be through this very bodily defect or weakness that the power of Christ is to be made manifest in us, as was the case with St. Paul.

GOSPEL : Mark 6 : 1–6. Jesus came to his own country; and his disciples followed him. And on the sabbath he began to teach in the synagogue; and many who heard him were astonished, saying, "Where did this man get all this? What is the wisdom given to him? What mighty works are wrought by his hands! Is not this the carpenter, the son of Mary and brother of James and Joses and Judas and Simon, and are not his sisters here with us?" And they took offense at him. And Jesus said to them, "A prophet it not without honor, except in his own country, and among his own kin, and in his own house." And he could do no mighty work there, except that he laid his hands upon a few sick people and healed them. And he marveled because of their unbelief.

EXPLANATION : According to St. Mark in this gospel episode, Jesus had been preaching and working miracles in Galilee for many months. He had spent most of the time in towns and villages around the Sea of Galilee. Before leaving Galilee he paid a visit to his home-town Nazareth where he was to meet with disappointment. He went into the synagogue on the sabbath day and began to preach there. His fellow-townsmen had heard of the extraordinary miracles he had worked around the other towns of Galilee; they had also heard of the huge crowds that listened to his preaching. Many of those who now heard him for the first time in their own synagogue, were astonished at his wisdom and learning. Where did he get it, he had not studied to be a rabbi and how did he work the miracles they had heard about? All these years they knew him. What was he but the local carpenter? They knew his mother and his relatives; he could not be the Messiah or anyone extraordinary. They began by being astonished at his preaching but they ended up by shutting their eyes to the truth and refusing to believe that he could be what others thought and said he was; he was their neighbor and they therefore knew better.

The reply of Jesus to their unbelief was to quote the saying for them : "a prophet is not without honor except in his own country." The rejection of Jesus as Messiah by his neighbors of Nazareth was a foreshadowing of his rejection by the leaders of the nation, which was to come later and for the same reason—unbelief.

his own country : More precisely this means his native town; the Greek word *patris* has both meanings. He had made Capernaum the headquarters of his Galilean mission but Nazareth was his home-town.

in the synagogue : On the sabbath most of the Jews attended a service of bible-reading with a sermon and prayers in their local synagogue. Synagogue means a gathering-place, hence our Greek word for church *ekklesie*, a calling-together.

astonished . . . carpenter : The amazement quickly changed to hostility founded on envy. How could one who was no better than themselves be so outstanding? Therefore, this carpenter did not have this wisdom, he did not work those miracles of which they had heard. "There is none so blind . . ."

brother of James . . . sisters : Jesus had cousins in Nazareth. Neither Hebrew nor Aramaic has a word for cousin, so brother and sister is used instead to denote a relative. That Jesus had no blood brothers or half-brothers or sisters is clear from the infancy narratives in Matthew and Luke. It is confirmed also by John 19 : 26–27.

They . . . at him : Being **only** one of themselves he could not have any extraordinary powers, therefore he was a fraud.

a prophet . . . country : He quotes a proverb to illustrate their frame of mind. In the apocryphal "Gospel according to Thomas" it reads : "no prophet is acceptable in his village, no physician cures those who know him."

could . . . work : Christ's power of working miracles was restricted and limited only by their lack of faith and their envy. The majority of them had made themselves unworthy to receive a miracle.

a few . . . people : Not all were affected by the virus of unbelief and envy.

he marveled : Our Lord was truly human and his human psychology is evident here. How could his townspeople be so blinded by their prejudices?

APPLICATION : What happened in Nazareth was a foretaste of the later reaction of the scribes and Pharisees, the leaders of the people, to Christ's claim to be the promised Messiah. What the people of Nazareth tried to do (Lk. 4 : 29–30), the religious authorities in Jerusalem succeeded in doing, because they were able to threaten the Roman governor with blackmail. Even in their wickedness and unknown to themselves, they were putting into action God's plan for mankind. It was necessary that Christ should die so that all men could live forever with God. Christ's death, followed by his resurrection, was the key that opened the door of eternity for the human race.

Unfortunately for the leaders of the Jews, the good end did not justify the evil intentions and evil means which they used. It is hard to understand the irrational opposition of the Nazarites on this occasion, and of the Pharisees of Jerusalem later. The people of Nazareth had heard nothing but marvelous reports of his wonderful preaching and outstanding miracles. One would therefore expect that if they were at all reasonable, they would rejoice on having one of their fellow-citizens admired by thousands and looked upon by so many as the long-promised Messiah. Instead, they turned against him in bitter hatred and there and then decided to put an end to his career (Lk. 4 : 29). Why? Because the demon of envy, a daughter of pride, laid hold of their hearts and minds. Why should a neighbor's son, and one of a lower status than many of them—a mere carpenter, be given this privilege while their sons were passed over? This could not be, their envy told them, and so they shut their minds against any proof to the contrary.

It was the same later in the case of the Pharisees. The same vices, pride and envy, darkened their intellects and prevented them from seeing the truth. They were the religious leaders of the people, or so they thought themselves to be. If the Messiah had come they felt that he should have come through them and with their approval. This impostor Jesus could not possibly be the Messiah. Not only was he not keeping the law as strictly as they kept it, but he was friendly with sinners and tax-gatherers. Furthermore, he was talking of some faraway kingdom in heaven and not of the earthly empire which they decided the real Messiah would establish. They had not only heard of his extraordinary miracles but had seen some of those who were cured. In Bethany only a few miles from Jerusalem Lazarus had been raised to life after four days in the grave. They tried very hard to deny these miracles (see Jn. 9: the man born blind), and they even thought of killing Lazarus to make the people forget the miracle! (Jn. 12:11.) Thus their pride and envy made them irrational. Nothing but the cruelest possible death of the one hated could satisfy their hatred. But that very death was Christ's road to glory. Lifted up on the cross he drew all men to himself as he had foretold (Jn. 12:32). Those on Calvary beheld the triumph of failure.

Would that all the opposition to Christ and his teaching, caused by human pride and envy, had ended with the Nazarites and Pharisees! Far from it. Pride and envy are still rife among us. All through the twenty centuries of Christianity, there have been proud men, men high in their own esteem. Not only would they not have Christ to reign over them, but they have tried to prevent his reign over even those who are gladly and proudly his subjects. Not content with dethroning Christ in their own hearts and minds, they have devoted all their energies to abolishing him and his Church from the face of our earth. Such enemies of Christ are still among us. They are more numerous than ever today but just as their predecessors failed in the past, so will these fail today. Christ will continue to reign and his Church will continue its mission of leading to heaven all men whose minds are free from sinful pride and therefore open to the truth.

Let us renew our loyalty to Christ today. He humbled himself so that we might be raised to the standing of sons of God. He shared our human nature with us so that we could share his divine nature. He died a cruel death on Calvary so that we could have an eternal life in heaven. We pray for light for those whose foolish pride has left them groping in darkness. Let us also ask the good God to keep us ever on the road of truth, the road of Christian humility which leads to the eternal home which Christ has won for us by his incarnation.

FIFTEENTH SUNDAY OF THE YEAR

FIRST READING: Amos 7:12-15. Amaziah said to Amos, "O seer, go, flee away to the land of Judah, and eat bread there, and prophesy there; but never again prophesy at Bethel, for it is the king's sanctuary, and it is a temple of the kingdom."

Then Amos answered Amaziah, "I am no prophet, nor a prophet's son; but I am a herdsman, and a dresser of sycamore trees, and the Lord took me from following the flock, and the Lord said to me, 'Go, prophesy to my people Israel.' "

EXPLANATION: Amos was a native of Judah. He was a shepherd and dresser of sycamore trees. He was sent by God to speak in his name to the people of Israel—the northern kingdom which had broken away from Judah in 930 B.C. He preached in Israel during the reign of Jeroboam II (783-743). He protested strongly against the religious abuses and lack of religion then rampant in Israel, and especially stressed the truth that religious worship without a morally good life had no value in the eyes of God. When he foretold the murder of Jeroboam and the exile of Israel he was denounced by Amaziah, the priest in charge of the sanctuary of Bethel, and was expelled from Israel. This expulsion is the theme of today's reading.

go flee . . . Judah: Amos is told very bluntly that he is not wanted and is to go back to where he came from. Amaziah calls him a seer, a prophet—most likely in a sarcastic and contemp-

tuous sense. The prophecy concerning Jeroboam's murder was twisted by Amaziah as a plot being hatched by Amos to assassinate the king. Hence the expulsion order.

eat bread there: The false prophets who were numerous in Israel earned their living by preaching their own words and not those of God. They were sycophants of the king. Amaziah, who was not better than they, implied that Amos was also a professional seer—prophesying to earn his livelihood.

never . . . Bethel: This was the national sanctuary of Israel, in opposition to the temple in Jerusalem. It was a sanctuary dedicated to Yahweh ever since the time of Abraham, but since the schism of the northern tribes pagan cults were practiced frequently there. It was now the king's sanctuary, and Amos, prophet of Yahweh, with his denunciations of injustice and irreligion, had no place in such a temple. He was not wanted there.

Amos answered : Amos denied that he was a prophet or one of the school of prophets who flourished in Israel. Thus he showed that he understood Amaziah's title of seer as being used in that false sense.

herdsman . . . trees : He was not prepared for this office of prophet nor did he seek it. He was a shepherd and cared for the sycamore trees which in Palestine produce a fruit something like figs. It is different from the Euro-pean and American sycamore.

the Lord took me : It was Yahweh himself who took him from his way of living.

go prophesy . . . Israel : He gave him the command to go to Israel and preach only what Yahweh would give him to preach. This was what he had done and for this he was being expelled, for neither the king nor the priests nor the false prophets of Israel wanted to hear the word of Yahweh.

APPLICATION : What happened to the prophet Amos in Israel eight hundred years before Christ, has happened again and again down through the centuries and is happening in our own day on a larger scale than ever before. This man of God was expelled and silenced because those in authority could not listen to the reproofs of the Lord which their injustices, inhumanity and irreligion so richly deserved. Had the king and his associates listened to the prophet and mended their ways, they would have saved their people from exile and their nation would not have been wiped off the map. But because they would not submit to the Lord their God, they were made slaves of the neighboring pagan nation.

The prophets who were sent to speak God's "word" were made to suffer and were silenced. The Word of God, the Son of God himself, who became man to lead all men back to their eternal Father, suffered even a worse fate. The pride and prejudice of the leaders of the Jews, God's Chosen People, had him condemned to a criminal's death as if he were an outcast from society and a blasphemer to boot. They would not accept the Son of God in human form—the "Word made flesh" came unto his own and his own received him not.

The Church which he founded to carry on and complete his work of redemption was threatened with the same fate. The Jewish authorities tried to strangle that infant Church in Jerusalem, in Palestine and even in far-away Damascus in Syria, but God's hand was raised in its defense—and its enemies failed. A few decades later the Roman emperors tried to do what the Jewish authorities had failed to do. But even though they persevered in their evil intent for almost three centuries, they too were fighting against the power of God—and they failed. Many saintly men and women gladly gave their lives for their faith but their deaths increased rather than diminished the number of Christians; for as St. Augustine said : "the blood of martyrs became the seed of Christians." The Church grew daily and spread through the Roman empire.

From the beginning of the fourth century down to the twentieth, there have been periods of persecution in different parts of the world. When compared, however, with the widespread disinterest in God and the things of God in most of today's world, together with the absolute rejection of Christ and God in very many parts of it, the irreligion and opposition to religion in the past were restrained and limited. Behind the iron and bamboo curtains today the destructive philosophy or folly of atheism is being imposed on more than a third of the world's population. God is excluded from the world he created; man is using the gifts of intellect and free-will, given him by God, to deny and destroy his divine benefactor. What is worse : two-thirds of the so-called believers are not shocked or disturbed by this sad behavior of God's children. The nominal Christian nations are indifferent as long as these atheistic ideas do not interfere with their own political or commercial interests. It's a sign of how little their belief in God and Christ affects their own daily lives and way of thinking.

Today we are living in a world in which the Creator and Lord of that world is given little or no say. Men think they can despise the road rules which he has so wisely laid down and still run human traffic successfully. Head-on crashes, wars and rumors of wars, the expensive build-up of armaments, the gross injustices inflicted on the weak, the inhumanity of men to their fellowmen are the visible proofs of the folly of such a philosophy. It is like trying to navigate a ship when the navigator has been thrown overboard. The world must come back to God and to his ten commandments. No society can survive without rules. The all-wise rules for human society are God's decalog. We can ignore them only at our peril. To expel God's prophets and shut our ears to his wise counsels may silence our troubled consciences for a moment, but this will not restore our social health or promote our true welfare. This world is not the sanctuary of any earthly ruler, nor the temple of any human king; it is God's temple, God's sanctuary where he expects his creatures to serve him devoutly and loyally.

SECOND READING: Ephesians 1:3-14. Blessed be the God and Father of our Lord Jesus Christ, who has blessed us in Christ with every spiritual blessing in the heavenly places, even as he chose us in him before the foundation of the world, that we should be holy and blameless before him. He destined us in love to be his sons through Jesus Christ, according to the purpose of his will, to the praise of his glorious grace which he freely bestowed on us in the Beloved. In him we have redemption through his blood, the forgiveness of our trespasses, according to the riches of his grace which he lavished upon us. For he has made known to us in all wisdom and insight the mystery of his will, according to his purpose which he set forth in Christ as a plan for the fullness of time, to unite all things in him, things in heaven and things on earth.

In him, according to the purpose of him who accomplishes all things according to the counsel of his will, we who first hoped in Christ have been destined and appointed to live for the praise of his glory. In him you also, who have heard the word of truth, the gospel of your salvation, and have believed in him, were sealed with the promised Holy Spirit, who is the guarantee of our inheritance until we acquire possession of it, to the praise of his glory.

EXPLANATION: Between 54 and 57 A.D. St. Paul preached the Christian faith in Ephesus, the capital of the Roman province of Asia Minor. So numerous were the converts he made here and in the surrounding districts, that Demetrius, a silversmith who made statues of the goddess Diana of Ephesus, began to lose trade. Demetrius raised a tumult. A great protest-meeting against Paul and the Christians was held but the town-clerk quietened the mob. Paul was not interfered with and the Christian faith continued to flourish. Leaving Ephesus, Paul went to Jerusalem where he was arrested and imprisoned for two years. Having appealed to Caesar, he was taken to Rome where he was kept under house-arrest for another two years before being released. This letter was written from Rome to remind his converts to continue to be faithful to the teaching he had given them.

Blessed . . . Father : Having introduced himself as their Apostle, he goes on now to proclaim the blessedness, the holiness of God, the Father of Jesus Christ. As in all his letters, he takes the dogmas of the divinity of Christ and the Trinity for granted.

blessed . . . Christ : God the Father has "blessed" us, has made us fortunate beneficiaries of his, because Christ has established a new brotherhood of man, and so made us all sons of God.

foundation . . . world : This plan of God to elevate us to sonship with himself through the incarnation of his Son is from eternity—before creation began.

sons . . . Christ : This was the real and primary purpose of the incarnation.

his glorious grace : This was an entirely gratuitous gift to us on the part of God. It came to us through his "beloved" Son, Jesus Christ.

redemption . . . blood : Sin had already entered the world and to a greater or lesser degree all men were sinners when the incarnation took place. Christ's shedding of his blood on the cross, caused by sinners, made complete atonement to God—his death was the perfect sin-offering for the sins of all men of all time.

riches . . . grace : This again is another gratuitious gift of God to us.

mystery . . . Christ : Our Christian revelation has made known to men God's eternal plan for their elevation and salvation. They are now heirs to heaven, to an eternal life.

fullness of time : That is the time of the incarnation, appointed by God from all eternity.

unite . . . him : Christ unites in himself all mankind, Jew and Gentile, Greek and Barbarian. He is the head, we are the members of his body, the Church.

heaven and earth : That is, the whole universe. Not only all men, but the whole of creation will benefit by the incarnation. Christ is the summit and the summation of all creation. When man becomes a loyal and loving son of God all creation returns to its true purpose of honoring God.

we who . . . Christ : St. Paul is probably referring here to the Jews who had the messianic hope for centuries; or he may be referring to the Jewish Christian converts of Palestine who were the first to accept the Christian good news.

praise . . . glory : The duty of every Christian is to thank and praise God all through his life.

you also . . . Spirit : The Gentiles from whom the vast majority of the Ephesian Christians came, were now equal to the early Jewish converts even though they had not been given the messianic revelations. They had accepted the Gospel, the good-news of their eternal salvation. They were "sealed" by the Holy Spirit in their baptism, that is, they were marked with a sign which proclaimed that they belonged to God.

guarantee . . . inheritance : The presence of the Holy Spirit in them is a down payment on the full reward yet to come. God who has accomplished the first part of his promise will complete his plan for us, if we do not impede him.

praise of his glory : Having reached our inheritance, our eternal abode with God, our every moment will be given to admiring and praising God's glory and perfection.

APPLICATION : In these opening verses of his letter, St. Paul recalls to the minds of his Ephesian converts the basic teaching, the fundamental and central meaning of the Christian faith which he had taught them. In his infinite love, God the Father planned from all eternity to make us his adopted sons, by means of the incarnation of his only begotten Son. "He destined us in love to be his sons through Jesus Christ, according to the purpose of his will." This is surely a tremendous truth—a truth that not only changes our whole outlook on life but our very nature itself. As intelligent creatures, the highest of all the other living beings that God put on this earth, we should have much to be grateful for. We have been given life. We are able to think and plan and provide for our needs, to enjoy the beautiful and seek after the good. We are able to study, control and put to our own use myriads of inanimate things, as well as the other animate beings God created. We have fellow humans with whom we can converse and share the joys of living. God had so arranged things that we were born into a human family where tenderness and love were showered on us during infancy and adolescence. When we came to the age of responsibility we could have formed a new family, a new association where in turn we would shower love and tenderness on our offspring who would, we should hope, look after us in our declining years.

Creation then was surely a marvelous gift given us by God. But just because of the special gifts he gave us which raise us above all other earthly creatures, could we really enjoy these few short years of life on this earth if we knew there was nothing but the gloomy grave awaiting us? If our sixty or eighty years were made up of days of unbroken happiness would we be content with that and nothing else. But as they are years heavily tinged with sorrow and sadness for so many would we not have less reason to be content with our fate? Good as God was to give us life would we not feel that we were somehow treated unfairly by Him?

However, once we know that God exists and once we know from revelation that he is a God of infinite love, we can see how it was in keeping with his love and thoughtfulness that he would arrange a future life for us in which the created gifts which he gave

us, would be used to the full capacity. This God did through the incarnation. We are made heirs to heaven because Christ, the Son of God, made us his brothers when he took our human nature and joined it to his divinity. We shall die to this earth and bid adieu to all its God-given gifts, but for the true Christian death will mean a change for the better, it will be the door to the true unending life. "Vita mutatur non tollitur," as we say in the requiem Mass: for the Christian "life is changed not taken away" by death.

The coming of Christ then has not only changed our outlook on life; we no longer see it in terms of days or years—we look on it from the angle of eternity. Christ's coming has also changed our very nature itself. We are no longer mere human beings, we are raised to the supernatural status of sons of God, we belong to God's heaven; God's home, is our home. Our life on earth is only a pilgrimage, a short journey, during which we work our passage to our everlasting home, our eternal fatherland.

We thank God for creating us and for putting heaven within our reach. We thank Jesus for humiliating himself in the incarnation in order to raise us up beyond our natural selves and for having shed his blood on the cross to wash away the one impediment that could keep us from heaven—sin.

GOSPEL : Mark 6 : 7–13. Jesus called to him the twelve, and began to send them out two by two, and gave them authority over the unclean spirits. He charged them to take nothing for their journey except a staff; no bread, no bag, no money in their belts; but to wear sandals and not put on two tunics. And he said to them, "Where you enter a house, stay there until you leave the place. And if any place will not receive you and they refuse to hear you, when you leave, shake off the dust that is on your feet for a testimony against them." So they went out and preached that men should repent. And they cast out many demons, and anointed with oil many that were sick and healed them.

EXPLANATION : Jesus had been quietly training his chosen Apostles for some time. They had heard his preaching, they had seen the miracles worked by him. Their future work would be to bring his teaching and the story of his life and miracles to all men. They had not seen all yet, nor were they as yet fully aware of who he really was, but they did know that he was laying the foundations of the kingdom of God among men. He now sends them out on a temporary mission; two by two they were to go to the neighboring villages and towns preaching repentance, casting out demons and healing the sick. They were to trust absolutely in God's providence; he would see to it that those to whom they preached would provide them with the necessities of life. **authority . . . spirits :** Many diseases, especially mental disturbances, were attributed by the Jews to possession by a demon. There were definite cases of diabolic possession during our Lord's ministry and later also. As he had come to set up the kingdom of God, which meant the destruction of Satan's kingdom, it was to be expected that Satan would resist. This resistance would be evidenced by the numerous cases of real possession of that time. But Jesus by his divine power overcame Satan's resistance. Satan, however, used his

human accomplices and injured Christ in his human nature as he was crushing Satan's head—as foretold in Genesis (3 : 15)—by his death on the cross. Here Christ gives to his Apostles power over the demons, when he sends them on their first mission.

nothing . . . journey : They were to take neither food supplies nor money to buy them, thus making them rely entirely on God's divine providence.

no bag : They were to be even worse off, from a human point of view, than the ordinary beggars, who carried a bag or receptacle in which they could store any extra food given them.

sandals . . . tunics : Sandals were the footwear of the very poor. Two tunics would be luxury when one sufficed.

enter . . . there : If accepted in a house, they were to remain there while their preaching continued in the village. To leave the home that accepted them would be to insult their kind host. Oriental hospitality set no limits to the sojourn of a guest.

not receive . . . hear : If a householder or a village or town refused to accept them or listen to their message, they were to depart immediately. To show that those who refused to accept them were no better than pagans, they were to wipe the dust off the soles of their feet at the door of the inhospitable householder, or at the end of the village if the villagers refused to hear them. This was an action performed by a Jew as he crossed from a pagan land into holy Palestine. By this action he signified that he was cleansing himself of all pagan contamination.

men should repent : The essence of their preaching was like that of John the Baptist—the kingdom of God was coming; men must prepare for it by repenting of their sins.

cast out demons : By the power which Christ gave them they commanded the demons to leave those whom they had possessed. Note that Mark clearly distinguishes the driving out of demons from the healing of the sick.

anointed with oil : Jesus did not include this action in his instructions; they could have healed without any anointing, but anointing with oil was very common in Palestine. The Church sees this action of the Apostles as the prefiguring of the sacrament of Extreme Unction, later expressed by St. James (Jm. 5 : 14).

healed them : Their expulsion of the demons and curing of the sick were extensions of Jesus' own ministry. In their preaching they were preparing men to enter his kingdom—the Church.

APPLICATION : That Christ the Son of God could have spread his Gospel of peace and love, his message of eternal salvation, to the whole world without human help need not be proved. He could, for instance, have written the Gospel in the sky—over each country in its own language. He could have gone to every part of the earth, after his resurrection, and taught his doctrine to all peoples, confirming his words with extraordinary miracles. Yet he chose the weaker but the more human way of evangelizing men—he sent their own fellowmen to bring them the message. This choice showed his divine love and understanding of weak human nature, much better and much more effectively than the use of any of the supernatural means which he could have employed.

God, and Christ is God, gave man the gift that we call freewill. Man is able to choose between alernatives. God wants man to choose heaven as his eternal home, but he wants him to choose it without compulsion or coercion. He will have volunteers in heaven not conscripts. The man who chooses heaven must choose the means for going there. If you choose a holiday resort for your summer vacation, you must buy travel tickets, book a hotel and save up the expenses necessary for the holiday. By appointing mortal men to bring the news of salvation, the news of heaven, and the means of getting there to all of us, Christ has given us the chance of exercising our freewill and therefore of meriting heaven. Refusal to accept would hardly be possible if Christ informed us miraculously or taught us in person. If some extraordinary individual could persist in refusing, his refusal would be utterly inexcusable.

Now, Christ has earned heaven for all men and not for Christians only. He has given his Church, with all its aids and its guaranteed truth, to those who will be his followers. For them the road of the Gospel is an absolutely assured way by which they will reach heaven, if they are faithful to the rules. But there are, and there have always been, millions and millions of men and women who through no fault of their own have not heard of the Church of Christ. There are other millions who have heard of Christ and his Church, but who, because of some personal kink of pride or because of their upbringing or surroundings, have not felt able to accept the Christian way of life. God is mindful of all these millions and wants them in heaven. If their present circumstances, their lack of knowledge of the Christian truths, or personal prejudice, brought on by circumstances beyond their control, prevent them from being convinced of the necessity of becoming Christians would God exclude them from heaven? Surely not. It was because he foresaw all those who could not freely accept his Gospel to the letter and who yet want to go to heaven, that he let other human beings, who could and would be doubted, preach and propagate his Gospel. Therefore, it would be inexcusable to refuse to listen to his own word if it were written by him in the sky or preached by himself personally. But men could be excused if they doubted his human agents, for some reasons which appeared to them as valid. In other words, the merciful Christ who humiliated himself and who submitted to the death of the cross in order to open heaven for all men, found ways and means of excusing those who would elect to trudge through the fields and over the hedges rather than travel on the royal highroad that he had laid down for them.

This is divine mercy in action. God wants every human being to be saved. There are no Jews or Gentiles in the Church; no pagans, Moslems, Jews or rationalists in heaven—the citizens of heaven are all children of God. While on earth they each served him according to their lights, under their own particular banners. "The Spirit breathes where it will." God's mercy and love can reach into the darkest corners and produce fruit from the most unlikely and apparently most neglected of orchards.

While we thank God from our hearts today for having been put on the road to heaven, let us remember in our prayers our fellowmen, God's other children, who are trudging along through the fields and hedges. May God continue to show his mercy and divine understanding toward them! May they meet us at the entrance to our Father's home where we shall be happy forever together!

SIXTEENTH SUNDAY OF THE YEAR

FIRST READING : Jeremiah 23 : 1–6. "Woe to the shepherds who destroy and scatter the sheep of my pasture!" says the Lord. Therefore thus says the Lord, the God of Israel, concerning the shepherds who care for my people : "You have scattered my flock, and have driven them away, and you have not attended to them. Behold, I will attend to you for your evil doings, says the Lord. Then I will gather the remnant of my flock out of all the countries where I have driven them, and I will bring them back to their fold, and they shall be fruitful and multiply. I will set shepherds over them who will care for them, and they shall fear no more, nor be dismayed, neither shall any be missing, says the Lord.

"Behold, the days are coming, says the Lord, when I will raise up for David a righteous Branch, and he shall reign as king and deal wisely, and shall execute justice and righteousness in the land. In his days Judah will be saved, and Israel will dwell securely. And this is the name by which he will be called : 'The Lord is our righteousness.' "

EXPLANATION : Jeremiah, who lived from 627 to 586 B.C., was called at the early age of 23 to the prophetic office. He prophesied in Jerusalem during the most critical period of Judah's history. The kings, priests and people were much more interested in politics than in Yahweh their God. They had been made subject to Babylon in 700 B.C. and had to pay an annual tax to this foreign power. About 630 they were engaged in intrigue with Egypt whose help they sought to set them free from Babylon. Jeremiah opposed this political scheme, foreseeing that Egypt would not help and that rebellion would bring nothing but the devastation of Judah and exile for its people. Abuses in the temple and in the city reached an alarm-

ing point. Jeremiah spoke out fearlessly against the disloyalty of the Chosen People of God, and foretold the destruction of the city and its temple and also the exile in Babylonia. Because of this he was imprisoned for a time. Later the people decided to kill him and he was dropped into a cistern, but a Cushite, a foreign servant of the king, released him with the king's permission but unknown to the court officials. Eventually (about 586) he was forcibly taken down to Egypt and, according to tradition, he was murdered there by his own people.

In today's seven verses, Jeremiah utters dire threats against the shepherds, the leaders of the people of Judah. Their neglect of the flock given into their care and their neglect of God was bringing exile on their people. God would avenge his people, bring back the "remnant" of his flock and set trustworthy shepherds over them. What is more, the era of the promised Messiah, the descendant of David, was at hand. Judah and Israel would live in security and peace under the new king of righteousness.

woe . . . pasture : Through their disloyalty to God, the king, courtiers, nobles and priests of the temple had brought terrible distress and misfortune on God's Chosen People who were the sheep of his pasture.

I . . . to you : Because they did not attend and care for the flock committed to them, God would exact a payment from them; they would suffer much more than the ordinary people in the siege of the city and the exile which was to come.

gather . . . my flock : Through Jeremiah God foretold that some—not all—of the people of Judah would return from the exile of Babylon and also from other countries to which he had scattered them. This return from the other countries was fulfilled in the messianic age when some of the Jews of the Diaspora accepted Christ and became the true people of God.

shepherd . . . care : In this new era those appointed as leaders by God would be interested in their true welfare for they would be loyal to God.

any be missing : Any of the new Chosen People who might be lost, will be lost entirely through their own fault. God's salvific will is universal.

raise up for David : The prophet said that the days were coming when the promise given to David (Sm. 7 : 5ff), and before that to Abraham (Gn. 12 : 2), would be fulfilled. The messianic king would soon come.

justice and righteousness : He would establish a kingdom wherein the rights of God and man would be respected by all.

Judah and Israel : These two sections of the Chosen People of old who had separated in the year 930 B.C. and had become bitter enemies would be united once more in happy fraternity in the new messianic kingdom.

Lord . . . righteousness : The Messiah, Christ the Son of God, has made us sons of God and therefore sons of justice and fidelity; he has likewise atoned for all the sins of the world. We rightly call him our Savior. He has saved us from sin and from eternal death. He will make us saints—we shall be numbered among his just.

APPLICATION : In the midst of the misfortunes and afflictions which were about to engulf his people—afflictions and misfortunes brought on them especially by their religious and civic leaders—Jeremiah had words of consolation and encouragement. Bright and happy days were in store for them. Some would return from the exile and live in peace in their homeland under more God-fearing leaders. But it is to the messianic age, to Christ's day, that the thoughts of the prophet were especially turned. The great day would come when the new Chosen People would have a king who would be justice itself, a king to keep them loyal to God, a shepherd to care for their real interests. As psalm 22 puts it : "The Lord is my shepherd, there is nothing I shall want. He guides me along the right path, he is true to his name . . . In the Lord's own house shall I dwell for ever and ever."

Both Jeremiah and the psalmist were looking into the future and beheld the coming of Christ and the age of the new

Chosen People. That these are messianic prophecies is clear from the fact that our Divine Lord himself applied the title of the true shepherd to himself: "I am the good shepherd, I know my own and my own know me, just as the Father knows me and I know the Father; and I lay down my life for my sheep" (Jn. 10 : 14–15).

We today are indeed fortunate to be living in the Christian era. We have seen the messianic prophecies fulfilled; we know that Christ has come and changed our world. We know that we are the sheep of his chosen flock, the members indeed of his mystical body. We know that he has put us on the right path, on the road to heaven and that as faithful Shepherd he is ever watching over us, moving us on when we are inclined to nibble at the forbidden grass by the road-side, bringing us back on his own shoulders when we stray from the path and get caught up in the briars and brambles of earthly attractions.

We Christians know all of this, but do we really appreciate what the good God has done for us? By sending his Son on earth as man, he made us heirs to heaven, brothers of Christ and adopted sons of himself. Heaven is now our destination, our only real purpose in life. Everything else is absolutely secondary and only of transitory importance. Yet how many there are who let these things of secondary importance get such a hold on them that they forget or ignore their one and only purpose in life? They allow the transitory things of this life to hold them back from reaching the endless life of heaven.

To help us to see the utter folly of such Christians let us suppose, for a moment, a poor man who had a great desire to go to Lourdes. He was given a free ticket with all expenses paid. He set out joyfully, say from Chicago. His first stop was New York. Here he became enchanted with the hustle and bustle of the great city's life. He visited many movie pictures and stage productions and spent so much time that he missed the pilgrim ship for which he was booked. He had not enough to pay for a ticket to Europe on another ship and so he missed seeing Lourdes. He ended his days in misery in New York, no longer enchanted by its attractions but driven to despair by the utter emptiness of what it had to offer. That man's fate was but a shadow of the irreparable loss of the Christian who lets the attractions of this world keep him from heaven.

He may find his days, his mind and his hands full of interesting worldly affairs, but he should realize that every time the clock strikes he is an hour nearer to his earthly end. After that what is there for him? What explanation can he offer when he arrives empty-handed and totally unprepared at the judgement seat? He cannot plead ignorance; he cannot plead lack of time; he could have provided for all of his earthly needs, while providing at the same time for his eternal future. He allowed himself to get so immersed in the things of this world that he gave no thought to his future. It has happened before and it will happen again. It can happen to us unless we frequently take a good look at our way of living and honestly and sincerely measure our daily doings by the standard of the Gospel. If frequently during life we judge ourselves and our actions with all sincerity we need not fear the judgement after death.

SECOND READING: Ephesians 2:13-18. But now in Christ Jesus you who once were far off have been brought near in the blood of Christ. For he is our peace, who has made us both one, and has broken down the dividing wall of hostility, by abolishing in his flesh the law of commandments and ordinances, that he might create in himself one new man in place of the two, so making peace, and might reconcile us both to God in one body through the cross, thereby bringing the hostility to an end. And he came and preached peace to you who were far off and peace to those who were near; for through him we both have access in one Spirit to the Father.

EXPLANATION: On St. Paul's relations with Ephesus and on this letter, see last Sunday. In today's six verses of this letter, the Apostle reminds his Ephesian converts that Christ has brought unity of brotherhood to Jews and Gentiles. Under the old dispensation a Jew could not associate with a Gentile—a state of cold war existed between them. Now Christ has brought peace to all Jews and Gentiles who accept him as their master. **far ... near:** The great majority of the Ephesian Christians were Gentiles or non-Jews. To the Jews, the Chosen People of God in Old Testament days, all Gentiles were utter outsiders; they were very far away from God. They did not even know of the true, the real God. **in the blood of Christ:** Because Christ became man and shed his blood on the cross for all men, without distinction, those Gentiles who accept Christ are no longer outsiders—they belong to God's family. **our peace ... one:** There is neither Jew nor Gentile in the Christian community. Christ united all and brought peace to all men who acknowledge him as their Savior. **broken ... wall:** There was a solid dividing wall separating the Jews from the Gentiles; it consisted of the Mosaic Law, religious privileges, their national and particularistic outlook. This separation had a material representation and reminder outside the temple of Jerusalem. Some distance from the temple a low marble wall was erected and on it were written notices warning any Gentiles that death was the punishment for approaching nearer to the temple. **hostility:** This was more than separation. There was hatred on both sides, the Jews despised and hated all Gentiles while the Gentiles in turn hated the Jews for their national and religious narrow-mindedness which, unfortunately, they often carried to excess. **commandments ... ordinances:** The old dispensation ended when the new law began. Christ abolished the Mosaic Law with the exception of the Ten Commandments, which were and are for all men for all time. All the additions which the rabbis had added to the commandments were abolished, as also were the cultic laws of the temple. The sacrifice of the New Law replaced the various sacrifices of the temple. **in one ... cross:** Christ's work of elevating and redeeming us culminated on the cross and in his resurrection. Because he became man, lived and died and rose again for us, he put an end forever to the hostility that had existed between the Jews and the pagan nations. He made them all brothers of his and of one another. **preached peace:** He preached the Gospel of peace between all men and made peace possible between all men and God. The Gentiles who one time were far away from God were now as near to him as were his Chosen People of old. They are part of the new Chosen People of the New Testament.

access . . . Father: Because of Christ's incarnation, death and resurrection we all have access to God our Father guided as we are by the Holy Spirit who is given to us in baptism. The Holy Spirit, the product of the reciprocal love of Father and Son, is the bond uniting us all in love with the Father and in love with one another.

APPLICATION: "He came and preached peace." In these five words, St. Paul sums up the ministry of Christ on earth. He preached peace. He laid down the foundations of peace. He reconciled men with God their Creator and Father, and reconciled men with one another. He taught men to be brotherly toward one another. When questioned by one of the Pharisees as to which was the most important of the commandments, he answered: "Love God with all your heart, all your strength and all your mind, and your neighbor as yourself." The two together are the essence of true religion "on these two depend the whole law and the prophets."

Long before Christ came on earth, the prophets had described the kingdom which he was to establish as a kingdom of peace. He was called the Prince of Peace (Is. 9); in his kingdom there would never again be war "men would turn their swords into ploughshares, their spears into sickles. Nation will not lift sword against nation, there will be no more training for war" (Is. 2; see also Is. 11; Ag. 2 : 8–10; Zech. 9 : 10). These prophecies, however, were not fulfilled in the kingdom that Christ set up on this earth, nor was that intended. The prophets were speaking of the final kingdom, the completion of Christ's work in heaven. There the perfect peace will prevail; there man will truly love his fellowman and all men will love God.

Christ did lay the foundations for peace between men and between nations even on this earth. He made us all his brothers; he made all men, no matter what their race or color, God's adopted sons and therefore members of the one family. But we must not forget that while Christ laid solid and secure foundations, the walls of the building were to be built of mortal, fallible men who could abuse the gift of freewill with which they were endowed. If all men kept the two great commandments, loving God with all their heart and loving their neighbor as themselves, peace would naturally follow. Such an if, however, is a capital "IF," for unfortunately, there will always be among us those who will fail to keep these basic commandments to the letter, and therefore there will always be violations of peace.

While we regret that even our fellow-Christians can and do break these commandments and act contrary to the teaching of their faith, we must not be scandalized at this nor must we say that Christ's teaching has failed. Christ laid the foundations for peace; he encouraged his followers to live in peace; he wished them this peace, but even Christ could not force man's freewill. He, being God, foresaw that the Christian peace which should reign in our world

L

would be broken many times. Yet, his forgiveness was ever available to those who failed to keep his law, and his grace and divine assistance were there to help all who suffered because of the violation of his law.

There will always be some who will be a menace and a threat to peace, because they have forgotten that God is their Father. Consequently, they do not look on their neighbor as their brother. There is still a majority of God-loving and neighbor-loving men and women among us, not only in the Christian Church but outside of it also, who want peace. It is up to them to make their voices heard before God, first of all in their daily, fervent prayers for peace; and then also in the councils of state where human decisions are taken.

We can all do more for the preservation of peace on earth than perhaps we realize. All true lovers of God and neighbor should instil this same love in their children so that they will grow up inspired by respect for the two greatest commandments—they will be peace-lovers. In our street, in our town, in our country, by word, by example and by prayer we can do much to spread love for the peace which flows from love of neighbor and love of God. If we turned our protest-marches, which so often are not inspired by true love of peace, into prayer-marches we might see better results. "More things are wrought by prayer than this world dreams of," said Tennyson long ago. He was but repeating what Christ had said centuries before: "ask and you shall receive." Peace in one's conscience, peace in one's home, peace with one's neighbors, peace between nations is one of the noblest causes to which one can dedicate one's energies and prayers. "Lord, make me an instrument of thy peace."

GOSPEL: Mark 6:30-34. The apostles returned to Jesus, and told him all that they had done and taught. And he said to them, "Come away by yourselves to a lonely place, and rest a while." For many were coming and going, and they had no leisure even to eat. And they went away in the boat to a lonely place by themselves. Now many saw them going, and knew them, and they ran there on foot from all the towns, and got there ahead of them. As he landed he saw a great throng, and he had compassion on them, because they were like sheep without a shepherd; and he began to teach them many things.

EXPLANATION: In the reading from St. Mark's gospel for last Sunday, we heard of the twelve Apostles being sent out two by two to the villages and towns of Galilee. They were ordered to preach repentance and to cure the sick and possessed. Today, St. Mark tells us of their return. They described their experiences to the Lord. He listened to their stories and then suggested that they should go to a quiet place away from the crowds to rest a while. He and the Apostles went by boat to some lonely part of the shore—but in vain. The crowd noticed where they were heading and running on foot they got there before the boat. Our Lord was not angry with the crowd, he pitied them. They needed a shepherd, and he preached to them words of hope and consolation.

all . . . taught : These were the miracles they had worked and the preaching they had done in the towns and villages which they visited.

rest a while : Notice the interest Jesus had in their material welfare. They were tired after their mission, they needed rest.

many . . . going : Their departure was noted and their destination was guessed. The news spread quickly and the crowds went in haste and got to the lonely place before the boat arrived.

head . . . them : Jesus himself was tired. His Apostles, too, were tired after their mission. He had planned a few hours, if not days, of rest for them and for himself, but when he saw the trouble the crowd went to, running a long distance to intercept him, in order to hear him preach, he took pity on them and forgot his own fatigue.

like sheep . . . shepherd : They were like stray sheep who needed someone to care for them—someone to teach them about God's love for them and his interest in their eternal welfare.

APPLICATION : In these few verses St. Mark very strongly brings out the compassion, the human understanding of Jesus for man. He first planned to give his Apostles a well-earned rest. They had evidently worked hard while out on their mission and a few days rest would restore their lost energy. He himself, too, must have been hard-pressed, preaching and dealing with the crowds. In the absence of the Apostles he had no one to help him—he too needed a rest. He, therefore, planned that he and they should go to a quiet corner of the Sea of Galilee where there was no village and where, therefore, they would not be disturbed.

The desire of the crowds, however, to see him and to hear him speak upset these plans. The people got to the quiet spot first. There they were waiting when the boat pulled to shore. He could have sent them away, but again his human compassion took over. Seeing these simple people of Galilee so anxious to hear about God and his mercy, he let them stay and began to preach the good news of forgiveness and hope to them. For the most part they were simple, unlettered villagers, shepherds and fishermen. They knew a little about the Law of Moses but only a little. There was no one but the local rabbi to teach them and the local rabbis were not very educated at the time. The doctors of the law, the great theologians were all in Jerusalem where they got the respect and the financial reward which they felt they merited. Hence the people of the country were more or less forgotten and neglected. They were, as our Lord described them, " like sheep without a shepherd," wandering about half-lost.

They were certainly fortunate, however, in finding the true shepherd who would lead them to the eternal pastures. Not only would he now sacrifice his rest to come to their aid but he would, later on, lay down his life for them and for all of us. We, like those poor people of Galilee, have so much to be grateful for. The compassionate Christ has had pity on us too, and has brought us into his fold. He knows all our infirmities and all our human weaknesses, and he is ever-ready to have pity on us and pardon us. Those people of Galilee were not saints, they were ordinary, run-of-the-mill, not over religious people. They cheated one another; they were often uncharitable to one another; they were not always chaste and pure; they prayed very little and perhaps only when they wanted some material benefit. Yet our Lord had compassion on them.

This should give us great confidence, great encouragement. Christ has not changed: he is the same yesterday, today and forever. He has the same compassion for us that he had for those Galileans; we too are often like sheep without a shepherd wandering half-lost through life. He is ever calling us to come to himself so that he will lead us to safe pastures. If only we would listen to his

merciful call! Today's Gospel is one such call : it goes out to every member of this congregation who has been lax in his or her religious life up to now. Christ wants us back on the high-road to heaven. All we have to do is to break with the past, with the earthly things that kept us from God. We can set out as freemen to follow Christ. He has left to his Church the holy sacrament of penance in which he guarantees us complete and entire remission of all past sins if we confess them with true sorrow. Let us not think that our sins are too big to be forgiven, that Christ could not have compassion on us because of our dreadful past. We can remember those Galileans; many of them were sinners as we are and he had compassion on them. He came to call sinners, he tells us. Let us answer his call today—tomorrow might be too late.

SEVENTEENTH SUNDAY OF THE YEAR

FIRST READING : 2 Kings 4 : 42-44. A man came from Baalshalishah, bringing the man of God bread of the first fruits, twenty loaves of barley, and fresh ears of grain in his sack. And Elisha said, "Give to the men, that they may eat." But his servant said, "How am I to set this before a hundred men?" So he repeated, "Give them to the men, that they may eat for thus says the Lord, 'They shall eat and have some left.' " So he set it before them. And they ate, and had some left, according to the word of the Lord.

EXPLANATION : We have here an incident from the life of Elisha, the prophet in Israel who inherited the mantle of the great Elijah. He prophesied in Israel during the second half of the 9th century. By anointing Jehu (842 B.C.) as king of Israel, he helped to bring about the overthrow of Achab's dynasty which had introduced the worship of Baal into Israel and had almost paganized the whole northern kingdom. Today's incident describes a miracle worked by Elisha.

man of God : This term was first applied to Moses who was God's representative during the Exodus period. Later it was applied to the prophets who were God's mouthpieces to the people.

bread . . . first-fruits : This was bread made from the first of the corn that had been reaped. In this case it was barley, as "twenty loaves of barley" are mentioned. According to Lv. 2 : 12 these first-fruits should be offered to the priest of the sanctuary, but to this man the prophet was God's real representative.

give to the men : Elisha, like Elijah, had many followers—the "school of the prophet" or the "sons of the prophet,"

they were called. They lived a form of religious life with their leader.

this . . . men : On this occasion the followers numbered a hundred and Elisha's servant, Gehazi, objected that twenty loaves of barley were not enough to set before a hundred hungry men.

give . . . men : The prophet merely repeated his order.

eat . . . left : The phrase "thus says the Lord," is not a quotation from scripture but a reference to the promise of a miracle made to him by God. The hundred would eat and would be satisfied. Some of the bread would be left over.

he set . . . them : The servant then did as he was told and the result was as the prophet had foretold, or rather as God had promised.

APPLICATION : This incident in the life of Elisha is chosen for today's first reading because the gospel story deals with our Lord's more astounding multiplication of the loaves (Jn. 6 : 1–15). Both stories have this in common : bread is multiplied miraculously in order to feed hungry men. The miracle worked by our Lord was greater in its result— five loaves satisfied five thousand men. This, however, does not alter the essence of Elisha's miracle. In both cases, God was producing more than the powers of nature could produce of themselves. This appears impossible only to those who have a warped idea of God and his essence.

There are such people, however, people who deny that God can in a particular case change the laws of nature which he himself has laid down. These people are not atheists, but their mental

concept of God is not derived from his revelation of himself which is the only human way of knowing the nature of God, but from their own preconceived ideas. They allow God to exist, but they have him interned, locked-up in his heaven, unable to engage himself in the affairs of the world he has created. This is surely a most arbitrary and high-handed way of treating God. They put outside his reach the world he has created : it concerns him no longer as he is unable to be concerned in it.

This, however, is not the truth about God as revealed by himself. In his revelation of himself, he has told us that he is able to alter his own laws of nature, for he has undoubtedly altered these laws time and again, but always for some very particular purpose. The stability and validity of the natural laws are not thereby weakened in any way, for God uses his power only very rarely and always for a very particular purpose, namely, to prove to men that he exists, that he knows their needs and that he has a very fatherly interest in them.

Ever since his first revelation of himself to Abraham, God has worked miracles and through them has convinced men of his existence and absolute power. Through their prayers, the prophets of the Old Testament obtained miracles from God. Christ, on the other hand, worked miracles by his own power because he was God. He did not have to pray for that power—it was his by nature. As God delegated his power of miracles in the Old Testament so did Christ give the same power to his Apostles when he sent them out to preach. This power was very effective in convincing men of the truth of Christ : that he was the Son of God, and of the truth of the Christian faith. As the Church spread throughout the Roman empire miracles became less frequent, for as St. Augustine says : "one waters a newly-planted sapling but once it has taken solid root it needs no further watering."

Holy men and women down through the history of the Church have had the power of miracles from God as a reward for, and a proof to others of, their sanctity. Apart from the marvels of God's love and interest in his children —marvels which in a broad sense can be called miracles—real miracles occur in our day too. God is still master of creation. Not everyone, however, that asks for a miracle needs it and not everyone that needs it gets it, for God has his own wise ways of making us earn our eternal salvation. The seriously-ill member of a family whose cure would earn the eternal gratitude of all connected with him, may be left uncured, for God sees that the charity and unselfish care bestowed on that sick person is the one and only way that will earn heaven for the other members of that family. Because he is kind and loving, God must refuse the requests often of those who are very close to him. It is because he loves us that he wants the best for us and wants us to reach heaven. If, therefore, the temporal favor we seek would hinder our progress on the road to heaven, God will not grant our request.

SECOND READING : Ephesians 4 : 1-6. I, a prisoner for the Lord, beg you to lead a life worthy of the calling to which you have been called, with all lowliness and meekness, with patience, forbearing one another in love, eager to maintain the unity of the Spirit in the bond of peace. There is one body and one Spirit, just as you were called to the one hope that belongs to your call, one Lord, one faith, one baptism, one God and Father of us all, who is above all and through all and in all.

EXPLANATION : On this letter to the Ephesians, see the fifteenth Sunday of the year. In this epistle, St. Paul lays great stress on Christian unity which is the essence of the faith. In today's six verses he gives a sevenfold formula of unity on which the various aspects of true Christian unity are based. If his readers preserve this unity they will prove themselves worthy of their Christian vocation, and fraternal love and peace will reign among them.

I . . . Lord : Paul is in prison in Rome because he is an Apostle of Christ. The leaders of the Jews in Jerusalem had him arrested as a disturber of the peace because he was preaching Christ (Acts 21–22).

a life . . . calling : He begs them to live according to the Christian faith which he has preached to them.

meekness . . . forbearing : That is humility, patience, bearing with one another's shortcoming.

in love : These virtues can only thrive where true fraternal love flourishes.

unity of the Spirit : They all have received the same Holy Spirit in baptism. Therefore, they all have the source of peace and unity within them.

one body : The Christians form one visible community, as Paul says in Romans 12 : 4 : "all of us, in union with Christ form one body, and as parts of it we belong to one another" (see also Col. 1 : 18).

one Spirit : The one Holy Spirit sanctifies, gives spiritual life to the Christian body.

called . . . hope : All are Christians because they all hope in the same eternal life to which their sonship with God gives them a right.

One Lord . . . baptism : They all love and obey the same Lord (Jesus Christ); they believe the same truths; they were all baptized into the same Christ (see 1 Cor. 10 : 1–18; Gal. 3 : 27).

one God . . . all : Having the same Father they all are brothers and therefore they form one family.

above all . . . all : This is a doxology which testifies to the transcendence and the omnipresence of God.

APPLICATION : What St. Paul asked of the Christians of Ephesus over nineteen hundred years ago, he is asking of us today. He is asking us to show ourselves worthy of our Christian vocation, worthy of the privilege Christ has won for us, namely, adopted sonship with God. The first Christian virtue that St. Paul recommends his converts to practice is humility : "with all lowliness and meekness" they are to conduct their lives. For a rational and reasonable man this virtue, which is simply admitting what we are, should not be a difficult one. What have we of any lasting value which we can call our own? All the qualities of mind and body were given to us by God. Our race or tribe or nation was not of our choice. If our family happens to have wealth or position of

importance, is this really something of which to boast or to be proud? What lasting value has wealth and worldly position? There is no apparent difference between Dives and Lazarus, between a millionaire and a beggar when laid out in death.

A proper estimation of himself should not be difficult for any sane man, but especially for a Christian who has the example of Christ before his eyes. Christ could have boasted : he had greatness itself, he was God but he hid his divinity; "he emptied himself of it" in order to live among us as man so that he could raise us up and make us fit for heaven. Having become man, he allowed men to despise and insult him, to strike him on the face and crown him with thorns; they spat on him and derided him while he was dying on the cross. He who could have annihilated all his enemies by one simple wish, patiently bore these humiliations for our sake.

With such a Master, with such an example, could we dare to look down on our fellowman and be overcome by the insults of some fellowman? Could we demand respect and special consideration from those of our neighbors who have less of this world's goods, or less gifts of mind or body than we have? If a sane pagan should not act thus, how much more unbecoming, how much more contrary to his vocation would it not be for a Christian to do so! A proud Christian is a contradiction in terms; the proud man is not following the humble Christ, he has joined the ranks of the Pharisees who put Christ to death.

The second virtue, and one which flows freely from humility and which Christ calls on us today to practice is "forbearance with one another in love": putting up patiently with the faults and foibles of our neighbors. As there are no two faces in the world exactly alike, so there are no two characters alike. Each one of us has his own peculiarities which make him uniquely himself. This is God's way of brightening our lives or as the old saying has it : "variety is the spice of life"; things would be very monotonous if we all acted in the same way always. But there is no danger of that, the danger is that this variety can become a source of irritation to some at times. That is where forbearance, based on love, is important; it prevents clashes of character. If I love all my neighbors—all those with whom I come into contact, if I realize that it is my Christian duty to help them on the road to heaven, I shall find it easier to put up with apparent defects and faults in their characters.

We must remember : what may often appear to us to be serious lapses in Christian behavior on the part of some neighbors, may not be sinful, in the eyes of God who sees all the circumstances. But even if there is no possible excuse for sin we are not our neighbor's judge. Do we have to condemn him or excommunicate him from us forever? Does not our Christian teaching tell us that we should do all in our power with true fraternal charity to show our erring brethren the error of their ways?

We are all on the road to heaven, there are lots of us, thank God, on that same road, and therefore some jostling and shoving are inevitable in such a crowd. God may be allowing that jostling and pushing so that the impatient Christian may yet overcome his impatience and be worthy of heaven. We are being trained, formed for heaven as we go along the road of life. All formation and training are a bit difficult, a bit trying. Let us accept this period of trial willingly because what we are striving for is worth all we can suffer—we are training to be saints for all eternity.

GOSPEL : John 6 : 1–15. Jesus went to the other side of the Sea of Galilee, which is the Sea of Tiberias. And a multitude followed him, because they saw the signs which he did on those who were diseased. Jesus went up into the hills, and there sat down with his disciples. Now the Passover, the feast of the Jews, was at hand. Lifting up his eyes, then, and seeing that a multitude was coming to him, Jesus said to Philip, "How are we to buy bread, so that these people may eat?" This he said to test him, for he himself knew what he would do. Philip answered him. "Two hundred denarii would not buy enough bread for each of them to get a little." One of his disciples, Andrew, Simon Peter's brother, said to him, "There is a lad here who has five barley loaves and two fish; but what are they among so many?" Jesus said, "Make the people sit down." Now there was much grass in the place; so the men sat down, in number about five thousand. Jesus then took the loaves, and when he had given thanks, he distributed them to those who were seated; so also the fish, as much as they wanted. And when they had eaten their fill, he told his disciples, "Gather up the fragments left over, that nothing may be lost." So they gathered them up and filled twelve baskets with fragments from the five barley loaves, left by those who had eaten. When the people saw the sign which he had done, they said, "This is indeed the prophet who is to come into the world!"

Perceiving then that they were about to come and take him by force to make him king, Jesus withdrew again to the hills by himself.

EXPLANATION : This miraculous multiplication of bread is given in the three other gospels also. In Mark, whose Gospel is not used, the account of this miracle follows immediately after last Sunday's gospel. At first sight therefore it would seem strange that John's description of this miracle is given today instead of Mark's. The reason for this change is that this miracle in John is but the introduction to our Lord's discourse on the Eucharist, which we shall hear during the next four Sundays.

multitudes . . . signs : Huge crowds followed him everywhere because of the miracles he was able to work. According to St. John miracles or "signs" were a proof of his power and glory.

passover . . . at hand : John is already thinking of the Eucharist—the theme he will develop in the discourse which

will follow this introduction. It was during the Passover feast that Christ instituted the Eucharist.

How . . . bread? : John tells us that our Lord asked this question to test Philip —and his fellow Apostles, that is, to make them realize the magnitude of the miracle he was about to work; "he himself knew what he would do."

two hundred denarii : That was two-thirds of a working-man's annual payment—a huge sum in any reckoning. This sum would only buy enough bread to give each "a little"—not enough to allow for some to be left over.

five . . . fish : Andrew, the practical man, had seen a boy with a small supply of bread and fish. But, as he said, what use would that little be among so many! Possibly this little boy, with an acute eye for business had followed the

Apostolic group on the chance that they might run short of food and then he could do a bit of business with them. Barley loaves and dried salted fish made up the ordinary food that the poor people took with them on a journey. It would seem as if the Apostles had no supply of food for themselves or, if they had, they were not sharing it. Judas, we must remember, was in charge of supplies.

make the people sit down : Our Lord was getting ready to work his miracle of mercy.

in number . . . thousand : There were about 5,000 men, the number of women and children is not mentioned. St. Mark tells us that the Apostles got the men to sit in groups of fifty and a hundred, evidently to facilitate the distribution of the food. This also made it possible to count the multitude.

Jesus . . . loaves : These were the five loaves that the boy had brought along.

had given thanks : This was the usual Jewish custom before meals. The Greek word used "Eucharistein" for giving thanks, is the very form from which the name Eucharist is derived. When about to institute the Eucharist at the Last Supper Christ gave thanks to his Father.

when . . . their fill : Each one got all that he could eat.

gather the fragments : This command was given in order to make the Apostles and the multitude realize the magnitude of the miracle of mercy which he had worked. The five loaves and two fishes fitted easily into one basket—but there were twelve full baskets left over when each of the 5,000 men plus women and children had eaten their fill. This command also taught them that the gifts of God must not be squandered or wasted.

people . . . sign : The miracle was evident and the multitude knew from whom it came, for they said :

prophet . . . come : He was the Messiah promised so often in their Old Testament books. This miracle-worker, Christ, is the promised One. But according to these people, their promised Messiah would be a political leader, one who would set them free from Rome and even put them over Rome.

take . . . king : They were determined to make him king even against his will; they evidently knew that his was not an ambition for a worldly kingdom.

he withdrew . . . himself : He escaped quietly from them. He knew their plans. He was the Messiah and their king, but his kingdom was not of this world. Note again his kindness and mercy : he did not rebuke them for their worldly ambitions and their slowness in understanding his teaching. Some, perhaps very many of them, would see the light in God's good time.

APPLICATION : Although Jesus had the intention of preparing the minds of the multitude for his discourse on the heavenly food which he would make next day, his principal motive in working this miracle was pity and compassion. He knew that they were hungry—they had been away from home all day and some for many days. They were willing to suffer this inconvenience but he did not want them to do so. Even though he knew there were some among them who would never accept him, and perhaps even some who would be among the rabble that demanded his crucifixion on Good Friday; yet he made no distinction. He had compassion on them all.

This miracle should surely convince us that Christ is interested in our daily needs too, just as he was interested in those of his contemporaries in Palestine. Our principal and only real purpose in life is to be saved and Christ is ever ready to help us. However, we have first to travel through our earthly life so, of necessity, we have to take a passing interest in the affairs of this world. We have to provide for our earthly needs and for those of any others who may depend on us. For many, in fact for the vast majority of men, this has always been and will be a struggle against great odds. Here, too, Christ is ever ready to help us. He has a true interest in our progress through life and if we turn to him trustfully and sincerely, he will help us over our difficulties.

This does not mean that we can expect or demand a miracle whenever we find ourselves in difficulties. If, however, we are true to Christ and to the faith in our daily lives, he will find ways and means of freeing us from difficulties which would otherwise overcome us. If we look back over our past we may notice occasions when we were saved from grave difficulties by some unexpected intervention. We may not even have called on Christ to help us but he knew our needs and he answered our unspoken request. Those five thousand hungry people had not asked him for food, but he knew their needs. He knew too that their needs were caused by their desire to be in his presence—so he gave them what they had not thought of asking for. If we are loyal to him we, too, can trust that his mercy and power will be with us in our hour of need. He may not remove the cause of our difficulty. Remember St. Paul who had some

bodily infirmity which he thought impeded his effectiveness as a missioner? Three times he pleaded with Christ to remove this infirmity, but Christ assured him: "my grace is sufficient for you." He would prove all the more effectively that he was Christ's Apostle by preaching in spite of that infirmity: "for my power is made perfect in weakness" (2 Cor. 12 : 7–9). Thus it may be that Christ will use the very difficulty from which we are suffering, to bring us and others into more intimate union with him. Many of the saints suffered great hardships and afflictions during their years on earth—these very afflictions were Christ's gifts to them. Without these, and the virtues of patience, faith and trust which they had to practice, they might not be among God's elect today.

We must rest assured then that Christ is intimately interested in our daily lives on earth. We must not expect that this interest of his will remove all shadows from our path. This would not be for our eternal good—and our eternal happiness is Christ's first interest in us. It should also be our own first and principal interest too. It will help us, too, to bear with our lot, if we look about us and see so many others who are worse off, or at least as badly off as we are especially with regard to the snags of life. Christian charity will move us to help them; we may not be able to give them any material help, but we can help to lighten their load by showing our sincere interest in them and by offering words of comfort and consolation. This is the only charity that the poor have to offer to their fellow-sufferers, but if it is Christ-inspired its effects will reach to heaven.

EIGHTEENTH SUNDAY OF THE YEAR

FIRST READING: Exodus 16 : 2–4; 12–15. The whole congregation of the people of Israel murmured against Moses and Aaron in the wilderness, and said to them, "Would that we had died by the hand of the Lord in the land of Egypt, when we sat by the fleshpots and ate bread to the full; for you have brought us out into this wilderness to kill this whole assembly with hunger."

Then the Lord said to Moses, "Behold, I will rain bread from heaven for you; and the people shall go out and gather a day's portion every day, that I may prove them, whether they will walk in my law or not. I have heard the murmurings of the people of Israel; say to them, 'At twilight you shall eat flesh, and in the morning you shall be filled with bread; then you shall know that I am the Lord your God.' "

In the evening quails came up and covered the camp; and in the morning dew lay round about the camp. And when the dew had gone up, there was on the face of the wilderness a fine, flake-like thing, fine as hoarfrost on the ground. When the people of Israel saw it, they said to one another, "What is it?" For they did not know what it was. And Moses said to them, "It is the bread which the Lord has given you to eat."

EXPLANATION : The Book of Exodus describes the liberation of the Israelites, God's Chosen People, from Egypt. The scene described in today's reading occurred in the desert of Sin between Elim and Mount Sinai. The food which the people had brought with them out of Egypt was now used up, and so they were hungry. They murmured against Moses and against God who, they said, had brought them there to die in the wilderness. God answered their complaint by giving them each day bread and meat to eat.

would . . . died : They thought that they were soon to die of hunger in the desert and they regretted having been freed from Egypt—better to live in slavery with full stomachs than to die of starvation. Why did not God kill them in Egypt?

I will . . . heaven : God's response was immediate. He did not bring them out of Egypt to die of hunger—they would eat and live.

a day's portion every day : Each morning enough for the day, and no more, was to be collected by each family, but on Friday morning, two portions, enough for Friday and the Sabbath, were to be collected.

prove them : This was a test of their obedience and trust in God's providence. They had to trust that he would send them enough each day, they were not to store up any supply for the future.

twilight . . . flesh : Each evening they would have meat to eat and each morning all the bread they needed. God would prove to them that he was able and willing to provide for their bodily needs.

quails . . . camp : The quails were migratory birds that left Africa for Europe in Spring, flying over the Sinai peninsula. They returned in Autumn by the same route. Being rather exhausted after their long flights over the sea, they were easily captured when they alighted in Sinai. Evening time was the best time to catch them as they settled down to rest.

a fine . . . thing : Next morning the people saw a thin yellow-white substance lying on the ground around their camp. This is a viscous substance exuded by the tamarisk trees, then very plentiful in that region. The sting of insects causes this substance to drop from the leaves. When it falls on the cool ground it hardens into a wafer-like substance but will melt again when the sun grows strong. It had to be collected early in the morning. This material is sweet and is still a favorite with Bedouin travelers but is much rarer now as the tamarisk trees are rare in those parts. The name "manna," given it by the Israelites, used to be derived from the Hebrew of "what is this"— man-hu, but it is generally thought now that the Egyptian name for the substance was "man", hence the Hebrew manna= this is man.

bread . . . you : Moses tells the people it is bread which the Lord has given them. Both gifts, the quail and manna, were natural products of the place, but the abundance of the manna and the alighting of the birds in the vicinity of the Israelites' camp was God's doing for his people. They were grateful for these gifts—for a while (Nb. 21 : 5).

APPLICATION : In spite of all the miracles that God worked to set the Israelites free from the slavery of Egypt, they were still far from trusting him. When their food supplies had run out and no food seemed available in the desert region where they were, they murmured against Moses and against God. They thought God was going to let them die of starvation. "Would it not have been far better to have remained reasonably well-fed slaves in Egypt rather than starve as freemen out here?" they said. As yet they did not realize that God had a loving Father's interest in them, that he intended to bring them into the land of Canaan, as promised to Abraham and his descendants. This he was doing in order to put his eternal plan for man's salvation—the incarnation— into action later on.

God did not reprimand them for their lack of trust in him, he knew they were as yet poorly formed spiritually. Instead, he immediately promised to provide for their bodily needs. That evening he would provide meat for them to eat and next morning they would be able to find a bread-like food in sufficient quantity to supply each day's needs. This provision of meat and bread-like food was a miracle of God's kindness for the people he had chosen to be the ancestors of his divine Son in his human nature. The two items of food were in themselves natural to the region—the quails were passing over the Sinai desert for six months every year, and the "manna" came naturally from the tamarisk trees. What was miraculous was the large number of quails which landed around the camp, and also the regular, abundant supply of the tamarisk product which was available each day.

Each day the people rejoiced for a while at the turn of events. They had an abundant fresh supply, but some months later they again murmured and complained against God : they longed for variety as they had only the same manna all the time (Nb. 11:5). They were surely an ungrateful, a stiff-necked, stubborn people, and nothing short of the infinite patience of God could have put up with them and continued to care for them. This he did, more for our sakes than for theirs. And it's here that this story of God's compassion has a lesson for us. Everything that God did in the Old Testament was in preparation for the New, in which his eternal plan for all men was put into operation. He chose Abraham so that from him would come Jesus "according to the flesh." He looked after Abraham's descendants and eventually established them as a people in the promised land. They were the people he had chosen to keep his name and his knowledge alive on earth, while all other peoples were serving empty idols. This Chosen People failed him again and again, but in spite of their disloyalty, he preserved a remnant of Abraham's descendants in Judah until the "fullness of time" had come—the time for sending his divine Son as man on earth.

This miraculous feeding of the Israelites in the desert therefore was an act of mercy for such ungrateful people. It was also, and more importantly, a step in the preparation for the immensely greater act of our elevation to sonship with himself—brought about by the incarnation. Think of it! God was planning for our eternal salvation over three thousand two hundred years ago when he saved the Israelites from starvation in the desert of Sinai! Consider how much we take our religion for granted; how little we esteem the privilege that is ours; what little thought do we give to all that God did in order to make us Christians.

God has no need of us in heaven; he is infinitely happy without us, but because of his infinite goodness he wants to share his heaven with us and therefore he has been making arrangements from the beginning of time to enable us to get there. But he does need our co-operation. He created us, as St. Augustine says, without our consent but he cannot bring us to heaven without our consent. Unfortunately, there are some men who will not cooperate in providing for their own eternal happiness. Let us not be of their number. Let us look back on history today, and see all that God has done for us in order to make us eternally happy. Let us thank him and make a sincere and heartfelt resolve to be faithful to his teaching in future, to follow the path he has appointed for us to lead us to him.

Thanks be to the good Lord for feeding the Israelites in Sinai, and for having had our eternal welfare in mind when he came to their aid!

SECOND READING: Ephesians 4:17; 20-24. This I affirm and testify in the Lord, that you must no longer live as the Gentiles do, in the futility of their minds. You did not so learn Christ!—assuming that you have heard about him and were taught in him, as the truth is in Jesus. Put off your old nature which belongs to your former manner of life and is corrupt through deceitful lusts, and be renewed in the spirit of your minds, and put on the new nature, created after the likeness of God in true righteousness and holiness.

EXPLANATION : St. Paul is urging the Ephesian converts to live as Christians. They must forget their Gentile past, which was a life of folly as far as their real purpose in life was concerned. They are now Christians, adopted children of God; they must live according to their new status in justice and holiness.

testify . . . Lord : The J. B. which reads : "In particular I want to urge you in the name of the Lord" and the New English Bible : "This then is my word to you, and I urge it upon you in the Lord's name," bring out the real meaning of this phrase. The RSV literally follows the Greek and Vulgate. St. Paul is addressing them as Christ's minister and not in his own name. It is Christ who wants them to live according to their new status.

futility . . . minds : They are no longer pagans whose lives are aimless, without real purpose and who know not God.

not . . . Christ : Their Christian instruction tells them what Christ expects of them.

assuming . . . heard : If they have learned the Christian doctrine, they know the truth about Christ and the change in their way of living which acceptance of that truth means.

put off . . . nature : Before their conversion they depended for direction on human resources, as sons of Adam, as mere men. This life of human weakness caused many moral infirmities and failures including spiritual death (Rom. 8:13).

put . . . nature : They are now incorporated into Christ himself—they are his brothers and sons of God and should act accordingly. This is a reminder of their baptismal liturgy. They took off their old clothes, were immersed in the water signifying their death with Christ, and then rising up (from the baptismal water) united to Christ. They were dressed in a new white garment. All this signified their change of life because they began a new manner of living on their baptismal day.

righteousness and holiness : Baptism made them new men—no longer mere sons of Adam but now sons of God through Christ. Therefore, they must live according to that new supernatural nature, in justice and holiness. This is what becoming a Christian means.

APPLICATION : St. Paul had to remind the Ephesians what Christianity meant. They were men and women who were close to the time of Christ. They had seen the many miracles worked by their Apostle and father in the faith. He was a saintly man and their teacher, if they needed a reminder. How much more do we Christians of today need such a reminder? This is the very reason that these words of St. Paul are read to us today : to remind us that we are Christians, that we are new men. We have a new outlook on life and therefore our way of living should not conform to the pagan ethos of our day, but should show to the world that we are sons of God. How many Christians today are doing that? How many of Christ's followers are bearing the true witness to him?

The western world, that is, all Europe and the Americas, is nominally Christian. However, for a large percentage of the citizens of these lands Christianity is only a label not a way of life. Many millions of these people have never learned the truth which is Jesus; they have not been taught the Christian faith. Other millions have learned the truths of the faith, in a modified form perhaps, but are not willing to carry out their Christian duties. The Eastern and Western schisms, the Greek and the Protestant revolts, can be blamed for much of this religious decay—but not for all of it by any means. There are many millions of unbaptized in the Christian countries of Europe which never had an Orthodox or Protestant infiltration. Laxity on the part of parents, and neglect of their duty on the part of pastors down through the years, have led such countries into this sorry state.

Africa, and Asia are two continents with about two-thirds of the world's population. They have still much pagan territory—and this after nineteen centuries of Christianity! There have been great efforts made by devout individuals and by dedicated groups but, by and large, the Christian countries have neglected their obligation of bringing the light of faith to their pagan fellowmen. The result would appear to be that what they were unwilling to share with their pagan neighbors, they also neglected for themselves.

Before we begin to take the mote out of our neighbors' eyes, let us make sure that we have not a beam in our own. Are we exemplary Christians; are we living up to the tenets and obligations of our faith? Are we just in our dealings with all men, truthful, chaste in thought, word and deed; are we, above all, charitable to our neighbor, carrying out the spiritual and corporal works of mercy wherever and whenever we can? Do we give a good example of what a Christian ought to be to those in our own homes and to all our fellowmen we meet during the course of the day? Not many of us can give a definite yes to all of these questions. God will, however, be merciful to us if our intention is to be good Christians—even though we may fail now and then in our efforts. Where there is good will and a good intention God will make allowances.

Parents : before God you have a grave obligation to lead your children on the right road to heaven. If they fail, through your fault, you cannot but fail yourselves. If they refuse to follow your teaching and example, pray often and with fervor for them. You want the best for them in this world and the next. There are many openings in this life, there is only one entrance, however, to happiness in the next—the gate of heaven. If they miss that, they have missed everything.

Let us all have a good look at our consciences today. We are Christians and should be proud of it. But to be true Christians, we must play our part, we must carry out our Christian duties. We must remember that we are now

sons of God, brothers of Christ, and
our lives must be in keeping with this
great dignity which Christ has won for
us; we must live in righteousness and
holiness.

GOSPEL: John 6: 24–35. When the people saw that Jesus was not there,
nor his disciples, they themselves got into the boats and went to Capernaum,
seeking Jesus.

When they found him on the other side of the sea, they said to him,
"Rabbi, when did you come here?" Jesus answered them, "Truly, truly,
I say to you, you seek me, not because you saw signs, but because you ate
your fill of the loaves. Do not labor for the food which perishes, but for
the food which endures to eternal life, which the Son of man will give to
you; for on him has God the Father set his seal." Then they said to him,
"What must we do, to be doing the works of God?" Jesus answered them,
"This is the work of God, that you believe in him whom he has sent." So
they said to him, "Then what sign do you do, that we may see, and believe
you? What work do you perform? Our fathers ate the manna in the wilderness: as it is written, 'He gave them bread from heaven to eat.' "

Jesus then said to them, "Truly, truly, I say to you, it was not Moses who
gave you the bread from heaven; my Father gives you the true bread from
heaven. For the bread of God is that which comes down from heaven, and
gives life to the world." They said to him, "Lord, give us this bread always."

Jesus said to them, "I am the bread of life; he who comes to me shall not
hunger, and he who believes in me shall never thirst."

EXPLANATION: After the miraculous multiplication of the loaves our
Lord sent the Apostles across the lake
to Capernaum. He himself disappeared
from the crowd as he knew they were
planning to proclaim him king. It was
a worldly kingship which he did not
want. Later, when the crowd missed
him and the Apostles, they set out by
boat to cross the lake. They found him
in Capernaum and asked him why he
had come there. He told them very
clearly that the free bread he had given
them was their principal reason for
seeking him and not his teaching or his
miracles as they should be understood.

St. John does not relate the institution
of the Eucharist at the Last Supper in
his Gospel; it was already well known
to all Christians and was described in
the other three Gospels. He gives instead
the long discourse on the Eucharist
which our Lord delivered to the multitude at Capernaum on the day after the
miracle of the loaves.
Rabbi . . . here: They knew he had not
come in the boat with the Apostles, and
no other boat had left the eastern shore.
Christ does not answer their question,
but instead shows that he knows their
hidden motives for searching for him.
food which perishes: All earthly food is

temporary in itself and in its effects; today's bread satisfies today's hunger only, one must eat again next day.

food . . . life : He is trying to raise their thoughts above physical necessities; physical bread can give only physical life, there is a heavenly bread which will give eternal life. This should be their principal concern.

Son . . . you : They knew he meant himself when he used the term Son of man—a half-hidden messianic title.

God . . . seal : All Jews believed in God the Father. They knew nothing yet of the Trinity of persons in that one God. Jesus, who is God as well as man, did not tell them this openly yet. But he told them that he was the One whom the Father was to send—the new Moses, the Prophet foretold for centuries. His miracles proved that he was from God, they were the "seal," the authorization of the Father approving his words and work.

doing . . . God : Christ has mentioned food that leads to eternal life, this evidently is something miraculous—the work of God—and so they ask what they should do to deserve such a miracle.

believe . . . sent : Of themselves they can do nothing toward eternal life but by believing, by accepting Christ as God's intermediary, they will be doing their part.

what . . . perform : They know he is claiming to be the One sent from God but they are demanding some greater miracle than one multiplication of loaves.

our fathers ate manna : They remind him that during the Exodus God supplied their ancestors with daily bread from heaven (they quoted Ex. 16 : 4), not only once but for years. Yesterday's miracle was very small when compared with that!

it was . . . heaven : The manna was not really bread from heaven (see first reading); it was an earthly food given by a miracle *quoad modum* not *quoad substantiam*.

my Father . . . bread : What God their Father is now offering them in the person of Jesus Christ is the true source, the real cause of eternal life. If they accept him and follow his teaching they will be on the road to the real life.

bread . . . heaven : He is telling them that he is the bread of true life, that he has come down from heaven to give eternal life to all who will accept him.

give . . . always : Their outlook is still earthly, they are thinking of an earthly bread which they need always for their subsistence—this is what they ask for. They have as yet no thought for eternal life.

comes to me . . . me : He now tells them explicitly that he is the "Bread of life" that has come down from the Father. Anyone who accepts him, believing and following his teaching, will have his hunger and thirst satisfied forever. He will have eternal life, where all earthly cares will vanish for evermore.

APPLICATION : The multiplication of the loaves which fed five thousand men was bound to recall to the minds of the multitude the bread from heaven which God had given to their ancestors in the desert. That it should do so was Christ's secondary intention in working the miracle; his first intention was to feed those hungry people. Next day when the crowds gathered around him again in Capernaum, hoping for another free meal rather than looking for religious instruction, he openly accused them of their worldliness. While they knew and admitted that he was the second Moses, the prophet from God (see last Sunday's gospel), and while they had heard him speak frequently of the new kingdom of God (see Mk. 5), their thoughts were still entirely worldly. The politically-minded wanted him to throw out the Romans and set up a new kingdom of David; the others were content with all the material benefits he could give them at the moment. Things spiritual and the everlasting life were far from their thoughts.

Christ told them how wrong their attitude to life was. They were concentrating all their thoughts and efforts on the things of this life, they should rather have given thought to the future life. Instead of looking for earthly bread which had real though transitory value, they should have looked for the bread which would bring them eternal life— "the food which endures." He could give them this; they had God's guarantee and seal for it—God sent him on earth so that men would accept him and believe in his message. They demanded further proofs; and referred to the manna given to their fathers in the desert. He answered them : the manna given to their fathers was not bread from heaven, it was earthly food which preserved earthly life, but God was now giving the true bread from heaven— Christ himself. He had come down from heaven; he was divine, and was to give them eternal life, if only they would believe in him.

Acceptance of Christ as God's intermediary with men was the first essential step on the road to eternal life. "It is my Father's will that whosoever sees (that is acknowledges him as Son of God) the Son and believes in him shall have

eternal life, and I shall raise him up on the last day" (6 : 40). Christ went on then in this discourse, as we shall see during the next three Sundays, to foretell the gift of the Eucharist wherein he gives himself as the spiritual food to all those who believe in him. The act of faith, the act of accepting him as God's envoy, God's Son in fact, is already the beginning, the first step, toward the eternal life he came to give us.

In today's reading we hear of the lack of faith of those Galileans, of their utter worldliness and lack of interest in their future life. We may be inclined to judge them severely. But we must not forget that as Jews they knew almost nothing about the future life. It was only with the full revelation given by Christ, that men learned of God's wonderful plan for them. Thank God, we have this full knowledge today; we know that this life is only a period of preparation, a few years during which we can make ourselves worthy to enter the real kingdom of God in heaven. We know that Christ was God's divine Son, who took our human nature in order to make us his brothers and therefore sons of God. We know that heaven is awaiting us, if only we accept Christ here and follow his teaching. Surely, we are infinitely more fortunate than were the Galileans we read about today!

Do we appreciate our good fortune; do we live up to the teaching which we know is true? Do we ever allow ourselves to get immersed in worldly affairs —forgetting that this earth is not our home, that we are only passing through? Unfortunately, many Christians do act in this manner. While they have the name of "followers of Christ," they are not following him, they have chosen the path of worldliness and earthly interests which will lead to a dead end. Have an honest, sincere look at your own Christianity today. Your eternity, the unending ages that come after your death, will depend on how you spend your fleeting years on this earth.

NINETEENTH SUNDAY OF THE YEAR

FIRST READING: 1 Kings 19:4-8. Elijah went a day's journey into the wilderness, and came and sat down under a broom tree; and he asked that he might die, saying, "It is enough; now, O Lord, take away my life; for I am no better than my fathers." And he lay down and slept under a broom tree; and behold, an angel touched him, and said to him, "Arise and eat." And he looked, and behold, there was at his head a cake baked on hot stones and a jar of water. And he ate and drank, and lay down again. And the angel of the Lord came again a second time, and touched him, and said, "Arise and eat, else the journey will be too great for you." And he arose, and ate and drank, and went in the strength of that food forty days and forty nights to Horeb the mount of God.

EXPLANATION: As today's gospel deals with the heavenly bread of the Eucharist, the reading from the Old Testament gives us a story from the life of the prophet Elijah in which it is narrated that an angel fed him miraculously. After the incident on Mount Carmel, when Elijah challenged the prophets of the pagan god Baal and proved that Yahweh was the only true God, he put the false prophets to death. Jezabel, the pagan queen, wife of Achab, then threatened to put Elijah to death. He left Israel and set out for Mount Horeb in Sinai. On the way he ran out of food and wished he were dead, but an angel awakened him and gave him a loaf of bread and a jar of water. This was repeated twice, and then Elijah, filled with new vigor, walked for forty days and forty nights without resting until he reached Mount Horeb.

take . . . life: Although he had proved that both Baal and his prophets were false and worthless, yet the fact that he was forced to flee from Israel and leave it in its idolatrous state was a depressing thought for Elijah. This, coupled with the fatigue and hunger, made him wish he were dead. He lay down and slept.

Arise and eat: An angel awakened him and told him to satisfy his hunger and replenish his strength.

a cake . . . water: It was not a seven-course dinner, but a luxurious meal for a hungry man in the desert. God had miraculously provided this food for him.

came . . . time : Having eaten enough Elijah, still tired, lay down again to rest. But the angel wakened him again and told him to eat and drink, otherwise he would not be able to make the journey to Horeb.

ate and drank : The prophet obeyed. That food, miraculously provided, gave him enough strength and energy to walk without further food, drink or rest all the way to Horeb, a journey of forty days and forty nights.

Horeb : Moses had received the Decalog at Horeb and it was here that the covenant—the pact between God and his Chosen People—was ratified. Elijah made the 300 miles journey on foot in order once more to re-establish this covenant which was neglected and violated by kings and people in Israel. God deigned to appear to him in a way that taught the prophet to act with gentleness and kindness toward his people when he returned to Israel.

APPLICATION : The miraculous feeding of the prophet Elijah on his journey through the desert is recalled to mind today, because the Gospel story concerns our Lord's promise of the miraculous bread which he will give to sustain his followers on their journey through life. That God provided for the bodily needs of his prophet, and that Christ did likewise for the simple people of Galilee, were but a foreshadowing of the spiritual food which Christ would leave to his faithful followers to sustain them during their journey through this life. Of this we shall hear more in today's Gospel. Let us now see what lessons there are for us in this incident in the life of the prophet Elijah.

Elijah defended the true religion in the northern kingdom against all the power of the forces which the pagan wife of king Achab had introduced into the country. Having won a great victory over the prophets of Baal on Mount Carmel, Elijah had to flee the country to escape the clutches of the pagan queen. He was on his way to Mount Horeb in Sinai hoping to contact Yahweh where Moses had received the covenant, the covenant which Israel had so seriously violated. On his way, however, weary from travel and short of food he grew despondent and lost heart. In spite of all his endeavors Israel was full of sin and idolatrous practices. His labors were in vain; he would be better off dead. He sat down under a broom tree and asked Yahweh to end his life.

Instead, Yahweh sent an angel to him with food to restore his tired body and mind—a food which gave him the strength to walk without ceasing until he reached Horeb. Here the gracious Lord appeared to him, and having shown him that he was not a God of fury but a God of mercy (1 Kgs. 19 : 9–12), he sent him back to continue his work. The reign of Jezabel, the pagan queen, would soon end, for God told Elijah to anoint Jehu as the next king of Israel. Elijah returned to Israel and with renewed vigor continued his work for the true religion of Yahweh.

Here is a story which has encouragement for all of us. Here we have a prophet, God's own chosen representative, a man full of zeal for God's honor and glory—a saint, and yet he was as human as the rest of us. He grew tired of fighting a losing battle, he fled from the front, he set out to get protection and consolation from God, but tiring of the long journey he became so depressed and so despondent that he wanted God to take him from this vale of tears. God was not disgusted with him, he did not think him a coward or a failure; instead, he renewed his energies and sent him back to fight on for the Lord.

There are few of us who do not have our moments, even days maybe, and weeks of spiritual depression. Our crosses seem at times to become unbearable; we feel like lying down under them and asking God to take us. This is exactly what this holy man did and we saw how kindly God dealt with him.

God will lift us up too, and if only we rely on him he will give us the strength to carry on. It is he who allows those crosses to come on us, but he does not want them to crush us, he wants us to use them to rise above our earthly weaknesses and to stay closer to him.

The next time I feel despondent, I shall not ask the good God to take me away from it all; I shall ask him to give me that new strength which he gave to Elijah—the strength to persevere, bearing my cross not only for forty days but for forty more years, if this should be God's means of assuring me my eternal salvation.

SECOND READING: Ephesians 4:30–5:2. Do not grieve the Holy Spirit of God, in whom you were sealed for the day of redemption. Let all bitterness and wrath and anger and clamor and slander be put away from you, with all malice, and be kind to one another, tenderhearted, forgiving one another, as God in Christ forgave you.

Therefore be imitators of God, as beloved children. And walk in love, as Christ loved us and gave himself up for us, a fragrant offering and sacrifice to God.

EXPLANATION : On this letter to the Ephesians, see the fifteenth Sunday of the year. In today's text, St. Paul urges his converts to live in peace, harmony and love with one another. They are children of God and therefore love should dominate their lives.

grieve . . . Holy Spirit : It is the Holy Spirit who keeps the Christian body united (4 : 4). Anyone who harms this unity grieves the Holy Spirit; it's a way of saying such an action is not pleasing to the Holy Spirit.

were sealed : In baptism they were marked as being the property of the

Holy Spirit; he took up his abode in them to sanctify them.

for . . . redemption : They had become Christians in order to attain to the redemption—the eternal life—which Christ had made available to them. It is at the moment of judgement after death that each one will know how he has fared. If he has lived as a faithful Christian that will be his day of redemption.

put . . . you : Paul tells them what they must avoid if they are to preserve true Christian unity. They must put away all bitterness, ill-feelings against a neighbor, all angry and defamatory words. Instead, they must :

be kind . . . forgiving : Always be ready to help one another, always ready to forgive a neighbor if he sins against us. **As God . . . you :** Their forgiveness could never equal this—God the Father pardoned us all our offenses and made us his adopted children through the incarnation, death and resurrection of his only-begotten Son. Such a price could never be paid by men, but they must keep this divine forgiveness ever before their eyes. If they do, they will find that forgiving their fellowmen is easier.

as beloved children : Through his infinite love God made them his children; they must try, in their limited human way, to imitate this love of God.

fragrant offering and sacrifice : It was for love of us that Christ—the Suffering Servant, foretold in Isaiah—laid down his life, suffering the cruel death of crucifixion so that we could have eternal life. He offered his human life as a sacrifice of atonement for the sins of the world—a sacrifice which ascended to the Father as a fragrant offering on our behalf. We should, therefore, try to imitate that love by being ever ready to help our neighbor, even ready to die for him, if necessary. St. John says : "In this we have come to know Christ's love, that he laid down his life for us; and we likewise ought to lay down our life for our brethren" (1 Jn. 3 : 16).

APPLICATION : Charity, love of neighbor, is the hallmark of all true Christians. We have it from our divine Lord's own mouth when he said : "by this will all men know that you are my disciples if you have love for one another" (Jn. 13 : 35). This is the basic virtue of Christianity which St. Paul is urging his recent converts to put into daily practice. First, he tells them what vices and failings they must avoid, and then he describes the positive things they must do in order to live in true charity with their neighbors. He then gives the reason why Christians must love one another, namely, that they are children of God and must imitate their heavenly Father who is Love; they are brothers of Christ who set them such a sublime example of true love.

What St. Paul urged on the Ephesians he is urging on us too. If charity was the hallmark of Christianity in the 1st century, it is still the same in the 20th. If the Ephesians were children of God

so, too, are we—thanks to God's mercy; if they should imitate their Father so, too, must we if we want to be found worthy of the dignity he has conferred on us. Christ died for us as well as for the Ephesians and this he did out of love for us; we must make some return for his sublime example of love.

How do we set about loving our neighbor in a truly Christian manner? St. Paul gives us some guidelines today. Avoid bitterness, he tells us. Bitterness is a feeling of dislike, of resentment which we develop within us against somebody who has done us a real or imagined wrong. Our Christian duty is to forgive a neighbor who has offended us, or who we think has offended us, for often the offense was not intended and the neighbor is not guilty. "Forgive and forget" is a truly Christian advice. One can forgive but still keep remembering the offense; this is not complete forgiveness and the retention of such memories makes one unhappy and develops a certain amount of bitterness against the offending brother. Cast your mind around among those neighbors against whom you have some resentment. Even if they did deliberately offend you, they have also offended God by that same act and that is far more serious; yet God will forgive them; should not you as his child do likewise? You have to turn to God pleading for forgiveness at times; you will obtain that forgiveness if you forgive your neighbor: "Forgive us our trespasses as we forgive those who trespass against us." If we refuse fully to forgive our neighbor what we are saying in that prayer is: "do not forgive me, Lord, as I do not forgive those who offend me."

St. Paul tells us to avoid "wrath, anger and clamor," in other words, uncharitable scenes and quarrels. Although "hot tempers" are especially attributed to Irishmen and redheads, the true fact is that men of all nationalities and colors of hair have their share of this unlovable commodity. It has to be kept in check, or it may lead us to say or do things to a neighbor which are the opposite of charitable. It is often said of a person that he would provoke the anger of a saint. It is not true: a true saint has control of his temper. What the saying really means is: "I am a saintly person but that neighbor's tongue or actions make me lose my temper." But that neighbor's behavior could have been the very test which would prove my sanctity and patience. No one deserves credit for being even-tempered and mild with those who are gentle and kindly in word and deed. It is in our dealings with the unkind and the uncharitable that we must avoid the uncharitable scenes mentioned by St. Paul. A true Christian, instead of paying such uncharitable neighbors back in their own coin, will try to make them better Christians by treating them kindly and charitably. St. Francis de Sales, speaking of charity, says one can catch more flies with a spoonful of honey than with a barrel of vinegar.

St. Paul goes on to tell us that we must be kind and tender-hearted to one another, not only forgiving any offenses our neighbors may have committed against us but taking them to our heart, making them feel that they are wanted. They are members of the one family and we should gladly sacrifice our own convenience in order to help them along in life. We may not be able to do much but if our "little" comes from a warm charitable heart it can and will work wonders.

GOSPEL : John 6 : 41–51. The Jews murmured at Jesus, because he said, "I am the bread which came down from heaven." They said, "Is not this Jesus, the son of Joseph, whose father and mother we know? How does he now say, 'I have come down from heaven'?" Jesus answered them, "Do not murmur among yourselves. No one can come to me unless the Father who sent me draws him; and I will raise him up at the last day. It is written in the prophets, 'And they shall all be taught by God.' Every one who has heard and learned from the Father comes to me. Not that any one has seen the Father except him who is from God; he has seen the Father, Truly, truly, I say to you, he who believes has eternal life. I am the bread of life. Your Fathers ate the manna in the wilderness, and they died. This is the bread which comes down from heaven, that a man may eat of it and not die. I am the living bread which came down from heaven; if any one eats of this bread, he will live for ever; and the bread which I shall give for the life of the world is my flesh."

EXPLANATION : Jesus goes on to foretell the Eucharist. In the previous section (last Sunday's Gospel) he told them that he was the bread that had come down from heaven. This meant more than that he was the Prophet or the Messiah. The crowd realized this and objected. How could he have come down from heaven? They knew well that he came from Nazareth and was the son of Joseph and Mary. John's readers knew the answer to this objection "born of a virgin," and so he did not give Jesus' answer. Jesus again stressed the need for faith which is a gift from God. Those who have that gift will come to him and believe in him. Once more he said that he was the bread of life, the bread which would give everlasting life, unlike the manna. Finally, he openly declared that not only was he the living bread from heaven, belief in whom is the beginning of eternal life, but his very body would be turned into the bread which would sustain those who believe in him. It was a direct foretelling of the Eucharist.

Jews murmured : St. John uses the term "Jews" to describe those in opposition to Christ. They now object to his claim to be from heaven.

father and . . . we know : How could he be from heaven? Mary is his real mother; they naturally thought Joseph was his real father.

unless . . . him : To accept Christ as being what he claimed to be required the grace of faith, a gift from the Father. This gift seems to have been offered them but instead of accepting it and responding to it they objected and murmured against his claim.

taught by God : He who accepts God's offer of faith will get further revelation from God (Is. 54 : 13).

he . . . Father : God is invisible to human eyes on earth. The Son has seen the Father and it is only through the Son made man, that men can see the Father through the eyes of faith.

manna in . . . died : The manna which the Jews called bread from heaven gave physical life only; the bread which is Christ will give real eternal life. As the synoptics and Paul do, John is also clearly connecting the bread of life with the redemptive death of Christ.

any man . . . bread : A man eats of this bread firstly by faith in Christ, by accepting him as being from God : prophet, Messiah and Son of God who alone has seen the Father; and secondly, by receiving him in the Eucharist.

live forever : He will be put on the road to eternal life because Christ became man and died and rose from the dead for that very purpose.

the bread . . . flesh : This is the climax toward which the discourse was leading. The Eucharist is foretold and its revelation is more astounding and more of a stumbling-block than anything he had said so far. "Flesh" in St. John stands for "body" which was used by Paul and the synoptics in this context.

APPLICATION : The main point of doctrine in this part of our Lord's discourse, as given by St. John, is the necessity for belief in Christ who has come down from heaven. It is only in the last verse of today's text that Christ explicitly states that he is about to give his own very body as their spiritual food to those who believe in him. The description of himself as "bread from heaven" and the vital difference between the effect of this bread and the manna given to their fathers in the desert, are a definite preparation for the announcement of the doctrine of the Eucharist.

However, before they could even think of accepting this teaching on the Eucharist they had first to accept Christ as divine, as the Son of God. This was not easy for Jews, for whom strict monotheism was the center of their faith. To admit that Christ was God would at first sight seem like admitting two gods. Secondly, even though Christ had worked extraordinary miracles, to all appearances he was still a mere man— and the prophets of old had worked miracles. True, Christ was evidently claiming to be more than a prophet; he claimed that he alone had seen the Father, that he had come from the Father. This claim of equality with the Father would be sheer blasphemy if it were not true; could God give the power

of miracles to such a great sinner?

Perhaps some of them argued along these lines and accepted his claim later on. Others remained stiff-necked and stubborn and could see nothing in him but a native of Nazareth, a humble Galilean like themselves, but one who had developed strange ideas about who and what he was. These Galileans began a long line of unbelievers which has stretched down through the centuries to our own day. The reasons for the unbelief are the same today as they were in the year 29 A.D. Man is proud of his intelligence; which he did not give to himself. Whatever he cannot grasp within the limited confines of that intellect, he treats as non-existent as far as he is concerned. If a God exists, a doubtful possibility to these great thinkers, we mortals can know nothing about him; he is beyond our ken and we can be of no concern to him.

If there ever was a Jesus of Nazareth, he could be only a mere man who suffered from grave hallucinations! But his miracles? A simple answer : there never were any. His disciples invented these stories later. But these disciples were willing to die for these inventions of theirs! Thousands of Christians were martyred rather than deny the divine claims of Jesus! More hallucination, no doubt! Nineteen centuries of Christian history can be shrugged off as easily as that by those who will not believe. If certain statements do not fit in with preconceived ideas then these statements are false; if certain facts do not agree with history, as the unbelievers understand history, then these facts never happened. So man's limited, finite mind remains the sole judge and arbiter of all truth.

We believe in a loving God, and in his divine Son, Jesus Christ, who came on earth to bring us to heaven, and in the Holy Spirit who completes the work of sanctification in us. Surely, we owe this Blessed Trinity a debt of gratitude! We can never fully repay it. Because of our Christian faith which has come to us from Jesus, we know where we came from, we know whither we are going and we know how to reach that destination. Of all the knowledge a human being can acquire on this earth, the above facts are the most essential and important. Any other knowledge is of temporary value. The knowledge our Christian faith gives us concerns eternity and our journey toward it.

Today, we must thank God from the bottom of our hearts for giving us the Christian faith. This faith means that "God out of the abundance of his love, speaks to men as friends and lives among them so that he may invite and take them into fellowship with himself," as Vatican II puts it. He did not put us on earth and leave us on our own with nowhere to go except to the grave. He sent his beloved Son on earth. He made us heirs to heaven and left to us, in his Church, all the instruction and aids we need to reach our inheritance. The unbelievers and free-thinkers may feel that they are free to do what they will here on earth, but we know that we have been given the freedom of the children of God for all eternity, if only we live according to the faith given us.

TWENTIETH SUNDAY OF THE YEAR

FIRST READING : Proverbs 9 : 1–6. Wisdom has built her house, she has set up her seven pillars. She has slaughtered her beasts, she has mixed her wine, she has also set her table. She has sent out her maids to call from the highest places in the town, "Whoever is simple, let him turn in here!" To him who is without sense she says, "Come, eat of my bread and drink of the wine I have mixed. Leave simpleness, and live, and walk in the way of insight."

EXPLANATION : The book which is called Proverbs is a collection of wise sayings and precepts to govern the daily lives of the lovers of wisdom and of

God. The book used to be attributed to king Solomon because he was regarded as the patron and inspirer of wisdom in Israel. Though some of the wise sayings in this book may have come down by oral tradition from Solomon, most of the material contained in it comes from later sources and the language and style point to a post-exilic (that is, after 500 B.C.) date for its final composition. In the verses taken from this book today, Wisdom is described as a person—a great lady who has built herself a mansion. She prepares a noble feast and sends out her handmaidens to call the "simple," that is, the non-prejudiced, the youth (see 1 : 4) of the town, to come and partake of her feast, namely: to learn wisdom from her. As bread and wine are mentioned as part of this feast of wisdom, the text was chosen to harmonize with the bread and wine of the Eucharist in today's gospel reading. **her house . . . pillars :** Wisdom is a rich lady who has built herself a perfect palace—the seven pillars denote perfection.

she . . . table : She has made ready a sumptuous banquet.

let . . . in here : She sends out invitations to partake of her meal to all in the town who are open-minded and, as yet, ignorant of true wisdom.

who . . . sense : This is a parallel to the above, the man who as yet knows not wisdom.

eat . . . wine : These were the staple foods in Palestine in those days. There were other items in the dinner, but these two give the essence of a meal.

leave simpleness : The meal is a metaphor or symbol of wisdom which this person wants to teach. If those who have not true wisdom come to her they will change from ignorance to knowledge.

walk . . . insight : Having learned wisdom they will walk, that is, they will live life as it ought to be lived; they will live a truly wise life in the spiritual, not the worldly sense.

APPLICATION : The sacred author of this book is personifying wisdom. By having wisdom seek to educate men he was, without knowing it, most likely foreshadowing the coming of God's Son on earth to teach men the way of salvation. But could the author, or any of his readers, have even vaguely imagined what the divine Wisdom eventually did for men in order to teach them the eternal truths? Because of the restricted revelation which the Jews then had of God the most that the readers of Proverbs could get from this book would be the necessity of keeping the Law of Moses, if they wanted to be successful in life. They had, as yet, no knowledge of the future life. Therefore, the best they could expect from God, if they served him faithfully, was prosperity, a large family and a long life in this world.

It is true that some of the messianic prophecies spoke of the unending happiness and the joys which would come with the messianic age. The world could not give these joys. All of these prophecies were necessarily couched in worldly terms and were therefore understood in the context of this world. The Jews had some vague hope of a shadowy existence after death in a place they called "Sheol," but it was a negative existence, a useless one in which they could neither give honor to God nor merit anything for themselves, and there was no hope of improvement.

We mention the sad lot of the Jews in order to make ourselves realize the blessings, privileges, knowledge of life here and hereafter which Christ has brought to us. Proverbs describes Wisdom as being anxious to communicate with the Jews; the Gospels tell us of the actual communications that the Son of God gave to us. Wisdom, according to Proverbs, built a palace in which she could refresh and instruct those anxious to come to her. Christ built his Church. It is the home in which his teaching, the deposit of faith, would be preserved for all men. Wisdom sent out her handmaidens to invite the citizens of Jerusalem to her banquet; Christ sent his Apostles to the four corners of the earth to call men to the heavenly banquet of eternal life.

One can get so accustomed to a good thing that one can fail to appreciate it. The blind man who gets back his sight appreciates this faculty to a degree that those who have always had their sight never do. The cripple who is cured esteems the new power given him far more than do the men who have always been able to move and walk. It is thus, too, with many Christians. We have had the gifts of our Christian faith from childhood and we take them so much for granted, that we seldom stop to think how much they mean to us. We even overlook saying a serious "thank you" to God for them.

Think of the poor Jews of old whose only hope of reward was in this life, and how little could they get of that same reward. Even if they lived to be a hundred, life would still be very short for them. Those who avoided serious diseases, and many of them did not, were still prone to plenty of the minor ailments, aches and pains, as well as family troubles and financial difficulties which made their life on earth anything but a paradise. And after all of these struggles and trials they had nothing like our eternal life to look forward to.

We have our struggles and difficulties in life, no one can escape meeting at least some of them, but we know that these trials can and do have an eternal value for us if we accept them and bear them patiently. Whether we are wealthy or poor will not trouble us very much if we are convinced Christians. We are "storing our treasures where neither moth nor rust consumes and where thieves do not break in" (Mt. 6 : 20). We are not too concerned about whether our life on earth will be a long or a short one; our concern is that it will be successful in earning heaven for us.

Wisdom in the person of the Son of God has instructed us. Let us "walk in the way of insight" on the Christian path laid down for us by Christ.

SECOND READING: Ephesians 5:15-20. Look carefully then how you walk, not as unwise men but as wise, making the most of the time, because the days are evil. Therefore do not be foolish, but understand what the will of the Lord is. And do not get drunk with wine, for that is debauchery; but be filled with the Spirit, addressing one another in psalms and hymns and spiritual songs, singing and making melody to the Lord with all your heart, always and for everything giving thanks in the name of our Lord Jesus Christ to God the Father.

EXPLANATION: There is a certain similarity between the lesson from Proverbs read today and these verses from St. Paul's letter to his Ephesian converts. In Proverbs, Wisdom is anxious to teach men how to walk according to the truth. St. Paul is urging his converts to live according to the Christian wisdom they have received: to live according to the will of the Lord. It would be utter foolishness for a Christian to do otherwise. He urges them to avoid drunkenness, to be full of the Holy Spirit and full of gratitude to God for all the gifts given them.

how you walk: To walk is a synonym in the New Testament for "to live."

not ... men: Those who had not the Christian wisdom—and there were still many in Ephesus—lived an unwise, foolish life as far as eternity was concerned.

days are evil: With pagans on all sides, these early days of Christianity were difficult times for the sincere Christian —there were temptations all about him.

will of the Lord is: It is true wisdom to know the will of God and to do it.

drunk with wine: Ephesus was in a wine-growing region. Evidently the Apostle knows that there are some of the converts who are inclined to over-indulge. This is sinful in itself and can lead to other sins.

filled with the Spirit: Those who were inclined to over-indulge in wine in order to enjoy life, are urged instead to be joyful in the Holy Spirit, that is, they should sing hymns and psalms with their fellow-Christians in order to show their gratitude to God.

in the ... Christ: This gratitude always and everywhere should be shown and offered to the Father through our mediator Jesus Christ—thus it becomes acceptable to the Father. We see the three persons of the Blessed Trinity implicated in our prayer in this verse 20. The Christian filled with and moved by the Holy Spirit offers his gratitude to the Father through the mediator Jesus Christ, the Son.

APPLICATION: St. Paul's words to the Ephesian converts: "look carefully how you walk," are words full of meaning and warning to all of us. On the day we were baptized we were made children of God, and set on the road to heaven. Since we came to have the use of reason and the power to make decisions, have we walked on that road or have we chosen paths of our own? If we have acted as wise men, as St. Paul says, we have stayed on that road, for to leave it is the act of a fool. The Christian who stumbles occasionally or who is inclined to "nibble at the grass by the road-side" has not left the royal road. If he repents of his lapses and uses the means Christ has given for washing away faults, he is able to go along at a better pace and make up for the time he lost.

It should console all of us, even the best among us, to know that Christ foresaw that the vast majority of us would stumble and fall now and then. This is why he left us the sacrament of penance, his gift of mercy and understanding for our human weakness. He knew we would need it. Even among the well-known saints in heaven, those we have all heard of and to whom we pray for help, there are few who had not some faults and failings. Some were big sinners before their conversion: St. Augustine and St. Margaret of Cortona, for instance. Others, more like ourselves, had their good and bad days early in life but gradually, aided by grace from God, they got rid of their failings and died in close friendship with him.

We would all like to die in God's friendship without a stain of sin. But there is only one sure way of securing this for ourselves and that is: to try to be always friends of God. To "try" is the operative word here; we may fail now and then but if we have the specific intention and desire of remaining in God's friendship we will get rid of our sins quickly and put ourselves right with God. If confession is not easily available, a fervent act of contrition, with the intention of going to confession as soon as possible, will wash away sin.

St. Paul mentions "making the most of the time," that is, we should use the years God gives us on earth to work for God's honor and glory and for our own eternal salvation. This does not mean that we should be always on our knees praying—this is not what God wants. What he wants is that we spend the days and years allotted to us following out faithfully and honestly whatever our vocation in life is, but doing it for God's honor and glory. We are to be honest, then, first and foremost in our work, whether we are our own masters or the employees of others. Sobriety and reasonableness in our recreation and sleep. Charity in word and deed towards our neighbors wherever we meet them. Short but heartfelt prayer morning and evening—offering the day's work and recreation to God while dressing in the morning and a sincere "pardon me, God, I could have been much better today," said at our bedside before retiring for the night. For the Christian who lives like this during the week, Sunday's Mass and devotions will be the high-light of his week. His Mass will be an offering of thanksgiving to God for all the graces given him during the past week, and a humble request for all the divine help he shall need during the coming week.

If a Christian who follows this rule of life were told: "you shall die on the sixth of next month," he would need to change nothing in his daily routine because he would be pleasing God every day, ready to meet not his judge but a Father whom he always loved and who always loved him.

GOSPEL : John 6 : 51–58. Jesus said to the crowd, "I am the living bread which came down from heaven; if any one eats of this bread, he will live for ever; and the bread which I shall give for the life of the world is my flesh."

The Jews then disputed among themselves, saying, "How can this man give us his flesh to eat?" So Jesus said to them, "Truly, truly, I say to you, unless you eat the flesh of the Son of man and drink his blood, you have no life in you; he who eats my flesh and drinks my blood has eternal life, and I will raise him up at the last day. For my flesh is food indeed, and my blood is drink indeed. He who eats my flesh and drinks my blood abides in me, and I in him. As the living Father sent me, and I live because of the Father, so he who eats me will live because of me. This is the bread which came down from heaven, not such as the fathers ate and died; he who eats this bread will live for ever."

EXPLANATION : The day after his miracle of the multiplication of the five loaves, which satisfied the hunger of five thousand men not counting women and children, our Lord took the opportunity of foretelling a greater miracle he was going to work for men. He was going to give his own body and blood to men to be the supernatural food which would sustain their spiritual life and energy during their earthly journey. Before the multitude to whom he was speaking at Capernaum could begin to grasp this extraordinary promise, he stressed the necessity of an unquestioning faith in him as one who had come down from heaven, as one who had "seen" the Father, in other words : as one who was in some mysterious way equal to the Father.

This necessary introduction has been given us by St. John in the gospels for the last two Sundays. Today, Jesus openly speaks of the great miracle of the Eucharist which he will work for them. He tells the people, and through them all his followers, that he will give them his flesh and blood to be their spiritual food and drink. The Jews understand him to speak in the purely literal sense (to "eat one's flesh" meta-

phorically was to slander one; obviously he could not mean that), but how could "this man," they ask, "give us his flesh to eat?" They have not believed that he came from God, that he is God in fact and so as a man he could not give his body to them to be their food. Jesus does not answer their objection, he simply goes on to repeat and emphasize the statement already made.

living . . . heaven : He has come from heaven, he is life, he is life-giving.

eats . . . forever : This bread from heaven will produce eternal life; ordinary bread gives temporal life.

bread . . . world : He is going to "give," to sacrifice, to offer up himself for the life of the world, that is, to provide eternal life for all men. This bread of which he is speaking is his own "flesh," his own human body, offered in sacrifice for the eternal life of men.

How . . . man : The Jews understood him to be speaking literally, which he was, but seeing in him nothing more than a man his saying had no meaning for them. Furthermore, they understood him as referring to his actual body as it was. They had no idea of a glorified body and as Jesus did not explain himself to them, they were not yet able to grasp the full truth.

unless . . . man : He simply goes on to repeat what he had said : they must partake of his body—flesh and blood—if they wish to have true life in them.

eats . . . life : Partaking of him will give them eternal life.

raise . . . day : On the day of judgement those who have partaken of his life-giving nourishment will be raised from the dead and enter eternal life.

abides . . . him : Intimate union with Christ will be the effect of partaking of his sacrificed body. Eating of the meats sacrificed to the gods identified the eater with the gods (see 1 Cor. 10 : 14–22).

I live . . . Father : Christ's human life is *from* the Father; he has his divine existence *in common* with the Father—this common life of the Father and Son will be shared by all those who partake of Christ in the Eucharist.

bread from heaven : Again he stresses the real difference between the food he is going to give and the food given to the Israelites in the desert. The "manna" could give only earthly life. Christ, the bread from heaven to be given in the Eucharist, will be the cause and source of eternal life. The fathers of the Jews in the desert all suffered earthly death, those who partake of the new manna, the Eucharist, will be assured of eternal life, after life on earth ends.

APPLICATION : About the year 90 A.D. when St. John was writing his Gospel, the doctrine and the practice of the Eucharist was so well established that the Evangelist did not deem it necessary to mention in his Gospel the actual institution of the Eucharist. Instead, he gave us this discourse at Capernaum in which our Lord foretold the institution of this divine gift to men. It is quite possible that John has joined together here two or more discourses given to different audiences and on different occasions, and it seems probable also that he has not given all our Lord said. As his Gospel reads now it would be asking too much of the Jews to expect them to really understand what Christ was promising. But as the whole doctrine of the Eucharist was common knowledge to all Christians of the year 90 A.D., John did not deem it necessary to go into details.

We, like the Christians of the year 90 A.D., have a great advantage over those Galileans to whom Christ spoke in Capernaum. We are convinced that Christ was the Son of God who had become man in order to make us sons of God. He died on the cross as a sacrifice of atonement to his Father for us and for our sins. He himself said : "Greater love than this no man hath that a man lay down his life for his friends." That is the greatest sacrifice a man can make for anyone. Christ, however, was more than man, he was God too; he was therefore able to do more for his friends. He was able to leave to his Church the power to repeat the sacrifice of the cross under the symbolic form of the consecrated bread and wine. By this repetition and recalling : "do this in memory of me," his followers could give infinite honor to the Father and renew the infinite atonement made on their behalf on Calvary. Furthermore, by partaking of this real sacrifice offered to God Christians could be united with Christ and with the Father in an intimate manner.

The Eucharist is a sacrifice and a sacrament. As a sacrifice it is the repetition, the re-enactment, of Christ's sacri-

M

fice of himself on Calvary. It is a sacrifice of infinite value for it is the same Christ, the God-man, who is offering himself, through the medium of his human representative, to his heavenly Father. It is a sacrament for it is a visible sign instituted by Christ to give us grace. Under the visible appearances of bread and wine, it is the source of all grace whom we receive within us. The staple human nourishment, bread and wine, are changed into the infinite source of our staple spiritual nourishment, the body and blood of Christ.

The Blessed Eucharist is a mystery in so far as our minds cannot understand how exactly Christ is present on our altars after the words of consecration. The very words given us by Christ himself have been said over the bread and wine. But while we cannot grasp how exactly this happens, we can have no room for doubt but that it does happen: for we have the solemn affirmation of Christ the Son of God that it is so. In today's Gospel he clearly says: "the bread which I shall give . . . is my flesh. He who eats my flesh and drinks my blood has eternal life." And during the course of the Last Supper "he took bread and blessed and broke it and gave it to them saying 'take, this is my body.' And he took a cup . . . he gave it to them and they all drank of it. And he said to them: 'this is my blood of the new covenant which is shed for many' " (Mk. 14 : 22). That the Apostles accepted his word and made this ceremony of partaking of the consecrated bread and wine the central act of the Christian worship from the very beginning of the Church, is fully proved in the Acts of the Apostles and in the writings of St. Paul. This has continued down to our day and will continue as long as men inhabit the earth.

For devout Christians the biggest mystery about the Blessed Eucharist is the mystery of the divine love that moved Christ to leave us such an intimate and such an effective memorial of the love he proved to have for us on Calvary. We certainly do not deserve this extra proof of his love. He opened heaven for us, he showed us how to get there, he did not leave us to struggle alone. His infinite and divine love made him find a means of remaining always with us in our tabernacles, and of opening the floodgates of divine mercy each time this sacrifice is offered on our altars. Furthermore, he wanted to give himself to us as the life-giving food which would give us the spiritual strength for salvation. The infinite love of Christ for us is the only explanation of this. And what return do we make for this love? We attend at the sacrifice of the Mass realizing that by active participation we are capable of giving infinite honor to God. Do we receive this truly heavenly food, the body of Christ, with the proper preparation? Do we visit Christ in the church where he ever remains ready to receive us and to listen to our requests?

If the Jews of old could boast: "For what great nation is there that has a god so near to it as the Lord our God is to us" (Dt. 4 : 7), how much more truly can we Christians make such a boast, for Christ our Lord has deigned to remain with us on our altars until the end of time.

TWENTY-FIRST SUNDAY OF THE YEAR.

FIRST READING: Joshua 24 : 1–2; 15–18. Joshua gathered all the tribes of Israel to Shechem, and summoned the elders, the heads, the judges, and the officers of Israel; and they presented themselves before God. And Joshua said to all the people, "If you be unwilling to serve the Lord, choose this day whom you will serve, whether the gods your fathers served in the region beyond the River, or the gods of the Amorites in whose land you dwell; but as for me and my house, we will serve the Lord."

Then the people answered, "Far be it from us that we should forsake the Lord, to serve other gods; for it is the Lord our God who brought us and our fathers up from the land of Egypt, out of the house of bondage, and who did those great signs in our sight, and preserved us in all the way that we went, and among all the peoples through whom we passed, therefore we also will serve the Lord, for he is our God."

EXPLANATION: Joshua, who succeeded Moses as leader of the Israelites, allotted their territories to the twelve tribes east of the Jordan and in the land of Canaan. He then called a general assembly of the tribes and got them to renew their acceptance of the covenant made between themselves and Yahweh at Sinai. This was a very suitable ceremony with which to begin their new settled life in the land given them by Yahweh. It took place in Shechem, a town of Samaria which already had associations with the Chosen People. Abraham had built an altar there (Gn. 12 : 6), Jacob had bought land there and had buried the idols brought by his followers from Mesopotamia under an oak-tree in that same place (Gn. 35 : 2). Yahweh's tent or tabernacle had been set up in Shechem; this coupled with the renewal of the covenant helped greatly to preserve the religious and political unity of the twelve tribes for the first three centuries of their life in Canaan. **presented . . . God:** The assembly took place in front of Yahweh's tabernacle. **choose this day:** As representative of the tribes Joshua challenges the leaders openly to declare their loyalty to Yahweh, or to the false gods of Mesopotamia which their ancestors worshiped before Abraham's conversion, or to the local Canaanite idols.

as . . . house: Representing the tribe of Ephraim, Joshua declared that Yahweh was and would remain his God.

The people answered: All gladly followed Joshua's example. They would not forsake Yahweh to serve other gods, for:

brought . . . Egypt: They have not forgotten what Yahweh their God has done for them.

great . . . sight: These were the numerous miracles he had worked in their favor. They were: the plagues in Egypt, the opening of the Red Sea, the feeding in the desert, the subduing of their enemies of their journey and in Canaan.

for he is our God: They all will continue loyal to Yahweh for he has been a kind God to them.

APPLICATION: It is possible and even probable that some of the twelve tribes had never been in Egypt and therefore had not taken part in the covenant of Sinai. This would explain Joshua's reason for re-affirming the Sinaitic covenant at Shechem, so that these tribes could take on themselves the covenant obligations and become fully integrated into the Chosen People. Even without this reason the re-enactment or re-acceptance of the covenant at this point in their history was of the greatest importance for the Chosen People. They had had the land of Canaan divided among them and were about to settle down as citizens with rights and duties in their *own* country. Hitherto, they had been slaves and nomads. Although their individual territories had been mapped out for them, most of the tribes had but a precarious foothold as yet on the land allotted to them. They had still many battles to fight before they could say that they owned their land.

Furthermore, they needed to renew their resolution to remain loyal to Yahweh for as yet their faith in the formative stage would often be threatened by the pagan idolatrous practices they would see on all sides of them. The pagan fertility gods of Canaan had attractions for agricultural people—they were supposed to make the harvests plentiful and produce rain when needed; these pagan idols were there among them. Yahweh was far away in heaven, above the skies. The idols *seemed* to answer the pagan people's prayers— Yahweh did not always do so. Therefore, the renewal of the covenant of Sinai at this moment in their history was of the greatest importance; to begin their lives as citizens of Canaan with a solemn dedication of themselves as a united people to the true God was setting up for themselves a standard, a banner, to which they could turn for strength in later life—if tempted to abandon their faith in the one and only God.

There is a lesson here for all Christians: at baptism we were made members of God's new Chosen People. A solemn covenant or pact was then entered into between us and the Blessed Trinity. God, through the Church, promised us the eternal possession of the true promised land—heaven, provided we kept our part of the covenant, that is, if we remained faithful to his laws during our days on earth. At our confirmation we renewed this covenant and promised to be loyal to Christ—even if that loyalty brought sufferings and death on us. We gladly became soldiers of Christ.

However, soldiers, tired of discipline and fearful of further battles, have been known to desert their colors and country. Many Israelites, in spite of all their solemn declarations of loyalty to God, turned away from him and put their trust in idols of wood and stone. Worse still, Christians who had a better and a fuller revelation of God in the person of Christ, have deserted God and Christ and their own eternal interests. Like the Israelites of old, they chose the earthly deities of pleasure and plenty; like the timid soldier they have resented discipline and hated the personal restrictions that the Christian code imposes on us all.

While we leave these to the infinite mercy of God, their desertion should make us examine our way of living the Christian life lest we, too, should fall away. We live today in a world which is, alas, ungodly and unchristian. This makes it all the harder for God's loyal people to live their religious life to the full, but at the same time, it demands of all of God's loyal subjects to let their light shine before men. Our world needs light and divine illumination. The faith of Christ, the belief in God and in a future life, is not only being attacked by enemies of Christ's Church, it is being hidden under a bushel, if not completely extinguished, by some who would still claim to be within the fold.

Let us ask God the Father, Son and Holy Spirit to strengthen our faith and baptismal covenant. We want to take up our permanent residence in the eternal promised land of heaven. Only the grace of God can keep us from being lost on the way.

SECOND READING: Ephesians 5: 21–32. Be subject to one another out of reverence for Christ. Wives, be subject to your husbands, as to the Lord. For the husband is the head of the wife as Christ is the head of the church, his body, and is himself its Savior. As the church is subject to Christ, so let wives also be subject in everything to their husbands. Husbands, love your wives, as Christ loved the church and gave himself up for her, that he might sanctify her, having cleansed her by the washing of water with the word, that he might present the church to himself in splendor, without spot or wrinkle or any such thing, that she might be holy and without blemish. Even so husbands should love their wives as their own bodies. He who loves his wife loves himself. For no man ever hates his own flesh, but nourishes and cherishes it, as Christ does the church, because we are members of his body. "For this reason a man shall leave his father and mother and be joined to his wife, and the two shall become one." This is a great mystery, and I mean in reference to Christ and the church.

EXPLANATION: St. Paul continues his exhortation to his Ephesian converts. Writing from his prison cell (see fifteenth Sunday), he urges them to make their home-life truly Christian. In today's extract, he sets up Christ's self-sacrifice for the Church as the model which all the members of the family should emulate in their mutual relations. Husbands and wives, parents and children, masters and slaves must all regulate their relations with one another, according to the example set by Christ. Today, Paul deals with the relationships between husbands and wives.

subjects . . . another : This mutual service sums up what he has already said in chapters 4 and 5 : 1–20 and also introduces what follows in the rest of the epistle.

reverence for Christ : This must be the true Christian motive for their mutual love and service; all selfishness is excluded.

wives . . . husbands : The husband is head of the family, the wife, children and slaves must recognize his authority but :

as to the Lord : A new motive for this respect and obedience is now given; Christian wives will see in their husbands the representatives of Christ in the home.

as Christ . . . Church : Christian marriage represents and symbolizes the union of Christ and his Church.

as Church . . . Christ : So the husband, representing Christ, is head of the Christian family.

is . . . Savior : Through his sacrificial death Christ made the Church worthy to be his bride (see 2 Cor. 11 : 2; Col. 1 : 22; Ap. 21 : 2–3; 9).

Husbands . . . wives : Husbands, if they are to be Christ's representatives, must act as Christ's representatives. Their dominion will be one of love, not of tyranny. "Christ loved the Church," and proved his love by sacrificing his life to purify her.

washing . . . word : The reference is probably to baptism and the profession of faith (the word), by means of which one becomes a part of Christ's bride, a member of the Church. There is also the background of the ancient middle-Eastern custom of the ritual bathing and preparation of the bride before the wedding.

without . . . wrinkle : This state of perfection can refer to the second coming. It was customary among the Jews to have a rather long interval between the espousals and the actual wedding. All Christians are espoused to Christ by baptism, it is only at the "parousia"—the second coming—that his actual spouses will be presented to him without any defect whatsoever, "without blemish." They will be his spouses forever.

their . . . bodies : As the members of the Church are made members of Christ's body, so the wife is as united to her husband as his own body is part of him. Note that she does not become a member of his body, as the Christian becomes a member of Christ's body, but he must regard her with the same love and esteem as he regards himself; "and no man hates his own flesh" so he must not hate or fail to love his wife.

for this reason : Genesis (2 : 24) is quoted as proving the sacredness of marriage. In that inspired approval there was hidden (mysterion) the symbol of Christ's union with his bride, the Church. "I mean in reference to Christ and his Church," as St. Paul puts it.

APPLICATION : While giving his Ephesian converts some very practical advice to govern the relationships between husbands and wives, St. Paul reveals to us that Christ has made all his faithful followers his bride. He,

Christ, is the divine groom; we the Christian Church, are his bride. In the Old Testament, the Chosen People are frequently described as the spouse, the bride of Yahweh. The Song of Songs or Song of Solomon, is generally interpreted as a poem describing this marriage bond between God and Israel. Now in the New Testament, Christ the Son of God has made his new Chosen People his bride. By becoming man he has become one of us, but under this symbol of marriage which is the closest union there can be between two individuals, he is represented as uniting us to himself by a bond greater than brotherhood. Could Christ have done more for us? What return do we make for such overwhelming love? Even the best of us must admit that we have indeed done very little.

Today, the spotlight is on husbands and wives. St. Paul calls on them to live in love and harmony. He tells the wife to be subject to her husband, not as a slave to one's master but as if subject "to the Lord." Her subjection is based on love and respect. Marriage has made them one with a unity that has no equal on earth. The husband is to love his wife as Christ loved the Church, and as Christ's love for the Church went so far as to sacrifice his life to save the Church, so must a true Christian husband be ready to sacrifice himself for love of his wife. St. Paul explains that the husband who truly loves his wife is loving himself, for by marriage husband and wife have become "one flesh." No man ever hates his own flesh and now that his wife is "one flesh" with him, he is loving himself when he loves her. The same holds for the wife.

This ideal state of perfect harmony in married life between husband and wife is not always easily attained but it must be the aim of all married couples. The example St. Paul sets before them is the mutual love of Christ and his Church. While Christ's love for his Church remains ever constant and unchanging, the same cannot be said for the individuals who form the Church; and no one knew this better than St. Paul. Christ himself foresaw that the many he had made his "bride" would fail sometimes in their obedience and reverence to him; but occasional lapses would not break the "matrimonial bond" between him and them. Therefore, he left the sacrament of penance, the means of erasing such defects, to his Church. Having purified themselves of their sins, these brides of his would return to him, renewed in love and loyalty.

Married couples, therefore, must not be surprised, much less despondent, if that perfect harmony and the idyllic love of their first years in marriage begins to show signs of tension and strain as the days go on. There will be lapses and disappointments on both sides, but this only proves that both are human : they are not yet saints but only learners of the art of sanctity. Here is where Christian charity and Christian forgiveness, obligatory on all Christians, are especially needed between husbands and wives. They must be ever ready to forgive and forget, and to do so quickly. Christ forgives us our sins the moment we sincerely ask for pardon; he does not make us wait for weeks while he sulks and refuses to deal with us.

Husbands and wives must imitate him in this readiness to forgive. When your partner seems to have insulted, neglected or offended you, think of your wedding day and honeymoon. Are you not to blame as much as your partner for this apparent lapse? With the passing of time you have taken your spouse too much for granted; perhaps, you are becoming selfish. Get back to your original loving enthusiasm, renew your wedding-day fervor, forget self for the moment and you'll find by your side the spouse with whom you walked arm-in-arm down the aisle that great day—one of the greatest days in your life.

GOSPEL: John 6: 60–69. Many of the disciples of Jesus said, "This is a hard saying; who can listen to it? But Jesus, knowing in himself that his disciples murmured at it, said to them, "Do you take offense at this? Then what if you were to see the Son of man ascending where he was before? It is the spirit that gives life, the flesh is of no avail; the words that I have spoken to you are spirit and life. But there are some of you that do not believe." For Jesus knew from the first who those were that did not believe, and who it was that should betray him. And he said, "This is why I told you that no one can come to me unless it is granted him by the Father."

After this many of his disciples drew back and no longer went about with him. Jesus said to the twelve, "Will you also go away?" Simon Peter answered him, "Lord, to whom shall we go? You have the words of eternal life; and we have believed, and have come to know, that you are the Holy One of God."

EXPLANATION: Last Sunday we read of the murmurs of objection among the multitude, the ordinary people. How could *this man*, they had said, give us his flesh to eat? They looked on him as a man who was promising to give them his human flesh, as it then was, to eat. Who could accept this? they asked. Christ did not explain, he simply went on to demand "faith in his word." He had come down from heaven, he was more than mere man, he had the words of eternal life. Today we read of objectors among his "disciples," the outer band of followers who had been continually with him for sometime now. They were a group distinct from the Apostles. Their reason for objecting was the same as that of the multitude: they thought he was a mere man. He knew of their lack of faith and told them so: "some of you do

not believe," but he made no attempt to remove this obstacle. He simply referred again to his divine origin and the divine knowledge he possessed.

He then put a direct challenge to the "Twelve"—the Apostles; Peter answered by professing for all their faith in him who had the words of eternal life. Peter did not say he understood what Christ meant by eating his flesh, but he was ready to accept it as coming from one who had the truth and was the Holy One of God.

Jesus . . . himself: His disciples were murmuring but not in his hearing, but he knew what their sentiments were without being told; this fact should have shown them that he was more than a *mere man*. **take . . . at this:** The power he has of giving his (glorified) body to be the spiritual food of his followers is but a consequence of the basic fact which they refuse to grasp—his divinity. His next words bring this out.

Son of man . . . before : This will be the culmination of the mystery of who the Son of man is. It will be the crowning act of the incarnation, death and resurrection and his return to heaven "where he was before," the final proof of his divinity (see Jn. 1 : 50; 3 : 11–15).

spirit . . . flesh : Faith in God's revelation is contrasted with worldly knowledge. These murmuring disciples have only human judgement, they are not enlightened by divine revelation, they have not faith which alone gives life—it is the beginning of eternal life.

words . . . life : His claim to be from God, and to return to him, as well as the doctrine of the Eucharist cannot be understood by earth-bound minds. The divine Spirit which produces "faith" is alone capable of giving life and meaning to his words.

knew . . . believe : Jesus knew who the unbelievers were from the very first day that they began to follow him, as he also knew his betrayer among the Apostles, but he gave them every chance to open their hearts to God's grace and change their minds.

unless . . . him : No one can be a true disciple of Jesus unless the Father gives him the grace of faith. But every man who "does what in him lies," who does his part to prepare himself, will receive that gift from the Father.

Will . . . away? : Jesus now puts this question to the "inner circle" of his followers, the twelve Apostles that he himself had chosen. Will they remain faithful or will they follow the deserters among the "disciples?"

Simon . . . answered : As in Mt. 16 : 17, Peter answers for the "Twelve."

the words . . . life : He does not say "we understand your promise of the Eucharist and therefore accept it." This he could not say, but instead he declares that they have "believed"; they have faith in Jesus and they know and have accepted him as :

the Holy . . . God : This title of itself could mean the Messiah only, but in the circumstances it seems very likely that it is used by John to convey a deeper meaning, which Jesus had for the Apostles after the resurrection. Because of their "faith," they are on the way to seeing in him the real Son of God. They know he has the words of eternal life, the truth which will lead them to eternity. They therefore accept his statement concerning his body and blood as food which produces eternal life, even though as yet, they know not how this may be.

APPLICATION : As we heard last Sunday, St. John was writing about the promise of the Blessed Eucharist at a time when Christians accepted the Mass and Holy Communion as the essential act of Christian worship. Very probably he omitted many details when describing this promise. The "disciples" who murmured evidently saw nothing but a man in Christ. It was very natural, therefore, that they could not accept his saying that they should eat his body and drink his blood. Thus it seems most probable that when Christ says they lacked "faith," he had given them sufficient proofs that he was more than a man. These individuals among the disciples, however, refused to open their minds to these proofs; therein was their guilt. Their minds were earth-bound and were determined to remain earth-bound. Faith is a gift of the Father, as Christ says to those disciples: "no one can come to me unless it is granted him by the Father," but the Father has offered them this gift and they have refused to accept it; otherwise they would not be guilty.

No one who accepts Christ for what he is, the Son of God in human form, has any difficulty in believing that he left us himself in the Eucharist as a sacrifice and a sacrament. This does not mean that we understand this gift of Christ in all its details—it was an act of divine power and as such beyond full human comprehension. However, we can understand enough about the actuality of the Eucharist because we accept the words of Christ, who "has the words of eternal life," even though its innermost nature escapes us. We are doing no violence to our intelligence when we accept as fact from a trustworthy witness what we cannot prove or confirm for ourselves. No more trustworthy witness than Christ ever existed. In Galilee he promised to give his body and blood— in the Eucharist—to be our spiritual nourishment — communion — and our means of offering an absolutely pleasing sacrifice to God every time his body and blood are made present by the words of his ordained minister. He fulfilled that promise at the Last Supper. He gave to his Apostles and their successors the power to repeat this act of divine love when he said: "Do this in memory of me."

When Simon Peter answered Christ's challenge—"will you too go away?"—he spoke not only for his fellow-Apostles that day with: "Lord to whom shall we go? You have the words of eternal life," but for all Christians who really believe that Christ was the incarnate Son of God. Peter, be it noted, made his act of faith before he was fully convinced of the divinity of Christ, but he was already convinced that Christ was close to God and spoke nothing but the truth.

We have the proofs of Christ's divinity which Peter and the Apostles later got. We have also the faith of two thousand years of the Christians whose belief in the Blessed Eucharist as a sacrifice and sacrament was at the very center of their Christian lives. We have also the noble example of many martyrs who gladly gave their lives in defense of this truth. Our faith may never be put to such an extreme test, but should it be, God grant that we will not be found wanting.

Many of us may need to examine ourselves as regards the full and effective use we make of that gift. Every time we attend at Mass do we realize that Christ is offering himself to his Father for our sanctification and the sanctification of the world? Do we realize that we, through his minister at the altar, are offering infinite thanksgiving, infinite atonement, infinite adoration, infinitely effective petition, to our Father in heaven through the sacrifice of his divine Son in the Mass? Are we always worthy to act this part, are our consciences fit to allow us to partake of this sacrifice in Holy Communion? A true Christian who realizes and appreciates what the Son of God has done and is still doing for him will try always to make himself less unworthy, for not even the greatest saint was *worthy* to partake of this act of divine love.

TWENTY-SECOND SUNDAY OF THE YEAR

FIRST READING : Deuteronomy 4 : 1-2; 6-8. Moses said to the people : Now, O Israel, give heed to the statutes and the ordinances which I teach you, and do them; that you may live, and go in and take possession of the land which the Lord, the God of your fathers, gives you. You shall not add to the word which I command you, nor take from it; that you may keep the commandments of the Lord your God which I command you. Keep them and do them; for that will be your wisdom and your understanding in the sight of the peoples, who, when they hear all these statutes, will say, "Surely this great nation is a wise and understanding people." For what great nation is there that has a god so near to it as the Lord our God is to us, whenever we call upon him? And what great nation is there, that has statutes and ordinances so righteous as all this law which I set before you this day?

EXPLANATION : Deuteronomy, meaning "second legislation" is the title given to the fifth book of the Old Testament, by the Greek translators (Septuagint). Most of the book is taken up with laws already given in the earlier books, but some of the historical events of the journey from Sinai to Transjordan find their place in it as well. The book contains three long discourses put in the mouth of Moses by the author. Having arrived at Mount Moab whence they could see Canaan, the land which was to be theirs, Moses—who was to die in Moab—called the people together and exhorted them to remember the covenant of Sinai and to be faithful to it when they settled in their homeland. Even if these discourses were not delivered by Moses but composed by a much later inspired author—as is commonly held today—they are still the word of God and have value for all time.

In the excerpt from Deuteronomy read today, the Chosen People are urged to carry out the laws God gave them. If they do, they will give good example to the pagan peoples among whom they live, and will make these pagans see how good God is to his Chosen People.

give ... ordinances : The tone and style of the Deuteronomist is exhortatory. "Shema": give heed or listen, indicates the opening of a liturgical address. Moses is naturally chosen by the author as the leader addressing the people. He had received the covenant and the commandments from God on Mount Sinai. He was a man with authority.

do them ... live : If they keep God's law God will keep them.

the God ... you : The land of Canaan

was already promised to Abraham. God is now about to fulfill his promise when he will lead Abraham's descendants into that land.

not . . . from it : They must not change God's laws but observe them as they are given to them.

your . . . understanding : In this alone will the Israelites be superior to the pagan nations among whom they will live in Canaan : in their knowledge of the true God and in their close association with him. The pagans will be superior in all the earthly skills and traditions but the Israelites' knowledge of God will astound these worldly-wise people.

what . . . there : This was a true boast. The Israelites, Abraham's descendants, were the only people then who not only knew the true God but had a covenant or pact with him which guaranteed them his almighty protection and help if they were faithful to their part of the covenant.

God . . . it : That God was with them had already been evident from the events of the Exodus and the journey to Moab. It would be evident again in their entrance to and occupation of the Promised Land.

whenever . . . him : If they are faithful to the covenant and call on God at any time in their history, he will come to their aid.

ordinances so righteous : Some of the pagan nations had some very fine civil legislation but Israel's civil legislation was part of the sublime covenant which bound them as a people and as individuals to the true God. The educated pagans must surely have wondered how a people as uncultured and as uninstructed in worldly knowledge at the Israelites could have acquired such a sublime theology. Because God had revealed himself to them they surpassed all others in this branch of learning—but in nothing else.

APPLICATION : Even though the book of Deuteronomy was written some centuries after the death of Moses it is quite possible that he spoke words of exhortation to the Israelites—exhortation to be faithful to their covenant with God —before they left Moab to enter the Promised Land. Whether or not Moses spoke the words given here, they were written by an inspired author and this exhortation was perhaps even more necessary for the author's contemporaries and their descendants, than it would have been for the Israelites of Moses' day. The memory of the Exodus and the part played by God in it, as well as all the assistance he gave to them during their journey from Egypt to

Moab (Transjordan), was still fresh in the minds of Moses' contemporaries. The temptation to forget God or to be disloyal to his commandments, would have been much less likely to impress these early Israelites—they badly needed God, they would remain close to him. It was much later, when their descendants had successfully settled in Canaan and through success had grown worldly-minded, that this temptation grew strong and made many Israelites forget their past and God's part in their history. The exhortation was more necessary in the later period than it would have been at the time of Moses.

These verses from Deuteronomy were selected for our reading today to remind us of our covenant with God, to remind us of all God has done for us and of what he expects of us in return. The boast of the Jews that God was very near to them was true, but with much more truth can we Christians make that same boast. God sent his divine Son to live among us and he raised us up to the dignity of adopted sonship. He made a new and everlasting covenant with us and sealed it with his own precious blood, shed on the cross of Calvary. He has prepared a place in heaven for us and there he will lead us if we cooperate with him. The old covenant made on Mount Sinai, the promised land of Palestine, the Chosen People of Israel were but pale shadows of what God had in store for all nations, Jews and Gentiles, when the "fullness of time" came with Christ.

The words of Moses : give heed to the commands of your Lord and God—keep them and do them, are words addressed to us today. Christ himself has summed them up for us very briefly : "love God and love your neighbor." If we do these two we are doing everything God expects of us. For any Christian who realizes all that God has done for him and the great future he has in store for him, it should not be hard to love such a good and kind Benefactor. It is to God that we owe our existence and every gift of mind and body we have in this life, and it is to his infinite generosity that we owe the promise of an unending happiness after death.

Loving our neighbor may be at times more difficult—there are people who seem very unlovable. However, we must see in our neighbors God's other children, our brothers in Christ, and be ever ready to overlook their faults and be willing to offer them the hand of friendship, as well as the helping hand if ever they need it. We are living in a world of tensions and strife. There is greater need than ever to foster the brotherhood of man. The lead should surely come from Christians whose faith teaches them that Christ has made all men his brothers and therefore sons of God. Race or color of skin can mean nothing to a true Christian. God is Father of us all and heaven is the end he has destined for all mankind. As Christians, all our endeavors should be directed to helping our brothers, our fellowmen, to reach that happy end. A narrow form of nationalism, or pride of race, or ancestry can have no place in the mind of a true follower of Christ. We are all made of the same clay, but the incarnation of God's Son has raised us up to a lofty dignity which carries with it the promise of a glorious eternal future. Our one desire should be to help all our neighbors, be they near or far, to share with us that glorious future.

SECOND READING: James 1:17-18; 21-22; 27. Every good endowment and every perfect gift is from above, coming down from the Father of lights with whom there is no variation or shadow due to change. Of his own will he brought us forth by the word of truth that we should be a kind of first fruits of his creatures.

Receive with meekness the implanted word, which is able to save your souls. But be doers of the word and not hearers only, deceiving yourselves.

Religion that is pure and undefiled before God and the Father is this: to visit orphans and widows in their affliction, and to keep oneself unstained from the world.

EXPLANATION: This epistle, together with six other books of the New Testament (Jude; 2 and 3 John; 2 Peter; Apocalypse and Hebrews) was not received as canonical by some of the Eastern and Western Fathers in the early centuries. But by the end of the fourth century it was officially accepted by the whole Church as canonical and inspired. The James to whom it is attributed is James the Less—one of the twelve Apostles (Mk. 3:18), also most probably the "brother" or cousin of the Lord (Mk. 6:3; 15:40). He was bishop of Jerusalem when the Council of Jerusalem was held and St. Paul mentions him as one of the "pillars" of the Church (Galatians 2:9; see 1:18; Acts 15:6-29). He was put to death by stoning on the authority of the High Priest Ananias, when the Roman governor's office was vacant in 62 A.D. We have testimony for this in Josephus Flavius (Ant. 29.9.1). This letter which is a series of sermonettes rather than a letter, is addressed to the "Twelve tribes in the Dispersion" (1:1), which most probably means the Judeo-Christians in Syria and Palestine. It is a Jewish-Christian exhortation closely following the Wisdom literature of the Old Testament. In the five verses we read from this epistle today, St. James exhorts us to be Christians in practice, not in theory; to "do," to live,

according to the law laid down for us, in other words, to put into practice the spiritual and corporal works of mercy. **every endowment . . . gift:** We have been given every perfection of body and mind by God from above, from heaven. **Father of lights:** It is the same Creator, who made the lights in the skies, the sun, moon and stars so visible and so necessary to every human being, who made us and gave us all the gifts we have.

no variation or shadow: The heavenly lights vary in their light-giving qualities but their maker, their Creator, is absolutely unchanged and unchangeable. **his . . . forth:** Our creation was a free act of his will, and our vocation as Christians "by word of truth" was a similar free act of his benevolence. **word of truth:** This is the revelation of himself that God gave to men. First he gave to the Jews a partial revelation and a preparatory stage, and now: the full revelation through Christ, the Christian gospel (see Eph. 1:13; 1 Pt. 1:23). **first-fruits of his creatures:** Now as Christians these convert Jews are born again through the gospel and they are but the beginning, the "first-fruits" of a new creation, a new race of men, a creation that will spread to all men of all nations.

with meekness . . . word: They are to

accept wholeheartedly and submissively the divine revelation and the gift of faith they received at baptism. This "word," this revelation, was implanted within them, it became part of themselves as the new creation.

able ... souls : It is the means of attaining eternal life. Christ has won that eternal life for them, it is up to them now to make sure that they will partake of it.

doers ... only : They must be Christians in action, in daily practice; it is not enough to say "I believe"—I must prove by my life that I believe.

deceiving yourselves : Any Christian who thinks that by accepting the gospel message without putting it into practice, will earn for himself eternal life is deceiving himself.

visit ... widows : Love of God is the greatest of the commandments and love of neighbor, Christ tells us : "is like unto this." But we show our love for God by real love for our neighbor, and so religion, the Christian religion, to be pure and undefiled—that is to be authentic and sincere—must produce works of charity. St. James mentions "orphans and widows," as those at that time most in need of charitable help—others in need are not excluded.

unstained ... world : As well as works of charity, the true Christian should preserve interior moral purity. The "world" is taken in its bad sense, in its opposition to God, and the many evil practices then in vogue; a Christian had to avoid these if his practice of Christianity was to be sincere and pleasing to God, his Father.

APPLICATION : The letter of St. James to his fellow-Jewish converts to Christianity is full of sound practical advice. Today's extract recalls to his readers' minds how indebted they are to the good God. It was he who gave them every gift of mind and body which they possess. Furthermore, as Jews they were given a limited revelation of himself, but now as Christians they have received, through Christ, all the revelation and helps they need to reach eternal life. They have been given the Christian gospel and the Christian faith and they have the honor of being the first to receive this divine gift.

The practical St. James, however, reminds them that they must use these gifts properly if they are to profit by them. They would be deceiving themselves badly if they thought they would earn heaven by simply professing their faith in God and his Son, Jesus Christ. They must act according to that faith; they must live as adopted sons of God and brothers of Christ by keeping and putting into daily practice the commandments they have learned from the gospel. They must as he says : "be doers of the word and not hearers only." In this he was but following his divine Master's warning : "It is not those who say to me, 'Lord, Lord,' who will enter the kingdom of heaven but he who does the will of my Father who is in heaven."

The Apostle then mentions two things that they must do in order to be truly Christian, truly religious in God's sight. They must care for the needy among them. He mentions orphans and widows as those most likely to be in need of help—spiritual and material. They must avoid the sinful practices of the worldly people among whom they were living.

This means that they must put the law of love of neighbor into daily practice and they must preserve interior moral purity in the midst of the moral laxity which then prevailed.

This letter of St. James, written about nineteen hundred years ago for the Christians of that day, has still a valuable lesson for us of the 20th century. We, too, need to be reminded often that the gifts of mind and body which we are fortunate to have are not our own—we did not give them to ourselves. We owe our existence and every natural and supernatural gift we possess to the good God who created us. He brought us into being, he gave us life in this world, in order to give us eternal life hereafter; for this reason he has given us the Christian faith which is the one and only true explanation of man's life on this earth.

We are surely privileged then for we have the true explanation of this life and a firm hope and divine promise of an unending future happy life. But we must never forget that in order to merit this divine promise we have a positive role to play: we must be Christians in practice. Being a Christian is like having a passport for heaven, but having a passport will not get one to the destination he wants to reach; he must take all the necessary steps to reach his desired goal. True, the Christian has divine assistance and aid in taking all these necessary steps, but he must cooperate with it. In other words, he must put the gospel teaching into practice every day of his life.

This is not beyond his strength; if it were, Christ would not have demanded it of him. Since St. James' day, millions have followed his sound advice and have reached heaven. The vast majority of them did nothing extraordinary—they kept their consciences at peace with God, avoiding the sinful temptations of this world. If they had an occasional lapse in a moment of weakness, they returned quickly to their loving Father. They loved God and proved that love by helping God's other children who needed help. If we keep these two commandments of love for God and love for our neighbor—the essence of the Christian gospel—we too will find heaven's gates open to us when our journey through this life ends.

GOSPEL: Mark 7:1-8; 14-15; 21-23. When the Pharisees gathered together to Jesus, with some of the scribes, who had come from Jerusalem, they saw that some of his disciples ate with hands defiled, that is, unwashed. (For the Pharisees, and all the Jews, do not eat unless they wash their hands, observing the tradition of the elders; and when they come from the market place, they do not eat unless they purify themselves; and there are many other traditions which they observe, the washing of cups and pots and vessels of bronze.) And the Pharisees and the scribes asked him, "Why do your disciples not live according to the tradition of the elders, but eat with hands defiled?" And he said to them, "Well did Isaiah prophesy of you hypocrites, as it is written, 'This people honors me with their lips, but their heart is far from me; in vain do they worship me, teaching as doctrines the precepts of men.' You leave the commandment of God, and hold fast the tradition of men." And he called the people to him again and said to them "Hear me, all of you, and understand: there is nothing outside a man which by going into him can defile him; but the things which come out of a man are what defile him." And when he had entered the house, and left the people, his disciples asked him about the parable. And he said to them, "Then are you also without understanding? Do you not see that whatever goes into a man from outside cannot defile him, since it enters, not his heart but his stomach, and so passes on?" (Thus he declared all foods clean.) And he said, "What comes out of a man is what defiles a man. For from within, out of the heart of man, come evil thoughts, fornication, theft, murder, adultery, coveting, wickedness, deceit, licentiousness, envy, slander, pride, foolishness. All these evil things come from within, and they defile a man."

EXPLANATION: Almost from the very beginning of Christ's public preaching in Galilee, the Pharisees and Scribes were in opposition to him, while the "crowds", the multitudes of ordinary Jews who followed him, daily grew larger. The Scribes and Pharisees accused him of "blasphemy" when he forgave the paralytic his sins. They criticized him for eating with tax-collectors and sinners in the house of Levi. They accused him of encouraging his disciples to sin because he did not prevent them from plucking ears of corn on a sabbath day. In today's episode, given by St. Mark, we have the same Pharisees and Scribes, accusing Jesus of collusion in sin, for he lets some of his disciples eat without first washing their hands. This was a violation of the tradition of the elders, they said, and of this tradition they were the staunch supporters.

Scribes from Jerusalem: These were the chief instigators of opposition to Jesus, and being from the center of religious authority, their opinions carried great weight.

hands . . . unwashed: The question here is of "ritual" cleanliness, it is not one of hygiene. According to the Talmud, the Jewish authority for traditional ritual observances, only priests were bound by this law of washing their hands before eating, but the Talmud dates from the fifth century A.D. The law of washing before eating was not then obligatory on all Jews. That it was, so long before that—at least in certain places and among certain pietists whose leaders were the Scribes—is highly probable. Mark had no need to invent this story, the opposition of the Scribes and Pharisees was abundantly evident without this incident.

many other traditions: St. Mark refers to the numerous other "traditions" orally handed down, which the Scribes and Pharisees had added to the Law of Moses.

why do your disciples: The Pharisees now accuse Jesus of encouraging his disciples to violate their (the Pharisees') traditions.

well . . . prophesy: Jesus' answer is that it was of their hypocrisy that Isaiah had prophesied seven centuries previously. "In vain do they worship me teaching as doctrine the precepts of men" (Is. 29 : 13).

you leave . . . God: This is a semitic mode of repetition, not a new charge. Christ does not mean that they deliberately violate the Law of God while emphasizing their own human, additional prescriptions but he says they have their priorities wrong. Human precepts may and must sometimes be broken, but the divine law never (on this see Mk. 3 : 1–6 : healing on the sabbath day; also Luke 14 : 1–5).

Hear . . . understand: Christ now addresses the "crowd," the ordinary people who had probably heard the remarks of the Pharisees, and explains the real meaning of cleanliness before God.

nothing . . . him: A man is not made unclean, sinful, before God because of some unclean thing he may swallow by eating with unwashed hands.

from . . . man: It is rather the evil designs that come from within, from a man's heart and mind, that defile a man and make him a sinner. He then adds a list of the many sins that men commit because of the evil designs they form within themselves. The evil begins within. This is the uncleanliness which men must avoid rather than the cultic impurity about which the Pharisees are so concerned.

APPLICATION: When Christ came on earth the Scribes and Pharisees were the religious leaders of the Jews. The Scribes, so called because of their knowledge of the Mosaic Law and the traditions added on to it, were the elite among the Pharisees who prided themselves on their strict, rigorous observance of the Law and the human traditions. The Pharisees had no time or no understanding for their fellow-Jews who often violated the scribal traditions—and even the Law of Moses itself sometimes. For this reason they kept themselves apart from the *ordinary* people and developed a proud superiority complex. They performed many acts of virtue but their pride and sense of self-sufficiency vitiated their good deeds (see the description of the Pharisee and the tax-gatherer in the temple, in Lk. 18 : 10–14). The opposition of the Pharisees and Scribes to Jesus began very early in his public life. It grew in strength daily until, with the help of the Sadducees, their arch-opponents, they finally nailed him to the cross.

The main reason why they opposed him so bitterly was his mercy, kindness and understanding for sinners. He ate with tax-gatherers and made one of them, Levi, an Apostle. He forgave the adultress and many, many others. While he certainly did not approve of sin, he never uttered a hard word against any sinner. He had come, as he said, to call sinners to himself and to repentance. This he did all through his public life. He objected to the Pharisees, not because of their strict observance of the Mosaic Law nor of their insistence on human traditions—although they sometimes carried this to an intolerable extreme. He objected because they despised the lowly people, the uneducated in the law and traditions—those, in other words, who did not belong to their own exclusive class. To the Pharisees all these were "sinners," while they themselves had the worst sin of all—the original sin of mankind, the sin of pride.

In today's encounter with the Pharisees, Jesus tells them that they are hypocrites: "they honor God with their lips but their heart is far from God"; they obey the Law and the traditions, not to please God, but to be seen and admired by men; their motive, self-glorification, vitiates every otherwise good act they perform. Christ then addresses the people—the crowds who most likely had overheard his dialog with the Pharisees—and he tells them that it is not legal or cultic uncleanliness that matters, but cleanliness of the heart before God. Eating with unwashed hands, or using unwashed vessels for drinking, does not defile a man, this does not make him less worthy before God. It is not from things outside him that a man incurs defilement but from his own innermost

self. Every serious sin against God and neighbor has its beginning within a man, in his intellect and will; the evil design is the forerunner and instigator of the evil deed.

The Pharisees should have known all this. They did know it. They knew very well that before a man breaks any of the commandments of God he must first plan and decide to break it; it was not their theology that was defective but their practice. They despised their neighbors and called fellowmen "sinners," because through ignorance they violated many of the man-made precepts the Pharisees had added to the Law of Moses. There were also fellow-Jews of theirs who violated the law itself, but it was not their right to judge or condemn much less excommunicate them, as they so often did in practice.

Christ condemned the Pharisees by word and deed. He was merciful, kind and understanding to all sinners. He forgave sin and promised forgiveness to all who would repent of their past misdeeds. Not only that: for he left to his followers for all time his sacrament of mercy and forgiveness, by means of which they could have their sins forgiven by his minister, acting in his name. Should we ever forget all he has done for us and disobey in a serious way any of his commandments, let us remember that we are not excluded from his company as the sinners were excluded by the Pharisees: we have banged the door on ourselves but he has given us the key with which to reopen it. Let us never be so foolish as to fail to use that key.

TWENTY-THIRD SUNDAY OF THE YEAR

FIRST READING : Isaiah 35 : 4–7. Say to those who are of a fearful heart, "Be strong, fear not! Behold, your God will come with vengeance, with the recompense of God. He will come and save you." Then the eyes of the blind shall be opened, and the ears of the deaf unstopped; then shall the lame man leap like a hart, and the tongue of the dumb sing for joy. For waters shall break forth in the wilderness, and streams in the desert; the burning sand shall become a pool, and the thirsty ground springs of water.

EXPLANATION : These verses from the prophet Isaiah (750 B.C.) are read to us today because one of the blessings of the messianic age—the healing of the deaf and dumb—which the prophet foretells, is described as happening in today's Gospel reading. Isaiah, as in all his messianic prophecies, has also other promises of happiness which his fellow Israelites will enjoy, when the great day of the Messiah shall come.

say . . . heart : Yahweh, God, tells the prophet to encourage the downcast. The times were bad, sin had darkened the world, but :

behold . . . recompense : God will come and avenge the wrongs his faithful ones have suffered, and will reward them for their fidelity in face of oppression and opposition.

He will . . . you : More than temporal liberation from oppression is implied

here, as the messianic context demands. **eyes . . . deaf :** Although the Messiah did heal the deaf and the dumb, the blind and the lame, there is more implied here than mere bodily cures. Men would see God and listen to God's saving word. The bodily cures were but a sign of the spiritual renovation that the messianic age would bring.

lame . . . sing : Men would again walk in God's way and would sing his praises with a new heart.

waters . . . wilderness : This is another image of the messianic blessings. Water and streams in the desert would be a material blessing without parallel, but streams of spiritual gifts and graces are still greater blessings.

burning . . . ground : The same image continues. Only a traveler in a desert could fully appreciate what pools and streams of water could mean.

APPLICATION : God chose the descendants of Abraham (1800 B.C.) as the people to whom he would reveal himself and through whom he would preserve that revelation while preparing for the coming of his Son as man on earth. He selected human representatives from among them who, acting in his name, would direct their civic and spiritual activities, and so keep them faithful to the covenant he had made with them on Sinai. Moses, Joshua and the Judges were civic and spiritual leaders who regulated the Chosen People's lives for nearly two hundred years. Samuel (1040 B.C.), the last of the Judges, was more a spiritual than a civic leader. He was the first of the prophets—a line of men chosen by God to speak his "word" to his people. It was he, under God's orders, who anointed Saul as first king of the Israelites.

The monarchy survived as the political and civic director of the Chosen People, down to 721 B.C. in the schismatic north, and until the Babylonian exile (587) in Judah. God, however, continued to send his prophets for nearly two hundred years more. The monarchy had failed in the break-away north (Israel). But even in Judah the line of David came under pagan influence— with a few notable exceptions—and led many of their subjects away from God. For their part, the prophets were faithful to their vocation and it is to them, under God, that we owe it that a "remnant" of the Chosen People preserved the knowledge of the true God in Israel until the "fullness of time" had arrived—the age predetermined by God for the coming of Christ.

Isaiah, of the 8th century B.C., was one of the greatest of these mouthpieces of God. As well as strong words of condemnation for the evil practices of kings and people—words that were badly needed, he had also words of encouragement and consolation for the faithful among God's people—they were needed too. Many of those good people, because of the evil which was rampant around

them, were beginning to doubt if God would fulfill the promises he made to Abraham and his descendants (Gn. 12 : 1–3), promises repeated down through the centuries. Had God forgotten them because of the disloyalty of so many among them?

Today's excerpt from the prophet gives a definite no to these misgivings. "Behold your God will come with vengeance (for the wicked) with the recompense of God he will save you." He goes on then to describe some of the blessings that this coming of God would bring them : spiritual blessings described in the image of material ones. The religiously blind would see God (in Christ); the deaf would listen to God's word; the lame would walk freely in God's paths; the dumb would pronounce God's praises. What was desert land, as far as the knowledge of God was concerned, would become fertile and fruitful in God's cause, flowing with streams and fountains of good works.

Today, perhaps more than ever before, devout Christians may, like Isaiah's contemporaries, be beginning to wonder if God has lost interest in them. Not only has theoretical atheism spread like wildfire throughout the world, but practical atheism seems to be getting a grip on some within the stronghold of the Church of Christ. What is God doing about it? people are tempted to ask. The answer of Isaiah to his contemporaries is the same answer that God gives to all good Christians today. God will fulfill his promises to us as he fulfilled them for his Chosen People of old. This period of doubting, of questioning, of permissiveness, will pass. There will be casualties but his Church will come forth from this passing crisis strengthened and renewed. Many who were blind will again see the light of faith, others who had closed their ears will again listen to the eternal truths.

Heaven is God's plan for us. If we remain faithful and loyal to him and his laws during life, no matter what those about us think or say, heaven will be our eternal home. While we do our best then to prove our fidelity to God and to Christ, let us not forget to pray sincerely and often to our loving Father to send his light and grace to those of our fellow-exiles who have put themselves in grave danger of missing their destined goal.

SECOND READING: James 2:1-5. My brethren, show no partiality as you hold the faith of our Lord Jesus Christ, the Lord of glory. For if a man with gold rings and in fine clothing comes into your assembly, and a poor man in shabby clothing also comes in, and you pay attention to the one who wears the fine clothing and say, "Have a seat here, please," while you say to the poor man, "Stand there," or, "Sit at my feet," have you not made distinctions among yourselves, and become judges with evil thoughts? Listen, my beloved brethren. Has not God chosen those who are poor in the world to be rich in faith and heirs of the kingdom which he has promised to those who love him?

EXPLANATION: On St. James and this epistle, see previous Sunday. St. James is here stressing the truth that fraternal charity can make no distinction of persons. Earthly wealth or position are no criterion for distinction in the Christian community. All are equal before God and therefore all must be equal in their Christian intercourse whether at their Christian religious gatherings or in their daily dealings with one another.

no partiality ... Christ: As Christians there was no distinction between rich and poor; therefore, all true Christians, if they really held the faith of Christ, should hold all their brethren in the same esteem.

faith ... glory: Jesus Christ is the God-man. Of his divinity James has no doubt. The "man" Jesus Christ who walked on earth is now God (Lord is the same as God) in his eternal glory. He is the Lord of glory.

if a man ... rings: St. James now illustrates how this "respect for persons" can take place. The "rich"—the well-dressed, and the "poor"—the "man in shabby clothing," must not be treated differently. The pagans and the Jews did this. A Christian must not so act.

become ... thoughts: The real worth of a man is in his conscience—only God can judge it. The man who judges is usurping God's right and is sinning by so doing.

Listen ... brethren: James now exhorts his fellow-Christians to imitate God who made no distinction between men when giving the gift of faith and the means of salvation.

chosen ... world: In fact God has shown a preference for those poor in worldly goods, because they, rather than the rich, were among the first to accept Christ and Christianity.

rich ... kingdom: They are no longer

poor, they are rich in the true sense, they are princes "heirs of God's kingdom."

promised . . . him : True love of God is the only guarantee of true eternal wealth.

APPLICATION : The words we have read from St. James' letter could have been written to almost any Christian parish in the world of our day. Yet, they were written over nineteeen centuries ago. This simply proves that human nature, even in Christians, has not changed with the passing of the centuries. There are still Christians who are "respecters of persons" and there are still Christians who because of their worldly wealth or position expect and demand special respect for themselves. This would be wrong even in a purely secular society, but in the religious brotherhood of Christians it is sinful and an offense against God whose children we all are.

St. James tells his fellow-Christians that giving special honor to the Christian who wears gold rings and fine clothes, while humiliating the poor man in shabby clothing is to pass judgement with evil thoughts—that is, to judge not on the real merit of a man but on one's own false criteria. God alone is able and has the right to pass judgement on a man's merit as a Christian. The Christian who usurps this right of God is sinning. Furthermore, to base one's judgement on the false worldly criteria or wealth status—which is what the "respecter of persons" does—is doubly sinful : it is usurping God's right and is a false judgement.

There are few of us who cannot profit from a meditation on these words of St. James. First of all, far too many of us are inclined to claim special consideration and credit because of our personal gifts of mind or body or because of the personal position of power or wealth which we happen to have attained. To such of us, St. Paul puts a very pungent and deciding question : "What have you that you have not received? If then you received it all as a gift why take the credit to yourself?" (1 Cor. 4 : 7.) As regards our personal qualities of mind and body, we did not give them to ourselves, God it was who gave them to us. If we have used them well and profited by them, we must still thank God. If our neighbors did not get these gifts, we have no right to think less of them because of that—God may have given them unseen gifts which will be more profitable in the final reckoning.

As regards position and worldly wealth, we have less reason still to exalt ourselves. There is always the great question-mark as to how we got them! And granted that everything was honorable and above board in our acquisition of wealth or position : neither is really of lasting value. The millionaire, president, or king of a country will get the same size grave as the pauper. Monuments and laudatory inscriptions will not help the dead man one bit once he has left this life.

We owe all we are and have honestly acquired to the good God; let us never forget it. Instead, let us thank him all the days of our lives. He has a bigger and a far greater gift in store for us— eternal happiness; let us not lose that through the infantile folly of pride. All men are God's children, he cherishes them all equally—even those who refuse to recognize him. They may have abandoned him, but he will not abandon them until they have breathed their last. As members of his family who recognize all that he has done for us let us do all we can to bring his prodigal children back to him, and help them to appreciate who their true Benefactor is. Thus we shall prove our own gratitude to him and strive to earn his esteem, the only esteem that really matters. We shall not be tempted then to seek glory from men, nor shall we encourage those who, in their childish folly, seek honors or adulation from us.

GOSPEL: Mark 7:31-37. Jesus returned from the region of Tyre, and went through Sidon to the Sea of Galilee, through the region of the Decapolis. And they brought to him a man who was deaf and had an impediment in his speech; and they besought him to lay his hand upon him. And taking him aside from the multitude privately, he put his fingers into his ears, and he spat and touched his tongue; and looking up to heaven, he sighed, and said to him, "Ephphatha," that is, "Be opened." And his ears were opened, his tongue was released, and he spoke plainly. And he charged them to tell no one; but the more he charged them, the more zealously they proclaimed it. And they were astonished beyond measure, saying, "He has done all things well; he even makes the deaf hear and the dumb speak."

EXPLANATION: The healing of a deaf and dumb man in the pagan district of Decapolis, as well as the exorcism of the daughter of Syro-Phoenician (pagan) woman in Tyre (7:24-30), show that the Gentiles, too, were to partake of the messianic blessing. Mark, writing for Gentile converts, would naturally be anxious to stress this point. Although Jesus did not preach his message openly among the Gentiles—he offered salvation firstly to God's Chosen People—he instructed and commanded his disciples to "go out to the whole world; proclaim the good news to all creation" (Mk. 16:16). In today's miracle, one of several similar ones worked among the Chosen People, the fulfillment of the messianic prophecy in Christ is especially stressed. The utter amazement of the crowd is emphasized and their comment: "he has done all things well" probably refers to God's creative activity (Gn. 1:31: "God saw all he had made and it was very good"). So, Christ was introducing a *new* creation; while "making the deaf to hear and the dumb to speak" was a fulfillment of Isaiah 35:5-6 (today's first reading).

Tyre ... Decapolis: The route described is hard to explain, but St. Mark's geography may be at fault. What he was stressing was a tour in pagan districts, which had great importance for his Gentile readers.

deaf ... speech: Although the man was deaf, he could utter some indistinct words. The Greek word *mogilalos* occurs in the Bible only here and in Is. 35:6. It seems to indicate "indistinct speech" and Mark's remark that after his cure: "he spoke plainly," confirms this interpretation.

they besought him: These were the

friends of the unfortunate man—most likely pagans as the place is in the region of the Decapolis.

aside . . . multitude : It was part of Christ's intention to preserve the messianic secret, which he revealed to his disciples only—and even to them by slow degrees (see Mk. 1 : 34; 44; 3 : 12; 5 : 43; 7 : 36; 8 : 20; 9 : 9).

fingers . . . tongue : These were all part of the healing technique of contemporary wonder-workers. In Jesus' case they were sacramental gestures in that they effected what they symbolized, he "opened" the man's ears, he loosed his tongue.

looking . . . heaven : This was a sign of Christ's intimacy with his Father rather than a plea for a miracle. He worked his miracles by his own divine power, always with the approval of the Father.

Ephphatha : It's an Aramaic word which means "be opened." Christ gives a direct command to the impeded tongue. The result was immediate.

spoke plainly : As said above the man suffered from a serious impediment of speech rather than from complete dumbness. That impediment now left him.

tell no one : Even to his chosen disciples it was only gradually that Christ revealed his messiahship. He did not want the people whose messianic ideas were political to get excited and stir up rebellion against the Roman authorities.

the more . . . it : The crowd disobeyed him and spread the news of the miracles far and wide.

astonished . . . measure : St. Mark here emphasizes very strongly the effect that this miracle had on the crowd. They were pagans—Gentiles, for the most part —and Mark, writing for Gentile converts, was showing that other Gentiles had been most impressed by the miracle of Jesus. It is possible that there were other miracles performed there by Christ on this occasion, and that Mark gives only the one miracle which fulfilled to the letter Isaiah's messianic prophecy.

he has . . . well : This is probably a reference to the first creation : when God saw that all he had made was "good." The Jews among the crowd would have some knowledge of the story of Genesis. The "all things" would seem to imply more than one miracle. However, the people of the Decapolis, bordering as it did on Galilee, would most likely have heard of Christ's miracles performed there.

deaf . . . speak : The prophecy of Isaiah was fulfilled. The messianic age had come.

APPLICATION : During his discussion with the Samaritan woman at the well of Jacob, our Lord told her that "salvation was to come from the Jews" (Jn. 4 : 22). This was in accordance with God's plan when he took Abraham from his pagan family and surroundings, and elected him to be the father of a Chosen People from whom God's blessing would come for all nations (Gn. 12 : 1–4). This was the historic beginning of "salvation" for men. It was, as yet, a vague generic promise but down through the following eighteen-century history of the Chosen People (Abraham's descendants) this blessing eventually became crystallized in the Messiah—the anointed and holy one of God. It was he who would introduce the messianic age of which the prophets so often had spoken, and it was in him that all peoples, Jews and Gentiles, would find their true "blessing."

It was right and fitting, therefore, that Christ should proclaim his kingdom and his Gospel among the Jews and in their promised land. Those who would accept him and his message would later spread the good news among the Gentile nations. This is what happened. His Apostles, including St. Paul, and the faithful disciples having done their best for their fellow-Jews, left Palestine and carried the great news of the incarnation—a blessing greater than any man could have imagined—to the pagan peoples of the then-known world. It was surely from the Jews that salvation came to us Gentiles.

While Christ reserved his preaching to the Jews according to God's plan, he visited some of the Gentile lands bordering on Palestine—Tyre, Sidon, Phoenicia, the Decapolis—and worked some miracles there. However, he did not preach to them. This exception—going into pagan lands—was evidently important to St. Mark, for he goes into details in describing the faith of the people of the place who asked for a miracle, and their enthusiastic reaction to Christ's power when he did what they requested. Mark himself knew very well that Christ was fulfilling the divine plan when he restricted his preaching to the Jews, and that he had given a command to his Apostles to bring his Gospel to all nations (Mk. 16 : 16). Possibly, however, some of his Gentile converts were questioning why Christ had not come to the Gentiles but spent all his public life in Palestine. In this short episode, Mark shows that Christ was interested indeed in Gentiles and showed his compassion for them by working miracles for them.

We have much for which to thank God the Father, Christ and the good Jews who preached the Gospel to our ancestors. We should not think of questioning why Jesus spent his short public life trying to convert his fellow-Jews. God thought of us from all eternity— the incarnation was his way of giving a truly satisfying meaning to the life of man—the masterpiece and master of all his creation. It has given us a new status in life, a new purpose and an end worth every effort we can muster to gain. Life, with its trials and troubles and its brevity, has a meaning, a profound meaning, for Christians—it is a short period of preparation for the future which awaits us after death if we use it properly.

Christ who carried out his Father's will even unto the death on the cross, deserves our unending gratitude. Eternity will not be long enough for us to thank and praise him. If ever we are tempted to be in any way anti-semitic let us first remember those of God's Chosen People who preserved the knowledge of God and trust in his promises until the time of their fulfillment had come. Secondly, we must never forget the Apostles and disciples of Christ who devoted and gave their lives in order to bring the Christian faith to us. The best way to show appreciation of a gift is to use it fully and gratefully. Let us make full use of the divine gift of salvation by living according to its teaching all the days of our lives.

TWENTY-FOURTH SUNDAY OF THE YEAR

FIRST READING: Isaiah 50:5-9. The Lord God has opened my ear, and I was not rebellious, I turned not backward. I gave my back to the smiters, and my cheeks to those who pulled out the beard; I hid not my face from shame and spitting. For the Lord God helps me; therefore I have not been confounded; therefore I have set my face like a flint, and I know that I shall not be put to shame; he who vindicates me is near. Who will contend with me? Let us stand up together. Who is my adversary? Let him come near to me. Behold, the Lord God helps me; who will declare me guilty?

EXPLANATION: In second-Isaiah we have a series of prophetic poems which describe the future Messiah (Is. 40–55). He is depicted as the faithful Servant of God (Ebed Yahweh). He is chosen by God before his birth; he has the "spirit" of God; he will instruct the nations in God's "justice"; he will do more than merely restore Israel—he will be a light for all nations so that God's salvation may reach to the ends of the earth. Because he is God's faithful, obedient Servant he will suffer death in the execution of his duty, but God will reward him. God will bring him back to life and bestow on him numerous spiritual offspring (53:10-12). Part of the sufferings which the Servant endured are mentioned in today's reading: but for the incredible tortures the Servant voluntarily endured "for us" see 52:13–53:12.

Lord ... ear: The Servant is speaking; he says that the Lord has made him his disciple—he has opened his ear to learn the words of instruction.

I was not rebellious: The Servant was obedient in all things to God: "Thy will not mine be done."

I ... backward: He did not run away in the face of difficulty or danger.

my back ... smiters: He allows his enemies to maltreat him; he submits to their scourges.

pulled ... beard: This was one of the greatest insults offered a man, humiliating as well as painful.

shame and spitting: He does not try to avoid these humiliations, for:

the Lord ... me: He knows he is working for God and God is giving him aid to undergo them.

therefore ... flint: He will courageously face his sufferings and will not flinch from them.

not ... shame: All the enemies' calumnies will be in vain, his justice will shine forth. God his vindicator is with him.

contend . . . adversary : He is so certain of final success that he challenges his opponents to do their utmost.
who will . . . guilty : Knowing that he is God's faithful servant and carrying out God's will, who can convict him of any evil? His case is safe in God's hands.

APPLICATION : Five hundred and fifty years before Christ came on earth, a prophet whom we call the second-Isaiah encouraged the Jewish exiles in Babylon with his descriptions of the great blessings which the Messiah would bring them (see chapters 43 : 44; 47; 51; 52). These blessings would be bought at a great price, bought for us by the shame, humiliations and death of the future Messiah. The prophet calls the Messiah the Servant of God—a servant faithful and obedient unto death, and because of his perfect obedience and fidelity he would be raised from the grave in glory and be given numerous offspring. This suffering and obedient Servant was Christ. Christ himself applied these prophecies to himself (see today's Gospel : also Lk. 24 : 26 etc.). He fulfilled these prophecies to the letter, and he did so for us and for our salvation. Our Creed says : "Who (the Son of God) came down from heaven for us men and for our salvation . . . suffered under Pontius Pilate, was put to death and was buried. The third day he arose from the dead, ascended to heaven and sits at the right hand of the Father."

This reading has been chosen for us to recall to our minds all that Christ has done for us in carrying out the Father's plan for our eternal welfare. God does not need us, he has infinite perfection and happiness in the community of the Blessed Trinity, but because his nature is goodness itself, he wants to share his perfection and his happiness with us his creatures. For that reason he decreed the incarnation of his divine Son from all eternity. Because sin had entered the world and man had rebelled against God, Christ when he came met with opposition, disbelief and hatred from the leaders of those who had been prepared for centuries to receive him—the Chosen People. Thus his life among us was a life of humiliations, persecutions and opposition which culminated in the death on the cross. But faithful and obedient Servant of the Father that he was, he bore it all in patience and in submission even unto death; but death could not hold him. He was raised in glory and returned triumphant to heaven to reassume the glory of his divinity of which he had "emptied himself" while on earth, as St. Paul tells us. With his glorified human nature he now occupies the chief place in heaven after that of God the Father.

We all know what meaning for us the incarnation has and the humiliations and sufferings it implied for Christ. The crucifix over the altar, the stations of the cross, the sacrifice of the Mass recall to our minds what Christ has done for us; but do we always react as we should to this sacred remembrance? Our first reaction should be sincere acts of gratitude to our Father in heaven and to his divine Son, for going to such lengths to give us eternal life. Christ died so that we should live eternally; he stretched out his arms on the cross in order to gather all men to his Father in heaven. We can do something in return. It should be our second reaction to remembrance of what the incarnation means : we can bear our own daily crosses patiently and gladly, for compared to the cross of Christ they are light indeed. A third way of showing our appreciation of Christ's suffering for us is to help our neighbor to carry his cross. We can all, and we all should, if we appreciate what the incarnation means, help to spread its fruits as widely as possible. As true apostles of Christ's faith we need never fear of becoming apostates.

SECOND READING : James 2 : 14–18. What does it profit, my brethren, if a man says he has faith but has not works? Can his faith save him? If a brother or sister is ill-clad and in lack of daily food, and one of you says to them, "Go in peace, be warmed and filled," without giving them the things needed for the body, what does it profit? So faith by itself, if it has no works, is dead.

But some one will say, "You have faith and I have works." Show me your faith apart from your works, and I by my works will show you my faith.

EXPLANATION : Today's reading from St. James' letter is a continuation of the practical guidance we heard two Sundays ago. Christians must "be doers of the word not hearers only." The Christian faith is not a series of theoretical truths, but a practical way of living based on Christ's revelation to us.

faith . . . works : Faith alone, that is, a mental acceptance of all revealed truths, is of no avail toward eternal life unless a man follows Christ in his daily living. This will demand the carrying out of the spiritual and corporal works of mercy. St. James stresses the corporal works today.

ill-clad . . . food : He mentions two of the corporal works of mercy : to clothe the naked and feed the hungry. These two necessities cannot be supplied by a theoretical command : "go in peace, be warmed and filled"—that is all a Christian who has faith without good works does for his needy neighbor. What does this profit the unfortunate needy brother or sister? Nothing.

faith . . . dead : That kind of faith, therefore, is as good as dead, it produces no good effect. It does not carry out the Christian law of charity and so does not help the neighbor. Nor does it help the so-called Christian whose faith begins and ends in his own intellect.

some . . . say : The RSV reading here is obscure. The J.B. reads : "This is the way to talk to people of that kind : 'you say you have faith and I have good deeds. I will prove to you that I have faith by showing you my good deeds— now you prove to me that you have faith without any good deeds to show.' " The Christian who puts his faith into practice especially by works of charity toward a needy neighbor, proves that he is a true Christian. The man who claims to have the Christian faith but does not practice a most essential part of it—good deeds— is not really a Christian.

APPLICATION: A pagan can recite the Creed from beginning to end from: "I believe in God the Father almighty" down to: "life everlasting, Amen," but he cannot recite it sincerely and with conviction and remain a pagan. To say: "I believe in God" and do nothing whatsoever about it means that I am not stating the truth; I am lying, when I say: "I believe in God." The "Apostles' Creed" is a brief synopsis of the Christian religion. When a true Christian recites this Creed he is affirming the central truths of his religion, and at the same time accepting the consequences which flow from these truths. This is what St. James means when he says that Christians must be "doers of the word and not hearers only." They must, he says, put their Christian faith into practice. A Christian must live his faith as well as believe it.

There is no need to labor this point; all who are sincere Christians know this; but most, if not all, of us can profit from a look at our daily actions in the light of St. James' words today. Is our faith really alive? Does it produce "good works," works of charity toward our needy neighbors? If it does not it is "dead," it produces nothing in this life and it will produce nothing, no reward for us in the next. There are Christians whose Christian faith is completely self-centered, it begins and ends with themselves. They say their prayers; they attend their Sunday Mass; they avoid grave sins or think they do; but they exclude all other men from their thoughts; they are blind and deaf to any appeals for spiritual or material help from any neighbor or charitable cause. They will try to justify their behavior by saying that they have enough to do to look after their own bodily and spiritual needs. They act as if they never

heard that the spiritual and corporal works of mercy were an essential part of the Christian code. Such Christians are rare among us, thank God, but they are not "doers of the word," and will meet some questions on their judgement day to which they will have no answers.

However, before we clap ourselves on the back and say: "thank God, we are not like the other Christians," we would all do well to look again at our own fulfillment of the corporal and spiritual works of mercy. Are we really doing all that our Christian faith expects of us to help our needy neighbors? To keep to the two corporal works of mercy mentioned by St. James, let each one of us ask himself or herself: "What have I done to clothe the naked and feed the hungry during the past month?" There are ill-clad and hungry people in the ghettoes and slums of every city in our land. There are millions of such unfortunate people in Asia, Africa and South America. These are calling on us, and beseeching us to come to their aid. Associations to help them have been set up by charitable Christians and charitable non-Christians in all the Western nations. These good men and women moved by the spirit of Christ and the brotherhood of men, depend on you and me to continue their good work. How much have we given to suffering neighbors or to these associations?

There may be some among us today who are struggling hard to keep off the bread-line themselves—God will excuse them from giving a helping hand, when their two hands are tied by their own poverty. But there may be others who should and could help, but do not. To these I would say: Limit severely your luxuries in food, drink and clothing while there are millions of hungry and half-naked brothers of yours—adopted sons of God. God is appealing to your Christian heart and conscience today, through these words of St. James. To refuse to listen to his plea will be to risk your eternal salvation. Remember Christ's own description of the judgement scene : "He will say to those on his left hand, I was hungry and you gave me no food . . . I was naked and you did not clothe me . . . depart from me into the eternal fire prepared for the devil and his angels" (Mt. 24 : 42-45).

"Be doers of the word and not hearers only, deceiving yourselves."

GOSPEL : Mark 8 : 27-35. Jesus went with his disciples to the villages of Caesarea Philippi; and on the way he asked his disciples, "Who do men say that I am?" And they told him, "John the Baptist; and others say, Elijah; and others one of the prophets." And he asked them, "But who do you say that I am?" Peter answered him, "You are the Christ." And he charged them to tell no one about him.

And he began to teach them that the Son of man must suffer many things, and be rejected by the elders and the chief priests and the scribes, and be killed, and after three days rise again. And he said this plainly. And Peter took him, and began to rebuke him. But turning and seeing his disciples, he rebuked Peter, and said, "Get behind me, Satan! For you are not on the side of God, but of men."

And he called to him the multitude with his disciples, and said to them, "If any man would come after me, let him deny himself and take up his cross and follow me. For whoever would save his life will lose it; and whoever loses his life for my sake and the Gospel's will save it."

EXPLANATION : In today's Gospel, St. Mark gives us two incidents in our Lord's public mission—both are intimately connected. Jesus had gone to the north-eastern corner of Palestine and on questioning his disciples as to whom the people thought him to be, received the various conjectures of the people. He then asked the disciples what they themselves thought, and Peter, acting as spokesman for all of them, declared that Christ was the Messiah. Jesus admitted the truth of Peter's declaration, but said he did not yet want this knowledge to be spread abroad among the people. Then to dampen any wrong political messianic enthusiasm, which this knowledge might arouse among the disciples, he went on to give the first prophecy of the passion and death which awaited him at the hands of his enemies. Later he told the multitude, and the disciples, that anyone who would truly be his follower must be prepared to suffer and even lose his earthly life if necessary, in order to gain eternal life.

Caesarea Philippi : This was a town just on the border of the extreme north-eastern corner of Palestine. The Tetrarch Philip had rebuilt the town (already called after Caesar) and added his own name to distinguish it from another

Caesarea on the west coast of Palestine.
who . . . I am : After a year or more of preaching and miracles, he knew they were forming some idea as to who he was. They had various ideas.
John the Baptist : Some of the people who evidently had not seen John, thought Jesus was the Baptist risen from the dead. Herod, whose conscience bore the guilt of John's murder—in fear and trembling one would expect—agreed with this opinion (Mk. 6 : 14–16).
Elijah : This man was the great prophet of Israel (c 900–850 B.C.), who had been taken up to heaven according to legend, and who would return again to prepare the way for the Messiah (see Mal. 3 : 1–21; Jn. 1 : 21–25).
one . . . prophets : Others thought that he was one of the prophets who had preached God's law to their ancestors.
But . . . you say? : Up to now only the demons had recognized him as the Messiah. Now the Apostles, through their leader Peter, proclaim their belief in him as the promised Messiah.
to tell no one : Even though the disciples declared that he was the Messiah, they had no clear idea yet as to what it meant —the title had political undertones for them also. Therefore, Christ ordered them to remain silent about who he was until the crucifixion and resurrection would make everything clear to them. Then they could and would preach the full truth to others.
Son of man . . . suffer : Christ's first prediction of his passion was made in this context in order to correct any wrong ideas of the Messiah that the disciples were forming in their minds. He was not to reign on earth as a glorious, triumphant king. Rather, he was to suffer many things and finally be put to death. He was the Suffering Servant of God, foretold by Isaiah.

after . . . again : Eventually he would triumph. His enemies would have a momentary victory, they would torture him and condemn him to death, but death would not hold him; he would rise again after three days.
said this plainly : Although this announcement of his sufferings, death and resurrection was crystal clear, it did not really register with the disciples. How could he who had such power from God be put to death and how could a dead man rise?
Peter . . . him : Peter, as always the leader, would not hear of anyone putting his Master to death. Later, in the garden of Gethsemani, he drew a sword to prevent Jesus' arrest. He "rebuked" him, that is : he told Jesus he could not admit the prediction he had made.
Get . . . Satan : The original meaning of Satan was an adversary or opponent. Later, it became the name of the chief opponent of men's salvation.
not . . . God : Peter, by wishing to prevent Christ's suffering and death, was opposing God's plan as laid down in the prophets, especially in the prophecies of the second-Isaiah (40–55; see today's first reading). Peter and his companions had as yet only a very human outlook on God's purpose in sending the Messiah.
called . . . multitude : Mark now adds some of the dispositions his true followers must have.
deny himself : The true Christian life demands that one is ever ready to sacrifice one's own convenience and pleasure if the gospel law so demands.
take up his cross : This can be taken metaphorically as : following Jesus on the road of suffering. From the very beginning, the Christian Church saw the cross as the symbol of Christ's redemptive action—something every Christian should be ready to imitate.

save . . . lose it : The contradistinction here is between temporal, earthly life and eternal life hereafter. He who will give his life, if called on, for Jesus and his gospel will receive eternal life; while the man who gains a few extra years of life here on earth by denying Jesus and his gospel, will lose eternal life.

APPLICATION : We need not be surprised at the slowness of the Apostles in grasping the messiahship of Jesus. He did not want the crowds who flocked to him to know this until later—after his resurrection—because they had the idea that the Messiah would be a political leader who would set them free from their subjection to pagan Rome. It was not until this occasion, near Caesarea Philippi, somewhat over a year after he had called them, that he admitted to his Apostles that he was the Messiah. He charged them not to make this fact known outside of their own limited circle. To forestall and erase any wrong ideas of a political leader which some of the Apostles might have, he immediately foretold the sufferings and death he would have to endure at the hands of the leaders of the Jews. He would be conquered and humiliated by his enemies but their victory would be short-lived —death would not hold him—he would rise triumphant on the third day.

To the Apostles this seemed incredible and Peter, their spokesman, told him so. This outlook of the Apostles is also very understandable. They had seen him work many miracles, God was evidently very near to him : how could God let his enemies humiliate and kill him? They did not know God's plan, they were fishermen and knew little if anything of the Old Testament messianic prophecies. Had they read of the Suffering Servant in second-Isaiah they would not have disbelieved the prophecy of his forthcoming sufferings, death and resurrec-

tion. And his mention of his resurrection after three days, which would prove that it was he and not his enemies who conquered, fell on deaf ears, because the idea of a resurrection of that kind was incomprehensible to them. We know how slow they were to accept his resurrection even after it had happened.

Although the message was only vaguely and dubiously grasped, Christ had forewarned his Apostles (he repeated this twice later : Mk. 9 : 9–10; 31–32 and 10 : 32–34), so as to prepare them for the scandal of the cross. While it did not really prepare them because they were still too worldly-minded, it did help to strengthen their faith once the facts convinced them of the resurrection. They then realized that their beloved Master was more than Messiah, that he was in fact the Son of God, who with knowledge aforethought freely accepted his humiliations and shameful death for their sakes and ours. They gladly gave their lives to bringing this news of God's great love for men to all nations. From being a scandal the cross became the emblem and the proud standard of God's love for mankind.

We are in the happy position of the Apostles after the resurrection of Jesus. We know how much God loves us; we appreciate the humiliation that the incarnation brought on his beloved Son and the sufferings and cruel death which the sins of the world, ours included, brought on the Son of God. All of this took place because God wished to make us his adopted sons and worthy of the

N

inheritance he had planned for us. For a faithful and grateful Christian, however, theoretical appreciation is not enough. Atonement has been made for our sins, but we have still a very important part to play. Our sins can be forgiven but we must truly repent of them before God will forgive them.

St. Mark adds some words of Christ which illustrate what practical form our appreciation and gratitude for Christ's sufferings should take. We must be ready to follow him on the road to Calvary. We must deny ourselves—deprive ourselves not only of sinful pleasure or gain, but even of lawful things at times, in order to be Christ-like. We must take up our cross and follow him. This does not mean that we must search for crosses —there are plenty of them in any good Christian's life—but we must gladly accept the crosses life brings us and see in them God's means of keeping us close to him.

Life on earth is very short, eternal life is endless. No thinking man, and certainly no true Christian, would risk losing the eternal life for the sake of a few paltry gains or a few extra years here below.

TWENTY-FIFTH SUNDAY OF THE YEAR

FIRST READING: Wisdom 2:12; 17–20. The ungodly said to themselves: "Let us lie in wait for the righteous man, because he is inconvenient to us and opposes our actions; he reproaches us for sins against the law, and accuses us of sins against our training. Let us see if his words are true, and let us test what will happen at the end of his life; for if the righteous man is God's son, he will help him, and will deliver him from the hand of his adversaries. Let us test him with insult and torture, that we may find out how gentle he is, and make trial of his forbearance. Let us condemn him to a shameful death, for, according to what he says, he will be protected."

EXPLANATION: On the book of Wisdom, see the thirteenth Sunday of the year. Today's extract describes the "ungodly" as planning to torture some righteous, just man, because he has condemned their mode of living. These "ungodly," as appears from the context, were apostate Jews: there were many such in Egypt where the book of Wisdom was written, and they probably represented to the author the wicked in general. The "righteous," or just man as described here has much in common with the Suffering Servant of God—

depicted by Isaiah, especially in the fourth Servant Song: 52 : 13—53 : 12. The "ungodly" are going to put him and God to the test. Will God fulfill his promise and stand by his Servant?

lie . . . righteous : The ungodly plan to capture the just man.

inconvenient . . . actions : Their reasons are clear. The just man is an embarrassment to them, he condemns their evil deeds.

sins . . . law : He reproaches them for their abandonment of the Law and therefore of God.

sins . . . training : That is, their apostasy from the faith of their fathers.

Let . . . happen : They have heard the just man claim that God is his protector; that he is God's son; that he is very dear to God. They want to put this to the test; will God save him from his adversaries when the climax comes?

insult torture . . . he is : He has claimed to be meek and gentle; insults and tortures will test that meekness; will he bear these tortures and insults with patience and equanimity?

condemn . . . death : It is God whom they are now putting to the test. Will God save his just one from their clutches? They have planned to put this righteous man to a cruel and shameful death—will God save him from it? Naturally, they could see no other alternative.

APPLICATION : St. Augustine says : "corruptio optimi pessima"—the best when corrupted becomes the most corrupt. The Jews who abandoned the true God and his law became worse than the pagans who never knew God. They also became the most bitter opponents of the observant Jews. The same holds today: the Christian who abandons his faith, as a general rule becomes a bitter opponent of Christianity—the deserting soldier always condemns his army! When the book of Wisdom was written there were renegade Jews in Egypt, and elsewhere. They despised and hated the God-fearing Jews, because they reminded them of their own apostasy; they would do all in their power to humiliate and exterminate them. When they got one such Jew in their clutches they plotted to jeer at him and mock him saying : "he claimed to be a son of God, let us see if God will deliver him from (us) his adversaries." That this could have happened there can be no doubt, and it may be that it is of some such incident or incidents that the words of Wisdom are to be understood in their literal sense.

The similarity of the ideas here expressed with the fourth Song of the Suffering Servant in second-Isaiah (52–53), which refers to Christ are so close that most of the Fathers of the Church saw in these words a typical prophecy giving the reasons for, and the fact of, the sufferings and death of Christ. He was the perfect Jew *par excellence*. He was an inconvenience and embarrassment to the Scribes and Pharisees and opposed their actions. He reproached them for sins against the law and against the true tradition (see Mk. 7 : 1–23 and Gospel for 22nd Sunday). He claimed to be the Son of God : this was the principal charge made against him at his trial (Mk. 14 : 61–64). "Let us condemn him to a shameful death," they say, "he will be protected" (by God). While he hung on the cross the passers-by and the chief priests and Scribes jeered him also: "he puts his trust in God," they said: "now let God rescue him if he wants him." For he did say: "I am the Son of God" (Mt. 27 : 42–43).

While some loyal Jews may have suffered injury and maybe death at the hands of Jewish apostates in Egypt, the words of the author of Wisdom were certainly fulfilled to the letter in Christ, the true Son of God, the perfect loyal Jew. The opposition of the Scribes and Pharisees which was manifest all through his public life and which culminated on Calvary arose from their jealous pride. In their proud estimation of themselves they alone were the true sons of Abraham. They heartily despised the tax-gatherers, the uneducated in the law and human traditions, and those guilty of human failings. All of these were sinners to be avoided at any cost. Christ who came to save sinners associated freely with these people, thus openly "opposing the Pharisees' action"; hence their plotting and their final resolve to get rid of him. They thought they had succeeded on Good Friday but Easter Sunday proved how wrong they were. He was indeed the Son of God.

Our Lord warned his disciples, and through them all of us, to beware of the leaven—the pride—of the Pharisees. Of all sins pride is the most injurious to the sinner and the most offensive to God. It was the first human sin and the source of all other sins. There is an inclination to pride in all men so we must be on our guard against it. If we try to remember always that everything we are, and everything we have is from God this would remove any cause for pride. If, furthermore, we remember that we are Christians, followers of the humble Christ, we can hardly be tempted, must less yield to the temptation, to be proud; for a proud Christian is a contradiction in terms. If we are Christians we cannot be proud, if we are proud we are no longer Christians.

Let us ever strive to imitate, in our own way, him "whose state was divine, but who emptied himself of his divine glory to assume the condition of a slave . . . and, being as all men are, he was humbler yet even to accepting death, death on a cross" (Ph. 2 : 6–8). He, Christ, is our leader and model; let us strive daily to follow him.

SECOND READING : James 3 : 16–4 : 3. Where jealousy and selfish ambition exist, there will be disorder and every vile practice. But the wisdom from above is first pure, then peaceable, gentle, open to reason, full of mercy and good fruits, without uncertainty or insincerity. And the harvest of righteousness is sown in peace by those who make peace.

What causes wars, and what causes fightings among you? Is it not your passions that are at war in your members? You desire and do not have; so you kill. And you covet and cannot obtain; so you fight and wage war. You do not have, because you do not ask. You ask and do not receive, because you ask wrongly, to spend it on your passions.

EXPLANATION : St. James, whose whole epistle is one of practical advice to his fellow-Jewish converts on how to live their newly-found Christian faith, has some eminently practical points in today's lesson for all Christians of all races and ages. Christianity is synonymous with unselfishness; we are not individuals in opposition to one another, we are members of the one body co-operating for the good of that body. Between such members there can be no jealousy, no hatred, no fighting, no coveting. Each member will live in peace, in sincerity, in justice, in truthfulness, in active helpfulness with all the other members. This is the rule of life for true Christians.

jealousy . . . ambition : The basic violation of the Christian code is concentration on self to the exclusion of fellow-Christians and fellowmen. The Christian who wants his fellowmen to prosper will not be jealous if they should so prosper; but the Christian whose first thought is for himself and his own welfare is moved by unchristian selfish ambition which makes him forget, and eventually despise his neighbor.

wisdom from above : Selfishness is worldly wisdom in its worst sense, but the wisdom from God—which we have in the Christian law—brings to the man who lives according to it : peace, security, gentleness, sincerity, mercy for all and kind deeds.

those . . . peace : "Blessed are the peacemakers." Those who live according to the Christian code must be men of peace; peace is the fruit of their Christian unselfishness, and by their example and peace among men; and this Christian word they will spread this Christian peace is the nursery of all good works. of all righteousness.

what . . . fightings : St. James pinpoints the cause of all wars and fightings whether they be family feuds, village quarrels, or global confrontations. It is the sinful cupidity, the covetousness on the part of an individual of something which another person has and which he lacks : "You desire and do not have, so you kill."

you covet . . . war : If unchecked this sinful, selfish ambition will and does lead the individual or group to violations of "peace," to war and killing in order to fulfill the unlawful desires.

wrongly . . . passions : They do not seek in vain the necessities of life—such a seeking would be just and fair—but the satisfaction of their "passion," of their covetousness by which they allow themselves to be driven. Their prayer, if it can be called prayer, is unheard by God because their requests are sinful, unjust (see Mt. 7 : 7–11 on prayer).

APPLICATION : The gospel of Christ is a gospel which preaches peace and harmony between man and God, and between man and man. Christ, the Son of God, who took our human nature made all men adopted sons of God. All men are therefore members of the same family—the family of God. Therefore, they should reverence and honor God their Father at all times and they should respect and love one another as brothers, which they are. Above all others, Christians should put this gospel truth into practice among themselves and then among all men. They know, from Christ's own lips, that love of God and love of neighbor are the two basic essential commands of Christianity. The man who keeps these two commandments keeps the "whole law and the prophets"—the whole of revealed religion.

Had Christians done this down through the twenty centuries of Christianity what a different world ours would be today! The vast majority of the peoples of this earth would be Christians. It is a religion, in practice so divine, and yet so rationally human: God, loved and obeyed by a family united in love. This would have convinced all heathens and would have kept Christians closely united and made the rise of agnosticism and atheism impossible.

However, there were lax, half-hearted and selfish Christians in the Church from the very beginning. They were there already in St. James' day which was less than a generation after the death and resurrection of Christ. Because of jealousy and selfish ambition, there existed disorder and every vile practice among those Christians to whom he was writing. The jealous and selfish ones resented others for having certain worldly goods or positions—goods or positions they lawfully gained. Why, say the jealous ones, should we not have these benefits? Let us take them; hence followed "wars and fightings" among fellow-Christians. What a scandal for their pagan neighbors and what a violation of the basic Christian law!

Unfortunately, St. James' letter did not eradicate these human weaknesses from human nature. There have been and there will be jealous and selfish people and nations who envy the success of others and, as is often the case, successful but selfish people who do not want others to equal them. Our own century has witnessed two world wars on a scale never seen before, and for what reason? Was there a just side in these wars? History will have difficulty in finding it. It is not always the invader, or so-called aggressor, who starts the evil of war. Jealousies and selfish interests have aroused hatred and animosity for years before ever the first gun-fire is heard.

Our world was never so divided and so lacking in true Christian brotherhood as it is today. Too many are lacking the necessities of life, while the well-to-do are smothering, in excesses and luxuries, their humanity and any brotherly love they have. The wealthy nations, jealous, ambitious and afraid of each other's ambitions, are squandering on war machines wealth that could save millions from starvation and slavery. Not only are professed atheists but ex-Christians also, forgetful that God is their Father and therefore they can no longer see all men as their brothers.

This is a time when true Christians must try to make their voices heard above the din and noise of the warmongers, who will remain safely at home filling their coffers, when war comes to claim millions of innocent lives. We want peace not war; we want to live in charity and unity with all men, not in enmity and hatred. Let us begin at home, by our charity and brotherly love. Let us make our own neighborhood a haven of peace and happiness and let us pray God to fill the hearts of all men with the same Christian spirit.

GOSPEL : Mark 9 : 30–37. Jesus and his disciples passed through Galilee. And he would not have any one know it; for he was teaching his disciples, saying to them, "The Son of man will be delivered into the hands of men, and they will kill him; and when he is killed, after three days he will rise." But they did not understand the saying, and they were afraid to ask him.

And they came to Capernaum; and when he was in the house he asked them, "What were you discussing on the way?" But they were silent; for on the way they had discussed with one another who was the greatest. And he sat down and called the twelve; and he said to them, "If any one would be first, he must be last of all and servant of all." And he took a child, and put him in the midst of them; and taking him in his arms, he said to them, "Whoever receives one such child in my name receives me; and whoever receives me, receives not me but him who sent me."

EXPLANATION : In St. Mark's gospel for last Sunday, we read of the disciples' profession of faith in Jesus as the promised Messiah. Jesus then went on immediately to give them his first prophecy concerning his sufferings and death. Today's reading from St. Mark gives us Christ's second prediction of his passion, death and resurrection. Between the two predictions he had given Peter, James and John in the scene of the Transfiguration a glimpse of the glory that was to be his after the resurrection. The reason for this would appear to be to encourage the Apostles, through their leaders, to bear the "scandal" which his passion and death would be for them sometime in the near future. A third prediction of the passion is given by St. Mark in 10 : 32–34. Although there could scarcely be any doubt in the minds of the Apostles as to what Jesus meant, yet we know that they did not grasp his meaning. His arrest and death on the cross came as a shattering blow to them. There were two reasons for this : firstly, their belief in a Messiah, glorious on this earth, who would subdue all enemies; and secondly, they thought Jesus would use the marvelous powers he had from God, proved by his miracles, to defend himself against all enemies. Furthermore, Mark's gospel written long after the passion and death of Christ gave an emphasis and a lucidity to Christ's prophecies which they had not for the Apostles at the time he uttered them. It was seen in its proper perspective as part of God's plan for us.

went . . . mountain : Jesus and his disciples left the Mount of Transfiguration—Mount Thabor according to an ancient Christian tradition—and went through Galilee.

he was . . . disciples : He did not want the usual crowds to know of his whereabouts, because he was trying to impress on his disciples that it was necessary that he should be put to death, but that he would rise again from the dead.

not understand the saying : Because of the reasons mentioned above, their minds could not grasp the possibility of any enemy overcoming him. That this should be part of God's plan "for us men and for our salvation," they did not yet know.

were . . . ask him : They were either ashamed to admit their slowness of intellect, or afraid that he should spell out in explicit detail a truth they had not the heart to hear. There have always been, and there always will be people who refuse to hear an unwelcome forecast.

who was the greatest : This shows how worldly, how earthly-minded his disciples still were. They dismissed his disturbing prophecy very quickly, and became engaged in arguing which of themselves was the most important and who would hold the principal post in the earthly messianic kingdom which they still

expected him to set up. Later—29th Sunday of the year—we shall hear of James and John asking for the chief positions in his kingdom.

if anyone . . . first : Christ did not reprove them for their worldliness; he knew their hearts, but he told them his kingdom would be one of service. The higher one's position was in it the more would he have to be the servant of others.

child . . . them : He made the child a symbol of his followers—they were as "little ones," as he said later in 9 : 42.

receives ... my name : Whoever accepts his disciples and followers and listens to their message, will be accepting Christ himself—and not only Christ :

but him who sent me : He would be accepting his Father who sent him on earth. Matthew, Luke and John express this saying more explicitly "anyone who welcomes you welcomes me, and those who welcome me welcome the one who sent me" (Mt. 10 : 40 see Lk. 10 : 16; Jn. 13 : 20).

APPLICATION : The Apostles were still very worldly-minded, they were full of the hope that Christ would establish an earthly messianic kingdom, that he would not only free their holy land from the hated pagan rulers but that he would set up a worldwide empire for the people of God. Many of the messianic prophecies of the Old Testament spoke of a worldwide kingdom; all nations would submit to the descendant of David; Jerusalem would be the magnet which would attract all peoples. The prophets, however, were speaking of the true messianic kingdom, the spiritual kingdom that Christ would establish. The Apostles were as yet unable to see

the true meaning of these prophecies. They took them as referring to a worldly kingdom. They had come to believe that Christ was the promised Messiah, therefore he would overcome all enemies and all opposition and set up this kingdom. How, therefore, could his enemies overpower him much less put him to death before he had accomplished his task? Thus they refused to believe his prophecies concerning his coming tortures and death.

Now, either in trying to understand what he had so plainly told them, or maybe in putting this disturbing thought far from their minds, they began disputing with one another as to which of them would have the highest post of honor in the earthly messianic kingdom which they had envisaged. How worldly but how human they were! We must not forget though, that they were not yet forget though that they were not yet were not yet really Christians—they needed the death and resurrection of Christ to make them what they became —his true followers and loyal disciples.

There was in the unformed Apostles a desire to turn Christ's kingdom into an earthly welfare state, rather than into a preparation for heaven? All Christians know that Christ suffered and died for their salvation, and that he asked his followers to take up their cross and follow him if they wished to be his disciples. The first generations of Christians fully understood this and faithfully followed him even to martyrdom. However, as time went on and opposition to the Christian faith disappeared, so too did the zeal and fervor of many Christians. For centuries we have had nominal Christians in Christ's Church : men and women who tried to make their paradise in this world, and forgot the everlasting heaven.

Our own age has seen an unprecedented increase in this falling away of Christians. Leaving aside the parts of Europe which are professedly atheist— but where in spite of the leaders there are many sincere and devout Christians —the number of lapsed and nominal Christians in the other Western countries is frightening. These non-practicing Christians, unwilling to carry their crosses, have decided to make this earth their paradise. They want prosperity, comfort and happiness in this world. The vast majority of them, of course, refuse to look to the future; it could be an unpleasant thought, yet they must see that in every town and village there is a mortician, an undertaker who makes a good living disposing of human "remains." Die they must; "and what then?" should be a question which overshadows their lives.

Many of these people who in practice have abandoned Christianity, try to salve their consciences by devoting any time they can spare to making this planet a better place in which to live. It is an excellent aim with a possibility of success—if the Fatherhood of God and the true brotherhood of man are upheld. But otherwise its a vain Utopia. If God, and Christ's teaching are left out of our reckoning, we shall ever have jealousies, enmities, hatred and wars. Christians have made war on Christians because neither side in the struggle was truly Christian. What chance then has the world when Christ and Christianity are banished from it?

Today's thought for each one of us is this : Christ became man, suffered and died as man, for our sakes. By his resurrection he conquered death and opened heaven for us. Heaven is our true destiny. Loving God and our neighbor and carrying our cross is the only way to reach heaven. Forget this "heaven on earth" doctrine; it does not and never will exist! Accept Christ and you are accepting the Father who sent him. He in turn will accept you.

TWENTY-SIXTH SUNDAY OF THE YEAR

FIRST READING: Numbers 11:25-29. The Lord came down in the cloud and spoke to him, and took some of the spirit that was upon him and put it upon the seventy elders; and when the spirit rested upon them, they prophesied. But they did so no more.

Now two men remained in the camp, one named Eldad, and the other named Medad, and the spirit rested upon them; they were among those registered, but they had not gone out to the tent, and so they prophesied in the camp. And a young man ran and told Moses, "Eldad and Medad are prophesying in the camp." And Joshua the son of Nun, the minister of Moses, one of his chosen men, said, "My lord Moses, forbid them." But Moses said to him, "Are you jealous for my sake? Would that all the Lord's people were prophets, that the Lord would put his spirit upon them!"

EXPLANATION: Moses, appointed by God to lead the Israelites out of Egypt, found this task more difficult as time went on. Three days after setting out from Mount Sinai—where they had spent some years and notwithstanding that God had provided them with water and food in the form of manna, the people "set up a lament that was offensive to Yahweh's ears." They blamed God for bringing them out of Egypt, where they had fish to eat as well as melons, onions and garlic; here in this desert they had none of these things— only the monotonous manna! Moses appealed to God saying he alone was unable to manage such a mass of people. God heard his plea and told him to select seventy elders—experienced men from among the tribes, whom God would appoint as leaders of the people under Moses. Moses selected the seventy men and brought them to the tent of Yahweh. There God gave them part of the spirit of Moses and they began to prophesy—a sign to the people that God had appointed them as his representatives.

At the same moment, two other men who had not come to the tent of Yahweh received the spirit from God and began to prophesy. Joshua, who was Moses's right-hand man and later his successor, objected to these two receiving the free gift from God. He wanted Moses to prevent them from speaking in God's name, but Moses would not—the more believers who had the spirit of God among the people the better it would be for all, was his answer. His task would be so easy: "if only the whole people of Yahweh were prophets."

Lord ... cloud : This was God's way of manifesting his presence in his special tent or tabernacle.

upon the seventy elders : They were given some of the spirit—the power and grace which God had given to Moses in Egypt, so that they would assist Moses in ruling and directing the people.

did so no more : They immediately spoke as God's representatives, perhaps with great religious enthusiasm, ecstasy, chanting and dancing as in 1 Sm. 10 : 11 and 19 : 20–24, but these external signs were no longer necessary once the people knew that they were God's representatives.

Eldad ... Medad : These two men were among the seventy selected by Moses but for some reason—perhaps they felt themselves unworthy of this honor?— they did not come to the tent of Yahweh. However, this did not prevent Yahweh from giving them his spirit.

Joshua : This loyal helper of Moses must have felt that getting the spirit of prophecy, while apparently disobeying Moses by not coming to the tent, they would be in some way in opposition to him, instead of being his helpers.

jealous ... sake : Moses had no such fears. He looked upon Eldad and Medad as his helpers and wished he had more.

APPLICATION : The close personal interest of God in his Chosen People— not only when bringing them from Egypt to Canaan, but all through their history— must strike even a casual reader of the Old Testament. He was a true Father to them, even though more often than not they proved themselves to be unworthy children. At times he had to chastize them as has any true father to chastize the children he loves, but his anger against them never lasted long. His constant aim was to make of them a loving and obedient family. In the desert, on their journey from Egypt to Canaan, he provided for their bodily and spiritual needs; while in Canaan he helped them to overcome their enemies and establish themselves in the land he had promised their patriarchs; and through his prophets he tried to protect them from the idolatrous practices of their pagan neighbors.

If one had read only the Old Testament story, and had never heard of the New Testament, one would surely find it difficult to understand why God—the God of the universe and of all nations— gave so much of his loving care to this one nation, while practically excluding all others. Such a reader would be like a man who read only the preface to a book while omitting the book itself. The Old Testament is in fact an introduction, a preface to the story of God's real love for *all men*. God picked Abraham and his descendants to prepare the way for the coming of his Son as man, in order to make all men sons of God and candidates for heaven. While favoring the Israelites then, he was preparing a far greater favor for all nations—he had not forgotten or neglected them. Through the Israelites they would receive the blessings he had planned from all eternity for the whole human race.

The incident described in today's reading shows God's interest in the temporal and spiritual welfare of the Chosen People in their desert wanderings. It is also a foreshadowing of the power of the Spirit which Christ would give to the new Chosen People—the Church, for its spiritual government and guidance. Moses and his assistants were types of Peter and the other Apostles. They and their successors would do for the Church of Christ what Moses and his helpers did for the Israelites—they would teach and guide it on the way of truth, they would lead it on its journey through this life to the gates of eternity.

The scene in Jerusalem on the first Pentecost day, when the Holy Spirit descended with visible signs and effects on the Apostles, was a replica of what happened in the desert to the Chosen People after they had left Mount Sinai; but the Jerusalem event had a meaning and a value which would extend through all time into eternity. The Church was to be taught the full knowledge of God as seen in the incarnation. It was to be taught the true destination of man. That destination was not Canaan or any other earthly kingdom, but unending life in God's kingdom. The Church was to be taught how to reach that goal. Peter and his assistants were given all the necessary helps which the members of the Church would need for their spiritual life.

God was good to the Israelites and near to them; he is much nearer to us and greater are the divine gifts he has given us. He did not visit us in a cloud, he came in the person of his divine Son and lived among us. That divine Son suffered torments and death in his human nature so that we could live forever. He founded for us a Church, a living institution in which we have all the helps we need, including infallible guidance, when necessary, from the leaders he has appointed for us. They are the successors of Peter and the Apostles. While we live loyally in the Church, striving in all sincerity to carry out its laws, we need have no fear for our eventual salvation.

Among the Israelites were some who resisted the authority of Moses and his assistants even though God had given his spirit to them. In Christ's Church also are some who challenge the authority of the divinely appointed leaders—the successors of Peter and the Apostles; the disobedient Israelites died in the desert, they did not see nor enter the Promised Land.

SECOND READING: James 5:1-6. Come now, you rich, weep and howl for the miseries that are coming upon you. Your riches have rotted and your garments are moth-eaten. Your gold and silver have rusted, and their rust will be evidence against you and will eat your flesh like fire. You have laid up treasure for the last days. Behold the wages of the laborers who mowed your fields, which you kept back by fraud, cry out; and the cries of the harvester have reached the ears of the Lord of hosts. You have lived on the earth in luxury and in pleasure; you have fattened your hearts in a day of slaughter. You have condemned, you have killed the righteous man: he does not resist you.

EXPLANATION: In these six verses from St. James' epistle, we have a very vivid description and strong denuncia- tion of the unscrupulous rich. While de- priving their workmen of their justly earned wages they have "fattened their hearts" on what did not belong to them. Worse still, because of the position of power which their ill-gotten gains secured for them, they are responsible for the deaths of innocent people. However, when they come to judgement the treasures they have laid up will be used as evidence against them and will bring their eternal condemnation.

weep . . . miseries : St. James tells them that miseries are coming on them which will make them weep and howl but not with repentance.

riches . . . garments : In antiquity, costly garments were usually the external signs of riches. However, both the riches and the garments will come to nothing very soon. St. James sees this already as having happened so he uses the prophetic perfect tense—so common in the prophets.

evidence against you : On the "dies illa," the day of wrath, this wealth or their ill-use of it, and the evil way it was amassed, will give testimony of their wickedness to the examining Judge. It will cause them to be condemned to "Gehenna," the place of torment and burning—according to the apocalyptic language of that time.

treasure . . . days : They have wasted their time collecting earthly treasures which will have no value on the judgement day—the day of the coming of the Lord as Judge, which was then expected at any moment.

wages of the laborers : This was one of the worst crimes that could be committed and one that cried to heaven for justice.

luxury and in pleasure : They had made this short life their heaven—getting every personal pleasure and selfish satisfaction out of it.

in a day of slaughter : Copying the image of Jeremiah (12 : 13), he says the unjust rich have prepared themselves as sheep are fattened for butchering, for the day of slaughter, or judgement day.

condemned . . . killed : The unscrupulous rich in the ancient world not only deprived laborers of their just wages, thus condemning them to starvation, but often they had the righteous man condemned to death—just because he was righteous and his way of living made their consciences uneasy.

APPLICATION : The unscrupulous rich to whom St. James is referring most likely were not Christians. He is, nevertheless, warning all Christians to beware of the danger of concentrating on the accumulation of earthly wealth, especially if that wealth is acquired through injustice to the poor and helpless who labor for them. At the same time, he is consoling his fellow-Christians who are suffering and are without hope of redress at the hands of the unscrupulous ones. The sufferings of the Christians will bring them an eternal reward, while the wealth collected by the rich will be as additional instruments in the punishment which judgement so very soon will inflict on them.

There is a reminder for all of us in these words of St. James. We have not here a lasting city; our purpose in life is not to collect the goods of this world in order to spend our years in luxury and pleasure, but to use this world as a stepping-stone toward our real goal in the life hereafter. Unfortunately, this earth with its wealth and pleasures, has a certain attraction for all of us. For some they become so alluring that they obscure, and sometimes exclude, the real purpose of life. While far from approving of this foolish mentality, we can nevertheless understand it. We are creatures of this earth, our life began here and here it would all have ended if God in his goodness had not planned otherwise. If this earth were the sole stage on which our life's drama was to run its course, then any sane man would try to get all he could out of this life. If death were the end, then surely we should try to pack all the pleasure and luxury possible into our few years on earth.

As Christians we know the true purpose of our life on earth. We know God's loving plan for us. An eternity of happiness awaits us after death, if we live according to the rules he has laid down for us. With such a future awaiting us, God is not asking too much of us when he demands of us to be relatively detached from the things of earth. "Relatively," we say, because we may acquire within reason the goods of this world according to our needs, and we may enjoy the pleasures of this life that are according to our state in life, not against the commandments.

For many the difficulty is to control "within reason" the acquisition of worldly goods and to see that these goods are acquired within the laws of justice. Today, in our Western world, because of the solidarity of laborers through their unions and associations, it is not quite so easy for employers to deprive their employees of just wages. What is often forgotten, however, is that the employees can and do at times act unjustly by failing, through idleness and unjustified abstention from work, to earn the wages given them. The worker, as well as the employer, is bound by the laws of justice.

It is perhaps in the underdeveloped countries today that the words of St. James are still literally fulfilled. There the unscrupulous are amassing wealth at the expense, and by the exploitation, of the poor and helpless natives. To our shame, many of these oppressors of the poor are Christian at least in name, but they have forgotten Christian justice and their true purpose in life. As individuals, we cannot do much to right such shameful wrongs, but there are groups formed or being formed in the Western world to promote world justice and peace; by joining such groups and helping them financially, if possible, we can do much to stop such seriously sinful violations of the Christian code and the code of simple human justice.

Today, let us examine our consciences in relation to this world's goods. Are we acquiring more than we need? Are we acquiring these goods justly? If we are employers: are we paying our workers a just wage? Are we treating them as fellowmen, fellow-Christians, fellow-travelers to heaven? If we are employees: are we earning justly the wages we collect? Have we an interest in our employer's business and property? Do we act justly toward all our fellow-workers? If each of us can answer "yes" to our questions we are laying up "treasure for ourselves in heaven where neither moth nor woodworm destroy them nor can thieves break in and steal them" (Mt. 6 : 21).

GOSPEL: Mark 9 : 38–43; 45; 47–48. John said to Jesus, "Teacher, we saw a man casting out demons in your name, and we forbade him, because he was not following us." But Jesus said, "Do not forbid him; for no one who does a mighty work in my name will be able soon after to speak evil of me. For he that is not against us is for us. For truly, I say to you, whoever gives you a cup of water to drink because you bear the name of Christ, will by no means lose his reward.

"Whoever causes one of these little ones who believe in me to sin, it would be better for him if a great millstone were hung round his neck and he were thrown into the sea. And if your hand causes you to sin, cut it off; it is better for you to enter life maimed than with two hands to go to hell, to the unquenchable fire. And if your foot causes you to sin, cut it off; it is better for you to enter life lame than with two feet to be thrown into hell. And if your eye causes you to sin, pluck it out; it is better for you to enter the kingdom of God with one eye than with two eyes to be thrown into hell, where their worm does not die, and the fire is not quenched."

EXPLANATION: In today's excerpt from St. Mark we have the incident of the exorcist who was not a follower of Jesus. The Apostles did not approve of this man, but Jesus said to let him be for "he that is not against us is for us"; the power of exorcism was from God. Mark then adds a collection of sayings on charity, avoiding scandal and the necessity of giving up what is most dear to us in life if it impedes us from entering eternal life.

casting . . . name: Although not as yet a follower of Jesus, the man was exorcizing, casting out demons in the name, that is, by the power of Jesus. John, one of the Apostles, thought this was wrong, that this exorcist was usurping power which was not his, but Jesus did not agree with this interpretation.

mighty . . . name: Any man who has this power, has it from God and therefore he is not an opponent of Christ; he will not be able to speak evil, condemn the activity of Jesus.

cup . . . Christ: Even a much smaller act of kindness than that of exorcism done to a fellowman because of Christ will have its heavenly reward—and a non-Christian could perform such an act.

causes . . . sin: Anyone who weakens the faith of Christ's followers, his "little ones" (see last Sunday's Gospel), would be better off if he had been drowned before he committed this sin of scandal. A shortening of one's earthly life is of little importance when compared with the loss of one's eternal life.

hand . . . eye: Not only must one avoid scandal—causing others to sin—but each true follower of Christ must be ready to sacrifice what is nearest and dearest to him rather than commit a personal sin. The cutting off of one's foot or hand or the plucking out of one's eye is not to be taken literally; this is a metaphorical way of stressing and indelibly impressing upon us that the kingdom of God, the future eternal life, is worth any sacrifice (see the parables of the pearl of great price and the hidden treasure). The thought here in terms of sacrificing part of the body rather than losing the whole life is similar to the idea expressed in

Mark 8 : 34 ff, under the images of taking up one's cross and of dying in order to live.

thrown . . . hell: Gehenna—the word is translated: "hell," was a valley west of Jerusalem which was, at the time of Christ, the refuse dump for the city. This explains the imagery of "the worm" —the maggots eating the offal; and the "fire" which was perpetually smouldering for the destruction of the refuse.

APPLICATION: There are two very practical lessons we must learn from today's Gospel: the grave obligation we have of not causing scandal to our fellow-Christians or indeed to any man or woman and secondly, the willingness we should have to sacrifice any earthly possession which is a cause of sin to us.

Scandal, the sin of being a cause or an occasion of another's sin, is doubly sinful involving one's own sin and the sin of the person scandalized. Scandal can be caused by word—that is, by teaching or propagating wrong doctrine or by giving sinful advice, and it can be caused by one's own sinful deeds which may be imitated by others. Those in positions of authority such as parents whose duty it is to bring up their children in the Christian faith, are especially liable to give scandal if they fail to live truly Christian lives. Christian parents who fail to live according to their faith will be held accountable not only for their own sins, but for the sins of their children and perhaps their children's children for generations to come.

Much, if not all of today's moral laxity and permissiveness can be blamed on parents who have failed to give the example of true Christian living in the home and in dealings with their neighbors. To children of such parents, Christianity is only a label; it does not inform or inspire their lives, hence they are only nominal Christians. It is true that there may be "black sheep" in the best of Christian homes. When, however, all the children of a home are "black sheep" the whiteness, the sincerity, of the parents of such a home must certainly be called into question. There may be many bad influences at work outside the home but the good example of truly Christian parents can counteract these influences. Let parents see to it that they will not be a cause of scandal and a cause of eternal loss to the children God put into their charge.

The second lesson for all of us in today's Gospel is that we should ever realize that eternal life is worth any sacrifice which we may be called on to make. The road we have to travel in life is not an easy one. As our Lord says in another place: "Enter by the narrow gate for the gate is wide and the way is easy that leads to destruction, and those who enter by it are many. But the gate is narrow and the way is hard that leads to life, and those who find it are few" (Mt. 7 : 13). We wish to reach heaven, therefore we must be prepared to follow Christ; we must not allow others to lead us astray but be prepared and determined to conquer and resist our own evil inclinations also.

The world and our own human nature will put many obstacles in our way. For that reason God gave us the Ten Commandments which spell out for us what we are to avoid and what we are to do if we wish to have eternal life. For many, keeping these commandments is no easy task—they make severe demands at times, but our Lord makes it crystal clear that we must endure the hardship because the prize, the reward, is everlasting happiness. When he said that we must be ready to deprive ourselves of a foot or a hand or an eye if they should be obstacles to us, he was speaking metaphorically: to stress that we must be ready if necessary to give up what is nearest and dearest to our nature. The less of earthly luggage we carry with us and the less of earthly attachments we give way to, the easier and safer will be our journey.

TWENTY-SEVENTH SUNDAY OF THE YEAR

FIRST READING: Genesis 2 : 18–24. The Lord God said, "It is not good that the man should be alone; I will make him a helper fit for him." So out of the ground the Lord God formed every beast of the field and every bird of the air, and brought them to the man to see what he would call them; and whatever the man called every living creature, that was its name. The man gave names to all cattle, and to the birds of the air, and to every beast of the field; but for the man there was not found a helper fit for him. So the Lord God caused a deep sleep to fall upon the man, and while he slept took one of his ribs and closed up its place with flesh; and the rib which the Lord God had taken from the man he made into a woman and brought her to the man. Then the man said, "This at last is bone of my bones and flesh of my flesh; she shall be called Woman, because she was taken out of Man." Therefore a man leaves his father and his mother and cleaves to his wife, and they become one flesh.

EXPLANATION: As the Gospel of today deals with the question of divorce, the reading from the Old Testament deals with the institution of marriage and shows that monogamy was God's rule from the very beginning. This section of Genesis dealing with the special creation of man and woman, the Fall and its effects, is from the Yahwistic author, one of the four sources which go together to make up the first five books of the Bible. The basic facts: creation of all things by God, the superiority of man over all other creatures because of the special gifts God gave him, the equality of woman with man—one complementing the other, their life-long union in monogamous marriage are historical truths; the details are not of the essence of the story.

that man . . . alone: If God did not express this true dictum he proved its truth by creating among all living species male and female, so that by their union they would continue to reproduce their species. He did the same for the human species.

helper fit for him: The author begins to stress the equality of the sexes. At the time he was writing (10th century B.C.), and for centuries before that, woman was looked on as an inferior being when compared with man. Polygamy and divorce had done much to introduce this wrong concept of woman.

out of the ground: All animals, birds and fishes came from the soil under God's direction.

what he would call them: To name a thing in the ancient days was to show one's mastery over it. By naming the animals, the man showed that he was their master; this was God's intention (see Gn. 1 : 26).

for the man . . . helper: None of these inferior creatures was fit to be man's helper.

so the Lord God: The author now gives a poetic description of the creation of woman—the details are added to stress not only that woman is equal to man, as was none of the other creatures, but that she is actually a part of him.

bone of my bone: These poetic words are put in the mouth of the man on seeing the first woman. Human nature is still much the same, today's young man calls the girl he loves his sweet-*heart;* she is part of his innermost self.

woman . . . man: This is a play on words in Hebrew which, of course, was not the language spoken by the first man or men. Man is *Ish* in Hebrew, woman *Ishah*—but the unity of the nature of man and woman is stressed.

cleaves to his wife: Here is the climax of the story. A man will leave his own home, his parents, to form a new home with his chosen wife (not wives). They will become one flesh for life. The indissolubility and the unity of marriage was the rule from the beginning.

APPLICATION: Although polygamy, that is one man with many wives, and divorce were widely practiced not alone among their pagan neighbors but also among the Israelites themselves. When the Yahwistic writer composed this source of Genesis, the author courageously expressed the will and intention of God in this regard. God intended woman to be man's helper and mate for life; she was not his slave or chattel. She was his equal and had a right to be treated as an equal. One of the many evil effects of polygamy and divorce was and is the lowering of the status of woman. Where polygamy is practiced, each wife is but a special slave in the household. She is a chattel which her lord can use when it suits him, but she has no claim on him. However, that one evil has disappeared "officially" from our Western world, but the worse evil of divorce, instead of disappearing, is on the increase.

Here again it is the woman who is humiliated, and sad to say there are women who agree to and encourage this humiliation of their own sex. Apart from the humiliation of woman there is a worse effect of divorce—it is a violation of God's law, as is clearly revealed to us in the text from Genesis that we have read; this text is again confirmed by Christ in today's Gospel. God created human nature in two sexes so that one would be a complement of the other and together they were given the power to reproduce themselves and thus continue the human race on earth. To do this—to procreate children and to educate them, is a life-long task and demands the greatest cooperation between husband and wife. Their task is no easy one, difficulties and differences of opinion can and do often arise; but it was God himself who gave married couples this vocation and with it he gives many consolations and moments of deep happiness and contentment as well.

Added to these divine blessings and to fulfill their duties, Christians have the graces of the sacrament which Christ instituted to help those who marry. Not only is their union blessed by God on the day of their marriage but the grace of the sacrament remains with them to aid them all through their married lives. Yet, there are many Christian nations today which have made laws permitting the dissolution of a valid marriage, and there are Christians who avail themselves of this legal loophole to get rid of the partner they took for life. They often enter a new matrimonial bond which not only has not the blessing of God but is directly against his will—as revealed in both the Old and New Testaments.

The nations who have passed this law which directly contravenes the law of the Creator, and the people who avail themselves of such a law are Christian only in name. Their outlook is purely and exclusively worldly, selfishness plays a leading part in their decision. They feel that all crosses must be removed from their paths, they do not wish to climb any Calvary.

Alone among the Christian communities the Catholic Church has stood firm against the violation of God's law in this matter of divorce, and firm, please God, it will continue to stand. Even among Catholics today, there are isolated voices raised here and there in favor of a relaxation of the indissolubility of marriage. The reasons they bring forward are humane—or is it humanist? They know of husbands and wives who are incompatible with each other, who are continually quarreling; would they not be better off materially and spiritually if they were separated? They can be separated, for the Church allows separation where things have become well-nigh impossible, and they may remain apart until peace descends once more upon them, as it often does.

However, this is not what our advocates of a relaxation of the laws of marriage want. They would go as far as allowing the separated partners to undertake a new union wherein they would each find a new happiness. Would they find that happiness? The history of the past few decades in the nations where the civil power allows divorce, with remarriage, would seem to prove the opposite. No, the Christian who violates the law of God for his own selfish happiness is not likely to get happiness in a new marriage venture nor can he hope to earn eternal happiness.

To our faithful husbands and wives I would say: continue in your fidelity. You have many trials and troubles, but they are the new crosses that will raise you up and keep you near God. Be quick to forgive and ever ready to forget. Even though one may be right in a row, let one not be too proud to be first to break the ice and reopen relations. Your marriage partner may not be an angel, but he or she is a saint in the making, and you are doing your part to make him or her just that. You, too, are on the road to heaven; you will kick some hard stones and hurt your toes many times during your journey, but when you see your reward you will realize how little you have done and how unprofitable a servant you have been.

SECOND READING: Hebrews 2:9-11. We see Jesus, who for a little while was made lower than the angels, crowned with glory and honor because of the suffering of death, so that by the grace of God he might taste death for every one.

For it was fitting that he, for whom and by whom all things exist, in bringing many sons to glory, should make the pioneer of their salvation perfect through suffering. For he who sanctifies and those who are sanctified have all one origin. That is why he is not ashamed to call them brethren.

EXPLANATION: On the Epistle to the Hebrews, see the fifth Sunday of Lent. In today's verses from this epistle, the writer who has been extolling the greatness of the incarnate Son of God "who is the radiant light of God's glory" and "who sustains the universe by his powerful command" and is "far above the angels" (1:1-4), now mentions the temporary humiliation Christ suffered in his humanity. But this was only temporary; he was again raised from death and crowned with glory and honor. It was God's wise decree that the Savior of all men should be made perfect in suffering and thus be the perfect "pioneer of salvation." He took our human nature and thus we are of the same human stock as he, and so he can call us his brothers.

was made . . . angels: He became man; therefore, in his human nature while on earth, he was lower than the angels.

we see . . . honor: After he had suffered torments and death for us he was raised in glory. He entered heaven to reassume all the glory of his divinity together with his glorified human nature.

taste . . . everyone: As man he endured death so that we could overcome the eternal death which would be our lot if the incarnation had not taken place.

fitting that he: God the Father decreed the incarnation so that we could become his adopted sons. He saw that it was right and fitting that the incarnate Son should be made perfect in his humanity through the sufferings which he endured for us.

pioneer . . . salvation: Christ was the leader, the first to rise from the dead. Thus he made possible our resurrection to eternal life. He was the pioneer, the first-fruits of all those that would follow him from earth to heaven.

who . . . sanctified: Christ who sanctifies us and we his followers have the same human nature in common. Because of this he can call us his brethren and need not be ashamed to do so for we are his brothers.

APPLICATION : The inspired author of this epistle sets out to strengthen the faith of his readers who had become lax in the practice of their faith (see 10 : 24). He recalls to their minds that Christ is high priest who has entered into the holy of holies—heaven—to make atonement for the sins of mankind, offering to God not the blood of sacrified animals but his own precious blood which he shed for mankind on Calvary. He does not enter into heaven alone; he enters rather as the pioneer, the leader of all the faithful ones who will follow him here on earth. He is God's own Son through whom the universe was created. He is, therefore, immeasurably above the angels. He condescended to become lower than they by taking our ordinary humanity here on earth. And this he did for love of us, to make us his brothers and heirs to heaven. He "tasted death" for all of us. Because of this, death can no longer hold us in its grip : we too shall rise from the dead as Christ did and we shall enter into the glory of heaven if we remain his faithful followers.

Surely, when a Christian realizes how much God has done for him in order to bring him to the eternal happiness of heaven, he cannot and should not find it too difficult to carry some few crosses in life. The author of this letter to the Hebrews compares our Christian life to a pilgrimage, to the heavenly sanctuary (4 : 16; 12 : 22). In days gone by, making a pilgrimage to some far-off shrine implied a willingness to make many sacrifices—but the thought of seeing the sacred place and kneeling in prayer there made the difficulties of the journey seem as nothing. Let us meditate more often on heaven. We too can make light of the hardships of the earthly journey.

If those in the past who have failed to merit heaven were given a second chance, do we think for a moment that they would let the difficulties and trials of life prevent them from reaching their eternal home? How gladly would they snatch up the crosses which perhaps we are throwing down? How cheerfully would they not forego the illicit pleasures of life, and how quickly would they not turn their backs on the treasures of this world, for now they see the full meaning of that warning : "what does it profit a man if he should gain the whole world and lose his (eternal) life?"

When tempted by our passions or by greed or by our pride and selfishness, let us look ahead and see ourselves at the judgement seat of God. It will help to cast these temptations far from us. I should imagine that the greatest shock those who are lost will get on their judgement day will be to realize the folly which moved them to exchange the eternity of happiness offered them for the empty baubles, the nothingness of this world's pleasures and gains. If one had all the possible pleasures of this life and never a pain or ache or sorrow of any kind, and had all the gold in Fort Knox he still would have to leave them all at death. What then?

The Son of God came on earth, emptied himself of his divine glory and lived a life of poverty and hardship among us. He let himself be put to death —the shameful death of a criminal and outcast—so that we could merit heaven. In order to reap the great, almost incredible, reward which he won for us, we are asked merely to accept the crosses life brings us and to plod along cheerfully on the road mapped out for us by our loving Lord. He has opened heaven for us, he has shown us the way there; he has left us all the aids we need on our journey. He cannot force our free-will, but is there a sane man or woman with such disdain for his or her own true interest as to refuse to follow him on the Christian road to eternal happiness? May God grant us all the grace to avoid such extreme folly!

GOSPEL : Mark 10; 2–16. Pharisees came up and in order to test Jesus asked, "Is it lawful for a man to divorce his wife?" He answered them, "What did Moses command you?" They said, "Moses allowed a man to write a certificate of divorce, and to put her away." But Jesus said to them, "For your hardness of heart he wrote you this commandment. But from the beginning of creation, *"God made them male and female." "For this reason a man shall leave his father and mother and be joined to his wife, and the two shall become one."* So they are no longer two but one. What therefore God has joined together, let not man put asunder."

And in the house the disciples asked him again about this matter. And he said to them, "Whoever divorces his wife and marries another, commits adultery against her; and if she divorces her husband and marries another, she commits adultery."

And they were bringing children to him, that he might touch them; and the disciples rebuked them. But when Jesus saw it he was indignant, and said to them, "Let the children come to me, do not hinder them; for to such belongs the kingdom of God. Truly, I say to you, whoever does not receive the kingdom of God like a child shall not enter it." And he took them in his arms and blessed them, laying his hands upon them.

EXPLANATION : In their role as opponents of Christ the Pharisees question him about divorce. Divorce was practiced among them to a limited degree, ever since the time of Moses. The Pharisees, therefore, must have heard rumors that Christ did not approve of divorce, and the purpose of their question would be to get him to admit this and so they could accuse him of contradicting Moses—their great lawgiver, and perhaps turn the people against him. His answer tells them that it is the law of God that must be kept and not dispensations from that law, forced from Moses by the laxity and worldliness of the Chosen People.

to test Jesus : This was to try to get him to make some statement that would, in this case, turn the people against him. **is it lawful? :** They had no scruples about using this dispensatiton which was forced from Moses. St. Matthew adds in this context : "divorce his wife for any reason"; this seems to fit in the context for there were big disputes among the rabbis at the time as to what excuse would be sufficient for a man to divorce his wife. The conditions laid down by Moses (Dt. 24 : 4) seemed to be vague; hence the disputes. **for . . . heart :** Jesus tells them that the exception which Moses allowed from God's original law was forced from him by the stubbornness and unwillingness of the Chosen People to keep the law of God in its entirety.

from the beginning: Jesus now proves from Genesis, one of the inspired books that were accepted by all Jews, that God intended marriage to be indissoluble—a union for life between one man and one woman. "What therefore," he said, "God has joined together, let not man put asunder." His answer to the Pharisees could not have been clearer or more definite.

he said to them: As was usual with them, when they were away from the crowd, the disciples questioned him.

adultery against her: The second woman whom the divorced man marries is not his real wife; any marriage relations with her are simply adultery, and by this adulterous association he is offending against his real wife whom he divorced.

she . . . husband: The same is true of a wife who divorces her real husband and unites herself to a second man, who is not and cannot be her husband. This second statement must have been in-serted by St. Mark himself, for a Jewish woman could not divorce her husband; this was the husband's privilege! But in Roman law—and Mark was writing for Gentile Christians—the wife as well as the husband could sue for divorce.

disciples rebuked them: The people were bringing their children to Jesus that he might lay his hand on them and bless them, but the disciples did not think it was right to trouble the Master in this way.

Jesus was indignant: He did not approve of the disciples' interference; he was glad to have the children come to him; they were truly innocent and fit to be members of the kingdom of God.

receive . . . child: All who would become true members of the kingdom of God, first on earth and then in its final sense, in heaven, must have the characteristics of children: innocence, humility, a trusting faith and complete reliance on God—just as children rely on their parents. The kingdom of God is a free gift of God: no man can ever deserve it but can simply and gratefully accept it.

APPLICATION: On the "divorce" section of this Gospel see today's first reading. Christ clearly states that from the very beginning, God's plan for marriage was that it should be a life-long unity of one man and one woman. Its purpose is the procreation of children and their education, as well as the mutual love and fulfillment of the husband and wife. These demand this life-long bond. Divorce, which tries to break this bond, breaks the law of the Creator who decreed what was best for the temporal and spiritual welfare of the human race.

The last four verses of today's Gospel describe an incident which is in no way connected with the previous discussion but which has a very useful lesson for all Christians. It describes Christ's love for children and while manifesting this love he stresses the need for all his true followers to be childlike. "I say to you, whoever does not receive the kingdom of God like a child shall not enter it." To receive the kingdom of God is to accept the teaching of Christ and live according to it in his kingdom on earth. He who does this will enter, after death, into the eternal kingdom of heaven. Christ says, however, that we must accept "like a child" : his kingdom on earth, his teaching and the Church he founded to carry on that teaching. It does not mean : in a childish way, an unthinking, uneducated way, but in a child-like way—a humble, grateful, receptive way. A child is unselfconscious, content to be dependent on others' care and generosity. Christianity is a gift of the generous God to us, we have done nothing and never could do anything to merit it. We must accept it simply and gratefully as a gift; we could never deserve it.

While Christianity is a religion of reason and conforms in all its aspects to the rational nature of man—its basis is the revelation of God who is the author and foundation of all rationality—yet it is the heart of man rather than his intellect which Christ means to capture. The assent of the intellect to the doctrine revealed by Christ is not sufficient of itself for a Christian to earn the eternal kingdom; faith is the total acceptance and *commitment* of the believer to God through Jesus Christ. The man of true faith commits himself to God with a filial childlike trust, assured that if he does all that in him lies God will do the rest.

Therefore, our Christian faith must be childlike, a trusting, humble and obedient faith. This is the kind of faith that will move mountains—the mountains that loom so large in the vision of too many Christians today—the mountains of doubt, selfishness, unwillingness to be subjected to authority. Christ asks us, if we would be his followers : to take up our daily cross and climb the way to Calvary after him. This daily cross is made of the troubles and trials of life from which no one can escape. They can be borne with reluctance and grumbling, or they can be accepted as the loving God's means of training us for the future life. Every true Christian accepts his trials in the latter way, for if he is true to his faith he knows that his years on earth are his apprenticeship to prepare him for his eternal life.

God is surely not asking too much of us when he asks us to live our Christian faith in childlike humility, candor and confidence during the days of our pilgrimage on this earth.

TWENTY-EIGHTH SUNDAY OF THE YEAR

FIRST READING: Wisdom 7:7-11. I prayed, and understanding was given me; I called upon God, and the spirit of wisdom came to me, I preferred her to scepters and thrones, and I accounted wealth as nothing in comparison with her. Neither did I liken to her any priceless gem, because all gold is but a little sand in her sight, and silver will be accounted as clay before her. I loved her more than health and beauty, and I chose to have her rather than light, because her radiance never ceases. All good things come to me along with her, and in her hands uncounted wealth.

EXPLANATION: On the Book of Wisdom, see the 13th Sunday of the year. In today's verses from this inspired book, the author says that he received the gift of wisdom from God, a gift which he esteemed as of greater value than all the riches this earth holds. Health and beauty of body are not to be compared with wisdom, which brings with it numerous other gifts.

I prayed . . . God: These are two parallel lines with the same meaning. Understanding, the power to discern truth, is the same as wisdom.

preferred . . . thrones: The gift of wisdom is far more valuable to a man than a king's scepter.

wealth as nothing: If asked to choose between wealth and wisdom, there would be no hesitation by the author. There is really no comparison between wealth and wisdom.

gold . . . clay: In general wealth consists of gold and/or silver, both of which are without value when compared with wisdom.

health and beauty: Even these two gifts, so important if one is considering life on earth, become unattractive to the author if asked to choose between them and wisdom; his vision is not bounded by the ends of this earth.

rather than light: He prefers wisdom even to the light which is so necessary for life and movement here on earth. The reason is that wisdom gives an unending radiance here and hereafter.

all . . . wealth: Wisdom brings with it the really good things for man's genuine welfare both in the present life and in the future. The really wise man has untold wealth.

APPLICATION: Though this Book of Wisdom was written over two thousand years ago, the message we have read from it today is so timely and practical for us Christians that it might well have been written last week! The reason is that real wisdom is unchangeable. It is a correct knowledge and understanding of the eternal truths that God has revealed to us and as these truths are unchanged and unchangeable so is our knowledge of them. The author clearly realized that reaching eternal life was the one and only aim worth striving for in this life; all his other occupations here below were only temporary and transient while eternal life is permanent and therefore well worth the sacrifice of all earthly attractions.

He was willing to forego all earthly wealth : gold, silver and precious gems, and all earthly power including a king's throne, rather than desert wisdom which would lead him to everlasting wealth. This is what all sane men would and should do when they are convinced that an unending life of happiness awaits them. No Christian doubts this. The very meaning of Christianity is a rule of life which directs our actions while on this earth, so that we shall enter heaven when we die. Christ did not come on earth without a purpose; he did not suffer and die in vain. He became man and suffered and died so that those who would follow him and keep the rules he laid down for them would enter into heaven when they breathed their last breath.

It was not then to make life here hard for us but to put eternal life within our reach that he commanded us to bear our crosses, our troubles and trials in life. He told us not to let ourselves be ensnared by the attractions of this world, its wealth, its positions of honor, its pleasures. But he did not forbid us to use wisely, that is, in moderation and within his rules, the pleasures, power and goods of this world. As Christians, we can enjoy the pleasures and happi-ness of family life; we can own property; we can accept positions of authority—provided always that these things will not come between us and our real life which is eternal life.

It is here that too many Christians fail. They let themselves become so absorbed in their pursuit of pleasure, or in the acquisition of wealth or power, that they leave themselves no time for the things of God, the things that really matter. If such people only stopped and asked themselves the question : during the two thousands years of Christianity did any of those who lost heaven because they became too absorbed in the things of earth, ever get real happiness and satisfaction out of their few years on earth? Was there ever a rich man who was truly happy with all he had, and deliberately stopped getting richer? Was there ever a pleasure-lover who could say that he was content with all the pleasure he had received? Did not these very pleasures interfere with his health and shorten the already too-short span he had to enjoy himself?

No, chasing after the will-of-the-wisp attractions of this life is not the occupation of a sane man, much less of the truly wise man—as a Christian is by his profession. We have been given a period of time here during which we can earn our future reward; any days, months or years wasted on other pursuits will be hard to replace. The mercy of God is infinite, and while there have been from time to time exceptional cases of death-bed conversions, the only sure way of passing our final examination is to have learned, during the years God gave us for this purpose here below, the answers to the questions we shall be asked.

SECOND READING: Hebrews 4:12–13. The word of God is living and active, sharper than any two-edged sword, piercing to the division of soul and spirit of joints and marrow, and discerning the thoughts and intentions of the heart. And before him no creature is hidden, but all are open and laid bare to the eyes of him with whom we have to do.

EXPLANATION: In today's two verses of this letter the author warns all Christians that nothing they do can be hidden from God for their innermost thoughts and intentions are known to him. They must, therefore, live, act and think as true Christians if they would enter into the rest that God has prepared for them—not in the promised land but in heaven (see 4:1–11).

Word of God: The reference is to the judgement of God or God as judge of men and not to Christ who is called the Word of God in St. John.

living and active: It is in the midst of us producing its effects.

sharper . . . piercing: It can penetrate and pierce into man's most interior and hidden recesses.

thoughts and intentions: This man can hide from his fellowmen but not from God; man's secret thoughts and plans are known to the all-wise God.

with . . . to do: The J.B.'s and C.V.'s translation: "to whom we have to give account of ourselves," is better than the above translation of the RSV. Man's innermost self is laid open and bare (uncovered) before God his judge and therefore any attempt at hiding anything from him is worse than useless.

APPLICATION: The sacred author of this epistle, writing for Jewish converts who presumably knew their history, is urging them not to make the same mistake as did their ancestors in the desert. They did not believe God's promise and they disobeyed him. For that reason they did not enter into the Promised Land of Canaan, they died in the desert. Now Christians through Christ have been promised and are made heirs of God's place of eternal rest, but unless they live their faith and obey God they too will end up like their disobedient ancestors in the desert.

Some of his intended readers may have been foolish themselves—pretending externally to be Christians while their thoughts and intentions were not. He reminds them of God's omniscience. He knows not only their external actions but their every thought and their most secret intentions. Therefore, external observance will not earn the heavenly rest for them, their heart and spirit must be in their daily observance of the Christian way of life.

There is a warning here for all of us and it is that not a single thought or action of our lives can remain unknown to the God who will be our Judge on our day of reckoning. We can fool ourselves, and fool our neighbors by carrying out the externals of the Christian law while in our hearts we have evil thoughts, evil intentions and sentiments of rebellion against our Creator. The Christian who behaves in this way is foolish in the extreme and he is fooling only himself. He cannot hide his wrong intentions or his rebellious inclinations from God who reads his heart and his mind. Unless he changes his relations with God and humbly submits himself to God's will he has little hope of entering the promised land of heaven.

Among us there are others who spoil and make useless those Christian acts that would earn heaven for them—by their refusal to repent of a sin or sins they have committed. To their friends and neighbors they may appear as model Christians but in the eyes of God they are proud and stubborn subjects who will not bend their knee to God and ask for the pardon which he is ever willing to give even to the greatest sinners. While they are in this state of sin they can earn no merit for heaven. Our God is a God of mercy, he has gone to incredible lengths to share his kingdom with us. He knows all our weaknesses and is ever ready to raise us up again when we fall—if we repent and turn to him. There is no sin we can commit, no matter how serious it be, that he cannot forgive and blot out if only we ask him to do so. Of those Christians whom God will have to condemn on the judgement day not one will be condemned because he sinned; but he will be condemned because he did not repent and ask God's pardon for his sins.

Let us never forget that God's eyes are always on us, not only to see our innermost faults but also to be ever ready to succor and help us. He is a loving Father and he will not give us a cross too heavy to bear. If, when we have crosses, we stay close to him and ask for his help he will most certainly answer our call.

GOSPEL: Mark 10:17–30. As Jesus was setting out on a journey, a man ran up and knelt before him, and asked him, "Good Teacher, what must I do to inherit eternal life?" And Jesus said to him, "Why do you call me good? No one is good but God alone. You know the commandments: 'Do not kill, Do not commit adultery, Do not steal, Do not bear false witness, Do not defraud, Honor your father and mother.'" And he said to him, "Teacher, all these I have observed from my youth." And Jesus looking upon him loved him, and said to him, "You lack one thing; go, sell what you have, and give to the poor, and you will have treasure in heaven; and come, follow me." At that saying his countenance fell, and he went away sorrowful; for he had great possessions.

And Jesus looked around and said to his disciples, "How hard it will be for those who have riches to enter the kingdom of God!" And the disciples were amazed at his words. But Jesus said to them again, "Children, how hard it is for those who trust in riches to enter the kingdom of God! It is easier for a camel to go through the eye of a needle than for a rich man to enter the kingdom of God." And they were exceedingly astonished, and said to him, "Then who can be saved?" Jesus looked at them and said, "With men it is impossible, but not with God; for all things are possible with God." Peter began to say to him, "Lo, we have left everything and followed you." Jesus said, "Truly, I say to you, there is no one who has left house or brothers or sisters or mother or father or children or lands for my sake and for the Gospel, who will not receive a hundredfold now in this time, houses and brothers and sisters and mothers and children and lands, with persecutions, and in the age to come eternal life."

EXPLANATION: The lesson in today's reading from St. Mark's Gospel is: How hard it is for the rich of this world, who are attached to their riches, to enter eternal life. However, although it is hard it is not impossible; God can give the grace to overcome this worldly attraction.

Good Teacher: By adding "good" to the usual salutation: Rabbi, Teacher, this man most probably was stressing the great esteem he had for Christ. Perhaps he accepted him as the promised Messiah when he asked how he could enter the "eternal life."

why . . . good?: The rich man had no suspicion that Christ was anything more than a man and therefore should not be called by a title which at the time was reserved for God—the only one who was good by his very nature. Of this Christ reminds the rich man.

you . . . commandments: This was a challenge to the man and to his understanding of the saving power of the Mosaic Law. The man's answer shows that he knew the Mosaic Law would not be sufficient to earn for him the eternal messianic kingdom. He had always observed the commandments and still felt that more was needed.

Jesus loved him: This probably means: "showed him some gesture of affection" as the aorist tense in Greek implies.

still . . . poor : This was a weighty demand—it meant more than giving alms to the needy which probably he already had done—but it was only a necessary prelude to a further demand : "come, follow me."

went . . . sorrowful : Although this man was anxious to gain eternal life, the pull of the wealth of this world was too strong. He could not do what Christ told him. He could not give away all of his great riches and follow Christ. Therefore he was sorrowful, for he feared he was putting eternal life beyond his reach.

how . . . be : Christ tells his disciples that one of the greatest barriers preventing entrance into heaven will be earthly riches.

disciples were amazed : Because worldly prosperity among the Jews was looked on as a sign of God's blessing on good-living people, the disciples could not see why riches should be a barrier to heaven.

camel . . . needle : This was a proverb expressing impossibility, and perhaps referred to some gate or passage so narrow that a camel could not pass through it.

exceedingly astonished : Christ's last statement seems to say that no rich man can enter heaven, but he goes on to explain to his disciples the full meaning of what he had said.

with man . . . impossible : No rich man could ever renounce all his wealth or use it with Christian detachment, unless God gave him the grace to do so; God can give that necessary grace.

Peter . . . everything : As usual, Peter speaks for the Apostles. Here, perhaps a little proud of himself and the others, he reminds Christ of their having left everything. It was not a lot indeed but yet it was all they had or could have had. Later they gave their lives, the greatest offering any men could make.

truly . . . hundredfold : Christ promises them that the eternal kingdom which they will inherit will be worth a hundred times more than all they have left.

now . . . persecutions : This verse is probably not part of Christ's promise but was added by Mark. It contrasts this life, its wealth or attachments—with persecution either threatening or present in fact—with the age to come, and eternal life—in peace and happiness without fear of any interference. This age to come is not only a hundredfold but a millionfold better than the present life.

APPLICATION : By coming to Jesus with his problem this man has done all Christians a good turn. We have learned from Christ's answer that over-attachment to worldly goods is one of the big obstacles to entering heaven. The man in this story was a good-living man, he kept all the commandments from his youth upward and he had an interest in eternal life, while many of his compatriots of that day had not. Reading this man's heart like an open book, Christ saw that not only was he fit for eternal life but that he was one who could have a very high place in heaven if he would leave everything and become a close follower of his. Not only would he become a saint, but he would lead many to sanctity.

The price to pay for this privilege, however, seemed too high to this "good man." "He had great possessions" and he was too attached to them so he could not accept Christ's offer, "his countenance fell and he went away sorrowful." Although his case was exceptional,

Christ saw in him the makings of a saint and he asked him to make an exceptional sacrifice, one which he did not and does not ask of all his followers; his remark to the disciples later : " how hard it will be for those who have riches to enter the kingdom of God" holds for all time and for all mankind.

This statement of Christ, however, does not mean that a follower may not possess any of this world's goods. He may possess and use those goods, but what he must not do is to allow them to take such a hold on him that he has no time for acquiring everlasting goods —the Christian virtues. Unfortunately, there are Christians whose whole purpose in this life is the accumulation of worldly goods. Concentration on such accumulation is wrong, but in many cases the methods of acquisition are unjust : defrauding laborers of their just wages; overcharging customers; cheating in business deals; giving false measures and many other devices which produce unearned wealth.

All this is far from Christian justice, and those who have let such sinful greed to regulate their lives are certainly not on the road to heaven. There are other sins, of course, which can keep us from heaven, but of all the sins a man can commit this irrational greed for the wealth of this world seems the most unreasonable of them all. How utterly inane and foolish to have spent a lifetime collecting something from which we shall soon be parted forever! The rich man's bank-book and his gilt-edged shares will be not only valueless in the after-life but they, if unjustly acquired,

will be witnesses for the prosecution at the judgement on which one's eternal future depends. While most of us are not guilty of such excessive greed for wealth, we all do need to examine our consciences as to how we acquire and use the limited wealth we have. There are very rich men who have acquired their wealth honestly and justly and who spend much of their wealth on charitable causes. Their wealth will not hinder them from reaching heaven. On the other hand, there are many in the middle and lower income-bracket who may be offending against justice through the means they use to acquire what they have, and in the little helps which they refuse to a needy neighbor. We may not be able to found a hospital for the poor, or pay an annuity to support the family of a disabled fellow workman, but we are not excused from bringing a little gift to our neighbors who are in hospital, or from supplying even part of a meal for the dependants of the injured workman.

Remember that Christ praised the widow who put a mite (a cent) into the collection-box for the poor in the temple area, and he also said that a cup of cold water given in his name would not go without reward. We need not be rich in order to be charitable; often our own exaggerated sense of our poverty can make us hard-hearted and mean toward our fellowmen who look to us for help. The true Christian, whose principal purpose in life is to serve God, will not overburden himself with unnecessary pieces of luggage; instead he will travel light and be ever ready to help others also to carry their burdens.

TWENTY-NINTH SUNDAY OF THE YEAR

FIRST READING : Isaiah 53 : 10–11. It was the will of the Lord to bruise him; he has put him to grief; when he makes himself an offering for sin, he shall see his offspring, he shall prolong his days; the will of the Lord shall prosper in his hand; he shall see the fruit of the travail of his soul and be satisfied; by his knowledge shall the righteous one, my servant, make many to be accounted righteous; and he shall bear their iniquities.

EXPLANATION : In today's short excerpt from second-Isaiah, we have a reference to the servant of God—as this prophet called the future Messiah. It is God's will that the Servant should suffer and offer himself as a sin-sacrifice for mankind. But his life will not really end in death, it will be given back to him again, he shall see the fruit of his sufferings in the many righteous ones whose iniquities he will bear.

will . . . him : It was God's plan that his Servant should suffer, not for any sins of his own but for those of mankind. The doctrine of expiatory vicarious suffering is clearly enunciated in these verses.

an offering for sin : It was a special sacrifice in the Levitical ritual offered to make atonement for sin.

he shall . . . days : Even though the Servant dies, as he must to offer himself as a sacrifice (and the two preceding verses 8–9 leave no doubt as to his death " for our faults struck down in death"), yet his days will be prolonged —death will not hold him. He shall live to see his offspring—generations of followers.

see the fruit . . . satisfied : He shall be pleased with the good results his sufferings produce in his fellowmen.

make . . . righteous : Many equals all. His expiatory sufferings and death will make all men "just."

he shall . . . iniquities : Because he bore the guilt of all men, mankind is therefore reconciled to God. "God has forgiven us all our sins . . . he has made you alive with Christ. . . The bond (sin) which stood against us, he has set aside, *nailing it to the cross"* (Col. 2 : 14–15; see Phil. 2 : 7; 1 Pt. 2 : 21–25).

APPLICATION : The lesson to be learned from these two verses of second-Isaiah (it would be well to read the entire prophecy, or Fourth Servant Oracle as it is called, in Is. 52 : 13— 53 : 12), is that God in his extraordinary, infinite love for us men and for our salvation, decreed that his divine Son in his assumed human nature, should suffer torture and death so that we might live eternally. The leaders of the Jews plotted his death, and forced the Roman authorities to condemn him to the shameful death of crucifixion, but this was all in God's plan for us before he created the world. Christ, the Son of God, knew this all along; he tried to prepare his disciples for the shock his death and sufferings would cause them by foretelling on three distinct occasions, that he would suffer and be put to death, but that he would triumph over death and rise again (see Mk. 8 : 31–33; 9 : 30–32; 10 : 32–34). In the garden of Gethsemani, as his hour drew near, he suffered agony because his human nature shrank from the tortures which he vividly foresaw; nevertheless he accepted what his Father had planned and humbly and submissively said : "yet not what I will but what thou wilt " (Mk. 14 : 36).

That Christ our Lord was the suffering obedient Servant foretold by the prophet is evident from the gospel story. He was "rejected by men, a man of sorrows and familiar with suffering . . . yet ours were the sufferings he bore, our sorrows he carried . . . he was crushed for our sins. . . We had all gone astray like sheep. . . Yahweh burdened him with the sins of us all. . . like a lamb that is led to the slaughter-house, like a sheep that is dumb before its shearers, never opening his mouth" (Is. 53 : 3–7). This prophecy had its literal fulfillment in Christ. This is testified by all four gospels. It is not so much the fact that one might be tempted to question, but rather the reason, the necessity, why it had to be thus. Could not God have found other ways of bringing men to heaven without subjecting his divine Son

to humiliations and sufferings?

God alone has the full and satisfying answer to this question, and part of our joy in heaven will be to learn the answers to this and to other theological questions which trouble us on earth. Both the Old and New Testaments indicate at least a partial answer to this particular question : when they tell us this was an effect of God's infinite love for us. We, of course, can form no adequate idea of what infinite love is and does. But even finite love, if true and meaningful, can and does go to great extremes for the sake of those loved. For instance, true patriots in all ages have never hesitated to sacrifice their lives for their country and their fellow countrymen. Their finite love was sufficient to move them to make the supreme sacrifice. God was not dealing with the preservation of a country's freedom or its liberation from an oppressor, he was dealing with the eternal freedom and happiness of the whole human race. The task was great, the end desired was of everlasting value, the life sacrificed was God's own Son in his human nature—but the love of God which his Son shared with him, was infinite and therefore capable of any sacrifice.

Furthermore, if we knew our own weak, lazy, human nature as well as God knows it, we would see another reason for the extraordinary manifestation of his love. The cross of Christ, the scourging at the pillar, the crowning with thorns, the cruel nails through the hands and feet, are reminders that will touch a chord even in the coldest Christian heart. With these reminders of God's love for us many of us are still all too slow to show our appreciation of all God has done for us. How much less responsive, how much less appreciative of what eternal life is worth, would such

Christians be, if God had opened heaven for them in a less impressive way?

Our Savior took human nature—an act of extreme humiliation, in order to make us his brothers and therefore sons of God. He came into a world of sin where God the Creator was practically forgotten. He told those who "had ears to hear," of God and of his desire to give unending life in his own eternal kingdom, to all who would follow the Christian precepts. He established a society—the Church—on earth which would continue until the end of time to proclaim God's mercy and love. He was tortured and put to the cruelest of deaths because of the opposition and hatred of some of the Jews among whom he lived. But as God, and with God his Father,

he foresaw all this and in the full knowledge that he would rise again, willingly accepted it notwithstanding the agonies it would cause him. While the resurrection made his life and death a success and an eternal triumph it did not make the pains of his passion any easier.

We may not understand what infinite love is, but we cannot fail to see the glorious effects that the infinite love of God has earned for us. We are citizens of heaven. We must expect to meet some obstacles on the way—there will be troubles and trials in our lives, but one look at our crucifix should make us realize how little we are asked to suffer for our own salvation when compared with what Christ has suffered to make salvation possible.

SECOND READING : Hebrews 4 : 14–16. Since we have a great high priest who has passed through the heavens, Jesus, the Son of God, let us hold fast our confession. For we have not a high priest who is unable to sympathize with our weaknesses, but one who in every respect has been tempted as we are, yet without sinning. Let us then with confidence draw near to the throne of grace, that we may receive mercy and find grace to help in time of need.

EXPLANATION : Last Sunday, the epistle to the Hebrews warned us to walk correctly in the presence of God, for the most secret thoughts of our mind are seen by him. Today, the epistle continues to urge us to stand steadfast in the faith, for our Leader and High Priest is none other than Jesus, the Son of God. He has offered full atonement for us and suffered more than we ever can; he understands our weaknesses and our needs. We can and must call on him with all confidence.

we have . . . priest : The high priest was

the head of all the priests and Levites who served in the temple of Jerusalem. He exercised supreme authority over the temple—and over the personnel of Yahweh's only legitimate temple—the temple of Jerusalem. He was the mediator *par excellence* between God and the people. He carried out the expiation rites on the Day of Atonement and entered the holy of holies on that day to sprinkle the Ark with the blood of the sacrifices. No other priest could enter there. Now, our mediator with God is Jesus, the Son of God, who has entered the real holy of holies, heaven, and pleads there for us.

hold . . . confession : Our Christian faith is solidly based on Jesus; let us continue to live up to it.

unable to sympathize : Our high priest, our mediator, is one who is well aware of all our weaknesses; he has lived the same life we live on earth and suffered far more.

tempted . . . sinning : The author knew of the temptations Jesus underwent in the desert, but all through his earthly life he suffered difficulties, and in his public life especially because of the opposition of the Scribes and Pharisees. Unlike us, however, he never gave in to any of these temptations—even his agony in the Garden ended in his triumph over the human fear of suffering.

confidence . . . grace : Therefore, we can confidently have recourse in our difficulties to the throne of God, for Christ is there to recommend our petitions to his Father. In 10 : 19–22, the author develops this theme : we have free access to God's sanctuary, to God, because by his death Christ opened for us the holy of holies.

in time of need : In time of need God will answer our prayers and give us the necessary strength to overcome our temptations and difficulties. Christ has won this guarantee for us.

APPLICATION : We Christians are God's chosen people of today. Compared with his Chosen People of the Old Testament, we have infinitely greater blessings and advantages. They knew of the existence of the one true and only God, the Creator of all things, and they knew he was interested in them. Although they knew that he existed they knew very little else about him, and their chief interest in him was to obtain from him all earthly blessings : health, wealth and progeny. They had only a very hazy idea of the future life or what it held for them, yet they did know they were chosen by God so that through them God would send a great blessing on all nations; somehow, sometime they would have a share in that blessing.

We Christians are indeed fortunate that we know much more about God and our real purpose in life. Through the incarnation we have learned that God loves us so much that he sent his divine Son to live among us in order to make us heirs to heaven. That divine Son of God suffered and died in his human nature in order to make perfect atonement to his Father in our behalf. This, surely, was divine love for us creatures. Not only did God make us heirs to his eternal kingdom through the incarnation, but he gave us his own divine Son to be our leader and intermediary between himself and us.

Unlike the Jews of old we know clearly what our real purpose in life is. It is not to be found on this earth, it is the eternal happiness that awaits us after death. Life on earth is but a preparation for the real life to come. This knowledge coupled with the assurance that Christ our brother is pleading for us at the throne of grace, should fill every Christian with courage and hope. Christ knows our weaknesses and should we give in to them and the temptations of life, he is ready to obtain from our Father in heaven pardon the moment we repent of our fall.

We are fortunate to have such a loving and all-powerful high priest who has entered heaven before us and is preparing a place for us. No true Christian can ever despair. God has proved how much he loves us, and how anxious he is to share his heaven with us. Christ, the Son of God, endured the humiliation of the incarnation and the sufferings and pains of his life on earth, and his cruel death on the cross, because he gladly cooperated with the Father in making us heirs of heaven.

With such an intermediary and helper how can we fail to reach our goal? With God and his divine Son on our side, who is against us?

GOSPEL : Mark 10 : 35-45. James and John, the sons of Zebedee, came forward to him, and said to him, "Teacher, we want you to do for us whatever we ask of you." And he said to them, "What do you want me to do for you?" And they said to him, "Grant us to sit, one at your right hand and one at your left, in your glory." But Jesus said to them, "You do not know what you are asking. Are you able to drink the cup that I drink, or to be baptized with the baptism with which I am baptized?" And they said to him, "We are able." And Jesus said to them, "The cup that I drink you will drink; and with the baptism with which I am baptized, you will be baptized; but to sit at my right hand or at my left is not mine to grant, but it is for those for whom it has been prepared." And when the ten heard it, they began to be indignant at James and John. And Jesus called them to him and said to them, "You know that those who are supposed to rule over the Gentiles lord it over them, and their great men exercise authority over them. But it shall not be so among you; but whoever would be great among you must be your servant, and whoever would be the first among you must be a slave of all. For the Son of man also came not to be served but to serve, and to give his life as a ransom for many."

EXPLANATION : Jesus had just given his Apostles the third prediction of the sufferings and death that awaited him in Jerusalem. These predictions fell on deaf ears as far as his Apostles were concerned. Two of their leaders, James and John, came forward to ask him for the principal places in the glorious kingdom they were sure he was going to set up when they reached Jerusalem. He was gentle with them for he knew they had not yet grasped that his kingdom was not of this world. He told them that if they would have a place in his kingdom they must imitate the sacrifice he was about to make to establish that kingdom —the path to glory is through suffering. Then he added that the leaders in his kingdom would not lord it over others as the Gentiles did; instead they would be the servants of those whom they would lead.

James and John : These two were among the first four disciples that followed Christ down by the Jordan in the days of John the Baptist. Later, he "called" them officially and they left their boats and nets and their father Zebedee.

at . . . your glory : They were not thinking of his glorious reign in heaven—as yet they could not accept that he would be put to death; much less, therefore, could they have any idea of his resurrection to glory. Yet our Lord's answer told them that it was in heaven that they would achieve the glory which they would have earned.

drink . . . baptized : Christ was here referring to the sufferings he was about to undergo. To drink the cup of suffering and to be immersed (baptized) in the waters of sorrow, were Old Testament figures of speech. Our Lord admitted that James and John would follow him through the path of suffering but told them the allocation of status in the glorious kingdom belonged to his heavenly Father.

when . . . heard it : The other ten Apostles were indignant that James and John should look for primacy of honor, not because they were looking for honor but because they wanted to be superior to "the ten." This was not to their credit either.

rule . . . Gentiles : Christ then explained to the Twelve together that the leadership they must exercise in his kingdom on earth in preparation for the reign of glory, was not to be like that of Gentile rulers who lorded it over their subjects. Instead it would be a humble service of love. They would be the servants of the Christian community, ever ready to help their fellowmen without counting the cost and without expecting any reward on this earth.

Son of Man . . . serve : Christ described himself as the Messiah—foretold by second-Isaiah—whose life would be that of a humble, obedient servant of God—obedient unto death (see Is. 52 : 13—53 : 12). He did not come to rule or to be served by others but to serve all and : **to give . . . ransom :** The giving of his life would be the means that would produce the righteousness of all—"many"—men. This is foretold in the Servant oracle in Is. 53 : 10-12. Christ's greatest service to all men was his atoning death for them (see today's first reading).

APPLICATION : Our own natural inclination most likely would be to react like the other ten Apostles and become vexed with James and John and to tell them what we thought of their selfish worldly ambitions. However, our Lord's gentle answer : "you do not know what you are asking" shows us that ignorance of the nature of the kingdom he was going to set up, was the cause of their very human ambitions. They, with the other Apostles, had still the common Jewish idea of the messianic kingdom. They thought the Messiah—and they were now convinced that Jesus was the promised Messiah—would set up a political kingdom in Palestine, oust the pagan Romans and eventually extend his kingdom to all nations. That this kingdom he would set up would be universal, extending to all nations, was indicated in almost all the messianic prophecies in the Old Testament, but that this kingdom would be spiritual not political, was not grasped by most of Christ's contemporaries including the Apostles.

Jesus, knowing that his Apostles still had this wrong idea, was gentle with James and John. He took this opportunity to tell them that he would set up a glorious kingdom but that his sufferings and death would be a necessary prelude to its establishment. He had already referred to his sufferings and death three times, but the mention fell on deaf ears. Their argument was: how could he suffer death when he has still to establish his earthly kingdom? The truth in fact was that it was by means of his sufferings and death that he would establish his glorious kingdom. He challenged the two Apostles then to know if they were willing to pay the price for a high place in his glorious kingdom: were they prepared to follow him through suffering and death? He accepted their affirmation, knowing it to be true, but told them their position of honor depended on his Father's decision. Once they realized the nature of his glorious kingdom they would be the last to look for positions of honor in it.

While no Christian today thinks that Christ came on earth in order to make us wealthy, happy and prosperous during our few years on earth, there are, unfortunately, many Christians who are unwilling to accept Christ's teaching that the way to heavenly glory is the way of the cross. "All this and heaven too" is their motto. It would, of course, be marvelous if all our days on earth were days of peace, happiness and prosperity to be followed by eternal happiness—when we "shuffle off this mortal coil." But any man who has the use of reason sees that our world is inhabited by weak, sin-inclined and usually sinful mortals, himself included—weak mortals who can and do disturb the peace and harmony that could regulate our mortal lives. There are "accidents" on our roads and highways every day of the year, frequently causing death or grave injury to hundreds. The rules of the road, if kept by all, would prevent ninety-nine per cent of such accidents—the other one per cent are caused by mechanical failure. Would any man be so naive as to expect that we could have even one day free from car accidents?

Because man has a free-will he is liable to abuse it by choosing what is sinful and wrong. Most of the crosses and trials we meet in life are caused by violations—by ourselves and others—of the rules of life and the laws of charity and justice. To prevent this abuse of free-will, God would have to deprive men of that essential gift which, with his intellect, makes him a man. Likewise, we could prevent all road accidents by removing the steering wheels from cars but then we would have no cars. Let us face the fact, almost all the hardships and sufferings which we have to bear in life, are caused by the unjust and uncharitable actions of our fellowmen: and even God himself, following his own wise pattern of life for men on earth, cannot prevent such evil actions.

Would God want to prevent all such injustices and all this inhumanity of man toward his fellowman? Not that he approves of it, much less causes it, but can he not have a purpose in permitting it? How would we, his children on earth, earn heaven if this world were an earthly paradise? What loving father would keep his children from school because they found it a hardship, and when they could be so happy playing at home all day and every day? School is absolutely necessary for those children's future, and it is because fathers are truly kind to their children that they compel them to undergo this temporary hardship. God is the kindest of fathers. He wants us all in heaven. He has mapped out the road which will lead us there. He allows these hardships to come our way so that we can prepare for our real future life.

With James and John, let us tell our divine Lord that we are ready to follow him on the path to Calvary; that we are ready to drink the cup of sufferings which he drank and to be immersed in the sorrows which he endured. He went through all of this for us; we are doing it for our own sakes. He carried the real cross—ours is light when compared with his; furthermore, he will help us to bear our daily trial and struggles. How could any Christian become weary and faint-hearted when he has Christ helping him on the road?

THIRTIETH SUNDAY OF THE YEAR

FIRST READING : Jeremiah 31 : 7-9. Thus says the Lord : "Sing aloud with gladness for Jacob, and raise shouts for the chief of the nations; proclaim, give praise, and say, 'The Lord has saved his people, the remnant of Israel.' Behold, I will bring them from the north country, and gather them from the farthest parts of the earth, among them the blind and the lame, the woman with child and her who is in travail, together; a great company, they shall return here. With weeping they shall come, and with consolations I will lead them back, I will make them walk by brooks of water, in a straight path in which they shall not stumble; for I am a father to Israel, and Ephraim is my first-born.

EXPLANATION : On Jeremiah, see the fifth Sunday of Lent. The prophet Jeremiah lived and preached during a troublesome and sad period of the Chosen People's history. Israel, the northern kingdom, had been overrun by Assyria in 721 and the people were taken into exile. Judah, the southern kingdom, survived until 587 when it was captured by Babylonia and the people were taken there to live a life of exile. The prophet told them that they had brought it all on themselves because of their disloyalty to their kind God who had given them this Promised Land to be their home. In today's excerpts, the prophet has changed from denunciation to consolation. He is speaking to Israel (the northern tribes) and promising them that the good God will lead a "remnant" of them out of exile and establish them once more in their own homeland. God will do this because, notwithstanding their forgetfulness of him, he is still a father to Israel.

sing . . . Jacob : Jacob is another name

for Israel (Gn. 32 : 28). There is reason for songs and shouts of joy in store for Israel.

chief of the nations : It is another description of Israel—the principal nation in God's eyes, as he says in verse 9 : "Ephraim is my first-born."

Lord has saved : The people who will sing with joy will declare why God has saved—brought back—his people.

remnant of Israel : Many would have become lost among the Gentiles during the exile, a (small) portion who retained their faith would return.

north . . . earth : Assyria was north-east of Palestine—it was at the end of the earth, in the estimatiton of Jeremiah and his contemporaries.

blind . . . travail : The return from exile will be so aided by God that even the least capable of traveling will be part of the caravan : for God will assist them miraculously.

weeping they shall come : The C.C.D. and J.B. have : "They departed in tears"—that is, when going into exile, but they shall return rejoicing. This fits the situation better—why should they weep when leaving exile?

walk . . . water : the journey homewards will be through miles of desert, but just as in the first exodus God supplied the Israelites miraculously with water, so in this second exodus he will act even more generously—they shall travel along the banks of continuously-running streams.

shall not stumble : God will smooth the path for them—there will be no hindrance in their way to hit or delay them.

father to Israel : Notwithstanding their past disloyalty he is still their father and still loves his children.

Ephraim first-born : Ephraim was the leading tribe in the northern kingdom and is often used in the prophets as a synonym for Israel. God loves Israel just as a father has a special love for his first-born son.

APPLICATION : While granting that the prophet uses some hyperbole in his description of the return of the "remnant" of Israel, as he also does in describing the return of Judah in the following chapters, the fact that God did forgive and bring back such unworthy children is proof beyond compare of his infinite mercy and love. His Chosen People in both the northern and southern kingdom (Israel and Judah) had insulted and betrayed him for centuries, before he allowed the pagan nations they imitated to take them into captivity. They were the very people to whom he had been a kind father for centuries. He had brought them out of Egypt, set them up in Canaan—a country he gave them to be their own, had protected them again and again from aggressive enemies; yet these ungrateful ones forgot all this and abandoned the living God for idols of wood and stone. For generations he tolerated their apostasy; he sent his prophets to recall them to their senses, but in vain; finally, as a last resort, he allowed both kingdoms to be overrun by pagan powers who took his people as slaves into exile.

Although his Chosen People had abandoned him, he did not abandon them. He watched over them in exile and when he found that their exile had wrought a change of heart in some of his rebellious children, he brought them back to their homeland where once more they could be his elected ones. There in the Promised Land of Canaan they remained until the time was ripe for the sending of his divine Son on earth—in the human nature which he was to take from these same Chosen People, as he had promised to Abraham and his descendants.

This prophecy of Jeremiah, then, foretelling the return of a remnant of the Chosen People from exile is not merely a bit of Bible history which we should learn, it is a reminder to us Christians that God was thinking of us and preparing the way for our salvation centuries before Christ came on earth. According to God's long-standing promise: the Messiah would be a descendant of Abraham, a son of David; he would be born in Bethlehem. But if some of the Chosen People had not been brought back from exile this could not have happened. Thus this return of the exiles, foretold by Jeremiah and later effected by God, was his preparation for the sending of Christ among us to be our Savior.

The first lesson we must learn from this bit of Bible history is, that God was planning for us and thinking of us from all eternity. We are not mere blobs of humanity groping our way in the dark on earth; we are individual human beings, very important in the eyes of God; individuals for whom he has planned a happiness, and he has been planning it from all eternity. The eighteen centuries of God's dealings with his Chosen People, as described in the Old Testament, are but a short chapter of the history of God's planning for our eternal happiness. However, it is a short chapter from which we can learn so much of his loving concern for us. If God has thought and planned for so long for our eternal happiness, surely we should be self-interested enough to make this, our eternal happiness, the governing thought of our short lives.

We, Christians, can surely "sing with gladness" today, as the prophet tells us, for the merciful and loving God has saved us. He has put us on the straight path to heaven, on a path made smooth and easy by the life, death and resurrection of his beloved Son whom he sent to lead us back to our merciful Father.

There is a second lesson for all of us in this prophecy of Jeremiah. It is: God's mercy is without limit and he is ready to bestow it on us at the first sign we give him that we need it. Most of us have offended God and perhaps deserted him for long periods. Like the Chosen People, we did not appreciate all he had done and was doing for us. We were unfaithful to him and went after worldly idols perhaps, getting ourselves swamped in worldly ambitions and pleasures. But we are dealing with the same God of infinite mercy and forgiveness who brought back the unworthy Chosen People from the exile that their sins had brought on them. Can we have any doubt that he will bring us, too, back from that self-induced exile which our sins imposed on us? He is waiting for our word of petition, our humble request for forgiveness to take us back to his fatherly bosom. In fact, he is sending out his fatherly appeals to us to return to the path of virtue. He is sending them in many ways and guises, telling us that he is still our Father—that we are his first-born. Today's reading is one of these loving calls. There may be other calls for us but there may not; let us not ignore this one—our eternal future depends on our response.

SECOND READING: Hebrews 5:1–6. Every high priest chosen from among men is appointed to act on behalf of men in relation to God, to offer gifts and sacrifices for sins. He can deal gently with the ignorant and wayward, since he himself is beset with weakness. Because of this he is bound to offer sacrifice for his own sins as well as for those of the people. And one does not take the honor upon himself, but he is called by God, just as Aaron was.

So also Christ did not exalt himself to be made a high priest, but was appointed by him who said to him, "Thou art my Son, today I have begotten thee"; as he says also in another place, "Thou art a priest for ever, after the order of Melchizedek."

EXPLANATION: Today's reading from the Epistle to the Hebrews is a continuation of last Sunday's theme: Jesus is our High Priest. The high priest of the Old Testament was the chief intermediary between the Chosen People and God. He brought their petitions and their repentance into God's presence through the temple sacrifices. He did not choose this office for himself, he was called by God to it through his ancestor Aaron, the first high priest of the Old Testament. Christ is our High Priest, our intermediary with God. He, too, did not take this office on himself—it was given him by God the Father, as the psalms show.

high . . . men: Aaron, and his descendants in the direct line were chosen from among their fellow-Jews to represent all the Chosen People in the offering of sacrifices to God. Christ is chosen from men in general, for he is the intermediary between all mankind and God.

for sins: There were other sacrifices besides those offered to make atonement for sins, but Hebrews is connecting the high priest especially with the Day of Atonement (see chapter 9): when the only sacrifices offered were sacrifices for the sins of the people.

can deal gently: The high priest of the Old Testament could understand the failings and weaknesses of his people for

he was one of them. The author of Hebrews says that our High Priest, Jesus, is able too to sympathize with all our weaknesses for he was tempted, as we are, yet without sinning (see last Sunday).

for his own sins: On the Day of Atonement the Jewish high priest offered sacrifices of atonement for his own sins and the sins of the people. In this Jesus differed: he had no sins to atone for, his sacrifice was for our sins.

Christ . . . himself: Like the Old Testament high priests who received this honor from God through Aaron, Christ was given this honor (which entailed humiliation and suffering) by his Father.

Thou art my son: The author now proves that it was God his Father who made him our High Priest by quoting two psalms: 2:7 and 110:4. In the first quotation God proclaims Christ to be his Son and in the second Christ is declared to be a priest forever. It was not from his sacrifice of himself on the cross alone, but from this sacrifice crowned by his resurrection and exaltation, that his priesthood was made perfect and permanent (see 9:24).

order of Melchizedek: Melchizedek was king and priest in the Jebusite city of Jerusalem when Abraham returned from his victory over the king of Elam and his associates (Gn. 14:18). He blessed Abraham and Abraham offered him tithes of all the booty he had taken. Hebrews stresses this fact to show that Christ, who is said in this psalm to be "a priest forever after the order of Melchizedek," was therefore superior to the Levitical priesthood—since they in their ancestor Abraham offered tithes to Melchizedek. Whatever may be thought about this king's priesthood that of Christ was forever (see 6 : 20 and the following chapters).

APPLICATION : Through the incarnation of his divine Son, God has given us a High Priest who offered, once and for all, his own body on the cross as a sacrifice for the sins of all mankind. He entered the real holy of holies on our great day of atonement and will remain there as our intermediary with the Father until the last man has been saved. It is of this basic truth of our Christian faith that the Epistle to the Hebrews reminds us today. As the author was writing to Judaeo-Christians, who knew the Jewish cultic regulations of the temple in Jerusalem, he uses terms connected with the temple cult to bring home to his readers the full meaning that the death and glorification of Christ have for them.

It was God himself who appointed Aaron, Moses' mouthpiece, to be the first high priest to have charge of the services of the Tent of the Meeting, when the Israelites fled from Egypt. His eldest son was to succeed him as high priest, and his other sons were also priests. This was to continue down through the ages. The high priest was the intermediary between the Chosen People and God. Once a year, on the Day of Atonement, he offered the sacrifice which made atonement for all the sins of the people. The high priest, therefore, had a very special place—the most important religious position—in the Jewish community. The Jewish converts to Christianity would understand very well what the author of this epistle meant when he called Christ our High Priest, appointed by God to make atonement for all the sins of the world. They already knew how this atonement was made. They knew who this high priest was— the Son of God who took human nature in which he could make this sacrifice which was of infinite value, and surpassed all the sacrifices offered by all the high priests of Jewish history. They knew that Christ's sacrifice on the cross was for all men—not for the Jews alone, but for each and every member of the human race for all time.

We, Christians of the 20th century, know all of this as did the Christians of the seventies of the 1st century. We know God has planned from all eternity to give us a place in heaven when we die. We know the humiliations and sufferings his divine Son endured so that we could be made worthy of this honor, and therefore we should know how important it is that we do the little expected of us in order to fulfill God's plan for us. Yet, there are many Christians today who are so entangled in the passing things of this world that they have no time or inclination to look to their eternal future. They live and act in this world as if it were to be their eternal world, and have no thought or time to prepare themselves for the future home which God has planned for them.

There will be a rude awakening when they are called to judgement. When they realize what they have lost, and when they look back on the follies and foibles on which they spent their days on earth, how they will despise themselves! Today, out of true Christian charity, let us pray that such deluded Christians will be very few in number.

GOSPEL : Mark 10 : 46–52. As Jesus was leaving Jericho with his disciples and a great multitude, Bartimaeus, a blind beggar, the son of Timaeus, was sitting by the roadside. And when he heard that it was Jesus of Nazareth, he began to cry out and say, "Jesus, Son of David, have mercy on me!" And many rebuked him, telling him to be silent; but he cried out all the more, "Son of David, have mercy on me!" And Jesus stopped and said, "Call him." And they called the blind man, saying to him, "Take heart; rise, he is calling you." And throwing off his mantle he sprang up and came to Jesus. And Jesus said to him, "What do you want me to do for you?" And the blind man said to him, "Master, let me receive my sight." And Jesus said to him, "Go your way; your faith has made you well." And immediately he received his sight and followed him on the way.

EXPLANATION : Jesus and his disciples, followed by a great multitude, were on their way from Galilee to Jerusalem. Three times already he had warned his disciples of what dreadful things would happen to him there, but they refused to listen and followed him gladly, expecting very soon to see him as the triumphant head of his new, political, messianic kingdom.

On his way through Jericho Jesus worked his last miracle of healing, as recorded in Mark. A blind man called on Jesus as "son of David," that is Messiah. He had such faith and trust in his healing powers that he refused to be silenced by those following Christ. He received the reward of his persevering faith. He was given not only his eyesight but the grace to become a follower of Jesus.

blind . . . roadside : He heard the noise of the crowd and naturally inquired what was happening. He had most probably heard of the miracles of Jesus in Galilee and Jerusalem, and had become convinced that he was the promised Messiah.

cry . . . say : He wanted badly to have his eyesight restored to him. Here was the One who could do him this favor. Although he did not know it, this was his last chance; Jesus did not pass through Jericho again.

cried . . . more : The attempts to prevent him from asking for this miracle only made him all the more determined.

Jesus . . . called him : Jesus heard his loud call for help and took pity on him. He asked the blind man to repeat his request when he was brought to him.

your faith . . . well : He believed that Jesus was the Messiah. His open confession that Jesus could heal him earned for him the miraculous restoration of his sight.

followed him : He got the spiritual grace to throw in his lot with Jesus. He did not know where Jesus was going, but he was convinced that he was the Messiah, the son of David, foretold by the prophets and therefore he determined to be one of his followers. That he became an outstanding member of the early Church, where Mark labored and wrote,

seems probable from the fact that Mark gives us his name : Bartimaeus, as if the name was known to Mark's readers. Matthew and Luke give the same story but do not give the blind man's name.

APPLICATION : This blind man of Jericho was one of the very lucky men in the gospel story. He got the last chance of appealing in person to Jesus for the gift of his eyesight. He used that chance in spite of opposition; his faith and trust in Jesus were so strong that nobody could stop him from expressing them. He made his request while proclaiming his faith. He got, not only what he asked—the physical gift, but a spiritual insight was added as well and he became a faithful follower of Christ.

Our Lord had passed through Jericho a few times during his public ministry. Jericho was on the route from Galilee to Jerusalem. Bartimaeus was very probably sitting on the roadside begging for alms on these occasions also, but influenced by the lack of interest of his fellow-citizens he, too, had no time for all this talk about a Messiah and a miracle-worker. In any case, it was only on the occasion of Christ's last journey through Jericho that his faith moved him to appeal aloud for help from the one and only person whom he was convinced could grant him his request. His appeal was heard.

There is a deep spiritual lesson for all of us in today's gospel story. Like Bartimaeus, many of us have been sitting by the roadside for years, not moving a foot toward our eternal destination. We have been blind to our true interests; our sole preoccupation seems to be to collect the paltry alms that this world would deign to drop in our laps. But we are even more to be pitied than

Bartimaeus—he knew that he was blind; we are not aware of our spiritual blindness—we think everything in the garden is rosy and colorful when we see only the colors we want to see and are blind to the things that really matter.

We said above that it is probable that Bartimaeus ignored the passing-by of Jesus on earlier occasions; it is certain that in our case we have ignored the presence of Jesus in the many reminders he has sent us up to now. That parish retreat we did not attend; that sudden death of a close friend; that illness of a near relative; that car accident from which we miraculously escaped; these and many other incidents are examples of the many times our loving Lord passed close to us—ready to cure our spiritual blindness; but we did not see him.

It is possible that our Lord saw Bartimaeus sitting by the roadside on his earlier journeys through Jericho. Perhaps he could not help him, for the blind man was engaged in collecting alms with no thought for the greater gift— the return of his eyesight. It is certain that our Lord has often been near to us, anxious to give us back our spiritual vision. But like Bartimaeus, we were so busy gathering up this world's paltry donations that we did not even think of the far greater grace we needed.

In the twenty centuries of our Christian history there have been some who have deliberately shut the eyes of their minds to the many calls to repentance which Jesus sent. This is a danger and a fatal mistake we can all avoid if we learn today's gospel message. This story of the blind man of Jericho was not inspired and preserved for some literary reason, but as an instruction for us. It is read to us today, to make us examine our consciences and see the true state of our spiritual standing in the eyes of God. Are we steadily moving on toward heaven, carrying out daily duties to God and to our neighbor, bearing life's crosses cheerfully—knowing that they come to us from a loving Father as part of our training for heaven? Or are we sitting idly by the roadside, engrossed and enmeshed in the affairs of this world, oblivious of our real purpose in life and turning deaf ears and blind eyes to all the danger signals that Christ our Savior regularly is sending out to us?

For some among us today this may be Christ's last call. Will we be so utterly disinterested in our own eternal welfare as to ignore it? For all of us it is a call to put our house in order. We may not have been sitting by the roadside, but have we been keeping faithfully to the road to heaven—marked out for us by our Christian faith? Let us all call on Jesus, son of David and Son of God today, to give us the grace to see ourselves as we are—and then to see ourselves as we ought to be. "Master, let me receive my sight."

THIRTY-FIRST SUNDAY OF THE YEAR

FIRST READING: Deuteronomy 6:2-6. Moses said to the people, fear the Lord your God, you and your son and your son's son, by keeping all his statutes and his commandments, which I command you, all the days of your life; and that your days may be prolonged. Hear therefore, O Israel, and be careful to do them; that it may go well with you, and that you may multiply greatly, as the Lord, the God of your fathers, has promised you, in a land flowing with milk and honey.

"Hear, O Israel: The Lord our God is one Lord; and you shall love the Lord your God with all your heart, and with all your soul, and with all your might. And these words which I command you this day shall be upon your heart."

EXPLANATION: Moses, having received the Ten Commandments from God on Mount Sinai, set about teaching them to the Israelites, God's Chosen People. He promised them temporal rewards if they remained loyal to their God who was the one and only God (verse 4), and would prove their loyalty by observing his commandments. To-day's excerpt from the book of Deuteronomy especially stressed the sincere, heartfelt love that the Chosen People should feel for God.

Fear . . . God : Fear in this context means reverence, not dread. The people should reverence and respect God.

your son . . . son's son : Down through all generations this reverence for God is demanded.

all . . . your life : This reverence for God was to be practiced in every way and at all times.

days . . . prolonged : This was a temporal reward. A long life was always looked on by the Israelites as a special blessing from God.

multiply greatly : A large family, another temporal blessing, was greatly esteemed by the Chosen People. God had promised Abraham a very numerous progeny—his descendants would be "as numerous as the stars in the sky" (Gn. 15 : 4).

flowing . . . honey : This was the land of Canaan which God had promised to give to the Chosen People to be their homeland. Compared with the desert, through which they had traveled since they left Egypt, it was a fertile land.

The Lord . . . Lord : Monotheism is here expressed as it is elsewhere in Deuteronomy (4 : 35; 32 : 39 etc.), as also is the oneness of Yahweh compared with the multiplicity of false gods about which they would hear in Canaan.

love . . . might : God must be loved with all the power a man possesses; by using the three terms : heart, soul, and might, Moses is emphasizing this obligation.

APPLICATION : The relationship between God and man is a relationship of love. God is love and because he is love he created the universe and made man the master and masterpiece of that creation. Love, like heat, is self-diffusive, that is, its nature is to spread itself out. The spreading out of God's love was creation; he made things and beings who could share his love with him. Chief among his created beings was man to whom he gave the capacity to appreciate love and to return it. Now, God could have given a limited portion of his love to men, that is, he could have let men, like the other creatures on earth, be content with whatever gifts of God's love they could receive in this world. In other words, earthly death could have been their final end.

However, God's love, being infinite, went far beyond this as regards men. In creating them, God gave them the faculties which place them away above all other earthly creatures. He made men capable of appreciating love and of reciprocating it—something the other creatures on earth cannot do. God saw that in the short space of this earthly life men could not satisfy the faculty for loving and being loved. He, therefore, planned for men a future life—a life wherein men could fully appreciate the immensity of divine love and return to the full that love according to our own created capacity.

In the "fullness of time," centuries and centuries after he had created man, God began to make preparations for putting his plan into action. By this time, men had more or less completely forgotten their divine Benefactor, but God had not forgotten them. He called Abraham out of the pagan land of Ur of the Chaldees, and made him a believer in the true God. He brought him over to

Canaan—promising to give his descendants that country as their fatherland. God did so in order to have one people on earth who would know and reverence him, and from whom his divine Son would take his human nature. The incarnation was God's loving way of making man fit and worthy to win the gift of the future life he had planned for him.

God took a special interest in the descendants of Abraham whom he made his own Chosen People. Having led them out of the slavery of Egypt he made a covenant or pact with them—through their leader Moses on Mount Sinai. God promised to bring them into the Promised Land of Canaan and establish them there; they on their part, were to keep the commandments he gave them. These commandments regulated their lives, their relationship with God and their neighbor. The basis of these relationships was a proper appreciation of all that God had done for them; this appreciation they would show and prove by their reciprocal love for him.

Unfortunately for themselves, the Chosen People did not always keep their part of this covenant of Sinai. Instead of loving God and thanking him for all his gifts to them, they became involved in worldly affairs and turned to the false gods of their pagan neighbors. The result : they were decimated by pagan conquerors and by exile. Notwithstanding their infidelity God was faithful to his promise. A remnant was saved and from that came eventually the human nature which the Son of God took on himself.

We may be shocked at the behavior of God's Chosen People who were never really grateful for all he did for them, but how much more blameworthy are we Christians, when we forget to love and reverence him. What he did for Abraham's descendants was but a shadow of what he has done for us. He made them his Chosen People—he has made us his adopted children. He gave them the land of Canaan—he has promised us heaven as our homeland. He gave them Moses to lead them out of the slavery of Egypt—he has given us his divine Son to lead us from the sin and slavery of this world to heaven. Moses, as leader of the stubborn Israelites, led a life of contradiction and troubles—Christ our Leader suffered the death of the cross for us.

We do owe so much more than the Chosen People to God; are we trying to repay that immense debt? Do we love God as we should?

SECOND READING : Hebrews 7 : 23-28. The priests of the old covenant were many in number, because they were prevented by death from continuing in office; but Christ holds his priesthood permanently, because he continues for ever. Consequently he is able for all time to save those who draw near to God through him, since he always lives to make intercession for them.

For it was fitting that we should have such a high priest, holy, blameless, unstained, separated from sinners, exalted above the heavens. He has no need, like those high priests, to offer sacrifices daily, first for his own sins and then for those of the people; he did this once for all when he offered up himself. Indeed, the law appoints men in their weakness as high priests, but the word of the oath, which came later than the law, appoints a Son who has been made perfect for ever.

EXPLANATION : The author of *Hebrews* continues to show the superiority of Jesus over the high priests of the Old Testament. They were many, he was one. They interceded daily for their own sins and the sins of their people. He interceded once for all for his people and he had no personal sins to atone for. On God's command it was the Mosaic Law that appointed the Old Testament high priests, it was God's oath which came later than the "law" that made Christ our high priest. The Levitical high priests were weak, sinful mortals, our high priest is the sinless, holy, divine Son of God.

many . . . death : Because they were mortal the term of office as high priest was limited and so of necessity there were many of them.

priesthood permanently : Christ's priesthood did not end in death. In fact, its efficacy really began when he rose from the dead. He is now in the inner sanctuary forever interceding for us.

near to God through him : He is permanently at the throne of God, ready to plead for all who want to approach God. There is no other approach except through him, for he is our sole intermediary.

holy . . . sinners : In his human nature Christ was the perfect man. He kept even the least of God's commandments and obeyed his every wish.

exalted . . . heavens : This refers to his ascension and glorification. As man he is next to God the Father in heaven : "sitting at God's right hand."

need . . . daily : Unlike the high priests who had to take part in and supervise daily sacrifices in the temple of Jerusalem, Christ had no need to do this.

once for all : Christ's one sacrifice on the cross was of infinite value because of his divine nature. Hence it was sufficient for him to offer this sacrifice once for all men and for all time.

law . . . men : On God's command Moses appointed the office of high priest of the Old Law. Christ is appointed directly by God, and his appointment is confirmed by God's oath : "God has sworn an oath which he never will retract, you are a priest forever of the order of Melchizedek" (Ps. 110 : 4; see also last Sunday's second reading).

APPLICATION : In today's first reading we saw how privileged we are when compared with the Chosen People of the Old Testament. These six verses from *Hebrews*, which form our second reading today are given over to the same theme: our high priest, our mediator with God, is incomparably greater and more efficacious than any intermediaries they had, for he is none other than God's own divine Son. But, lest we be tempted to see discrimination or acceptance of persons on the part of God, we must realize that God's plan for man's salvation was put into operation gradually—as he found men's minds fit to receive his revelation.

The Israelites, whom God selected to be the recipients of his partial revelation in the Old Testament times, were evidently more worthy of this honor than any of their contemporaries. Yet, they were only a few steps removed from paganism and were ever in danger of reverting to it. However, God dealt with them mercifully and patiently. He quickly forgave their many lapses, and again and again he protected them from their pagan enemies during their twelve hundred years in Canaan. Even when the exile—which their disloyalty brought upon them—should have ended their history as a separate race forever, he brought back a "remnant" to Jerusalem and Judah from whom the promised Messiah took his human nature.

His revelation of himself to them, and of his great purpose for man, was partial and limited because they were not yet sufficiently developed in their religious outlook. They were given only a vague idea of life after death. The rewards promised for fidelity to him and to his commandments were temporal, earthly rewards. But running like a golden thread through the tapestry of their history, was the promise and, therefore, the hope of a great blessing to come through them for all mankind. The prophets gradually developed this promise and hope. By the time Christ came—as the fulfillment of that promise first made to Abraham—sharing in this blessing was much more important to the true, loyal chosen ones of God than were temporal rewards or blessings.

While thus preparing his Chosen People for the incarnation God was also preparing the pagan nations for the coming of Christ. The following were all preparations for the speedy spread of the gospel when Christ came : Alexander's conquest of the known world toward the end of the 4th century B.C.—with the consequent spread of the Greek language; the rise of the Roman empire which strengthened the unity of its various subjects by sound laws and safe means of travel; the decline in almost all parts of the empire—the then known world—of the belief in the pagan gods. In these and in many other ways, God was patiently and wisely preparing the world for the astounding act of divine love toward mankind which was revealed in the incarnation.

We are Christians today because God wanted it so from all eternity. He worked quietly and efficiently down through the ages to make this possible. As regards our knowledge of God and the purpose he has for us, we are much better informed than were the Chosen People and the pagan nations of the past. But they will be judged according to their knowledge; their religious ignorance will excuse many a fault. We, on the other hand, will be expected to make a return to him in proportion to the many talents he has given us. Our excuses at the judgement seat will be very few and very flimsy. Our Judge will be the very Son of God who made himself our high priest, in order to open heaven for us and make our entrance there safe and relatively easy. He is ever present, pleading our case at the throne of mercy. The Christian who turns his back on Christ his advocate during life, will surely find it hard to face him as his judge when he comes to die.

GOSPEL : Mark 12 : 28–34. One of the scribes came up to Jesus and asked him, "Which commandment is the first of all?" Jesus answered, "The first is, 'Hear, O Israel : The Lord our God, the Lord is one; and you shall love the Lord your God with all your heart, and with all your soul, and with all your mind, and with all your strength.' The second is this, 'You shall love your neighbor as yourself.' There is no other commandment greater than these." And the scribe said to him, "You are right, Teacher; you have truly said that he is one, and there is no other but he; and to love him with all the heart, and with all the understanding, and with all the strength, and to love one's neighbor as oneself, is much more than all whole burnt offerings and sacrifices." And when Jesus saw that he answered wisely, he said to him, "You are not far from the kingdom of God." And after that no one dared to ask him any question.

EXPLANATION : At the time of Christ, the Jewish rabbis spent most of their time expounding and examining the Mosaic Law. Very often this resulted more in mental gymnastics than in spiritual or religious uplift. There were various schools of thought among them and often heated discussions. One of the questions frequently debated by the rabbis was : which of the ten commandments was the most important? This is the very question a Scribe—a man well-versed in the law—puts to Jesus in today's gospel reading. From the context it is clear that unlike other tendentious questions put to him by Scribes and Pharisees, this question is put by an honest Scribe who is sincerely anxious to get an honest and true answer.
Jesus answered : Knowing that his questioner was sincere Jesus gave him a frank answer, telling him that the two primary and essential commandments were to love the one true God and to love one's neighbor as one loved oneself.
Hear O Israel : Jesus quoted Deuteronomy 6 : 4–5 for the first commandment : the love of the one true God; to this he added the second greatest commandment : true love of neighbor, which he quoted from Leviticus 19 : 18.
you . . . Teacher : The Scribe, honest man that he was, accepted and approved of the answer. He had himself come to the same conclusion and recognizing Jesus as a sound, sincere rabbi had come to him for confirmation of his opinion.
that he is one : The Scribe went on to praise Jesus for emphasizing the oneness of the true God who has no equal or no contender for this position.
with . . . heart : This one and only God is to be loved with all the love of which man is capable.

one's . . . oneself : In Leviticus this commandment was binding on one Israelite in relation to his brother Israelite. In Christ's mind, of which the Scribe is approving, neighbor meant not only a fellow-Jew but any man, all men. (See Luke 10 : 29–37, where the story of the Good Samaritan is given by Christ when, having stressed the primacy of this commandment, he is asked : who is my neighbor?)

much sacrifices : The Scribe emphasizes that without true love of God and neighbor, the external signs of worship offered to God are useless. These services are of value, if they are motivated by a sincere interior love for God, which of its nature includes love of neighbor.

not far . . . God : The kingdom of God was the messianic kingdom which Christ was setting up on earth and which would have its completion and perfection in heaven. The wisdom shown by this Scribe proved to Jesus that he was very close to becoming a member of his kingdom. All that was wanting was the acceptance of Jesus as the promised Messiah. Did he accept Jesus later? We are not told, but many of the Jewish priests and Scribes did become Christ's followers after his resurrection and the descent of the Holy Spirit.

dared . . . question : This statement is hardly in its correct context here. Matthew 22 : 46 and Luke 20 : 40 place this sentence in more suitable contexts.

APPLICATION : The personal lesson which comes over loud and clear for every sincere Christian from today's gospel, is that the solid foundation of our Christian religion is love of God and neighbor. As our Lord says : "there is no other commandment greater than these." All the other commandments are expansions of these two and indications of how we are to put these two commandments into daily practice. For example : why am I forbidden to murder my neighbor? Simply because he belongs to God; it was God who gave him his life, and God has commanded me to love and respect him. Taking his life is interfering with God's rights, and disobeying him as well. Likewise, the prohibition of idolatry, refraining from insulting God's name, keeping the Sabbath day holy are the principal ways of indicating how we should love God.

One may ask : how can I love God? He is infinitely perfect, he needs nothing from me, what therefore can I do for

him? I can understand loving my neighbor—for a neighbor can need help, advice, encouragement and consolation. I can prove my love by giving these to my neighbor, but God has no such needs. It is quite true that true love is not theoretical but pragmatic, it means doing some good for somebody. While the infinite God has no needs that I can supply, he has claims on my service, on my respect, on my gratitude—claims so basic and so great that I must be ready to suffer persecution and even death rather than deny or dishonor him (Mt. 5 : 10; Lk. 6 : 23). It was God who gave me existence and every gift that I have. It was God, through the incarnation of his own divine Son, who made me his adopted child and heir to heaven. Everything that I am and have and hope to be, I owe to God's generosity; therefore, he has an unquestionable right to my gratitude, my reverence, my respect— these are the ways in which I can show my love for him.

The keeping of God's commandments, the prayers of thanksgiving, praise and petition which daily we offer, the attendance at Mass and other liturgical functions, these are the means God gives us of showing our love, our recognition of total dependence on him and our gratitude for all he has done and is doing for us. God does not need any of these signs of our submission and reverence and respect, but we need them absolutely, for they are the means he has given us of fulfilling his purpose in creating us—to share his eternal glory with him. To love God then, is not an obligation imposed on us by some demanding superior but a privilege granted us so that we can become worthy of the greater gifts he has in store for us.

Loving our neighbor—and in the Christian code this means all men no matter what may be their color, race or religion—is, according to our divine Lord, another most effective way of proving to God that we love him. Because of our common humanity we should be inclined to help our fellow-men, our neighbors, but the Christian law spiritualizes this natural inclination, by commanding us to help our neighbor because he is God's child. We are all fellow-children of God, members of the one family. Our heavenly Father loves each one of us and wants our salvation. If we love our common-Father we will do all we can to help his other children also to attain salvation. It will earn for us God's favor.

If we observe these two commandments we are "fulfilling the whole law and the prophets,"; we are serving God and showing our gratitude to him for all his goodness to us. The Christian who is following Christ in love is already active in the earthly kingdom of God and traveling safely toward God's eternal kingdom of peace and happiness.

THIRTY-SECOND SUNDAY OF THE YEAR

FIRST READING : 1 Kings 17 : 10–16. Elijah, the prophet, arose and went to Zarephath; and when he came to the gate of the city, behold, a widow was there gathering sticks; and he called to her and said, "Bring me a little water in a vessel that I may drink." And as she was going to bring it, he called to her and said, "Bring me a morsel of bread in your hand." And she said, "As the Lord your God lives I have nothing baked, only a handful of meal in a jar, and a little oil in a cruse; and now, I am gathering a couple of sticks, that I may go in and prepare it for myself and my son, that we may eat it, and die." And Elijah said to her, "Fear not; go and do as you have said; but first make me a little cake of it and bring it to me, and afterward make for yourself and your son. For thus says the Lord the God of Israel, 'The jar of meal shall not be spent, and the cruse of oil shall not fail, until the day that the Lord sends rain upon the earth.'" And she went and did as Elijah said; and she, and he, and her household ate for many days. The jar of meal was not spent, neither did the cruse of oil fail, according to the word of the Lord which he spoke by Elijah.

EXPLANATION : In this reading from the first Book of Kings we have one of the many miracles attributed to Elijah, the great prophet who preached in the northern kingdom between 900 and 850 B.C. Because of the willingness of a poor destitute widow to help him—when she and her son were reduced to the last handful of meal—the prophet guaranteed that her jar of meal and her cruse of oil would not run out until the famine which then raged in Israel had ended. His word was fulfilled because it was the word, the promise, of God.
bring . . . bread : The prophet's need was not very great but in the case of the

morsel of bread it was more than this poor widow could spare.
a handful . . . jar : This was all she had left. She was about to bake this last little cake for herself and her son.
so that . . . die : They would eat this last bit of food and then resign themselves to death by starvation.
Fear not : The prophet tells her it will not be so. He has the word of the Lord, the God of Israel, that the little meal and oil she has will last until the famine is over, even though she uses it daily.
went . . . Elijah said : She believed the word, the promise, of God which the prophet gave her and :

jar ... spent : God fulfilled his promise. Although she used them daily the jar of meal and the cruse of oil never diminished. She and her household were never short of food during the famine. God rewarded the generosity she showed when dire poverty stared her in the face.

APPLICATION : "Anyone who welcomes a prophet because he is a prophet will have a prophet's reward; and anyone who welcomes a holy man because he is a holy man will have a holy man's reward. If anyone gives so much as a cup of cold water to one of these little ones because he is a disciple, then I tell you solemnly, he will most certainly not lose his reward" (Mt. 10 : 41–42). These are the words of Christ, the Son of God, when recommending his poor disciples to the charity of the people. Doubtless his mention of prophet and the cup of cold water, would recall to the minds of his hearers the story of Elijah and the kind-hearted widow of Zarephath. Elijah was one of the most popular and best-remembered prophets of the Old Testament. On another occasion (Lk. 4 : 25), our Lord reminded his doubting hearers in his home-town of Nazareth how God sent Elijah to this good widow of Sidon, who was not one of the Chosen People, although there were many widows in Israel then in need of help but unworthy of it. They would not have shared their last morsel of bread with a stranger even though he was God's representative.

The lesson of today's reading—re-emphasized as it is by our divine Lord's own word—is clear for us. We must be charitable towards a needy neighbor, not only when we have some superfluous goods which we can give away, but even when we have only the bare essentials for ourselves. We are expected to share these with one who has not even that little. But is not this demanding too much of us? Can Christian charity command us to shorten our own lives in order to prolong those of a needy neighbor for a few days or weeks? The answer is very clearly "yes" : we must be ready not only to risk our own lives in order to save that of a neighbor but we must be ready to lay down our lives willingly, if needs be, to save a neighbor. "Greater love than this no man has, that a man lay down his life for his friends" (Jn. 15 : 13); this is the ultimate in Christian charity, our Lord tells us. He put it into practice for us and he expects us to be willing to imitate him should the need arise.

We are grateful to God that Christ has had followers who fulfilled his command to the letter. They gave their lives to save others. Their noble sacrifice not only earned eternal life for them, but inspired many with a new love for God and neighbor. While making this earth a better place in which to live, it put heaven within the reach of many who would otherwise not have attained it.

Most of us will never have the privilege of being called on to make the supreme sacrifice for our neighbor's sake —but we are all called on to sacrifice some of our possessions to help a neighbor in need. Today's story emphasizes that we must be ready to share even our scanty means with one in greater need. It also adds that God will not let such charity go unrewarded. The widow of Zarephath and her son could have had one last modest meal before they died of the famine, but her generosity made her share even that little with a stranger.

She was rewarded : the little supply she had never diminished and she lived in frugal comfort all through the famine.

God can never be outdone in generosity. All we have and all that we are we owe to his kindness. If we show our willingness to share with those who are in want, he will not forget our charity— he will not see us in want.

SECOND READING : Hebrews 9 : 24–28. Christ has entered, not into a sanctuary made with hands, a copy of the true one, but into heaven itself, now to appear in the presence of God on our behalf. Nor was it to offer himself repeatedly, as the high priest enters the Holy Place yearly with blood not his own; for then he would have had to suffer repeatedly since the foundation of the world. But as it is, he has appeared once for all at the end of the age to put away sin by the sacrifice of himself. And just as it is appointed for men to die once, and after that comes judgement, so Christ, having been offered once to bear the sins of so many, will appear a second time, not to deal with sin but to save those who are eagerly waiting for him.

EXPLANATION : The Epistle to the Hebrews continues with its description of Christ as the high priest of the New Testament and his superiority over those of the Old Testament. Today's reference is to the Day of Atonement—one of the most important of the Old Testament ritual services—which was held only once each year. On that day the Jewish high priest entered into the inner sanctuary or holy of holies and sprinkled the blood of the sacrifices on the Ark of the Covenant. This was part of the atonement he was making for his own sins and the people's sins, committed during the preceding year. This ritual was repeated annually because, being a mere human act, it did not atone for all sins for all time. Christ our high priest offered himself in sacrifice once for all, for his sacrifice had infinite value. He was God and the holy of holies he entered on our great day of atonement, was not the inner sanctuary of the temple in Jerusalem but heaven itself,

the very abode of his Father. His second coming will be on our judgement day when he will reward those who were loyal to him and bring them into the eternal kingdom of his Father.

not sanctuary . . . hands : Christ our high priest, bearing the precious blood of his sacrifice, did not enter the inner sanctum of the Jerusalem temple which men had built; he entered God's own sanctuary in heaven.

on our behalf : He had no sins of his own to atone for—his sacrifice of himself was "for us men and for our salvation."

offer . . . repeatedly : His sacrifice was sufficient to atone for all men's sins for all time—because he was the Son of God in human nature.

at . . . age : When the time appointed by God arrived and the age of preparation —the Old Testament period—had ended Christ came and died for us.

to . . . judgement : As it is God's plan for men that they close their life on this earth when they come to die, so also is it his plan that each one will be examined, judged on how he lived that life in relation to God.

not . . . sin : The second coming of Christ in glory will not be to remit or forgive sin but to reward his faithful followers who are eagerly awaiting his coming.

APPLICATION : The author of the Epistle to the Hebrews is evidently writing to Jews who had become followers of Christ. Again and again he stressed the superiority of the Christian religion over that of the Old Testament which they had left. The Jewish high priesthood, appointed by God through Moses, was one held in great esteem and importance all through Old Testament times, but especially after the return from Babylon—when the high priest became their political as well as their religious leader. It was the high priest who regulated all the services of the Jerusalem temple. On their great annual Day of Atonement, he alone could offer sacrifice for the sins of the people and for his own sins. On that day, he alone could enter the holy of holies—the inner sanctuary of the temple in which were kept the tables of the commandments in the Ark of the Covenant. This Ark was called God's throne on earth. The Ark was missing from the inner sanctuary since before the destruction of the temple by the Babylonians (587 B.C.), because the prophet Jeremiah hid it in a cave on Mount Nebo according to 2 Mc. 2 : 4–8. The high priest, however, still carried out the ritual of the Day of Atonement. He entered the holy of holies and sprinkled the blood of the sacrifices where the Ark used to rest. This ritual was repeated each year.

The author of *Hebrews* says that Christ, our high priest, was superior in every way to the Jewish high priest, important though he was in the eyes of religious Jews. Christ did not have to repeat his sacrifice annually, his offering of himself as atonement for the sins of the whole world, of Jews and Gentiles, sufficed once for all. His sacrifice, unlike the temple sacrifices, was of infinite value. It was not the blood of goats and oxen that Christ offered to his Father, but the sacred blood of his body which he, the Son of God, assumed in order to become one of us and to be able to die for us. It was not into the inner sanctuary of the Jerusalem temple that Christ sent his precious offering, but into the real holy of holies, the eternal throne of his Father in heaven.

Therefore, there is no real comparison between the Jewish high priesthood and the real effective priesthood of Christ. Any effectiveness which the intermediation of the Jewish high priest had, or any value which the temple sacrifices could claim, came to the Chosen People from God's loving mercy which had the incarnation in view. They were types and the shadows of the real intercession, the real sacrifice which God's Son would offer not only for the Chosen People of old but for all mankind and for all time.

Do we Christians really appreciate the favors and the blessings God showered on us by sending his divine Son in human nature? By the fact of the incarnation we became brothers of Christ and adopted sons of God. This was the fulfillment of God's eternal plan for mankind. In the meantime sin had entered our world. To atone for the sins of the world the incarnate Son of God willingly accepted to undergo his passion and death by crucifixion so that his heavenly Father would remit the spiritual death our sins merited. Thus we would be able to share in the eternal inheritance which the incarnation won for us.

Do we really appreciate the greatness of God's love for us in planning this eternal future happiness for us and at such cost—the humiliation, sufferings and death of his only-begotten Son? With a future such as this, could we be so foolish as to let anything or any person on this earth come between us and the eternal crown God has prepared for us? Let St. Paul, the man who loved God with every fiber of his being, and

gladly spent his life to bring the knowledge of God's love for us to all the world, answer for us: "I consider that the sufferings of this life are not worth comparing with the glory that is to be revealed to us . . . If God is for us who is against us? He did not spare his own Son but gave him up for us all . . . Who shall separate us from the love of Christ? Shall tribulation, or distress, or persecutions or famine or nakedness or peril or sword . . . nothing will be able to separate us from the love of God in Christ Jesus our Lord" (Rm. 8 : 18 ff).

St. Paul is in heaven. We shall be there too if we follow his advice.

GOSPEL : Mark 12 : 38–44. In his teaching to the people, Jesus said, "Beware of the scribes, who like to go about in long robes, and to have salutations in the market places and the best seats in the synagogues and the places of honor at feasts, who devour widows' houses and for a pretense make long prayers. They will receive the greater condemnation."

And he sat down opposite the treasury, and watched the multitude putting money into the treasury. Many rich people put in large sums. And a poor widow came, and put in two copper coins, which make a penny. And he called his disciples to him, and said to them, "Truly, I say to you, this poor widow has put in more than all those who are contributing to the treasury. For they all contributed out of their abundance; but she out of her poverty has put in everything she had, her whole living."

EXPLANATION : There are two separate incidents in today's Gospel: Christ warns the people to beware of and not to imitate the hypocrisy of the Scribes; the widow whose tiny contribution to charity was in fact more generous than the large donations of the rich. She gave the penny which she could ill afford to give, while the others gave of the superfluity.

Beware . . . Scribes : The Scribes were

well versed in the Mosaic Law but, unfortunately, they prided themselves on this superior knowledge and also on their strict observance of its letter. They despised all the other Jews who knew little about the Law and did not always keep it to the letter. In so doing, the Scribes were violating one of the two basic precepts of the Law—love of neighbor.

long . . . salutations : They wanted to be

noticed by people and to be saluted reverently wherever they went among them.

in the synagogue : Even in the place of prayer they had to have the highest places—and the seats of honor at feasts.

devour widows' houses : They played on the gullibility of pious widows of wealth with financial profit to themselves.

pretense . . . prayers : In order to attract attention and admiration, they lengthened their public prayers. Because of their motive, however, their prayers had no value in God's sight.

greater condemnation : They succeeded in fooling some of their fellow-Jews but they could not fool God.

opposite the treasury : Jesus sat near one of the receptacles for alms in the temple-area and observed those who gave alms.

rich people . . . sums : Many people generously gave of their abundance.

a poor . . . penny : The poor widow's gift was made up of two of the smaller copper coins then in circulation : they equalled about one penny or one cent.

has put in more : He called his disciples and said to them that the poor widow had contributed more than all the other donors. They gave out of their abundance—they would not miss what they gave, but the widow gave her all. She had nothing left. This indeed was generosity.

APPLICATION : Our Lord's severe condemnation of those Scribes whose exaggerated opinion of their own importance made a mockery of the religion they professed to live, is a serious warning to all his followers not to look for the praise and esteem of their neighbors when doing their good works, but rather to hope for God's praise and esteem in the future world. In another context, he said to his followers : "Because of practicing your piety before men in order to be seen by them, for then you will have no reward from your Father who is in heaven . . . when you give alms do not let your left hand know what your right is doing . . . and your Father who sees in secret will reward you . . . when you pray go into your room and shut the door and pray to your Father . . . who sees in secret and will reward you" (Mt. 6 : 1–6).

It is hardly necessary to say that our Lord is not referring to community prayers or services here. What he is condemning is the hypocrisy of the Scribes, who lengthened their garments and their prayers not in order to give glory to God but to earn the glory of their fellowmen for themselves. Pride was their predominant vice—the vice which caused the fall of angels and of man. It so governed their lives that even their best actions were vitiated by it. There is a strong inclination to pride in every one of us. The reason is that we have great gifts from God and great capabilities; but we are tempted to claim the credit for these gifts and capabilities for ourselves—whereas we owe them all to God's generosity.

A proud Christian is surely a contradiction in terms. A Christian is a follower of Christ whose humility can never be equalled. He was God as well as man. While on earth he emptied himself, as St. Paul puts it, of his divine glory so that he could be like one of us. A follower of Christ should not try to make display of gifts which are not his own, nor try to exalt himself above his neighbor because of something he has which was not given to his neighbor. If Christ wanted to be, and indeed was like the least one among us, we must never try to raise ourselves above our neighbor. Love of neighbor is the second of the two essential commandments—there can be no true love of neighbor where there is pride.

The second incident in today's Gospel story highlights true humility and true charity. The poor widow, forgetful of herself and of her own needs gave her all, her last penny, to help others who were in need. She made this sacrifice without publicity and without seeking the praise of her neighbors. It is this deep contrast between her outlook on life and on religion, and that of the Scribes in the first that connects the two incidents. While the Scribes sought to earn the respect and praise of their fellow-Jews—as well as all the financial gain they could come by—from the practice of the externals of their religion, this poor widow's religion was practiced in secret and it was to God alone that she looked for any reward that he might deign to give her.

As we saw in today's first reading: we can be sure that she was not left without the reward she deserved. The widow of Zarephath was given a temporal reward. The same generous God did not let the similar act of supreme generosity on the part of the widow in Jerusalem go unnoticed. Christ's judgement on the Scribes implies this: They will receive the greater condemnation for their pride, and abuse of religion for their own temporal gain. On the other hand the widow's religion was an act of complete self-renunciation: "she has put in everything she had, her whole living."

We may never be called on to share our last morsel with a starving neighbor but if we are, we must remember that Christ gave his very life for us and has asked us to do likewise, if necessary. It may never be necessary for us to make this supreme act of self-renunciation. If, however, we are sincerely practicing our religion, we must be ever-ready to help a neighbor in need even if this cuts into our hard-earned reserves. The greater the sacrifice, the greater the reward.

THIRTY-THIRD SUNDAY OF THE YEAR

FIRST READING : Daniel 12 : 1–3. Michael, the great prince who has charge of your people, shall arise. And there shall be a time of trouble, such as never has been since there was a nation till that time; but at that time your people shall be delivered, every one whose name shall be found written in the book. And many of those who sleep in the dust of the earth shall awake, some to everlasting life, and some to shame and everlasting contempt. And those who are wise shall shine like the brightness of the firmament; and those who turn many to righteousness, like the stars for ever and ever.

EXPLANATION : The Book of Daniel is not named after its author—who is unknown—but after its principal protagonist, who is described as living in Babylon during the last years of the Babylonian empire—and their first successors, the kings of the Medes and the Persians. The general consensus today is that this book was written in the second century—about 166 B.C. before the death, in 164, of Antiochus, the savage persecutor of the Jews. It was written with the purpose of encouraging the Jews to remain faithful to their religion in spite of the bitter persecution they were enduring, and also in spite of the attraction for many of them of the higher worldly culture of pagan Hellenism. The stories about Daniel in the first half of the book are intended to show the mastery of the God of the Jews over all nations. He has supreme dominion over all the world and so he "removes and installs kings" as he wishes (2 : 21). The author is more concerned with the moral of his stories than with their historical exactitude. In the rise and fall of nations God is directing history toward the establishment of the kingdom of God on earth and later in heaven. In the second half of this book, the author presents the first clear example of apocalyptic writing which was further developed during the succeeding centuries. Angels are much in evidence in this second part and the doctrine of the resurrection of the body is clearly taught for the first time in the Old Testament. The author does not speak of the Messiah as an individual, he speaks clearly of the messianic kingdom which is to come. His mention of "one like the son of man" (7 : 13), refers to the kingdom rather than to the personal Messiah. Our Lord used this title "Son of Man" —sixty times in the four gospels—almost exclusively to describe himself. The Book of Daniel was the last link in the long chain of preparation in the Old Testament for the coming of Christ in the New.

Michael . . . arise : The patron angel of

the Jews (10 : 13; 31; Apoc. 12) will come at some unspecified time—the end of the world—to take up the cause of the faithful ones among his people.

a time of trouble : The last days of this world are always described in apocalyptic literature as times of catastrophe never before experienced (see Mt. 24 : 4–31; Apoc. 13 and today's gospel).

people delivered : The faithful among the Chosen People of God will be delivered from these disasters.

name . . . written in the book : Only if they have already proved themselves faithful and thus have got their names written in the book of life (see Ex. 32 : 32; Ps. 69 : 29; Is. 4 : 3).

sleep . . . awake : Sleep is a euphemism for death. The dead will come back to life, but not all will come back to a life of eternal happiness; some will come back from death to an everlasting life of contempt : they will have God's contempt and their own. This is the clearest expression of the belief in the bodily resurrection of the dead in the Old Testament (Ps. 16 : 9–11; 49; 15; Is. 26 : 19 are not quite so explicit). The mother and her seven sons, martyred by Antiochus IV, were aware of and surely strengthened by this truth enunciated in Daniel (see 2 Mc. 7).

those . . . wise : The good Jews who know and keep the law of God and who teach others to do likewise ("those who turn many to righteousness," is a parallelism to "those who are wise") will shine like the stars in their new eternal life. They will have special glory.

APPLICATION : The Church begins and ends her liturgical year with lessons that remind us of our end and the end of the world. In the new liturgical arrangement, the Feast of Christ the King is celebrated on the last Sunday of the year and therefore the Church places the reminder of death, judgement and resurrection on this the penultimate Sunday. Today's reading from the Book of Daniel puts before our eyes the fact that this world will have an end marked by great upheavals and disasters. However, these will be followed immediately by a new and everlasting existence. This new life will be one of unending joy and happiness for those who are found worthy. For the others who did not think of it or prepare for it, it will be a life of unending shame and sorrow.

Here, surely, we have a solemn reminder of what is ahead of us and of what we ought to do about it. Every businessman worthy of the name annually takes a serious look at his business affairs to see how he stands. If he finds that all is going well he resolves to continue or to improve things if improvement is possible. If his business is going down, he will search for the causes of this decline and resolve to do all in his power to check the defects that are causing the decline. Today, we are all called on to make this stock-taking of our progress or decline. Our duty to have this stock-taking is of infinitely greater importance than that of the businessman. If his business fails it is not the end of him, he can find other ways of making a living. He has other options open to him. If we fail to be prepared for heaven, we have no second chance, our failure is final and for all eternity.

This is a thought that should make us stop and think. We have one life only on earth—a life of a few short years. Our real life, the eternal life of happiness or misery depends on how we spend these years on earth. We can waste them and arrive empty-handed at the end of our journey, or we can spend them well and hear the welcome words : "Come you blessed of my Father, possess the kingdom prepared for you," when we die. To which class would we like to belong when our end on earth comes? The choice and the answer is entirely in our hands, no one can make this decision for us. Our dearest and nearest will be helpless in this regard. Generously and gladly God will help us but we must cooperate with that help. In baptism he has already given us our passport to heaven. Each day in the sacraments and prayers of his Church he is offering us the necessary travel expenses. Again and again through his ministers he advises us to stay on the right road, but all in vain if we refuse to accept these gifts.

The rules of the road to heaven, the regulations which God asks us to keep, are not severe sacrifices or tasks beyond our power to fulfill. His ten commandments are not impossible or unreasonable restrictions, but rather rules which make life on earth civilized and happy. Where they are observed we have peace and harmony between neighbors and nations. Where the Fatherhood of God is revered and kept in mind, the brotherhood of man is recognized and his rights respected, there is true fraternity on earth. Somebody has said that if God did not exist it would be necessary for us to invent him—if life on earth was to be liveable. But he does exist and in his goodness and mercy he has made life on earth liveable and reasonably enjoyable —by laying down the sound rules which should govern our lives as rational creatures.

God is not a tyrant who will take pleasure in punishing those who ignore him and his laws. Rather is he a loving Father who wants all his children to share his eternal happiness. Therefore, his laws are not imposed on us as restrictions and burdens but as helps to guide us safely to our eternal home.

Today's lesson from Daniel is one of God's ways of reminding the forgetful ones of him and their own eternal destiny. Let them wake up and take stock of how they stand in relation to God; are they on the right road or are they wandering in the wilderness from whence they may never return?

SECOND READING : Hebrews 10 : 11-14; 18. Every priest stands daily at his service, offering repeatedly the same sacrifices, which can never take away sins. But when Christ had offered for all time a single sacrifice for sins, he sat down at the right hand of God, there to wait until his enemies should be made a stool for his feet. For by a single offering he has perfected for all time those who are sanctified. Where there is forgiveness of these, there is no longer any offering for sin.

EXPLANATION : The author of *Hebrews* continues to compare the priesthood of Christ with the Jewish priesthood. The temple priests offered the same sacrifices of goats, sheep and oxen day after day. But these sacrifices could not remove the barrier that stood between man and God—the barrier of sin. Any graces resulting from these Jewish sacrifices were obtained in view of the real sacrifice that was to come. This was a once for all sacrifice, a sacrifice of infinite value because it was God's Son who offered his assumed human body to make atonement for the sins of the world. By his incarnation Jesus made men heirs to heaven; by his death he made men fit for the inheritance. The priestly office of Jesus, therefore, was of infinitely greater importance than that of the whole history of the Levitical priesthood.

offering repeatedly : The same sacrifices of animals and fruits of the earth were offered day after day, year after year in the Jerusalem temple.

never . . . sins : The Jewish sacrifices were ordered by God and accepted by him as a token of the Chosen People's submission to him. By sacrificing part of their property, animals and fruits of the land, they were proclaiming their dependence on God for all. These sacrifices had no intrinsic value of their own.

Christ . . . sins : This was a true sacrifice, of infinite value, because of the divine Person offering it. It was more than sufficient to make atonement to the Father for all the sins of the world.

sat . . . hand : In his human nature Christ was given the place of honor at the right hand of the Father in heaven. When he finished his work of redemption he was seated in glory.

enemies . . . a stool : His victory over the enemies of men's salvation would be gradually completed. They would be prostrate and powerless before him while he placed his foot on their necks to indicate complete control. This was the custom of triumphant monarchs of the time.

single . . . perfected : Christ's offering of himself on the cross was sufficient to obtain eternal sanctification for all mankind.

those . . . sanctified : Not all men would avail of this divine bounty and mercy, but those who would believe in and accept this merciful plan of God would receive their eternal reward.

no longer . . . sin : Christ's one act of self-sacrifice on the cross is sufficient for all time. It need not be repeated. The objective forgiveness for sin has been obtained for all men, but each man must apply the sacrifice of Christ to himself in the sacramental order. Hence the purpose of the Mass, the "memorial" of the sacrifice of the cross, in which "we proclaim the Lord's death until he comes" (1 Cor. 11 : 26).

APPLICATION : "By the mystery of this water and wine may we come to share in the divinity of Christ who humbled himself to share in our humanity." This prayer, which the priest says when mixing a drop of water with the wine in the chalice at the offertory of the Mass, gives in a nutshell the profound meaning that the incarnation of Christ has for us. The drop of water is our human nature; it is absorbed in the wine—the divine infinity; and it shares in the incredible glory of becoming the precious blood of Christ. When the Son of God took our human nature, he made us capable of becoming sharers in the eternal glory, and happiness of the Infinite God.

If only we could fully realize what the loving God has done for us through the sending of his Son to "dwell among us," we would never stop praising, thanking and loving him. We are mere creatures, higher than all the other creatures on this earth because of the extra gifts he gave us—but still mere creatures—nothing in comparison with the omnipotent and infinite God. Out of an infinite goodness which our minds cannot even begin to grasp, he raised us up to the status of adopted children. He had no need of us, he did not require our company or our adoration, he is infinitely perfect and happy in himself. Yet, out of sheer benevolence he wished to confer on us a gift which we are to value and appreciate with our intelligence and freewill—but a gift which we could never even dream of expecting.

To give us the gift the incarnation took place : "the word was made flesh and dwelt among us." Christ became our brother; we became, through him, adopted sons of God and therefore heirs to heaven. The sins of mankind which had corrupted the world brought about the death of Christ on the cross—"a death he freely accepted." Through that death and as our representative and senior brother, he made a perfect atonement to God the Father for all our sins. His triumph over sin and death was our triumph; ever since his ascension, the incarnate Son of God is in the seat of glory in heaven, interceding for us sinners; he is preparing a place for us, his brothers, which will be ours when life on this earth ends.

Therefore, there is no comparison, as the epistle to the Hebrews stresses, between the intercession that the Levitical priesthood could make for the Chosen People of the Old Testament, and the intercession that Christ has made and continues to make for us. The sacrifices they offered were but shadows and symbols of the real sacrifice offered by Christ. Any value which they had derived from the true sacrifice which was to come. The members of the Chosen People who did God's will earned heaven through the merits of Christ and only after his ascension. Because of God's loving generosity these infinite merits of Christ were applied to all Jews and Gentiles, who, before Christ, lived according to their lights. They will be applied to all who have lived since his incarnation, provided they act according to the revealed or the natural knowledge of God which is given them.

We know this and our gratitude to God should be boundless. The years left to us on earth are long enough to enable us to earn eternity. Those who have weaknesses, temptations and trials must never forget that they are not on their own; they are not left to fend for themselves; they have Christ, their brother, in heaven pleading with the Father of mercies on their behalf. With such an advocate, with such a defending counsel, we cannot lose our inheritance, provided we do our best to be true and loyal to him. God grant that we shall never be among the ungrateful ones but rather that we may willingly and gladly co-operate with God to earn the eternal merit won by Christ.

P

GOSPEL : Mark 13 : 24–32. Jesus said to his disciples : "In the days after the great tribulation, the sun will be darkened, and the moon will not give its light, and the stars will be falling from heaven, and the powers in the heavens will be shaken. And then they will see the Son of man coming in clouds with great power and glory. And then he will send out the angels, and gather his elect from the four winds, from the ends of the earth to the ends of heaven.

"From the fig tree learn its lesson : as soon as its branch becomes tender and puts forth its leaves, you know that summer is near. So also, when you see these things taking place, you know that he is near, at the very gates. Truly, I say to you, this generation will not pass away before all these things take place. Heaven and earth will pass away, but my words will not pass away.

"But of that day or that hour no one knows, not even the angels in heaven, nor the Son, but only the Father."

EXPLANATION : As we said above in the application of today's first reading, the Church wants to remind us that this universe will come to an end one day. Then will come the general judgement, when Christ will gather his faithful followers from the four corners of this earth. In the verse which precedes today's gospel text, our Lord had mentioned the destruction of the temple of Jerusalem— which happened forty years later in 70 A.D.—and the end of this world. The Apostles asked him when these things would take place. As regards the end of the world he could not tell them—since this was not revealed to him as man. However, some of those then alive would live to see the Jerusalem temple razed to the ground by the Romans. He warned them to be ever vigilant living according to the truths he had taught them.

sun . . . stars : Our Lord uses the apocalyptic imagery of the Old Testament when it describes the "Day of Yahweh" (see Am. 5 :18–20; Is. 2 : 12ff; Jer. 46 : 10). Its end having come, the whole universe will break up.

Son of Man . . . glory : Christ frequently used the title "Son of Man"—taken from Daniel 7 : 13—to describe himself. Here he tells his disciples that when the present world ends he will come in "power and glory" to judge mankind. His second coming will be very different from his first when he came in humility and meekness.

send . . . angels : The angels will be his servants—his messengers. He will use them to collect his faithful from the four corners of the earth.

from the fig tree : The lesson to be learned from the fig tree : as sure as the summer follows spring so will the judgement follow our sojourn on earth, and it is nearer than any of us imagines.

this generation . . . away : Here Christ is referring to the destruction of the temple. Many of those living in the year 30 witnessed in the year 70 the fulfillment of his prophecy.

my word . . . away : The created universe "heaven and earth" will end one day, but the truths which Christ brought to man will continue to have their effects all through eternity.

only the Father : The time of the end of the world is the Father's secret. It was not to be revealed to men, hence it was not given to Christ as man.

APPLICATION : There are some obscurities in this extract from St. Mark. Firstly, because Christ was discussing and answering questions on two distinct topics : the destruction of the temple and the end of the world. Secondly, because we may not have the "ipsissima verba" of Christ here, as many exegetes suggest. The message we must learn from today's gospel comes across without any ambiguity or doubt : we must always be ready to face our judgement for we know not the day nor the hour when we will be called from this life. When or how this world will end is of no great importance to us; what is important is that we shall leave this world very soon and our eternity will depend on the state of our consciences at the moment of our departure.

This is the steadying thought the Church, in her wisdom, wishes to put before our minds today. We all know that we must die someday. We are strangers and pilgrims on this earth; we have not here a lasting city, as St. Augustine says. No sane person among us will try to deny this and yet, many of us are so immersed in the things of this world that we forget or try to forget that we must leave this world soon. This is very natural : life is a precious gift and as our earthly life is the only one of which we have experience our every inclination is to hold on to it at all costs. Even when our intelligence tells us that it can, in spite of all our endeavors, end very soon we try to convince ourselves that that "very soon" is really in the distant future.

We have God's word for it and the example of Christ's resurrection to a life of glory. Let us appreciate the truth that our death on earth is not the end of life but rather the beginning of the true life that will never end. As the liturgy says in the Mass for the Dead : "Life is changed (by death) not taken away." Our death is the doorway through which we pass into the unending life. The years on earth are a gift of God to enable us to earn the infinitely greater gift which in his loving mercy he has prepared for us from all eternity.

God in his mercy is calling on each one of us to be ready when our call comes. We can do nothing about the when or the where of that call, but we can do much about the state of our relationship with God when death comes; in fact, aided by God's grace we can ensure that all will be well with us. We cannot avoid a sudden death, but we can avoid an unprepared death by striving always to live in peace with God. This does not mean that we must be always on our knees praying to God and that we must take no interest in the things and the joys of this world. Far from it. God wants us to use the things of this world, but to use them so that they will not hinder us on our journey.

A very practical way to see how we stand in relation to God and to the things of this world, is for each one of us to ask himself today : "How would I fare if I were called to render an account of stewardship tonight?" This is the practical question that God, through today's readings, is asking us to put to ourselves. If, to our dismay, we find there are several things which have to be put right before facing our judge we will start right away to put them right. We may get another chance, another warning, and we may not. If we value our eternal happiness we will take this warning; we will put our books in order; we will make peace with God and our neighbors—and with God's grace we will do all in our power to persevere in this good resolution.

Q

THIRTY-FOURTH OR LAST SUNDAY OF THE YEAR
SOLEMNITY OF CHRIST THE KING

FIRST READING : Daniel 7 : 13–14. I saw in the night visions, and behold with the clouds of heaven there came one like a son of man, and he came to the Ancient of Days and was presented before him. And to him was given dominion and glory and kingdom, that all peoples, nations, and languages should serve him; his dominion is an everlasting dominion, which shall not pass away, and his kingdom one that shall not be destroyed.

EXPLANATION : These verses are part of some visions which Daniel had in the night and for which he got the explanation next day (Dn. 7). There were visions of the four kingdoms or empires whose rulers are described as beasts. These kingdoms were those of Babylon, Media, Persia, Greece. Finally he saw the worst of them all—the reign of Antiochus Epiphanes who tried to destroy the Jewish religion. But the "Ancient of Days" stepped in and set up a new king and a new kingdom. The kingdom was for all nations—for Gentiles as well as Jews—and one that would be everlasting. **one . . . man :** In Hebrew and Aramaic "a son of man" means a man, but here it signifies some man who is mysteriously more than man. That he was an individual is attested to by early Jewish apocryphal (Enoch and 2 Esdras), and rabbinical writings but especially by our Lord who applied this title to himself. At times, he used it to express his lowly state (Mt. 8 : 20; 11 : 19; 20 : 28), at

other times to proclaim the definitive triumph of his resurrection (17 : 19), of his return in glory (24 : 30), and of his coming in judgement (25 : 30). In this way, the title puts a veil over—and hinted at—the sort of Messiah Jesus was. His final explicit avowal before the Sanhedrin left no doubt as to the meaning for him of this title.

Ancient of Days : The rulers of the pagan kingdoms are described as beasts coming out of the abyss; the ruler of the eternal kingdom, however, is like a man and comes "with the clouds of heaven" —that is, comes from God who is described as the Ancient of Days—he who was there before time began.

presented before him : After his resurrection, Christ appeared in glory at the throne of the Father, his mission on earth accomplished (see Jn. 17).

dominion . . . kingdom : He was then made king of the new universal, spiritual kingdom—the Church—which begins on earth but has its completion and perfection in heaven.

people . . . languages : All mankind was made subject to his rule.

everlasting . . . destroyed : Unlike all earthly kingdoms, the kingdom of Christ will last forever. On earth his Church will last until the last man has been saved : "the gates of hell will not prevail against it," and in heaven those who served him faithfully will have an unending kingdom of happiness.

APPLICATION : Today's feastday was instituted as a rallying-call to all Christians to acknowledge the sovereignty of Christ our King over all earthly powers, kingdoms and peoples. This call was very necessary in an age when worldliness and earthly ambitions were drawing the minds of men further away from God and Christ, and from their own eternal interests. Our twentieth century has seen not only pagan countries denying the existence of God and a future life but nations that were once Christian have been forced to live under atheistic regimes which forbid the public practice of religion. It was to counteract and stem this growing infidelity that Pope Pius XI instituted the feast in honor of Christ the King; he wanted to remind Christians of the fidelity and loyalty they owed to Christ who by his incarnation had made them adopted children of God and future citizens and heirs of the kingdom of heaven.

Today's extract from the Book of Daniel, written two centuries before Christ came on earth, tells us that the son of man would receive from God his Father, dominion and sovereignty over all peoples, nations and languages. He would be the king of kings and the lord of glory and his kingdom would last forever. Many other messianic prophecies in the Old Testament give Christ the Messiah the title of King. The prophet Nathan promised King David (c. 1000 B.C.) that a descendant of his would come "who would establish his throne forever" (2 Sm. 7 : 16). Isaiah says of the future Messiah : "he will sit on David's kingly throne, to give it lasting foundations of justice and right" (Is. 9 : 6–7; see 1–5). In the prophet Jeremiah we read : "a time is coming, the Lord says, when I will raise up from the stock of David a faithful scion at last" (Jer. 23 : 3). To crown and confirm the Davidic typology, the Virgin Mary is told by the angel that the child she is to conceive " shall be known as the Son of the Most High; the Lord God will give him the throne of his father David . . . and of his kingdom there will be no end" (Lk. 1 : 32).

We are called on today to honor Christ our King. The other feasts of our Lord which we celebrate throughout the year remind us of all that Christ has done for us, but today's should call to our minds what we are to do for him in return. Unlike the kings of earthly kingdoms who rightly expect their loyal subjects to die for them and their nation if need be, our King, Christ, died for us in order to make us free citizens of his kingdom. He does expect us to be ready to die for him and for his kingdom if the occasion should arise, and down through his Church's history many of his loyal subjects have gladly done so. But from the vast majority of his subjects, Christ does not demand this supreme sacrifice. What he does expect and demand is not that we should die for him but that we should live for him.

This we can and should do by faithfully living our Christian life day by day.

The loyal, honest citizen of any country will keep the law of the land of which he is a citizen. A Christian has double citizenship : he is a citizen of his homeland and he is a citizen of Christ's kingdom. He must, therefore, be loyal to his country and loyal to Christ but as the Christian law commands obedience to the lawful civil authority the two obligations are identical in many cases. As Christians, however, we have some extra duties to perform above and beyond what our country demands of us. These can be summed up briefly in the double commandment of charity, love of God and love of neighbor.

While most civilized states have laws preventing their citizens from publicly insulting God or religion, and all states prohibit citizens from injuring their neighbor in his person or in his property,

the Christian law demands a positive approach. The Christian is bound to love, reverence and obey God. The first three commandments spell out for him how this is to be done. Likewise, the Christian rule of life not only forbids a Christian to injure his neighbor, it commands him positively to help his neighbor—in fact to love him as he loves himself.

How loyal are we to Christ? Are we worthy citizens of his kingdom on earth and so working our way toward his eternal kingdom in heaven? Our answer is the answer to the question : do we sincerely love God and our neighbor? Only we can give a true answer to this question and it is we ourselves who will reap the reward or suffer the eternal consequence of the positive or negative answer which our consciences give to this vital question.

SECOND READING : Apocalypse (Revelation) 1 : 5-8. Jesus Christ is the faithful witness, the first-born of the dead, and the ruler of kings on earth.

To him who loves us and has freed us from our sins by his blood and made us a kingdom, priests to his God and Father, to him be glory and dominion for ever and ever. Amen. Behold, he is coming with the clouds, and every eye will see him, everyone who pierced him; and all tribes of the earth will wail on account of him. Even so. Amen.

"I am the Alpha and the Omega," says the Lord God, who is and who was and who is to come, the Almighty.

EXPLANATION : Apocalypse, a Greek word meaning uncovering or revelation, is the name given to the last book of the New Testament. Tradition dating from St. Justin (165 A.D.), and widespread by the end of the second century, says that its author was St. John the Evangelist. The very different style of writing and

the different vocabulary when compared with St. John's Gospel and Epistles may be explicable when we consider that the apocalyptic literature was very different from ordinary literature. It became a very common type of writing among the Jews of the last two centuries before Christ. It uses a lot of symbolic imagery and language, mostly borrowed from Old Testament prophetic books. Visions occur frequently but need not be taken as having been objective; nor must the symbolic imagery be interpreted literally. The general theme of St. John's Apocalypse is best interpreted as eschatological, that is, as referring to the end of the world and the events that precede and accompany it. On the other hand, the brief letters to the seven churches are practical contemporaneous advice as the occasion demanded. The four verses, read from this book today, refer to the supreme kingship of Christ who founded a kingdom for us. In this kingdom he has made us priests dedicated to the service of God his Father. He will come a second time to judge all men.

Jesus . . . witness: Jesus is our witness of God. He has revealed God to us and God's plan for us, and as a faithful witness he gave his life to prove the truth of what he preached and revealed to us.

first-born of the dead: But death did not hold him, he rose from the dead "the first-fruits of those who have fallen asleep (died)" (1 Cor. 15 : 20). He conquered death not only for himself but for all men.

ruler of kings on earth: At the resurrection of Christ, God the Father glorified him in his humanity and gave him dominion and power over all creatures. Everything in heaven and on earth was made subject to him. As he said to his Apostles before his ascension: "All authority in heaven and on earth has been given to me" (Mt. 28 : 18; see Dan. 7 : 14; Rom. 14 : 9; Phil. 2 : 11; Eph. 1 : 20–23). Here, in this one sentence, we have the essential points of our Christian faith: the incarnation, death, resurrection and glorification of Christ, the Son of God.

To . . . us: Because of his love for us —a love which will continue for all time —he has freed us from our sins; his sacrifice of himself on Calvary made atonement to his Father for all the sins of the world.

made us a kingdom: He established his messianic kingdom. Its first stage is the Church on earth. Its perfection is the eternal kingdom of heaven.

priests . . . Father: Christ was our great High Priest (see Epistle to Hebrews), who offered the perfect sacrifice. We Christians are members of his mystical body and therefore partake in his priesthood. Our Christian lives, if truly lived, are a continual reoffering of the perfect sacrifice of Christ.

glory . . . ever: This is a doxology thanking Jesus for all he has done for us.

coming . . . clouds: He will be seen coming in the clouds of glory to judge all men, as foretold in Daniel 7 : 13 (first reading today).

every . . . him: This judgement will be universal.

everyone . . . him: His second coming will not be a cause for joy for those who caused his passion, either physically or morally, by their sins.

tribes . . . wail: The pagan nations which persecuted Christ's Church will then bemoan their errors but too late.

Alpha and Omega: These are the first and the last letters of the Greek alphabet. Here the phrase means the beginning of all things and the end toward which all things created are destined.

is . . . come: That is the eternity of God; he began all history and he it is who will terminate it.

the Almighty: This corresponds to "the God of hosts," the "God of power" of the Old Testament.

APPLICATION : As one would expect on this special feastday of Christ our King, the readings chosen from sacred Scripture stress the kingly glory and dignity of Christ after his triumph over sin and death, while they also remind us of how much we owe him. This kingly glory will be visible to all men at his second coming—a vision which will delight his faithful ones but which will strike terror into his enemies. In his Apocalypse St. John reminds us first and foremost of all that Christ has done for us. During his life among us, he has revealed his loving Father. It was his own divine love that made him come as the incarnate Son of God and give his life for us. He triumphed over death and continues to love us in heaven. He established his messianic kingdom, in which we, his subjects, are given the power and the privilege of serving God with a true service—for he has joined us to himself who alone could give fitting service to his Father.

John then reminds the faithful followers of Christ and Christ's opponents as well that Christ will return in glory and majesty to demand a reckoning from each one. This is a sobering thought for all of us. Each will have to stand before the tribunal of Christ one day and see one's life work laid bare. On that day we shall see all our thoughts, words and actions as they really were. Here on earth, our prejudices and our pride and selfishness can minimize our faults and exaggerate our virtues, but in the presence of the omniscient Judge we will see ourselves as we truly are. We shall have no excuses to offer because we will see the emptiness, the folly of the excuses with which we silenced our consciences here below. Instead of making too much of our good deeds and our virtues, we will realize how little we have done for him who humbled himself even to the death of the cross for our sakes. The saints of God regretted that they had not done more for the Savior and King who had gone to such lengths in order to bring them into his heavenly kingdom.

We thank God that the dread moment has not yet arrived. We have still time left in which to put our conscience and our spiritual affairs in order. Today's feast gives each one of us the opportunity of seeing how we stand in relation to Christ. Are we loyal subjects faithfully trying to carry out his laws? Are we sincerely grateful to him who put heaven within our reach, showed us the way to go there and is daily helping us? If so, let us promise that with the help of God's grace we will continue to be loyal and grateful.

If, on the other hand, some of us will have to admit to ourselves, and to Christ, that we have been far from faithful and too often entirely ungrateful for his divine love and mercy we still have a chance to put things right before our judgement day arrives. Christ is ever ready to forgive and welcome back the prodigal sons. Today our King is calling to us to return home to him who "loves us and has freed us from our sins by his blood." He died on a cross so that we should have eternal life. He is ready to forgive and forget all our past disloyalties, if only we will turn to him and ask for forgiveness. Our verdict on the day of our judgement will depend on the decision which we take today. Our eternity of happiness or of misery depends on that verdict. With our eternal future at stake should we allow the trivial, transient things of this life to come between us and Christ, the King of Kings?

GOSPEL : John 18 : 33–37. Pilate said to Jesus, "Are you the King of the Jews?" Jesus answered, "Do you say this of your own accord, or did others say it to you about me?" Pilate answered, "Am I a Jew? Your own nation and the chief priests have handed you over to me; what have you done?" Jesus answered, "My kingship is not of this world; if my kingship were of this world, my servants would fight, that I might not be handed over to the Jews; but my kingship is not from the world." Pilate said to him, "So you are a king?" Jesus answered, "You say that I am a king. For this I was born, and for this I have come into the world, to bear witness to the truth. Every one who is of the truth hears my voice."

EXPLANATION : The Sanhedrin or the highest governing body of the Jewish people at that time, had condemned Jesus as guilty of blasphemy, because he claimed to be the Son of God. For this crime they judged him deserving of death. Because they wanted him to die the most shameful and painful of deaths, they brought him to Pilate who would pass the sentence of crucifixion. The accusation they produced to Pilate was not the religious one mentioned above, but a trumped up political charge. As St. Luke puts it : "We found this man inciting our people to revolt, opposing payment of the tribute to Caesar, and claiming to be Christ, a king" (Lk. 23 : 2). Pilate was not impressed by their accusation. He questioned Jesus about his kingship and Jesus admitted that he was a king but that his kingdom was not of this world.

Are you . . . Jews? : Pilate saw there was something false about the Jewish accusation and so he questioned Jesus the prisoner, in order to get the true facts.

or did . . . it : Jesus knew that Pilate did not suspect him of being a leader of a revolt against the Roman authorities who were then in Palestine. As governor, Pilate had his agents around the country. He wondered therefore why Jesus should ask him this question. As Messiah, Jesus was a king—the messianic descendant promised to David, but he was not a king in the Roman sense of the word.

what . . . done? : Pilate again showed that he did not accept the accusation of the chief priests who handed Jesus over to him for condemnation. He, therefore, asked Jesus what he had done to merit this treatment from "his own nation," his fellow-Jews.

Jesus answered : Jesus told Pilate that the priests' accusation about his claim to be King was not a true one in the sense that they wished Pilate to understand it, but he was a true king and was founding a new kingdom which was a spiritual kingdom, one not concerned with political causes. His "kingship was not of this world."

you . . . king : Jesus agreed with Pilate's statement. That Pilate understood Jesus' kingship to be something other than political is clear from his later attempts to free Jesus.

bear . . . truth : He had come into the world as man to teach men the fundamental, real truths concerning God and man.

who . . . hears : Christ's message would be accepted gladly by all lovers of truth and likewise would be rejected by all those who preferred the darkness of ignorance. Whether Pilate was impressed or not by this statement, history has proved how true it was.

APPLICATION : In today's two previous readings we have seen that the prophets foretold the kingship of Christ and the Apostle John described him as the founder of our kingdom who one day would judge all mankind. In today's gospel, we have our divine Lord's own statement that he is a king—the king of a new and everlasting kingdom which is not of this world. He made this statement to the Roman governor to whom he had been handed over by the priests and leaders of the Jewish people to be put to death by crucifixion. Long before, he had foreseen this death and had accepted it as part of his Father's plan for making atonement for the sins of mankind. He knew Pilate did not believe that he was the leader of a rebellion against the Roman authorities, but he did not try to influence Pilate's decision in his favor for he wanted the will of his Father carried out to the letter.

Five centuries before, the prophet second-Isaiah had described the Messiah who was to come as the Servant of God who suffered torments on our behalf. The prophet says : "He was despised and rejected by men; a man of sorrows and acquainted with grief . . . surely, he has borne our griefs and carried our sorrows, yet we esteemed him stricken, smitten by God. But he was wounded for our transgressions, he was bruised for our iniquities; upon him was the chastisement that made us whole, and with his stripes we are healed. We like sheep have gone astray . . . and the Lord has laid on him the iniquity of us all. He was oppressed and he was afflicted, yet he opened not his mouth; like a lamb that is led to the slaughter, like a sheep before its shearers he opened not his mouth" (Is. 53 : 3–7). Had Pilate known this prophecy he would not have been surprised that Jesus uttered no word in his own defense. His Father had sent him to raise up mankind and to make atonement for men's sins; his death on the cross was that supreme act of atonement and without objection he accepted it.

The kings of this earth demand of their subjects that they should be ready, if necessary, to lay down their lives to defend their king and realm. Men have always accepted this and millions have gladly given their lives to defend their country and rulers. We have a king who laid down his life for us and set us an example unlike that of any earthly king. Following his Father's will, he did this to make us worthy to share in the Father's eternal kingdom. The incarnation, which made us adopted children of God, and the crucifixion, which obtained remission of our sins, surely prove to us the love and the esteem in which God holds us. It should also show how important is our future life. Christ did not come on earth to make us healthy, happy or prosperous in this world; he came to open heaven for us where we could be happy forever. This was God's purpose in creating us. This is his purpose for us still. All our other interests in this life are secondary when compared with this.

In honoring Christ today as our King, let us especially thank him for all the humiliations and sufferings he endured on our behalf. If our Christian way of living makes some demands on us let us not forget how trivial they are when compared with what Christ's earthly life cost him. He made these severe sacrifices for us; we are asked to make our small offerings for ourselves. Our self-interest alone should inspire us, but our gratitude to Christ should especially move us to play our part. Let us promise to be grateful and loyal subjects of his for the rest of our days. He has made us members of his kingdom on earth—the Church—and is preparing a place for us in his everlasting kingdom. Let no one be so foolish as to forfeit an eternal happiness because of some earthly attachment to the passing things of this world.

FEAST OF THE ASSUMPTION OF THE BLESSED VIRGIN MARY

FIRST READING: Revelation 11:19; 12:1-6; 10. God's temple in heaven was opened, and the Ark of his Covenant was seen within his temple. And a great portent appeared in heaven, a woman clothed with the sun, with the moon under her feet, and on her head a crown of twelve stars; she was with child and she cried out in her pangs of birth, in anguish for delivery. And another portent appeared in heaven; behold, a great red dragon, with seven heads and ten horns, and seven diadems upon his heads. His tail swept down a third of the stars of heaven, and cast them to the earth. And the dragon stood before the woman who was about to bear a child, that he might devour her child when she brought it forth; she brought forth a male child, one who is to rule all the nations with a rod of iron, but her child was caught up to God and to his throne, and the woman fled into the wilderness, where she has a place prepared by God. And I heard a loud voice in heaven, saying, "Now the salvation and the power and the kingdom of our God and the authority of his Christ has come."

EXPLANATION: On the authorship and literary style of the Book of Revelation see the 34th Sunday of the year above. The apocalyptic literature was full of imagery and visions which need not be taken in the literal and objective sense. In these verses, taken from Revelation today, John is describing the beginning of the messianic era, in which the powers of evil, represented by a dragon, would fight bitterly to hinder the victory of the Messiah. This dragon tries to kill the Messiah at birth but fails. The Messiah fulfills his mission and triumphantly reaches the throne of God. The woman, representing Mary the mother of Christ, and also the Church, will likewise triumph. When the dragon has been conquered the reign of God and of Christ will begin.

God's temple in heaven: In a vision John sees God's throne in heaven. In his earthly Temple in Jerusalem the Ark of the Covenant was his throne. At the time of the Babylonian exile Jeremiah hid this Ark in a cavern in Mount Nebo and it was not to be rediscovered until the messianic era had come (see 2 Mac. 2 : 4–8). John is very probably referring to this.

a woman clothed with the sun . . . twelve stars: John has before his mind both Mary the virgin Mother of Christ the Messiah, and the Church, the new Chosen People of God. The pangs of childbirth refer to the sufferings of the early Church, as does the later flight into the desert. The sun covering the heavenly woman, with the moon under her feet and the twelve stars as her diadem, are images which together attempt to describe the glory of Mary, the mother of the triumphant Messiah. The twelve stars also symbolize the twelve tribes of Israel whose place is taken by the new Israel with the twelve Apostles as its leaders. Thus it applies to the Church.

dragon . . . ten horns: These are apocalyptic images to describe the opponents of the messianic kingdom. Isaiah refers to Rahab and the dragon who were hacked to pieces by the Lord (Is. 51 : 9) and Leviathan the writhing serpent whom the Lord will punish with his powerful sword (Is. 27 : 1). The fourth beast in Daniel's vision has ten horns (Dn. 7 : 7). John draws on these images to describe the opponents of the Messiah and his kingdom, the Church.

dragon stood before the woman: He meant to devour the woman's child at birth. Herod comes to our mind here, but so do the Sanhedrin, and Saul before his conversion, and the Roman emperors who did everything possible to destroy and devour the infant Church.

to rule . . . nations: He was to be King of the world, a King who would be as a shepherd over his flock.

with . . . iron: There is a reference here to psalm 2 where the Messiah is said to break the power of the impenitent pagan nations with a rod of iron, and so win freedom for his Chosen People.

caught up: John moves directly from the birth of the Messiah to his ascension. In Acts (1 : 2; 11; 22) the ascension is described as a "taking up," a "taking away from" the Apostles. It was God the Father who took him up to heaven.

woman fled into the wilderness: St. John is here speaking of the infant Church which had to go through its period of persecution and formation just as the Chosen People of old had to go through their desert before entering the promised land. This was God's plan and therefore a success. The blood of the martyrs became the seed of Christians.

kingdom . . . God: When Constantine the Roman Emperor became a Christian (311 A.D.) freedom was eventually given to God's kingdom on earth.

authority of his Christ: Christ's authority as head of the Church was then publicly admitted.

APPLICATION: This text from the Book of Revelation or Apocalypse was chosen for the feast of the Assumption of Our Lady, because of the close link between Christ our Messiah and Savior and his blessed Mother. John stresses it in these verses. In God's plan for our elevation to divine sonship by adoption,

Mary was chosen from all eternity to be the Mother of his divine Son's human nature. She was thus intimately connected with her son in the carrying out of this divine plan. As this plan was to be opposed by sin, and by Satan, the head and representative of all sinners, it was to be expected that opposition would concentrate on his blessed Mother, as well as on her offspring, Christ the Messiah.

In chapter three of Genesis this opposition was already foretold in the poetic description of the first sin of disobedience, attributed to the wiles of Satan. God said to the serpent, who represented Satan, as the Dragon in Revelation does : "I will put enmity between you and the woman, between your offspring and hers" (Gn. 3 : 15). St. John in his apocalyptic imagery, describes this opposition. We know from the Gospel story how Mary suffered with her divine Son. The culmination of that suffering was the three hours of incredible and indescribable agony she had to bear while her beloved one slowly shed his life's blood on the cross.

Today, on the feast of our Blessed Mother's triumph, we can omit the tragic events of her life and, like St. John, pass quickly to the victorious outcome of the struggle between the Dragon and the Messiah, a victory in which Mary had played her part. In return she received a reward far exceeding any earthly pains which she had endured.

Today the Church celebrates Mary's assumption into heaven which took place immediately after her death. She was then given the same glorified existence which her divine Son's human nature had been given by the Father at

his moment of death, and which all the elect will be given at their moment of resurrection. We believe that, after Christ, she has occupied the next highest place of glory in heaven from the moment that her earthly life ended. This has been the constant belief of the Church from the very beginning, a belief confirmed and guaranteed by the infallible declaration of Pope Pius XII in 1950.

Mary was Mother of Christ, the God-man and our Savior. She cooperated with him in his salvific mission. She suffered, as we saw above, because of our sins. She saw her beloved Son suffer and die on the cross for our sins. She is now enjoying eternal glory in heaven. Is it likely that she could lose interest in us, her other children who are brothers of Christ? No, her divine Son has not lost interest in us and therefore his blessed Mother cannot fail to be interested in our eternal welfare. We can feel certain that she will intercede for us if we ask her, and we can rest assured that her intercession will not be ignored.

Let us honor her today in the manner in which she wants us to honor her, that is, by thanking God for all the graces which he conferred on her, graces which flowed from her privileged position as Mother of Christ. Her immediate assumption into heaven was the crowning grace and the divine reward which the infinitely loving God conferred on the woman whom he had chosen to cooperate in the messianic mission of his beloved Son. For having been made sons of God and heirs to heaven we owe a debt of thanks, after God, Father, Incarnate Son and Holy Spirit, to the Mother of God and our Mother.

SECOND READING: 1 Corinthians 15:20-27. Christ has been raised from the dead, the first fruits of those who have fallen asleep. For as by a man came death, by a man has come also the resurrection of the dead. For as in Adam all die, so also in Christ shall all be made alive. But each in his own order: Christ the first fruits, then at his coming those who belong to Christ. Then comes the end, when he delivers the kingdom to God the Father after destroying every rule and every authority and power. For he must reign until he has put all his enemies under his feet. The last enemy to be destroyed is death. "For God has put all things in subjection under his feet."

EXPLANATION: In this chapter of his first letter to his Corinthian converts St. Paul is proving that we shall all rise one day from the dead. Evidently some of the converts were doubting this. St. Paul refutes this false idea by reminding them that one of the basic doctrines of the Christian faith, which they had accepted, was Christ's resurrection. For his proofs of this basic fact of the faith see verses 1-11 of this fifteenth chapter.

the first fruits ... fallen asleep: As the appearance of the first fruits was a sign and proof that the rest would follow, so the resurrection of Christ was a proof that all men would be raised from the dead one day. In the New Testament death is often compared to a sleep (see Jn. 11:11; Acts 7:60; 13:16; 1 Cor. 7:29; 11:30, etc.). This figure of speech was so common among the early Christians that the Greek word "koimeterion," which meant a dormitory or sleeping-place, came to mean the Christian burial-place. Hence our English word "cemetery."

In Adam all die: St. Paul accepted the literal interpretation of Genesis 3:5-19, and so Adam's physical (not spiritual) death was a punishment for his disobedience. This punishment was incurred by all his descendants.

In Christ ... alive: Christ by his death and resurrection has earned for all men, all the descendants of Adam, a resurrection from death. As St. Paul says later in this chapter, our risen bodies will be different from our present bodies: "What is sown (buried) in the earth as a perishable thing is raised imperishable, sown in humiliation, it is raised in glory; sown in weakness, it is raised in power, sown as an animal body it is raised as a spiritual body" (15:42-43).

at his coming ... belong to Christ: Christ has already risen. At the *parousia*, or second coming of Christ, at the end of time, all those who belong to him, that is, those who were loyal to him in life, will rise in glory as he did. He does not say what will happen to those who were disloyal.

destroying ... rule: Having completed his salvific mission as the incarnate Son of God, and having brought all the elect to the glory of the eternal life, he will have conquered all evil. He will then hand over the kingdom he has won to the Father.

he must reign: The end of the world will see the end of his kingdom on earth. All his opponents will be subjected to him, if not willingly, then to their own eternal loss. All his elect will be transferred to the heavenly kingdom of his Father.

APPLICATION : St. Paul says in the verse that immediately precedes today's reading (15 : 19): "If it is for this life only that we had hope in Christ, we of all men are most to be pitied." How true this is! If all were to end for us in the grave how foolish we would be to deprive ourselves of any of the pleasure, power or wealth of this life! What folly it would be for any man to mortify himself, to keep laws that were restricting his personal liberty, to waste time on prayer and other practices which produced no earthly pleasure or gain! In other words, being a Christian would mean taking on oneself unpleasant obligations which earned nothing for us but the grave!

However, St. Paul proves in this same chapter that there is a life beyond the grave, an eternal life which Christ has won for us and which God has planned for us from all eternity. We shall all rise from the dead and enter into this new life. Christ's own resurrection is the proof that this will be so. We have another proof of this basic truth of our faith in the feast we are celebrating today. This proof has been infallibly defined by the successor of St. Peter, the head of the Church.

Our blessed Lady, Mother of Christ and our Mother, has been raised from the dead and is now in heaven in a glorified state next to the incarnate Son of God who is her Son also. The blessed Mother is one of us, a mere creature who was made of flesh and blood as we are. She differs from us in this, that because of her honored and most special relationship with God's incarnate Son she received greater graces than any other human being, and she cooperated with these graces. If we cooperate with them each one of us is guaranteed enough graces and favors to win our own resurrection to the eternal life.

As the resurrection or assumption of our blessed Lady is a further proof and guarantee that we too shall one day rise in triumph from our graves, so also is it a source of greater confidence and hope for each one of us. She, our Mother, is in heaven. She is interested in each one of us. She has influence with her Son and with the Holy Trinity. She will use that influence on our behalf if we ask her. This fact of her power of intercession has been proved again and again down through the history of the Church. She has obtained material blessings for thousands. The spiritual blessings she has obtained for those devoted to her are innumerable. They will be known to all only on the last day.

Today, then, let us thank God first and foremost for the incarnation, for sending his Son on earth as a man in order to lift us up to sonship with his Father. Then let us thank him for choosing this human Mother—one of ourselves—for his incarnate Son, and for giving her all the graces necessary for the position he gave her in life. She suffered with her divine Son on Calvary and that suffering was for us. She, like her beloved Son, wants us in heaven. She is able and willing to help us to get there. At the wedding feast in Cana she successfully interceded with him to save a bridal pair from temporary embarrassment. Will she not be even more successful still in her intercession to save all her devoted children from eternal embarrassment, now that she is with her Son in heaven?

All that is needed is trust and confidence on our part. Let us ask her today, on this great feast of her triumph, to be ever watching over us, directing and encouraging us to persevere in our loyalty to her divine Son. Let us resolve to follow her example and climb our Calvary as she climbed hers. If we do so, the day is not far distant when we too will rise from the dead and join her and him in the home prepared for us through the incarnation and the infinite love of God.

GOSPEL: Luke 1 : 39–56. Mary arose and went with haste into the hill country, to a city of Judah, and she entered the house of Zechariah and greeted Elizabeth. And when Elizabeth heard the greeting of Mary, the babe leaped in her womb; and Elizabeth was filled with the Holy Spirit and she exclaimed with a loud cry, "Blessed are you among women, and blessed is the fruit of your womb! And why is this granted me, that the mother of my Lord should come to me? For behold, when the voice of your greeting came to my ears, the babe in my womb leaped for joy. And blessed is she who believed that there would be a fulfillment of what was spoken to her from the Lord."

And Mary said, "My soul magnifies the Lord, and my spirit rejoices in God my Savior, for he has regarded the low estate of his handmaiden. For behold, henceforth all generations will call me blessed; for he who is mighty has done great things for me, and holy is his name. And his mercy is on those who fear him from generation to generation. He has shown strength with his arm, he has scattered the proud in the imagination of their hearts, he has put down the mighty from their thrones, and exalted those of low degree; he has filled the hungry with good things, and the rich he has sent empty away. He has helped his servant Israel, in remembrance of his mercy, as he spoke to our fathers, to Abraham and to his posterity for ever." And Mary remained with her about three months, and returned to her home.

EXPLANATION : The Angel Gabriel told Mary that she was to be the mother of the Messiah. Mary's big problem was how this could be, because she intended to remain a virgin. The Angel told her that God's power would do this, because the son whom she would conceive and give birth to would be the Son of the Most High. As a proof of this power of God the Angel told her that her cousin Elizabeth, who was barren and then quite advanced in years, had conceived, and was already in her sixth month "for God's promises can never fail."

Mary accepted the Angel's word saying : "I am the maidservant of the Lord, let it be done unto me as you say." The incarnation took place at that moment.

Mary's first thought was to visit, congratulate and help Elizabeth. Without hesitation she left for Elizabeth's and Zechariah's house, which was in the hill country of Judah about five miles west of Jerusalem, a four days' journey from Nazareth.

Elizabeth . . . filled with the Holy Spirit : On hearing Mary's greeting, Elizabeth was inspired by the Holy Spirit and proclaimed Mary as the most blessed of all women and Mother of God. She feels how unworthy she is that the Mother of her Lord (God) should visit her. John the Baptist, the baby in her womb, also recognized the presence of the Son of God and of his Mother, and leaped in Elizabeth's womb.

Mary said : We have now what we know as the "Magnificat," Mary's hymn of praise to God, who is about to fulfill the messianic promises which he had made to Abraham and his descendants. The Son of God has become man so that all men could become sons of God. It is very likely that Mary did not compose this hymn verbatim as St. Luke gives it. However, it certainly expresses her feelings. There is gratitude for the infinite love and mercy of God toward the humble and lowly. These will be filled with good things (the fruits of the incarnation) while the selfish and proud will not share in his generosity. She realizes how unworthy she is of the great things he has done for her. She prophesies that all ages will call her blessed because God, through his mighty power, had made her Mother of his incarnate Son.

She remained with her : Although St. Luke does not say so expressly, it is evident that Mary remained until the Baptist was born, so that she could be of help and comfort to her cousin.

APPLICATION : "All ages to come shall call me blessed" was a prophecy uttered by our Lady and was not a boast. She who was chosen by God to be the Mother of his incarnate Son, saw in herself nothing but a maidservant, completely and entirely unworthy of the dignity conferred on her. Elizabeth had called her "blessed among women" but Mary attributes this blessedness to the "greatness of the Lord" who had "looked on his servant in her lowliness." She had no doubts about her own unworthiness and her unfitness for the dignity conferred on her by God, but she recognized how great, how sublime that dignity was. She had been made the Mother of God.

Her prophecy has been fulfilled from the very first days of the Church. She has been given the highest place among all of God's creatures—Queen of Angels and Queen of all Saints—right through the history of Christianity. In giving her this place of honor above all other angelic or saintly creatures, we are but following God's own initiative—he made her the Mother of his divine Son and gave her all the graces which that position of unparalleled dignity demanded. When we honor her it is really his infinite love for, and his unbounded generosity toward, the human race that we are honoring. It was for us men and for our salvation that the Son of God came down from heaven. It was for us that he chose Mary as his Mother. She was but the human intermediary in God's plan of salvation for mankind.

Today's feastday of God's Mother and ours is the climax and crowning of all the other graces and honors which God conferred on her. The assumption or the transferring of our blessed Lady to heaven, in her glorified but identical, total personality, immediately after her death on earth, was not only the triumph of Mary but a triumph for all humanity. Where the Mother is, there will be all her loyal children. She played a large part in the redemption-work of her divine Son on earth. She continues in heaven to play a very effective part in applying the fruits of that redemption to all her children. If we follow Mary we are following Christ. If we remain close to the Mother we can never wander away from her Son. If we put ourselves under the mantle of her protection, Christ will shelter us from the enemies of our salvation. If we call on her to intercede for us our petitions will be answered by Christ.

This climax of all God's gifts to Mary —the assumption into heaven, not of her separated soul, but of her total person, is a gift which God has ready for all of us, provided we imitate Mary on earth and be loyal to her Son and God's Son. We cannot expect the same degree of heavenly glory which is hers, but we shall be perfectly happy with what we shall receive. All eternity will not be long enough for us to thank the Blessed Trinity, Christ in his humanity and his Blessed Mother who did so much to save us.

FEAST OF THE IMMACULATE CONCEPTION

FIRST READING: Genesis 3:9–15; 20. After Adam had eaten of the tree, the Lord God called to the man, and said to him, "Where are you?" And he said, "I heard the sound of thee in the garden, and I was afraid, because I was naked; and I hid myself." He said, "Who told you that you were naked? Have you eaten of the tree of which I commanded you not to eat?" The man said, "The woman whom thou gavest to be with me, she gave me fruit of the tree, and I ate." Then the Lord God said to the woman, "What is this that you have done?" The woman said, "The serpent beguiled me, and I ate." The Lord God said to the serpent, "Because you have done this, cursed are you above all cattle, and above all wild animals; upon your belly you shall go, and dust you shall eat all the days of your life. I will put enmity between you and the woman, and between your seed and her seed; it shall bruise your head, and you shall bruise its heel."

The man called his wife's name Eve, because she was the mother of all living.

EXPLANATION: In the preceding verses (2:4—3:8) the Yahwehistic source of this part of Genesis has described the temptation of the woman (later called Eve) by the serpent. She succumbs and tempts the man (ha-adam). As soon as they had disobeyed God's command given in 2:16–17, they realized their guilt and tried to hide from God.

where are you : God knows where he is, but he wants them both to come forward and admit their guilt.

afraid because I was naked : This answer implies that because of their disobedience, concupiscence of the flesh had now entered the world of humans. In their state of innocence it had no place in their lives (as 2 : 25 clearly states : "the man and his wife were both naked and they felt no shame").

eaten . . . to eat : They had eaten of what was called the "tree of knowledge of good and evil" and were therefore conscious of evil. They had disobeyed a test of obedience which God had given them and they now felt a sense of guilt.

the woman . . . with me : Not only has man lost his friendship with God but his love and friendship for his wife has changed. He throws the blame on her, while at the same time blaming God for giving her to him, "you put her here with me!"

the serpent beguiled : The woman in turn puts the blame on the serpent, who had certainly tempted her, although she was free to reject his suggestion.

said to the serpent : It is clear from God's condemnation of the serpent that there is more than an irrational animal in question. Some of the punishment applies to the animal, some to a rational being hidden in and symbolized by the serpent.

cursed . . . cattle : Because of his poisonous fangs all other animals avoid the serpent.

upon your belly you shall go : This and "dirt you shall eat" are symbols of humiliation for an intelligent being, not for the animal who was made as a crawling creature and appears to eat dirt but does not.

enmity between you and the woman : A perpetual hatred will exist between the tempter and the woman (Eve in the context), between his (seed) offspring (followers and helpers) and the woman's (seed) offspring, that is, all mankind.

It shall bruise your head : The Hebrew word for seed (offspring) is singular, hence *he* will strike could be used here.

bruise its heel : The image of the serpent, while it means the tempter, is still used. In this struggle the descendants of the woman will have the victory, for the serpent's head is his most vulnerable part. The seed of the woman will also suffer but not fatally.

Eve . . . mother of all living : In the preceding verses the Hebrew word used for "woman" was "ishah" derived from man="ish." Now we are told that the man changed her name to "Hawwah," Heva in Latin, Eve in English, and the reason is because it is from her that the human race, the living="Hay" will spring.

APPLICATION : "I will put enmity between you and the woman and between your offspring and hers." These words of God addressed to the serpent, the evil tempter, immediately after the sin of disobedience committed by the first parents, have been called the proto-Evangelium or "first good news" of hope for the human race. These verses from the Book of Genesis have been chosen for today's feastday, that of the Immaculate Conception of Mary, because she was chosen by God to be the human Mother of his incarnate Son, and was conceived free from any stain of the sin handed down from the first parents. From the first moment of her human existence she was "full of grace" and God's "highly favored daughter."

In Mary, therefore, this "first good news" had its first fulfillment. Satan had no part in her. The serpent had lost his power in her case. This was because of the privileged position God had allotted to her. She was to be the Mother of the long-expected Messiah—Savior, who would finally crush the serpent's head.

This victory, already won in the moral sense, had still to be won on the physical plane. As foretold by this first prophecy and promise of eventual salvation for the human race, the serpent could still inflict pain and suffering. Using his offspring, his human agents, he had Christ condemned as a criminal to the cruel death of the cross. Christ's blessed Mother suffered with him. She stood beneath the cross during his three hours of death-agony. She knew that he was the innocent victim of Satan's wiles, and of the sins of mankind. She had to listen to the jeers and the insults of those very men whom he had come to save, and for whom he was laying down his life.

Yes, the serpent could and did use his poisonous fangs but they failed to save him from defeat. The sufferings of Jesus and of his blessed Mother were the very means foreseen by God to con-quer sin and Satan, and to win eternal life and freedom for all the children of Eve. Satan unwittingly played the chief role in his own undoing. Calvary was the stage where the "triumph of failure" was enacted. The death of the Savior brought eternal life to men.

If Eve was given her name because she brought all living human beings into this world, how much more so can Mary be called the source of life for all men? Eve brought men into a world of misery, a world of suffering, a world of sin. Mary brought Christ our Savior, the author of eternal life into this world. Through him she brought to all those who will become his brothers through faith, and therefore her children, the assurance of an everlasting life and happiness, joy and unending peace and love.

We honor our sinless Mother on this great Feast of her Immaculate Conception. Though we are sinners, let us ask her to spread her mantle of purity and grace over us. She loves us because she suffered with her beloved Son for us. She wants his triumph on Calvary to be as full and complete as possible. She is able and willing to help us to gain the victory which he won for us. All that is needed is that we turn to her as humble suppliants. She will pray for us sinners now and especially at the hour of our death.

SECOND READING: Ephesians 1:3-6; 11-12. Blessed be the God and Father of our Lord Jesus Christ, who has blessed us in Christ with every spiritual blessing in the heavenly places, even as he chose us in him before the foundation of the world, that we should be holy and blameless before him. He destined us in love to be his sons through Jesus Christ, according to the purpose of his will, to the praise of his glorious grace which he freely bestowed on us in the Beloved.

In him, according to the purpose of him who accomplishes all things according to the counsel of his will, we who first hoped in Christ have been destined and appointed to live for the praise of his glory.

EXPLANATION: From his prison in Rome (about 63 A.D.) St. Paul wrote this letter to his converts in Ephesus. He had preached the Gospel to them some eight years previously and the Christian message had since spread to the neighboring cities and towns. The purpose of this letter was to recall to their minds the basic Christian truths and to encourage them to remain faithful followers of Christ.

Blessed be the God and Father: St. Paul has taught the doctrine of the Blessed Trinity to his Ephesian converts (Jews and Gentiles). They have accepted it without question, although for Jewish converts especially this was not easy.

of our Lord Jesus Christ: The Jesus who had lived and died recently in Palestine was "Christ," that is, the promised "Messiah." Furthermore, he was "Lord," that is, God. We have, therefore, in this single verse the doctrine of the Trinity, God the Father, God the Son (the Holy Spirit is mentioned later on) and the doctrine of the incarnation. Jesus, the man they all knew about, was also God, the Son of God the Father.

blessed us in Christ: Through Christ, that is, through the incarnation of his Son, God the Father had bestowed every spiritual blessing in the heavens

(where the Christians would receive their full reward) on the Ephesian Christians.

chose us in him: Through the medium of the incarnation, Christians (and all men of good will) have been predestined by the Father to share in eternal happiness.

before . . . the world: As Scotus teaches, God's plan for sharing heaven with us by making us his adopted sons through his divine Son's incarnation was from all eternity, and not a remedy necessary because of men's sins.

through . . . Christ: Through his Son's adoption of our human nature we were predestined to be elevated to the status of adopted sons of God. The prayer which we say in the Mass points to this: "through this mystery of water and wine may we come to share in the divinity of Christ who humbled himself to share in our humanity."

according . . . will: The only explanation of this infinite generosity on the part of God the Father toward us mere creatures is his will and pleasure.

glorious . . . Beloved: Unending praise and thanksgiving should be man's response and reaction to the favor which the Father, in the mystery of the incarnation, has planned for us through his beloved Son.

In him . . . appointed: St. Paul is referring first to the Jewish converts. While they were still Jews they were the first to have hope in Christ the Messiah. They praised God for his mercies. Then in the following verse (13) he addresses the Gentiles : "you too . . . became incorporate in Christ. . ."

APPLICATION : The Christo-centric doctrine of St. Paul expressed above occurs too in all of his greater Epistles, especially in the captivity Epistles (Colossians, Ephesians, Philippians). It is closely connected with the Feast of the Immaculate Conception which we are celebrating today. God planned from all eternity to make man, the masterpiece and master of creation, his adopted son, and heir to his own eternal happiness. He was to bring this about through his divine Son's adoption of our human nature. Man would then become a brother of Christ and there-fore a son of God by adoption. Christ, the Son of God in human nature, the God-man, is the pivotal point in all of God's creative activity. In him, through him, and for him all creation came into existence. In him and through him all mankind, the whole human race, was destined for eternal life.

But man, realizing the many gifts which he had, and forgetting the one who gave them to him, grew proud of his own capabilities and wanted to be his own master. He rebelled and sin came into the world. Despicable and mean as it was on the part of man, it did not stop God from carrying out his eternal plan. The incarnation could still have taken place. When the "full-ness of time" as St. Paul calls it, was approaching, he called Abraham from his pagan homeland and made him the Father and Founder of a Chosen People. This People would prepare the world for the fulfilling of the "mystery" which he had planned from all eternity.

As the prophecies given to his Chosen People had foretold, Christ was to be born of a virgin, a descendant of Abraham and of David. She was a virgin and intended to remain a virgin. Today's Gospel makes that clear. When told by the angelic messenger, whom God sent to her, that the conception of this child would take place through the power of the Most High she humbly accepted the role to which God had appointed her.

Mary the virgin of Nazareth, the humblest of the humble who would have been the last to expect any such dignity, became the Mother of Christ. She thus played the leading human part in the fulfillment of God's eternal plan for the human race. As she said herself : "God who is mighty has done great things for me." When he chose her, before time began, for this sublime dignity of motherhood of his incarnate Son, he decreed to preserve her free from any stain of the sin committed by the First Parents. She was conceived "Immaculate," pure and free from any human stain. She was "our tainted nature's solitary boast," as the Pro-testant poet Wordsworth puts it.

This befits one who was to bear for nine months in her womb the world's greatest mystery; God's greatest gift to humanity, the Son of God clothed in human nature, Christ, God and Man. He was the perfect man and God as well. His Mother, the creature who was nearest and dearest to him, was the most perfect of creatures—the most favored daughter of God.

Had sin not entered the world, hers would still be the highest dignity that a creature could be given—the Motherhood of God. Her preservation from the stain of sin was but a consequence of that dignity. But in the imperfect, sinful world into which she was born it was an added, lustrous gem in her crown of glory.

We congratulate the Immaculate Mother of Christ and our Mother on this special privilege of exemption from the guilt which all of Eve's children incurred and incur. While doing so let us turn with gratitude to the God and Father of our Lord Jesus Christ. He chose her and prepared her to be the proximate means through which he was to give us every blessing in heaven.

We shall all be saints in heaven one day enjoying unending happiness. For this we give thanks to the infinitely loving Father, to the Holy Spirit, to God's incarnate Son, and to the Immaculate Virgin Mother who played and still plays such a big part in bringing us to our eternal heritage.

GOSPEL : Luke 1 : 26–38. The angel Gabriel was sent from God to a city of Galilee named Nazareth, to a virgin betrothed to a man whose name was Joseph, of the house of David; and the virgin's name was Mary. And he came to her and said, "Hail, full of grace, the Lord is with you!" But she was greatly troubled at the saying, and considered in her mind what sort of greeting this might be. And the angel said to her, "Do not be afraid, Mary, for you have found favor with God. And behold, you will conceive in your womb and bear a son, and you shall call his name Jesus. He will be great, and will be called the Son of the Most High; and the Lord God will give to him the throne of his father David, and he will reign over the house of Jacob forever; and of his kingdom there will be no end."

And Mary said to the angel, "How can this be, since I have no husband?" And the angel said to her, "The Holy Spirit will come upon you, and the power of the Most High will overshadow you; therefore the child to be born will be called holy, the Son of God. And behold, your kinswoman Elizabeth in her old age has also conceived a son; and this is the sixth month with her who was called barren. For with God nothing will be impossible." And Mary said, "Behold, I am the handmaid of the Lord; let it be to me according to your word." And the angel departed from her.

EXPLANATION : In these thirteen verses St. Luke gives us a brief account of what we call the Annunciation or the message of the Angel Gabriel to Mary. He told her that she was to be the Mother of the Messiah, Son of the Most High. When the angel solved the problem concerning her virginity, she humbly accepted the role that God had planned for her. At that moment of acceptance the incarnation took place. The Son of God began his human life in the chaste womb of the Blessed Virgin.

Angel Gabriel : He is the same divine messenger who had announced the birth of the Baptist to Zechariah (Lk. 1 : 11) and the seventy weeks of years to Daniel (Dn. 9 : 21).

city . . . named Nazareth : A hamlet of no importance, never mentioned in the Old Testament, and not held in much esteem by Jesus' contemporaries (Jn. 1 : 46).

a virgin betrothed to . . . Joseph : A young girl of marriageable age which also meant at that time physical virginity. Although she was betrothed to Joseph, with his consent, she could have an intention of perpetual virginity. Many scriptural writers hold this view even though it would have been an unusual intention in Palestine at that time.

The virgin's name was Mary : Luke's repetition of the qualification "virgin" seems to imply something more than the fact that she was as yet unmarried.

Hail . . . grace : The CCD translation of the Greek: "Rejoice O highly favored daughter" brings out the angel's meaning better than the old form "Hail, full of grace." He is bringing her great good news. It is a time for rejoicing, and he tells her that she is a highly favored daughter of God, a statement that must have surprised one so humble as she.

The Lord is with you : As the sequel shows, this implies some special prerogative, the divine maternity. God is working through her to fulfill his messianic prophecies.

she . . . be : Because of her lowly opinion of herself she wondered at this greeting. What was she but an unknown young girl engaged to an unknown carpenter in an unknown and despised village? Why should she be favored by God?

do not . . . Mary : The angel notices her amazement and goes on to explain.

favor with God : He has already told her that she is God's favorite daughter. Now he explains why.

conceive . . . and bear a Son . . . Jesus : There is a reflexion of the Immanuel prophecy here. Isaiah says : "the virgin is with child and will soon give birth to a son whom she will call Immanuel" (Is. 7 : 14). It was the father's right to name his child. Here Mary, and the virgin mother in Isaiah, name the child. This would seem to exclude human paternity. The angel gives Mary the name which means "Yahweh (God) will save." Immanuel means "God is with us." Jesus was God incarnate.

Great . . . Son of the Most High : The angel now describes the Son to be born of Mary in messianic terms (see Is. 9 : 6; Dn. 7 : 14) especially in

throne of . . . David : This refers to the prophecy which Nathan made to David, that he would have a successor on his throne and that throne would be established for ever (2 Sm. 7 : 13; 17).

over the house of Jacob forever : The house of Jacob refers to the Chosen People. Mary's Son will reign forever over a Chosen People of Jews and Gentiles. It will be more than an earthly kingdom, it will have no end.

since I . . . husband : Unlike Zechariah (1 : 18) she does not doubt the word of the angel but admits that she cannot understand how a virgin, while remaining a virgin, can be with child.

Holy Spirit . . . Most High . . . overshadow you : God's power will do this. As shown in the Old Testament, there are reminiscences of God's power and presence here (see Gen. 1 : 2, the Spirit of God hovered over the waters before creation began; the Tabernacle was covered with a cloud to show the presence of God (Ex. 40 : 35), and so was the newly-built Temple of Jersualem (1 Kgs. 8 : 10)).

be called . . . the Son of God : The title Son of God means more than the Messiah here. The child will be conceived by the action of God *hence* he "will be" the true "Son of God."

your kinswoman Elizabeth : The angel tells Mary of Elizabeth's good fortune as a proof of God's power and a guarantee that God's power would be forthcoming in her own case. She had not asked for a proof.

I am the handmaid of the Lord : She had been chosen to be Mother of the Lord, Mother of Christ, God's Son, but she fully realized her lowliness and her nothingness in relation to God. However, she accepted what God had willed for her; with the help of his grace she would fulfill his wishes.

Let it be done to me as you say : I accept whatever God wants of me : A fitting close to an interview between the humble Mother of God and God's angelic messenger.

APPLICATION : God planned to bestow an eternal, heavenly life on man, the highest of the creatures whom he placed on this earth. This heavenly life will be supernatural, quasi-divine. We shall still be human beings, creatures of God, finite in our powers, but we shall be free from all defects to which our human lives on earth are subject. Death and all its preliminaries and consequences will have no further place in that heavenly life. There will be no more sicknesses or ailments, no more mental or physical pains, no more partings from relatives and friends; "all tears shall be wiped away."

There will be no more vices, hatred, jealousy, anger, lust, deception, egoism, pride and prejudice. All the evils that make the life of man a burden for himself and for his neighbor on this earth, will remain in our graves when we rise from the dead.

Not only will all evil and sources of evil be removed but we shall have all that is good. First and foremost, with the grace of the beatific vision, we shall see, in a limited but satisfying way, the glory and the beauty and the perfection of the Blessed Trinity. As the Triune God is infinite, there will be something new for us to enjoy in him for all eternity. Next we shall converse with and enjoy Christ glorified, who has brought about our glorification.

Finally, we shall be in the intimate company of our blessed Mother who has played such an important part in the drama of our redemption and our glorification. We, her children, for whom she suffered so much will then be able to render her the praise and the thanks that she deserves from us.

Today, on this great feast of her Immaculate Conception, let us turn to her with hope and confidence. We are commemorating the graces and blessings which God gave her to fit her for the dignity he had chosen for her. She, like her divine Son, wants all of us in heaven. Like any human mother she wants nothing but the best for her children. But, as in any human family, the children must cooperate. Otherwise, all the Mother's desires and hopes will be in vain.

If we expect to be in heaven with her we must try to imitate her on earth. Above all she was humble and unselfish, pride had no part in her make-up. She was chaste and pure to a degree we cannot expect to reach. But even if from afar, each of us in his or her own vocation in life, can follow her. Chastity, the proper use and respect for God's gift of sex, can and must be practiced, not only in a life of virginity consecrated to God's service but also in the married state. Obedience was another of her outstanding virtues. She welcomed and carried out the will of God even when it meant offering her beloved and only Son on the altar of the cross for our sakes. Those humble, submissive words of hers : "Let it be done to me as you say" should be always in our hearts and ready on our lips, when God asks some sacrifice of us.

Love of God and neighbor were the mainspring of her life. Her unhesitating acceptance of motherhood of the Savior of the human race proves both her love for God and her fellowman.

Most of us have much leeway to make up if we wish to come in any way near to her in the practice of these basic commandments. In heaven, we have a most powerful advocate, a Mother who loves us with a love greater than the love that any earthly mother can have for her child. If we call on her she will hear our prayer. When we begin to stumble on our upward climb she will stretch out her hand to steady us. When we fall and injure ourselves, she will lift us up and heal the wound if only we ask her. Even if, as sometimes happens, we should turn our back on her and on her divine Son, she will not turn her back on us. She will be praying and waiting patiently for our return.

With such a Mother, the Immaculate Virgin Mary, in heaven, looking down on us, what true Christian can ever have any doubt about safely reaching heaven?

FEAST OF ALL SAINTS

FIRST READING: Revelation 7:2-4; 9-14. I, John, saw an angel ascend from the rising of the sun, with the seal of the living God, and he called with a loud voice to the four angels who had been given power to harm earth and sea, saying, "Do not harm the earth or the sea or the trees, till we have sealed the servants of our God upon their foreheads." And I heard the number of the sealed, a hundred and forty-four thousand sealed, out of every tribe of the sons of Israel.

After this I looked, and behold, a great multitude which no man could number, from every nation, from all tribes and peoples and tongues, standing before the throne and before the Lamb, clothed in white robes, with palm branches in their hands, and crying out with a loud voice, "Salvation belongs to our God who sits upon the throne, and to the Lamb!" And all the angels stood round the throne and round the elders and the four living creatures, and they fell on their faces before the throne and worshiped God, saying, "Amen! Blessing and glory and wisdom and thanksgiving and honor and power and might be to our God for ever and ever! Amen."

Then one of the elders addressed me, saying, "Who are these, clothed in white robes, and whence have they come?" I said to him, " Sir, you know." And he said to me, "These are they who have come out of the great tribulation; they have washed their robes and made them white in the blood of the Lamb."

EXPLANATION: St. John here describes two visions which he had of the elect on earth and of the countless numbers of martyrs in heaven. The chosen ones of God on earth are the new Israel, the successors of the twelve tribes. They are about to suffer persecution. Marked with the seal of God on their foreheads, they will be given the supernatural strength to bear their sufferings.

In the second vision he sees the huge crowd, countless numbers in heaven wearing white robes as a sign of their victory over their enemies. They surround the throne of God and the "Lamb," Christ, and sing their praises. **seal of the living God:** A sign or mark that indicates those who are loyal to the true God, the living God. **the four angels:** Described in 7:1 as standing at the four corners of the earth, holding back the winds which would destroy the earth.

do not harm . . . till : The four angels are commanded to prevent destruction until God's chosen ones are marked with God's seal. This would give them the strength to persevere.

I heard the number : John could not count them but he was told their number, a symbolic number : the twelve tribes multiplied by twelve and then by a thousand. One hundred and forty-four thousand, that is an immense number.

from . . . tongues : He now sees the countless numbers of saints in heaven.

before . . . the Lamb : They stand in the presence of the throne of God and before the Lamb, the paschal lamb who is the Savior Jesus Christ. He is the suffering servant of Isaiah who was led like a lamb to the slaughter (see Ex. 12; Is. 53 : 7; Jn. 1 : 29).

salvation . . . God . . . the Lamb : They are singing the praises of God and of his incarnate Son who brought them salvation.

elders . . . four living creatures : The elders represent the saints in praising and worshiping God. The number twenty-four is probably taken from the twenty-four priestly classes in I Chronicles 24 : 1–9.

Four living creatures : These are the four animals in Revelation which symbolize the noblest (the Lion), the strongest (the Bull), the swiftest (the Eagle) and the wisest (the Man) of God's creatures. From the second century these four animals have been taken as symbols of the four Evangelists.

worshiped God : All the inhabitants of heaven adore, worship and praise God.

washed their robes . . . in the blood of the Lamb : Having suffered for Christ and shared in his crucifixion, they are now in glory with him.

APPLICATION : This vision of St. John is chosen for today's reading in order to encourage us to persevere in our Christian faith. Firstly, those on earth (ourselves) have to be prepared to meet opposition in our Christian lives. From the very beginning Christ had his followers and opponents. Christ, the innocent lamb, was "led to the slaughter and opened not his mouth." As our representative and Savior he saw that the perfect obedience which he was to give to his Father demanded that his enemies' wicked plan should be carried out. Likewise, during the first three centuries of the Church thousands of his followers had to give their lives for his sake and for their faith. In the intervening centuries, up to and including our own day,

thousands have been put to death because of their loyalty to Christ.

If not for most of us today, at least for many, it is not a quick martyrdom that is threatening us, but a subtle persecution which is trying to make us disloyal to Christ and to our Christian principles. Under various pretexts the enemies of Christ and of God are trying to undermine our faith. Open atheism is not the most dangerous of these enemies. Few sane men can be convinced that there is no God or nothing for man but the grave. That is the fate only of the dumb beast. The dangerous enemy is the one who, in theory, admits that there is a God and a future life, but that what we do in this life has no connexion with God or our future. We are free agents, they say. We can and should do what we like. Why should we accept any restrictions on our personal liberty? Why keep the commandments? Why control our natural instincts? We should get all the pleasure and wealth we can in this life and the next will look after itself.

Today, we are reminded that every Christian on earth and everyone who wants to go to heaven must face opposition. But St. John tells us that the followers of Christ are given the necessary graces to face and overcome this opposition. Their foreheads are imprinted with the seal of the servants of God. Try to remember this when the advocates of earthly pleasures, the agents of the powers of evil, are using their wiles to make you forget that you are God's chosen servant. His grace is there for the taking. The Christian who perseveres is he who lives his daily life at peace with God and neighbor, drawing on the sources of God's grace—prayer and the sacraments.

Another source of encouragement for us today, on this the feast day of all of God's saints, is the countless numbers John saw in heaven. These countless numbers were men and women of flesh and blood like ourselves. They had the same weaknesses, the same human inclinations, the same faults and failings in many cases as we have. They never forgot God, they never gave up trying to live the Christian life. They died at peace with God and so went to heaven. Many good-living Christians would almost laugh if they were told that they will be saints. Yet, that is what they will be. The reason why they would laugh at this statement of fact is the wrong idea that some spiritual writers have given us of the essence of a saint. The few saints who are canonized by the Church, and whose lives are written to encourage and inspire us, were exceptional individuals. We have no written lives of the ordinary men and women who were not exceptional in any way but who lived in God's friendship and died in his grace. They now are saints in heaven.

Christ died to save all mankind. His death on the cross was not for St. Paul or St. Augustine or St. Francis only. It was for plain Mrs. Murphy and Franz Allesmanner and Signora Benvenuta also. They didn't work miracles or do anything extraordinary, but they fully lived the very ordinary, humdrum daily Christian life. Thanks to God's infinite mercy and thanks to the Lamb of God who takes away the sins of the world, there are countless saints in heaven today. One day soon you and I, please God, will increase their number. There are close relatives of each one of us in heaven. Let us ask them and all the other millions today to intercede for us. We are anxious to get to heaven and we are anxious to do the things that will get us there. Each day we have to meet much opposition. This will obtain for us God's grace and "we shall overcome." We too will be saints in heaven praising and thanking the good God who brought us there.

SECOND READING : 1 Epistle of John 3 : 1–3. See what love the Father has given us, that we should be called children of God; and so we are. The reason why the world does not know us is that it did not know him. Beloved, we are God's children now; it does not yet appear what we shall be, but we know that when he appears we shall be like him, for we shall see him as he is. And everyone who thus hopes in him purifies himself as he is pure.

EXPLANATION : The Apostle and Evangelist St. John wrote this letter to the churches of Asia Minor to encourage them to remain faithful to Christ who was the Son of God. There were heretics and heresies arising here and there. There were proud men who questioned the divinity of Christ and the true love of God for mankind. In the verses read today he tells them (his readers) and us that God has made us his children and that if we live as true children we shall see him in heaven later on as he is.

what love the Father has . . . us : The love of God for man is the central theme of all John's writings. Through that love God has sent his Son to become "flesh," to become one of us. Because Christ the Son of God is one of us, we have become brothers of Christ and therefore sons, "children," of God.

the world does not know us : The enemies of God, the followers of evil are the "world" for John. They cannot recognize Christians as children of God for they do not recognize Christ as the true Son of God.

what we shall be : John states that we are God's children now. What we shall be, that is, what changes will take place in us, when we leave this earth, John says he does not know. It has not been revealed. We shall still be the same individuals, the same "we" both now and in the hereafter. But we shall be changed so that we can "see God as he is" and live an eternal life.

we shall be like him : This much John knows : we shall be like God in some limited way. St. Paul says we shall be spiritual bodies, we shall be transformed, the corruptible will become incorruptible, the mortal in us will become immortal (1 Cor. 15 : 53).

for we shall see him as he is : We shall be in God's presence in the future life. We shall never be able to comprehend God, for our knowledge will still be finite, but, with the aid of the grace of the beatific vision, we shall more and more understand God's infinite qualities for all eternity.

Everyone who . . . hopes : Because he wants to reach heaven and spend an eternity of happiness with God, every true Christian must strive to keep himself "pure," that is, free from *all* sins (not impurity only).

APPLICATION : We are celebrating the Feast of all Saints, that is, of the millions of men and women who are today in heaven. St. John's words are intended to help us to persevere in our heavenward journey. The great, encouraging thought that John puts before us is the fact that God the Father has already placed us more than half-way on our road to heaven by making us his adopted children through the incarnation. No father can forget his children. He is ever ready to protect, help and guide them. Could the heavenly, all-powerful, all-loving Father forget his children? Their adoption caused the humiliation of his beloved Son in taking human nature and the sacrifice of that same beloved Son on the cross of Calvary.

A human father can be inhuman and desert and neglect his human children. God can never be unGodlike. He cannot change his nature which is Love itself. He cannot forget us, his adopted children. This is surely an encouragement for us. At times we may find the uphill climb to heaven hard. But if we remember the all-loving, omnipotent Father who is watching over us, we can never despair, no matter how dark our nights of struggle and sorrow may seem.

We must never forget that a loving father may have to appear severe at times in order to be truly kind. The human father has to correct his child at times. He has to make him learn obedience, to do things necessary for his health and soundness of body. If he is to prepare him to face life and earn his living he has to make him study his lessons, a thing most children would gladly avoid. Most of this discipline can appear cruel to the unthinking child. Instead it is true love and kindness.

So it is with our heavenly Father's dealings with us. We would all love to be free from all temptations, free from all anxieties, free from all physical pain but our loving Father sees otherwise. He sends us these messengers of his love in order to prepare us to face our true life and earn for ourselves an eternal living in the future. When we are looking down from heaven on the troubles and misfortunes that we thought no kind God should let us suffer, we shall see their purpose. We shall heartily thank God for having provided them to help us on our way to heaven.

The reward for a few years of very limited suffering here on earth will be an eternity of happiness in the company of God and all his saints. As St. John says, we have only a limited revelation as to the nature of our existence in heaven, but we have enough knowledge of heaven to make us exert all our endeavors to get there. We shall be in the presence of God, the source and author of all that is good and enjoyable. We shall see the Son of God in his human nature. In him we shall understand the love of God for us which brought about the incarnation and all that it entailed for Christ of humiliations and sufferings for our sake. We shall be in the company of our blessed Mother and all our fellow human beings who will be intimately united with us in singing the praises of God, our common Father. Added to these joys will be the certainty that this state of happiness will last forever. Never again shall anxiety or suffering enter our lives. Pain, death and separation from those we love will never again cast a shadow on our existence. We shall feel safe with God for all eternity.

God grant that every one of us will meet in this happy state some day in the future!

GOSPEL: Matthew 5:1–12. Seeing the crowds, Jesus went up on the mountain, and when he sat down his disciples came to him. And he opened his mouth and taught them, saying:

"Blessed are the poor in spirit, for theirs is the kingdom of heaven. Blessed are those who mourn, for they shall be comforted. Blessed are the meek, for they shall inherit the earth. Blessed are those who hunger and thirst for righteousness, for they shall be satisfied. Blessed are the meriful, for they shall obtain mercy. Blessed are the pure in heart, for they shall see God. Blessed are the peacemakers, for they shall be called sons of God. Blessed are those who are persecuted for righteousness' sake, for theirs is the kingdom of heaven. Blessed are you when men revile you and persecute you and utter all kinds of evil against you falsely on my account. Rejoice and be glad, for your reward is great in heaven."

EXPLANATION: These verses we read today from St. Matthew's Gospel are what we call the "Beatitudes." The name comes from the Latin word "beatus= blest" with which each of the sayings begins. In the Old Testament the term "blest" or "happy" was understood of material happiness, earthly prosperity, but as a reward for carrying out the law. As given here in Matthew the statements made by Christ mean the following: the blessedness and happiness which are in store for those who do what is right and put up with sufferings and injustices are the spiritual blessings and happiness of God's eternal kingdom. Hence the suitability of these verses for today's feast. The saints have their blessed state of eternal happiness because they carried out what is recommended in the " Beatitudes."

poor in spirit . . . heaven: That is, those who are really poor, through no fault of their own. Such were the vast majority of the people of the Roman Empire at the time. It is not so much the lack of temporal wealth that Matthew emphasizes, but the servile conditions under which they had to live. Christ says that they will be rich and independent in the kingdom of God later in heaven

mourn . . . comforted: This refers in general to all who have heavy burdens to bear such as pain and grief, in this world. In particular it may refer to the pious Jews of that day who grieved over the lowly state of Israel which was caused by the sins of the Chosen People. Their sorrow will be changed to joy because the messianic kingdom has arrived. Our Lord applied the words of Isaiah to himself, words in which the prophet foretold that the humble, the broken-hearted, the prisoners, the mourners would all be comforted and freed when the Messiah would come (see Is. 61 : 1–3 and Lk. 4 : 18–21).

who hunger and thirst for righteousness: Those who are anxious to serve God truly. The Pharisees boasted of their holiness because they kept the letter of the Old Law. Christ insisted that his followers must do better than that. They must serve God in spirit and truth. The law of the love of God and neighbor covers much more than the letter of the commandments (see Mt. 5 : 20–6 : 34). Those who will fulfill God's law sincerely and truly will have their abundant reward in the next life.

Blessed . . . mercy: Compassion for one's neighbor, and a willingness to help him in his need, is one of the basic principles of the law of charity which is so much stressed by Christ. Those who are really merciful and kind to their neighbor will find that God will deal mercifully and kindly with them.

pure . . . shall see God: The true service of God is not the external ritual of purity by ablutions which the Pharisees stressed, but the service given by a sincere God-loving heart. Our Lord quotes Isaiah to the Pharisees whom he calls hypocrites: "well did Isaiah prophesy of you. This people pays me lip service, but their heart is far from me. They do me empty reverence making dogmas out of human precepts" (see Is. 29 : 13 and Mt. 15 : 7–9). Those who follow Christ's teaching will "see God," that is, they will be in his kingdom in heaven.

peacemakers . . . sons of God: Those who foster love among men by settling quarrels are true Christians. Peace was a mark of the messianic age and was the special gift of Christ to his disciples (Jn. 14 : 27).

persecuted for righteousness' sake: Those who suffer because of their love for God and for their loyalty to Christ his Son, will have the eternal reward of heaven, God's kingdom.

revile . . . account: This is an expansion of the previous beatitude, but those who suffer all these false accusations and insults do so because of their fidelity to Christ, who is God as well as man. Their reward in heaven will be great.

APPLICATION: The eight Beatitudes are a résumé of the Christian charter. They are the boundaries within which the Christian life is successfully lived. We are celebrating today the Feast of All Saints, that is, of all those who have lived their Christian life according to the ideals that Christ placed before them in the Sermon on the Mount. They have succeeded. They have reached heaven because they followed the rules which Christ laid down for them. They loved God and they showed that love in their daily living. They kept his commandment not only according to the letter but in spirit and in truth.

They bore the trials and troubles of life patiently, as part of God's plan for their sanctification. They loved their neighbor and proved it by their deeds of charity and mercy. They forgave those who persecuted and injured them. They lived in peace with God and with their neighbor. They helped to promote peace among their fellowmen wherever and whenever they could.

Some of the saints whose feasts we are celebrating today were outstanding in their sanctity. They lived their lives of mortification far beyond what was required of them. They loved God with an intensity that is not expected of ordinary mortals. They served their neighbor with a life-long dedication. They set an example and made an impression on the life of their contemporaries which will never be forgotten. God be thanked for such noble examples of saintly Christians!

But there are millions of others in heaven, saints of God also, who did nothing except their ordinary Christian duties. They did them sincerely and willingly. Their names are not inscribed in the Church's Martyrology but they are written in the "Book of Life" in heaven.

Most of us can only admire the first group from afar and thank God for the graces which their very saintly lives obtained, and are still obtaining, for the Church of God. However, we can all feel a little more confident today because of the lesser saints. What they did, we can do. Where they succeeded we too can succeed. With the help of God's grace and the assistance of the major and minor saints in heaven we will and we shall succeed.

Heaven is the eternal home that God has planned for all men of goodwill. It was to raise us up to sonship with God that Christ came down and lived and died as a man on earth. It was to help us on the way that he founded the Church and gave her the sacraments that sinners and weak mortals would need on their road to heaven. God knows the material of which we are made. He knows too how to make something far greater out of that same weak material. He has done so already with millions of very ordinary human beings. He is doing it daily and will continue to do it.

All that is needed is that we put ourselves in his hands. That he fashioned Adam out of a lump of clay may be a fact or a poetic description. What he can and will make out of me is a saint, a citizen of the kingdom of eternal happiness if only I will let him. May God give me the sense and the grace to do just that, so that when I close my eyes in death, I shall see God and become one of the millions of saints whose feast I am honoring today. So be it.